WITHDRAWN

OXFORD
UNIVERSITY PRESS
LONDON : AMEN HOUSE, E.C. 4
EDINBURGH GLASGOW LEIPZIG
COPENHAGEN NEW YORK TORONTO
MELBOURNE CAPETOWN BOMBAY
CALCUTTA MADRAS SHANGHAI
HUMPHREY MILFORD
PUBLISHER TO THE
UNIVERSITY

PALIMPSEST OF AQUILA'S GREEK TRANSLATION OF THE OLD TESTAMENT

Description of this plate will be found on pp. xi–xii

The Legacy of
ISRAEL

Essays by Sir George Adam Smith, Edwyn Bevan
F. C. Burkitt, R. T. Herford, A. Guillaume
Charles *and* Dorothea Singer, Rev. Canon Box
W. B. Selbie, N. Isaacs, L. Roth, A. Meillet
Laurie Magnus, C. G. Montefiore

Planned by the late
I. Abrahams
and edited by
Edwyn R. Bevan & Charles Singer

With an Introduction by
The Master of Balliol

OXFORD
At the Clarendon Press

296
B571l

28597

Corrected Impression of 1928
First Edition 1927
Printed in Great Britain

PREFACE

THE *Legacy of Israel* deals with the contribution that has come to the sum of human thought from Judaism and from the Jewish view of the world. It is not in any sense either a history of the Jewish people or an exposition of Judaism, and it is concerned with these topics only in so far as discussion of them may be necessary for the clear setting forth of the proper theme of the volume. It is a companion to *The Legacy of Greece* and *The Legacy of Rome*.

Some of the subjects discussed in this volume demand not only statement of fact, on which common agreement should be attainable, but also judgements as to value, on which differences of opinion may often prevail. It has, however, seemed practicable to give a survey of the field which should aim at commanding general assent from unprejudiced students of history. Each writer in the volume is, nevertheless, solely responsible for his own contribution.

The book, as originally designed, was under the joint editorship of Dr. Abrahams and Dr. Bevan. These two planned the general outline and read together several of the chapters. Dr. Abrahams died in October 1925. Dr. Charles Singer, who had already been a contributor to *The Legacy of Greece* and *The Legacy of*

Rome, then joined Dr. Bevan as editor. Dr. Abrahams had originally arranged with Dr. Singer that he should also contribute to *The Legacy of Israel*. Since the death of Dr. Abrahams considerable changes have been introduced by the editors, both into the plan of the book and into the panel of contributors.

Dr. Abrahams felt—and the present editors agree with him—that the mechanism by which Hebraic thought passed to the mind of Christendom, especially during the Middle Ages, is a closed book to most modern readers. It is in accordance with the original design of Dr. Abrahams that considerable space is given to this topic. In this sense the book is a companion volume to *The Legacy of the Middle Ages*, in which this topic is hardly touched upon. On the other hand, the purely Biblical record of Israel is in the background in the present work, for that subject is more fully discussed in another companion volume of the series, *The People and the Book*.

The attention of readers is drawn to the appreciation of the great qualities of Dr. Abrahams as scholar and man of letters at the close of the chapter contributed by Canon Box (p. 374). The chapter that was to be contributed by Dr. Abrahams himself was not left in such a state that it could be used. The gap has been filled by Dr. Montefiore with an Epilogue that bears, however, no relation to the fragment left by Dr. Abrahams. The Epilogue contributed by Dr. Montefiore differs from the other articles, as he himself clearly indicates, in that it expresses a definite religious standpoint.

The illustration of the volume has been mainly the work of Dr. Singer. An attempt has been made to make these illustrations a truly integral part of the volume, so that reference to them will assist in its comprehension. Many of the descriptions of the illustrations are perforce of considerable length. Owing to the difficulty of 'making up' a book of this type, some of these descriptions are placed in the *List of Illustrations* at the beginning (p. xi to xxxiii). The reader will, it is hoped, find his task considerably lightened by frequent reference to this list, in which, also, the sources of the figures are acknowledged. Among the objects, monuments, and pictures reproduced are several which, it is believed, will be of special interest to English readers. The volume owes a particular debt to the generosity of the *Gesellschaft zur Erforschung jüdischer Kunstdenkmäler*, who have lent eight originals from which figures are taken.

The editors would like to express their especial thanks also to the Rev. Professor Guillaume, who has read the proofs and has arranged the spelling of the Hebrew and Arabic names. In doing this he has borne in mind the needs of readers who have no knowledge of the Hebrew or Arabic languages, and he has adopted the simplest method of transliteration, avoiding the use of diacritical points.

It is evident that a Glossary of difficult and foreign terms is essential for the proper use of the volume by most readers. The reader is advised to refer frequently to this Glossary.

E. R. B.
C. S.

CONTENTS

LIST OF ILLUSTRATIONS . . . xi

PROLOGUE. By A. D. LINDSAY, C.B.E., LL.D., Master of Balliol College, Oxford . . . xxxv

THE HEBREW GENIUS AS EXHIBITED IN THE OLD TESTAMENT. By the Very Rev. Sir GEORGE ADAM SMITH, D.D., LL.D., Litt.D., F.B.A., Principal of Aberdeen University 1

HELLENISTIC JUDAISM. By EDWYN R. BEVAN, O.B.E., D.Litt., LL.D., Honorary Fellow of New College, Oxford, Lecturer on Hellenistic History and Literature at King's College, London . . 29

THE DEBT OF CHRISTIANITY TO JUDAISM. By F. C. BURKITT, D.D., F.B.A., Norrisian Professor of Divinity, Cambridge University . . . 69

THE INFLUENCE OF JUDAISM UPON JEWS IN THE PERIOD FROM HILLEL TO MENDELSSOHN. By the Rev. R. TRAVERS HERFORD, B.A., Late Librarian of Dr. Williams's Library. Author of *The Pharisees*, &c. 97

THE INFLUENCE OF JUDAISM ON ISLAM. By the Rev. ALFRED GUILLAUME, M.A., Professor of Hebrew and Oriental Languages in the University of Durham 129

THE JEWISH FACTOR IN MEDIEVAL THOUGHT. By CHARLES SINGER, M.D., D.Litt., F.R.C.P., F.S.A., Lecturer on the History of Medicine in the University of London, and DOROTHEA WALEY SINGER 173

HEBREW SCHOLARSHIP IN THE MIDDLE AGES AMONG LATIN CHRISTIANS. By CHARLES SINGER 283

HEBREW STUDIES IN THE REFORMATION PERIOD AND AFTER: THEIR PLACE AND INFLUENCE. By the Rev. G. H. Box, D.D., Rector of Sutton, Hon. Canon of St. Alban's, Late Professor of Hebrew and Old Testament Exegesis, King's College, London 315

THE INFLUENCE OF JUDAISM ON WESTERN LAW. By N. ISAACS, M.A., Ph.D., S.J.D., Professor of Business Law, Graduate School of Studies, Harvard University 377

THE INFLUENCE OF THE OLD TESTAMENT ON PURITANISM. By the Rev. W. B. SELBIE, D.D., Principal of Mansfield College, Oxford . 407

JEWISH THOUGHT IN THE MODERN WORLD, By LEON ROTH, Officier d'Académie Française, M.A., D.Phil., Lecturer on Philosophy in the University of Manchester 433

INFLUENCE OF THE HEBREW BIBLE ON EUROPEAN LANGUAGES. By A. MEILLET, Professor au Collège de France, Directeur d'Études à l'École des Hautes Études, Paris 473

THE LEGACY IN MODERN LITERATURE. By LAURIE MAGNUS, M.A., Author of *A Dictionary of European Literature. An Introduction to Poetry, A Primer of Wordsworth, &c.* 483

EPILOGUE. By C. G. MONTEFIORE, D.D. . . 507

GLOSSARY 524

INDEX 533

LIST OF ILLUSTRATIONS

Frontispiece. PAGE OF PALIMPSEST OF AQUILA'S TRANSLATION OF THE OLD TESTAMENT FROM HEBREW INTO GREEK. (*See p.* 86.)

Reproduced by permission of the Syndics of the Cambridge University Press from Professor F. C. Burkitt, *Fragments of the Books of Kings*, Cambridge, 1897.

Aquila is said to have been a connexion by marriage with the Emperor Hadrian. A pagan by birth, he was converted first to Christianity and then to Judaism. Aquila's translation was made in the first half of the second century A. D.

The manuscript, of which a page is here reproduced, was transcribed in the sixth century, probably during the reign of the Emperor Justinian (reigned 527–65). It is a *Palimpsest*; that is to say that when the book of which it is a single leaf was no longer wanted, it was taken to pieces, the sheets of valuable vellum on which the Greek work of Aquila had been written were washed so as to obliterate the script as far as possible, and a new work was then written on the old leaves on top of the obliterated writing. In this case the new work is in Hebrew. It consists of religious poetry by Yannai, a writer of the seventh century.[1] The Greek letters of the underlying text of Aquila fortunately show through and can be read.

The translation made by Aquila is excessively literal. It follows the Hebrew word for word, being, in fact, what would now be called a learned 'crib' rather than a piece of literature. This is well illustrated by the leaf here reproduced which contains 2 Kings xxiii. 15–19. It will be noticed that the Greek writing is in two narrow columns with no divisions between the words. The later Hebrew work, which is written over it, is distributed quite differently upon the page; it is in a much smaller script and moreover shows spaces between the separate words.

The first five lines of the left-hand column correspond to 2 Kings xxiii. 15b. Transliterated into ordinary Greek characters and with the words divided, we read:

$\kappa\alpha\iota\ \kappa\alpha\iota\gamma\epsilon\ \sigma\upsilon\nu\ \tau o$ and moreover *with* the
$\theta\upsilon\sigma\iota\alpha\sigma\tau\eta\rho\iota o\nu$ [2] altar [2]
$\epsilon\kappa\epsilon\iota\nu o\ \kappa\alpha\iota\ \sigma\upsilon\nu$ that and *with*
$\tau o\ \upsilon\psi\omega\mu\alpha$ [3] $\kappa\alpha\tau\epsilon$ the exaltation [3] he de-
$\lambda\upsilon\sigma\epsilon\nu\ \ldots$ molished ...

[1] See the edition by I. Davidson, *Mahzor Yannai*, New York, 1919.
[2] Hebrew את המזבח.
[3] Hebrew את הבמה, Authorized version translates *high place*.

συν (= *with*) governs the Dative case in Greek. Nevertheless, συν το θυσιαστηριον and συν το υψωμα, which are in the Accusative not the Dative, are no mistakes of the scribe, since an Accusative with συν was regularly used by Aquila to indicate that the particle *eth* (את, which merely denotes the Accusative), here stands in the Hebrew. This is so peculiar and non-Greek a construction that the decipherment of the three words συν το θυσιαστηριον was in itself sufficient to suggest that the text was Aquila's translation.

The proper name of the God of Israel is written יהוה (i. e. JHVH = *Jahveh*, misread as *Jehovah*) in the Hebrew Bible. Out of reverence this word was not pronounced by the Hebrews, who used instead the word *Adonai* (i. e. ' Lord '). The old Greek version of the Old Testament, in agreement with this custom, translated יהוה by *Kyrios* (i. e. ' Lord '). Aquila, however, retained the Hebrew name in his Greek translation, and, moreover, he continued to write it not in Greek but in Hebrew letters. But the Hebrew letters which he used for this purpose were not the Hebrew letters familiar to modern readers, such as can be seen, for instance, in the work written over Aquila's Greek text. The script employed by Aquila for writing the Holy Name was the *old* Hebrew script akin to the letters on the Moabite Stone set up by Mesha, King of Moab in the time of the prophet Elisha. (Fig. 4.) These old letters are akin to those found on Hebrew coins from an early date and until the time of Aquila.

An instance of the practice by Aquila of using the old Hebrew letters for the Holy Name is to be seen in the Greek text of the frontispiece in the left-hand column, last line but two. The vellum is torn here, but the two letters יה, shaped something like FE reversed, are clearly seen below to the left at the spot indicated by an asterisk. That Aquila had adopted this plan was told us by the Christian scholar Origen (third century A.D.), but till the discovery of this manuscript, every one supposed that Origen was mistaken.[1]   F. C. BURKITT.

Figs. 2 & 3. STATUES OF THE CHURCH AND SYNAGOGUE. *facing p.* xxxvi.
From the porch of Strasbourg Cathedral.

These two magnificent allegorical figures are among the finest specimens of Christian art of the thirteenth century.

To the left stands the *Church*, looking sternly at her sister. She

---

[1] A full account of this palimpsest has been given by the author of this note in his *Fragments of the Books of Kings according to the translation of Aquila from a MS. formerly in the Geniza at Cairo*, Cambridge, 1897. For the meaning of the word *Geniza* see the glossarial index at the end of the volume.

wears a crown which she has taken from the head of the Synagogue, as it is said, *And thou, prince of Israel, whose day is come, saith the Lord God; Remove the diadem and take off the crown* (Ezekiel xxi. 26). In her left hand she holds the chalice, which has come to her also from the Synagogue. With her right hand she plants the banner of the cross firmly on the ground.

To the right stands the Synagogue. Her head is downcast and her eyes veiled, as it is said, *For unto this very day, at the reading of the old covenant, the veil remaineth unlifted; which veil is done away in Christ* (2 Corinthians iii. 14). Her banner is supported not by a cross but by a spear, but the staff is broken and is no support, as it is said, *For behold the Lord, the Lord of Hosts, doth take away from Jerusalem and from Judah the stay and the staff* (Isaiah iii. 1). In her left hand the Synagogue still grasps a fragment of the tables of the commandments, emblem of the Old Covenant.

This representation of the figures of the Church and Synagogue was a common convention of medieval art. Similar treatment of this theme is seen for instance in Fig. 41 facing p. 252 of this volume. C. S.

Fig. 4. THE MOABITE STONE, NOW IN THE LOUVRE AT PARIS.
facing p. 1.

This remarkable monument was discovered at Dibon (Numbers xxi. 30), in the territory of Moab, four miles north of the river Arnon. Soon after it was found a squeeze was taken of it. This was fortunate, for the stone was broken into pieces by the Arabs of the neighbourhood, before it could be brought to Europe. The fragments were, however, recovered and the squeeze made it possible to piece them together.

The Moabite Stone is the oldest historical inscription in any dialect nearly allied to Hebrew, and is the most valuable monument of Palestinian history. Its language and phraseology differ but slightly from Hebrew. The date of the Moabite Stone is about 850 B.C. The following description and translation is by Dr. S. A. Cook. It is taken, by permission, from the *Cambridge Ancient History*, vol. iii, pp. 372–3.

'The style of the inscription indicates that Moab was no rude land; the same could no doubt be said also of Edom, Ammon, and other states.

'In it Mesha, a wealthy sheep-owner who had been forced to pay a heavy tribute of wool to Ephraim (2 Kings iii. 4) tells how, through the help of his god Chemosh, he recovered his cities, particularly those north of the Arnon, and sacked the Israelite sanctuary at Nebo, devoting 7,000 inhabitants to Ashtor-Chemosh. To commemorate his victory he built a "high-place" to Chemosh in Kerekhoh, possibly a suburb of his city, like the Zion of Jerusalem. The inscription runs as follows:

"I am Mesha, son of Chemosh king of Moab, the Daibonite. My father reigned over Moab for thirty years, and I reigned after my father. And I made this high-place for Chemosh in Kerekhoh a high-place of salvation, because he had saved me from all assailants, and because he had let me see my pleasure upon all them that hated me. (Psalm cxviii. 7.) Omri was king of Israel and he afflicted Moab for many days, for Chemosh was being angry with his land (2 Kings xvii. 18). And his son (i. e. Ahab), succeeded him, and he also said, I will afflict Moab. In my days said he thus, and I saw my pleasure on him and his house. And Israel perished with an everlasting destruction; now Omri had taken possession of the land of Mehdeba (Numbers xxi. 30). And it (i. e. Israel) dwelt therein his days (viz. twelve years) and half the days of his son, forty years; and Chemosh restored it in my days. And I built Baal-Meon (Joshua xiii. 17), and I made in it the reservoir, and I built Kiryathen (Numbers xxxii. 37). Now the men of Gad had dwelt in the land of Ataroth (Numbers xxxii. 34) from of old; and the king of Israel built for himself Ataroth. And I warred against the city and seized it. And I slew all the people of the city, a gazing-stock to Chemosh and to Moab. And I captured thence the altar-hearth of Dawdoh and I dragged it before Chemosh (compare 'before Jahweh' 1 Samuel xv. 33) in Keriyyoth (Amos ii. 2). And I settled therein the men of Sheren (1 Chronicles v. 16, Sharon) and the men of Makharath, And Chemosh said unto me, 'Go (compare Joshua viii. 1), seize Nebo (Isaiah xv. 2) against Israel'. And I went by night and warred against it from the break of dawn unto noon. And I seized it, and slew all of it, 7,000 men and male sojourners and women and female sojourners and maidens. For to Ashtor-Chemosh had I devoted it (Deuteronomy ii. 34, Authorised Version 'utterly destroyed'). And I took thence the vessels of Yahweh,[1] and I dragged them before Chemosh. Now the king of Israel had built Yahas (Jahaz, Numbers xxi. 23), and dwelt in it, when he warred against me. And Chemosh drove him out (Joshua xxiv. 18) from before me; and I took of Moab 200 men, all its chiefs. And I brought it (i. e. them) against Yahas, and seized it, to add it unto Daibon. I built Kerekhoh, the wall of the Woods and the wall of the Mound (or Ophel, 2 Chronicles xxvii. 3). And I built its gates and I built its towers.

---

[1] This is the earliest instance of the Divine Name in this spelling outside the Old Testament.

List of Illustrations

And I built the King's house, and I made the two reservoirs for water in the midst of the city. Now there was no cistern in the midst of all the city, in Kerekhoh; and I said to all the people, Make you every man a cistern in his house. And I cut out the cutting for Kerekhoh with the prisoners of Israel. And I built Aroer, and I made the highway by the Arnon. I built Beth-Bamoth, for it was overthrown. I built Beser (Deuteronomy iv. 33) for ruins had it become. And the chiefs of Daibon were fifty, for all Daibon was obedient. And I reigned over an hundred chiefs in the cities, which I added to the land. And I built Mehdeba and Beth-Diblathen. And Beth-Baal-Meon; and I took thence the sheep-masters ... the sheep of the land. And as for Horonen, there dwelt therein ... and Chemosh said unto me, Go down, fight against Horonen (Jeremiah xlviii. 5) And I went down ... and Chemosh restored it in my days. ...'

The inscription dates after the weakness of Israel, but whether it is just before or after the rise of Jehu it is difficult to determine.'

In Dr. Cook's translation he has indicated a number of difficult and alternative readings. Some of them turn on philological and historical points with which we are not here concerned. Others are due to the injuries that the stone has received and the consequent gaps in the inscription itself. In our version we have chosen from among Dr. Cook's readings. Those interested in the details of the readings are referred to Dr. Cook's original.   C. S.

Fig. 5. TRIUMPHAL PROCESSION WITH TEMPLE SPOILS FROM THE ARCH OF TITUS AT ROME.   *description p.* 28. *facing p.* 28.

Fig. 5a. PLATES BEARING JEWISH EMBLEMS FROM THE CATACOMBS AT ROME.   *p.* 68.

Fig. 6. RESTORATION OF HELLENISTIC SYNAGOGUE AT CAPERNAUM.
     facing p. 68.

From H. Kohl and C. Watzinger, *Antike Synagogen in Galilaea*, Leipzig, 1916.

The remains of a lime-stone building at Tell-Hûm, more stately than any other so far discovered in Western Palestine, were examined for the German *Orientgesellschaft* in 1905, and identified as the Synagogue of Capernaum. This seems to have been erected about A. D. 200, but it was an ampler reconstruction of an older Synagogue, which may well have been the one in which Jesus preached. The south side of the building, at which the reader looks in the figure, was built facing the lake, and was crowned by a pediment, that had in it the three entrance doors and the principal window. The interior resembled a basilica, minus the apse; along three sides ran a two-storied colonnade, the upper story being probably for women.

Along the two side walls were stone-benches. The other seats for the congregation and the raised platform for the ministrants and the Rolls of the Law were no doubt of wood. If, as is supposed, the platform was in the middle of the building, so that the reader of the Law had his back to the entrance doors, and the congregation sat beyond the platform facing the reader, they would, during their worship, have looked out through the open doors over the lake towards Jerusalem and the Temple.

Outside the Synagogue to the East was a courtyard with a colonnade on three of its sides, probably for washing before worship. The irregular position of the doors on the north wall of the courtyard seems to indicate that in the older Synagogue the courtyard had not been rectangular, but had been made so to fit the new building of A. D. 200. One remarkable feature of the decoration of the Synagogue is the representation of living animals, which the Judaism of Jerusalem in the days of Herod regarded as sinful. In Rabbinical literature the inhabitants of Capernaum are referred to as heretical. (The Synagogue of Chorazin had even representations of men.)

See H. Kohl and C. Watzinger, *Antike Synagogen in Galilaea*, Leipzig, 1916. E. R. B.

Fig. 7. SMALL SCHOLA OR SYNAGOGUE. *p.* 96.
From a mosaic of the fifth century known as the 'Capitoline plan' at Rome.

Fig. 8. *AUTO DE FÉ*. Photograph, Roig. *facing p.* 96.
From a painting of about 1500 in the National Gallery at Madrid.

Auto de fé ('Act of faith') is the Spanish title (Portuguese *auto da fé*) for the proclamation and execution of a judgement by the Inquisition. The public ceremony was often a state function, attended by king and court. The Inquisition formally handed over the victims to lay functionaries for execution, with instructions to spill no blood. Hence was adopted the method of burning.

Autos de fé were first held in the thirteenth century, reached their maximum under the Inquisitor Torquemada (1420–98) and were common till 1745. The last public burning was at Valencia in Spain in 1826, when a Quaker and a Jew were victims. The Inquisition was abolished in Spain in 1834.

Contemporary pictures of *autos de fé* exhibit amazing callousness. In the foreground of this figure, two naked victims tied to stakes are about to be burnt. In front of them are two other victims on whom a confessor presses repentance, holding a crucifix before their eyes. Behind on a dais, sheltered by a canopy, sit the officers of the Inquisition, who exhibit benign expressions. The attendant to the right of the President bears a large cross. The President is adorned with a halo, and the artist has, perhaps, meant to represent St. Dominic himself. The name of St. Dominic and of the Dominicans is associated with the Inquisition in an especial way. The office of Inquisitor in all countries was usually held by a Dominican. C. S.

Fig. 9. DOMESTIC PASSOVER CELEBRATION. *between pp.* 110 *and* 111.

From a fourteenth-century Hebrew MS. of the Domestic Passover Service, in a Spanish hand. British Museum, Or. 2884.

The picture shows men, women and a child seated at a table. Two of the men are clean shaven. The table is covered with a white cloth, an unusual feature in the Middle Ages and specially connected with the celebration of the Passover. An animated discussion is proceeding, in which the women and the child are participating, according to custom. Two dogs gambol in the foreground. C. S.

Fig. 10. SCENE IN A SYNAGOGUE. *between pp.* 110 *and* 111.

From a fourteenth-century Hebrew MS. of the Domestic Passover Service, in a Spanish hand. British Museum, Or. 2884.

The floor of the building is occupied by a crowd of 14 men who wear praying shawls. Two hold books. Some are bearded and some are clean shaven. A number of lamps hang from the ceiling. The main feature of the building is the central reading desk, raised on pillars and reached by a staircase. From it an elder or rabbi is declaiming from a scroll or draped book. A similar central reading desk may be seen in Figs. 43, 53, and 80. The entrance and tiled roof are drawn as though the walls of the building were transparent. C. S.

Fig. 11. THE BODLEIAN BOWL. *facing p.* 114.

The so-called 'Bodleian Bowl' was 'found in an old mote in Norfolk' about 1696. It passed into the hands of Dr. John Covel (1638–1722), Master of Christ's College, Cambridge. In 1722 it was purchased by Robert Harley, first Earl of Oxford (1661–1724). It subsequently became the property of Dr. Richard Rawlinson, the non-juring bishop, who died in 1755 bequeathing it to the Bodleian Library where it has since remained.

The bowl is finely cast of bronze, 9¾ inches high and 30 inches round the widest circumference. It is very substantial and weighs 11 pounds. It has two handles and three hoof-shaped feet. Handles and feet belong to the original casting. Over the feet are grotesques of a bird (which can be seen in our figure), a stag, and a circle containing a flowery pattern. The workmanship is of the thirteenth century and is French, a fact confirmed by the fleur-de-lis under each handle. One of these is seen to the left of the figure. Round the widest part runs a Hebrew inscription in high relief.

Both the use of the bowl and the interpretation of the inscription have been much discussed.

As regards use. The most likely suggestion is that it was used in the Synagogue for collecting alms for distribution in Palestine.

As regards interpretation of the difficult Hebrew. Dr. Abrahams translated it somewhat as follows:

'This is the gift of Joseph, the son of the Holy Rabbi Jehiel—may the memory of the righteous holy be for a blessing—who answered and asked the congregation as he desired in order to behold the face of Ariel [i. e. Jerusalem, cp. Isaiah xxix. 1, 2, 7, also Ezekiel xliii. 15, margin], as is written in the Law of Jekuthiel [i. e. Moses] "And righteousness delivereth from death" (Proverbs xi. 1).'

The question remains as to the identity of Joseph son of Jehiel, mentioned in this inscription. It seems probable that Jehiel was Rabbi Jehiel of Paris, who had a controversy with Donin of La Rochelle (see pp. 294–5). Jehiel of Paris suffered such persecution in France that in 1257 he left for Palestine with his son Joseph who was subsequently buried there. Three hundred disciples accompanied Jehiel thither and many came from England. These English disciples explain the presence in this country of this thirteenth-century relic. The first recorded Palestinian envoy commissioned to collect money for the Holy Land was a pupil of Jehiel.

These notes are from two articles by Dr. Abrahams in the *Transactions of the Jewish Historical Society of England*, v. 184, London, 1905, and *Miscellanies of the Jewish Historical Society of England*, London, 1925, where further bibliographical references can be found. C. S.

Fig. 12. CLIFFORD's TOWER, YORK. *facing p.* 120.
From an engraving by Joseph Halfpenny (1748–1811), in his *Fragmenta Vetusta*, York, 1807.

In this tower the Jewish population of York, men, women, and children, took refuge in 1190 against a mob uprising, led by a Premonstratensian monk. The account of what then happened is thus given by the chronicler, William of Newbury:

'The taking of the tower became certain. It was clear that the fatal hour was nigh. The Jews, braced by despair, had little rest, discussing what they should do.

'Now there was there a certain old man, a famous Doctor of the Law, who had come from beyond the sea to teach the English Jews. When asked his advice, he replied, "God, to whom none shall say 'What doest Thou?' (Ecclesiastes viii. 4, Daniel iv. 35), orders us now to die for his Law. Death is at the door, unless, perchance, which God forbid, you think of deserting the sacred Law for this brief space of life, and choose to live in dishonour. Since then we must prefer death to a dishonest life, we ought to select the easiest and most honourable form. If we fall into the hands of the enemy, we die at their will and amidst their jeers. So since the life which the Creator gave us, He now asks of us, let us yield it to Him devoutly with our own hands."

'Many embraced his advice, but to others his words seemed hard. Then he said, "Let those whom this plan pleaseth not, seat themselves apart from this holy assembly, for to us this life on earth is now nothing, through our love of the Law of our fathers." Many withdrew, preferring to try the clemency of enemies rather than to perish with friends.

'Soon, at the instance of this mad elder, lest the enemy be made rich by their wealth, they burned their possessions. Fire being set to the roof, they prepared for the sacrifice. Those whose courage was most steady took the lives of their wives, the famous Joce cutting first the throat of his dear wife Anna, and then of his own sons. And when this had similarly been done by the other men, that wretched elder cut Joce's throat last, so that he might be more honoured than the rest. [The rabbi then killed himself.]

'The fire had now spread to the tower, and those who had chosen to live fled to its extremity. At daybreak the crowd collected to storm the castle. The wretched remnant of the Jews, standing at the gates, declare with tearful voice the slaughter of their people. Throwing down their bodies as proof, they called out "Behold the corpses of men guilty of their own death. We refused to do the like, preferring to try Christian clemency. God has preserved us that we may be one with you in religion. For, our trouble giving us sense, we recognize Christian truth, and desire its charity, being prepared for the sacred baptism.

as you demand. Receive us as brothers, let us live with you in the faith and peace of Christ." '

'Hearing this, many of our men were horrified at the madness of the dead and pitied the living. But the leaders, among whom was a certain Richard, with the truthful surname, *Evil Beast* [Malabestia = Richard Malebysse], were unmoved. Speaking fair words and promising the wished for grace of the Faith, so that they should come out, they seized them, and though they demanded the baptism of Christ, those cruel butchers destroyed them. Of those thus slain, I would say that, if there was no deceit in their demand for sacred baptism, their own blood baptized them when defrauded of the result of their petition.'

The speech of the rabbi is doubtless apocryphal, but there is no doubt of the character of his advice and of the general accuracy of the record. For the documents of these events see J. Jacobs, *Jews of Angevin England*, London, 1893, from whose translation ours is abbreviated and slightly modified.

The 'teacher from overseas' to whom William of Newbury refers was the French Rabbi, Yom-tob of Joigny near Auxerre. *Yom-tob* means literally *day good* (i.e. good day). An acrostic poem by this brave rabbi forms part of the Jewish Liturgy. The last two lines begin with the words *yom* and *tob*. They seem prophetic and have been thus translated by I. Zangwill:

DAY by day,   Stronghold they   Seek in Thee
GOOD One! let   Stronger yet   Thy word be 'Forgiven'.

C. S.

Fig. 13. A GHETTO OF SOUTHERN TYPE. SIENA.
between pp. 122 *and* 123.
From a photograph kindly lent by the *Gesellschaft zur Erforschung jüdischer Kunstdenkmäler*.

Fig. 14. A GHETTO OF NORTHERN TYPE. PRAGUE.
between pp. 122 and 123.
From a photograph kindly lent by the *Gesellschaft zur Erforschung jüdischer Kunstdenkmäler*.

Figs. 13 and 14 of existing or recently existing buildings give a good idea of the squalor of medieval ghettoes.

Fig. 15. MUHAMMAD'S JOURNEY TO HEAVEN.   *facing p.* 128.
From a MS. in the British Museum. Or. 4535.

The Islamic legend of Muhammad's *Miraj*, or Ascension, has had a long and fascinating history. Beginning with a comparatively simple story, it was rapidly enlarged and was finally mystically allegorized by Ibnu-l-Arabi in his *Futuhat al Makkiyya*.

The *Miraj* has been interpreted by some Muhammadan expositors as non-corporeal and the prophet's experience has been described as that of a dream or vision only. A popular version is that the prophet was transported by night from Mecca to Jerusalem, thence through the 'seven heavens' to the presence of God, and thence back to Mecca. The 'seven heavens' is a conception related to the seven crystalline spheres of the seven planets. (Compare Fig. 24, p. 195.)

The story bears a close resemblance to several Jewish *Midrashim*. One tells of the transformation of Moses into a fiery angel and his ascent through the seven heavens. Another tells how, before his death, Moses was translated into heaven and the heavenly Jerusalem was revealed to him. Somewhat similar stories are to be found in the Jewish apocryphal books known as *The Assumption of Moses* and *2 Enoch*. For further information on Jewish legends of this type the reader is referred to these works and to the introductions to them in R. H. Charles, *The Apocrypha and Pseudepigrapha of the Old Testament*, Oxford, 1913.

Our picture of the Islamic version of the legend portrays the features common to most of the versions of the *Miraj*. The prophet, mounted on the mysterious celestial animal, neither horse nor ass and with a human head, is seen passing through the seven astronomical heavens, on his way to the throne of Allah. The great irregular cloud, with which Muhammad and his steed are surrounded, corresponds in Islamic art to the halo in Christian art. In Islamic art it is usually flame-like, and is seen in more manageable proportions round the head of Joseph in Fig. 16. Muhammad is escorted by a group of angels.

Portrayals of Muhammad are very rare, and here the face has been left blank in deference to religious scruples. Compare the second commandment: 'Thou shalt not make unto thee any graven image, or any *likeness* of anything that is in heaven above, or that is in the earth beneath, or that is in the water under the earth.' This likeness was interpreted in Islam to apply most especially to the human form.

A. Guillaume.

Fig. 16. THE HANDSOME JOSEPH. B.M. Or. 1368.   *facing p.* 148.

Fig. 17. JONAH AND THE WHALE.   *facing p.* 148.
From a MS. in the Edinburgh University Library.

Fig. 17a. SIGNATURE OF MOSES MAIMONIDES.   *p.* 171.
From a 12th cent. Bodleian MS. (MS. Huntingdon 80.)

List of Illustrations

Fig. 18. PANEL OF THE FRANKS' CASKET. FALL OF JERUSALEM AND CAPTURE OF THE TEMPLE. *between pp.* 172 *and* 173.

Fig. 19. PANEL OF THE FRANKS' CASKET. FINDING OF ROMULUS AND REMUS AND THE SHE-WOLF. *between pp.* 172 *and* 173.

A full description of Figs. 18 and 19 is given on p. 172. The negatives from which Figs. 18 and 19 were taken were kindly lent by the Trustees of the British Museum.

Fig. 20. SPHERES OF INFLUENCE ABOUT A. D. 750. *p.* 178.

Fig. 21. SPHERES OF INFLUENCE ABOUT A. D. 1150. *p.* 179.

Fig. 22. SPHERES OF INFLUENCE ABOUT A. D. 1500. *p.* 179.

Fig. 23. MAP TO ILLUSTRATE THE RECESSION OF ISLAM IN SPAIN. *p.* 183.

Fig. 24. MEDIEVAL DIAGRAMS OF THE STRUCTURE OF THE UNIVERSE. *p.* 195.

Fig. 25. THE PRIMUM MOBILE. *facing p.* 198.

From a fourteenth-century Provençal MS. in the British Museum. Harley 4940. Of a text by Armengaud (see pp. 234–5 and 306).

The terrestrial world, made up of the four *lower elements*, namely *earth*, *water*, *air*, and *fire*, is in the centre. The four *lower elements* are represented by four rectangles in the central core. Around this central core are spheres of the *higher elements*, namely (*a*) *water*, represented as a dark circle with small white circles upon it, (*b*) *air*, represented by a circle with diapered patterns separated radially by broad white bands through which descend celestial 'influences', such as lightning, &c., (*c*) *fire*, represented by a zone with a wavy line and dots. Around these higher or upper elements is a dark circle, with small white circles upon it. This is the sphere of *ether*. Beyond this again is a broad zone with asterisk-like markings. This is the *starry firmament*. The movement of this starry firmament is caused by angels who are here shown, hard at work, turning the handles of an obliquely set crank. The obliquity is intended to indicate the obliquity of the ecliptic. See also Fig. 24 and pp. 194, 196, and 198. C. S.

Fig. 26. MAP TO ILLUSTRATE THE RECESSION OF ISLAM IN SPAIN. *p.* 203.

Fig. 27. A GENERAL VIEW OF TOLEDO, AS SEEN ACROSS THE TAGUS. *facing p.* 204.

From José Amador de los Rios, *Monumentos históricos*.

Fig. 28. A STREET IN OLD TOLEDO. *p.* 207.

From a pen and ink sketch by Mr. Hector Corfiato.

List of Illustrations xxiii

Fig. 29. DETAIL OF A SYNAGOGUE AT TOLEDO. *p*. 213.
Built in 1357 by Samuel Abulafia (1320–60).
Reproduced by permission from a drawing in the possession of the *Gesellschaft zur Erforschung jüdischer Kunstdenkmäler*.

Fig. 30. MAP OF ITALY IN THE FIRST HALF OF THE THIRTEENTH CENTURY.
p. 215.

Fig. 31. GREEK, SARACEN, AND LATIN NOTARIES AT WORK. *p*. 217.
From the MS. of Pietro da Eboli, *Liber ad honorem Augusti*. Codex 120 in the Civic Library at Berne. The MS. has been reproduced for the *Instituto Storico Italiano* by G. B. Siragusa.

Fig. 32. THIRTEENTH-CENTURY SYNAGOGUE OF SOUTH ITALIAN TYPE AT TRANI. *p*. 219.
From a drawing kindly supplied by the *Gesellschaft zur Erforschung jüdischer Kunstdenkmäler*.

Fig. 33. SCENES FROM A MS. OF 1282 OF THE TRANSLATION BY FARRACHIUS OF THE *LIBER CONTINENS* OF RHAZES. *facing p*. 222.
This MS. is at the *Bibliothèque Nationale* at Paris, (Lat. 6192) written in 1282. The MS. is of French or of North Italian workmanship. It was written at the order of Charles of Anjou and the representations of Farrachius (Faradj ben Salim) appear to be of the nature of portraits. If this is the case, they are the first portraits of a Jew that we possess other than caricatures. See *Gazette archéologique*, vol. xi, and M. Steinschneider, *Hebräische Uebersetzungen*, p. 974, and Virchows *Archiv* xxxix. 296. For further description see p. 222. C. S.

Fig. 34. THE DEATH-BED OF WILLIAM II OF SICILY. *p*. 223.
From the same MS. as Fig. 31.

Fig. 35. ARMILLARY SPHERE CONSTRUCTED IN THE THIRTEENTH CENTURY FOR ALFONSO THE WISE OF CASTILLE BY HIS JEWISH ASTRONOMERS.
facing p. 224.
The figure has been taken from Manuel Rico y Sinobas, *Libros del Saber de Astronomica*, 4 vols., Madrid, 1863–7, vol. ii, *De las armellas*. Owing to the absence of perspective it is difficult of interpretation. There is a good description and restoration of it by F. Nolte, *Die Armillarsphäre*, Erlangen, 1922, p. 28. In our figure, however, the ecliptic ring, the equator, the polar ring, and the 'sights' can be easily distinguished by their positions and legends. A number of other graduated circles can also be made out. C. S.

Fig. 36. FRANCE AT THE BEGINNING OF THE FOURTEENTH CENTURY. *p.* 225.

Fig. 37. RECONSTRUCTION OF A SPHERICAL ASTROLABE OF ALFONSO THE WISE. *p.* 227.

Reproduced, by kind permission of the authors, from H. Seemann and T. Mittelberger, *Das kugelförmige Astrolab nach den Mitteilungen von Alfons X von Kastilien und den vorhandenen arabischen Quellen,* Erlangen, 1925, p. 68.

Figs. 38 & 39. MAPS OF SPAIN (38) AND ENGLAND (39). *p.* 229.

From a Portolano map in the *Bibliothèque Nationale,* prepared by a Jewish cartographer in 1375. For description see p. 228.

Fig. 40. FOURTEENTH-CENTURY SYNAGOGUE OF NORTH ITALIAN TYPE AT SIENA. *p.* 231.

From a drawing kindly lent by the *Gesellschaft zur Erforschung jüdischer Kunstdenkmäler.*

Fig. 41. JESSE TREE, FROM A TWELFTH-CENTURY BIBLE. *facing p.* 252.

Permission for reproduction has been given by His Grace the Archbishop of Canterbury. The photograph from which the plate is printed has been kindly lent by the Comte Alexandre de Laborde.

The manuscript was written in England, perhaps at Canterbury, in the first half of the twelfth century. It is now in the Library of the Archbishop of Canterbury at Lambeth Palace. The *Jesse Tree,* in which scriptural personages are represented as springing out of the body of Jesse, is a common medieval convention, though in certain aspects the treatment in this figure is unique.

Jesse lies on the ground, sleeping with his fathers. On either side of him below is a crowned figure bearing a scroll. These are his descendants, the Kings David and Solomon. From his body springs a trunk, supporting the Virgin. At the summit, as a flower, is the figure of Christ surrounded by seven doves, representing the seven gifts of the Holy Spirit. Christ is supported by St. John the Baptist and St. John the Evangelist, who occupy the two upper corners and also bear scrolls.

The trunk gives off three sets of branches. In the lowermost are seen four prophets. One can be identified as Isaiah, for he bears a scroll on which is written *Egreditur virga de radice Jesse et flos de radice eius ascendet.* 'And there shall come forth a rod out of the stem of Jesse, and a Branch shall grow out of his roots.' (Isaiah xi. 1.) The other three prophets cannot be identified. They bear scrolls which have not been inscribed.

In the central branches, on the left 'Mercy (carrying a vase of balm) and Truth have met together'; on the right 'Righteousness and Justice (carrying scales) have kissed each other' (Psalm lxxxv. 10).

In the upper branches, on the left, the crowned Church carries the cross, and is supported by two prophets, perhaps Moses and Aaron, since they wear no haloes. On the right the Synagogue is being exhorted by Moses (who wears horns in the traditional manner) and by Isaiah. Nevertheless, a hand from Heaven draws a veil over the eyes of the Synagogue, as it is said, 'But their minds were hardened; for unto this very day at the reading of the old covenant, the same veil remaineth unlifted; which veil is done away in Christ. But even unto this day whensoever Moses is read, a veil lieth upon their heart. But whensoever it shall turn to the Lord, the veil is taken away.' (2 Corinthians iii. 14–16.) Compare Figs. 2–3, after Prologue.

For a description of this manuscript see Eric Millar, *Bulletin de la Société française de Reproduction de manuscrits à peintres*, viii. Paris, 1924.
C. S.

Fig. 42. VESTIBULE OF THIRTEENTH-CENTURY SYNAGOGUE AT RATISBON.
between pp. 260 and 261.

From an engraving by Albrecht Altdorfer (1488–1538), a pupil of Albrecht Dürer. Original kindly lent by Dr. Max Simon of Berlin.

This Synagogue was built in 1210 and destroyed in 1519, when it was replaced by a Church. Albertus Magnus (pp. 259–64) was Bishop of Ratisbon from 1260–3 and must have known this Synagogue. The building is of the Gothic type. Above the engraving is the inscription:

PORTICUS SINAGOGAE	The Vestibule of the Synagogue
IUDAICAE RATISPONENSIS	of the Jews of Ratisbon
FRACTA 21 DIE FEBRUARII	Destroyed 21st day of February
ANNO 1519	in the Year 1519

and below is the monogram **AA** of Albrecht Altdorfer. C. S.

Fig. 43. INTERIOR OF SAME SYNAGOGUE AT RATISBON, AS IS REPRESENTED IN FIG. 42. *between pp. 260 and 261.*

Original kindly lent by Dr. Max Simon of Berlin.

The interior of the building which, like all medieval synagogues, was extremely small, is nearly filled by the reading desk. This structure bears about the same relative size to the building as a whole as is exhibited in figures 10 and 53. From these three figures the minuteness of the medieval synagogues can be gathered.

Above may be read the inscription:

ANNO DOMINI MDXIX	In the Year of the Lord 1519
IUDAICA RATISPONI	the Ratisbon Jewish
SYNAGOGA IUSTO	Synagogue, by the just
DEI IUDICIO FUNDITUS	Judgement of God, was utterly
EST EVERSA	Overthrown

and below the monogram of the artist **AA** for Albrecht Altdorfer, as in Fig. 42.
C. S.

Fig. 44. St. Thomas triumphs over Averroes. Photograph, Brogi.
facing p. 266.

Altar-piece by Francesco Traini in Sta. Catarina at Pisa. For description see p. 265.

Fig. 45. Nicholas of Lyra writing at a desk. *facing p.* 282.

From MS. 30 in the John Rylands Library at Manchester.

This MS. consists of the *Postilla super omnes libros bibliae* of Nicholas of Lyra. It was completed in 1402 at the Franciscan convent of Pesaro by Ugolino Marini Gibertuzzi.

Fig. 46. Roger Bacon. *facing p.* 282.

From a MS. (Bodley 211) written about 1450 in Northern France.

Fig. 47. Hebrew and Samaritan alphabets in Early Latin Manuscripts. For description see p. 290. *p.* 291.

Fig. 48. Old Synagogue at Worms, first built 1034. *facing p.* 294.

Photograph kindly supplied by the *Gesellschaft zur Erforschung jüdischer Kunstdenkmäler*.

The old Synagogue at Worms is one of the oldest buildings of any kind in the whole of Germany. In spite of the accidents that have befallen it, the original appearance of the building has altered comparatively little. Rashi certainly worshipped here, but the building close to the Synagogue and known as the 'Rashi chapel', has nothing to do with Rashi and was erected long after his time. A drawing of the interior of the old Synagogue is shown in Fig. 53, p. 314.
C. S.

List of Illustrations xxvii

Fig. 49. THE 'JEW'S HOUSE' AT LINCOLN OF THE TWELFTH CENTURY.
facing p. 298.

The oldest stone house in England. Reproduced, by permission of Messrs. Bowes & Bowes, from R. Farren, *Cathedral Cities*, 1896.

The so-called 'Jew's house' on the west side of Steep Hill at Lincoln is probably the earliest stone dwelling house in England. It dates from the earlier part of the twelfth century and still preserves its old street front. There is a rich entrance doorway. The first-floor windows light the principal room, which was invariably on this floor in medieval houses. The ground floor was used for service and stores but has since been turned into a shop. The walls are throughout about $2\frac{1}{2}$ feet thick. No trace of the original staircase has survived. The house as a whole presents much the same appearance as when Robert Grosseteste was Bishop of Lincoln. Careful measurements of the house are given by F. Haes, *Transactions of the Jewish Historical Society of England*, iii. 185, London, 1899. C. S.

Fig. 50. LINES OF POINTED HEBREW WITH ROGER BACON'S TRANSLITERATION AND TRANSLATION. *p.* 302.

From a MS. of the *Opus Majus* of Roger Bacon, now in the Vatican (Vat. 4086). This MS. was written about 1400. It is reproduced from a photograph presented to the British Museum by His Eminence Cardinal Gasquet.

Fig. 51. TRANSLITERATION INTO MODERN TYPE OF FIG. 50. *p.* 303.

Fig. 52. A PAGE FROM THE BIBLE OF THE HOUSE OF ALBA. *facing p.* 312.
A medieval Demonstration in Favour of Religious toleration.

The miniatures in this volume have been reproduced in facsimile in the *Biblia de la Casa de Alba* by Jacobo Stuart Fitzjames, Duke of Berwick and Alba.

Fig. 53. INTERIOR OF A SYNAGOGUE AT WORMS, BUILT 1034. *p.* 314.

Fig. 54. ERASMUS ABOUT 1531. *facing p.* 314.
From an oil painting by Hans Holbein; now in the Metropolitan Museum, New York. Originating from Freiburg i. Breslau, the picture was successively in the possession of Sir John Norris, Edward Banister, the Arundel Collection, the Family of Howard of Greystoke, and Pierpont Morgan.

Fig. 55. GIOVANNI PICO DELLA MIRANDOLA. Photograph, Alinari.
facing p. 320.
From a portrait by an unknown artist in the Uffizi Gallery at Florence.

List of Illustrations

Fig. 56. JOHANN REUCHLIN. *facing p.* 340.
From L. Bechstein, *Zweihundert deutsche Männer in Bildnissen und Lebens beschreibungen*, Leipzig, 1854.

Fig. 57. JOHANN FROBEN. *facing p.* 340.
From H. Lempertz, *Bilderhefte zur Geschichte des Bucherhandels*, Cologne 1854.

Fig. 58. JOHN SELDEN. *facing p.* 354.
From a portrait by Lely in the Bodleian Library at Oxford.

Fig. 59. EDWARD POCOCKE. *facing p.* 354.
From a portrait in the Bodleian Library at Oxford.

Fig. 60. HOUSE IN 'THE STRAND', LONDON, WHENCE MANASSEH ISSUED HIS PETITION TO CROMWELL. See Fig. 67 between pp. 406 and 407. *facing p.* 366.
From *Transactions of the Jewish Historical Society of England*, vol. iii, London, 1899, p. 147, reproduced by kind permission of Mr. Lucien Wolf, President of the Society.

Fig. 61. MANASSEH BEN ISRAEL, age 28. *facing p.* 366.
From an engraving of 1642. See description of Fig. 67.

Fig. 62. I. ABRAHAMS. *facing p.* 374.
From a painting by M. Cohen in the possession of the Liberal Jewish Synagogue, London, reproduced by kind permission of the Council of the Synagogue.

Fig. 63. ORNAMENTAL HEBREW LETTERS FROM THE RABBINIC BIBLE OF DANIEL BOMBERG (Venice, 1517–18). *p.* 375.
Reproduced from D. W. Amram, *The Makers of Hebrew Books in Italy*, Philadelphia, 1909.

Fig. 64. BOOK PLATE OF WILLIBALD PIRCKHEIMER DESIGNED BY DÜRER. *p.* 376.

Fig. 65. SHRINE FOR THE SCROLLS OF THE LAW, CONSTRUCTED IN 1472 FOR A SYNAGOGUE AT MODENA. *facing p.* 377.
Photograph by *Les Archives Photographiques d'Art et d'Histoire*.
This fine piece of Renaissance walnut wood-carving is now in the Cluny Museum. Such a shrine forms the main part of the furniture of a Synagogue, and is placed at the Eastern end. The front and sides of this shrine are decorated with inscriptions in Hebrew characters which may be thus translated:
Consecrated to the Lord.—For out of Zion shall go forth the Law and the word (Isaiah ii. 3)—*The Law of the Lord is perfect, restoring the soul;*

the testimony of the Lord is sure, making wise the simple. The precepts of the Lord are right, rejoicing the heart (Psalm xix. 8–9)—*A glorious throne, set on high from the beginning is the place of our sanctuary* (Jeremiah xvii. 12).

The date of the Shrine is given by a Hebrew inscription on its lower part which may be thus translated:

This Shrine was wrought in honour of the Most High and Sublime in the fifth millenium in the year BLESS the Lord, O my soul (Psalm ciii. 1) *Hallelujah.*

The word BLESS בָּרְכִי is a chronogram. The points of its letters yield the number 232, for 5232 *Anno Mundi*, i. e. in the Jewish Era which is supposed to date from the Creation, indicating A. D. 1472.

For description see E. Haraucourt, *Musée des Thermes et de l'Hotel de Cluny. Catalogue des bois sculptés et meubles*, Paris, 1925, p. 94.   C. S.

Fig. 66. TITLE-PAGE OF THE *DECRETUM* OF GRATIAN.   *p.* 406.

Francis Gratian was a Camaldulian monk, who worked at Bologna. About 1148 he compiled his immense *Concordia Discordantium Canonum*, which became known as the *Decretum Gratiani*. This work of Gratian has exercised the greatest influence on the development of Canon Law. It soon became accepted as the standard manual, both for teaching and for practice. It was studied throughout the Middle Ages, and enjoys very great authority to this day. Some idea of the popularity of the work may be gathered from the fact that about fifty editions of it appeared before the year 1500. It is still being printed.

Our figure is from the back of the title-page of an edition of Gratian which appeared at Lyons in 1509. The centre of the picture exhibits the monk Gratian in his library writing his *Decretum*, inspired by a crowd of his predecessors, each of whom holds open his book. Around the margins are allegorically represented the Jewish and Christian writers from whom Gratian was considered to have derived the basis of his work. Each of them holds an open book. In the left-hand column, from below upwards, are Jeremiah, Isaiah, David, Job, and Moses; in the right, Paul, Mark, Luke, Matthew, and John. The four corners are occupied by the four doctors of the Church, St. Ambrose and St. Gregory below, St. Jerome and St. Augustine above.   C. S.

Fig. 67. JEWISH PETITION TO OLIVER CROMWELL IN 1656, WHICH LED TO THE LEGALIZATION OF JEWISH RESIDENCE IN ENGLAND.
between pp. 406 *and* 407.

About the middle of the seventeenth century certain groups of Puritans in England began to take interest in the Jews. A number of Jews had secretly been settled in the country since the beginning of the sixteenth century. They gradually declared their religion. Manasseh ben Israel (Fig. 61), a distinguished Hebrew scholar resident in Holland who had knowledge of English, was invited over to put their case to the English government. He arrived in London in 1655 (Fig. 60), and presented to Cromwell his petition, signed by himself and by six leading Jewish residents in London. It is now in the Record Office in London, and it bears the Protector's signature. Cromwell referred it to a special committee who rejected it. Nevertheless, the Protector supported the Jewish claims which, within two years, obtained legal sanction.

The petition runs as follows:

'To His Highnesse Oliver Lord Protector of the Commonwelth of England, Scotland and Ireland and the Dominions thereof.

The Humble Petition of The Hebrews at Present Residing in this citty of London whose names ar underwritten

Humbly sheweth

That Acknolledging The manyfold favours and Protection your Highnesse hath bin pleased to graunt us in order that wee may with security meete privatley in owr particular houses to our Devotions, And being desirous to be favoured more by your Highnesse, wee pray with all Humblenesse that by the best meanes which may be, such Protection may be graunted us in Writting as that wee may therwith meete at owr said private devotions in owr Particular houses without feere of Molestation either to owr persons famillys or estates, owr desires Being to Live Peacebly under your Highnes Governement. And being wee ar all mortall wee allsoe Humbly pray your Highnesse to graunt us Lisence that those which may dey of owr nation may be buryed in such place out of the cittye as wee shall thinck convenient with the Proprietors Leave in whose Land the place shall be, and soe wee shall as well in owr Lifetyme, as at owr death, be highly favoured by your Highnesse for whose Long Lyfe and Prosperitty wee shall continually pray To the allmighty God

      Menasseh ben Israel
      David Abrabanel
      Abraham Israel Carvajal
      Abraham Coen Gonzales
      Jahacob de Caceres

Abraham Israel de Brito
Isak Lopes Chillon

OLIVER P[rotector]
Wee doe referr this Peticon
 to the Consideracion of the Councill.
  March the 24th.'
   165⅚   C. S.

Fig. 68. MEDAL TO COMMEMORATE THE EMANCIPATION OF PROTESTANTS
 AND JEWS IN HUNGARY, 1781.   *p.* 431.
From F. Szecheny, Catalogue of Hungarian coins in the National Institute at Szegedin 1807–10.

Fig. 69. SEVENTEENTH-CENTURY DRAWING OF BAS-RELIEF ON ARCH OF
 TITUS, SHOWING PROCESSION BEARING TEMPLE SPOILS (cp. Fig. 5).
                                                         p. 432.

Fig. 70. BARUCH SPINOZA.   *facing p.* 450.

Fig. 71. SPINOZA'S WORK-ROOM AT RHIJNSBURG.   *p.* 453.
From a drawing prepared for the *Jewish Encyclopaedia* and reproduced by kind permission of Messrs. Funk & Wagnall, New York.

Fig. 72. SOLOMON MAIMON.   *facing p.* 460.
From a contemporary stipple engraving by W. Arndt from an original kindly lent by the *Gesellschaft zur Erforschung jüdischer Kunstdenkmäler*.

Fig. 73. IMMANUEL KANT   *facing p.* 460
From a contemporary engraving.

Fig. 74. ILLUSTRATION FROM BLAKE'S *BOOK OF JOB*, 1825. *facing p.* 472.
'When the morning stars sang together and all the sons of God shouted for joy.'
There is, perhaps, in the whole history of art no more remarkable instance than Blake of continuous inspiration by the phrases of the Hebrew scriptures. The interpretation of the pictures of Blake is often difficult. In this instance, however, the meaning of the artist is clear. The account we give is taken with permission from the work of Mr. Joseph H. Wicksteed, *Blake's Vision of the Book of Job*, London, 1910, who rightly observes that in this glorious design the passion and splendour do not depend for their appeal upon any accurate knowledge of the meaning of the details. Pp. 101–2.

' In this great design, where Blake touches the height of his genius, and, indeed, of genius itself, he shows the perennial act of spiritual

Creation ever going on in the 'Bosom of God, the Human Imagination', and the fusion of this with Universal reality beyond.

'The rolling layers of cloud divide the design into the four great worlds of vision, united by the Divine Being who appears as before, in the spiritual likeness of Job. Below is the world of time and space; the world as it appears to our bodily senses, shut off from everything but the earth. Above this opens the eternal world within. Here dwells the spiritual Creator, the light of life that illumines the whole universe, but can only be known in its true subjective reality in the here and the now and the me. This inner world is divided into two. Beneath the Deity's right arm there rides forth the sun of the mind, driving the horses of instruction; while beneath his left arm the moon of poetic, or woman's love, controls and guides the serpents of corporeal desires. Between these and the seraphs above, we have a glimpse into the empty abyss representing the void of Nature—the unknown, where we cannot trace the presence of the Divine humanity. But beyond this again is the universe of stars—the infinite life beyond our life, multitudinous in sea and air and the countless generations of men, with which our Eternal Being, bridging the gulf of Nature, links us in sympathy and spiritual unity. The seraphs are the Sons of God, the poetic emanations of the Divine-Human imagination. These, mingling with the Morning Stars, adjoin 'Man to Man' and waken harmonies of so intense a joy, that it seems to tremble on the verge of a great sob, in which the eternal grief of the universe is merged in its eternal rapture. "Excess of joy is like excess of grief".' C. S.

Fig. 75. INSCRIPTION AT NARBONNE.   *p.* 481, *description p.* 482.

FIG. 76. SYNAGOGUE OF SPANISH AND PORTUGUESE JEWS, LONDON, BUILT 1701.   *facing p.* 483.
From an eighteenth-century painting by M. Belisario in possession of the Synagogue.

Fig. 77. SÜSSKIND OF TRIMBERG SINGING BEFORE A BISHOP. *facing p.* 496.
From a MS. of about 1300 in the Maness collection in the University Library at Heidelberg.

Süsskind of Trimberg was a Jewish Minnesinger of the thirteenth century (p. 496). A number of his writings have survived, and he takes a definite position in the history of German literature.

In our miniature Süsskind has a long beard and hair and wears the pointed hat customary with Jews in Germany at the period. He is singing before a bishop, who is enthroned on a dais and bears an

List of Illustrations   xxxiii

episcopal staff. Over the bishop floats a banner with a cross, while two Gothic arches indicate that the scene is within the walls of a palace. Above are written the words *Süsskind der Jude von Trimperg*.

Some of the songs of Süsskind have been translated into English in G. Karpeles, *Jewish Literature*, Philadelphia, 1895. An account of Süsskind will be found in the *Jewish Quarterly Review*, vol. xv, p. 60. London, 1903. An account of the MS. will be found in *Die Manessische Handschrift, Minnesänger und Zeit der Hohenstaufen, gesammelt im 14. Jahrhundert von Rüdinger Maness u. Maneck*. Facsimile edition by R. Sillib and others. Leipzig, 1926–7.   C. S.

Fig. 78. JEWISH HOUSE AT TOLEDO OF THE FOURTEENTH CENTURY, FORTIFIED AND ALMOST WITHOUT WINDOWS. Photograph, Roig.
facing p. 498.

Fig. 79. MOSES MENDELSSOHN. *facing p.* 502.
From L. Bechstein, *Zweihundert deutsche Männer in Bildnissen und Lebensbeschreibungen*, Leipzig, 1854.

Fig. 80. HEINRICH HEINE. *facing p.* 502.
From a contemporary engraving.

FIG. 81. PRINTER'S MARK OF GERSHON BEN MOSES SONCINO. *p.* 505.

Fig. 82. BABYLONIAN WEIGHT IN FORM OF LION WITH CUNEIFORM INSCRIPTION. On the base is graven in the *old* Hebrew script the words מנה מלך = royal maneh. *p.* 522.
From F. W. Madden, *A History of Jewish Coinage*, London, 1864.

Fig. 83. A VISION OF THE TEMPLE. *p.* 523.
From a Hebrew Domestic Passover Service Book printed at Amsterdam in 1695.

PROLOGUE

THERE is a necessary difference, as is noted by several of the contributors, between this book and the companion volumes which have preceded it—the *Legacy of Greece* and the *Legacy of Rome*. Greece and Rome, as they are meant in these titles, came to an end; their legacies were what they passed on to other civilizations.

Most of us, who are not Jews, think of the legacy of Israel in the same way—as something which Israel passed on to what was not Israel—to Christianity. When we think of the elements which have gone to make up the civilization of modern Christendom we compare the part played by what Israel handed down to us with what we have been given by Greece and by Rome. Rich legacies they all are, though very different in character—and they are all, so conceived, strictly legacies.

Principal Adam Smith's, Professor Burkitt's, and Dr. Selbie's Essays in this book are concerned with the legacy of Israel as so understood. But most of the book is concerned with something which is in its way different: the legacy to our civilization given by that blinded figure with the broken staff set up in the porch of

Strasbourg Cathedral, a photograph of which is reproduced on the opposite page, by the Israel which persisted as a separate community though scattered all over Europe, and which still persists. It is concerned therefore with something which is not strictly a legacy but rather gifts which a living community has in the past given to civilization.

If the account of these gifts is to most of us unfamiliar, it is a story full of interest. Even if we begin with the assumption that Israel was a community which fulfilled its historic mission in the first century, we learn from this volume how much our civilization has got from the fact that Israel persisted, a separate unabsorbed community, in both the Christian and the Muhammadan worlds. Not only did its continuity with the Israel of the past enable it to preserve Hebrew learning and scholarship in such a way that all through the centuries Christian scholars have gone to Jews for the sources of their understanding of the Old Testament, but—and this is a more surprising fact—Israel, because it was one community living in both the Christian and Muhammadan worlds, was the carrier of Greek and Arabic thought to medieval Christendom.

The two characteristics which have above all marked out this Israel throughout its long history have been its devotion to the law and to the community, and to both of these as the command and the special concern of God.

FIGS. 2, 3. CHURCH AND SYNAGOGUE, STRASBOURG CATHEDRAL

For description see pp. xii–xiii

Devotion to a law may easily become legalism, and devotion to a community which is conceived as specially chosen or marked out by God may easily produce exclusiveness and spiritual pride. Israel has always made its law a law of righteousness and has, therefore, served a law whose essence was a following after something more universal than a merely legal system could give : its community has been thought of as having its nature and purpose from a God who was the God of the whole earth, and, therefore, much more than the God of the community. Hence have come out of Israel evil and good—evil when the accidental, historical, and personal aspects of the law or the community have been given a false importance and significance because God and the world have been thought of as existing as it were for their sake ; but great and wonderful good as time and again the noblest spirits of Israel, armed with a certainty and a calm unshakable conviction, such as training in devotion to a law and membership of a strong community give, have left behind all the trammels of ceremonial valued for its own sake and all national exclusiveness, and have made the whole world and the depths and heights of human nature bear witness to the divine, and have uttered a message more universal than perhaps the teachers of any other people. These were not mindful of that country out of which they had come, and yet it was the country out of which they had come which made them seek a heavenly city whose builder and maker was God.

Time would fail to note how this universalism breaks out again and again in the Old Testament and in the teaching of the Rabbis—not to speak of the Gospels or the Epistles of St. Paul. I wish rather to illustrate what seems to me the special greatness of Israel's thought by considering for a moment two great Jewish writings which, though separated in time by more than two thousand years, seem to me to have something common in their greatness, the Book of Job and the Ethic of Spinoza, the one as great in form as in its imaginative content, the other a philosophical treatise which in form is repellent and obscuring.

If to be religious means, as it sometimes is thought to mean, to take desires as facts, to suppose the world is what man would like it to be, to insist on keeping some part of life outside the sphere of truth and relentless honesty, then these two books must be among the most irreligious books ever written. They both are attacks on the orthodox religion of their time. It is hard to believe that the Book of Job can have been more kindly received by any contemporaries who perceived its religious significance than was the Ethic of Spinoza. Both books are thoroughly sceptical in the good sense of that word—there is no fact they are not prepared to face and acknowledge: nothing into which they are not ready to inquire. Yet though each of them goes the whole way with the scientific spirit, making no qualifications and holding back nothing, each is inspired by an intense moral earnestness and above all by a deep sense of reverence for the omnipotence and the infinity of God. There is a world of difference between the dramatic passion and the poetic imagery of the Book of Job and the austere and ordered reasonings of Spinoza's Ethic; but in that rare combination of unflinching truthfulness and religious reverence the two books are alike, and in the strength of that combination they breathe an assurance of trust and confidence which is the more precious because it has been so hardly won.

Spinoza was excommunicated by the synagogue of Amsterdam, and it may be that many would hold that what is called his pantheism is not typical of Jewish thought. But we know that along with his knowledge of contemporary scientific thought he was profoundly influenced by the philosophy of his own people. However that may be, what I have tried to indicate as the peculiar qualities of his greatness are not found in anything like the same degree outside Jewish thought, and the achievements of those combined qualities, whether in the Book of Job or the Ethic of Spinoza, seem to me no small part of the legacy of Israel.

A. D. LINDSAY.

Fig. 4. MOABITE STONE

For description see pp. xiii–xv

THE HEBREW GENIUS

AS EXHIBITED IN THE OLD TESTAMENT

§ 1. *In General*

THE origins of the Hebrews, the breed or breeds from which they sprang, the traditions they inherited from pre-historic ancestors, the earliest impressions they received from the civilizations of that already old world, upon which they emerged into history, are all still obscure enough to allow of differences of opinion regarding them. And this is even true, though far less so, of the exact degrees of the people's indebtedness to the various empires with which they afterwards came in contact. But whatever traditions the Hebrews brought with them into history and whatever modifications the race, their ideas and institutions, subsequently experienced under foreign influence, there cannot be doubt or question of the substantial identity of the people throughout their long history or of the specific qualities and force of character by which that identity was maintained. Indeed, the main impression from a study both of the earlier and of the later stages of their history is not more of what they brought with them out of their successive environments and racial relations than of what they left behind and turned their backs upon; not more of what they actually did inherit or borrow from other peoples—even where such inheritance or borrowing is most evident—than of what they outgrew or rejected in the systems of culture into which they were drawn or which their conquerors tried to impose upon them. Thus while the desert origin of the Hebrews appears indisputable,[1] and, as we shall see, left its effects on the people's temper to the end, how soon and how far they rose beyond

[1] Hos. ix. 10; Jer. ii. 2; Deut. xxxii. 10, cf. i. 28 ff.

it is manifest from the absolute contrast in which their character and history stand to those of their nearest kindred among the Semites—Ishmael, Edom, Moab, and Ammon. From the desert the Hebrews came up into a world overrun by the Babylonian and Egyptian civilizations, and they settled in a land with whose people they shared, in addition to what was virtually the same language, the same environment teeming with economic and religious distractions. Yet though often yielding to the example of the Canaanites, and borrowing not a little from them, they were never absorbed. Their critical struggles with the Philistines only served to bring their tribes more closely together. And so throughout their later history, whether in alliance with Phoenicia or with Aram, or under Assyrian, Babylonian, Egyptian, Persian, or Hellenic dominion, whether left in peace to the seductions of their new home or harassed by enemies and sometimes terribly reduced in numbers, or driven into exile, their national individuality ever rallied, and their separate identity was maintained to a degree hardly matched in history. Of their singularity and aloofness as a people they themselves became conscious very early—*a people dwelling alone, nor reckoning itself with the nations* [1]—and remained conscious.

The sheer vitality of the breed, both physical and spiritual, has been so intense and, despite demoralizations and disasters sufficient to have shattered other peoples, has been so enduring as to imply sources of blood and of brain uncommonly rich and vigorous. Of this indeed we have very early evidence. That from the first the fibre of the race was hardy and their spirit heroic, save for the selfishness of some of them, is seen from the Song of Deborah,[2] in the strength and sweep of its religious enthusiasm, its instinct for rule and order, its scorn of the delinquent tribes and its praise of the voluntary discipline of the rest of them, their valour and self-sacrifice in

[1] Num. xxiii. 9.   [2] Judges v.

devotion to their God and the commonweal. That fire never died out of the nation. Though often slumbering it was ready, almost always, to flare up at the breath of a prophet. Though its embers were scattered by foreign oppression and drenched by the tears of the people themselves, as in the beginning of their great exile, a time of regathering and rekindling would surely come round, and then—as with the revival of the national consciousness and hope which beats through the prophecies of the Second Isaiah—the flames burst forth purer and more brilliant than before. To whatever source we may ascribe those inspirations, it is clear that the fuel necessary to them, the sheer human material indispensable for their display to the world and their tradition to later ages, was of marvellous strength and exhaustless powers of replenishment and endurance.

Two of the most formidable of the many adverse influences, to which the unity of the Hebrews was exposed, were the diverse nature of the land of their settlement and the looseness of the political form, the tribal organization, bequeathed to them by their nomadic forefathers. In its various soils, levels and temperatures, and its divergent avenues upon the world beyond, the little land of Canaan opened to its inhabitants different lines of culture and ideals of life, tempting them to sacrifice the national unity and interests to local economic advantages, just as the Song of Deborah describes, or to the local religious influences deplored by Jeremiah: *according to the number of thy cities are thy gods, O Judah*.[1] Hospitable to various ethnic types and cultures, Palestine has always been a land of tribes and of sects, and very seldom, if ever, the country of one nation with one religion and under one king. It is not surprising that in such a land the incoherence of the tribal life of their ancestral deserts should have continued to beset the Hebrew confederacy and lead, as it notoriously did, to frequent disruptions and secessions. Even when the distinctions and rivalries of the

[1] Jer. ii. 28.

tribes faded, it was only to be replaced by the bitter factions into which the Jewish people broke up during the Greek and Roman periods. That the national and spiritual identity of Israel survived these formidable dangers is, apart from all considerations of the unifying power of their faith, proof of their racial vigour and tenacity.

It is difficult to measure the degree of political genius to which the Hebrews attained. They originated no political institutions. Their local authorities were the same as throughout the rest of the Semitic world, tribal or family judges from whom there was right of appeal to the representative of the Deity at the nearest sanctuary; and in general their jurisprudence developed on lines parallel to, though on a higher ethical level than, those common to all Semites. The later appointment of a court or courts of ultimate appeal in Jerusalem followed naturally upon the establishment there of the Monarchy and the centralization in the Temple of the national worship. The Monarchy itself was confessedly founded in imitation of other nations.[1] The social and political philosophy of the people expressed in the Book of Proverbs and other parts of the Old Testament certainly equals but hardly excels in native shrewdness that of other races. The *wisdom of Solomon* has become proverbial through both the East and the West, and, whatever may be said of his luxury and extravagance, it was he who besides developing the internal economy of his people brought them into close contact with civilization and its arts, widened their horizon, and led their energies abroad in other directions than those of war and conquest. Yet, though his father's and his own influence succeeded in founding a long dynasty, this failed to secure the unity of the kingdom. On the other hand no loftier ideals of kingship have been offered to the world than by the Hebrew prophets, nor any finer deliverances on the rights and responsibilities of the people.

[1] 1 Sam. viii. 5; Deut. xvii. 14.

Nor should the splendour of the prophets' conception of the unity of all human history under Divine Control dazzle our eyes to the keenness and accuracy of their personal observations and estimates of powers and potentialities in the world around Israel, and the consequent soundness of most of their political and military forecasts in contrast to the fickle and short-sighted policies of the statesmen of their time. Again, whatever be the defects of Deuteronomy, we must allow no inconsiderable degree of political faculty to the attempt which the Book embodies to recodify the national laws in accordance with the ethical ideals of the prophets and the principle of the single national altar. Nor can we ignore the enormous influence which the theocratic system of the Old Testament exercised upon Christendom from Augustine up to, at least, the end of the eighteenth century. Throughout that long period the constitutional history of Israel was appealed to by political philosophies and systems of every kind: champions of the Throne and champions of the People, defenders of the Divine Right of Kings equally with advocates for their arraignment and deposition, the persecutor equally with his victims, the professors of non-resistance and the instigators of rebellion, those who believed in the subjection of the civil power to the spiritual, and those who maintained the former's independence of every ecclesiastical control. It was, of course, the Divine authority ascribed to the Hebrew Scriptures by all the controversialists alike, which educed so universal if so discordant an appeal to the political principles and patterns that those Scriptures record; but some credit for constructive ability and ingenuity, if not for genius, is due to the nation which under whatever inspiration, human or divine, elaborated a political system and bred examples of political virtue of such lasting influence on the kingdoms and empires of the other side of the world.

The tribal character of the gods of the Semites (to use a

convenient if not wholly accurate name for the peoples to whom the Hebrews were most akin) ensured the association of religion with the practical life of the tribe, the discharge of justice and government and the waging of war. It was favourable to the growth of a communal conscience, which, coupled with the fear of the more or less mysterious deity, exercised a certain degree of moral restraint on the individual, and was a powerful incentive to courage and devotion. But in these effects the ethical force of the Semitic religions appears to have spent itself. They remained on the one hand particularist or selfishly tribal, and on the other concerned with private conduct only so far as this directly affected public interests. There can have been little feeling for humanity as a whole and no profound sense of the spiritual value of the individual.[1] Of this system the Hebrews inherited both the practical advantages and the limitations, but, by whatever inspiration, they gradually grew away from the latter, developing not only higher standards of public justice and ideals of social purity, but an ethic which embraced at once more penetrating and articulate claims on the inner life of the individual and a sympathetic and generous attitude to other races. Here it is not possible to follow their moral progress in detail, but the following outline may be traced. Even the narratives and poems which otherwise reflect a primitive stage of moral development neither spare the frauds and follies of Hebrew individuals or tribes, nor ignore the virtues of foreigners; as in the tales of Abimelech's generous treatment of the deceitful Patriarchs, or the condemnations of the cruelty of Levi, Simeon, and Benjamin and of the immorality of Reuben.[2]

[1] To this there were exceptions, as e.g. in the introduction to the Code of Ḥammurabi and in the Babylonian Penitential Psalms, but how far these examples influenced Hebrew ethics it is impossible to say. As is well known the Hebrew conception of Babylon was of a remorseless, cruel, arrogant, and wholly immoral power.

[2] Gen. xii. 10 ff., xx, xxvi. 1 ff., xlix. 4, 5–7, 27 ; Judges iii. 15 ff., xix, xx. 1–5.

The magnanimous and forgiving spirit of David's elegy on his enemy and persecutor, Saul, is wonderful in so rude an age and so hunted a man.[1] The acknowledgement by the Aramean envoys of the mercifulness of Hebrew kings may not be mere flattery,[2] for it was some of these who refused to enforce the law of the vendetta, accepted throughout the Semitic world as both just and necessary, and who broke the custom of putting to death the children of criminals along with their guilty fathers.[3] In the earliest days of the Monarchy we find Samuel's insistence on obedience as better than sacrifice, Nathan's searching indictment of David, Elijah's denunciation of the injustice of Ahab, and in the tale of Micaiah-ben-Imlah and Ahab a personal conviction of the truth prevailing, even at so inferior a stage of prophecy, over tribal sentiment and all its subtle temptations to flattery—the prophet, observe, being helped to his moral victory by the instinct for truth in the king himself.[4] It is unnecessary to recall how this ethical strain in the Hebrew genius—whether slender or strong always persistent—developed at last into the incomparable ethics of the writing prophets; or how under the influence of these (as a comparison of the earlier Hebrew codes with Deuteronomy proves) the national Law not only eliminated from the ritual gross and cruel practices formerly sanctioned by the Hebrew religion or borrowed from the heathen; but achieved a greater thoroughness in applying its high principles both to the whole range of the national economy and administration and to the inner life of the individual, along with a finer equity and a more tender humanity.[5] An extraordinary power of moral discrimi-

[1] 2 Sam. i. 19 ff.   [2] 1 Kings xx. 31.

[3] David, 2 Sam. iii. f., cf. xvi. 5 ff., xix. 16 ff.; Amaziah, 2 Kings xiv. 6, which is more probably the precedent, than the consequence, of the obviously later law, Deut. xxiv. 16.

[4] 1 Sam. xv. 22; 2 Sam. xii; 1 Kings xxi, xxii.

[5] For details of the similarities and the differences between the Deuteronomic Code and (1) the Code of Ḥammurabi, (2) the consuetudinary law of

nation and selection emerges in the bold distinction which even the earlier of the great prophets make between the piety that is of the heart and shows itself in purity, meekness, and loving-kindness, and the worship that is merely outward and formal, between the truths which because of their moral power still live and those which once lived but have exhausted their virtue and are dead. But the same genius for eliminating the immoral and discarding the unworthy is conspicuous in the manner in which Israel elevated and transformed what they borrowed from other peoples, as, for instance, the Babylonian scheme of the Universe and accounts of its creation and the origins of man. In their treatment of these there are both an ethical and an intellectual originality which fully acquit the Hebrews from the charge of being the mere middle-men of the spiritual world. According to Jeremiah the duty of a prophet was *to bring forth the precious from the vile.* These words might well stand as a motto for the bent of the Hebrew ethical genius till at least the end of the prophetic period.

This ethical development was concurrent with an advance to higher conceptions of the character of the Deity. While long retaining the tribal form of their religion, the ancestral identifications of their God with certain physical phenomena such as the thunderstorm, and other mythological elements, the Hebrews—admittedly from the time of Moses onwards—came to see in Him attributes of righteousness, faithfulness, holiness, and mercy far above what other peoples of their world have told us of the Deity. The question is not now before us, whether their high conceptions of God were the consequence of the superior moral sense of the Hebrews or whether conversely their ethical development was due, as they themselves testify,

the Arabs, and (3) the earlier Hebrew Codes in the J and E documents of the Pentateuch, the reader is referred to recent Commentaries on Deuteronomy.

to the impressions of Himself which their God made upon them through the events of their history and the minds of their prophets. But it is significant that Israel's moral growth never outran the character of their national God. Other races have achieved ethical progress at the expense of their religion. But Israel never found their God wanting at any crisis of their history, or discredited by any fresh ethical experience or problem which their spirit encountered—however much for a time their faith in His righteousness might be shaken by their sufferings or by the injustice and cruelty that prevailed among themselves or in the world about them.

The qualities, habits, and general attitude of the Semitic mind, as exposed not only in ancient documents but by those Semites who still inhabit their ancestral deserts, are simple and of simple explanation. The discipline of the desert bred in the race not only a keen observation of natural phenomena, but a mental alertness and practical curiosity towards every stir and happening of human life upon it, forcing the mind to face and question facts and to an immediate responsiveness to all that was ominous and alarming. As Amos, the earliest of the great prophets and the nearest to the desert, impresses upon us by a few vivid illustrations,[1] it was precisely such qualities and habits of mind which with Hebrew prophecy were translated to the spiritual sphere and applied to religion. The earliest name for the prophets was *seers*, and to the end they called themselves *watchmen, waiting looking listening* for events and sounds, divine or human, and especially responsive to the bearing of these on the life of their own tribe or nation. They were the sentinels of Israel, ever growing in appreciation of the wider issues of history, but first of all zealous for the awakening, the defence, and the interests of the people to whom they belonged. It was natural to so practical a bent of mind to throw off very early the states of ecstasy to which oriental

[1] Amos iii. 3–8.

religion has ever been prone, and in concentration upon the real life about it to regard with scorn all magic and trafficking with ghosts. On the other hand, the power of sustained argument and speculation is not native to that type of mind, and no branch of the Semitic race has achieved it save under the discipline of foreign philosophies or science ; nor did ancient Israel do so till very late in their history. Yet the steady advance of the Hebrews towards an absolute monotheism brought with it inevitable intellectual consequences in the conceptions of a universe of law and reason and the favourable influences of these on the logical faculties.

The foregoing survey of the general features and forces of the Hebrew genius prepares us for a closer study of the Literature and Religion.

§ 2. *Literary*

Neither the language of Israel nor the styles of their literature were of direct revelation, but like those of other peoples were gradually developed by the opening of the eyes and ears of the people to the scenes and sounds of nature and of human life, by the beating of their hearts in response, by a growing sensitiveness to rhythm and music, and by practice, long and laborious, in the art of giving to their sensations, passions, and experiences proper utterance in suitable measure and cadence—all of course under the inspiration of those thoughts of God and of His world by which, through their prophets, the mind of the nation was elevated and its vision enlarged.

Hebrew may be called primarily a language of the senses. The words originally expressed concrete or material things and movements or actions which struck the senses or started the emotions. Only secondarily and in metaphor could they be used to denote abstract or metaphysical ideas. There is a prevalence in them of the harder, heavier consonants, including a greater variety of gutturals, than Western alphabets contain.

Much use is made of the explosive letters, and the doubled consonant exerts its full value both for phonetic and grammatical reasons. Thus, though the liquids and softer gutturals also abound in the vocabulary, it is urgency more than beauty, emphasis more than melody, which strike the ear as characteristic of Hebrew. So far the language was suited to a people who first heard the voice of their God in thunder and tempest, who primitively were warriors and minstrels of war, excited to battle-cries, curses, and prayers for vengeance on their foes; and who were destined to become a people of prophets and enforcers of truth as well as of poets and singers. One remembers the summons to the prophet to *call with the throat*.[1]

Few abstract terms exist in ancient Hebrew and no compound words. Abstraction and constructive power are almost as absent from the grammar and the syntax as from the vocabulary. That subordination of clause to clause in which the subtlety and flexibility of other languages appears is hardly found, but to the end, both in prose and verse, the clauses are almost invariably strung together by the bare copulas *and* and *then* in a co-ordination which requires both skill and spirit to redeem it from monotony.

Such were the means of expression afforded to the poets, prophets, and historians of Israel. What changes they made in the vocabulary and grammar we are without enough material to trace. Signs of literary genius are rather to be traced in the growing deftness of their use of so defective an instrument, and in the high styles of verse and prose which they ultimately achieved with it. Up to at least the end of the exile their literature proves a growing fineness of ear and mastery of poetic form, with increasing power to mould so concrete and sensuous a dialect to the utterance both of the subtler thoughts of man and the sublimest truths about God; despite the fact that the psychology in which the introspective Hebrew was so

[1] Isa. lviii. 1.

expert had to be stated in the terms of a very rudimentary physiology. No small ability was required to train so unpromising a tongue to the definition and enforcement of the most spiritual ethics, or to proclaim a Gospel for mankind in what was the dialect of a few small tribes of herdsmen, peasants, and warriors. Nor may we forget that not only the spiritual substance but the very styles of the literature of Israel have impressed themselves on some of the greatest of modern literatures. The vivid simplicity of Hebrew narrative and the majestic eloquence of the prophets did much to mould the youth of our own and of the German language and the styles of our earliest writers. Even granted that the elevation of so provincial and so comparatively poor a language is mainly due to the sublime and universal truths communicated to its religious writers, yet their gradual achievements of music and of style speak also of a native alertness, soundness of instinct, and patient conquest of their difficult material, which amount to a good degree of literary genius.

The singers of Israel played little with rhyme, which was mostly confined to proverbs and popular catches, but along with the writers of prose they skilfully used the opportunities for assonance, which their vibrant and sonorous vocabulary afforded, and impressively reproduced the sounds and movements of nature, the dull roar of masses of men and the clash and turmoil of battle. In the following lines, for instance, which render the tumult of the peoples in terms of stormy seas, the slow lift and roll of the billows is brought out by the long vowels, while the doubled consonants echo their boom and crash and hissing sweep along the shore :

> Hôi h^{a}môn 'ammîm rabbîm
> Kah^{a}môth yammîm yeh^{e}māyûn
> Ush$^{e'}$ôn l$^{e'}$ummîm kabbîrîm
> Kish$^{e'}$ôn maîm yishshā'ûn
> L$^{e'}$ummîm kish$^{e'}$ôn maîm rabbîm yishshā'ûn

which can be but faintly reproduced in English with our weaker words *waters* and *peoples*, that trickle rather than surge, as their Hebrew equivalents do,

> Woe, the booming of peoples multitudinous!
> Like the booming of seas they boom,
> And the crashing of nations immense
> As the crash of waters they crash—
> Nations as the crash of vast waters are crashing.[1]

Or take Deborah's ear for a charge of horses

> 'Az hāl^emû 'ikk^ebhē sûsîm
> Dah^arôth dah^arôth 'abbîrau
> Then thudded the hoofs of the horses,
> Gallop on gallop of his stallions.[2]

There are countless instances of the like.

In contrast to such forcible verses there are many in which the gutturals and liquids have been woven into exquisite melodies, as in the last verses of the Forty-third Psalm or in these lines from the Twenty-third,

> Yahweh Ro'î lo'-'eḥs-ar
> 'Al-mê m^enûḥôth y^enah^alēnî
> The Lord is my Shepherd, I shall not want,
> By the waters of restfulness He leadeth me,

or the opening couplet of the Fortieth of Isaiah,

> Naḥ^amû, naḥ^amû 'ammî,
> Yo'mar '^elôhêkhem.
> Comfort ye, comfort ye my people,
> Sayeth your God.

It would be hard to find in any language words that more gently woo the broken heart of a people. I do not know whether Handel had heard the original Hebrew, but he has caught its music in the bars with which his *Messiah* opens.

We have only to compare the rude verse of the Song of Deborah, one of the very earliest of Hebrew poems and

---

[1] Isa. xvii. 12 f.: a revised text.   [2] Judges v. 22.

metrically as irregular as some of our ballads, with the finished and stately forms of the poetry of the Second Isaiah or the Book of Job; or only to follow the development of the Hebrew Ḳinah or Elegy from one of its earlier efforts in David's Lament over Saul and Jonathan up to the elegies of Jeremiah, to see how skilfully the singers of Israel worked for and how far they won a mastery of regular metre, yet used this with a freedom, of which great poets in all languages have availed themselves, in order to emphasize a central thought or reach a climax or effect a surprise by single lines of greater length than their fellows or by a broken or arrested line. That Hebrew poets were ever ready to subordinate rhythm of sound to the rhythm of meaning, that they were controlled more by the urgency of their subjects than by metrical consistency, is significant—characteristic of men who felt it their first duty to deliver the truth.

As we have seen, the primitive measures of the Song of Deborah are already instinct with poetic genius: force, passion, and music, sweep of vision across both storm and battle, and power of scorn whose vivid flashes imperishably light up the characters of whole tribes, the dramatic encounters of individuals, and in a climax, as weird as it is pathetic, the figure of Sisera's mother mumbling to herself of the *spoil* of *women, divers colours* and *embroidery* which her son is to bring home and which we already know he never will. And thus onwards the early Hebrew poetry, in addition to that keenness of observation of scene and incident which we have found characteristic of the Semitic mind, exhibits a strength of conception, and faculties of wonder and worship, even before the people had reached the full monotheism, which as with other races gave their imagination of the universe its widest range and greatest sublimity and endowed them with their loftiest powers of satire and scorn. But, whether through their early or their later verse, we see in the Hebrews native poetical talents of no mean order, rising by the inspiration of a religious faith to heights of contemplation and of worship, to which our world may well look back with envy and longing.

Before we leave the nature-poetry of the Hebrews we may also note its tender feeling for the gentler forms of the world's life, as well as its occasional humour or playfulness about animals, as in certain of the Proverbs, and perhaps even in that verse in which, amused by the heavy gambols of whales or porpoises in the ocean, the Psalmist[1] (on a possible reading of the text) ventures to speak of God as having created Leviathan in order to *sport with him therein*.

Passing to the prose of the Old Testament we find two very different styles both bearing proofs of no small degree of literary genius—that of the narratives in Genesis and the Books of Samuel, and that of Deuteronomy.

To the narratives great tribute has been paid by modern masters of their art. Especially memorable are Goethe's admiration of the tales of the Patriarchs and Tolstoy's judgement that the story of Joseph is the model of what story-telling should be. The originality of these narratives cannot be doubted. Their style bears no marks of foreign influence, and all that has been recovered of the Egyptian literature of travel and adventure is not comparable to them—does not approach them in simplicity, charm, or dramatic power, far less in moral feeling and insight. For their main lines the Hebrew narratives have the careers and fortunes of individuals, and when separated from the additions that later editors have imposed on them they prove marvellously true transcripts of human life and character. With equal faithfulness they reflect the primitive morality of the times with which they deal, and record the vices as well as the virtues of their heroes, aware of the complexities of human character and showing a fine sense of proportion in portraying these. Even in the story of

[1] Ps. civ. 26; cf. Job xli. 5.

Balaam, the governing aim of which is a national one, namely to contrast the irresistible purpose of Israel's God for His people with the futile endeavour of the powers, from Pharaoh to Balak, to frustrate it, what subtlety is shown in depicting this conflict in the mind and conduct of Balaam, with all the mixed religious experience and fluctuating conscience of that ambiguous and most interesting pagan! This is worked out with a simplicity that must not be allowed to hide from us the psychological power by which it is informed.

But the richest flowering of the Hebrew genius for narrative is found in the histories of Saul and David, originally (as is admitted) by a contemporary writer or writers, but subsequently edited into their present form. When they have been relieved of the dogmatic additions imposed upon them, their natural beauty and piety become fully apparent. As Professor Robertson Smith says, there is none of that 'artificial' or 'mechanical conception of Jehovah's rule in Israel which prevailed more and more among the later Jews and ultimately destroyed all feeling for historical reality and at the same time all true insight into the methods of the Divine Governance, but the Divine Spirit guides the action of human forces without suppressing or distorting them'.

The stories reveal a very rare combination of equal intimacy and detachment. There is no sparing of the faults and errors of their heroes, and the keen insight into the complex characters of these and the sympathy felt for them develop through a simple tale of the consequences they brought upon themselves to the outlines of a great tragedy, or rather of two tragedies, of which they are the central figures, while surrounded by lesser personalities whose passions and blunders contribute to the general effect. There is no intrusion of miracle nor arbitrary interference by the Deity, but a simple faith in God's justice and His discipline of families and individuals; and things work themselves out naturally as the issues of men's right or wrong actions yet conditioned by forces over which the men themselves have no control. Thus throughout we have that mingling of sternness and of pathos, of the rigid development of moral consequence and the inevitable addition of accident or fate which form the essence of great tragedy. Let us keep in mind that all this vivid recital of events, this revelation of character and its consequences, with their tragic culminations, were accomplished through a medium of expression so defective in construction and flexibility as we have seen the Hebrew language to be.

Other and more elaborate styles of prose appeared in Israel, of which the most original and powerful is that of the Book of Deuteronomy, a style of mysterious source but of immediate and prolonged influence on the national literature. The rhythm is unlike the rhythm of any other prose in the Old Testament. It may have been the invention of one man; but so haunting and infectious is its music that it was caught up by a school or schools of writers and developed and even exaggerated (as textual criticism has shown) to an extent which indeed its peculiar cumulative structure provoked. Deuteronomy retells the earlier history of Israel and, under the influence of the great prophets, re-enforces the ancient truths and laws of the national religion with a fresh original rhetoric, inspired by an imagination more full of colour and by a warmer zeal than those of the earlier Hebrew histories and codes. It is lavish in resonant words and phrases, and in musical repetitions; urgent and expansive, yet frequently falling back from its urgency in order to explain, qualify, or refine. The music of its phrasing overcomes all feeling of redundancy. As I have said elsewhere, ' Deuteronomy is like a flowing tide upon a very broad beach, the long parallel waves dashing, withdrawing and dashing again '.

One other feature must be noted. Unfamiliar with the idea of evolution the Hebrew mind fixed upon results rather than processes. Things which came into being only gradually appeared to it as the offspring of a word, of a moment. Just as physical phenomena, now known to be of age-long development, are described in the first chapter of Genesis as happening in a day, so in Deuteronomy the effect of centuries of ethical influence on the law and ritual of Israel is presented as a single discourse of Moses, the first mediator of that influence. To the Hebrew, as to many other Easterns, power and authority were personal and immediate, the effect of a single fiat or proclamation, and secondary causes were ignored.

So much for the literary lines of the Hebrew genius, and now to follow the religious to which we have already found the others so closely linked.

§ 3. *Religious*

Whatever be the form or degree of our faith in a direct Divine Revelation to Israel we must acknowledge that the moral and spiritual truths, of which the nation has proved to be the minister to mankind, were not solely due to operations upon the mind of the people from without or above, under which the native faculties of their psalmists, prophets, and wise men remained wholly passive. As the records show, the religion of Israel was not only the approach of God to man but also man's quest after God. 'The Hebrew thinker', it has been truly said though only with part of the truth, ' came down from his thoughts of God upon the world rather than rose from the world up to his thoughts of God.'[1] It is also true that the convictions which individual Hebrews reached during their search after God were recognized by them as due to personal encounters with Himself and to the articulate impression on their minds of His Nature and Will, often in direct contradiction to their own thoughts and their own wills.

[1] A. B. Davidson.

Nevertheless it is equally true that the energy and sincerity of the quest largely depended on themselves—on the alertness of their eyes, ears, and hearts to the phenomena of nature and the happenings of history, and on the quickness of their consciences to react to their experience of life. The quest was carried through by the patient thinking out of all these elements, a process in which the thinker often felt left to himself, unaided from on high, troubled by questions and doubts wholly his own, and stirred by the revolt of his intellect or moral sense against beliefs or doctrines which had satisfied as divine previous generations or still so satisfied the mass of his contemporaries. All this led to argument and expostulation with God Himself in which the thinker asserted his individuality, pled against the Divine righteousness the reality of his opposite experience of life, and though finally submitting struggled to the last to preserve his independence, as did Jeremiah and Job and more than one Psalmist. Of Jeremiah it may be said that the man would not be mastered, but when mastered was not crushed. He questions each moment of his own sufferings, each moment of his people's oncoming doom. He debates with God on matters of justice. He wrestles things out with God, and emerges from each wrestle, not halt and limping like Jacob of old, but firm and calm, more clear in his mind and more sure of himself.

The biographer of David declares that for His purpose of giving a king to the people *the Lord sought Him a man after His own heart*,[1] sought, it would appear, for one already, by natural gifts and disposition, fitted for higher inspiration and guidance; and another Old Testament text states the Divine condition for the gift of fuller light to be *if thou prepare thine heart*. Again, the shrinking Jeremiah heard God say to him *Be not dismayed lest I make thee dismayed*; and his Parable of the Potter illustrates how the Divine designs for nations and individuals, the shaping of them for this or that form of service,

---

[1] 1 Sam. xiii. 14.

depend on the raw material God finds in them when they come into His hands.[1] No other nation of the ancient world has more explicitly declared man's own responsibility for his religious inspiration and for his serviceableness to the Kingdom of God, or has bequeathed to us so many examples of this.

Encouraged by such emphasis upon the part man himself has to play in religion, upon the place in it of his native powers, with all the contributions to these from the ordinary sources of family piety, pride in the history and institutions of his people, and the influence of his physical environment, we turn for illustrations to the richest treasury of the religious genius of the Hebrews and consider what may be called the natural strength of the Psalms.

In these, of course, there is much that is merely racial, displaying the hereditary qualities of the Hebrews—a people sprung from ancestors whose life in the desert had bred in them a long patience of hunger, broken by fits of rancour and ferocity; a race untrained for sustained argument and speculation and primarily interested in the phenomena of life and the influences of religion in so far as these were of practical bearing on the fortunes of their people; to whom religion from time immemorial had been a tribal or national concern, and their most definite ideas of God as the god of a particular people; gradually drifting, as desert tribes still do, from the pastoral life to agriculture, with the herdsman's and peasant's shyness towards towns and their ways, and yet at last concentrated with all their politics and worship upon one city, that they grew to revere as their only Home, Temple, and Mother, whom the bitterness of her destruction and their long exile from her only made the more indispensable to their faith and hope. All these hereditary tempers and economic and political experiences form the ground-tones of the Psalter. The ancient rancour of the desert breaks out in the cursing Psalms; the tribal form of

[1] Jer. i. 17, xviii. 1 ff.

religion persists in the focussing of the Divine Purposes on this single people; the fairest and most frequent figures of the poetry are drawn from the tents and marches of the nomads, from the pastures of the flocks and duties of the shepherd, and from the fields and furrows of the husbandman; but over all those landscapes and figures rise dominant the towers and bulwarks of the City with the musical name, Yerushalayim, and the Temple with its smoke of sacrifice, and the long lines of pilgrims coming up through the land chanting their Songs of Ascents.

And yet 'the eternal human' is there too; else the Psalter had never become the liturgy of so many other races. Its racial and national forms are by reason of their vitality so flexible that other nations, far off both in time and in space, have readily used them, even to the details of the terminology, to express their own aspirations and struggles for liberty, their migrations and exiles. The Psalmists in being, as we shall presently see, so heartily their own Hebrew selves, most fully lay bare the universal human gifts, failings and needs, passions and dreams. And they break away too, like the prophets, from the national religion, and express the revolt of the individual from many of its dogmas: from the belief that suffering is ever proof of the guilt of the sufferer and of the punishing purpose of God, from the creed that material sacrifice and ritual are what the Deity demands of men, and from that hopeless outlook beyond the grave which the Hebrews shared with the rest of the Semitic world.

The most obvious quality of the Psalms is their wholeheartedness, their natural, untamed and unstinted expression of all that is in the heart of man. *Bless the Lord, O my soul, and all that is within me bless His holy Name!* For more than blessing did the Psalmists' souls respond to this call. 'I may truly name this book', says Calvin, 'the anatomy of all parts of the soul; for no one can feel a movement of the spirit which is not reflected in this mirror. All the sorrows, troubles, fears, doubts, hopes, pains, perplexities, stormy outbreaks, by which the souls of men are tossed, are depicted here to the very life.' And Matthew Henry says, 'In other portions of Scripture God speaks to us, but in the Psalms men speak to God and their own hearts'. In what other literature is there a collection of utterances which discover human nature with such sincerity and thoroughness?

This frankness emerges in many forms. The darkest is its expression of hate. Under national or personal persecution the passion for justice grew awful in the heart of the Hebrew and he did not mitigate his anger before the Lord. *Let his children be fatherless and his wife a widow, neither be any to have pity on his fatherless children. Let them be as chaff before the wind and the angel of the Lord driving them on. Break their teeth, O God, in their mouth ; let them melt as water that runneth apace. Daughter of Babylon, Happy be he that dasheth thy little ones against the rocks.*[1] This is the delirium of the conscience, a delirium of the conscience produced by a famine of justice. Such outbursts are pathological, of course, but authentic proofs that the Psalms are the utterances of real men and not of tamed creatures performing a part.

The frankness of the Psalter is also evident in its expression of doubt. Belief was not easy to the Psalmists and they let us feel so. One symptom is the sudden interjection or disjunctive particle on which some Psalms open, making clear that they are breaking away upon their flights of faith from the grip of doubt or fear. *Ah but my soul waiteth upon God, ah but He is my rock and my salvation. Nevertheless*, says another singer after telling us what his doubts had been, *nevertheless continually I am with Thee*. These interjections and disjunctive particles speak volumes.

[1] These may be matched by several of Jeremiah's outcries, xvii. 18, xviii. 21–23, &c.

Sometimes it is the silence of God, and His seeming indifference towards flagrant injustice or cruelty, which weigh heavily upon the Psalmists, with in consequence their feelings of the vanity of righteousness and piety. Yet glimpses break through of the patience of the Divine Providence and assurances of the omnipotence of righteousness. On these the doubter rallies his spirit, and—this is significant of the honesty of the Hebrew mind—confesses how much of his doubt was due to his own ignorance, impatience and short temper. *For my heart was in a ferment and I was pricked in my reins; so brutish am I and ignorant, I was as a beast before Thee.*[1] In the history of the human mind is there an instance of doubt more candid than this? so honest a confession that the blame of men's pessimism and cynicism is not to be all put upon their hard experience of life, but may be, at least partly, due to their own short and envious tempers.

The veracity of the Hebrew Psalmists is nowhere more thorough than in such self-examination and faithful dealing with their souls—their passion and prayers to be searched and known and shown to themselves, and their call upon their own faculties to work with the Spirit of God to this end: *my reins also instruct me in the night seasons.*[2] In uttering their sense of sin their realism burns to a degree that sometimes scorches their art. The cowardice of sin, the breach of trust towards God and man, the personal shame, the curse on body and soul, all the workings of a guilty conscience, are rendered with a power that no mere dramatic aim, however high, could have achieved but only utter truth to human nature and to a man's experience of this in himself. No wonder that the Psalm-book of that little Hebrew people should have become the confessional of half mankind.

Over against such confessions of sin and folly the frequent asseverations of self-righteousness in the Psalter stand in con-

[1] Ps. lxxiii. 21 f.   [2] Ps. xvi. 7.

trast and indeed in apparent discordance. But many of these are obviously in the name of the Nation as a whole, and due to the national consciousness of a higher morality than that of their heathen neighbours or oppressors. They are very natural protests against the cruel afflictions which Israel suffered, even when honestly striving in the main to follow justice and fulfil the Law of their God. Others of these asseverations cannot be thus explained. They are clearly the utterances of persons urging their individual righteousness, which they do to a degree that would be offensive but for two considerations. First, we must remember that with very few exceptions even the most religious of Hebrews enjoyed no hope of any life, beyond this brief and transitory one, in which to vindicate themselves or be vindicated by Providence. So far their assertions of innocency or perfect obedience are natural and command our sympathy. And, second, these assertions may be viewed as just another side (from the frank confessions of sin) of that distinctive contribution which the Hebrew genius has made to the history of religion: the development of the place of the individual in religion, as the real human unit thereof, the emphasis of his spiritual claims and rights as against the Nation and even God Himself. If this emphasis be regarded as overdone by some Psalmists of the more complacent and self-satisfied kind, when urging their own righteousness, in such cases we only see once more the proof that the Psalmists were not tamed creatures performing parts, but real men pouring out what they actually felt, however narrow or however exaggerated this might be.

The Psalter's reflection of the loneliness of the human spirit is a signal instance of the experimental genius of the Hebrew mind, appealing as it does to both aspects of that universal experience of man—the loneliness of the deep and the loneliness of the height, the solitude of pain or doubt, temptation or sin, and the solitude of high unshareable responsibility. For the former of these Religion and Poetry in every age have given relief by peopling the battlefields of the heart and conscience, on which a man so often feels left to himself, with the memories of other spirits who have fought and conquered there; but the Psalter brings besides the assurance that even there the solitary struggler or defeated man shall find God's own Presence with him. Indeed, Hebrew faith has left to mankind no finer witness than the readiness in which it received and the fullness in which it has transmitted, by prophet as well as by psalmist, the gospel of the Divine participation not only in human sorrow and suffering—*in all our affliction He was afflicted*—but even in the shame and trouble of men's guilt, and in spiritual agony for their redemption and holiness. It is remarkable that a religion, which forbade the representation of the Deity in human or other earthly form, never hesitated in its poetry or prophecy to image Him as a Father full of pity, or as man's fellow in spiritual struggle, or even as a mother in travail for the birth of her children.

But while the Psalms thus redeem man's spirit from the loneliness of the deep they do not forget that of the height: the solitude of a great decision, of lofty office or lonely leadership. It is perhaps a king who cries out, *when my heart is overwhelmed lead me to the Rock that is higher than I.*

Again, the Psalms are full of a natural sympathy with the forces and beauties of God's world, and of the free enjoyment of all that is stored therein for the use of man. To creation they resort, sometimes to feel her streams and cataracts loosening the floods of their own gathered memories and regrets; sometimes to lift their eyes above all the littleness and despair of life to the horizons of new hope, the thresholds of coming salvation, which her hills present to their imagination; sometimes to draw peace to their hearts from her order and calm; sometimes to exult in her stormy energies and clamours, and to bring the swell and gladness of all her music into their praise of her Creator. How frank is their joyful acceptance of the boons, pleasures, and fruits of physical life: fertile fields and flocks; corn and oil and wine; fatness, fragrance, and richness of colour; the vigour and litheness of the body, fair faces, strong arms, and nimble feet; the fruitfulness of marriage and the joy of children! We have already noted how Hebrew poets linger over the movements of all forms of animal life, and their playfulness with its more uncouth shapes and gambols.

All these, then, are the bolder features of the Hebrew genius displayed in the Psalms, some of which have in error been looked upon as offences and scandals, yet all of which are proofs of their sincerity and genuineness. Carlyle used to say of his father, that he did 'not know of any man whose spiritual faculties had such a stamp of natural strength'. We may ascribe the like not only to the Hebrew Psalmists but to the Hebrew Prophets. They have that stamp of natural strength which sends their spiritual witness home to our hearts with power. Thorough and genuine as they are in their confession of human nature and experience, how can we doubt their records of intimate communion with the Spirit of God or the convictions which this gave them of the Divine Power and Mercy, of God's own seeking for the souls of men, of His readiness to forgive and His prevailing help to the weakest will that turns to righteousness? How impressive and of what guidance to our own generation, drifting from the assurance of immortality, is the way in which some Hebrew Psalmists rose, above the hereditary inability of their race to believe in a life beyond the grave, upon their experience of the love, the truthfulness, and the reasonableness of their God in this one!

No survey of the Hebrew genius is complete without reference to the Book of Job. Ours can only be brief, for a whole chapter were needed to estimate the literary power alone in which its author surpasses the rest of the Old Testament. The Book has been called a Drama and offered as proof that the Hebrews at last achieved one of the very great dramas of literature, if not the greatest of all. And indeed its use, like Shakespeare's, of the frame of an old story, its delivery of dialogues between contrasted characters and the vividness in which these characters gradually but passionately reveal themselves, might justify the designation. Yet the speeches are rather separate poems than parts of dialogue, though woven into a dramatic whole round the conduct and fate of a single personality and the confronting of his soul with the power of the Deity. But it is really indifferent how we define the form of the Book of Job. There Hebrew poetry, scattering on its flight its richest treasures of reflection and music, soars to its highest glory.

As regards the substance of the Book, we see in it the liberation at last of the religious genius of Israel from all national limits and prejudices. The scene is laid in, and the personages are gathered from, a land and atmosphere beyond those of Israel. Even the name of the national God is confined to those fragments of the old story of the hero which the author has preserved in the prologue, epilogue, and some formal headings of other sections of the work. But the stage and the personages selected are only the outward signs of an inward spiritual revolution: the bold effort to win the way out of all religious provincialism into that world of the spirit, of which men of every tribe and race are natives and citizens. In effecting this advance the author develops what, as we have seen, Hebrew prophets had already maintained, the right of the individual soul to measure its experience of life against doctrines of the Divine justice. He articulates more clearly the protests of psalmists and others against the dogma that human suffering is proof of human guilt; yet discards not only rigid doctrines of retribution but *all* human attempts to define the Divine will and duty. Never has the inadequacy of these attempts been so powerfully exposed in face of the infinite power and inscrutable wisdom of God as revealed in Creation. The author's ethical insight and skill in the analysis of character is conspicuous in his conception of his hero as afflicted not only by physical distresses, but by the sorer agony of having his honesty questioned and his character torn up by those who had been his friends; yet there is equal power in showing how so terrible a fate is discipline, stirring a man to deeper knowledge of himself, and without further attempt to solve the problems raised—a reserve which itself is a mark of power—in describing Job's ultimate repentance and surrender to God.

On those heights we may leave the religious genius of the Hebrews.

GEORGE ADAM SMITH.

Description of Fig. 5

BAS-RELIEF FROM ARCH OF TITUS

This arch was erected at Rome in celebration of the victory of Titus over the Jews, culminating with the fall of Jerusalem and the destruction of the Temple in A. D. 70. (A seventh-century Anglo-Saxon reminiscence of these events is shown in Fig. 18 between pp. 172 and 173.) The bas-relief here represented is in the passage of the arch.

The scene is occupied by a procession of laurel-crowned Roman soldiers bearing three standards. The soldiers wear no arms but carry on their shoulders the spoils from the Temple. In front is the golden table of shewbread (Exodus xxv. 23; 1 Kings vii. 48; 2 Chronicles iv. 19, and elsewhere). Crossing the table are two of the sacred silver trumpets (Numbers x. 2; 2 Chronicles v. 12, and elsewhere). Behind is a pediment on which stands the golden seven-branched candlestick (Exodus xxv. 31; Numbers viii. 2, and elsewhere). This bas-relief is now much defaced. A drawing made in the seventeenth century, when it was in better state, is shown in Fig. 69 on p. 432.

C. S.

FIG. 5. TRIUMPHAL PROCESSION WITH TEMPLE SPOILS FROM ARCH OF TITUS

For description see p. 28

HELLENISTIC JUDAISM

ACCORDING to a calculation made by Professor Eduard Meyer [1]—exceedingly doubtful, of course, as all such calculations must be, but still as probable as any we are likely to get—the whole people of Israel, before the Assyrian and Babylonian captivity, putting together Ephraim and Judah, numbered about three-quarters of a million. Six centuries later the Jews in the Roman Empire are calculated to have numbered something between four and seven millions. Israel, a scattered and subject people, had become a far more important factor in the world—numerically at any rate—than Israel, when comprised in two little Palestinian kingdoms under independent kings. It seems probable that in the Roman Empire out of every thousand men seventy were Jews—a higher percentage than is shown even in the United States to-day, where the Jews number only 36·8 in the thousand. To some extent this great increase of the people whose God was the Lord had come about through the accession of proselytes; in Palestine the Hasmonaean kings had forcibly incorporated Edomites and Galilaeans, and in the cities through which the Jews were dispersed many in those days of religious doubt and confusion sought shelter under the wings of the Divine Glory; their children became merged in the Jewish community; but mainly, no doubt, the increase was due to the natural growth of families. Jewish families seem in general—for whatever causes—to have been larger than Gentile families; [2] and the

---

[1] Under 'Bevölkerungswesen' in J. Conrad's *Handwörterbuch der Staatswissenschaften*.

[2] The causes are not perhaps to be sought exclusively in the morals of the pagan world, since even after the empire had become Christian, St. Jerome notes that the Jewish community was prolific in a peculiar degree

practice of 'throwing out'[1] unwanted infants, so common a measure of 'birth control' amongst the Greeks, was an abomination to the Jews.

Over all the lands round the Eastern Mediterranean the Greeks, in the days after Alexander, had spread their dominant culture; then Rome had come upon the scene, adopted the Greek tradition in literature, thought, and science, and added thereto its own genius for government and law, so that a culture half Hellenic became imposed upon the Latin West, and under that double Greco-Roman predominance the traditions of the other Mediterranean peoples had lost prestige and power. The oldest tradition of all, the one most associated with ancient greatness, the Egyptian, merely lingered on as a doctrine transmitted in an unknown tongue in a close corporation of priests in one province of the Empire, or penetrated in a weak adulterated form, with the Hellenized cult of Isis and Sarapis, to other Mediterranean lands. As a factor in the future European and Near-Eastern world the Egyptian tradition would count for very little. There was only one tradition in that Mediterranean world which did not go down under the predominance of Greece and Rome, which met them with equal power and showed a unique stubbornness of resistance— the tradition of Israel. Judaism might indeed enter into various combinations with Hellenism, in which the Jewish tradition underwent notable modification, but it always gave as well as received, and in the end, Greek intellectual culture and Roman imperial sagacity had to accept the supremacy of a Hebraic religion.

An exceedingly odd people, not only odd, unlike all other

'Usque in praesentem diem pullulat filios et nepotes' (Comm. on Isaiah xlviii. 7).

[1] Ἐὰν ἦν ἄρσενον, ἄφες, ἐὰν ἦν θήλεα, ἔκβαλε. Pap. Oxyrh. iv. 744. In the famous 'Hippocratic Oath' abortion is abjured, but Dr. Singer believes this document not to be older than the first century A.D.

peoples, but holding fast to their peculiarities, cherishing them, separating themselves deliberately and persistently from the general body of mankind—that was the first aspect which the Jews presented to the Greeks. But the oddity did not in the first instance repel: on the contrary it seemed rather interesting. A community of 'philosophers' was the way the Greeks put it, when the little Jewish state established under its High Priests on the uplands of Palestine first came within their purview. Aristotle's disciples, Clearchus and Theophrastus, were the first Greek writers—so far as we know—to speak of them, at a time when the peoples of Nearer Asia had only just come under Macedonian rule. Greek philosophers were fond of describing imaginary republics in which life was regulated by some novel system of law. Well, here was a real community with a mass of peculiar ordinances which seemed to constitute a system of life always going on with that stability and rhythm the Greek ideal required. 'They spend their time', wrote Theophrastus, 'conversing on divine matters and observing the stars at night, calling upon the Divinity the while, as they do so.' The Jews must certainly have told Greek inquirers that their relation to the Divinity was one of peculiar intimacy. And if a Greek witnessed the worship in a Jewish synagogue, he may well have been impressed. What were these people doing, what were they saying and reading aloud in a tongue he could not understand? They were conversing on divine matters. There was nothing like that in the worship of a Greek temple. The nearest thing he knew to it was the talk in a philosophic school. A 'nation of philosophers'!

Hecataeus of Abdera, a Greek historical writer, contemporary with Theophrastus, described the community in Jerusalem—the symmetry and punctual discipline, twelve tribes to correspond with the twelve months, the young men trained, as at Sparta, to courage and endurance. The Greeks in those days were inclined rather to idealize this strange people they had just come to know than to decry them. Strange they certainly were, Hecataeus did not attempt to deny that. Their founder Moses—' a man of extraordinary sagacity and courage '—had deliberately made their customs unlike those of other peoples in order to keep them a nation apart. And there was some excuse for it. The Jewish exclusiveness was the answer to the intolerance of the Egyptians who had driven them out of Egypt in the days of old. No Antisemite note as yet. But it was all very well to find the Jewish peculiarity and exclusiveness something curious and interesting when you looked at it from far off, there on the grey hills of Judea; it was quite another matter when you had this people close beside you, in your own city. And this came about more and more in the days of Alexander, as the Jewish Dispersion grew in all the cities of the Mediterranean world. Then it was—it could hardly be otherwise—that the exclusiveness, the assumption of religious superiority, began to mean trouble. Why do these people, the Greek townsmen complained, fix themselves here in our midst and expect us to treat them as neighbours, when they hold themselves apart from all the social amenities of our city, shun our festivals, avoid gymnasium and theatre? In a society for which occasions of communal enjoyment meant as much as they did for the Greek city-states, such exclusiveness, such obstinate unsociability in a particular set of people, could not fail to create resentment and hatred. And the Jews could justify their aloofness only by explaining that all the festivities and amusements in a Greek city involved some offering of homage to gods which were foul idols—whereby they only made matters worse; for the Greek townsman, even if not deeply religious, was sensitive regarding the honour of his city's gods. ' Great is Artemis of the Ephesians! '

It was perhaps in Alexandria that Antisemitism had its beginning; the number of Jews here was considerable almost from the city's foundation. Things did not, so far as our

Hellenistic Judaism

knowledge goes, come to actual pogroms till Roman times, but Antisemitism in literature began as early as the reigns of the first Ptolemies. The first Greek book we know of in which the Jews were held up to odium was not written by a Greek, but by an Egyptian, Manetho, who wrote, under the patronage of the Ptolemaic court, a history of his people for the Greek public (early third century B. C.). He gave currency to the story that the Jews were descended from a section of the Egyptian people which had been expelled from Egypt because they were afflicted with leprosy and scrofula. The enmity between Jews and Egyptians was of old standing, and more bitter than the enmity between Jews and Greeks. About a hundred years later (just about the time when Antiochus Epiphanes was trying to suppress the Jewish religion in Palestine) a Greek called Mnaseas wrote against the Jews; the popular belief that the Jews kept the image of an ass's head in the Temple was perhaps first set afloat by Mnaseas. In the last century before the Christian era the principal Greek men of letters, Posidonius and Apollonius Molon, were Antisemitic, though, curiously enough, the historian Timagenes, although an Alexandrine, does not appear to have been so, to judge by what has been transmitted of his work through Trogus and Justin. Literary Antisemitism went on after Egypt had passed under the Romans, represented especially by the vain pedant, Apion, who is chiefly remembered because the short apologetic work of Josephus came to be called *Against Apion*. But in the first century of the Christian era Antisemitism at Alexandria passed from literature into violent action, in the pogrom of A. D. 38, described for us by Philo; fighting between the Jews and Greeks occurred in 66 and ended in a great massacre of the Jews by the Roman troops; after the destruction of Jerusalem in 73, Jewish Zealots from Palestine tried to stir up a revolt in Egypt, which was choked by the Romans in blood; finally in 115 a regular racial war between Jews and Gentiles broke out in Egypt, the Jews apparently this time the aggressors, and was not stamped out till terrible atrocities had been committed on both sides. After the last flare-up of Jewish nationalism, in the rebellion of Bar-Kochba (A. D. 132 to 135), had been suppressed in Palestine, Antisemitism expressed itself mainly in heavy taxation, till the Empire became Christian. Then, the very fact that the new religion of the Empire started from Hebraic presuppositions brought the other Hebraic religion into collision with the State in a new way: Judaism appeared as a wicked perversity: the old Paganism, in matters of religion, had been comparatively easygoing. The Antisemitism of the Christian Empire took the form, not of pogroms, but of the subjection of the Jews to various disabilities; honorable careers, open to them under the Pagan emperors, were henceforth closed to them—the army, for instance. Pagans had had no objection to resorting to Jewish physicians; Saint John Chrysostom declared that a Christian had much better die.

The Antisemitism of the Pagan world sprang simply from the resentment felt by Greek city populations at a set of people who refused to share in their social interests and amusements. Morose separation—*odium generis humani*—that was the ever-recurring charge. But, generally speaking, while the Jews were unpopular with the Greek man in the street, they found protectors and patrons in the kings. If rights and immunities were accorded them in the cities of the Greek world, that was because the kings brought *force majeure* to bear upon the cities to secure them. The Hellenistic kings who ruled different tracts of what had been Alexander's empire saw in this far-spread people an element which might serve their purposes. The Greek city-states with their ineradicable desire for independence, their political passion, were apt to be troublesome to the ruler in whose sphere of power they were situate. In a huge straggling realm, like the Seleucid, embracing a great number of heterogeneous elements, the problem of binding it together under the supreme government was a difficult one. A people who had little interest in the political rights of the cities wherein they sojourned—so long as they were left in peace to practise their religion and follow their business—who were loyal upholders of the powers that be, because order and security were what they chiefly needed in this world, and who, finally, though diffused through the cities, to some extent kept in touch with each other as a single community—such a people offered just the kind of cement which the ruler of a realm without national coherence wanted. In every city of his realm there would be this element on the side of the government.

Also, the Jews made good soldiers. We are too liable to think of the Jews in those times as just like the Jews of medieval and pre-emancipation times—people addicted peculiarly to finance and usury, with little aptitude, or rather opportunity, for agriculture and war. It was in Christian Europe, after so many walks had been shut to them, that the Jews betook themselves on a large scale to the handling of money, and developed those exceptional capacities which some people suppose to inhere in the Jewish nature as such. In the ancient world the Jews had no special reputation as financiers or usurers. Josephus, at the end of the first century A. D., was able to write—he was speaking of the Jews of Palestine, 'We are not a commercial people; we live in a country without a seaboard and have no inclination to trade'.[1] If you put together all the things said against the Jews in the remains of Greek and Latin Antisemitic literature, you never find that they are attacked as usurers.[2] Think of the contrast with the Antisemitism of

---

[1] Josephus, *c. Ap.* i, § 60.

[2] We have, indeed, one document which might seem to contain such an implication—a letter, recovered from the dust of Egypt, written in A.D. 41 by a Greek merchant to a friend in Alexandria who is hard put to it to find money to meet his obligations. 'Whatever you do,' the merchant writes,

medieval and modern times! In Palestine, the Jews seem to have engaged principally in agriculture. In Egypt large numbers of them were enrolled in the Ptolemaic army, and many of them were apparently granted, as military colonists, plots of land which they might cultivate in the intervals of active service. In the letter from Antiochus III to Zeuxis, the governor of Asia Minor,[1] we see 2,000 Jewish families transported from Babylonia to Lydia and Phrygia. They are to serve as a military colony, being settled especially in the fortified towns and other places which command the lines of communication, in order to hold down the Greek and native inhabitants who have shown signs of revolting against Seleucid rule. What fighters the Jews could be was seen in the war of independence against the son of Antiochus III. Julius Caesar and the early Roman Emperors followed the policy of the Hellenistic kings in patronizing and protecting the Jews, in insisting that Alexandria and other Greek cities should grant the Jews in their midst liberty to follow their religion and their customs unmolested.[2] Expressions of loyalty to the kings and emperors on the part of Greek cities regularly took the form of rendering them divine honours. The Jews were especially dispensed from sharing in these public acts, and allowed to express their loyalty in ways which did not offend their conscience—praying and offering sacrifice *for* the human ruler, not *to* him.

Till the mutual goodwill subsisting between the imperial

'keep clear of the Jews' ($\beta\lambda\acute{\epsilon}\pi\epsilon$ σατὸν ἀπὸ τῶν Ἰουδαίων). But we have to remember that the letter was written just after the enmity between Greeks and Jews in Alexandria had culminated in a pogrom; that, probably, not any general ill-fame of the Jews as usurers, was the reason why a Greek in Alexandria might do well, at that moment, to keep clear of the Jews.

[1] Josephus, *Archaeol.* xii, §§ 148 ff. Doubts have been thrown on the genuineness of the letter, but there is nothing to show that it is not genuine. Eduard Meyer accepts it as such.

[2] Whether the Jews had the status of 'citizens' of Alexandria is a vexed question. See H. I. Bell, *Jews and Christians in Egypt* (1924).

government and the Jews gave place, in the course of the first century A. D., to that bitter enmity which led to the destruction of the Jewish state in Palestine, it was only occasionally, in consequence of the eccentricity of particular rulers and of some special circumstances, that kings or emperors showed hostility to the Jews. The first instance would be that of Ptolemy IV Philopator (in 217 B.C.), if we could take the substance of 3 Maccabees as historical.[1] Leaving that problematic narrative aside, the episode of Antiochus Epiphanes (in 165 B.C.) stands out as a strange landmark in history. The Jews had long known what it was to be subject to Gentile rulers, to have to meet their demands for tribute, to be removed at their will from one country to another, but they had never before experienced the attempt of a Gentile ruler to suppress their religion by forcible persecution. Antiochus IV, with his theatrical vein, was enthusiastic for the externals of Hellenism ; no doubt too, he was influenced by the impatience felt generally by the Greek city-populations at the obstinate separation of the Jews, and thought that this barbaric nonsense could be disposed of, if only the ruler gave the Jews plainly to understand by drastic action that he would stand it no longer. We must remember too, that numbers of the richer and more ambitious Jews had voluntarily embraced Hellenism, and they may well have represented their faithful countrymen to Antiochus not only as passively obstinate, but as actively intolerant. The faithful in Jerusalem had no doubt made things in various ways unpleasant for the Hellenizers, and when Antiochus resorted to force against the faithful, he may have

[1] There is an able defence of the historical character of 3 Macc. by Dr. Abrahams in the *Jewish Quarterly Review* for October 1896. It seems to me, however, much more probable that if the elephant story has an historical basis, the Ptolemy in question was Euergetes II, as Josephus says. If Philopator had tried to penetrate into the Temple, as 3 Macc. affirms, the silence of Daniel (ch. xi) in its review of the doings of Ptolemies and Seleucids would seem to me inexplicable.

considered that his persecution was directed against the persecutors. The result was, of course, far different from what Antiochus had anticipated—a revolt which the Seleucid power was unable to suppress, and the establishment of an independent Jewish state in Palestine under the priestly Hasmonaean dynasty for seventy-nine years (142 to 63 B.C.). Yet that was not really the most important result of the persecution. That May day of 142, indeed, when the victorious Jewish nationalists entered the citadel of Jerusalem ' with praise and palm branches and with harps and with cymbals and with viols and with hymns and with songs ', must have seemed to them the coming of the kingdom of God; yet we, who look back, can see that it was not really of great consequence, either for the inner life of the Jewish community, or for the mission of Israel in the world, that the Jewish state in Palestine won seventy-nine years of precarious political independence under worldly kings, before Rome was ready to take over the heritage of Alexander in the East. But the persecution had an effect upon the inner life of the Jewish people far more important than its transitory political consequences.

There shone out in that intense moment the sterner and sublimer qualities which later Hellenism, and above all the Hellenism of Syria, hardly knew—uncompromising fidelity to an ideal, endurance raised to the pitch of utter self-devotion, a passionate clinging to purity. They were qualities for the lack of which all the riches of Hellenic culture could not compensate. It was an epoch in history. The agony created new human types, and new forms of literature, which became permanent, were inherited by Christendom. The figure of the martyr, as the Church knows it, dates from the persecution of Antiochus; all subsequent martyrologies derive from the Jewish books, which recorded the sufferings of those who in that day ' were strong and did exploits '.[1] After this, their religion

---

[1] This paragraph was written twenty-four years ago in my ' House of Seleucus ' : at Dr. Abrahams's request I re-embodied it in this chapter.

would have for the Jews a new consecration. Further, the experience of having to face martyrdom made a new conception of life beyond death common amongst the Jews. It is questionable how far before this the idea of personal immortality, of a hope for the righteous on the other side of death, had gone with the Jewish faith. Traces of it in the Old Testament are faint. But from now onwards unquestionably the outlook of the pious in Israel received this great extension, even if the conservative circle of the priestly aristocracy at Jerusalem, the Sadducees, as they were called, would have none of it. True, Rabbinic Judaism was of another temper than those visionaries who composed the Jewish apocalyptical literature flung abroad in the century before, and the century following, the Christian era, but the belief in personal immortality beyond the grave—that, at any rate, the Rabbis took over as a fixed article of orthodox Judaism for the time to come.

In the clash between Hellenism and Hebraism at Jerusalem as the books of the Maccabees represent it to us, Hellenism appears as something purely evil—the embodiment of the world principle at enmity with God, a matter of sensuous idolatrous pomps, impious gaieties, pride of power. When the faithful in Zion saw Hellenism like that, they did not see it altogether untruly. In many of its representations Hellenism did mean just that. That there were other elements in Hellenism, of whose value the faithful in Zion had probably no conception, is also true. Few of the Jews in Palestine, it is likely, had any knowledge of Greek beyond one or two phrases of everyday use, and the difference in language alone would cut them off from any possibility of appreciating those riches of human thought and feeling embodied in Greek literature and the Greek intellectual tradition. Men who spoke only Aramaic could judge Hellenism only by its outside.

The case of the Jews dispersed through the cities of the Greek world was wholly different. Greek became their mother-tongue. In Egypt, where the Jewish element was stronger than in any other Mediterranean country outside Palestine and Syria (125 Jews in every thousand about the Christian era), it was necessary, apparently as early as the reign of Ptolemy II (283–246 B. C.), for the Law to be translated into Greek in order that its contents might be kept in the memory of the Egyptian Jews. They became, most of them, quite incapable of reading or understanding their Scriptures in the original Hebrew.[1] A myth conveniently developed amongst the Egyptian Jews declared that the Seventy Translators of the Law had been as directly and verbally inspired as Moses; the translation was as good as the original. In the course of the next century or two the rest of the Old Testament was translated into Greek for the benefit of the Greek-speaking Jews and, being added to the translation of the Pentateuch, came to form that version of the Jewish scriptures which we know to-day as the Septuagint.

But Jews speaking Greek and living in daily contact with their Greek fellow-townsmen could not remain ignorant of the intellectual and spiritual heritage of Greece. In Alexandria indeed, that part of Hellenism which consisted in idolatrous pomps and impious gaieties was even more conspicuous than it can have been to the Jews of Jerusalem. In no city of the Greek world were these things more in evidence than in this great Levantine city of riches and merchandise. Processions with the images of Isis and Sarapis, of Dionysos and Aphrodite and Adonis, passed continually along its broad streets: its population went mad about chariot-races or the latest musical star. But in Alexandria the other elements of Hellenism were also close at hand. It was the city of the Museum, the greatest university of the Greek world for literature and science, royally endowed, the city with the world's largest library. In days

[1] A man so profoundly devoted to Judaism as Philo never even discovered that the Κύριος of the Septuagint represented the Hebrew IHVH.

when literature was embodied throughout the Mediterranean world in rolls made of papyrus fibre, a plant found in any quantities only in the country of the Nile, it was natural that Alexandria was a chief place for making the books with which the Mediterranean lands, as a whole, were supplied. In no other city would the Jewish townsman see more continually passed from hand to hand those little rolls containing the wisdom of the Greeks, would he more often hear the immortal words, written in Athens a century, two or three centuries, before, read aloud; hundreds of young Jews, if for no other reason than the necessity of learning how to read and write Greek correctly, according to the standard of educated society, must themselves have unrolled and studied those Gentile writings.

And then something happened in their souls unlike anything which had happened in Israel before. There was no doubt a clearly marked principle, laid down in the Law, which had given their fathers sufficient guidance in their dealings with Gentiles. 'After the doings of the land of Egypt wherein ye dwelt shall ye not do; and after the doings of the land of Canaan, whither I bring you, shall ye not do: neither shall ye walk in their ordinances' (Leviticus xviii. 3). But here was something of quite a new kind. Imagine what it must have been to a young Jew, whose mind was filled from his infancy with the solemn exhortations of the Law, the rich imagery of the prophets, the cries of Psalmists after the living God, when, for the first time, he heard read, or read himself, the utterance of Plato, quite different from anything in his own books, and yet so thrilling in its deep passion for justice and temperance, in its faith that behind the world movement there was a Power which cared for good. Or, it may be, he would make acquaintance with some living Greek Stoic whose philosophy really governed his life—some one who made you feel by the touch of his personality, by some strange power in his eyes that nothing except goodness and inner freedom was worth desire.

Here surely the young Jew, loyal to his God, would find something akin, something which drew him by its likeness to his own ideals of righteousness, and yet something, in other respects, unlike, dissonant, Gentile. He might well be perplexed. It was impossible simply to turn your back on all that as you had done on the fantastic superstitions of Egypt or Canaan. You could hardly cast out Hellenism of that kind as evil. And yet was it safe to let it creep, with its subtle subduing power, into a mind which ought to be consecrated to the Law?

The inner conflict which the Jews of the Dispersion had to go through in their contact with Hellenism was in a way more difficult than the conflict of the martyrs at Jerusalem, where good and evil had been seen so plainly marked off in white and black. And we to-day, whether we are Jews or Christians, may regard the Hellenistic Jews of two thousand years ago as bearing the first brunt in a conflict in which we too are engaged. For their problem is still in a way our problem. In the civilization of the European peoples the Hebrew and Greek traditions have entered into combination, but their mutual adjustment still raises questions on which men are not agreed. Both in the Jewish community and in Christian community to-day there is an opposition between Traditionalist and Modernist, Orthodox and Liberal, which really springs from the old difficulty, how to harmonize the claims of the God of Israel with the claims of intellectual culture—an opposition which exists not only between man and man, but often within the individual himself.

When we take up what remains of Jewish Hellenistic literature—especially the works of Philo of Alexandria—we may be sure that behind this smooth-flowing stream of discourse there is a long history of doubt and questioning, of struggle and controversy, in the society from which it comes. What had gone on for centuries in the heart of the Jewish community at Alexandria is covered with silence for us now, without record.

But we hear echoes occasionally through the writings of Philo of the disagreements and arguments by which the Jewish community had been exercised in the attempt to solve its standing problem, to find the true adjustment between the two traditions of Israel and of Greece. It was plain, of course, to an Alexandrine Jew who remained faithful to his God at all, that certain things in the Greek tradition he must firmly repel—the worship of the popular gods, or the practice of exposing infants, or perversions of the sexual instinct. But that left a margin of things upon which religious Jews might differ. There was the theatre, for instance. Some of the Rabbis condemned all attendance at a Greek theatre; it was the 'seat of the scorners' spoken of in the first Psalm; Philo, on the other hand, apparently went to see performances of the great Greek dramas, as something permissible, nay profitable. To draw the line, to say exactly how far a loyal Jew might participate in the interests of the surrounding Greek society, must often have been exceedingly difficult. The pain of conscientious scruples, friction between parents and children, divisions between friends—all those things which our analogous problems cause to-day, must have been known well enough two thousand years ago in Alexandria.

And if it was a problem what you might admit of Hellenism, it was also a problem what you must retain of the Hebrew tradition. To-day the difficulty largely comes as a conflict between religion and science, because our modern civilization is scientific to a far greater degree than the ancient Hellenism. It was the aesthetic, rather than the scientific, element in Greek culture which made the difficulty in those days. To a man who had the Greek view of the world many practices involved in the Jewish religion seemed uncouth, barbarous, ugly—especially circumcision. The Hellenistic Jews took the line of defending their peculiar practices as figurative. Jews were forbidden, they explained, to eat birds of prey in order that it might be impressed upon their minds how wrong it was to domineer over their fellow-men: they were ordered to eat animals with cloven hoofs, in order that they might be reminded to make the proper ethical distinctions; circumcision signified the cutting off of passions and ungodly opinions, and so on. But this was a very precarious line. For if you once defend an external practice, simply because it is useful as a symbol, it is very hard to assert it as obligatory for all times and all places. And we find, indeed, that some Liberal Jews of those days went so far as to throw over the external practices which seemed absurd from the Greek point of view. The source from which Strabo drew his account of Judaism appears to have been derived from some such circle. The original teaching of Moses, he says, was a pure ethical monotheism—or rather, as he describes it, pantheism—all that God required was clean living and righteousness, and the objectionable external practices were just a later adulteration of the religion, brought in after the successors of Moses had fallen into superstition. Philo speaks of Jews in Alexandria who maintained that the ritual and ceremonial practices might be discarded, because all that mattered was the spiritual truth they were intended to inculcate. Philo disagreed with them, and he argues that these parts of the Law should still be literally observed. But his argument shows how far he had himself gone towards the position he condemns. For he condemns those who give up the external practices chiefly on the ground that by so doing they isolate themselves, as individuals, from the general life of the community, and create unnecessary offence—not on the ground that the practices in question are an inscrutable command of God.

Whatever view Jews or Christians to-day may take of that ancient controversy, it is plain that the problem of finding the right line was a difficult and painful one for the Hellenistic Jews. In the sphere of religious thought, Philo's writings

Hellenistic Judaism

show us the most elaborate attempt at a synthesis. Much in that attempt cannot but appear fantastic to us to-day, yet it remains an attempt of extraordinary interest, and later on had a marked influence upon Christian thought. To take Philo as a philosopher is, I believe, a mistake [1] and leads to an unfair estimate of his value. So much in his writing is taken from Plato, or the Stoics, often he so obviously tries to write like Plato, that it seems, at first, the natural thing to take Philo too as a writer of philosophy. But the essentially philosophic interest in Plato, the desire to find a theory of the universe which can stand the scrutiny of rigidly logical reason, is not Philo's interest. He is a religious preacher. He uses philosophical terms and ideas for a homiletic purpose. His interest is in a particular kind of religious experience, emotional experience. He has to turn men's desires towards that, and tell them how they must rule their inner life in order to attain it. The life of the soul, the hindrances which prevent its reaching the beatific vision, the wrong directions in which it may so easily turn—that is Philo's province. He is a spiritual director. If anything in his writings still has value to-day, it is in the field of psychology and of practical religion—not of metaphysics or systematic theology.

The experience which for Philo is the crown of the religious life, that to which everything else leads up and is subsidiary, is the experience which is ordinarily described as 'mystical'

---

[1] I had forgotten, when I wrote this, that in Mr. Claude Montefiore's fine chapter on 'Hellenistic Contributions' in his 'Old Testament and After' he says more than once, 'Philo is a philosopher.' But I hope there is not as grave a contradiction between my view and his as might appear from this. The term 'philosopher' is used with different shades of meaning. I only mean that Philo's interest is not to get a rational explanation of the Universe. Mr. Montefiore himself writes (p. 485): 'Philo is not a mere philosopher in the sense of a man who has a mere intellectual curiosity to know the truth.' If you leave out the 'mere', that is precisely what I wanted to say.

in the special sense of that word. As a matter of human psychology, it is beyond controversy—whatever value you may attach to the experience—that certain people under certain conditions do go through an experience which, they say, cannot be adequately described in words to those who have not themselves been through it. But they can tell us certain of its characteristics ; and the accounts given of it by different people in different ages, and belonging to different races, so correspond, that we cannot take the mystical experience, as such, to be something peculiar to any one race or form of religion. One characteristic is that the individual seems to be lifted out of his ordinary life of successive thoughts and feelings ; the flow of time ceases ; the soul is absorbed into an eternal Now. Another characteristic is that the individual seems to come into direct contact with some tremendous Reality; he has a sense of extraordinary intellectual clarity, the Universe lies before him an open book. And the experience is accompanied by a wonderful expansive joy. In what Philo tells us of the mystical experience these characteristics are distinctly marked.

'If any yearning enters into thee, O Soul, of inheriting the good things of God, thou must leave, not only thy " country "—that is, the Body—and thy " kindred "—Sense-perception, and the " house of thy father "—thy Reason—but thou must even run away from thy *self*, " go out from " thy *self*—inspired by a kind of prophetic afflatus, like those possessed by the Corybantic or Bacchic frenzy. For the mind, in this condition of frenzy, no longer in itself, but exalted and maddened by heavenly love, led along by the One Really Real, pulled upwards towards Him, while truth goes in advance and removes impediments, so that the Soul may travel along a plain road—behold, this is the inheritance ! ' (*Quis Rerum Divinarum Haeres*, §§ 69, 70.)

'When the Soul, through the whole extent of its words and works, is spread out flat and filled with God, then the call of the Senses ceases, all the troublesome and ill-omened noises—the voices of Sight and Sound and Smell and all Sense-perception—they all cease, when the Mind " goes out " from the City of the Soul, and refers her doings and her thoughts to God.' (*Legum Allegor*. iii, § 44.)

'To what soul does it belong to hide and put away evil, save to the soul to which God has been made manifest, which He has counted worthy of His unutterable mysteries? For He saith, "I will not hide from Abraham my servant the thing which I do." Even so, O Saviour, Thou hast shown Thy own works to the soul which yearned after beauty and *hast hid from it nothing of all Thy works*.' (*Legum Allegor.* iii, § 27.)

Now one thing which seems immediately obvious is that when Philo gives to the mystical experience this place in religion, his affinity is rather with Plato than with the Old Testament. For in Plato the religious-mystical vein is there as well as the philosophical vein, and it was that element in Plato upon which Philo laid hold. Philo's language in describing the mystical experience is clearly suggested by Plato's language in the *Symposium* and the *Phaedrus*. Even Aristotle held that the highest state of man is not that of moral action, but that in which he contemplates ecstatically absolute Being, his activity being then most like God's. Philo is in this respect Greek, not Hebrew. For one may consider it a thing especially notable in the religion of the Bible, both the Old Testament and the New, how slight the mystical element in it is. There are experiences like the visions of Isaiah and Ezekiel, and the rapture of St. Paul 'to the third heaven'—but such things are quite subordinate and incidental. The essence of religion is not there, but in the conformity of the human will to God's will in practical everyday life. 'He hath shewed thee, O man, what is good; and what doth the Lord require of thee, but to do justly, and to love mercy, and to walk humbly with thy God?'[1] 'Not every one that saith unto me Lord, Lord, shall enter into the kingdom of heaven, but he that doeth the will of my Father which is in heaven.'[2]

The mystical experience does not seem, of itself, to have necessarily any spiritual value. It may be induced by particular drugs, after the way of certain Oriental mystics. The sense

[1] Micah vi. 8. [2] Matthew vii. 21.

of immense knowledge which it gives does not mean necessarily any extension of real knowledge. Different ways may lead up to it, and its value seems to depend on the way by which it is reached, upon the whole life of the soul which forms its context. For although the person who goes through it seems to be taken quite out of his ordinary life, he is himself made what he is by his ordinary life, with its series of voluntary choices and reactions to the Universe, and according to his general attitude to the Universe will be the effect of the mystical experience upon his subsequent life—different, for instance, in the case of a theist and in the case of a pantheist. Various kinds of interest may find in the mystical experience a moment of intense concentration, which will afterwards raise their power over the soul. With Plato the mystical ecstasy was connected with the contemplation of true general concepts for which his whole life was a search; with an artist it may be induced by the revelation of some visible beauty; with a musician by some wonder of sound. We must ask then, in the case of Philo, what was the attitude to God, with which he rose to the mystical experience, and to which that experience gave an indescribable consecration? And here the answer must be, that it was essentially, and all the time, Hebrew, Old Testament, not Greek.

The abasement of the creature before the Creator, the adoring gratitude to Some One who gives by a distinct act of His will to the unworthy, to whom every good that a man has, material or spiritual, must be ascribed; at the same time Some One who will receive from the human creature the expression, poor as it may be, of his thanks and love and praise—all that, so central in Old Testament religion, was also central in the religion of Philo. The mode by which he thought to come into contact with God was Greek, but the God with whom he desired to come into contact was the God of Israel.[1]

---

[1] I cannot think that Siegfried is right in accusing Philo of having

Hellenistic Judaism

Philo, as has been said, must be thought of as a religious preacher, a director of souls. And the religion he sought to develop in men, was, in the essential character of its attitude to God, Hebraic. But again he borrowed largely from the Greeks in forming a method of soul-cultivation, of training, *askesis*. The Greeks first had turned their eyes inwards, observed the processes of mental life, distinguished and classified the faculties and activities of the soul. A scheme for methodical training of the inner life would be impossible apart from some articulated psychology, and that the old Hebrews had not possessed. A rich inner life indeed is implied in the Psalms, but it was spontaneous and *naïve* in its expression, not curiously introspective. Philo had the Greek psychology ready to hand, and he could use it to frame rules for the systematic training of the Soul to receive the vision of God. The psychological observations of which Philo's writings are full are often in themselves interesting; sometimes they are apt to seem to us commonplace only because since Philo's time they have been so frequently repeated in religious literature that they have come for us now to be truisms. An anthology from Philo might find many sentences of psychological import worth recording. Take for example the following:

'Often we have an agreeable taste and do not know what causes it; we smell sweet smells and have no idea what they are: even so, the

---

abandoned the God of Israel for an empty abstraction. It is true that Philo sometimes calls God ἄποιος 'without qualities', but it seems to me quite plain that Philo did not mean by this that He was without positive character. He means that no description we may attempt to give of God by assigning attributes to him (Righteousness, Goodness, &c.) is adequate to the Reality. One may set against Siegfried's view Mr. Montefiore's words: 'Not least is he Jewish in the most fundamental portion of his teaching—his doctrine of God. It is not the impersonal divine Reason to which Philo is constantly seeking to draw near, which he yearns to understand, for which he feels reverence and love, but it is the living God.' Surely that is profoundly right.

Soul has often a sense of joy, but cannot tell what it is that has made her glad.' (*Legum Allegor.* iii, § 173.)

Instructions for the conduct and development of the spiritual life have formed throughout the centuries a regular branch of Christian literature. Books of this kind continue to be issued to-day. Philo is the first master in this line; the earliest Christian writers who follow it wrote under his influence; here, too, we can trace in Christianity the heritage of Judea—the heritage of Judea and of Greece combined.

Philo's heart, his attitude to God, his religion, remain Hebrew. But Philo's Hebraism, genuine as it is, carries on only part of the older Hebraism. We may, I think, say that the three essential elements of the Hebraic view of the world are: (1) an apprehension of God as righteous Will, Some One who does definite 'mighty acts' in the world-process; and hence (2) a conception of the world-process as a process in Time, which embodies a Divine plan beginning in God's mighty act of creation and leading up to a great consummation in the future; (3) an association of the Divine plan with a Divine community, a 'people of God' chosen to be the vehicle of God's purpose, so that the ultimate consummation is a communal bliss, the community redeemed, blessed, and glorious. In these three respects the Hebrew view offered a singular contrast to the Greek view for which: (1) God, when once the primitive and naïve polytheism had been left behind, tended to become immovable Being, to which men might indeed strive to attain, but which did not do particular acts in the world-process; (2) the world-process was a vain eternal recurrence, a circular movement, leading nowhere; and (3) deliverance was attained by the individual when he detached himself in soul from the world, not through his incorporation in a Divine community of the blessed.

When now we look at Philo we see that he has the first element finely and strongly, though in a somewhat changed form. God is for him an essentially righteous and beneficent Will who does mighty acts, but the mighty acts which Philo cares about are not done in the broad field of history, but in the Soul. God ' plants virtues ' in the Soul. The precepts of the Law which warn the children of Israel not to take any credit to themselves for the conquest of the land of Canaan are transferred by Philo from the literal fields of the Holy Land to the inner life. It is the supreme sin when a man says of his virtues ' I planted these '. Because Philo remains Hebrew all the time, he takes all that man attains in the inner life to be concrete acts of God's gracious Will, and prostrates himself in adoration and gratitude and confession of his own nothingness in a way quite foreign to the Greek man of virtue. But the second and third elements of the Hebraic tradition are dim in Philo. He believes, of course, in a general way—in the way the Stoics believed—that the course of the world is governed by God's providence: one special tract of his, which we have in an Armenian version, the *De Providentia*, is directed to defend this belief. But the Hebrew conception of a particular world-plan embodied in a Divine community—that Philo has only dimly. There are a few—very few—' Messianic ' passages in his writings; passages in which he indicates his hope that some day the people of Israel will be gathered by God, and the people of Israel be extended to include the multitude of the nations—for ' Israel ', Philo insists, means ' the man who sees God ', and any man of any nation who attains the beatific vision is to be taken as belonging to Israel in as full a sense as those who are physically children of Abraham—but such hopes are indicated by Philo only faintly and vaguely. His abiding interest is not directed to the future, but to what God does now in the individual human Soul.

And in order to see rightly the place which Philo occupies in the history of Hebraic religion, it is important to notice that the two elements which have almost faded out in his religion are carried on strongly in Christianity—though, of course, in a form of which Judaism disapproves. For the essential elements in Christianity are : (1) the belief in mighty creative and redemptive acts of God; (2) in a world-plan initiated and carried out by such acts and leading up to a great future consummation; and (3) in connecting the world-plan with a Divine community, whose perfection in heavenly bliss is the end to which the whole creation moves. Whilst, therefore, we may say that Philo, in so far as he does not put forward additions to the old Hebrew view which are as unacceptable to Judaism as those of Christianity, represents a *purer* Jewish type, we may say, on the other hand, that, inasmuch as elements of the Hebraic view, which have almost faded out in Philo, are carried on strongly (though in a changed form) by Christianity, Christianity is in that sense more *fully* Hebraic than Philo.

The two things which mainly make Philo's religion appear fantastic to modern men are his far-fetched method of allegorical interpretation applied to Scripture, and his theories of intermediate beings between God and the world, especially the Logos. With regard to the first we must remember that it will not have seemed equally fantastic to his contemporaries, whether Jews or Greeks. To Philo the Scriptures, as he read them in Greek, were an oracular utterance, with characteristics which the Greeks habitually attributed to oracles. To any one who had had a Greek literary education the language of the Septuagint must have seemed generally uncouth and very often obscure. But that was just what inspired utterances, according to the Greek view, tended to be. 'The Sibyl,' Heraclitus had said, 'uttering with frenzied mouth things unsmiling, unbeautified, unperfumed, reaches with her voice through a thousand years by reason of the god.' It was also an established idea that oracular utterances were commonly couched in figures and allegories. When the Delphic oracle spoke about a 'mule' being king of the Medes, it did not mean a mule in the literal sense, but a man of mixed Median and Persian stock. And so on. You had to dig below the apparent meaning to find the real meaning of the god. Amongst the Hebrews too, the prophets sometimes spoke in allegories not unlike those of a Greek oracle—where, for instance, Ezekiel describes how 'a great eagle with great wings and long pinions came to Lebanon and took the top of the cedar and carried it into a land of traffic and set it in a city of merchants', meaning the King of Babylon's coming into the land of Israel and his carrying off the king and princes of Judah. Perhaps the old Hebrew 'wise men' really used to cloak their teaching in difficult parables to a greater extent than we should suppose if we went simply by what remains of that branch of Hebrew literature, for the exordium of the Book of Proverbs, describing what their disciples must be trained to do, says that it is 'to understand a parable and a figure, the words of the wise and their dark sayings'—their riddles (ḥîdôth). Neither to the Greeks nor to the Jews, therefore, in Philo's time can it have seemed an altogether baseless suggestion that the whole of these crabbed oracular books were to be taken as ancient divine wisdom hidden under a system of curious riddles or symbols.[1]

Such a theory was just what was needed in order to provide

[1] It has been observed as strange that Philo brings in so little any part of the Old Testament beside the Pentateuch. Perhaps one reason is the psychological law which Philo once points to—that men are more interested in finding that which is hidden than in taking knowledge of that which is obvious (*De Decalogo*, § 1). The spiritual lessons of Psalmists and prophets were there for who runs to read; it was precisely because so much in the Pentateuch was externally unattractive that Philo was excited to break through (as he conceived it) the outside crust. Just as Sir Thomas Browne said that there could not for him be too many paradoxes in religion, so one feels that for Philo it was a peculiar delight when a passage in its literal acceptance was contradictory or absurd. Here you could be triumphantly sure that there was a profound inner meaning.

relief for the people who wanted still to regard as divine the sacred lore come down from the past, and who at the same time found much in the tradition, if understood literally, offensive, or trifling, or absurd. It was such an obvious expedient to say 'allegory' that it had been taken independently, long before Philo, both by Greeks in regard to their ancient myths and by the Indians in regard to theirs. And if it was also taken to some extent in the Rabbinical schools with regard to parts of the Old Testament—such as the Song of Songs—that need not be due to any outside influence. In the case of Philo, on the other hand, since Alexandrine Jewish circles drew so largely from Greek philosophy, we may feel sure that Greek suggestion did count for something in the application of the allegorical method to the Pentateuch. Lest, however, we should hastily identify Philo's method with that of the Greeks, we must notice the different kinds of meaning which have been extracted at different times from sacred traditional stories and documents, on the theory that they are symbols.

They may, first, be taken as symbols of the physical processes of nature. When the Greeks tried to give an explanation of their myths as allegory, it was usually this kind of meaning they found in them. Poseidon was a symbol of water, Apollo and Hephaistos of fire, Hera of the air, Artemis of the moon, and the battles of the gods round Troy were a parable of the strife of the elements. We have the little book of the Stoic Cornutus, a generation later than Philo, in which there is a systematic exposition of the Greek myths, mainly as physical allegories. Now this method, common in the Greek schools, had been followed, before Philo, in the Jewish schools of Alexandria. He refers now and again to his predecessors who had explained the 'tree of life in the midst of the garden' as the heart in the midst of the body, and the two Cherubim who guarded the gate of Eden as the two hemispheres, and their flaming sword as the sun.

Hellenistic Judaism

Philo himself, though he does not repudiate this method of interpretation as altogether wrong, is profoundly dissatisfied with it. That is not the most valuable meaning, he holds, which the Scriptural allegories can be made to yield. He takes them as symbols of the inner life of the Soul, of faculties and virtues and vices, of God and the abiding Powers of God, the Logos, Wisdom. Interpretation of this kind is also occasionally found amongst the Greeks. The first Greek writer (so far as we know) to advance the allegorical method, as applied to Homer—Theagenes of Rhegium in the sixth century B.C.—found meanings of this kind, as well as physical meanings, in the mythology: Leto stood for forgetfulness, Ares for folly, Athena for Wisdom.[1] But the Greeks never followed up this line at all far; with them the physical explanation held the field. It may be that, while Philo was not original in believing the Scriptures to be allegories, he was original in developing his own system of interpretation according to which they were allegories of Man's Soul and of the great spiritual Powers. And when we point to the formal resemblance between Philo's allegorizing and the allegorizing of the Greek schools, we must not overlook this important difference between them. Even Philo's own Jewish predecessors had not, as we have just seen, struck out Philo's path—not all of them at any rate.

There is yet a third kind of allegory which has been found in Scripture. The figures of the Old Testament and the ritual laws have been held to symbolize, not physical objects and processes, not abstract qualities and faculties of the soul, but concrete individual persons, or groups of persons, and concrete actions and events regarded as of singular importance and worth for the spiritual history of mankind. That is the kind of meaning which the early Church found in Old Testament 'types'. And just as the formal resemblance between

[1] See Paul Decharme, *La Critique des traditions religieuses chez les Grecs*, pp. 270 ff.

Philo and the Greek allegorizers ought not to lead us to overlook the difference between them, so the formal resemblance between Philo and the Epistle to the Hebrews, or certain passages of St. Paul, ought not to make us say 'This is just the Alexandrine procedure over again'. There is a profound difference. With Philo Melchizedek symbolizes the Logos, a general constituent of the Universe; with the writer of the Epistle to the Hebrews Melchizedek symbolizes an individual Man, Jesus: again, with Philo, Sarah stands for Virtue in the abstract, with St. Paul for a concrete community, manifested in time—the Church. And when we look at the Rabbinical allegorizing, we see that it too belongs to this third kind. The Bride in the Song of Songs symbolizes no abstract or general quality, not even the Soul in general, but a quite concrete community, manifested in time—the people of Israel. In Psalm xix the sun symbolizes the kingdom of David, the moon the Sanhedrin, and the stars the sages and their disciples.[1] Thus, here again, we find Rabbinical Judaism and Christianity agreeing in their presuppositions against Philo. And that is not accidental. It is because they both hold fast to the original presuppositions of the Hebraic world-view—the importance of the time-process, the importance of the individual and the concrete—unique moments, unique actions, unique personalities of transcendent value. For the Greeks the general was important, the particular and concrete of interest only as an example of the general type or law: to the Greek, the rationalist, view, uniqueness is something uncomfortable; it has somehow to be got rid of by the apparently unique being discovered to be an example of a general law after all. When Philo makes the books of Moses allegories of things general and abstract, we see that he has passed through the schools of the Greeks. And yet God is still for him a real Person, and God's acts done upon the soul are still concrete acts of divine grace. Philo's heart is Hebrew still.

[1] See Dr. I. Abrahams, *The Glory of God*, p. 33.

Hellenistic Judaism

The second thing in Philo which seems fantastic to modern men is his theory of intermediate divine beings between God and the world, especially the Logos. It seems a strange ' sport ' in Hebrew monotheism. There has been a good deal of discussion whence Philo derived notions of this kind: from the old Egyptian religion, some have suggested, with its idea of the Word of Power which goes forth from the god and brings the world into being; from Persian Zoroastrianism, others have thought, with its *Yazatas* and its six *Amshaspands*, semi-personified divine qualities, which attend upon the supreme God; from Heraclitus, Plato, and the Stoics, others again have maintained; or, simply, from the Hebrew Wisdom literature, with its poetically personified figure of Hokmah. Perhaps we shall never be able to answer that question with any certainty; but it seems to me possible to say with much greater assurance why such notions, wherever Philo may have got them from, had spiritual value for him.

If you take Philo as a philosopher, and take his ideas of the Logos and the Divine Powers as intended to give a rational explanation of the Universe, they seem indeed fantastic and arbitrary. Why should he start with such a supposition as that God cannot come into direct contact Himself with the material world? How unnecessary! But approach his teaching from the psychological side, and it all seems to fall into its place: it is simply a transcript into metaphysical terms of what for Philo was a matter of psychological experience. The direct apprehension of God Himself remember, was, for Philo, attained only in the mystical elevation. And the soul could get that only by separating itself from the distractions of the manifold world, from bodily feelings and appetites, from the interests of every day. Even ordinary religion recognized this in a way. You have to shut your eyes in order to pray; you must shut out the world if you desire to come into contact with God. When Philo says that God is separate from the world, cannot come into contact with the world, he means that *you*, in order to come into contact with God Himself, must separate yourself from the world. You cannot find God in the world; you can find Him only in the mystical elevation, apart from the world. You then enter, as it were, a plane of being in which you meet with God; that is where, in this sense, He is; He is not in the world, in the sense that you cannot find Him there.

But here comes a difficulty. Is it true that God is not in the world? Is the whole world not interpenetrated by God, full everywhere of the evidence of His Power, His Goodness, His Glory? And, if this is true, why must you go away from the world, shut out the world, in order to find Him? That is the question, and Philo's answer to it in effect is: ' Yes, the whole world in one sense is full of God; in your commerce with the world you meet at every turn with the evidences of God's Power and God's Goodness, but the kind of contact with God which you get in that way is not the direct contact with God *Himself* which you get in the mystical experience. You see in the world rather a reflexion of God's attributes, an " image " of Him. God Himself is something more than His attributes, more than Power and more than Goodness, you cannot describe in words the Reality which you know directly in the moment of mystical contact, but, as compared with that, the Power and the Goodness revealed in the ordinary world are only a shadow of Him.' It is this inferior revelation of God in the ordinary world— a revelation, one might perhaps say, at second-hand—which Philo means by the Logos. A man who never had the mystical experience might still know God in a way, might see the Power and Goodness displayed in the world, and make an inference to God, but he would not come into direct contact with God Himself, as the mystic does.

Looking at the matter in this way, we can understand what Philo means, when he says—so strangely, it might seem to any one who took such a sentence by itself—that ' the Logos is the

Hellenistic Judaism

God of the imperfect', and that only those who have attained to wisdom have the One Supreme for their God.[1] And we have only to think how such a sentence contrasts with anything which Christians later on could write about their 'Logos' to see how far removed Philo's Logos really is from the Logos of Christian theology, even if Christian theology at this point was influenced in its mode of expression by Philo. But if Philo says that the God revealed in Nature and the World is an inferior God, we may understand here by 'God' the image of God produced by Nature and the World in the mind of a man, that which for him is 'God'—just as we might say to some one who had a particular conception of Shakespeare '*Your* Shakespeare is a very imperfect representation of the real Shakespeare'. Philo speaks, that is, as if grades in the apprehension of God were grades in the Divine Being, or, to repeat what was said just now, he transcribes psychology into terms of metaphysics.

It may be asked whether Philo believed that these grades in the human apprehension of God corresponded with grades really existing in the Divine Being. And that is a very hard question to answer. Many passages of Philo, no doubt, seem to imply that he did believe these grades in the Divine Being really to exist apart from the mind of man. On the other hand, in one place he expressly says the opposite, as regards the distinction between the One Supreme and His Powers of Lordship and of Beneficence. He explains the three Strangers who appeared to Abraham at Mamre as the One Supreme and His two attendant Powers, manifesting themselves to the soul of the Learner, and he adds:

'The One in the midst, attended by His two Powers, presents to the mind's vision sometimes the appearance of One and sometimes the appearance of Three—of One, when the mind has been perfectly purified, and has passed beyond, not only the plurality of numbers,

[1] *Leg. Alleg.* iii, § 207.

but even the duality which is next to unity, and has pressed on to the Idea which is without mixture, without complexity, and altogether independent of anything outside Itself; of Three, when the mind has not yet been initiated into the Greater Mysteries, but is still a worshipper in the Lesser Mysteries only, not capable as yet of apprehending the One apart from something else, but only by the things which the One does, creating, ruling.' (*De Abrahamo*, § 122.)

In all that Philo says of the Soul, of its training for the vision of God, of the dangers it has to avoid and the grace it receives, there is nothing to limit the application to the soul of a Jew rather than that of any other member of the human family. In that sense he rises far above any national exclusiveness. Yet he certainly believed that the way to God marked out by the Mosaic Law was the best, or the only satisfactory, way to find Him, and so he would no doubt have considered that any Gentile who desired to reach the mystic vision would do well to take on him the yoke of the Law. If you call that Jewish particularism, Philo was a particularist in that sense. Only he insists that it is not a question of race; the vision is attainable by any man who will take the right way; any man may become 'Israel', the man 'who sees God', and no Jew has ever spoken more warmly about the welcome to be given to proselytes. They are to be regarded as in no way inferior to those who are Jews born—very much superior, indeed, to Jews who walk unworthily of their calling.

It is the impression of large kindliness, embracing all the world, of assurance and serenity, of joy in God, which abides with us, when we come away from the writings of Philo, and helps to raise our own temper. And it sets all this in strange relief, when we remember that 'hatred of the human race', moroseness, gloom, were the charges commonly brought in those days against the Jews! Perhaps we may miss in Philo the tension, the stress, the conflict, which can hardly be absent from the utterance of those great spirits who wrestle profoundly with the evils and the problems of this strangely various world. In Philo[1] it is all too smooth-flowing, too confidently serene. Had he ever felt, one wonders, the jar of those contradictions which have exercised the greatest thinkers and given to their ultimate convictions a worth which they could not have had, less painfully won? When, for instance, you emphasize, as Philo does, that every good thing to which a man attains is by pure Divine grace, without any merit on the man's part at all—that, as a Christian hymn puts it, ' every virtue we possess, and every victory won, and every thought of holiness are His *alone* '—and at the same time are concerned, as Philo is, to assert the reality of the human will, of free acts of choice, so that in every bad thing we do God has no share at all, you are really at close quarters with a frightful philosophical difficulty—a difficulty which has tried hundreds of religious thinkers in many ages. Philo seems to have no sense of the difficulty; the tranquil copious river of his discourse flows over it, as if it were not there at all. But to meet philosophical difficulties is not really his business; he has simply to induce in men a particular attitude of Soul, and unquestionably Jewish and Christian religious teachers have commonly told men, as a matter of practical instruction, to give God all the glory for everything good in them and take to themselves all the blame for everything bad—however the apparent contradiction is to be philosophically explained.

Philo's writings are no doubt the greatest among the literary products of Hellenistic Judaism left to us. The remains of its

[1] Regarding the chronology of Philo's life, we only know that he was an old man in A. D. 38. His brother Alexander had close relations with the house of Herod, and his brother's son, Marcus, was the first husband of the famous Berenice, who appears in company with her brother, King Agrippa, in Acts xxv—a curious link between Philo and the New Testament. Berenice, who here listens to St. Paul, must often in her youth have listened to Philo. Another son of Alexander was the apostate Tiberius Alexander, Prefect of Egypt (see p. 105).

literature, apart from Philo, have, generally speaking, small original value. They include, of course, a number of translations of Hebrew or Aramaic books, which have considerable interest for us to-day, because the originals are lost—the First Book of Maccabees, the Psalms of Solomon, Judith, Tobit, the Fourth Book of Ezra, &c., and one may include Ecclesiasticus in this connexion, although a good part of the original Hebrew has been recently rediscovered—but such translations can hardly count as products of Hellenistic Judaism, where the version has no literary worth of its own apart from the original which it reflects. The greatest translation of all is the Septuagint version of the Old Testament. That was destined certainly, as the Bible of the early Christian Church, to be an important factor in the fashioning of the future, and is of great importance to us to-day as a means of recovering the original text of the Hebrew writers, where the Massoretic text has gone wrong, but the Septuagint has no claim to be, as a Greek work, a great addition to Greek literature, in the way the English Bible was a great addition to English literature, or Luther's Bible to German. Of the works composed originally in Greek by Hellenistic Jews, one cannot regard either the Second or the Third or the Fourth Book of Maccabees (all three, of course, independent works) as great literature, or the Letter of Pseudo-Aristeas, or the forged Sibylline Oracles—though all of them, apart from their intrinsic quality, are useful as documents to the historian. The epic poem written by Philo 'the Elder' with the history of Jerusalem as its argument and the Greek drama composed by a certain Ezekiel on the subject of the Exodus are lost, but from the fragments quoted one does not gather that the loss is a great one. Beside Philo, only two Jewish writers of the Greco-Roman age have made a contribution of intrinsic value to world literature by works composed in Greek—the author of the Wisdom of Solomon and the historian Josephus.

Wisdom in its outlook has obvious affinities with Philo. It is generally taken to be older than Philo, to represent an earlier stage of Jewish Alexandrine thought. But perhaps its appearance of being more primitive and simple is due only to its being a poem, whilst Philo is in prose, and to the author having chosen a form of poetry modelled on old Hebrew poetry, not on the Greek poetical tradition. He was wise to do this. If, like the dramatist Ezekiel, or the writers of the Sibylline Oracles, he had attempted to write verse in the Greek epic or dramatic manner, he would probably, like them, have produced only an insipid conventional imitation; as it is, he has produced something much greater, something to which the simpler structure of Hebraic expression gives an antique dignity, while there is just enough influence of Greek literature to enrich the vocabulary and give greater flexibility and rhetorical effectiveness. The poet has a passion and fire wanting to Philo; he falls short of Philo's benevolent serenity. He is not above dwelling with gratification upon the punishments inflicted by God upon the Egyptians. But one feels that when he asserts his hope for that which lies beyond death, there is an urgency in this assertion just because he has felt so painfully how the appearances of the world seem to justify the mockers who in this world gather the rosebuds while they may, and laugh the children of God to scorn. It is with the supreme effort of faith that he rises to seize and hold fast the great hope.

> But the souls of the righteous are in the hand of God,
>   And no torment shall touch them.
> In the eyes of the foolish they seemed to have died;
>   And their departure was accounted to be their hurt,
>   And their journeying away from us to be their ruin:
> But they are in peace.

That magnificent chapter by some old Hellenistic Jew still often sounds with a solemn pathos in the churches of England on occasions when the faithful dead are commemorated. The book of Wisdom is not the least thing in the legacy of Judea.

Philo, Wisdom, Josephus—these, as has been said, are contributions of intrinsic value made by Hellenistic Judaism to the literature of the world, and if the other literary products of Hellenistic Judaism are either of poor quality, or valuable only because they transmit in a Greek version products of Hebraistic Judaism, we must remember that the importance of Hellenistic Judaism is not to be measured simply by what has survived of its literary output. Whatever view we may take of Christianity, it was certainly an event of immense moment in human history when the Greco-Roman world cast aside its old religions to adopt a religion built on Hebraic presuppositions, and in the preparation for that development, in the transmission of all that the Greco-Roman world took over of the Hebraic tradition—the fundamental ideas and standards of value, the great body of religious literature—the part played by Hellenistic Judaism was of capital importance. It is well known that before Christian missionaries appeared in the field, during the century which preceded the Christian era, and the earlier part of the century which followed it, there had been a great work of Jewish propaganda in the Greco-Roman world. When the first Christian missionaries, themselves Hellenistic Jews, went out to preach, they found everywhere in the cities of Asia Minor and Greece to which they came a body of Gentile proselytes, or semi-proselytes, attached more or less closely to the Jewish synagogues. When they based their message on belief in the One God who had made Himself known to Abraham and Moses and spoken through the Hebrew prophets, they found large numbers of Gentiles to whom this foundation was already familiar. It would seem that especially amongst women, often women of high social position and influence, Judaism had gained adherents, and that is easily understandable, if one considers that for men, in these

Hellenistic cities where the gymnasium was the centre of social life,[1] circumcision had peculiar terrors. Probably those forms of Hellenistic Judaism which disparaged the external observances and ritual ordinances had especially drawn proselytes, and such proselytes would be all the more ready to receive a gospel which told them that the old Law, having served its purpose, was now definitely abrogated in the community of the Messiah.

Christians were in the position of having to explain to Gentiles that the Jewish Law was really of divine origin and authority, and was nevertheless not to be literally observed. The arguments used by Hellenistic Jewish apologists were here ready to their hand: the Law was a mass of symbols and shadows. Some early Christians took the line of saying that God had never intended the Jewish external ordinances to be literally carried out; it was carnal misunderstanding on the part of the Jews which had taken the figures of the Law in this gross literal way,[2] and that, as we have seen, is just what had apparently been maintained in those Hellenistic Jewish circles from which Strabo drew. But this was not the line taken by the main body of Christian opinion: according to that it had been quite right to observe the Law literally before the coming of the Messiah; only now the time of symbols and shadows was over, because the reality to which they pointed was come. Yet, as one can see from Justin's *Dialogue with Tryphon*, Christians had their difficulties at this point, because, if circumcision was an external rite, so was baptism.

The Christian Church inherited the great problem of Hellenistic Judaism, how to find the right relation between Hebraic religion and Greek philosophy and culture. Just as there had been amongst the Jews, so now amongst Christians

---

[1] For the importance of the gymnasium in the Greek society of those days see Wilcken, *Archiv für Papyrologie*, v (1913), pp. 410–416, and cf. 1 Macc. i. 14, 15.

[2] *Epistle of Barnabas*, x. 9; *Epistle to Diognetus*, iii and iv.

there were those who were for repudiating pagan culture, as wholly evil, and those who were for finding a harmony which embraced both. The great attempt to establish a synthesis for the Christian Church was made at Philo's Alexandria, by the Christian teachers Clement and Origen, and made on lines for which the works of Philo were extensively drawn upon. Philo, when the Jewish community had forgotten him, had almost the status of a doctor of the Church.

Hellenistic Judaism, soon after Christianity had begun to spread in the Roman Empire, faded away. There must still have been large numbers of Jews, scattered in the Empire, whose mother-tongue was Greek, but they ceased to produce any distinctive literature in Greek, and they ceased to win more than an inconsiderable number of proselytes. The Judaism which survived was the Judaism whose religion, at any rate, had Hebrew or Aramaic for its medium. That Judaism had no use for the books written in Greek by the Hellenistic Jews, and it soon forgot all about them. They were preserved only by the Christian Church. The Septuagint, which for Philo and his contemporaries had been directly and verbally inspired, was discredited when the Christians drew controversial arguments from its text. New translations of the Old Testament into Greek were made for Jews who did not understand Hebrew, but these, too, in a few generations were dropped and forgotten, though Aquila's Greek translation was used in the Byzantine synagogues in the age of Justinian. The Jewish Rabbis, all the world over, went back to the original Hebrew scriptures.

It has been sometimes thought that masses of the Hellenistic Jews became Christians. But, if that were so, it would be odd, as Dr. Abrahams has observed, that we do not hear of more men of Jewish origin amongst the prominent members of the Church. If the Hellenistic Jews did not become merged in the Christian Church, they must have ceased, for all religious purposes, to be Hellenistic. That special variety of Judaism which existed in the centuries just preceding the Christian era, and in the first century after it, and which we call 'Hellenistic Judaism', ceased to exist. But if it was a branch which withered, it did not die without leaving spiritual seed. Whether any influence of Hellenistic Judaism upon the later Rabbinical Judaism can be traced is a question upon which I am not competent to have any opinion. But I gather from discussions of the subject by Siegfried and others that, whilst it is possible to point out quite a large number of points of contact, which cannot be accidental, between Philo and the Rabbis, it is usually difficult to say with any certainty whether Rabbinical Judaism was influenced by Alexandrine Judaism, or whether, on the other hand, Alexandrine Judaism here embodies a bit of Palestinian tradition which reappears later on in the Rabbis. The obvious affinity again between some of the ideas in Philo and ideas embodied in the medieval Cabala need not mean that the Cabala derived anything from Philo. The affinity may come from their both drawing upon the same sources—traditions in Judaism, whether peculiar to Judaism or more widely current in the East, Platonism, Pythagoreanism. However that may be, there can be no doubt as regards the influence of Hellenistic Judaism upon the Christian world. I cannot do better than end with a sentence from a living French historian, whom no one can suspect of being too favourable to the Jews:

'La communauté juive d'Alexandrie a pris dans l'histoire des religions une place éminente; elle a exercé sur les destinées de l'humanité une influence dont les effets sont encore présents.'[1]

EDWYN BEVAN.

[1] A. Bouché-Leclercq, *Histoire des Lagides*, iii. 149.

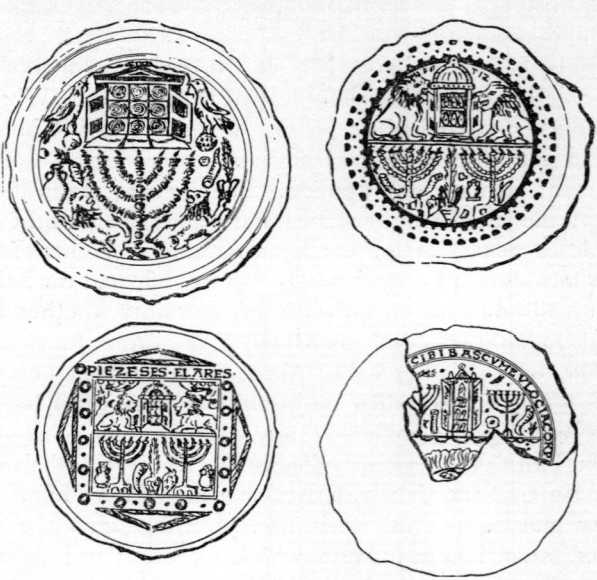

FIG. 5A. PLATES BEARING JEWISH EMBLEMS FROM THE CATACOMBS AT ROME

Many of the interments in the catacombs at Rome dating from the early Christian centuries were Jewish or Judeo-Christian. At that period it was customary to present to a friend, on festive occasions, a glass cup in the bottom of which was a gold plate containing some emblem or expression of goodwill. These plates were frequently placed in the tomb at death, the vessel being previously broken. Sometimes, as in our figure, such plates reveal a Jewish origin. We here see the shrine for the scrolls of the law (see Fig. 65), shown open with the scrolls exposed, the seven branched candlestick and the sacred trumpets (see Figs. 5 and 69), doves as symbols of the Divine Spirit, the lions of Judah and other Jewish emblems.

C. S.

Fig. 6. RESTORATION OF HELLENISTIC SYNAGOGUE AT CAPERNAUM

For description see pp. xv, xvi

THE DEBT OF CHRISTIANITY TO JUDAISM

§ 1

To estimate the extent and value of the debt of Christianity to Judaism the first requisite is some clear ideas as to what main parts of Christianity are derived from other sources. This is all the more requisite in an Essay intended chiefly for an English-speaking public, for English-speaking Christianity is in some respects more Judaic than European Christianity generally. The generally Biblical tone of English religion ever since the Reformation has given it a Judaic, not to say Semitic, cast and this to some extent obscures the non-Judaic system out of which historically it was derived.

It is the old historical Catholicism with which we must first deal, the orthodox and Catholic system of Religion, which so long dominated Europe and is far from being dead at the present day. This great system grew up and in its essential features was developed before the Roman Empire became Christian, it co-existed and flourished with the Christian Empire, and when that perished it was the Church that inherited and incorporated all that survived of Imperial Rome. The fact that the chief personage in the Christian Hierarchy is the Bishop of Old Rome is certainly not part of the debt of Christianity to Judaism. Even more striking is the fact that the second personage in rank is the Bishop of New Rome, the Patriarch of the upstart capital Constantinople. The Bishop of Jerusalem, the mother-church of Christendom, though he is reckoned to be the legitimate ecclesiastical successor of S. James 'the Brother of the Lord', is only the fifth in rank. Here clearly is a non-Jewish, imperial element, something derived from the fact that Christianity became a dominant world-religion, a great feature of the Roman world-power.

But prominent as this hierarchical and political element has been at certain periods no one would take it for the essential feature of Christianity. What is Christianity? Let us take first two familiar features of historic Christianity, neither of which is specifically Jewish, though like almost everything Christian they contain some Jewish elements, some features inherited from Jewish ancestry.

From one point of view Christianity may be regarded as a Creed, as a belief about God and Man and their relation to one another. 'The Catholick Faith is this: That we worship one God in Trinity, and Trinity in Unity; neither confounding the Persons, nor dividing the Substance.... Furthermore, it is necessary to everlasting salvation, that (a man) also believe rightly the Incarnation of our Lord Jesus Christ.' Is this, is any of this, part of the Church's debt to Judaism? Surprising as it may sound, I would say, 'partly, Yes'. But it is also quite clear that there is in these famous and uncompromising sentences a great deal that is not Jewish. There is an element of legal acumen which is chiefly Roman, and an element of comprehensive thinking, or rather argumentation, which is mainly Greek. Christian Theology is not Judaic, either in its conclusions or its processes. But on the other hand some of its fundamental premises are directly derived from the religion of Israel. No better illustration of the double strain can be given than is afforded by the very document I have just been quoting. The author of the *Quicunque Vult* feels himself compelled by his dialectic, by the Greco-Roman argumentation which he uses, to acknowledge Son, Spirit and Father each to be God and Lord, but in the very act of enunciating this dogma he is pulled up by an irreversible *tabu* taken over direct from Judaism and confirmed by the Gospel: 'we are forbidden by the Catholick Religion to say There be three Gods or three Lords.'

But far more fundamentally than as a Creed Christianity

may be regarded as a Way of Salvation. The striking likeness of some Christian rites to those practised in certain of the so-called Mystery-Religions did not escape the observation of Justin Martyr, the Christian Apologist in the second century, and this likeness has been the subject of many learned treatises in the present day. It is indeed unmistakable. And it is more than a mere external similarity. Whatever be the cause of the resemblance between the Eucharist and the rites of Mithra, the Christian Religion *is* a cult whereby the worshippers, who have all been individually admitted members of the Society by a holy rite, believe that they obtain the favour of Heaven now and a happy immortality hereafter by partaking of a Sacred Meal, whereby they get in some way communion and fellowship with the God whom they worship. The Christian Sacraments are certainly not part of the inheritance taken from Judaism. They are not derived from the Temple worship, nor (except in certain minor details) from the services of the Synagogue.

The Hierarchy, the Creeds, the Sacraments,—when we make abstraction of these things from Christianity, what is left? I am inclined to answer with S. Paul upon a somewhat similar issue 'Much every way!' But this answer needs a good deal of historical explanation. Furthermore, our abstraction and separation of the Jewish and non-Jewish elements in a living Christianity must not be thought of as a surgical operation, but rather as the tracing of features in a child characteristic of each separate parent. 'What God hath joined together let not man put asunder': the Christian Church has always regarded itself as the true Israel, the heir of the promises of God made of old, a claim which at least shows that the Christians thought of their Religion as legitimately descended from pre-Christian Judaism.

It is easy to enumerate the Jewish elements in Christianity. They are two: Jesus and the Bible. Let me begin by explaining what I mean to exclude by naming these in this way. I mean to exclude Jewish *Tradition* generally. The Church took over what it believed to be the Holy Scriptures, the Oracles of God committed of old to the Jews, but took them over without note or comment, without an exegetical tradition. And it is much the same with what Christians know about Jesus. Knowledge of Jesus is derived from the Gospels, works written by Christians for Christians, with a minimum of explanation about things that do not directly concern the matters immediately in hand. Christians in general know about the Judaism contemporary with Jesus from the Gospels and from the Gospels only. In many ways they are good historical sources, almost contemporary, vivid, life-like. But they assume the Jewish background, rather than describe it. What is the result? In not a few cases that which was once a paradox has become a commonplace. To most Christians 'Pharisee' is only another name for a hypocrite, 'Sadducee' for a worldly unbeliever, while 'publicans' and 'sinners' are half-expected to say or do something noble or disinterested as soon as they appear on the scene. The famous Tale of the Pharisee and the Publican (Lk. xviii. 10–14), whether it be regarded as a 'parable' or a record of something seen, has lost its point to-day to all but historical students. When it was first narrated it was meant to startle, if not to shock.

So it has come to pass that the doctrine of the Fatherhood of God has even been regarded as the great new revelation of Jesus to men. Yet 'Our Father in Heaven' is certainly a phrase of Jewish religion, however much fresh vitality may have been put into it by Jesus. The sixth petition of the Eighteen Benedictions, the oldest non-Biblical formula of Synagogue worship, begins both in the Palestinian and the Babylonian forms with the words 'Our Father, forgive us, for we have sinned'. The same title also is given to God in the prayer for understanding according to the Palestinian recension

The Debt of Christianity to Judaism

(no. 4), and in the prayer for repentance according to the Babylonian recension (no. 5). That Jesus felt Himself to be peculiarly God's Child, set apart for a peculiar mission and in such a special relation to God that he often spoke of God as *his* Father, is clearly set forth in the Gospels, particularly in Matthew and John, but when he taught the disciples to say ' Our Father ' in their prayers it was no innovation, nor was it meant as an innovation. ' Our Father ' is part, no inconsiderable part, of the debt of Christianity to Judaism.

As I said above, it is impossible entirely to separate the Judaic and Greco-Roman elements of Christianity, for they grew up side by side and are inextricably intertwined. A sort of chronological sketch of the development of Christianity from the point of view of its relation to Judaism will perhaps be more useful than a mere analysis.

Three stages can, I think, be distinguished: that of the first set of Gentile converts, that of the second set, and lastly that of the constituted Catholic Church. These stages are purely artificial divisions, made for the student's convenience. In the actual course of events they shaded imperceptibly one into the other. Perhaps it will make my meaning clearer if I label them *Cornelius*, *Clement*, and *Ignatius* respectively.

Cornelius.—This is the stage chiefly reflected in the Acts and in the Epistles of Paul. What was the religion of these first Gentile converts? They had ' turned to God from idols, to serve the living and true God, and to wait for His Son from heaven, even Jesus, which delivereth us from the Wrath to come ' (1 Thess. i. 9, 10). These well-known words cannot be too often quoted. They are a compendium of the earliest Christian belief, and they are wholly *non*-Graeco-Roman. The name ' Jesus ', and the words ' Son, which delivereth us ', belong to the new Christian part of the belief, to the ' Gospel ' ; the rest is purely Jewish. The one true God and the Wrath to come—to come very quickly—these conceptions the Christian missionaries shared with the Jews generally. A generation later, it is true, a leading school of Jewish thought, that of Johanan ben Zakkai, began to believe that the circumstances of the Wrath to come had not been revealed to man, but this belief (or rather, abandonment of belief) was only arrived at under the pressure of severe and unexpected misfortune. That it was not the general view of Jews in the period covered by the Gospels and Acts is in my opinion proved by the very fact of the Jewish War. 'They thought that the Kingdom of God should immediately appear' (Lk. xix. 11), as the Christians undoubtedly did. The Kingdom of God—that is another Jewish idea, foreign to the Gentile world of the time.

Well, these converts to Christianity, spoken of in 1 Thessalonians, had no doubt been attracted to Judaism before they were converted to the new form of Judaism proclaimed by Paul and Silas. This we know to have been the case with Cornelius the Centurion, and he must have been typical of many others. In the case of the converts to Christianity, the new Message had come to them unencumbered by certain stumbling-blocks of ordinary Judaism, and lit up by a new and romantic devotion.

Paul seemed to the people of Athens to be a setter forth of new and strange Gods, because he proclaimed to them 'Jesus' and 'the Resurrection'. The last term has a double meaning: undoubtedly part of the Christian message was that there was coming, soon coming, a Day when all men should rise again from the dead with their bodies and give an account to God (or His Vice-gerent) of their works whether good or evil. This idea, in the then Greco-Roman world, was wholly Jewish. It is the Jewish equivalent for the doctrine of the immortality of the soul in which many schools of Greek thinkers had come to believe. But the Christian message contained also a new and surprising development of this belief. It was the belief of the Christian missionaries that Jesus their Master had been

The Debt of Christianity to Judaism

seen alive in a real body after his death but before his departure to Heaven, where he now was, and that in that very body he would come again to reward his faithful followers and to mete out a just judgement upon all wrong-doers. In this way Jesus had brought the true knowledge of immortality to men and women, for those who joined his followers and disciples in the right way would themselves be endowed with an immortality similar to that of Jesus. Whether they lived or died now their future was assured.

This of course was new : it was not Judaism, though it might be Jews who were announcing it. The documents of the New Testament are unanimous as to the enthusiasm and conviction with which they came to their work of conversion. A new spirit was fermenting in their society : they and their converts together felt themselves endowed with a new life.

No doubt this was the master-impulse of the new Religion. The new spirit was its own witness. At this distance of time we judge of the objective value of the enthusiasm of the Believers according as we ourselves are believers or not, but of the fact of the enthusiasm there can be no two opinions. But besides this master-impulse there was another feature in the Christian propaganda. Judaism had obviously a good deal of attraction for many serious people during the century that preceded the Destruction of Jerusalem. But it also had many features that repelled outsiders. In the first place it was, in practice if not in theory, intensely national. In theory it was the worship of the One God, who made the whole earth and all men were His creatures. In practice it meant the cultus of an alien Oriental nation, centred at Jerusalem, and to join the Jews meant also observing a number of *tabus*, which shut out a civilized Greek or Roman from ordinary society, *tabus* most of which were apparently irrational or tiresome to carry out, and some of which were actively distasteful to non-Orientals. It was different if you had been born a Jew. Then these *tabus* and observances were part of your national heritage : it was a privilege and a pleasure to perform them, they were associated with the pride of ancestry and hallowed with the remembrances of childhood. But to heathen inquirers after a newer and a purer religion the yoke of the Law was unattractive. Why should a man not eat pork and hare ? Why must he be idle one day in seven ? And, above all, why must he be circumcised ? Ethnologists now tell us that the Covenant of Abraham is very much older than Abraham's day, date him when we will, but so far as I know it never has been a European practice. It was difficult for a people unaccustomed to such a rite to embrace a Religion that insisted on it.

It is not my purpose in these pages to sketch the history of Paul and Paulinism. St. Paul's own objection to the Law was not that it was burdensome but that it did not remove the Evil Inclination.[1] In his letters we are able to study the mental processes of a very original and independent thinker, who combined a remarkable theory of ethical anarchy with very sound practical instincts, the whole suffused with tremendous religious enthusiasm. But, so far as we can judge, the vast majority of the Christian Converts took very little interest in St. Paul's arguments. The argumentation was necessary for Paul himself : to retain his moral integrity it was supremely necessary that he should convince himself that the Old Law was no longer binding, though it was just and good. The converts, I venture to think, were generally content to know that their Apostle was convinced. At a later period first Marcion, then Augustine, then Luther, had their ideas cleared and focussed by the arguments of Paul, and the peculiar Pauline theology has reappeared in their writings, but to most early Christians Paul was the great Missionary Apostle rather than the casuist and psychologist—and that Christians were

[1] The ' other law in the members' of which St. Paul speaks in Rom. vii. 23 is exactly what Jewish psychology calls the *yétser ha-ra'*.

not expected to keep the Jews' Law was taken by the second generation of converts almost as a matter of course.

The net result was what I have called 'Cornelius': a class of Gentile converts to Christianity who found in the new Tidings from Judaea 'a not impossible Religion', a Religion moreover that carried within it a strange and infectious enthusiasm and hope.

Clement.—The next stage I have called 'Clement' after St. Clement of Rome, who wrote the well-known Epistle to the Church at Corinth about the year 95. In some ways 'Hermas' might have been a better name, though he is later in date. What I have in mind is a stage just previous to full Catholicism, in which the Christians find the Jewish element in the faith regulative and stabilizing, though it is now no longer the main controlling factor.

The period about which I am speaking is the period during which the Gospels were written, roughly speaking the last third of the 1st century. It is a period during which, contrary to all expectation, the first generation of Christians were dying off one by one and a new generation, the children of Gentile Christian parents, were growing up in Christian homes. Moreover the old norm of which, so to speak, Christianity was the new version disappeared. The Jewish State, the sacrifices, almost the whole society depicted as the background to the Gospel tales, vanished away; the Rabbinical Judaism organized by Johanan ben Zakkai and his followers was a fresh development in which the Christians had no share. The new Christians of this period, whether converts or the children of Christians, had not been Jews or semi-Jews first and Christians afterwards. Their whole religion as Christians was connected from the beginning with the Church, not with the Synagogue, and they needed to be taught those ideas and doctrines in which Jews and Christians agree as well as those in which they differ.

This was the public for which our Gospels were written.

Mark's vivid sketch of what he had seen as a boy, and of the tales he had heard from Peter, turned the Gospel into a Biography; and others turned the track which Mark had blazed into a highway. Different as the Four Gospels are in other respects, they all agree in this that they tell a Jewish tale, a tale of what had happened in Judaea and Galilee thirty and fifty and sixty years ago. It is a tale in which the actors are Jews living in their own land while they were still a nation. The aspirations, the ethics, the customs, the passions of the *dramatis personae* are Jewish—and this tale, almost from the days when the books which tell it first appeared, has always been regarded as containing the essence of Christianity.

As I said above, the commonplaces and the paradoxes of the Gospels are equally familiar to Christians, so that they do not sufficiently regard the paradoxes as paradoxical. But how much less would Christians have known of Judaism if the Gospels were not familiar! How much less familiar would certain Jewish ideas be if they were not set forth in the Gospels! How much less the debt of Christianity to Judaism would have been if the Four Gospels, however inadequately interpreted, had not been established in their place of honour!

And along with the Gospels there were the Holy Scriptures, the writings which Christians were beginning to call the *Old* Testament. The influence of these ancient writings on the new Gentile Church was enormous. In certain respects, I venture to think, their salutary influence is often not realized in modern times. For various reasons the attention of scholars has been mainly directed toward the errors and misapprehensions into which Christians fell, or tended to fall, by the use of the Old Testament, while the errors and misapprehensions to which they would have been exposed if the Old Testament had not been there to guide their ideas are forgotten.

It is true that the Christians studied the Old Testament under grave disadvantages. As I said above, they took over the

The Debt of Christianity to Judaism

bare text, without any exegetical tradition. They took the Bible as current among Greek-speaking Jews, in the current translation, which was often most inadequate and in some books frequently misleading in detail. The place of what modern scholars would regard as a sound exegetical tradition was taken by an *a priori* prejudice that everything in every part when properly understood was a prophecy of Jesus Christ and of the Christian Church. To most of the conceptions that during the past century have so profoundly modified our view of the Bible and of the history of Israel they were utter strangers. They had very little idea of what we mean by evolution and development, either in the physical or the moral sphere. That which seemed trivial or shocking they often allegorized into ingenious theological mysteries. Thus they often took as literal historical fact things that we cannot accept as such, while they explained away literal *tabus* upon certain sorts of food into counsels to avoid intercourse with sinful or dangerous characters.

All this is what immediately strikes the modern investigator when he observes the use of the Old Testament by Christians, forgetting how much of his own sound knowledge of the Past comes from his familiarity with the Old Testament records. This is not a fanciful plea. We have examples in History of what happened when the Old Testament was unduly disparaged. The time was not yet ripe for a scientific exegesis, and the results of the alternative to the Catholic use of the Bible is seen in Marcion and in the Gnostics.

Marcion is the great example of a Christianity that was determined to owe no debt to Judaism at all. He rejected the authority of the Old Testament and also everything in the Gospel that seemed to him to be a Jewish corruption. What is the result? It is impossible not to speak of Marcion's Religion with respect and sympathy, for Marcion was a very able and earnest thinker and organizer, one who had imbibed something of the spirit of Jesus and so much of the teaching of St. Paul, that he still has something to teach us to-day. Marcion is rightly regarded as a Heretic, but he is not 'Less than Arch-angel ruin'd,' the greatest Christian of the second century.

But by repudiating his Christian's debt to Judaism he has lost monotheism and all sense of unity and purpose in this world and in human history. His Jesus is no live being of flesh and blood, for the flesh and blood of Jesus was Jewish, and Marcion would have none of it. His system is a sort of triangular duel between evil Matter, heartless Law, and non-natural Grace, a religion which has no contact with family life in this world.[1]

And above all the Religion of Marcion is unhistorical. To Marcion Jesus with his Redemption comes on to the earth as a Stranger. In discussing the historicity or unhistoricity of certain parts of the Old Testament it is easy to forget its generally historical character, at least till we get back beyond the age of Moses. The anarchy of the time of the Judges, the establishment of a Kingdom under Saul, David, and Solomon, the two realms of Israel and Judah, the Captivity in Babylon, the Return—all this historical outline is given in the Bible, whether we read it in Greek or in Hebrew. And with this is bound up the impassioned utterances of Prophets and Psalmists, who amid much that was admittedly obscure were constant in their insistence that God, the One true God, had chosen Israel, but only that Israel might exhibit justice and mercy. It was not only Jesus who considered that love to God and neighbour was a compendium of the Law and the Prophets. A somewhat similar story is told of Hillel, and the Gospels themselves are not unanimous whether it was Jesus who formulated this conclusion with the approval of a Jewish Scribe

---

[1] The absolute opposite to Marcion's Religion is that which is expressed in the well-known saying of R. La'zar Chasmah that *Kinnīm* and the indications of *Niddah* were essentials of the Law (*Aboth*, iii. 28).

The Debt of Christianity to Judaism

or *vice versa*.[1] The point is, that Jesus and the Scribe agreed. There was a new element in the Religion of Jesus, a new impulse, a new enthusiasm, what the men of that age called a new Spirit, but it was not altogether a new Religion. Marcion denied this, but neither the Catholic Christian nor the modern historian agrees with him.

It was much the same with the religion which underlies the various Gnostic systems which sprang up during the second century. In all of them the emphasis is laid on some imagined Plan of Salvation from the contamination of matter, and is shifted away from that historical development of religion which really had made the Tale told in the Gospels possible. One has only to compare the account of Christianity, and what led up to it, in the *Apodeixis* of Irenaeus with any of the Gnostic systems to see how much nearer the Church kept to historic truth than the Gnostics did. It is not fair only to consider those parts in the Church's account that we no longer accept, when we estimate the value and the influence of the Old Testament: we must also bear in mind that it is only because of the Old Testament that the Church preserved through the ages any consciousness of what had happened in the past and prepared the way for Jesus.

To go back to what was considered at the beginning of this section, the period that I have called 'Clement' was marked by a general weakening of the original connexion between the Christian movement and living Judaism. The majority of the Christians were now Gentiles who had had no connexion with Judaism apart from their Christianity. But the influence that was lost in this way was made up by the Jewish character of the literature read by Christians and accepted as authoritative by them. Apart from this literature Christianity at this period must have been very much like one of the many Mystery-Religions, like the cult of Mithra or of Isis. But the Jewish

[1] Contrast Lk. x. 26–28 with Mk. xii. 28–33.

character of the sacred writings received by the Christians as in some way divinely inspired gave a peculiar character to the religion of Christians and endowed it with a Jewish element that it still retains.

Ignatius.—I have called the third stage by the name of S. Ignatius of Antioch, because rough and unformed as are his Letters they do express the theology of the Catholic Church. His own attitude to 'Judaism' is quite markedly defined: 'If anyone interpret Judaism to you do not listen, for it is better to listen to Christianism from a man who is circumcised than Judaism from one who is uncircumcised' (*Philadelphians*, vi). It is not quite easy to see what he means by Judaism preached by an uncircumcised teacher: obviously it is not a propaganda conducted by Jews, and I fancy Ignatius uses the word for false or separatist doctrine generally. In any case the Religion of Ignatius represents that form of orthodox Christianity which owes least to Judaism. He does not quote the Old Testament. He is chiefly concerned with loyalty to the Church organization, to the approved local Bishop, who alone can conduct a valid Eucharist, for if anyone forsake the Bishop he is deprived of the Bread of God, of which Ignatius says that it is the 'Drug of Immortality'.[1] Ignatius, so far as we know, was the first to use this notorious expression.

The exaltation of the ecclesiastical Hierarchy, the immense stress laid on the sacred ritual Meal, the whole tone of the Ignatian Letters—all these things make the reader feel that he is dealing with a Greco-Roman 'Mystery-Religion', rather than with a peculiar if legitimate development of Judaism. Harnack says somewhere that at the end of the third century, in the times of Aurelian and Diocletian, there was only one Religion in the Roman Empire: the difference between the Christians and the Heathen of those days was only a difference of mythology. We may say something the same of the difference

[1] φάρμακον ἀθανασίας, *Ephesians* xx (end).

The Debt of Christianity to Judaism

between the Religion of Ignatius and that of the Mysteries of Mithra or of Isis, or the old Mysteries connected with the name of Orpheus. The sacred story accepted by Ignatius was the Jewish sacred story, supplemented by the Gospel. In the case of Ignatius and the circle of Antioch generally we may say this was the Gospel 'according to Matthew': other circles used other similar writings, and a generation after Ignatius' day the greater Churches came to accept the Four Gospels that are now Canonical. But with such documents for Archives a limit was set to speculation. However interpreted, the letter of the Jewish Bible remained a standard to which Christians could and did appeal. The Debt of Christianity to Judaism is Jesus and the Bible.

§ 2

It remains now to touch upon the gradual recovery of a better text and a more scientific interpretation of the Old Testament, because in a very special sense it is the portion of the Debt that the church owes to Rabbinical, post-Christian Judaism. I cannot help feeling that it is a chapter in the history of Religion creditable both to Jews and to Christians, because the net result has been the building up of a scientific exegesis that prepared the way for the great reconstructions of ancient history that our own age has witnessed.

Let us begin by seeing what sort of an Old Testament the Church started with. There was no formal selection of documents. Luke xxiv. 44 enumerates the Scriptures as consisting of the Law, the Prophets, and the Psalms. This corresponds roughly with the Jewish division into Law, Prophets, and 'Writings'. About the Law there was no controversy. It consisted of the Five Books of Moses, which had been very well rendered into Greek about two centuries or so before the Christian Era. The 'Prophets' according to the Jewish reckoning include also Joshua, Judges, Samuel, and Kings, but

Daniel belongs to the 'Writings'. In the Greek Daniel was reckoned among the Prophets from quite early times (Matt. xxiv. 15), but the Historical Books formed a class by themselves. Of these Joshua seems to have been translated at the same time as the Pentateuch; the others have been transmitted in Greek with very extensive and surprising variations. The Greek text of all the books is of great interest to modern scholars, who use it as a basis for conjectural emendations of the Hebrew, but as a translation it is bald and unintelligent. What we have in our Greek MSS. is not the original stage: traces of an earlier stage of translation can be detected, in which a good deal of the more secular and less edifying parts of 2 Samuel and 2 Kings was left out.[1] The Prophets were all translated into Greek in a most inadequate way. It is possible that the Greek of Jeremiah and Ezekiel contains some readings representing a better Hebrew text than the Masoretic, but as a translation it is poor. The Minor Prophets rarely differ from the Masoretic text except for the worse. Worst of all is Isaiah, the Greek of which is very often unintelligible.

Of the 'Writings' (or Hagiographa) the Church had from the beginning Psalms, Proverbs, Job, the latter in a version in which some 400 lines of the original had been left untranslated. The historical literature of the Return was represented by what we call *First Esdras*, i. e. a rather free translation of the most interesting part of Chronicles-Ezra-Nehemiah. Of most of the rest of the 'Writings' there is no trace among the earliest Christians. On the other hand they possessed some other books which the Palestinian Jews did not receive, such as Enoch, the Wisdom of Solomon, the Wisdom of Jesus ben Sira, some tales such as Tobit and Judith, and the Books of

---

[1] See Dr. Thackeray's Schweich Lectures *The Septuagint and Jewish Worship*, pp. 16–28. A trace of the use of this early incomplete version seems to me to survive in the Christian tale called 'The Ascension of Isaiah'.

The Debt of Christianity to Judaism

Maccabees. The titles show how miscellaneous this set of books was. They were all accepted uncritically as true histories or as works of the authors whose names they bear. Jude quotes Enoch i. 9 as the prophecy of 'Enoch the seventh from Adam'. The most practically useful of them all, curiously enough, was the work of Ben Sira, called by Western Christians *Ecclesiasticus*, because it was found useful as a sort of manual of behaviour for Catechumens.

All these books had one characteristic in common. They had been Jewish books, written by Jews for Jews. There were a certain number of books in the same style, written by Christians in imitation of this Jewish-Greek literature, such as the *Ascension of Isaiah* and the *Rest of the Words of Baruch*, but none of these succeeded even in becoming Deutero-canonical.

Such was the earliest Christian Bible. No definite list of its contents can be given, because the limits were uncertain. Many books had a very restricted circulation, and a few of the books now reckoned among Old Testament 'Apocrypha', such as *Second Esdras* ('4 Ezra') and the *Fourth Book of Maccabees*, were not even written till after the destruction of Jerusalem.

The story of the interaction of Jewish and Christian Learning opens with a period of mutual distrust. The reorganization of Judaism under Johanan ben Zakkai and the early Talmudists was above all things a learned movement. It became an accepted principle that the tradition of the Elders must be deduced from Scripture. In following this out the methods of exegesis were often fanciful, but the principle demanded a closer definition of the Canon and a stricter fixing of the text. The Law and the Prophets were fixed before the Destruction of Jerusalem, but the complete list of the other Writings was not universally agreed upon before the time of Akiba, who died about 135. And with the more rigorous methods of exegesis practised by Akiba, who saw in every variation of a Hebrew expression some nuance of doctrine, the old slipshod

Greek version used by the Christians fell out of favour among Jews. The second Christian century is marked by a whole series of translations of the Scriptures into other tongues by Jewish scholars, which came in the end to have a great influence on the Bible used in the Church.

Aquila of Pontus, a Greek convert to Judaism, is said to have been a pupil of Akiba. He produced a new translation of the Hebrew Bible, in which an attempt is made to render the Hebrew word for word into Greek with mechanical consistency. The result of course is extremely uncouth, and to a Greek who knew no Hebrew must often have been unintelligible, but Aquila was a real scholar who must have had a good knowledge of the learned Jewish tradition as to the meaning of the Hebrew. His work in fact is a learned and often ingenious ' crib '.

Symmachus, a Samaritan (or an Ebionite), was also a convert to Judaism. His translation also follows the Jewish tradition in general, but in contradistinction to that of Aquila aims at a less slavish following of Hebrew syntax and a greater regard for Greek idiom. He wrote a little before the end of the second century.

Theodotion, probably an Ephesian, is also said to have been a proselyte to Judaism, and is usually dated about the middle of the second century, but there are a good many unsolved problems connected with the nature and the date of his work. His aim is said to have been not to differ greatly from the ancient Greek version: ' Theodotion ' may therefore be regarded rather as a revised Septuagint than as a new translation.

The difficulty is that neither Aquila, Symmachus, or Theodotion, or the original Greek translation first adopted by the Church, survives in a pure form. What we have is the product of more or less learned revised texts, together with occasional notes as to the renderings adopted by Aquila or Symmachus or Theodotion in particular verses. Aquila even in mere fragments is always recognizable by his peculiar style, but Theodotion is much less individual. There are, further, a number of indications that some readings which we know as Theodotion's existed long before his time, especially in certain books.[1] A discussion of these questions would be much too technical here, but it may be conjectured that partial revisions of single books were current, some from very early days, and that Theodotion incorporated much of this older work into his comprehensive revision.

As I said above, the interaction of Christian and Jewish Learning begins with mutual distrust. The first that we hear of the matter is in Justin Martyr's *Dialogue* with the Jew Trypho, where Justin quotes Isaiah vii. 14 ('Behold the virgin shall conceive') from the old Greek translation with $\dot{\eta}\ \pi\alpha\rho\theta\acute{\epsilon}\nu o\sigma$, though he knows already, before Trypho tells him, that the Jews say the Hebrew term should be rendered $\dot{\eta}\ \nu\epsilon\hat{\alpha}\nu\iota\sigma$ (*Dial.*, §§ 43, 67, 71). Justin will have none of it, of course, and he retorts by accusing the Jews of having cut out various prophetic references to Christ (§ 72).[2] Very much the same point of view is maintained by Irenaeus, who tells us (*adv. Haer.* iii. 21, 1) that Theodotion and Aquila, the Jewish proselytes, have substituted ' young woman ' for ' virgin ' in Isaiah vii. 14, but they are not to be followed.

The deduction seems obvious. Church writers know that Jewish scholars do not accept the old Greek translation, but Christians need take no notice, for it is only a matter of unbelieving prejudice. The deduction, I say, seems obvious, but closer observation shows it to be wrong. And the first witness

---

[1] In particular it has been noticed that the text of Daniel as quoted in the New Testament sometimes agrees better with Theodotion than with what Origen edited as the genuine LXX.

[2] One of these is the famous addition to Psalm xcv (xcvi.) 10, ' Tell it out among the heathen that the LORD hath reigned *from the Tree*,' a curious interpolation which long survived in Latin Psalters.

to this is Irenaeus himself. Justin Martyr a little after the middle of the second century had quoted Daniel from the old Greek version,[1] but Irenaeus quotes from the version of Theodotion.[2] Irenaeus wrote about 180. A few years later Tertullian, writing in Latin and in Roman Africa, still uses the old version of Daniel, but Cyprian in the middle of the third century uses Theodotion,[3] though traces of the old version survive here and there in the *Testimonia*. In other words we may say that only a couple of generations after Theodotion's revised version appeared the Church had adopted it for the book of Daniel and rejected the old version.

What happened wholesale in the case of Daniel seems to have happened piecemeal in other books, notably in Isaiah. In the matter of Isaiah vii. 14 indeed the Church kept to the old rendering: it seemed to fit the traditional interpretation so well that nothing could shake its position but a real knowledge of Hebrew, such as none of the Church Fathers possessed. But in most matters connected with the text of the Old Testament the Church was singularly willing to accept the verdict of Jewish scholarship, even at the cost of abandoning famous proof-texts. The *Epistle of Barnabas* had cited Isaiah xlv. 1 as a prophecy of the Christian Messiah, because the text was then read 'The Lord said to my Christ the Lord', i.e. with κυρίῳ instead of Κύρῳ (= Cyrus). This error survived for long in Latin, but it has quite disappeared from our Greek MSS. of Isaiah.[4] In Isaiah ix. 5 ff. the titles of the Wonder-

---

[1] See e.g. the long quotation of Dan. vii. in *Dial.*, § 31. A few readings agree with those found in 'Theodotion', but it must be remembered that what we call the 'LXX' (or old Greek version) of Daniel is represented by a single codex transcribed by Origen. In ancient times, no doubt, the text of this version was as little fixed as other much-read books of the Old Testament.

[2] See especially Dan. viii. 25, quoted in *adv. Haer.* v. 25, 4.

[3] See *De Op. et elem.* 5 (Hartel, p. 377).

[4] A similar error is ἱμάτια 'garments' for ἰάματα 'healings' in Isa.

child had been most inadequately rendered in the old version, but most of our MSS. also contain a fairly literal rendering ('Wonderful Counsellor', &c.), inserted into the middle of the old version, the insertion in this case being adapted from Aquila, not from Theodotion.

In the less read portions of the Scriptures the changes were even more drastic. The Book of Enoch, notwithstanding the protest of Tertullian,[1] was tacitly abandoned, because it was found not to be in the Jewish Library: in the fourth century Jerome tells us that the Letter of Jude was generally rejected because it quoted the Book of Enoch 'which is apocryphal'. On the other hand the Church seems to have taken Canticles and Ecclesiastes from the new Jewish translators. If I may be allowed a conjecture I should say that the text of both these books, as read in what is commonly called the 'Septuagint', is Theodotion's revision of Aquila's learned crib and that variant readings of 'Theodotion' are so rarely quoted for these books because the text we have *is* Theodotion. However this may be, there is very little evidence for the use of Ecclesiastes and Canticles by Christians before the time of Aquila. Chronicles also, and the literal version of Ezra-Nehemiah (commonly called in Greek, Ezra B), seem to have been taken bodily from Theodotion, though the old version of Ezra (Ezra A, called in English *First Esdras)* continued to be copied as a separate work.

The net result of two generations of haphazard revision of Christian Bibles by Jewish revised versions was anarchy and confusion in the text. It was to remedy this that the unwearied Christian scholar Origen prepared his *Hexapla*, an edition of the books of the Old Testament with the various translations in parallel columns, together with the Hebrew in the original

lviii. 8, which (with $ἱμάτια$) was a favourite proof-text for the resurrection of the body. But nearly all our MSS. now read correctly $ἰάματα$.

[1] Tert. *de Cultu Feminarum* I. 3.

and in a Greek transliteration. The column containing the 'Septuagint' also contained a Greek rendering of the passages left out from the old Greek translation. These were marked by Origen with an asterisk (⁙) while the passages in the old Greek translation which had no equivalent in the Hebrew were marked with an obelus (÷). The passages under asterisk were mostly taken from Theodotion, notably the 400 lines left out by the old translation in Job. Other passages, especially in the historical books, were taken, or rather adapted, from Aquila. Where the current text seemed to Origen to be definitely faulty, corrupted by the negligence of scribes, he seems to have corrected it without any mark, e. g. in such places as those mentioned above (Isaiah xlv. 1 *κυρίῳ* for Κύρῳ, lviii. 8 *ἰάματα* for *ἱμάτια*).

It is difficult to write about these matters without going into details that confuse rather than illustrate the general results. In the case of the *Hexapla* the very success of the work accomplished by Origen has contributed to obscure its influence. The fact is that all our MSS of what is often called the Septuagint—the name properly applies only to the Pentateuch—with the exception of some Latin fragments, may fairly be called post-Hexaplaric. A complete transcript of Origen's gigantic compilation seems never to have been made, except for the Psalms, but the original MS. was preserved for centuries at Caesarea, where it was used as a standard for correcting old copies of the Bible and for preparing new ones. It was freely used by Eusebius and Jerome and other fourth century scholars. The errors that Origen had corrected disappeared, those that he had left standing remained. Important variations still remained in Christian Bibles, but a good many of these arose from observing or neglecting Origen's critical marks. Some, who wished for the old text untouched by Jewish innovations, transcribed what was under obelus, but omitted what was under asterisk: in some such way arose the Sahidic text of Job[1] and the greater part of the Old Testament text of Codex Vaticanus (B). Others included everything, leaving out the critical marks. But the queer old corrupt texts disappeared, or only survive as isolated duplicate readings.

Further, the *Hexapla* emphasized the limits of the Canon of Scripture received by the synagogue. A few well-established favourites among the books not accepted by the Rabbis stood their ground, such as the 'Great Wisdom' of Solomon and the work of 'Jesus the son of Sirach', but the general result was to unify the Scriptures received by Jews and Christians.

Nevertheless the Church believed itself still to be using the venerable translation of the Seventy, and the tale that originally applied only to the Greek version of the Pentateuch was now popularly believed to have been told of all the Books. The 'Septuagint' was popularly believed to be a version of the Law and the Prophets and the rest of the Books made by seventy Elders working independently in separate cells but under the influence of the same Holy Spirit. What seemed to be errors were inspired variations, implying subtle mysteries. Something in fact like this is the theory set forth by Augustine, and he was only echoing what was generally believed by Churchmen.

We must bear all this in mind, if we are to appreciate the magnitude of the revolution effected in the West by Jerome through his new translation of the Hebrew Bible into Latin. That which is now called the Latin Vulgate is not, strictly speaking, a new translation. S. Jerome calls himself *trilinguis*, but his knowledge of Hebrew was not profound. On the other hand he had a fine command of Latin and a feeling for language generally that guided him whether to choose Aquila or Symmachus or Theodotion as the basis of his new version. For certain books also he was coached by a Rabbi, as he himself tells us. The result is a really admirable rendering of the Old

[1] 'Sahidic' is the Coptic dialect of Upper Egypt: most books of the Bible were translated into it from the Greek in the third or fourth century.

Testament, reflecting the higher levels of Jewish linguistic scholarship in the age immediately preceding the work of the Masoretic punctuators.

Equally remarkable is the acceptance of this fine work by the Latin-speaking Church. Jerome had begun under official patronage, but his patron Pope Damasus died in 384 when he was still occupied with a revision of the New Testament: the new version of the Old Testament was made while Jerome was at Bethlehem and the party in power at Rome was opposed to him. He had devoted and wealthy friends and a well-deserved reputation for learning, but he had no official position and he had made many enemies even among scholars. His work was calculated to arouse theological prejudice of every kind, and it had nothing to recommend it, except its scientific merit that it was a better translation made from what was on the whole a better text.

It made slow progress at first. The whole work was completed about 403 A. D., and it was not till some fifteen or twenty years had passed that it won its first important victory. This was the approval of S. Augustine, who in the second edition of the *De Doctrina Christiana* recognized that if you want to know the literal words of Old Testament Revelation and the literal facts of Old Testament History you must go to the presbyter Jerome's new revised version rather than to the text then in ecclesiastical use, inspired though it be.[1] After this it gradually came into favour, but the earlier stages of its reception by the Latin-speaking Churches has yet to be written. What is certain is that by the time of Gregory the Great, who died in 604, it had won its way into general recognition.[2]

---

[1] See *De Doct. Christ.* iv. 16 and my article in the *J. Th. St.* xi. 258–268.

[2] The best illustration of this is found in the fact that the words of several of the Anthems in the Gregorian Antiphonary (or musical portion of the Mass-Book) are taken from the New Version. A notable example is *Rorate*, an Anthem for Advent, which is taken from Jerome's rendering of Isaiah xlv. 8.

§ 3

During the greater part of the Middle Ages the Church learned nothing fresh from Jewish sources. Learning was at a standstill where it had not actually slipped back, and for centuries Biblical scholarship was confined to preserving or restoring the true text of Jerome's version, or to copying extracts from his commentaries or those of his contemporaries. Meanwhile in the East a new stage of Semitic study had opened out. The conquests of Islam led to the grammatical study of Arabic by Aryan Persians and by Syrians who had learned something of linguistic structure from the Greeks. The Arabic language lends itself particularly well to this kind of investigation and the result was Arabic Grammar, a fine analysis of a then living language closely akin to Hebrew. The Oriental Jews soon perceived the analogy, and a new more scientific study of Hebrew was the result. On the one hand the traditional pronunciation of the text was securely fixed by the invention of the vowel-points and accents, on the other the literal meaning was brought out by a series of Commentators, the most illustrious of whom were perhaps 'Aben-Ezra' (pp. 209–211) and David Kimhi.

Once again the Synagogue had something to teach the Church. As early as the time of Roger Bacon some doubts as to the correctness of the current version had arisen,[1] but the first attempt on a large scale to interpret the Hebrew Bible more exactly to the Western world is connected with the almost forgotten name of Simon Atumano (i. e. the Ottoman), Latin Archbishop of Thebes in Boeotia from 1366 to about 1385, who prepared a trilingual edition of the Bible in Hebrew, Greek and Latin, of which part of the Greek column survives in Simon's autograph in a codex known as the *Graecus Venetus*.[2]

---

[1] On the medieval knowledge of Hebrew see article by Dr. Singer, p. 283.
[2] See G. Mercati, *Simone Atumano* (Studi e Testi 30), Rome, 1916.

More fruitful was the rise of Humanism, one feature of which was the study of Hebrew by Christian scholars, of whom the pioneer was Johann Reuchlin, a German scholar and jurist of distinction, who published in 1506 the first Hebrew Grammar not written by a Jew.[1] Mention also should be made in passing of Elias Levita, a learned Jew who lived a good part of his laborious life (1468–1549) under the protection of enlightened ecclesiastics, to some of whom he taught Hebrew while steadily refusing to give up his ancestral faith. The new study met with opposition, notably from the Dominicans of Cologne, but in this matter the Popes favoured the New Learning.

Two causes contributed to the progress of Hebrew studies. The Reformation professed to base its doctrines on the Bible, apart from Church Tradition, and consequently the Reformed theologians of every variety felt impelled to study the text in the original: Roman Catholics followed suit, and in a couple of generations a knowledge at least of Biblical Hebrew was as much a possession of the Christian as of the Jewish scholar. But it was not, I believe, interest in grammatical exegesis or theological controversy that most strongly impelled men of the Renaissance period to take up the study of Hebrew: it was the belief that in the mysterious theosophical writings known as Cabala, and particularly in the book called *Zohar*, the Jews possessed a Key of Knowledge which unlocked the greatest problems, from the doctrine of the Trinity to the mystic Harmony between each single Man and the Universe. Only by a knowledge of Hebrew and 'Chaldee' could the secrets of the *Zohar* be revealed, and Reuchlin and his friends spared no pains to master it. In less than a century the discoveries of Copernicus and Galileo had once for all demonstrated the baselessness of the old speculations of this sort, whether they

---

[1] *De rudimentis Hebraicæ linguæ* (Pforzheim, 1506). Reuchlin's later treatise *De Accentis et orthographia Hebræorum* (1518) is said to be a much better book.

were due to a cosmologist of the second or of the fourteenth Christian centuries. Now the *Zohar* is a curiosity for scholars, but, though its Light was little more than a will-o'-the-wisp, enthusiasm for it played a great part in encouraging Christians to master the language of Canaan.[1]

§ 4

Protestant thought and practice, and especially the English and Scottish varieties of it, have or used to have a Judaic air, but this was due entirely to a following of the Old Testament, and it differs from the influence of the Old Testament on the early Church in its conscious antiquarianism. The Genevan model was a Reconstruction from an ancient literary source, whether that source was the Church of the Apostolic Age or the ancient Israelitish Theocracy, and for that reason the details of this reformed Genevan model, or of the somewhat different Anglican model, are to be regarded as a debt to Judaism. The principles of selection from the Old Testament as to what was, or was not, binding for Christians were not Jewish at all, and any special resemblance between Jewish and Protestant systems, as compared with the Catholic system, is external and as it were fortuitous, being due merely to the common use of one external authority.[2]

But there is one special point in which all forms of Christianity, both Catholic and Protestant, have been influenced by Judaism, which deserves separate notice here. The religion of Judaism, above almost all others, was dominated by a sense of Divine Purpose, manifested in Time. God had set the world going so many years ago, and He was going in His good time to bring it to an end, whenever His Purpose had been accomplished. Reality, on this view, was a grand Drama, a Play to be performed once for all and never repeated, so that some single Events were decisive moments in the Divine Plan of

[1] See article by Canon Box, pp. 327–328. [2] See article by Dr. Selbie, p. 407.

things. To God, it is true, a thousand years are as one day and one day as a thousand years. Yet, though our clocks may be imperfect instruments for measuring duration, the succession of Events is really there. The Christians took over this set of ideas from Judaism, and it still dominates every Christian philosophy. To the Christian, one Event, at least, the Incarnation, is central: a certain state of things preceded it and a different state of things followed it.

Many philosophers, I believe, hold this whole conception to be unphilosophical; as philosophers they are the spiritual children of Greece. My point is, that the Christian Church did undoubtedly believe in the reality and the eternal significance of Time. Right or wrong, wise or foolish, it is part of the debt of Christianity to Judaism.

F. C. BURKITT.

FIG. 7. Small synagogue or schola from a mosaic of the fifth century known as the 'Capitoline plan' at Rome.

FIG. 8. AUTO DE FÉ

From a painting of about 1500

For description see pp. xvi–xvii

THE INFLUENCE OF JUDAISM UPON JEWS

FROM HILLEL TO MENDELSSOHN

A QUESTION so far-reaching and so elusive as that implied in the title of this chapter could hardly be answered with any approach to accuracy unless the facts of Jewish life were observed over a long period of time. Only so can the permanent factors be distinguished from those which were but transient and local. The period from Hillel to Mendelssohn, extending over nearly eighteen centuries from the beginning of the Common Era, would seem to furnish an adequate basis for an answer. It has, moreover, a very special fitness for the present purpose since it begins with the rise of Talmudic Judaism, and it ends with the awakening of the desire for emancipation, the claim of Jews to an equal share with non-Jews in modern intellectual, social and political life. During the whole of this long period, the religion whose principles found expression in the Talmud and the cognate literature was the dominant factor in Jewish life and thought, the chief and often the only bond of union among Jews. No period of history can be marked off by any hard and fast line from the age which preceded or from that which followed it; but the period at present chosen for survey corresponds with remarkable closeness to such a clear demarcation. What will be found within its limits grew out of the experience of Jewish people in earlier times; and Judaism as it is to-day bears the marks of the treatment endured in the Middle Ages and later. Nevertheless, during the period now before us, Jewish life and thought, religious and ethical, intellectual, literary, social and economic, present characteristics which justify the choice of the period for study, when the purpose in view is to estimate the influence of Judaism upon Jews.

The question implied in these words may be more clearly stated thus: 'What sort of people did Jews become by reason of their Judaism?'

More particularly, having in view the special period with which we are at present concerned, we may state the question in this form: Given the Jews as they were at the beginning of the period, what sort of people did they show themselves to be at the various stages of that period as the result of their being Jews? The question is deeply interesting, and of the first importance for any true understanding of the meaning of Judaism as a factor in the history of mankind. Some answer is certainly possible, and an attempt will be made in the following pages to furnish an answer. But to state the question at all is to raise several preliminary questions which must first be answered.

If the influence of Judaism upon Jews is to be estimated with any approach to accuracy it will be necessary to distinguish between the original character of Jews at the beginning of the period, if any such can be defined at all, and the special features which were developed in that original character as the result of the contacts and the treatment of various kinds to which Jews were exposed. Non-Jews also of course were subject to various influences, religious, economic, and other, in the course of those same centuries; and some influences affected both Jews and non-Jews in a sense equally, while yet they produced very different results. Thus, the Black Death in 1348–1351 devastated all Europe, and spared neither race nor creed; but its indirect effect upon the Jews, for many a year after its immediate force was spent, was far other than its effect on Christians in the same countries. And the difference was due precisely to the fact that the former were Jews, and the latter were Christians; the former lived under a set of conditions governing their mental and spiritual life different from those which applied in the case of Christians.

Thus, the influence of Judaism upon Jews is observable not only in the actual types of character which it tended to produce, but also in the differences between Jew and non-Jew, living side by side under the same general conditions.

In what has been said hitherto, and in the very statement of the question to be answered, it has been assumed, unavoidably, that there is a certain unity among Jews, in virtue of which it is permissible to make general assertions about them. Beyond all doubt there is such a unity, to the extent that propositions may be made which are true of all Jews and not true of any Gentile, whether Christian or heathen. But when it comes to defining that unity and saying precisely in what it consists, and upon what basis it rests, the case is not so simple. The choice must be made between two alternatives, which are these: Is Judaism mainly based on unity of race, or mainly on unity of religion? In other words is a man a Jew because he comes of that particular Semitic stock which once had its seat in Palestine and its capital city in Jerusalem? Or is he a Jew because he professes the religion whose founder was Moses, whose record is in the Hebrew Scriptures, whose fuller development is in the Talmud and the Midrash? These are the two, and the only two alternatives; and in stating them no attention is paid to any variation of type in the racial development or in the character of the religion. Race or religion? Which of these gives the real clue to Jewish unity? We will take them in order.

At the beginning of the period under survey there were Jews in many parts of the Roman Empire, not counting those in Palestine; and in Babylonia the descendants of those carried into captivity formed the largest collection of Jews in the dispersion.[1] There was a numerous community of Jews in Alexan-

[1] See article by Dr. Bevan, pp. 29-30.

dria, and another in Rome. Probably every considerable town in the Mediterranean regions contained some Jews. The missionary journeys of Paul took him into many cities of Asia Minor and Greece; and everywhere he came into contact with Jews. If, as seems probable, he began his missionary work in each place by speaking in the synagogue, he would naturally direct his steps to towns where he expected to find Jews. He had the intention of going to Spain; presumably, with the same expectation.

The Jews living in the towns and regions here indicated were probably of ultimate Palestinian origin, the descendants of persons who had once lived there. But in some cases certainly the separation from the mother country was of long standing. The Babylonian Jews had been settled in that country for full six centuries; and though they called it the Golah (Exile) it was none the less their native land, and they remained there. Much the same is true, though in a lesser degree, of the communities in Alexandria and Rome, in Antioch, Athens and elsewhere. The first settlers or colonists, or transported immigrants, however they came to be in the place, grew and multiplied there without directly, still less continually, renewing their connexion with the mother country. To this may be added the fact that after the war of Vespasian which ended with the fall of Jerusalem in A. D. 70, and again after the war of Hadrian which ended with the overthrow of Bar Kokeba in A. D. 135, large numbers of Jewish captives and fugitives found their way to different parts of the Empire. Some Jewish settlements in Europe, known in later times, may have owed their origin to this cause. Moreover, wherever the Roman armies went, a certain amount of trade went also; and it is quite likely that some Jews were amongst the traders. In all these ways the presence of Jews in the different parts of the then known world may be explained, and for such as have been mentioned a connexion with Palestine, more or less remote, is not improbable.

But, on the other hand, it must be remembered that at all events in the early part of the period there was a certain amount of proselytizing, whereby Gentiles came over to Judaism. The Jewish religion had power to attract some at least of those who found no satisfaction in the heathen cults; and Horace and Juvenal, though they did not themselves feel the attraction of Judaism, were quite aware of its existence, and of the fact that some yielded to it. The Talmud is not without hints that certain well-known teachers were of heathen ancestry; and a court scandal of the conversion of a great Roman nobleman to Judaism (or Christianity) seems to underlie the story of Flavius Clemens in the reign of Domitian.

Moreover, apart from individual cases, which were probably fairly numerous, there was one instance where the people of a whole kingdom had before their eyes the conversion to Judaism even of their own King and Queen. This was the little kingdom of Adiabene, in Mesopotamia, whose Queen Helena and her son Izates embraced the Jewish religion in the reign of Claudius (A.D. 41–54). It is impossible to say how far their example was followed by their subjects; but the effect must have been considerable, and Josephus[1] speaks of the Adiabeni as Jews.

A more important case is that of the kingdom of the Chazars in South Russia, where not only the rulers but certainly a large number of the heathen population definitely adopted the Jewish religion. This more or less Jewish kingdom had already flourished for a considerable time (some centuries, according to the then King) when an account of it reached Hasdai ibn Shaprut at the Moorish court of Spain about the year A.D. 960. The Chazars, dwelling in what is now Russia, seem to be a likely source for a proportion of the immense Russian Jewry of later times, though this proportion has been much exaggerated by recent controversialists.

To these cases of conversion of Gentiles to Judaism must

[1] *Wars*, Pref., § 2.

be added the evidence of the mixed marriages between Jews and Christians which went on all through the Middle Ages. The practice was condemned and forbidden in the decrees of Church councils and synods, with a frequency which shows the persistence of the evil as the Church regarded it. And obviously the grievance was that Christians became Jews; if Jews on marriage had become Christians the Church would have raised no objection.

In all these cases of conversion there can be no question of Palestinian ancestry, and it is accordingly vain to assert a racial unity of Jews. As they are to-day, even allowing for intermarriages amongst themselves, the Jews, so far as racial origin is concerned, are as mixed a people as any in Europe or elsewhere. If there are to be found in them characteristics more or less common to all, they are not due to identity of race.[1]

The other possible basis on which to found a theory of Jewish unity is religion, and the experiences which grew out of it. During the whole period the Jewish experiences had much in common, and this was a consolidating force. The Jewish religion itself retained the same fundamental principles, with whatever difference of local detail. A Jew who was familiar with what was taught in Pumbaditha and Sura in Babylonia was of a very different type from a Jew of Metz or Rothenburg in Central Europe; a Jew accustomed to the strict Talmudism of Northern France in the age of Rashi would find much even to disapprove in what was taught in Spain or Italy. And, so far as ritual detail was concerned, the *minhag*, or customary method, of fulfilling the prescriptions of the Torah, the 'minhag' varied not only from land to land but even from town to town in the same land.

But these were only surface differences. Fundamentally, for Jews of all types, the Jewish religion was in principle the same. And Gentiles who became Jews, in the manner already indicated, while they could not change their racial origin, did

---

[1] See article by Dr. Singer, pp. 177 and 180.

change their religion, and in doing so they accepted the ground principle of Judaism.

The Jewish religion throughout the whole of the period is based upon two main principles, the assertion of the undivided unity of God and the paramount duty of obedience to His declared Will. If either or both of these were denied there could be no Judaism. In the accounts of Jewish martyrdoms, recorded in the Memorial Books of German and French Communities, the term constantly used is that the martyrs gave their lives for the sake of the Divine Unity, as being the *ultima ratio* of their religion. And that sacrifice was the last act of unflinching obedience to the Divine Will. Nothing in Judaism was more fundamental than these two principles. The rite of circumcision and the observance of the Sabbath were the indispensable requisites of any profession of Judaism, affording two most clear and explicit proofs of loyalty to its ground principles.

Judaism accordingly was a strict monotheism, and its source of revelation was the Torah, the entire body of divine teaching focussed in the Pentateuch and irradiating the whole realm of life, thought, feeling and action. In that revelation was made known the Will of God, as well as (in some degree) his nature; and that is why the Torah is all in all to Judaism, since without it there would be no knowledge of the One Supreme God, and no possibility of learning or doing his will.

The Talmud gave expression to both these fundamental principles of Judaism, and during the whole of the period it was the chief, though not the only, formative element which determined the main lines of the development of Jewish life. That part of the Talmud which was concerned with defining the manner of obeying the divine will was known as the *Halakah*, and was the only part to which, in theory, strict obedience was required. The authority of the Talmud rested upon the character of the teachers whose words were recorded in its pages, and whose teaching was accepted for the guidance of Israel.

But its authority was one which could never be, and certainly never was, enforced and imposed upon Jews always and everywhere. The strict Halakah, which *Tannaim* and *Amoraim* in the early centuries of the period had elaborated with so much toil and patience, was incomplete even when they passed away. Completed it could, of course, never be. But in the ages which followed the closing of the Talmud, from the early sixth century down to the end of the period (or even down to the present day), there has never been any central authority which could give for all Jewry an authoritative interpretation of the Halakah. A last act of the kind, and it was not a declaration of Halakah though it was an act affecting all Jews everywhere, and received as such, was when the Patriarch Hillel II (A. D. 330–365) made public the rules for fixing the calendar, by which all the religious festivals of the Jewish year are regulated.

But although there was not and could not be during the period a uniform and consistent development and application of the Halakah throughout all Jewry, the principle underlying it was never abandoned, the principle that the doing of the divine will was the paramount duty of the Jew as Jew. And this is the reason why, amid all local and temporary variations in the outward expression of Judaism in ritual observance, the Jewish ethic kept at the same high level right down the centuries. As has been finely said : [1]

'There have been comparatively long periods during which Jews produced neither poets nor philosophers, neither imaginative writers nor historians ; long and dark periods during which the light of science was obscured and the refinements of literary style and culture obliterated or ignored. These gaps are inexpressibly sad ; but they would have been sadder still in their practical effects, but that they are all bridged over by a broad and solid structure against which the friction of internal faction and the stress of external storm were equally powerless. There is hardly any " local colouring " in the arches of this ethical bridge ; there is absolutely no variation in its high moral level.

[1] I. Abrahams in the *Jewish Quarterly Review*, Old Series, iii, p. 444, London, 1891.

Whether the particular moralist be philosopher or stock-Talmudist, whether he hail from a country in which the Jew was persecuted or from one in which he was free ; whether he wrote at a time of general enlightenment or at a period of wide ignorance, whether the inspiring fount of his thought were Aristotle or Hegel, though the details will reflect differences in environment, though the style of expression varies with prevailing taste, though the abstract conception of Judaism often changes, yet the Jewish code of morality is without variation, and the noblest ideals form that code.'

In the Jewish ethic the spirit which created the Halakah lives immortal ; and in the Judaism which inspired the Talmud, the Judaism not of the early centuries alone but of the whole period under review, religion and ethic are but two aspects of one and the same spiritual conception, if indeed they can be separated.

When therefore we speak of the influence of Judaism upon Jews, we are speaking of the influence of the Jewish religion upon those who held it, and not of the influence of any common racial ancestry upon its scattered posterity.

We are now in a position to understand the meaning of the fact, observable throughout the whole of the period no less than before and after it, that the Jews were always felt to be in some way different from those in whose midst they lived, were regarded as to some extent aliens from the common life of their time and country. Was this due to their race or their religion ? Not to their race, because if a Jew gave up his religion and adopted that of his neighbours whether Gentile or Christian, his neighbours, ultimately at least, felt no objection to him on account of his race. Tiberius Alexander, who was made governor of Alexandria in the reign of Vespasian, is a case in point. He gave up his Jewish religion and received high promotion at the hands of Rome, in spite of his Jewish origin. And he gave significant proof of the thoroughness of the change by the fact that he himself directed the Roman troops against the Jewish rebels in the city. Racially he remained as he had been; in everything else he was a Roman and a heathen. The case of Paul proves the same truth conversely. He never changed his racial origin and prided himself on being a Pharisee of the Pharisees, but that did not avail against Jewish anger when he taught things contrary to the Jewish religion. And, while Paul was technically a Roman citizen, he was as far as any Jew from being accepted as one of themselves by the people of the 'countries round about'.

Again, all through the Middle Ages the persistent efforts of the Church were directed to the conversion of the Jews. A Jew could instantly save himself from persecution and death by being baptized. And once he had in this manner become a Christian, the Church took no further interest in him except to see that he did not relapse. Whatever he had been, racially, before baptism such he necessarily remained afterwards. It was his religion which he had changed. The whole objection to the maranos or crypto-Jews of Spain and Portugal in the days of the Inquisition, was not that they were of Jewish birth, because many of the highest nobility in Spain and of the clergy as well had Jewish blood in their veins; it was that they were suspected of keeping up in secret the observances of the Jewish religion. The Inquisition warred not so much against other religions, as against those who were relapsed heretics, as the Inquisition regarded them.

It is true that the objection felt to the Jew was also, in the Middle Ages, based on economic grounds, the Jew being commonly regarded as an extortionate usurer. But there would not have been this ground of complaint unless the Jews were already regarded as a people apart; for the same charge of extortion was brought against Christians also, with even more justification.

It was clearly therefore some cause other than that of racial origin which gave rise to and perpetuated the sense of unlikeness between Jew and non-Jew and prevented the assimilation of the former with the latter. The Jewish religion affords a complete explanation by showing that a Jew who remained faithful to his religion could not be assimilated under ancient and medieval conditions; until the modern period he perforce remained to some extent an alien, even in his native country.

For the Jew, by reason of his religion, was debarred from taking part in any social act which implied recognition of Gentile or later Christian religion. Recognition indeed there might be on the part of the Jew, at all events of Christianity. Jews have never denied that Christianity was a real religion. But when public acts involved the offering of a sacrifice, the invocation of some heathen deity, or later when they were associated with Christian rites or worship in a Christian Church, the Jew could have no part in these things. And considering how closely the symbols and formulae of religion were associated with the common life alike of heathen and Christian countries, it is evident that the Jew could not, if he were consistent, accept the symbols or utter the formulae. He could only stand aloof, and thereby proclaim the fact that in a matter so vital as religion he was not at one with his neighbours, he was in their eyes an alien however he might wish to be accepted as one of themselves.

Moreover, his religion made it impossible for him to eat and drink either with heathen or Christian, except under precautions as to the preparation of his food which did not affect his neighbours. The Jew has always been socially inclined; and it was often the case, during the Middle Ages and later, that Christians partook of Jewish hospitality and were glad to do so. The Church strongly disapproved of the practice, as is shown by the repeated prohibitions and censures contained in decrees of councils. The fact that the prohibitions were repeated so often shows how ineffectual they were. But the Jew could scarcely accept the hospitality of his heathen or Christian neighbours without disregarding the dietary laws which were bound up with his religion.

In regard to eating and drinking the Jew might honestly wish that it was possible for him to be socially at one with his neighbours. But it was not so in regard to his religion. Rarely at any time had he the desire to exchange his religion for that of heathen or Christian. This goes without saying so far as all heathen religions are concerned, considered as possible substitutes for Judaism. But it is no less true in regard to Christianity, so considered. As I have shown elsewhere,[1] Judaism and Christianity are incommensurable, and the Christian religion could offer nothing to the Jew which he regarded as better than what his own religion already afforded. Now his own religion laid the primary stress upon *doing* the Divine Will; *that*, before everything else. The necessary corollary of this axiom is a pure and lofty ethic, such as Judaism has always had. Christian theology repelled him at every point, by its assertion of the doctrine of the Trinity, the Deity of Christ, the sacraments; but, even more, Christian morality, as he saw it around him and suffered the effects of it, was to the Jew an abomination and a horror. Christianity showed itself to Jews in its most repulsive form, whatever it might look like to its own adherents. The Church from the beginning had given the first place to right belief. Without that no one could be saved, on Christian lines. The conversion to Christianity of pagan Europe left the pagan morality but little changed for ages afterwards. When one thinks of the state of things in regard to common social morality disclosed in the pages of Chaucer or even Shakespeare, whose country was presumably no better and no worse than other countries, and when one remembers the stern passion of chastity which is one of the fundamentals of the Jewish ethic and practice, it is not wonderful that the Jew should shrink from the Christian who was known to him, and who was so often disloyal to his own exalted moral code. The Christianity that was offered him, or forced

---

[1] R. T. Herford, *The Pharisees*, London, 1924, p. 214.

upon him at the cost of suffering or death, was not recommended by the character of the persecutors who were its advocates or the mobs who took the word from them.

Moreover, the Jew in virtue of his religion set great store by education. Not every Jew was learned, but all respected learning. No Jewish community throughout the period before us but had some scholars, some who would teach and some who would learn. Most Jews could read and write in ages when amongst Christians only the clergy could do so, and of them not all. In the pursuit of knowledge, not excluding secular learning, Jews were in no danger from any ecclesiastical censure as were the pioneers of secular learning amongst Christians. Doubtless there were those who considered that the Talmud contained all that a Jew needed to study, and others who, as in Spain and Italy, sat at the feet of Aristotle and studied philosophy and science. Maimonists and anti-Maimonists might denounce each other, and this or that Rabbi might excommunicate an opponent, or invoke external authority against him; but, when all was said and done, there was nowhere a Jewish Pope, still less a Jewish Inquisition, to force heretics into silence. The Christian Pope, and much more the Christian Inquisition, provided an object-lesson which the Jew could readily understand.

The attitude therefore of Jews towards Christians was not only one of moral aversion, but of intellectual incompatibility; not pride or scorn but simply the recognition of the difference between knowledge and ignorance. And both the moral and the intellectual attitude were due to the Jewish religion.

Here then we have the root-cause of that unlikeness between Jew and non-Jew which made assimilation impossible, and which led the heathen and much more the Christians to regard the Jews as aliens in their midst and to treat them accordingly. Such deep-lying cause could not be overcome by any mutual good-will or desire to be on friendly terms with each other. Apart from definite grounds of dislike or repulsion, the natural inclination of mankind is to friendliness. Jews and Christians often lived on good terms with each other until the era of persecutions began. And probably even in the darkest days the Jew would have been glad if Christians would allow him to be friendly with them; feeling as he did that the country he lived in was as much his native land as it was that of his neighbours, and that apart from his religion he was by nature very much what they were.

That claim was never recognized. The feeling of unlikeness, which caused the Jew to be regarded by Christians as an alien outsider, persisted throughout the whole period, being intensified when the Church brought her forces to bear on the task of conversion, when the economical conditions of the time drove Jews into the position of moneylenders, and reaching its height when the policy of segregation was introduced in the institution of the ghetto. It was this sense of unlikeness which made the Jew the immediate object of suspicion on the occurrence of any notable crime or public calamity. He was at the mercy of every rumour which accused him of ritual murder, committed for the sake of obtaining Christian blood to be used in the celebration of the Passover;—a charge which if it were not so horrible would be merely absurd, in view of the Jewish horror of eating blood. In the time of the Black Death rumour flew through Central and Western Europe saying that the Jews had poisoned the wells, and that the disease was their work. The aloofness of the Jew made it easy to believe that he was a sorcerer; he could read books in an unknown language, he knew things that other people did not know. Jewish physicians were in request everywhere, the Church frowned on them, but they were to be found at the court of every sovereign from the Pope downwards. And Jewish physicians in spite of, or even by reason of, their eminence were feared and suspected in an age when medicine and magic were thought to be not unrelated.

It was partly a cause and partly a result of Jewish 'otherness' that although they were citizens of the country in which they

FIG. 9. DOMESTIC PASSOVER CELEBRATION

From a XIVth-century Hebrew manuscript in a Spanish hand

For description see p. xvii

FIG. 10. SCENE IN A SYNAGOGUE
From a XIVth-century Hebrew manuscript in a Spanish hand

For description see p. xvii

lived they were dealt with by exceptional laws, or by the mere caprice of their rulers, not having such protection as the ordinary laws afforded to the ordinary citizen. They were often, as in Germany, France, and England, regarded as the personal property of the king, being agents for collecting his revenue, and victims in the process of paying it in. They were forced into this position because they were not under the Church law which forbade lending money at interest. Someone had to do it, as an economic necessity, in times when money on credit was urgently needed for building, for wars, and for the spendthrift extravagance of courts. The Jews, being aliens, were forced to do it, and were everywhere hated for doing it. Financial ability came only by long practice; it was not natural to the Jew who under other conditions has given ample proof of his proficiency in handicrafts, to say nothing of agriculture, which in Bible times as in those of Josephus was his chief occupation.

In all these ways the Jew was made to feel his aloofness from the rest of his fellow-citizens; such was their way of marking the fact that he did not, could not, or would not assimilate with them. And the root-cause of it all was his religion and the demands which it made upon him.

We shall therefore take this fact of aloofness, inability to assimilate, as our guide in studying the period with which we are concerned, and shall inquire in what way Jews in this country or that, in such and such circumstances reacted to their environment. It might be said that this is to answer the question what was the influence not of Judaism but of non-Judaism upon Jews? In a sense it is so; but the answer to the question depends after all on the influence upon the Jew of his Judaism, in virtue of which he reacted to his environment in a manner different from that in which he would have reacted if he had not been a Jew.

We shall make no attempt to give an historical survey of the period. The history of eighteen centuries cannot be compressed into a few pages; and even if it were possible to do so, the attempt would be useless for the purpose of this chapter. The history must be read independently, and no better guide can be found than the volumes of Graetz.[1] We shall consider Jewish life from three different points of view, first as seen in the mass when a large number of Jews inhabit a country; second, in the local community, and third in the individual experience of particular Jews. To this survey, illustrated by examples chosen here and there over the wide field inclosed within the period with which we are concerned, the remainder of this chapter will be devoted.

'Dispersion', *Diaspora*, is the name applied to the residence of Jews outside Palestine. Dispersed, scattered, they have always been, not merely in the local sense of being found in many countries and in many cities and villages of those countries, but in the deeper sense of having no central authority, whether political with a seat of government, or even religious with a central synod or ecclesiastical head. There have been communities large or small, ranging from the *Golah*, the great Babylonian Jewry which succeeded to the prestige of Palestine from the fourth or fifth century, down to some little handful of Jews in a village. Each of these communities had some method of regulating its affairs, both internally and in relation to other communities so far as that was possible or occasion demanded. The only authority recognized was that of eminence as a teacher or as a man of commanding influence in his country. Obviously such authority could only be exercised where the man who wielded it was known. The *Geonim*, the religious heads of the Babylonian schools after the closing of the Talmud (sixth to tenth centuries), were appealed to for decisions upon ritual and legal questions by Jews living in other lands; but what they gave was instruction and advice, they had no power to enforce obedience to their decisions. In Northern France in the eleventh century the great Talmudist Rashi held a somewhat

[1] H. Graetz, *History of the Jews*, English translation, 5 vols., London, 1901.

similar position. He was revered as the greatest teacher of his time, and his fame spread far; but it never placed him in any position of control over Jews even in his own country, let alone those of distant lands where his name was hardly known. The same is true of Maimonides in the twelfth century, the greatest genius of medieval Jewry. His word carried more weight than that of any man, in his own time and for long afterwards. But so far was he from being in any sense a governing authority for all Jews, that one of the fiercest controversies which has ever raged in Jewry was that between the Maimonists and the anti-Maimonists: those who followed him in the inclusion of philosophy and science amongst the proper subjects of *Jewish* study, and those who would restrict it to the Talmud.[1]

These are three pre-eminent examples of what is to be found on a small scale in countless instances. It only amounts to saying that, in the absence of any central authority, either council or ruler, the Jews of any community would apply for advice to the most eminent teacher known to them, whether the Rabbi of the chief community in their land, or the revered head of some school in a distant land to whom they could send a letter and a deputation. More than this was not possible when Jews were scattered in so many lands; and although Jewish traders did something to promote exchange of thought as well as of goods, and could thus bring Jews of widely sundered lands into conscious fellowship with each other, they could not establish any kind of unity amongst Jews, social, economic and least of all political. They could have done nothing at all if there had not been already the unity of religion described above. The unity which is the object of anti-Semitic dread has never existed. There never has been and there is not now any central authority, ruler, public council or secret conclave, anywhere or at any time, which could speak or act in the name of all Jews in all lands, much less impose commands upon them, or dictate, let alone

[1] On Rashi see article by Dr. Singer, pp. 283–285, 293.

enforce, a common policy. In the *Golah*, the great community of Jews in Babylonia, there was, under the Persian Kings, a tolerated autonomy in domestic affairs, and a recognized Head, the *Resh Galutha*. But this 'Head of the Captivity' was by no means sovereign even over the Jews of that country; and he had no authority over Jews in other countries except by the prestige of his office, as being the most eminent Jew of his time in the then known world. He held a place at the Persian court not unlike that of one of the great tributary princes of India in relation to the British Raj.

Jews in other countries had no central organization comparable to that of the Persian Jewry under the *Resh Galutha*. Even where a considerable number of Jews were living in the same country, as in Egypt or Germany, France, Spain, or Italy, there was never any recognized head of such a group. It was often convenient for the civil government—Emperor, King, or baron—to deal in Jewish matters with some eminent Jew; and naturally the advice of such a Jew would count for much with those on whose behalf he acted. The famous Isaac Abarbanel at the court of Castile held some such position, not by official appointment but in actual fact. And Rabbi Joselmann of Rosheim was the frequent intercessor with the Emperor Charles V on behalf of his Jewish subjects in Germany. He has left a most interesting journal relating his adventures in that capacity; a journal on which it would be tempting to dwell if the space at our disposal allowed.

Perhaps the nearest approach to the self-government of the Persian Jews under the *Resh Galutha* is to be found in the *Council of the Four Lands*, known as the *Waad*, which virtually governed the Jewry of Poland, Lithuania, and Galicia for nearly two centuries, until it was suppressed by the Polish Diet in 1764. The Waad was a council of deputies from all the chief local communities concerned; and it acted as a kind of Supreme Court, on the one hand to decide on appeal disputes between one com-

FIG. 11. BRONZE BOWL USED BY ENGLISH JEWS IN XIIITH CENTURY AS RECEPTACLE FOR ALMS FOR PALESTINE

For description and interpretation of Hebrew inscription see pp. xvii–xviii

munity and another, and on the other hand to take measures for the safeguarding of Jewish rights when threatened by the civil power, and to maintain the strict discipline which was necessary for the self-preservation of the Polish Jewry. It had, as the means of enforcing its authority, the ban of excommunication solemnly pronounced and strictly carried out against recalcitrants.

There was no other case on so large a scale as the Waad in Poland. But it was often found possible and useful for the Rabbis and *Parnassim*, or wardens of neighbouring communities, to meet from time to time for consultation on matters affecting the common welfare or the common danger. Thus, the communities in Provence kept in close touch with each other for such purposes; and in the Rhineland the three communities of Metz, Speier, and Worms formed a group by themselves.

In all these local and partial groupings of Jews, large and small, there was no other unity than that of religion, no other unity which included all Jews everywhere. And it is remarkable that even the religious unity was not carried so far or felt so strongly as to allow of a central ecclesiastical organization. The attempt was made, in 1538, by the Rabbi of Safed in Palestine, Jacob be Rab, to reintroduce the rite of ordination in such a way as to make Palestine the seat of religious authority for all Jews everywhere. The authority of Maimonides was claimed for the proposal, but even his great name was not sufficient to carry it to success. That success would have implied that every Rabbi in future, in every Jewish community throughout the known world, would have had to depend directly or indirectly on Palestine for the right to hold his office. The plan came to nothing in 1541. It originated with Jacob be Rab in Safed; it was denounced by Ibn Habib, the head of the College in Jerusalem. When even the Jews of Palestine itself were ranged on opposite sides in the controversy it was out of the question to expect the assent of all the Jewries of other countries.

Of any comprehensive unity amongst all Jews there is not a trace, and there never has been, except that of the common religion. There is, indeed, the unity of suffering and the unity of compassion. The chief era of persecution which began with the first Crusade in 1096 brought sorrow and misery upon the Jews in well-nigh every land where the Church could make its authority felt; and Jews were moved by their own sufferings to keen pity for those of their brethren. When the expulsions of Jews from England in 1292, from France in 1306, and Spain in 1492, sent thousands of homeless wanderers adrift, the Jews of other countries did all they could to help and shelter them, ransom them from captivity, keep them from starvation, not knowing but that their own turn might come next. That was the only way in which Jews as a whole acted together. It was a real unity, and it had no other basis than that of the religion which taught them pity in a pitiless world.

And here is seen one effect of the alienation between Jews and Christians explained above. In the Christian view, whether that of the civil ruler or that of the dominant Church, the *Jews* as a whole, wherever they might be, were regarded as a single body to be dealt with *en masse*, or at least in as large a number as circumstances would allow. If a king decreed the expulsion of all Jews from his dominions, the blow was aimed at them as a collective whole; but it fell upon them as local communities and the several members of those communities. In the Jewish view there was no such civil unity, nor the possibility of establishing it. If there had been, even in a single country, the decrees of expulsion or of persecution might have had a very different result from that which in fact they had. In like manner the economic position of Jews, oppressed on the one hand and protected as agents of the revenue on the other, might have been very different if the Jews, say, of France or Spain or Germany, had had in their several countries anything to call a political unity. Jews in those and the other countries were in their own view just citizens of their country, subject to its laws and not maintaining nor attempting to maintain any kind of *imperium in imperio* to divide their allegiance. They were not recognized as citizens on an equality with the other citizens, being, indeed, subject to all manner of disabilities; but they could only submit, having no collective means of redress, nor even a voice which could speak for them all. So it remained to the very end of the period under consideration; and so it remains to the present day, for while Jews have been admitted to some share, sometimes a complete share in the civic and political life of their country, they have never established, nor sought to establish, nor dreamed of establishing a political unity for the Jews of any one country, let alone for those of the whole world.

We pass on to consider Jewish life as it appears in the local community as distinguished from the whole Jewish population of a country. The local community is the real unit of Jewish life, the group of persons living in close proximity to each other and having its centre and focus in the synagogue. It is true that in a large community there might be more than one synagogue, but that does not affect the principle involved in the fact that it was the synagogue on which the unity of the local group depended. That this was so is one of the many results of the Jewish religion and of the sense of alienation which, as already explained, it tended to produce. The Jews were always in a minority in whatever country they inhabited; but, if that were all, they might have been distributed evenly among the rest of the population without forming noticeable groups. Wherever they came they brought with them a religion which was not that of the people in whose midst they lived, and which in proportion to the strength of their adherence to it prevented their assimilation to their neighbours and exposed them to treatment varying from unfavourable remark to violent persecution. Jews therefore naturally drew together, both for mutual encouragement and for mutual defence, so far as defence might be possible. They naturally made the synagogue the centre round which they grouped themselves, because the synagogue was the place where their religion influenced them most strongly.

It was sometimes impossible for a very small local group of Jews to have a synagogue, but no community was complete until it had one. Not merely for the purpose of common worship, because prayer could be offered though there were no special building set apart for the purpose, nor even as many as ten men to join in it. The synagogue was not exclusively a place of worship, it was for the furtherance of every activity in which the religion of the Jew found expression. Teaching and learning were directly fostered by the synagogue, and all the charities of the community were managed from that centre. It would take far more space than this chapter will allow to describe in detail the communal life of Jews in the period before us. The reader is referred to Abrahams's *Jewish Life in the Middle Ages*,[1] which is a mine of information on the subject and to which the present writer is greatly indebted. Assuming what is there stated in detail we can only endeavour to trace some effects of the influence of Judaism upon Jews when seen in the local community instead of in the mass.

The natural cause of the local grouping of Jews was no more than the fellowship of like with like amidst a crowd of dissimilars. Before the era of persecution began the instinct of self-preservation seldom came into play. Jews, though living in close association with each other, still were able to mingle in the common life around them to a considerable extent. But, from the time when persecution began, the local grouping of Jews gradually came to have another meaning, no longer beneficial but injurious to the community. So far as Europe is concerned there were few if any outbreaks of violence on the part of Christians against Jews until the eleventh century, notably

[1] Philadelphia, 1911.

during the first Crusade, when the turbulent horde of armed men marching towards the Holy Land massacred and plundered many Jewish communities along the Rhine and the Danube on their way. These massacres were more in the nature of pogroms than of systematic persecution; but they were significant of the way in which the mind of Christendom was hardening towards Jews as being not only aliens but enemies of the Christian faith, and was making ready to enforce that opinion by violence. It is true that the Church, through its responsible leaders, did not commit itself to the policy of persecution and massacre. It sought the conversion of the Jews; and, if they would not accept baptism, at least they should be allowed to live as standing witnesses to the wrath of God and the truth of the Christian religion. Yet it was only a natural deduction from such premises when the Jews were made the victims of fanatical violence and unrestrained brutality as often as opportunity offered or an excuse could be found. Such were never far to seek, in times when rumour was powerful through the lack of general knowledge, and when the Jew, as shown above, was necessarily an object of suspicion. So for centuries the Jew lived in a constant state of alarm, and often of acute suffering, never knowing but that he might be driven from his home or see it burnt over his head, or be butchered by a mob of ruffians, or sent wandering, with wife and children, to find shelter if he could and if not to die of starvation. There is a book in Hebrew with the significant title of *Emek Habacha*, the Valley of Weeping. It gives in a series of annals the record of all the massacres known to the writer from the earliest times to his own (middle of the sixteenth century). Every page of that terrible book is, as it were, soaked in blood and tears; and not the least impressive feature in the recital is the way in which the story of horror is told with a dull monotony in which all separate incidents are merged in one long agony of grief. The Memorial books of many communities in France and Germany record the names of those from their midst who died for their faith. There also is to be found the same blunted sensibility due to the strain of suffering; and incidents are recorded without remark which are beyond belief and intolerable to quote.

This may be sufficient to indicate the nature of the treatment to which the Jew was liable at any time say from the eleventh to the sixteenth century. It is not that persecution was continuous. In any given country, and still more in any one community, there were often long intervals of comparative safety. But always and everywhere there was for Jews the feeling of insecurity, and the knowledge of the danger which was never far away. Even in times of comparative ease and safety the Jew was always living on sufferance, at the will or caprice of the sovereign power whatever that might be. And one of the most essential tasks of the local community was to organize the life of its members so as to maintain its vitality amidst those perilous conditions. So long as the community could hold together there was a haven of refuge for its harassed members, where they could find the solace and strength of their religion and live their own life unmocked by the hard and cruel world. The Jew found the only freedom for the higher life of the spirit in the synagogue and perhaps even more in the home, the Holy of Holies for the Jew in all ages of his wanderings.

The influence of his Judaism upon him amid such conditions was to strengthen in him his allegiance to it, as indeed is usually the effect of persecution; but it also had the result of making him an unconquerable optimist, in spite of such trials of his patience and frustration of his hope as have seldom been laid upon any victims of religious intolerance. So it is seen that in the life of the community, in its times of comparative tranquillity, there was provision for social enjoyment which hardly seems possible to people with such memories and such haunting fears. The more the Jews were thrust out from the fellowship of their

FIG. 12. CLIFFORD'S TOWER AT YORK IN 1807

This tower was built in 1068 and was the scene of the massacre of the entire local Jewish population in the year 1190

For further account see pp. xviii–xx

Christian neighbours and driven in upon themselves the more strenuously they sought to develop their own life amongst themselves, and to provide as best they could what was refused to them outside.

The antagonism of Christian to Jew showed itself in its most extreme form as persecution, and gradually shaped a policy intended to give practical effect to the separation between the adherents of the two religions. And the two significant expressions of that policy were the institutions of the wearing of the yellow badge and the compulsory seclusion of the ghetto. The former dates from the year 1215, when the Lateran Council at the instigation of Pope Innocent III ordained that Jews in all countries should be required to wear on their dress a mark to distinguish them from Christians. The pretext was the desire to prevent illicit intercourse between Jews and Christians of opposite sexes, an evil of whose existence there is but slight evidence. The effect was to make visible and tangible the fact that Jews and Christians were separated, and to disclose the Jew as being literally a marked man, to the hostile observation of Christians wherever he might be. The enforcement of the decree varied in different countries and from time to time, according to the zeal or otherwise of the ruling power. But, exceptions apart, the obligation to wear the badge was on the whole general in Middle and Western Europe from the thirteenth century till far on in the period before us. It is easy to see how this usage added to the general sense of insecurity of the Jew, in addition to wounding his self-respect by pointing him out to public obloquy as an enemy to God and man. Without it he might have a chance of passing quietly on his own errands without attracting notice. That protection was taken from him; and every one who had a gibe or a curse or a blow for the Jew, a wrong he could inflict or a hate that he could let loose, knew his victim when he met him. That the Jews could endure under centuries of such treatment is proof of the influence of their religion upon them, when they could have saved themselves at once by giving up the struggle and being baptized. But no men and women however brave and devoted could remain exposed to centuries of the kind of treatment symbolized by the yellow badge without showing the effects in their mind and character. The Jew could never retaliate, he could only submit; and if the Jew in literary description by the Christian and in common imagination is often a cringing and despicable figure, it should be remembered how he became so, so far as he did actually become so. The traits of character are those which the Christian ancestors of the one bred in the Jewish ancestors of the other.

The policy of actual separation of Jew from Christian, of which the yellow badge was the first visible symbol, was carried a long way farther by the institution of the ghetto (Figs. 13 and 14). That name in common usage denotes a restricted quarter of some city within which the Jews of that city were forced to live. Ghettoes did not come into existence at one and the same date. The most conspicuous example is the ghetto of Rome which was definitely established in 1556. But there had been others earlier, as in Prague (Fig. 14) and elsewhere. Jews in any locality, as shown above, naturally tended to congregate together; but till the institution of the ghetto such congregating was so far voluntary that it was not usually required by law. Legal compulsion to reside there made the Jews' quarter a ghetto. And legal compulsion required that so far as possible the ghetto should be cut off from the surrounding city, if not always by an enclosing wall at least by gates at the entrance of its streets. Within the narrow enclosure thus marked out the Jews of the city were compelled to live, and however much their numbers increased they were not allowed to extend their boundary. For unsanitary conditions and over-crowding the worst slum of a modern city would be preferable to a medieval ghetto. Under some such conditions the majority of Jews in Europe

Fig. 13. A GHETTO OF SOUTHERN TYPE. SIENA

Fig. 14. A GHETTO OF NORTHERN TYPE. PRAGUE

were forced to exist during three centuries (*c.* 1400–*c.* 1700), the dreariest period in all Jewish history. Perhaps no more deadly injury has ever been inflicted upon any considerable number of human beings than that inflicted by the ghetto, or rather by those who devised it. For though it is true that Jews living in ghettoes did succeed in keeping up their life as a community inspired by their religion, though their continued existence under such conditions was a miracle of faith and perseverance, the fact remains that the ghetto life was an unnatural life, a forcible interference with the normal intercourse of men with their fellowmen, aggravated by brutal oppression and fanatical hatred. Being an unnatural life it worked ill both to those who enforced it and to those who suffered under it. Both Christian and Jew were made to accept, as one of the settled factors in social and national life, that there should be a permanent barrier between them, not to be surmounted or removed. To the Christian the ghetto was a cage where certain dangerous and repulsive animals were confined. To the Jew it was the prison in which he was shut up from the free world outside, where as a man he ought to have been allowed to take his part. True, the ghetto afforded him a certain measure of protection; for its gates, if they shut him in, at the same time shut the Christian mob out. And within its gloomy shelter he did his best to live the life which as a faithful Jew he desired to live. Within the ghetto there was found room for study, for charity, and even for social festivities. In that prison there were no jailers, and the prisoners kept order amongst themselves, succeeding to a wonderful degree in keeping alive the communal consciousness of religion as their uniting principle.

To do so much was a great thing; and if the ghetto period cannot compare in mental activity with the great days of the Talmud schools in Northern France under Rashi and his successors in the twelfth century, or the brilliant era of the Spanish poets and philosophers which ended with the expulsion in 1492, what wonder since the first requisite was wanting, the freedom to exchange thought with their fellow men and to move to and fro through the world ? The Jew as he is to-day is the descendant of those who suffered the unnatural constraint and distortion of their lives in the ghetto ; and most if not all of the traits of character which are thought to mark the Jews as an alien people, and disagreeable at that, are the effects not of racial origin but of that Christianity which drove them apart and kept them apart, branded them with a badge of shame, herded them into ghettoes, or drove them helpless and unpitied from one land to another, the victims through the centuries of those who professed the gospel of peace and brotherly love.

To give any indication of the influence of Judaism upon Jews considered as individuals is not easy, though it be the most interesting part of our study of the period. There is of course an immense literature ; and every book that is written is in a sense evidence as to the mind of its writer. Some general indication of the Jewish response to the influence of religion is afforded by the ethical literature which has never been unrepresented in any age in which Jews wrote at all. When it is remembered what were the outward conditions under which Jews for the most part lived, as indicated above, the attitude of the Jewish mind towards the Christian tormentors is truly remarkable. Over and over again the Jewish moralists teach the lesson of charity and forbearance, of strictly honourable and truthful conduct, of kindness and helpful service to Christian as well as to Jew. The hymns in the synagogue uttered the grief and the longing for deliverance of tortured Israel, but seldom if ever the note of hatred against the oppressor. The cry for vengeance was uttered, but yet only by men who remembered that 'vengeance is mine, saith the Lord'. And in controversial writings, or books intended for the instruction of Jews in their religion, the difference in tone between Jewish and Christian polemics is as the difference between light and darkness. Compare Maimonides with Eisenmenger.

Yet, while this is true, it is also true that Jewish literature but seldom takes the form of autobiography. Very much even of the Bible is anonymous. The prophetical books contain the work of others beside the men whose names they bear. The Psalmists reveal the depths of their religious experience, but not in a single case their own name. And in the medieval literature, though great names abound they are the names of men who said very little about themselves. The Jew, however strongly marked his own individuality might be, seldom if ever forgot that he was a member of the community. If he wrote it was something which should benefit the community, and only comparatively seldom did he write about himself. It is remarkable how scanty are the biographical details which can be gleaned from the works of even the most eminent Jewish writers of the Middle Ages, and a complete biography of any one of them, as the term is understood at the present day, would be out of the question.

The opportunity therefore is very seldom afforded to the student of the Jewish literature in any part of our period of learning from a writer's own words what his religion meant to him and what was its influence upon him.

Apart from some few small fragments (contained in medieval texts edited in the *Revue des Études Juives* and other journals) there are two notable examples of real autobiography to be found within our period. One is the life of Solomon Maimon, the other the Memoirs of Glückel Hameln. Maimon and Glückel illustrate in strongly contrasted ways the influence of their Judaism upon them. Maimon was born and bred in Poland amidst conditions which gave him no outlet for the imperious craving of his mind for wider knowledge. The story of his life is the story of a violent revulsion from Judaism, at all events in the form presented to him in his early training. How far he retained any of its higher meaning it would be hard to decide. His main desire was to study philosophy and incidentally to confute Kant. His introduction to Mendelssohn places him at the very end of our period; and he was one of those who showed how the new spirit was beginning to stir in the Jewish mind, narrowed and darkened by three centuries of enforced isolation. A man of profound genius and most disordered life, he stands in his right place between the old order and the new, unable to find peace in either.

Maimon with his uncouth garb and Yiddish speech standing amid the brilliant company in Mendelssohn's *salon* was a visible symbol of the profound change which was coming to pass in Jewish life.

Glückel Hameln, a century earlier, knew nothing of any such possibility of change. The story of her life (1645–1724) is the self-revealing confession of one who found in her religion all the help, comfort, and joy that her soul longed for. She was just a woman of the people, the wife of a business man, married young and left a widow with a large family before she was fifty. She wrote the account of her life in her old age, as she says to drive off sad thought and while away the night hours when she could not sleep. She wrote for the sake of her children and grandchildren, that they might learn from what she had found as she went through the world. The story which she tells, so far as its events were concerned, might have been told of hundreds of other lives. What makes her book so deeply interesting is the unconscious disclosure which she makes of her own mind. Her religion was intensely real to her, and it took the form of fervent gratitude to God for all his mercies to her, of humble submission to his will, and of a deep sense of her own sinfulness. 'Who knows', she says, 'what is good for us sinful men, whether that we should live on earth in great wealth and enjoyment, and spend our time in this transient world in mere pleasure, or whether it is better for us that the heavenly Father should have us always in his gracious keeping in this sinful world, so that we may have our gaze always set on heaven and may cry to our loving Father with all our heart and with flowing tears. Thus I feel assured that the faithful gracious God will have mercy on us and redeem us from our long sad exile.' Such as those words indicate she remained throughout her long life, a very humble-minded woman whose love to God and trust in Him were ' her light and her salvation '. She had no time to sit and indulge in pious meditation. She had to look after her growing family and her household, and she helped her husband in his business, so that he did nothing without consulting her. After he was dead she bore the burden by herself with great toil and growing weariness. Through it all she was just the same, in prosperity and in adversity. Trust in God was the sheet-anchor of her life; she was filled with wonder and gratitude for his goodness, and thought that if she were not a poor ignorant woman she might serve him better. There is not in the whole book a single harsh judgement on any one whom she thought to have done wrong. Of one who had brought heavy losses upon them in business, by what certainly seems gross dishonesty, she says, ' I will not name him because he is dead; and I will not blame him, for I cannot read his thoughts, and it may be that he did what he did with good intention'. But she is warm in her praise of those whom she respected, and of none more so than the men with whom in her later years she did business. She went through life as a brave, capable woman, a sort of working saint with not the slightest idea that she could ever be thought a saint.

This is only a glimpse into one Jewish life, and the book which affords it is, so far as I know, the only one of its kind. But it is fitting to place at the end of this study of the influence of Judaism upon Jews the figure of Glückel Hameln, and to reflect that after seventeen centuries of 'sad exile' Judaism could produce such a life amongst the rank and file of Israel. She was not of those who made great contributions to learning, she was no scholar or philosopher or poet; what she wrote was not in Hebrew but in the Yiddish which she always spoke, the language in which she thought and loved. She was just herself, one of her people, sharing in their life, their hopes, their fears, their aspirations, their undying trust in God.

And is it not true that in some sense she is a type and representative of her people through all the centuries of their dispersion? For, apart from any contributions made by Jews to the general welfare of the world, as shown in other chapters of this book, the chief significance of the presence of the Jews in the midst of Christendom is that they should simply be and continue to be such as their religion made them.

Israel has done much and suffered much, and surely more remains for him to do. But perhaps the most important function that he has fulfilled in the world is that he has been what he has been, and has stood unshakable to bear witness, at the cost of life and death, to the truth committed to him.

R. Travers Herford.

Works bearing on the subject of this chapter.

H. Graetz, *History of the Jews*, English translation, 5 vols., London, 1901.
M. Güdemann, *Geschichte des Erziehungswesens und der Kultur der Abendländischen Juden*, 2 vols., Vienna, 1880–1888.
I. Abrahams, *Jewish Life in the Middle Ages*, London 1896.
I. Loeb., *Réflexions sur les Juifs*; posthumous essay in the *Rev. des Études Juives*, xxvii, xxviii.
Many Hebrew texts in the foregoing Journal, the *Jewish Quarterly Review* and others. The *Emek Habacha*, by Joseph ha Cohen, edited by Letteris, Wien, 1852. *Zichronoth Glückel Hameln*, Yiddish text, edited by D. Kaufmann, Frankfort a. M., 1896.
Solomon Maimon's *Lebensgeschichte*, 1792.

FIG. 15. MUHAMMAD'S JOURNEY THROUGH THE CELESTIAL SPHERES

For description see pp. xx–xxi

THE INFLUENCE OF JUDAISM ON ISLAM

Not the least valuable part of a man's legacy to his successors is known as the 'good will': it is intangible and indispensable; intangible because it exists only in association—the reputation of the original owner and his wares; and indispensable because the new-comer can only hope to prosper by trading on the accepted merits of his predecessor. It was the fortune of the founder of Islam to secure this 'good will' at the beginning of his ministry, and it stood his successors in good stead in their subsequent relations with the educated populations of Syria, Mesopotamia, and Egypt.

At first sight the relation of Judaism to Islam is complicated by the presence of Christianity, an intermediate legatee; but the complication is not real because those writings, doctrines, rites, and traditions which were taken over by the Christians from the Jews, with or without acknowledgement, must in all fairness be credited to their original owners and authors. It is of little moment that certain beliefs flourished side by side in Jewish and Christian communities in the Arabian peninsula when it is a commonplace that Christianity as a way of salvation 'cometh of the Jews'. Therefore in this chapter though it may appear that certain ideas or rites, which were demonstrably existent in Judaism centuries before the rise of Islam, are tinged with Byzantine Christianity, nevertheless the genius of the people with whom those ideas and rites originated will be held to have prevailed, and the existence of similar phenomena in contemporary Christianity will be ignored.[1]

---

[1] Since these pages were written Mr. Richard Bell's *The Origin of Islam in its Christian Environment*, London, 1926, has appeared. He ignores the influence of Judaism.

Whatever be the world's opinion as to the Arabian prophet's sincerity there can be no doubt as to his stupendous ability. The Kuran may be held to support the assertion of Muslims that Muhammad was ignorant of letters (though his contemporaries thought otherwise and it is incredible that a prosperous merchant was unable to read a bill of lading), but as a man of affairs he has seldom been surpassed. The earliest chapters of the Kuran are eloquent of a soul conscious of the overwhelming might and splendour of a transcendent God: they inevitably produce an impression of the depth of the writer's feeling and the urge of his message of judgement to come. No other motive is obvious. So much cannot be said of the later Medina *suras* or chapters. The early chapters take no side in the wretched strife between Jew and Christian. Arabia was then the home of Jews and Christians, and early in his career Muhammad was profoundly affected by the teaching common to both. It is highly probable, to judge from his later development, that he felt keenly the religious inferiority of his race, and he sought to ally himself now with one and now with the other monotheistic religion. The conclusion he came to after an acquaintance of some years was that both were right in their prediction of resurrection to judgement, of paradise and hell, of the ministry of angels and other matters; that Judaism would never be a universal religion nor commend itself to the Arabs in the form in which he knew it; and that Christianity as taught in Arabia was in many respects indistinguishable from idolatry. Further, he perceived that the strength of both systems lay in their possessing revealed books. For him these books had a fascination which he never entirely succeeded in shaking off. Thus while Jews and Christians in mutually accusing one another of tampering with the text of the Old Testament afforded Muhammad the opportunity of levelling a similar taunt in later days against them both, Muhammad seems to have accepted without hesitation, as do

Muslims to the present day, the principal miracles of the Old and New Testaments. The plagues of Egypt, the fountain of water struck from the rock by Moses, stand side by side with the miraculous birth of Jesus, son of Mary, and are *de fide* in the Muslim community.

The position of this remarkable seeker after God was not without its difficulties. Jews openly regarded Christians as abominable blasphemers against God, while Christians looked on Jews as murderers of the Son of God. Yet both religions claimed to be true. The genius of Muhammad lay in his appreciation of the state of affairs. He searched for common ground on which to construct a Church which he probably hoped would include all monotheists. The common ground was the religion of Abraham, who was ignorant of the law of Moses and certainly no Christian. It is not impossible that Muhammad borrowed this appeal from Moses to Abraham from Christians. The keen interest he took in theology may have led him to inquire of Christian priests, who are more than once mentioned in the Kuran, why it was that Christians did not keep the law of Moses, and he may have found one who was able to tell him of the famous argument of Saul of Tarsus that the promises were to Abraham. ' Know therefore that they which be of faith, the same are sons of Abraham. And the scripture, foreseeing that God would justify the Gentiles by faith, preached the gospel beforehand unto Abraham, saying, In thee shall all the nations be blessed. . . . A covenant confirmed beforehand by God, the law, which came four hundred and thirty years after, doth not disannul, so as to make the promise of none effect ' (Gal. iii. 7–8, 17). Whether this conjecture of the present writer be true or not, it is certain that Muhammad, like Saul of Tarsus, was driven to find some justification in revealed books of his attitude towards Judaism ; and if he did not consciously follow Christians in postulating Abraham as the ideal servant of God, at all events the coincidence is remarkable. It is interesting to observe that, though the Meccan *suras* contain numerous references to Abraham, they do not assign him that position of paramount importance he obtained as the result of the more accurate information Muhammad acquired when he mixed daily with the flourishing community of Jews in Medina. The genius of Muhammad perceived that Abraham lifted the reproach of heathenism from the Arab race. For Abraham, ' the friend of God ', the saint of Jews and Christians alike, was the father of Ishmael the progenitor of the Arabs. One step more and Abraham and Ishmael are claimed as the founders and builders of the Ka'ba at Mecca and the historical basis of Islam is assured. By this masterly stroke Muhammad made a powerful appeal to the conservatism of the Arabs. Islam was not an innovation, it was not an adaptation of Judaism and Christianity, as his fellow tribesmen asserted; it was a return to the original religion of Abraham and Ishmael who prayed at the Ka'ba that they and their posterity might ever remain Muslims.

Before we endeavour to trace the steadily increasing influence of Judaism on Muhammad and his successors, it may be well to consider the expansion of the Jewish Diaspora in the Arabian peninsula. Commercial relations on a large scale between Palestine and Arabia certainly go back to the days of Solomon; and many books of the Old Testament, particularly Job and Proverbs, which are strongly marked by the presence of Arabic words, show that the connexion was steadily maintained. The Jewish genius for commerce probably accounted for the presence of Arabian Jews at Jerusalem at the Feast of Pentecost vouched for by Acts ii. 11. In all probability these Jews came from the neighbouring Nabatean kingdom, though there is no reason to confine the activities of Jews to the north of Arabia when history and legend agree in tracing them to the southernmost confines of the peninsula. By the seventh century Jews were firmly entrenched in Al Hijr, Al 'Ula, Taima, Khaibar,

Taif, and Medina; and the south had known a Jewish hegemony. Local conditions at Mecca, the centre of a heathen cultus and a community largely parasitical, were not likely to attract so many Jews; yet, as the half-way house of merchants plying between the Yemen and Syria, Mecca could hardly have been entirely neglected by them. Whole tribes seem to have gone over to Judaism and accepted monotheism before the rise of Muhammad; but as all information from Jewish sources is wanting, it is impossible to say what was the status of Judaism in Arabia at this time. In default of such evidence some have felt themselves free to condemn the Jews of Arabia as ignorant and unorthodox. But the abundant material which Muhammad obtained from them serves to show how baseless such an assertion is. A just critic will not play the judge when the defendant's case has not been heard.

The following pages will demonstrate the wide range of the Arabian Jews' knowledge both of the Old Testament and of *midrash* or homiletic narratives. Further, it must be remembered that the Kuran can only supply us with Biblical and midrashic stories as they were remembered and repeated by Muhammad; it is too late to inquire whether the informants are prepared to accept responsibility for the stories from scripture and tradition in the form in which they exist in the Kuran.

But after all external evidence for the place and importance of Jews in the life of Arabia in the seventh century is scarcely needed, for the majority of the chapters of the Kuran witness to the depth of the impression they made on the Prophet's mind. He can never let them alone: appeal, argument, rebuke, denunciation, and cursing are successively addressed to them; they can never be ignored. Provided that it can be established that Muhammad imbibed Jewish doctrines, and that he was in a high degree indebted to the oral traditions of the Rabbis, the question, What particular individual taught him? is of no more practical importance than an inquiry as to who prepared a contemporary prelate for confirmation. The impression the Kuran makes on the reader is that its Jewish fibre has been spun from hearsay and scraps of information gathered from conversation with different persons. The extraordinary solecisms of the Kuran, e. g. the confusion of Miriam, the sister of Aaron, with Mary the mother of Jesus, are probably due to Muhammad's obtaining information from synagogue proselytes of his own race rather than from men of Jewish descent.

The origin of the Jewish community in Arabia is most obscure; there is every indication that their sojourn had been exceeding long, and the spread of Judaism among the Arabs was marked by breadth rather than depth. Thus they were not able to offer that determined and united opposition to a new religion for which they have ever been conspicuous. Indeed it has been the misfortune of Jews to suffer most intensely through the optimism implicit in their faith. A people who fervently believe in the advent of a heaven-sent deliverer who will usher in a reign of universal peace, justice, and prosperity, is to some extent at the mercy of any person who claims to fulfil that role. Intense and expectant hope in a coming Messiah cost the Jews innumerable proselytes in the Roman period; and five hundred years later their Arabian converts went down before an Arabian prophet who claimed to be God's last messenger to man whose coming was foretold in their own scriptures. Muslim *hadith* or tradition records the implacable opposition of the true Jew to Muhammad and his message, and Muhammad's death in the course of a few years at the hands of a daughter of Abraham. But *hadith* also records the accession to the new faith of many ' Jews ' like 'Abd Allah ibn Salam, Salman the Persian, and others.

The Kuran itself indirectly bears witness to the presence of Jews behind the scenes, inasmuch as Muhammad boldly reproduces the taunts of the Kuraish that he was composing a message partly from his own mischievous imagination and partly from stories long familiar which were dictated to him. 'The unbelievers say: This is nothing but a fraud which he hath fabricated; and other people have helped him therein. But they say that which is unjust and false. And they say: Tales of the ancients which he has had written down, dictated to him morning and evening!' (xxv. 5). A second passage is even more significant: 'We also know that they say it is only a human being who teaches him. The tongue of him at whom they hint is foreign while this is in plain Arabic' (xvi. 105). The cap fits, and Muhammad himself puts it on. He admits that he knows who it is that is referred to; but he denies that that person can possibly be the source of his information on the ground that he speaks a foreign tongue. History has shown that the Arab mind is a strange mixture of credulity and shrewdness; and the Kuraish, whose voice cannot now be heard, refused to believe on the double ground that they had heard all this before and that Muhammad's instructor was a foreigner of the race which had consistently propagated this teaching.

The dictum that a prophet is without honour in his own country was certainly true of Muhammad, for those who knew him best in Mecca were not 'converted' until the sword was the sole alternative. The reasons why these men refused to believe are preserved in the Kuran in the passages just quoted. They had heard—how could they not have heard when the city of Medina and the neighbouring wadi oases swarmed with Jews—of all the principal points of Muhammad's preaching, one God, Hell, Paradise, and the Day of Judgement. They were not impressed when they heard these doctrines in the rhymed prose of the ordinary Arabian seer, especially when he was obviously associated closely with a member of a foreign nation notorious for holding those views.

At a comparatively early period of his public ministry Muhammad eagerly sought the support of the Jews. He claimed to confirm the Torah and to be the prophet whose coming had been foretold in Deuteronomy. And it is not surprising that he should have received a certain measure of support and encouragement from local Jews. One who attested the truth of the Law was surely one who was prepared to keep it and to further the spread of Judaism : the Kuran refers to the Jews' pleasure at Muhammad's preaching. We need look no further for confirmation of the theory that Muhammad learned of the Jews, for his claim that the Jews ' recognize him as they do their own children ' is a clear proof that he had close personal relations with them and discussed his preaching, the nature of prophecy and history, and the coming Messiah. The subsequent relations between Muhammad and the Jews of Arabia culminating in their slaughter and banishment are not germane to our subject, and we may now examine the extent of Jewish influence on the Kuran.

It will be convenient to survey the effect of Judaism on the Kuran generally, in doctrine and cultus, and to separate where necessary the biblical from the talmudic element; the advantage of this last course being that any lingering suspicion that the predominating influence is Christian will be dispersed.

First, then, the general influence in doctrine. The one central dogma of Islam is that there is no God but Allah *la ilaha illa'llah*. It has become a habit with some writers to ascribe a quasi-magical power to the desert in effecting this belief : with them the desert has become the peculiar habitat of monotheism—a desolate waste creating a craving for oneness. The truth is that the desert—at any rate so far as the Arabs are concerned—has nothing at all to do with monotheistic belief, as a glance at any page descriptive of the religion of pre-Islamic Arabs will assure the reader. Monotheism in form and content comes from Judea. It may be conceded that the Arab has been more belligerent, but he is certainly not more vehement, in its defence than the Jew. The daily cry of the *Muadhdhin* was familiar to Jews centuries earlier, and is found in those very books of the Old Testament—Psalms and Isaiah—which exercised a paramount influence on Muhammad's mind.

It is not to be thought that the Kuran adds nothing to, or modifies nothing in, the Old Testament conception of God. Islam, despite the infusion of an enormous number of ideas demonstrably foreign in origin, has always succeeded in being itself, whether at its inception, or during the reign of the earlier caliphs when the inrush of foreign culture was fiercest, or at the present day. True though it is that Judaism has been the most generous contributor to its fundamental doctrines and its everyday praxis, Islam has made of its borrowed material something that is not and never was Judaism. The body is there but the spirit has departed. If the Old Testament is brought under contribution the thought is severed from its members: the generous breadth of vision and the self-effacing heroism of the Hebrew prophet are lost or obscured in the self-centred pronouncements of the Arabian prophet. If Talmud and Midrash exercise sway, the keen-witted discussions of critical rabbis are lacking, and Jewish lore has changed its distinctive colouring for a coat of many colours. Thus, if our purpose is to indicate what Islam holds that once was Jewish, it is not maintained that Islam has left the borrowed garments unchanged. The Kuran is the creation of one man whose strong individualism marks its every page; and with the possible exception of the Joseph *sura*, which is more fully discussed below, all that the author heard he gave forth to his followers in his own way.

Of general resemblances in doctrine and mode of doctrinal representation we may cite the following. God in the Kuran, as in the Old Testament, is transcendent, omnipotent, omniscient. In both books these ideas are sometimes somewhat paradoxically expressed in anthropomorphic terms. In the Kuran the gulf between God and His creatures is wider: angels are more frequently interposed between Him and men, upholding His glorious throne. Here the divergence is only from biblical theology: to later Jewish thought this teaching was perfectly familiar. God created the heavens and the earth in six days: man was formed from earth and to earth he returns. He fell from his original high estate through listening to the wiles of the devil. Man has continued to sin against God and has for the present lost paradise; but he is not necessarily estranged from God. Muhammad follows the Law rather than the Prophets in equating sins against the moral with sins against the ceremonial law, and on the assumption that both codes emanate from God he is right in so doing: he agrees with the Law and the Prophets in regarding idolatry, or the association of other gods with Allah, as the most heinous crime of man. The way of salvation is Repentance, Faith, and Good Works: the pious will meditate night and day on Allah and His revealed word. It was a noble thought which prompted Muhammad to sum up the godly life in the word *Islam*, patient submission to the decrees of God and acceptance of His will. In this all-embracing term he numbered the 'goodly fellowship of the prophets' from Noah even unto Jesus.

The many personages which appear again and again in various *suras*, with the exception of the few figures taken from the New Testament and one or two names which cannot be identified with certainty, are Old Testament characters; and the space and importance allotted to them are out of all proportion to what is given to other personages. A comparison of the biographies is most instructive: it illustrates the limitations of Muhammad's knowledge and gives the impression of a student striving, and on the whole successfully, to assimilate information he is gaining from instructors. In some places the text of the Kuran is only intelligible if we refer back to the midrashic source of Muhammad's information; and all the earliest Muhammadan commentators showed their good sense by going to the same source for their explanatory notes as their master before them. In other places information is given and amplified in later *suras*; in almost all it is clear that Muhammad never had an inkling that there was any difference between tradition as enshrined in holy scripture and the fanciful stories in Jewish *haggada*.

Muhammad follows the Biblical story of the fall of Adam pretty closely though there are some curious inaccuracies. Adam was created of clay and his wife was formed from him; there is no mention made in the Kuran of Adam's rib as the material. Adam becomes God's vicar (*khalifa*), and gives names to everything. He is tempted by the devil, and, in spite of a divine warning of the evil one's intention, he succumbs and is cast down from paradise (which Muhammad located in the heavens) to earth where he repents and is restored to God's favour. The famous passage proclaiming the divinity of man made in God's image wherein God speaks in the royal plural had been interpreted by Philo as the gracious condescension of the Creator who would commune with His angels. And both Kuran and Midrash claim to know what was said in the heavenly council. The angels express surprise that God should create one who will commit sin and disorders in the earth. God replies that He knows best; and proves to them that their knowledge is inferior to man's knowledge. The further statement of the Kuran that Iblis, the devil, alone of the angels refused to do Adam homage is hardly likely to be of Jewish origin, for man ' is made a little lower than the angels '.

The story of the world's first murderer affords a most informing example of the influence of the Jew behind the scenes. The quarrel between Cain and Abel follows pretty closely the Biblical account in its main details; but the Kuranic conclusion contains a remarkable addition. God sent a raven which scratched in the ground to show Cain how to hide his crime. Cain thereupon repented of his evil deed. Muhammad continues thus: 'For this cause we commanded the children of Israel that he who slayeth a soul shall be as though he had slain all mankind; but he who saveth a life shall be as though he had saved all mankind alive.' Here his dependence on Midrash is patent. In the first place the appearance of the raven who was seen by Adam and Eve to bury its mate in the ground is quite naturally recorded in Jewish tradition, and is in keeping with the early chapters of Genesis. One of the functions of Genesis is to explain the origin of many human customs and phenomena, and tradition rounds off the Biblical account of the first death with an explanation of the means taken to dispose of the first corpse: it answers the question, Why are the dead buried? A slight difference between Kuran and Midrash is that in the latter the sorrowing and perplexed parents saw the raven's act; in the former, Cain the murderer witnessed it. But the sequel is extraordinary. The *halakic* rule of the Kuran just quoted appears in the *Pirke de Rabbi Eliezer immediately after* the narration of the burial of Abel and in its characteristic Rabbinic phraseology and exegesis. The word blood is used in the plural, not in the singular, from which is deduced: 'He who slayeth a soul . . . shall be as though he had slain the whole world; and he who saveth a soul from Israel the scripture imputes to him the saving of the whole world.' It is impossible to doubt that Muhammad has borrowed both *haggada* and *halaka* just as they stood side by side in their Jewish setting.[1]

Passing over the nebulous figure of Enoch (Idris), who was exalted to a 'lofty place'; Noah, now among the prophets

[1] Cf. A. Geiger, *Was hat Mohammed aus dem Judenthume aufgenommen?* (reprint) Leipzig, 1902, p. 101 f.

The Influence of Judaism on Islam

and preachers as in Rabbinical writings; the building and destruction of the tower of Babel; we come to the greater figure of Abraham.

The title *Khalil*, the friend of God, which the Old Testament confers upon Abraham, is confirmed by the Kuran, and is still commemorated by Jewish and Muhammadan pilgrimages to the place of that name in Palestine. Those who are familiar with the pseudepigraphical works ascribed to the patriarch by the Rabbis will not feel surprise when they find Abraham cited in the Kuran as an author. In the book of Genesis Abraham is called by God to leave his father's house and kindred and journey to the land of promise. It is elsewhere in the Old Testament explicitly affirmed that Abraham's ancestors were idolators; and the break which Abraham makes with the past is represented as a mysterious venture of faith which is wonderfully vindicated by Jehovah. Abraham is for all time a type of simple obedience and noble trust.

Jewish *haggada*, like the contemporary apocryphal gospels, often attempts to explain the mysteries or obscurities of the sacred text. The attempted embellishment of the intentional reticence and restraint characteristic of the inspired writers often mars rather than enhances the effect produced by the reading of scripture. Nowhere is this more apparent than in the story of Abraham's response to the call of the one true God. The Kuranic passage [1] is worth quoting at length to illustrate Muhammad's method: 'Of old we gave unto Abraham his direction for we knew of him. When he said to his father and to his people "What are these images to which ye are devoted?" they said: "We found our fathers worshipping them." He replied: "You and your fathers have been in obvious error." They said: "Art thou come to us in truth or art thou of those that jest?" He said: "Nay your Lord is Lord of heaven and earth Who hath created them both, and I am one of those who witness

[1] *Sur.* xxi. 52.

thereto; and by God I will surely plot against your idols after you retire and your backs are turned." So he broke them in pieces save the largest of them, if haply they might return to it. They said: "Who hath done this to our gods? Verily he is a wrongdoer." They said: "We heard a youth named Abraham talking about them." They said: "Then bring him before the eyes of the people if haply they may witness." They said: "Hast thou done this against our gods, Abraham?" He answered: "Nay but this the largest of them hath done it; so ask them if they can speak!" So they returned to themselves and said: "Verily ye are the wrongdoers." Then falling into their former error (they cried): "Thou knowest that these cannot utter!" He said: "Do ye then worship to the exclusion of God what can neither help nor harm you at all. Fie on you and what ye worship to the exclusion of God. Can it be that ye do not understand?" They said: "Burn him and come to the aid of your gods if ye are men of action!" We said: "O fire, be cold and to Abraham a safety!" And they wished to plot against him so we made them the losers.'

The position of these verses in the *Sura* of The Prophets makes it obvious that Muhammad had a definite method in making up the stories he drew from his Jewish associates. It does not require much imagination to see that he is putting the Meccan idolators' excuse for their polytheism in the mouth of Abraham's contemporaries. It would probably be a fair inference to assume that the origin and provenance of the gods of the Meccan pantheon had long been forgotten by the Arabs, a race notorious for a contempt for archaeology while fiercely conservative and tenacious of custom. Muhammad's message is the same as he conceived Abraham's to have been, and though he was not yet an iconoclast he doubtless cherished the design, afterwards fulfilled on his triumphal return to Mecca, of destroying the images in the Ka'ba. The

Kuran in the passage we have just cited only contains a brief *résumé* of the Rabbinical account of Abraham's destruction of the people's idols. The grim humour of the Midrash is not reproduced. The Midrash on Genesis tells us that when a woman brought an offering of fine flour to set it before the idols, Abraham's patience was exhausted; and taking a staff he smashed all the idols save the largest, into whose hand he thrust the staff that had been the instrument of their destruction. When his father returned and demanded an explanation, Abraham told him that the idols had quarrelled among themselves as to who was to eat the flour-offering first, and that the biggest had smashed the others with the staff which he still held in his hand. Terah, his father, enraged, asks why he invents this foolish story, as though the idols had understanding. Abraham replies: 'Do not thine ears hear what thy mouth uttereth?' His father then delivers him to Nimrod, who casts him into a fiery furnace whence he is delivered by God.[1]

The Kuran differs profoundly from the Old Testament in the treatment of its characters. The stories of the patriarchs and prophets in their original setting are straightforward narratives, which, even if composite in origin, carry the reader forward from the birth to the death of the hero, and present a consecutive, or fairly consecutive, series of events. Not so the Kuran. There the characters are introduced to serve their turn as successful preachers in antiquity of the doctrines promulgated by Muhammad in the present. Thus in an entirely different context we find Abraham entertaining the angels. Contrary to the Biblical story, it is asserted that the messengers did not eat of Abraham's roasted calf, so that he withdrew from them in dismay. But this detail is not of Muhammad's invention: already the Talmud has given the story a Docetic turn and asserts that the angels did not eat and drink: they merely seemed so to do.

[1] Geiger, *op. cit.*, p. 119 f.

In one *sura*, the twelfth, Muhammad really addresses himself to the task of setting forth the life story of a prophet.[1] The *sura* entitled Joseph is in some respects the most interesting in the Kuran, because it keeps to the point and is comparatively free from those digressions and anacoloutha which mar so many of the later revelations. For its own sake it deserves a more detailed examination, and no chapter in the Kuran can better illustrate the weight of Jewish lore and exegesis which bore upon the Prophet's mind. In the beginning of this *sura* there is a self-conscious note in the emphasis which is laid on the assertion that the revelation has been set down in Arabic, that perhaps its hearers may understand. The statement, put into the mouth of Gabriel, the Hermes of Islam, that Muhammad has hitherto been heedless of its import, can only mean, when read in conjunction with the preceding verse, that the history of Joseph was known to Muhammad and his contemporaries and that they cared little about it, presumably because it was not a genuine Arabian tradition. This latter difficulty Muhammad swept away for all time. Even in this, the best attempt at a biography of a former saint and prophet, the limitations of Muhammad as a biographer plainly appear; for the story opens thus: When Joseph said to his father: 'O my father, I saw eleven stars, the sun and the moon bowing down to me,' the reader is not helped by any introduction to an intelligent grasp of the situation: indeed it is doubtful whether it could ever have been put in its proper setting without the labours of the commentators, who drew extensively from Jewish sources.

The narrative, it is true, unwinds to a certain extent in the telling, but it could only be the composition of a man ignorant of letters. It would be tempting to suppose that much of the Kuran has been lost, were it not that it has an inner unity

[1] Cf. Israel Schapiro, *Die haggadischen Elemente im erzählenden Teil des Korans*, Teil I, Berlin, 1907.

The Influence of Judaism on Islam

which forbids this assumption; and tradition, which, *ex hypothesi*, ought to give supplementary sayings on the innumerable obscurities in the Kuran due to omission, very seldom provides anything to the point. The commentators who really elucidate the sacred text of Islam do not draw their material from any *agrapha* of the Prophet: they go behind him to his source—the oral tradition of the Jews. The interpretation of Joseph's dream, which is self-apparent in Genesis, is clear to the commentators, though it is anything but clear from the text of the Kuran. It is not stated in this chapter that Joseph had eleven brethren, though a later verse pictures Joseph's parents prostrating themselves before him. Moreover, what of Joseph's mother who had died long before? Muhammadan exegetes follow haggadists in explaining that his foster mother is meant. It is not unlikely that Muhammad himself was ignorant of the early decease of Rachel. Genesis records the fact that Jacob's partiality to Joseph and Benjamin was patent to his brethren and the direct cause of their hatred. The Kuran adds the interesting comment of the brethren: 'Our father is in obvious error.' Here Muhammad is in agreement with the Rabbis who choose this text for a sermon to warn their people of the sin and danger of preferring one son to another, the suffering of the nation in Egypt being due to this sin of their ancestor.

According to the Kuran, Joseph, while lying helpless in the pit, receives a revelation that he will yet live to remind his brethren of what they have done. This is a detail which has no support in Genesis, but Haggada has much to say on the point. There Joseph is cast naked into the pit, and an angel clothes him magically from an amulet suspended from the patriarch's neck. Elsewhere we read that the garment made by God for Adam descended to Jacob. Doubtless the commentators of the Kuran, who explain that Abraham was cast naked into the fiery furnace and was there clothed by Gabriel in a silken garment which the flames could not scorch, have another version of a story which was still a part of oral tradition. This garment, they say, became an heirloom which Joseph wore round his neck as an amulet.

It is not altogether certain whether the writer of Genesis meant it to be understood that Potiphar was a eunuch. Muhammad certainly implies that he was childless when he makes him suggest to his wife that they should adopt Joseph as a son. The commentators follow Jewish exegetes in affirming the reason of Potiphar's childlessness. The steadfastness of Joseph under strong temptation has won for him the position of a St. Anthony among Jews and Muhammadans alike. To the Jews he is Joseph The Righteous *par excellence*, just as Abraham is The Friend. To Muslims he has become, through a misunderstanding of the Hebrew word *saddiq*, Joseph The Truthful (the meaning of the word in Arabic), and his reputation as a veracious interpreter of dreams stands as high as his fame for continence. The story of Joseph's resistance to temptation is told in Genesis with simplicity and restraint. ' My master hath kept back nothing from me, but thee, because thou art his wife : how then can I do this great wickedness, and sin against God ? ' Joseph is an honourable and a deeply religious man. But to some of the Haggadists a reason other than that given by Joseph seemed imperative ; and we find his refusal to fall into sin attributed on the one hand to fear of hell fire, and on the other to a mysterious apparition which met his eyes at the very moment he was about to abandon resistance. Muhammad, too, seems to have felt the need of both these motives to explain a self-control so unexampled. Joseph, says he, would have given way had he not seen the ' sign (or, plain evidence) of his Lord '. The Kuranic word is a strange one and invites comment. What was the sign ? The Talmud asserts that Jacob appeared at the window uttering warning and reproach. He smote Joseph on the breast and

The Influence of Judaism on Islam

his passion went forth at his finger tips. This explanation is repeated almost verbatim by the commentators; and it can hardly be doubted that they were filling up the gaps their master left in his narrative, either accidentally or by design. A provocative atmosphere of mystery often lingers round passages in the Kuran, a hint that the speaker could say more if he pleased or willed; the present passage is a fair example of many.

Some curious additions to the narrative will be found in the Kuran at this point. Joseph's innocence is established; but nevertheless his master determines to imprison him. The truth of the matter leaks out; and the other women of the city mock at Potiphar's wife. To justify her former weakness she invites them all to a banquet. She hands each of them a knife, and then summons Joseph, who is within hearing, to show himself suddenly to them. 'And when they saw him they were amazed at him and cut their hands and said: " By God! this is not a man! This is nothing but a noble angel!"' This addition to the Biblical narrative has been lifted bodily from *haggada*.

Before Joseph's brethren make their second visit to Egypt their father cautions them not to enter by one gate but by different gates. The command is explained in *haggada* as due to fear of the evil eye. This explanation is accepted by the commentators, and evidently by Muhammad himself, though he prefers to hint at secret knowledge possessed by Jacob alone which induced this caution.

As an interpreter of Judaism Muhammad must be held to have failed. At this stage of his career (the last verse of this *sura* claims that ' this is no new tale of fiction, but a confirmation of previous scriptures ') he certainly would seem to have desired to pose as the restorer of ancient paths; the disingenuous character of his methods, while apparent at once to the Jews, was concealed from his own countrymen. He claimed to obtain his knowledge from on high, while every instructed Jew must at once have recognized the source of what he said, what he hinted at, and what he concealed. In this last category it is significant that the same Jewish sources from which Muhammad so freely draws his material for the story of Joseph, tell how Gabriel comes to Joseph to impart to him secretly the knowledge by which he confounds his detractors and obtains temporal power.

The extent of Jewish influence on the Kuran has been by no means exhausted; every Old Testament character mentioned therein is dealt with in the manner dictated by Jewish exegesis, whether it be Moses or the Queen of Sheba; and the fabulous elements of the Kuran are almost always to be traced to Jewish sources.

When we turn from the Kuran to the lawyer's handbooks we find that the laws and customs prescribed by the Kuran are often translated into everyday practice according to the Law of Moses as it is developed and expanded in the Talmud.[1] This development came about naturally and without pressure: the anxious efforts of the doctors of the law in Medina to establish the beliefs and practices of Muhammad as the faithful Muhammadan's standard in this life, resulted in very many ways in approximating Islam to Judaism; and then, by a compensatory reaction, in making arbitrary deviations therefrom. An example was afforded them by the Prophet himself, who had at first prayed with his face turned towards Jerusalem and enjoined his followers to do the same. But later, when he had abandoned all hope of a religious alliance with the Jews and found them for the most part antipathetic to his schemes of enrichment by forays and brigandage, he changed the *Kibla* (direction of prayer) from Jerusalem to Mecca. Not a little pressure has been exerted by Judaism in this negative way.

A new sect or a new religion must always use the legacy

[1] T. W. Juynboll's *Handbuch des islamischen Gesetzes* (Leiden, 1910) is a most useful summary.

FIG. 16. THE HANDSOME JOSEPH, POTIPHAR'S WIFE, AND HER FRIENDS

FIG. 17. JONAH RESTING UNDER THE GOURD WITH THE WHALE IN FRONT OF HIM

From an Arabic manuscript in Edinburgh University Library written in 1306 A.D.
The main incidents in the story of Jonah are faithfully
recorded in the Kuran, Suras 10, 37, and 68

The Influence of Judaism on Islam

bequeathed by its predecessors; but, unless it has boldness to eschew much, it stands to lose all in the absorption of its devotees in the mother religion. Fear of this result is always more potent in the professorial than the popular breast, as the violent reaction of official Protestantism from Catholicism, of Islam from Judaism, and indeed of Judaism from Hellenism, will prove. That which is good and attractive in itself will gain a hold on the affections of the multitude despite all formularies and confessions, so that formularies must be cancelled or interpreted anew. Not the least attractive feature of Islam is its generous receptivity. Difficult as it is to prove a negative, it is probably true to say that no attitude of mind or soul in Judaism and Christianity is, or has been, unrepresented in Islam : animism, prophetism, legalism, scholasticism, chiliasm, asceticism, and mysticism have all claimed their adherents and won an accepted position within the system of life which is Islam.

The early history of the development of the Islamic Church is not much clearer than the origin of much that is vital in the organization of Christianity to-day. After the death of the Prophet, Islam is cast upon the world like a seed, and one can but admire the amazing tenacity and fertility of the germ. The old idea that hordes of semi-savages went forth in resistless numbers from the deserts of Arabia, sword in right and Kuran in left hand, has been for ever dissipated by the researches of modern historians. The truth is that, apart from the comparatively small number of men who had come under the personal influence of Muhammad and were loyally devoted to his person and principles, the Arabs knew little and cared less about Islam. Moreover, the most important of Muslim conquests, Syria, the stronghold of the Umayyad caliphs, was won by the defection of the *Christian* Byzantine auxiliaries. Had it not been for the disaffection rife among these disciplined Arabs of the marches trained in the finest military organization of antiquity, it is likely that the religion of Muhammad would have gone the way of other minor Eastern heresies. Hunger and covetousness, far more potent forces than fanaticism, drove the Arabs from their arid peninsula to the fair places of the earth.

Researches into this, the evolutionary stage of Islam, are anything but complete; but they serve to show the religion of Muhammad as it stands in the Kuran in conflict with the superior civilizations of Byzantium and Persia. Unlike the Germanic hordes who overran the Roman Empire, the Arab princes were men who had long been familiar, from caravan journeys to Syria, with the organization of the Byzantines: the frontier guards, the customs, the postal system, engineering, hydraulics, and the whole system of provincial administration; and whatever the rude and untutored native of the interior thought about Western civilization, he was not allowed to wreck it. When the Arab princes set foot as conquerors in the ancient cities of Jerusalem and Damascus they did not come to destroy but to enjoy.

The earlier rulers of the house of Umayya showed no little ability in carrying on the administrative system of their predecessors. Far from it being true to speak of Muslim fanaticism at this time, it was, on the contrary, perhaps the only period in Muhammadan history when a genial tolerance towards non-Muhammadans was permissible or possible. There is an adequate reason for this: Islam as an organized state religion did not exist. Of course it was there in *esse*; but the legionaries were indifferent to it, the caliphs blasphemed it, and those who fain would accept it to escape paying the poll-tax on non-Muslims could find few to tell them what it was. Well-authenticated stories are current of would-be Muslims greeting the Almighty with the salutation common among fellow Muslims, and of Arabs of Basra at the end of the first century not knowing the form of daily prayer!

The Influence of Judaism on Islam 151

Here was the opportunity of the older religions. Arabs had been forced to employ Jews and Christians in high offices in the state because they alone possessed the necessary knowledge of administration. They had to be called in as experts and specialists in all that concerned the arts and sciences. And whatever the high-born Arab with his age-long pride and independence thought, he was gradually forced to a position of inferiority. The logic of facts prevailed, and once again the conquerors were vanquished by the superior culture of the conquered.

There is a vast literature of religious polemic containing the arguments of Jews, Christians, and Muslims; but little, if any of it, belongs to the early days of Islam. Still it is of value in showing the lines on which religious controversy ran, and it undoubtedly witnesses to the interest a later age had in such questions. The rise of the earliest Muslim sects points to the great influence exercised by Judaism on Islam, and it would be remarkable if the followers of the older monotheistic religions, who gained by their intelligence such a moral superiority in the community, had not directed to a very considerable extent the course of religious thought and custom among the Muslim peoples. A large number of Jews accepted Islam at a time when their academies in Mesopotamia were active centres of theological learning. But they exacted their price. They compelled Islam to conform to the religion of their fathers in all essentials. Prayer, ceremonial cleanliness, domestic and sexual hygiene—vital matters to the Jew—were settled and established on a basis almost always to his liking.

A most fortunate accident has preserved to us traces of this external influence. Muslim jurisprudence, a most comprehensive subject which embraces all that a believer should think, do, and be, cannot stand alone inasmuch as it is religious law, and therefore requires divine, or quasi-divine, sanction. Perhaps, owing to the sacred character of law among all primitive peoples who seem to have regarded legislation as a divine prerogative, it is illegitimate to postulate Jewish influence; but nevertheless, the astonishing similarity between the content and form of the Talmud and *Hadith* (the traditions as to what the Prophet said and did, on which all law not already promulgated in the Kuran, is theoretically based) calls for comment. In Judaism all law explicitly and implicitly was revealed to Moses on Sinai; and the subsequent labours of the Rabbis were held merely to extract the full meaning of the law originally given by God. This is a defensible and intelligible position.

But when Muslims began to formulate their laws it is significant that the idea of framing the lives of the community on a quasi-sacred basis was not present to their minds. The earliest legislators, it is true, recorded the practice of the Prophet where it was known, or thought to be known; but they did not scruple to use their own intelligence and their knowledge of the existing customs of their countrymen in compiling their law books. But inasmuch as the Arab conquests wrought a revolution in the habits and lives of the people, the practice of the Prophet was in many matters no guide at all.[1] There was, therefore, danger that the law of the community might rest on no sacred basis and remain purely secular. The danger was the greater because practice obviously approximated ever more closely to the laws and customs of Jews and Christians. What was to be done? The difficulty only existed in the minds of the religious. Law books had long been in use throughout the Muhammadan Empire before pious doctors succeeded in providing them with an apostolic background. An enormous number of *hadith* or traditions was current in

[1] The difficulty is still felt by pious Muslims. The Prophet certainly forbade the taking of usury. Did he mean to forbid investing one's money in a limited liability company? The question is a burning one at the present time.

The Influence of Judaism on Islam

the empire in the third century of the Hijra, partly because the historical Muhammad had been transformed in the passage of the centuries into a wonder-working all-powerful interceder with God, and men were highly esteemed who knew, or claimed to know, details, however insignificant, of his life ; and partly because there was a commercial value in tradition : he who could relate a number of traditions which were unknown to the hearer could exact a high price for his information. The encouragement thus given to forgery and invention produced an enormous crop of spurious traditions which have now perished. But enough remained to fulfil the design of the religious, which was nothing less than the compilation of a corpus of traditions of the authentic words and deeds of Muhammad which should give divine sanction to the law of the community.[1]

Orthodox Sunnis acknowledge six collections of traditions as canonical, and through them all law goes back to the Prophet of God. Tradition, however, preserved more than mere *hadith* confirming praxis. It is of enormous value in that it is quite oblivious of contradiction, and records the views of the warring sects, the discordant ambitions and the different beliefs of the many peoples under Muhammadan rule. We have in *hadith* a more or less faithful picture of the intellectual and cultural ferment of the first centuries of the Hijra. *Hadith* is an authoritative exposition of Islam as Talmud is of Judaism ; and the more deeply they are explored, despite superficial differences, the plainer does the similarity become.

The place of *halaka*, or rule of life, is taken by the legislative sections, wherein folklore, anecdote, and historical notes are freely interspersed, just as *haggadic* and *midrashic* strands run at will through the length and breadth of Talmud. Another general resemblance is the citation of authorities. In the place of ' Rabbi A in the name of Rabbi B used to say '

[1] Cf. the present writer's *The Traditions of Islam*, Oxford, 1924.

we have a much longer chain of authorities which always ends in the Prophet or one of his associates. Before we pass to some of the customs and laws bequeathed by Jews to Muhammadans we may notice one or two other points of general resemblance between Talmud and Hadith. The most fundamental of these is the exaltation of oral tradition to the rank of the inspired word of God. In Talmud it is familiar in the statement that whatever may be deduced from the Torah by the Rabbis was revealed to Moses on Sinai: in *hadith* it appears in the form, 'What is in agreement with the Kuran is from me, whether I have actually said it or not'. Another most striking similarity is in the choice of subjects, which, allowing for the different background of Kuran and Torah respectively, is extraordinary. It is hardly likely that this latter similarity is due to the collectors of canonical tradition: indeed that may be said to be impossible. It can therefore only be due to the influence wielded by Judaism during the period when the doctrines and laws of Islam were being codified. So profound was the effect of Judaism on the younger religion as to make it impossible to determine the limits of the latter except in the categories of the former.

The extent of Jewish influence on the Kuran has not yet been explored to the full: still less have the great range of Muhammadan tradition and the encyclopaedic compass of the Talmud been traversed by a competent scholar undaunted by the vast expanse of territory opening before his eyes. The most that the present writer hopes to do is to follow in the footsteps of those who have ventured into this territory and to record beside their finds some small incursions of his own.

Even the tourist in Muhammadan countries is impressed by the atmosphere of prayer in which seemingly the meanest Muslim lives: any one who has spent but a few weeks in Cairo will have found the humble *bawwab*, with his forehead pressed to the floor, going through the postures of prayer meticulously

The Influence of Judaism on Islam 155

prescribed by Islamic ritual; no novel on the Near East is complete without its reference to the haunting cry of the 'muezzin', the voice from the minaret. But few have the knowledge or imagination to see the prototype of this somewhat ostentatious piety in the worship of the synagogue in their own country.

Perhaps the caution uttered in the beginning of this chapter ought to be repeated here: it must not be supposed that Islam has slavishly imitated Judaism in every particular. Far though Islam's founder carried his followers on the path to Tiberias or Pumbeditha, they succeeded in preserving the genius of their own race amid the enormous changes which an alien creed and attitude to life imposed upon them. Here we shall follow some of Professor Mittwoch's steps in tracing the origin of the prayers and cultus of Islam to its home in the very heart of Judaism.[1]

First of all, what is meant by Prayer? It is not personal thanksgivings or petitions. These have their place in the believer's devotions, but they are no necessary part of the same. Prayer is a carefully defined ritual act which must be performed by all Muslims with the same bodily postures and the same ejaculations made in the same order. Some scholars have assumed that the Muslim rite is an adaptation of Christian worship; but this inference must now be abandoned. Though it is always possible that something may have been borrowed from the Church, the genesis of daily and festal prayer among Muslims can only be clearly identified in the synagogue. The similarity is present in the terminology, posture, time, character, leaders, and status of prayer in Judaism and Islam. The

---

[1] The exhaustive comparison made by this scholar, though of great interest to specialists, cannot be given here and must be studied in the author's own work, *Zur Entstehungsgeschichte des islamishen Gebets und Kultus*, Berlin 1913: only the principal points of resemblance between Jewish and Islamic prayer will be noted.

pious Muslim prays no less than five times a day. The close correspondence of the names of these prayers in Arabic and Hebrew and the existence of threefold and sometimes fivefold prayers in Jewish worship point to the obvious conclusion, and it is worth while noticing that the Kuran knows nothing of fivefold prayers. The Islamic *Kira'a* is the synagogal *Keri'a*, and the constant assertion that 'God is Greater' is a substitute for the Hebrew 'God is Blessed'. Prayer is incumbent on women and slaves and children who can understand the import of their words. On the other hand it must not be performed by persons under the influence of drink. Muhammad's prohibition became redundant in a later age, because when wine-drinking was prohibited by the sacred law it was thought unseemly to contemplate the necessity of the earlier prohibition. The latter belongs to Jewish law. The preliminaries essential to prayer are ceremonial cleanliness and proper orientation—Jerusalem to the Jew and Mecca to the Muslim. The first of these requirements is more fully discussed below.

The serious Muslim's worship is no arbitrary exercise: it follows the course carefully prescribed in the *Sunna* which classified his duty in prayer under eighteen points. The first and the most important of these is found in Judaism, Christianity, and Islam alike under the names *Kawwana, Intentio,* and *Niyya*. There is, of course, a different *nuance* in each religion; but the fundamental purpose is the same—the devout concentration of the suppliant on the Deity and on the words and acts of the prayer to follow. It may not be out of place here to express the hope that a more widely diffused knowledge of the three great monotheistic religions of the world may lead in this age of widening intellectual interests to a liberal appreciation of the merits of these three systems of faith and worship among their respective adherents. Literary and historical criticism applied to religion are purposeless unless they contribute to a better understanding; *tout comprendre c'est tout pardonner*.

Emphasis is placed by all three religions on a realization of the majesty of the Deity; perhaps the following three sayings can be left to speak for themselves: (Talmud), 'When ye pray realize before Whom ye stand': (New Testament), 'Pray to thy Father which is in secret . . . and use not vain repetitions': (Hadith), 'Whenever we climbed a height or descended into a valley we lifted up our voices and shouted Allah Akbar! [the indispensable ejaculation in ritual prayer]. The Apostle of God approached us and said: ' Restrain yourselves men! For ye do not call to one who is deaf or absent but to one who hears and sees.'

Prostrations in prayer, which form so picturesque a symbol of piety in the Orient, are a relic of Judaism now only known from the Talmud. Prostration has its practical difficulties in colder climates where other clothes are worn, as medieval Arab writers already note. The greeting of peace in the Muslim rite has its counterpart in the Jewish Tefilla and the Christian Eucharist. Public prayer in which the whole community joins is as strongly enjoined in the canonical writings of Islam as in Judaism and Christianity. The two daughter religions have broken away in entirely different directions in ecclesiastical organization. Islam is more closely akin to the organization of the synagogue which was originally very elastic, while Christianity has been profoundly influenced by the Old Testament sacerdotal tradition. Islam has no priesthood and no pope. Its doctors, like the Rabbis, have no influence beyond that which their own merit and reputation for sacred scholarship can attain for them, though decisions of the supreme authority in canon law have the same weight as those of the Gaons of the early medieval period.

The methods of announcing services or festivals in the Near East were bells, clappers, and trumpets. The latter were sounded by the synagogue authorities from the roof-top, while bells, of course, were in the tower. The minaret is the architectural equivalent of the latter, but the muezzin's call to prayer has close affinities with the Jewish liturgy; just as the sermon-bidding prayer which is artificially divided into two parts corresponds with the reading of the Law and the Prophets in the synagogue. Indeed, in the earliest days of Islam a reading from the Kuran formed one part of what is now a double sermon, and the pause the preacher makes merely to sit down, rise, and begin again, corresponds with nothing but the pause during which the synagogue reader sat while the sacred law was rolled up. Now this practice of delivering the *khutba* (sermon) standing is not primitive; there are tendencious traditions extant which seek to show that it was; but the Umayyads, who are blamed by later theologians for haranguing the worshippers in the mosque while comfortably seated, seem to have followed the custom of their race and the precedents then existent; it would seem, therefore, that there must have been a time (probably in some definite area) when Jewish influence was paramount. This is a subject which cannot be satisfactorily investigated until the colossal bulk of Islamic tradition has been brought under control by the concordance now in preparation at Leyden; but it is one deserving of close attention, for the post-Muhammadan influence of Jews on the very centre of Islam, an influence which in many respects changed and modified the system in many important particulars, is of very great interest. The Muhammadan traditionists often hand down pseudologia of the Prophet which show a peevish irritation against the influx of Jewish and Christian customs and doctrines, and they could be made to throw light on the question as to when and where the custom or doctrine was introduced.

A second line of inquiry is the origin of the Muhammadan laws of ritual cleanness. All who are familiar with the requirements of the Levitical code will realize that the subject is not one which readily offers itself for discussion in any language but the original; but the writer would make one or two observations at this point. First it may be doubted whether Western civilization, which permits a considerable proportion of its population to live in indescribably filthy conditions, has gained by a reticence which is often synonymous with criminal silence. Practically all that Jewish and Muhammadan law demands as a religious obligation in the way of personal cleanliness is imbibed in early training, or adopted instinctively by the cultured, in Western civilization. And as the cultured never come in actual contact with those who are ignorant of the unwritten law of cleanliness, delicacy forbids even the mention of such things. The wisdom and reason of Judaism in this matter cannot but be apparent to those who work or have worked among the poorest classes. Though we do not propose to pursue this inquiry in any detail, it is just to demand that teaching which is urgently needed by millions of the ignorant should not be ignored because it is unpalatable and unnecessary to the cultured few.

Further it is believed, without sufficient warrant, that the Founder of Christianity rejected the whole category of the clean and the unclean. But the instinct which inspired men of old to ascribe an imperative demand for personal purity to the Deity was a sure one which the common sense of this nation approves in a familiar proverb. A positive passion to fulfil the sacred law—an ambition which has often been condemned without a hearing—led the Rabbis into issuing meticulous instructions as to cleanliness which, like our own conventions, could only be observed by those who had the necessary leisure and means. Consequently in Judaism, as later in Islam, the great majority of the community did not keep the law as it was interpreted by the few. The reaction of the Christian Church was violent and unbalanced; and when the hygienic tradition of the Romans all but perished with their empire, there was no body of teaching to put in its place.

The Muhammadans, on the other hand, adopted all the essentials of the Jewish law of the clean and the unclean.[1] The *hadith* faithfully preserves traditions put into the mouth of the Prophet which are placed on record as the pattern for the true believer's imitation. Many of these have not become Muhammadan law: they represent the attempts of Jews to compel Islam to comply with the Mosaic law.

It will have been seen from the foregoing that the Jews achieved a large measure of success in moulding the course and conduct of Muhammadan prayer to their liking and in accord with their traditional rite; and if we were at liberty to pursue the present subject in all its details it would be seen that the laws of cleanliness have been even more profoundly influenced.

The Muhammadans had, and still have, a most useful theological principle which if fearlessly applied would enable them to adapt their religion to most of the currents of thought in the modern world. Students of Islam will have observed how enormous have been the changes in the mental outlook and theological equipment of Muslims during the present century. These changes are fraught with tremendous possibilities because of the principle of Ijma' (best rendered, perhaps, Catholic consent): this principle in brief is that the practice of the Islamic world is what the majority believe, or want it, to be. We are not concerned with the present-day application of the principle, as it can hardly be said to be influenced from Judea; but its importance in the evolutionary period of Islam was supreme. It was Ijma' which produced tradition, not tradition which produced Ijma': that is to say, that many customs and beliefs had become settled, many more were still fluid and contending for existence with rival theories when

[1] Cf. A. J. Wensinck, 'Die Entstehung der muslimischen Reinheitsgesetzgebung', *Der Islam* v, 1914, pp. 62-80.

the need for an authoritative apostolic basis for society was felt. Demand created supply, and consequently the canonical traditions of Islam are full of sayings and recorded doings of the Prophet Muhammad which essay to prove that he fulfilled the Law of Moses. It would be most interesting and instructive to know what proportion of these secured a permanent place in Muslim jurisprudence compared with the number which were rejected. Certainly the number of the former is very high. And seeing that Ijma' was the deciding factor in the compilation of Muhammadan law, Jewish influence must have been extremely powerful to have entrenched itself in popular belief and practice before it coined apostolic assent in canonical tradition.

The subject of the purity laws has been carefully and accurately studied by Professor Wensinck,[1] and we follow his lead. In general, as would be expected, the Islamic law is less rigorous than the Jewish. The fifteenth chapter of Leviticus, which deals with various categories of uncleanness, very definitely lays down the principle of contagion. Thus an unclean person defiles a person or object; and whosoever touches that person or object is *ipso facto* defiled. In Islam, however, the ritual defilement is not passed on to the third party. Nevertheless the question was raised and debated keenly before a decision was come to. Often the tone of the protest or contradiction shows that Jewish teachers have been propagating their doctrines. Thus it had been asserted that a dead body caused defilement, and commentators admit the existence of rival opinions; but the matter is settled with the dictum ' A Muslim never causes defilement, be he alive or be he dead! ' Typically Jewish is the teaching that the carcass of a slaughtered animal over which the name of God has not been pronounced is unclean, as also the attitude to dogs and swine.

Uncleanness is to be removed by washing or bathing. Of

[1] *Op. cit.*

course it is not maintained that the Arabs learned what is a universal instinct from the Jews, but merely that the ritual form, restrictions, and preliminaries are all peculiarly Jewish.

Personal cleanliness evidently appealed to Muhammad, for already in the Kuran we find directions as to ritual washing with water, and, where water is not procurable, with sand. This latter is an edict of the Rabbis; but perhaps the practice was not borrowed from them but was a traditional custom of the Arabs. A close correspondence exists between Talmud and *Hadith* in the careful definition of the quantity of water necessary for ritual bathing or washing. The point was felt to be of such importance that we find it asserted that Muhammad or his wives had vessels specially constructed to contain the precise amount of water required for ablutions. This is an imitation of the recorded practice of Rabbi Nahman. The same discussions occur as to the quantity of water which will suffice for the ritual purification of more than one person; of water partially contaminated by foreign substances, and so on.

It is most interesting to find that all these enactments are opposed by traditions also claiming to emanate from the Prophet. These latter were promulgated by the descendants of the old Arabs who knew nothing of such laws and restrictions and detested them: in fact by resting on some of these antinomian utterances it is possible for the Muslim, did he wish, to rid himself of all ordinances. Jewish requirements as to bathing or washing before prayer are also those of Islam. The bathing of the convert to Islam and the Friday bath likewise correspond to the baptism of proselytes and the sabbath bath. The former, of course, is the parent of Christian baptism. Washing, a lightened form of ritual bathing, is one of the most important of the outward observances of Islam; and is performed in precisely the same order as the Jewish rite: first the face, then hands and feet, are washed, and the name of God is pronounced. Imitation is even carried to the point of pre-

The Influence of Judaism on Islam

scribing that the right side must be washed first and that the washing must be threefold.

We propose to pass rapidly in review a few more points in Jewish and Muslim jurisprudence which prove how profoundly the one has influenced the other. In the first place, the Muslim conception of law is peculiarly Jewish. True, all ancient law was held to be divine in origin; but only Judaism and Islam trace their law to a Prophet and credit him with the refinements and legal niceties of an age incredibly remote (be it in time or culture) from his own. Again, there is a striking similarity in the structure which can only be due to imitation. The Talmud grew up round the Old Testament; but its legal core has not always any obvious connexion with the teaching of the prophets who are sometimes taken to task therein. A life of legal righteousness was possible—though hardly so common as many suppose—without reference to the great ethical principles of the prophets; and men could live with the legal supplement as their principal guide. The development of Islam followed very similar lines. There the legal supplement in a few enturies was enshrined in the books of jurisprudence (*fiqh*) which were the believers' guide, and the traditions on which legal maxims were presumed to rest became merely an object of study to devout theologians. They had nothing to do with ordinary life, the affairs of which were fixed by the particular *fiqh* school to which the Muslim belonged. In the following notes only the abiding influence of Jews on the present practice of Muhammadans will be noted: the greater influence in traditions which have not been given effect to in Muhammadan law must be disregarded.

A certain elasticity is still existent in Islamic law in that new circumstances requiring an authoritative interpretation are determined by *fatwas* or decisions pronounced by the supreme authority on sacred law. Such a practice, no doubt, arose naturally in course of development; but it is difficult not to see the prototype of this legal artifice in the Responsa of the Geonim, though it must be admitted in this case that the form of the Jewish Response has been coloured by the style of contemporary Muhammadan Muftis.

Not all the enactments of Muslim law are of equal stringency: that is to say all are not absolute commands or absolute prohibitions. The recognition of this difference is perhaps the nearest point a Muslim reaches towards the Western conception of a gulf lying between the religious and the secular, inasmuch as he recognizes that certain acts or austerities belong to a religious sphere. Such acts are called *mandub*, commended, or *mustahabb*, desirable. The law falls into five of these categories: the obligatory, the commended, the permissible, the disapproved (i. e. not punishable by law but disliked by the religious), and the forbidden. The familiar categories of the *Mizvah*, *hobah*, *issor*, *mizvath 'aseh*, *lota 'aseh*, *reshuth*, and so on, will instantly occur to the mind of the Talmud scholar as the origin of this classification.

Another point of similarity is the derivation of law by inference and analogy. Hair-splitting ingenuity in this exercise is as common in the Muhammadan legal supplement as in the Talmud, and though philologically the Muhammadan term *kiyas* cannot be derived from the Hebrew *hekkesh*, doubtless the one suggested the other. Thus it is established that the Prophet forbade usurious transactions in gold, silver, corn, barley, dates, and raisins. But legists say that these are merely specimens of categories designed to cover every conceivable case of usury and thus to make the rule an absolute prohibition. The way in which this dictum was dealt with so as to make it an absolute prohibition is strongly reminiscent of Jewish *halaka*. It was argued that gold and silver indicated that everything which could be weighed was intended; others judged that everything that had value was included, and thus the law was made much more stringent in much the same way as some of the rabbinic rules were evolved. These rules obtained by deductions of this kind were fiercely opposed by some legists. The following may serve as a specimen of an argument which might well have found a place in the Talmud: 'Which is the greatest crime in the sight of God, murder or adultery? Answer: Murder. Objection: But murder is tried at the mouth of two witnesses while adultery requires four.' Consequently analogy (*kiyas*) is a faulty guide.

To descend to some particulars. The attitude to marriage and its laws is in many respects similar. The intimate side of married life is fully discussed in Jewish and Islamic manuals of law in much the same way; but here we shall deal only with the public or external features. There is general agreement in principle that celibacy is disgraceful and contrary to the law of God: marriage in both religions is not merely a state 'commended' it is obligatory. According to the great Jewish scholar, Maimonides, the command to be 'fruitful and multiply' is the first obligatory enactment of the Torah.

Here I may translate the remarks of a contemporary Egyptian lawyer who displays a scholarly interest in the origin of his country's laws and notes the great influence of the Talmud thereon: 'He who studies the prescripts of the three religions with laws of celestial origin, Judaism, Christianity, and Islam, will perceive that they agree in recognizing that marriage is a matter imperiously decreed by divine law and human nature; and that the reason for its promulgation is the procreation of children and the perpetuation of the human species. But these religions differ as to the command being absolute and obligatory. Jewish law is extremely firm in asserting its absolute necessity and Islamic law comes near thereto. But the Christian religion is not firm in asserting that marriage is obligatory; it manifests a certain compliance in the matter acting on the saying attributed to Jesus (on him be peace!), which inspires a desire to cut off the worship and put an end to the service of the Creator and asserts the superiority of continence over marriage for those who can practise asceticism, even though they are otherwise fitted for marriage.'

It may be a little precarious to postulate Jewish influence on marriage customs and laws, but in certain particulars, as for instance, the adoption (*inter alia* with the curious addition of the 'milk-relationship', i.e. a foster-sister and so on) of the Jewish table of kindred and affinity wherein marriage is incestuous, and the insistence on the presence of two witnesses to establish the validity of a marriage, Muhammadan law is obviously of Jewish origin. Possibly we ought to add the function of the *wakil* or arranger of marriages, a person invested with far more authority than the mere bringing together of the interested parties. The *wakil* (or *wali*) is generally the woman's nearest male relation.

Judaism has bequeathed very little of its divorce laws to Islam. There are many sayings in the canonical traditions of Islam which I can only attribute to Jews, like 'Nothing is so hateful in the sight of God as divorce'. These still stand as an indication of the more excellent way. But Islam has chosen its own course in this matter, and the revolting practice of compelling a wife who has been divorced with a threefold formula in a sudden fit of anger or for any cause, trivial or weighty, to consummate a 'marriage' with a third party and be divorced by the latter before remarrying her first husband, is of course abhorrent to Judaism.

Muhammad wrought an amelioration in the hapless state of fatherless daughters by decreeing that they were to have a share of the patrimony, though only half the share of a son. This is very similar to Jewish law which prescribed no fixed share to the daughter. Her brothers inherited the estate of their deceased father. The daughter was entitled only to maintenance therefrom. The same holds good of widows.

The attitude of Jews and Muslims towards vows is somewhat similar. The Talmud says that he who vows sins, though he fulfil his vow; the same strong deprecation is to be found in Islam despite the fact that vows were extremely common in the pre-Muhammadan era. Jewish jurisprudence provides for the annulling of the vow by three teachers or one ordained teacher. Islam prescribes an atonement, or rather expiation, *kaffara* (the word is obviously borrowed from the Jews) which takes the form of largesse to the poor, or, where the vow is taken by a poor man, a three days fast.

In connexion with oaths a comparison between the Jewish *Korban* (Mark vii. 11–13), the dedication of property to a sacred purpose in such a way as to make it impossible for it to be acquired, inherited, or applied to any secular purpose by any one, and the Muhammadan system of *wakf* is most instructive. The laws in regard to the slaughter of animals already commented upon, are strikingly similar in the qualifications of the slaughterer, and the severing of the wind-pipe and gullet of the animal, together with the mention of the name of God at the time of slaughter. Further similarities will be found in the custom of washing the dead and of reciting sacred texts while various parts of the body are being washed.

It would only be tedious to pursue this subject in further detail. Marks of Jewish influence will be found in practically every chapter of Muslim jurisprudence, and more especially in the Hadith Literature which forms its alleged justification. As would be expected, in the two centuries or so when Islam was being built up into a rigid system of life, Jews could only be advisers. They were not in a position to dictate the laws and beliefs of their conquerors. Those who are persuaded that Muhammad was all his later life under Jewish influence, and that (whatever additions and modifications he may have made from his observation of Christians) he and his followers, while persecuting the people of the book, drew more and more freely from their book, will not marvel that the humane influence of Judaism has gone so deeply and is yet so thoroughly disguised by the Arabian colouring it has received.

To deal at all adequately with the debt of Islam to Judaism in *haggada* and the Old Testament point of view, a large book would be necessary. Every Muslim writer of the first centuries who would appear in the guise of a learned man had to acquaint himself with the Biblical genealogies of his race, and too, with the further particulars of the lives of those otherwise mysterious personages, David and Solomon. And as it was felt essential that history should begin with the foundation of the world all histories began with Adam and Eve. It will readily be understood how the compulsion which lay upon Muslim scholars to go to Jews and Christians for all theological and archaeological learning forced them to respect the writings of the conquered. The biblical legends of the Muslims drawn from these sources are innumerable; and it hardly seems worth while to quote them here as many of them have been translated into various European languages.

It is not so generally known that many of the stories which are familiar to youth in the pages of *The Arabian Nights* are found in germ in the Talmud. The origin and transmission of popular stories and nursery tales are problems which seldom permit of a definitive solution, so that one can hardly postulate Jewish influence without some reserve. Thus, when we find the roc of nursery days performing his terrifying function under the *nom de plume* of *bar yokani* or *ziz* in the Talmud, and Rabbi Yannai, and not an Arabian sorceress, turning a woman into an ass, we cannot assert that the relationship is one of filiation. Still the close correspondence between Jewish and Islamic legend, coupled with the strong religious atmosphere in which these fables subsist in the two literatures, creates a strong presumption that the immediate source is Jewish.

In the realm of the miraculous it is noteworthy that one of the earliest signs said to have been wrought by Muhammad was the tree which advanced and receded at his command in order to prove his apostleship. As is well known, Muhammad himself frankly declared that he was a man like his hearers. But after his death his followers were at a disadvantage in disputations with Jews and Christians who possessed prophets with miraculous powers. The difficulty could be effectively coped with since none can call on a dead prophet to work a miracle. And in a circle where miracles are expected and required one man's word is as good as another's. Many of Muhammad's 'miracles' are imitations of some of the acts of Jesus recorded in the New Testament, such as the feeding of crowds of people from a loaf and so on. The miracle of the tree seems to be an imitation of the tree which consistently withdrew its shade from all or any of Abraham's idolatrous guests. With equal consistency it vouchsafed its shade to all true monotheists and thus enabled Abraham to make many proselytes.

No notice is taken here of the most valuable services rendered by Jews to Muhammadans in the realms of philosophy and medicine, because the part played by Jews was that of carriers. Valuable as their contributions were, they were not specifically Jewish, and Christians naturally shared the credit of encouraging and fostering the growth of science.

It is, I think, possible to trace one of the greatest literary achievements of the Christian Church to Jewish influence on Muslim writers. The subject is one which the present writer has not had leisure to examine systematically; and, therefore, the following remarks are made with some reserve owing to the disputed date of some of the Jewish sources. All who are familiar with the general scheme of Dante's immortal poem will remember the principal details of his vision: the gigantic funnel descending from Jerusalem to the bowels of the earth with its sevenfold strata and subdivisions; the seven heavens in which the blessed live according to their spiritual status; categories of sin requiring a special stratum in hell; the conversations of Dante with the inhabitants of hell and heaven; the ablutions in Purgatory; the gigantic eagle (in Judaism and Islam a cock) formed of myriads of angels who hymn the praise of God. These and very many other Dantean ideas and symbols of a more subtle kind have been traced to the writings of Islamic traditionists and particularly to the Spanish Arab, Ibnu-l-Arabi (died 1240).[1] All the essential characteristics of Dantean and Arabian eschatology just cited will be found in Jewish literature, some in the Talmud, some in the later medieval *midrashim* and *cabala*. To the Arabs belongs the fame of the mystical conception of God and the beatific vision given us in the *Paradiso*, as also the allegory of moral regeneration in the ascent to the heavenly spheres. But the genesis of these ideas is Jewish. As it is seldom easy at first sight to equate the terse directness of the rabbinic writings with the stern loquacity of the Kuran, so it is only by gathering sentence by sentence the sayings of the rabbis, often embedded in foreign contexts, that one is able to achieve a connected story. But, inasmuch as the process of borrowing without acknowledgement the eschatological doctrines of the Jews began with Muhammad himself (cf. the 'punishment of the grave') and continued throughout the era of apostolic tradition in Islam, and seeing that the more extravagant stories of *haggadic midrash* circulated orally for centuries before they found a permanent home in Jewish literature, it is reasonable, and indeed necessary, to infer that it is the treatment of the material, not the substance, which Arabian writers can claim as their own.

It has been an endeavour in the foregoing pages to approach the subject without bias or prejudice; and if a preponderating weight has been attributed to the influence of Jews it has seemed to the writer the only possible conclusion from the

[1] The discovery is due to Prof. Miguel Asín y Palacios, cf. *La Escatología musulmana en la Divina Comedia* (Madrid, 1919), now tr. under the title *Islam and the Divine Comedy* (London, 1926).

evidence. The enormous value of the legacy bequeathed by Jews to Christians and Muhammadans alike makes it incumbent on the present writer to express the hope that a more generous recognition of the services of the testators will be forthcoming and that Jewish scholars will be accorded the grateful assistance of those to whom they taught the *reshith hokmah*.

ALFRED GUILLAUME.

BIBLIOGRAPHY

S. Munk, *Mélanges de Philosophie Juive et Arabe*, Paris, 1859. I. Goldziher, *Muhammedanische Studien*, Halle, 1888. M. Steinschneider, *An Introduction to the Arabic Literature of the Jews*, London, 1901. A. Geiger, *Was hat Mohammad aus dem Judenthum aufgenommen?* (Reprint). Leipzig, 1902. D. B. Macdonald, *Development of Muslim Theology, Jurisprudence, and Constitutional Theory*, London, 1903. R. A. Nicholson, *A Literary History of the Arabs*, London, 1907. I. Schapiro, *Die haggadischen Elemente im erzählenden Teil des Korans*, Teil I. Berlin, 1907. T. W. Juynboll, *Handbuch des islamischen Gesetzes*. Leyden, 1910. R. Dozy, *Spanish Islam. A History of the Moors in Spain*, English translation, London, 1913. E. Mittwoch, *Zur Entstehungsgeschichte des Islamischen Gebets und Kultus*, Berlin, 1913. A. J. Wensinck, 'Die Entstehung der muslimischen Reinheitsgesetzgebung.' *Der Islam*, V. 1914, pp. 62–80. Nöldeke-Schwally, *Geschichte des Qorans*. 2 vols. Leipzig, 1919. A. Guillaume, *The Traditions of Islam*, Oxford, 1925.

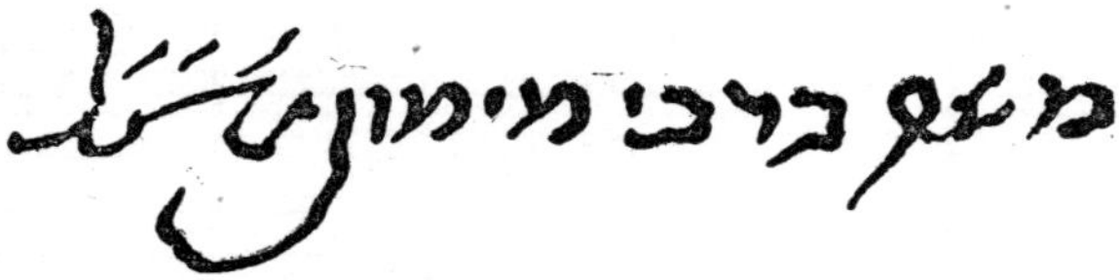

FIG. 17 A. Signature of Moses Maimonides. From a twelfth-century manuscript in the Bodleian Library at Oxford.

Description of Franks Casket Figs. 18 and 19.

Figs. 18 and 19 represent two faces of the so-called *Franks Casket*. This important relic is Northumbrian carving in whale's bone, of about A.D. 700. It was presented to the British Museum in 1857 by its Director, Sir A. Wollaston Franks (1826–97). Taken together, the two panels exhibit a consciousness on the part of the Barbarian artist of his double legacy, from Hebraic and from Classical sources.

Fig. 18

The panel shown in Fig. 18 is divided into an upper and lower division. Each division is divided into a right and left half by an arched central structure. Around the panel is an inscription, mostly in the Anglo-Saxon language but with a few words of Latin. The Anglo-Saxon words are written in the Runic or old Teutonic letters but for the Latin words Latin letters of Anglo-Saxon type are used.

In the upper division, on the left, Jerusalem is being stormed by Roman soldiers in armour. Over this scene is written in Runic letters and Anglo-Saxon language the words: HER FEGTATH TITUS END GIUTHEA SU(MAE), which may be translated, *Here fight Titus and some Jews*. On the right the Jews are seen fleeing from the city. Over this scene is written in Latin letters of Anglo-Saxon type and in the Latin language the words: HIC FUGIANT (for FUGIUNT) HIERUSALIM AFITATORES (for HABITATORES), which may be translated, *Here the inhabitants fly from Jerusalem*. (Compare description of bas relief on Arch of Titus, p. 28.)

In the lower division, on the left, sits a tribunal, with the Anglo-Saxon word DOM = *judgement*, written in Runic. The judge is on a throne, the prisoners below him and armed officers on either side. On the right Jews are led away prisoner, with the Anglo-Saxon word GISL = *hostage* also written in Runic.

The arched structure in the centre represents the Temple. Within it may be seen the Ark of the Covenant, supported by two staves passed through rings (Exodus xxv. 12–15 and xxxvii. 3–5, and 1 Kings vii. 6–8). On either side of the Ark are two bird-like figures representing the Cherubim. Their heads are repeated above the Ark and on either side of the Mercy Seat. Above the Cherubim, and on the centre of the roof of the Temple is a rudely carved dove, representing the Divine Spirit, for it is said that the Almighty communed with Moses ' above the Mercy Seat, from between the two Cherubim which are upon the Ark of the Testimony ' (Exodus xxv. 22). Below the Cherubim the pattern is continued into a representation of the *brazen sea*, standing upon oxen ' with their hinder parts inwards ' (1 Kings vii. 25).

Fig. 19

In the centre of the panel a she-wolf lies on her back suckling Romulus and Remus. Above stands another wolf. The whole scene is set in a thicket of trees through which armed warriors approach from either side. Around the panel is written, in Runic letters and in the Anglo-Saxon language, the words: OTHLAE UNNEG ROMWALUS AND REUMWALUS TWŒGEN GIBROTHAER AFOEDDAE HIAE WYLIF IN ROMAECAESTRI, which may be translated: *Far away were exposed Romulus and Remus, brothers twain. A wolf in Rome-city fed them.*

C. S.

FIG. 18. PANEL OF EARLY ENGLISH CASKET (about 700 A.D.)
Showing fall of Jerusalem and capture of the Temple by the Emperor Titus

For description see p. 172

FIG. 19. PANEL OF EARLY ENGLISH CASKET (about 700 A.D.)
Showing the finding of the twins, Romulus and Remus, and the She-wolf

For description see p. 172

THE JEWISH FACTOR IN MEDIEVAL THOUGHT

	PAGE
I. THE NATURE OF THE JEWISH FACTOR	
§ 1. *Introduction*	173
§ 2. *Hebraeo-Arabic Thought*	184
II. TRANSMISSION OF THE JEWISH FACTOR	
§ 3. *Transmission in the Earlier Middle Ages*	202
§ 4. *Transmission in the Later Middle Ages*	215
(a) *In the Sicilies*	215
(b) *In Castille*	222
(c) *In Aragon*	226
(d) *In North Italy*	228
(e) *In France and Flanders*	233
(f) *In England*	237
§ 5. *The Link with the Renaissance*	238
III. CHARACTERISTICS OF MEDIEVAL LATIN THOUGHT	
§ 6. *The Course of Scholastic Philosophy*	245
§ 7. *The Medieval Latin Aristotle*	249
IV. RECEPTION OF THE JEWISH FACTOR	
§ 8. *Jewish Elements in Twelfth-Century Scholasticism*	251
§ 9. *Jewish Elements in Thirteenth-Century Scholasticism*	257
(a) *The Preparation for St. Thomas Aquinas*	257
(b) *St. Thomas Aquinas*	264
(c) *The Later Thirteenth Century*	271
§ 10 *The End of the Middle Ages*	276

I. THE NATURE OF THE JEWISH FACTOR

§ 1. *Introduction*

THE modern world has three main roots in antiquity, Greece, Rome, and Israel. In previous members of this series, the *Legacy of Greece* and the *Legacy of Rome*, one of us has tried to place before the reader certain attitudes to the world around him inherited from these ancient civilizations. There are special obstacles in our way if we seek to treat Israel in the same manner.

Chief among these difficulties is the fact that the Legacy of Israel is only to a very slight extent a part of the external world. It would, of course, be easy to draw up a list of individuals of Hebrew origin who have made important contributions to our science, our art, our literature, our philosophy. But we cannot thus discern any Jewish legacy of true cultural distinctness, for it might justly be said that these men owed their eminence to the great European civilization in which they had been nurtured, and not to a narrower and less significant Jewish training. There is, however, a deeper sense in which our European science, art, literature, and philosophy owe a debt to Israel. It would indeed be fantastic to suggest that in these departments the debt is comparable to that owed to Greece and Rome. Our debt to Israel is in the main in another realm and is, in the main, a religious one. Yet if we search the foundations of the modern way of thinking, even external to the department of religion, we shall discover a real Jewish factor. This factor is, however, particularly intricate and far more difficult of presentation than are the Greek and Roman elements.

Such influence on thought, other than religious thought, as can be called specifically Jewish was exercised mainly in the period that preceded the great classical Renaissance. It is in the earlier 'Revival of Learning', that of the thirteenth century, that this influence may be most clearly discerned. Without Jewish aid this earlier Renaissance would have been long delayed and would have assumed a different form. Without the earlier Renaissance the more familiar classical and humanist revival of the fifteenth and sixteenth centuries would have been retarded. The one movement was historically, intellectually, and spiritually the preparation for the other.

The Nature of the Jewish Factor

A leading characteristic of our modern European world is its division into great nationalities, each of which contains within itself widely diverse ethnic elements. With these great nations lies the guardianship of our modern civilization. Without them, as our world is at present, civilization surely could not be. Nationality is based ultimately upon the consciousness of those who inhabit the different countries. Men of the same nation share certain elements of civilization which dwellers in other countries do not possess, or possess in very different proportion. The great nations of the West have, without exception, arisen on the débris of the tribal system. Each contains, in fact, the remains of many tribes of widely different origin, and each has exhibited great powers of tribal absorption. In this respect the great nations of the West differ fundamentally from most of the smaller nations, some of which are but tribes under another name.

The great nationalities, however, are comparatively modern growths. If we look into the medieval past, we find a very different face upon affairs. The Western world, it is true, was divided, but its divisions were largely without the national sense with which we are familiar. They were, in effect, little but vast estates, each governed by its own peculiar laws. Beneath the surface the tribal units persisted. A close parallel to this artificial welding of unmixing factors may be seen to-day in many oriental countries.[1]

Yet if we glance at the social fabric of the medieval world, we find that while men of different country, race, and surroundings were certainly in some senses far more sharply separated from one another than in the modern world, there are other respects in which they were more closely linked. There was a

---

[1] A good illustration of the unmixed character of the elements in a medieval society is given by the history of Sicily. Thus we have a formal edict issued at Catania in 1168 that the local Latin, Greek, Saracen and Jewish populations shall each be governed by its own laws. Cp. Fig. 31, p. 217.

common religion and ritual dictated by a universal and ruling Church. There was but one language for works of learning. There was the basis, at least, of one common law. The link of the West was the *Latin culture*.

But though the West was thus united in medieval times, it was very clearly marked off from the East. Over against the great concrete mass of Christendom was set another and even more concrete power. We are in the great days of Islam. The link of the East was the *Arabic culture*.[1]

Let us not here be beguiled by any of the old formulas, of which 'the changeless East' is one of the most familiar and one of the most untrue. For some of the centuries that we have to consider those relations of East and West to which we are nowadays accustomed were wholly reversed. In our time Orientals accept the value of Western civilization, and they accord it the sincerest form of flattery. The Oriental recognizes that in the Occident are science and learning, power and organization, public spirit and public justice and honest business capacity. The Oriental will gladly admit the Occidental as his physician, his paymaster, his engineer, nor is he wholly unwilling to receive him as his teacher or his judge, though he may repudiate his religion and despise his philosophic outlook. The world of the tenth, eleventh, and twelfth centuries was far other. Then it was the Westerner who admired while he feared. The Occident knew full well that science and learning lay with Islam. Despite the boastings of the Crusaders, the superiority of the Oriental in those days in arms and administration had been sufficiently tested. The Occident had felt the weight of his arm, and the impression that it had made is enshrined in our language in such Semitic words as 'arsenal' and 'admiral'. Nor was it

[1] The term *East* is here used in the familiar cultural, not in the accurate geographical sense. A glance at the maps contained in Figs. 20-22 will show that the medieval Islamic world was largely south and even west of the medieval Christian world.

The Nature of the Jewish Factor

in affairs and in war alone that Islam excelled. Philosophy and science, medicine and law, lay there beyond the confines of Christendom. The Western mind was awakening from its secular slumber. There was a longing for the intellectual treasures held by the East. And yet Europe was haunted by a fear and repugnance for Eastern religion and Eastern thought similar to that which the East now often feels for the West. Such was the stage whereon, during the Middle Ages, the Jewish role was played. These are the conditions under which the Jews acted as the intermediaries between Orient and Occident.

A modern poet has assured us that 'East is East and West is West and never the twain shall meet'. Away with these cobwebs! The well-ordering of history has no place for them. In the pages which follow we shall find East very often meeting West. The question as to whether East and West are indeed so diverse, demands an investigation of the history of the cultures which these two words connote. That investigation must be so searching as to extend to their origins. Now Arabic thought, like Latin thought, Arabic culture, like Latin culture, comes from Greece. The Eastern culture with which we have to do in these pages differs from the Western culture mainly in this, that it is derived more directly and at an earlier date from the Hellenic fountain head. Greek thought, as we shall find, was in the charge of men of Arabic speech for centuries before it reached the Latins, and the first effective contact of the medieval West with Greek thought was in translations from the Arabic. These translations were conveyed largely through Hebrew channels.

The Jewish carriers represent perhaps the most continuously civilized element in Europe. European Jewish thinkers in numbers were consciously developing Hellenic philosophy and discussing Plato and Aristotle, the Stoics and Plotinus, while the rest of Europe was, as yet, in its barbaric incoherent child-

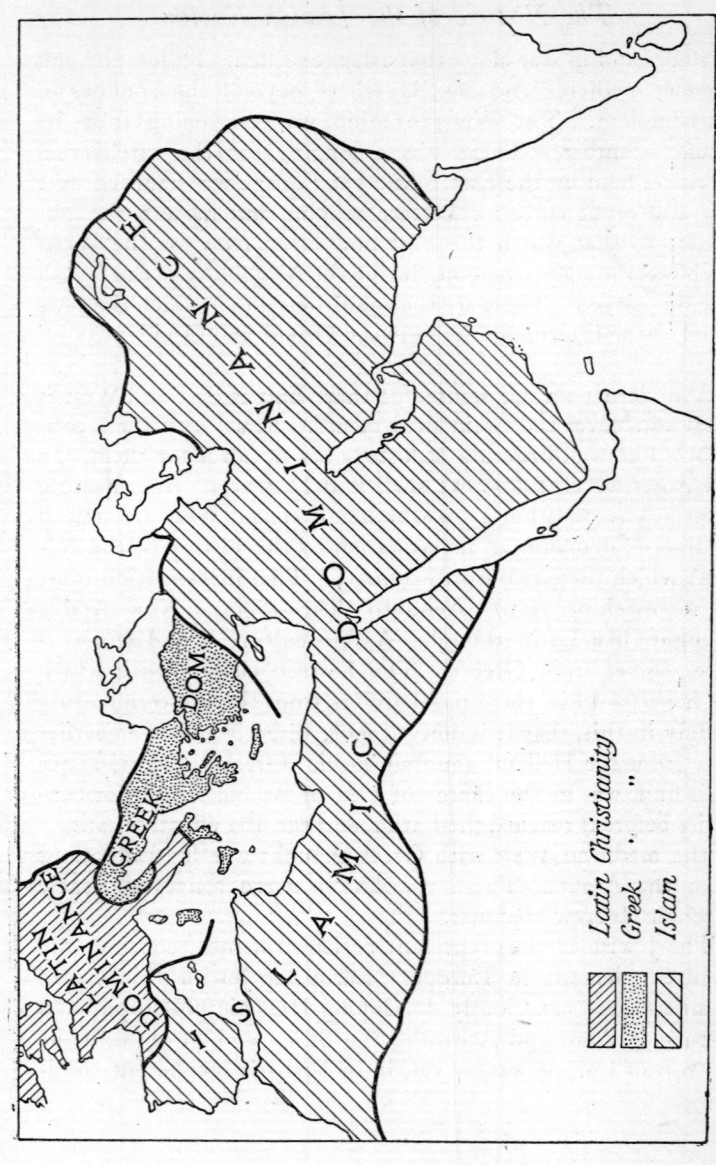

FIG. 20. Spheres of Influence about 750 A.D.

Fig. 21. Spheres of Influence about 1150

Fig. 22. Spheres of Influence about 1500

hood. A reasonable claim may be made for the Jewish communities of Southern France, the Iberian Peninsula, and the Rhineland, as having had the longest and most ancient continuous civilized history in Europe outside the classical zone. In a cultural sense the Jews were the first Europeans. In a racial sense—if indeed there be a Jewish race [1]—the reader may be reminded that the Jews had settled in Western Europe before many of its most typical inhabitants had emerged from Asia and before others had crossed the Central European Plain or had traversed the North Sea to invade the West.

From the first impact of the Arab hordes on the Byzantine Empire in the seventh century till the Turks were rolled back from the gates of Vienna a thousand years later, the dominion of the Crescent ever waxed.[2] During the five centuries of Abbasid rule at Bagdad (749–1258) the Islamic world developed its great intellectual system. The language, the law, the religion of the Kuran came to reach from the frontiers of China to the Atlantic. Although Islam was only for a short time even nominally under the suzerainty of a single Caliph, yet the Arabic-speaking world acquired an intellectual homogeneity which was in some ways even greater than that of the Latin West. The Latin and Arabic cultures competed for universal domain, while Greek civilization was as between the upper and nether millstone (Figs. 20–22).

The main intellectual basis of this imposing Eastern civiliza-

---

[1] The conception of a Jewish *race*, in the biological sense, seems to be based on a misunderstanding. The word race is often used very loosely, but there is both anthropological and historical evidence against the existence, at the present time, of a Jewish race in the biological sense.

[2] There were recessions of Muslim rule in Spain continuously from the end of the eighth century, in South Italy and Sicily in the eleventh century and in the Near East during periods of the Crusades and notably the twelfth century. These recessions were compensated in other directions and there was a general advance of the Muslim sphere of influence which was hardly checked even by the terrible disasters of the Mongol invasion of the thirteenth century; cf. Figs. 20–23.

The Nature of the Jewish Factor

tion was the brilliant revival of learning that spread from Bagdad in the ninth and tenth centuries. In that great Renaissance, the wisdom of ancient Greece played a part comparable to that which it served in the better known Western Renaissance of the fifteenth and sixteenth centuries. Greek writings and Greek ideas gradually found their way into Arabic. In this cultural development the leading part was played not by Arabs, but by Syrians, Persians, Jews and others who were neither of Arab race nor domiciled in Arabia. Many were not Muslim by faith. A multitude of the works in Arabic produced by this culture was ultimately rendered into Latin. This literature is described as *Arabian*. It is the Arabian literature, product of this culture, rather than merely literature in Arabic, that specially concerns us here.

The Eastern Renaissance, spreading from Bagdad, though comparable in many ways to the later Western Renaissance of the fifteenth and sixteenth centuries, differed from it greatly in the character of the material selected for transmission. In the West the revival of classical learning was mainly in the hands of men of letters. It was essentially 'humanist', and the poets, historians, orators, and writers of *belles lettres* of antiquity were especially studied. The Renaissance in Europe, surrounded by the models of classical architecture and sculpture, reacted profoundly also on the arts. The direction assumed by the Eastern revival of learning under the Abbasids was very different.

In estimating this difference we must recall certain differences of environment. All graphic art was forbidden to the Muslim as to the Jew. Eastern architecture developed without any direct dependence on 'classical' models. The form of literature in Arabic, as in Hebrew, was affected hardly, if at all, by Greek literary methods and style. It was on philosophy and the positive sciences that the Arabic writers and their Jewish exponents chose to concentrate. Aristotle was even more fervently followed than in our own scholastic ages. Platonic and Neoplatonic writings were also studied to some extent, while the sciences of mathematics, astronomy, astrology, geography and medicine, of which the Latin West as yet knew naught, were eagerly pursued at Bagdad and were rapidly diffused throughout the Muslim world. Once this material became available among the Arabic-speaking peoples it was developed along characteristic lines which may be regarded as the *Arabic version of Hellenism*. These lines were, in effect, *Scholasticism*. The scholastic system came to the Latins largely from Islam, and from Islam it was largely brought by Jews.

Looking back upon his medieval heritage the modern man is apt to be contemptuous of the scholastic spirit. He thinks of the endless and exhausting discussion about what seem to him mere words, nor can he fail to reflect that scientific method has given him a much more effective instrument for the acquisition of knowledge than was possessed by his medieval predecessors. Should he take up a medieval philosophical work he will probably lay it down in weariness before he gains an inkling of its meaning. To one educated in physical science the medieval neglect of the observational element will be particularly distasteful. Almost equally repellent to him will be the covering of every development by an appeal to authority.

The severity of the modern reader's judgement, induced by the combined operation of fatigue and disgust, is liable to distort his historic perspective. He tends to judge Scholasticism as though it were developed in the environment of his own time. Yet reflection will convince him that the scholastic age was a necessary prelude to the development of modern Western culture. The Western mind had sunk into ineptitude during the centuries that preceded the scholastic revival. Systematic thought had ceased to be ; philosophy had wholly vanished ; science had perished ; even the love of nature was

The Nature of the Jewish Factor 183

submerged; the very instinct for intellectual consistency was languishing. But still beyond the sunrise trickled the ancient spring of Hellenic wisdom. From those healing waters man could still renew his youth, and it was the Wandering Jew who bore westward the magic draught.

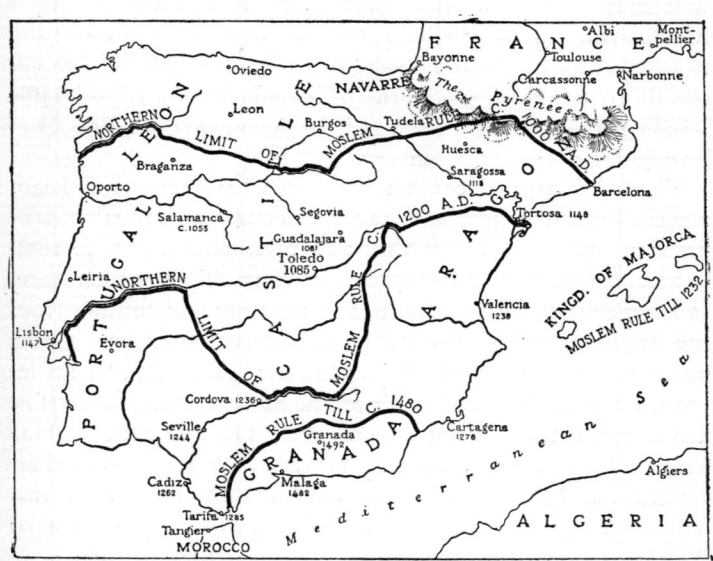

FIG. 23. To illustrate the recession of Islam in Spain. The figures after the names of the towns are the dates of their conquest by Christendom.

When we seek by what means the Arabic-speaking Jewish world could influence the Latin West we shall discern two main areas of contact (Fig. 23 and Fig. 30, p. 215).

One of the areas with which we are concerned is Southern Italy and Sicily, the old *Magna Graecia* (Fig. 20, p. 178). Throughout the Dark Ages this was a battle-ground of various conflicting interests. Here for centuries the Byzantine Empire, ensconced for safety on the Adriatic seaboard, disputed the mastery with native chiefs and Saracens. The predominating language of this territory was Greek. The faltering hold of the Byzantines gave an opportunity, however, for the entry of other tongues. A Latin dialect was spoken in many places. Arabic secured a firm foothold, notably in Sicily, and was spoken and written there for centuries after the island ceased to be under Muslim rule (cp. Fig. 31, p. 217). Nor were Latin, Greek, and Muslim cultures the only competitors. Material and literary remains combine to tell of the development of a considerable Jewish element in this region and the documents take us back at least as far as the sixth century.

The other area of contact between Christianity and Islam was the Iberian peninsula. The Saracen was here gradually withdrawing southward under Christian pressure (Fig. 23, p. 183), but leaving behind extensive remains of his language, literature, and civilization. From this area translations and versions from the Arabic passed northward in an increasing stream. Great numbers of Jews had been settled here from remote, indeed from pre-Christian, antiquity. During the Saracen domination they had adopted Arabic as their vernacular. The literature of these Spanish Jews bears evidence of the very high standard of their civilization. They set their mark deep on the Arabic-Latin translations of Spanish origin and thereby profoundly influenced Western scholasticism. Before we discuss that influence, we must, however, consider firstly the nature of Hebraeo-Arabic thought, and secondly the mechanism of its conveyance.

§ 2. *Hebraeo-Arabic Thought*

The Arabic language was cultivated by the Jews from the time of the great Saracen conquests. From the eighth century onward it was familiar to all who dwelt in Muslim lands. Thus Arabic literary methods rapidly reacted also on the Hebrew language and Hebrew developed largely on the Arabic model, in grammar and idiom as in literary form. Moreover, even in

The Nature of the Jewish Factor

Jewish circles, Arabic tended to replace Hebrew for secular purposes. A secular literature continued for many centuries to be produced by Jews in both Hebrew and Arabic.

Among Jews in Spain, Arabic continued in general use until the end of the twelfth century. Spanish Jews preserved some living acquaintance with that language two hundred years and more beyond that time. Even when Arabic had ceased to be spoken by Spanish Jews, it remained in use for learned purposes by Jewish scholars in the West. After the beginning of the thirteenth century, however, the output of original literature in Arabic by Jews ceased to have any great value, though important scientific works in Hebrew continued to appear. Moreover, an active process of translation from Arabic into Hebrew persisted for ages.

The development of the Hebraeo-Arabic literature, so far as contact with the West is concerned, is in three main departments: Philosophy, Mathematics, Medicine. The Mathematical and Medical systems of the Latin Middle Ages, of which our own are but natural outgrowths, were not only influenced by this 'Arabian' material, largely transmitted by Jews, but were actually founded and based upon it. Indeed it would be fair to represent medieval European Mathematics and Medicine as mere special developments of the Arabian system. Nevertheless, we must here pass lightly over these departments and devote ourselves mainly to Philosophy.

The Jews, after the advent of the Muslim conquests, were deeply affected by the version of Greek thought that passed into Arabic. To understand this system we must know something of its sources. These can be set out as (*a*) Aristotelian and (*b*) Platonic.

The Aristotelian writings on which the Arabic authors depended were in part apocryphal, with but little of the spirit of the master in them. These writers possessed, however, the genuine *Logical*, *Physical*, and *Biological* works of Aristotle, as well as his *Metaphysics* and his great treatise *On Soul*. The *Politics*, *Rhetoric*, *Poetics* and *Ethics* were also available, but they stand in the background and are less heard of.

As regards Plato. The Arabic writers, like the Latins, studied most eagerly what seems to us the darkest and most obscure of all his dialogues, the *Timaeus*. They had also the *Republic* and the *Laws*. Far more read, however, than the true Platonic writings were products of certain of Plato's successors of the so-called *Neoplatonic* school. Islamic thought has been epigrammatically, though a little unfairly, described as 'Aristotle seen through Neoplatonic spectacles'. It is that, but it is a great deal more.

Although the actual sources of Islamic thought can be thus reduced, it must be remembered that these comparatively simple factors were received through a wide variety of channels. Thus the Syriac-speaking Nestorian Christians were early teachers of Islam. They conveyed especially the text of Aristotle, and the versions of the medical writers such as Galen and Hippocrates, besides many mathematical and mechanical works, e.g. of Euclid, Hero, and Archimedes. The Jacobites or Monophysite Christians were the chief introducers of Neoplatonic ideas, largely of a mystical character. Persian Zoroastrianism reacted on the Syriac transmitters, and Jewish thought itself had a large influence on Islamic Philosophy.

Thus the Arabic literature accessible to the Jews became extremely complex in nature though simple in ultimate origin. The Hebrew thinkers seized on this material and developed it along characteristic lines. Moreover, many Jewish philosophical works in Arabic were intended not only for Jews but for the larger Arabic-reading public, and were widely read throughout the Arabic-speaking world. Furthermore, it fell out that certain non-Jewish schools of Arabian philosophers had strong affinities with Jewish thought, and deeply affected and were affected by Jewish thinkers. So much is this the case that there is a group of later writers, nominally Muslims, whose works, as

The Nature of the Jewish Factor

regards both their content and their treatment by the Latin West, can only artificially be separated from the writings of those who were more distinctively Jews. Thus Jewish thought and Muslim thought, so far as Philosophy was concerned, became almost inseparably linked. This Hebraeo-Arabic movement gave rise to a portentous mass of writings. We can consider only a very few outstanding and typical figures.[1]

The earliest Jewish philosopher of the Western school was Isaac Israeli of Kairouan, known to the Latins as ISAAC JUDAEUS (c. 855–955). Like most of the thinkers of the Hebraeo-Arabic group, he practised as a physician, and was deservedly one of the best-known of his craft of the whole Middle Ages. We possess a number of his medical works, and it is only as a physician, not as a philosopher, that Maimonides had regard for him. Isaac is described by a Muslim historian as a man of the highest character who, though much occupied about the court, was indifferent to wealth and personal advancement. He is said to have lived unmarried—a very unusual thing among medieval Muslims or Jews—and to have died at over one hundred years of age.

This many-sided man wrote a number of philosophical treatises. Only two have survived in any degree of completeness. That *On definitions* contains an account of some of the favourite terms used later by the Latin scholastics and adopted by them from him. His larger work *On the elements* is an exposition of Aristotelian physics. We have also fragments of his *Book of Soul and Spirit*. This shows a Neoplatonic scheme in which creation is represented as taking place in a series of *emanations*. From God emanates a ' splendour ' which gives rise to the rational soul. From this emanates a lesser splendour or spark which produces the vegetable soul. From this again comes the material world. The whole system may be described as a

---

[1] The names are chosen for the influence that they came to exert on the Latin West. No judgement is implied of their importance either for the general history of philosophy or for the development of Judaism or of Islam.

mixture of the Neoplatonist Plotinus and of Aristotle. Isaac's influence is to be seen not only on Latin writers but also on the Arabic author Avicenna.

The Muslim AVICENNA (980–1037) was born near Bokhara, son of a Persian civil servant. He was a marvel of precocity and gave himself ardently to study from his earliest years. He took especially to Medicine and Philosophy, and rose to a high position at court. Despite his enormous and untiring industry in every department of thought, he was of dissolute character and particularly addicted to wine. This is said to have been the cause of his premature death.

Few men have possessed the power of codification to so great a degree as Avicenna. His writings greatly impressed Jewish thinkers in every department. In philosophy it is as a logician that Avicenna was most influential, although he also takes an important place as a codifier of Aristotle and a writer on Metaphysics. Logic, as Avicenna treats it, has a much wider significance than that usually associated with the word. It includes for instance not only the method of reasoning but also the construction of discourse which shall persuade or stir the soul or imagination. In other words, it includes Dialectic, Rhetoric, and Poetic. Nevertheless its power is chiefly negative. It does not discover truths, but helps man to use well those he already has. In Physics and in Psychology Avicenna presents fewer original departures. His work known as the *Canon of Medicine* was, however, the most widely read of all medical works in the Middle Ages, alike in the Arabian and the Latin world.

In Metaphysics Avicenna had certain special views developed along Neoplatonic lines. Very strange to modern eyes, but familiar in various forms to his contemporaries, is Avicenna's doctrine of Emanations which we have already encountered in Isaac. Beings are classified in the orthodox fashion in a scale the bases of which are the three types of soul of the Aristotelian system, the *vegetable*, the *animal*, and the *rational*. This same scale is continued to man and beyond man to the region of the stars. At the top of the scale is the *Necessary Being* who is perfect unity and from whom emanates a *First Cause*. From the First Cause emanates the *World of Ideas*. This World of Ideas is a series of pure *Intelligences* which animate *Celestial Bodies*. The highest body thus animated is the sphere of fixed stars. From this is emanated a soul which animates the outermost planet. This in its turn emanates a soul for the next planet and so on till we get to the innermost or lowest planet, the Moon. From this lowest celestial body is emanated the so-called *Active Intellect* which animates the sublunary or mundane world in which we live. The reader may be reminded that the conception of higher souls in the stars goes through Greek philosophy, both Aristotelian and Platonic, while the immutability of the heavens was held by all to the time of Galileo.

After Avicenna the future of Arabian thought in general and Jewish thought in particular lay in the West and especially in Spain.

The first outstanding representative of philosophy among the Spanish Jews was SOLOMON IBN GABIROL known to the Latins as AVICEBRON (*c.* 1021–*c.* 1058). This very original writer was born at Malaga, and after a wandering life he died at Valencia before he was forty years of age. He was active as poet, exegete, grammarian, and in many other capacities. To us he is important for his work the *Fountain of life*. This most remarkable treatise introduced Neoplatonic thought among the Arabic-speaking people of the Spanish peninsula. The *Fountain of life* shows no trace of its Jewish origin. There is, for instance, no quotation from or reference to the Bible in it. It thus had little effect upon the scholastic development of the Jews themselves, though its influence on cabalistic writers, both Jewish and Christian, has long been well recognized.[1] The work of Avicebron was widely read in Latin Europe for centuries. The

---

[1] On the cabala and on Avicebron's influence upon it see pp. 324–328

identity of Avicebron, the author of the *Fountain of life*, with ibn Gabirol, the Jewish theologian, was unsuspected until revealed about the middle of the nineteenth century.

The *Fountain of life* derives its name from its consideration of *Matter* and *Form* as the basis of all existence and the source of life. It sets forth four principal doctrines. Firstly, it separates the *First Substance*, or God, from that which is created. Secondly, all created things are constituted of *Matter* and *Form*, which are always and everywhere in the relation of essence and attribute. Thirdly, this holds true not only of the physical, but also of the spiritual world. Matter is intelligible or spiritual, not corporeal. Fourthly, there are but three categories (*a*) *First Substance* or God; (*b*) *Matter and Form* comprising the world; and (*c*) the *Will* as intermediary. Will is neither attribute nor substance, Avicebron being so pure a monotheist that he cannot brook the thought of any attribute of God, lest it mar His utter unity and uniqueness. In this respect he is in the line of Hebrew tradition, and it is interesting to observe that a poem by him has entered the Jewish liturgy.

An important Spanish Jewish thinker who flourished in the century following ibn Gabirol was ABRAHAM BEN EZRA (1092–1167). It is, however, convenient to defer to another place what we have to say concerning him (pp. 209–211).

Significant and typical of Hebraeo-Arabian thought are the works of Averroes and Maimonides. The writings of these two men not only form the crown of this literature but are also of the greatest importance for the development of Latin thought. The active lives of Averroes and Maimonides extended over the latter half of the twelfth century. They were therefore contemporary with the early translators into Latin that adventured into Spain (pp. 202–214). Moreover, they immediately preceded the great period of Arabian impact on Latin thought.

AVERROES (1126–1198) was born at Cordova, son and grandson of a legal officer. He himself held the office of judge but also studied and practised medicine. All the time that he could spare from his duties he gave to the preparation of his very voluminous philosophical writings. These earned him the enmity of orthodox Muslim theologians, some of whom regarded him as having gone over to the Jews. It is indeed a fact that no writer exerted greater influence than Averroes on the course of later medieval Jewish thought, though he did not so wholly determine it as some would have us believe. His writings were burned by royal decree, and the latter part of his life was passed in disgrace and something very like imprisonment.

Averroes was the greatest of all the Western Muslim philosophers and one of the most influential thinkers of all time. He placed his thought in the form of a long series of commentaries on the works of Aristotle, whom he exalted above all other men. Despite the enthusiasm of Averroes for Aristotle, his teaching was basically, though unconsciously, modified by Neoplatonism.

The Averroan doctrine that caused most discussion was his teaching concerning *the eternity of the World*, which some of his interpreters have represented as a denial of creation. There can be no doubt, however, that Averroes did accept the idea of creation, though with him it is not that creation out of nothing demanded by the current theology of Islam, Christianity, and Judaism alike. In this matter Averroes is really an *evolutionist* in the true sense of the word; that is to say, he believes not in a single act of creation but in a creation renewed every instant in a constantly changing world, always taking its new form from that which has existed previously. The world, though eternal, has a *Mover* or *Agent*, constantly producing it and, like it, eternal. This mover can be realized by observation of the eternal celestial bodies which have a perfected existence only through their movement. Thereby may be distinguished two forms of eternity, that with and that without cause. Only the *Prime Mover* is eternal without cause.

A very important point in the Averroan philosophical

system is the distinction between *Soul* and *Intellect*. The Intellect is not merely the highest kind of Soul but differs from all other kinds of Soul in nature as well as in degree. It alone is absolutely free from matter, and is indeed in certain senses opposed to matter.

It is usually said that Averroes taught the unity of souls, and regarded the discontinuity of souls as apparent, not real, so that their survival as separate units after death was impossible. The Muslim philosopher Algazel (1058–1111) had accused the school, of which Averroes was the last and greatest member, of denying the resurrection. Averroes repudiates the charge, but it was very freely made and is deducible from his views. There are passages in which Averroes seems to put the orthodox view with his tongue in his cheek. He claims that the denial of resurrection is nowhere to be found in the writings of his school. Religious law, he says, which precedes philosophy, has always held the doctrine of the resurrection. He adds that philosophy teaches happiness only to the wise few, while it is the aim of religion to teach the crowd; but that the special class of philosophers to which he himself belongs arrive at complete existence and perfect happiness only by associating with the crowd. In this debate there were two renowned philosophical works by the two protagonists of the two schools of thought. Algazel had written his *Destructio philosophorum* as an attack on these irreverent thinkers. Averroes rejoined with his *Destructio destructionis*. The two works were famous throughout the Middle Ages.

Jewish philosophy proper culminates with MOSES BEN MAIMON, called MAIMONIDES (1135–1204). He was born at Cordova, and educated by a learned father and under Arabic masters. When he was thirteen years of age Cordova fell into the hands of the fanatical Almohades. Maimonides fled and, after leading a wandering life in Spain, Morocco, and Palestine, he settled in 1155 in Cairo where the rest of his life was passed.

The Nature of the Jewish Factor

He practised as a physician with great success and was attached to the court. He has left an account of his manner of life in a letter, which gives a vivid and pleasing impression of the conditions of existence in the East in the Middle Ages. The works of Maimonides, both medical and philosophical, became widely known not only among Arabic-speaking peoples, but also among the Latins and among the Jews themselves. On all three he exerted much influence.

It was the view of Maimonides that there is and can be no conflict between truths discerned by reason and those inculcated by revealed religion. For him the truths discerned by reason are to be sought first and foremost in the Aristotelian writings. He was persuaded that both the written and the oral Law, which go to make up the Jewish sacred canon, contain philosophical material, and that this harmonizes with Aristotelian philosophy. The conflict between religion and philosophy is, he held, due to a misinterpretation of one or both. Particularly the anthropomorphic passages in Scripture were to be interpreted not literally but as having an allegorical and inner meaning which, rightly understood, would prevent this conflict. God being incorporeal, these anthropomorphisms could not be interpreted in any other way. Arising out of the question of anthropomorphisms is his treatment of the *Divine Attributes*. The ascription of attributes to God, he held, arose also from biblical misinterpretation. Attributes, being attempts to ascribe to an object properties not inherent therein, could not be applied to God in whom all things were inherent.

Maimonides set forth a complete philosophical system which included metaphysics, physics, and ethics. All alike, he considered might be decided by reason, but the conclusions of reason were, in fact and in experience, coincident with the conclusions of revealed truth. His most famous work, in which his philosophy is set forth, is his *Guide for the perplexed*.

Very important for subsequent developments of philosophy

among the Latins was the view that Maimonides held of the angels and their relation to the so-called *Separate Intelligences*. The existence of these *Intelligences* he proves from the motions of the celestial spheres. To understand his arguments we must digress to describe the Aristotelian world system, or rather what Maimonides regarded as that system.[1]

The Universe in the Aristotelian system was spherical, with the Earth fixed in the centre, and the heavens revolving round it. Matter, of which the World in which we live is made up, is composed of the four elements, *earth*, *air*, *fire*, and *water*. These substances, however, as we encounter them in our imperfect world, are not in their pure elemental form. Each has in it mixtures of the other three, the one whose name it bears predominating. The elements in their purer form are arranged in concentric hollow spheres, like skins of an onion, around the spherical Earth. Of these elements *earth* is heaviest. Hence its natural place is lowest, that is at the centre of the spherical Universe. When away from the centre its natural motion is in a straight line toward its own place, that is toward the centre. This explains the action of gravitation. *Water* is next heaviest; its natural place is just above earth. Both earth and water tend to fall toward the centre. Above the water, which laves the surface of the earth, is the hollow sphere of *air*, concentric with that of earth and water. The natural motion of air is in an opposite direction to that of earth and water, that is, in a straight line outward, toward the circumference of the universe. It cannot however go outward beyond the sphere of the lightest and purest element, namely *fire*. The

---

[1] Aristotle's account of the structure of the Universe is chiefly to be found in his *De coelo* and *Meteorologica*. These works were available in an Arabic translation prepared from the Syriac by the Syrian Christian ibn Honein of Bagdad (died 911). Maimonides, however, probably relied chiefly on the secondary account by Avicenna.

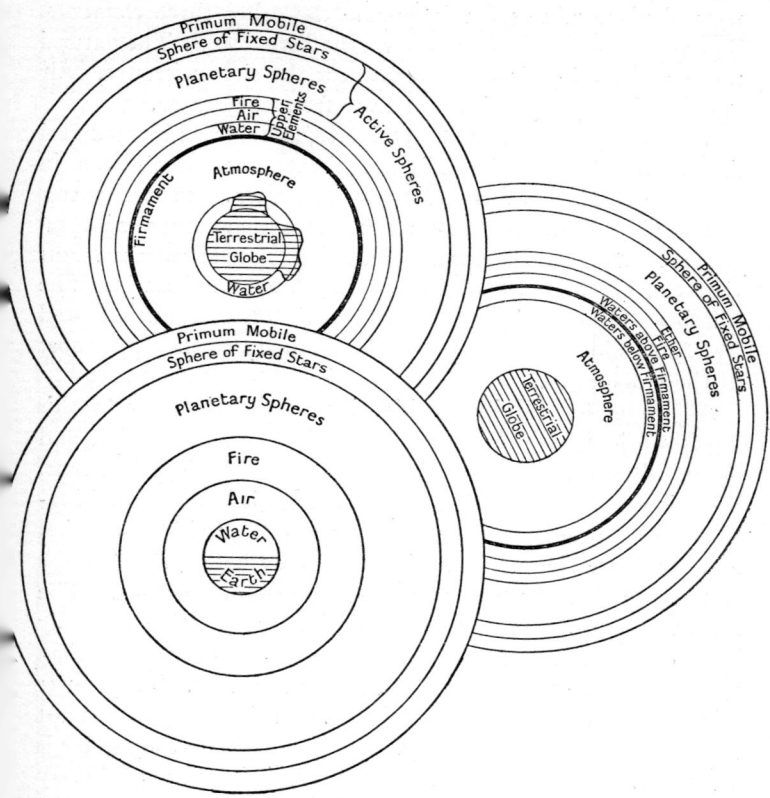

FIG. 24. Three typical medieval diagrams of the structure of the Universe. The uppermost accords fairly with the scheme of Maimonides, the lowermost with that of Dante. A separate planetary sphere was believed to exist for each planet including the Sun and the Moon. For simplicity, however, we have avoided displaying separately the various planetary spheres.

natural place of this fire is outside the other three elements. There it too forms a hollow sphere, the *Empyrean*.[1] The natural motion of fire is also outward towards the circumference. Air and fire thus both tend to rise away from the centre.

The exact structure of the Universe, as depicted by medieval Arabic and Latin writers, is not always the same—even in the same writer—and is seldom entirely clear. In this matter Maimonides is neither better nor worse than other medieval writers. We give diagrams (Fig. 24, p. 195) of variant forms that can be elicited from such works, Arabic and Latin. The number of these might be multiplied. The account adopted by Maimonides may be referred in the main to the uppermost of these diagrams.

All things formed by combination of the elements in this lower world in which we live are subject to generation and decay. But while nothing in our lower world is permanent, there is yet no annihilation, for all change is but a recombination of these four elements. The causes of all this generation and decay are the motions of the heavenly bodies that occupy spheres outside the sphere of the outermost element. The lowest of these heavenly bodies is the moon. The heavenly bodies themselves are composed of something even purer than the elements in their pure form, to wit the *ether*. They differ from things composed of the four elements in that they are not subject to generation or decay. The only change they suffer is *movement*. Yet this movement is different from the sublunary movement in our lower world and from the motions of the elements there. The motions of the four elements, as we have seen, are naturally *in straight lines*, either toward the centre (*earth* and *water*), or toward the circumference (*air* and *fire*). On the other hand, the heavenly bodies *circle* eternally round the

[1] The position and nature of the *Empyrean* was a subject of dispute in the Middle Ages. Most Christian writers (e.g. Dante) place it beyond the fixed stars and make it the abode of God and the angels.

FIG. 25. THE ANGELS AS PRIMUM MOBILE

From a Provençal manuscript of Armengaud Blasius of the XIVth century

For description see p. 198 opposite, and for further details see p. xxii. For Armengaud see pp. 234–5

centre. The heavenly bodies are set in a series of concentric transparent spheres. These revolve and carry the heavenly bodies with them in their movement. Outermost of all is the sphere that carries the fixed stars.

It is important to note that the Aristotelian Universe is finite. God himself sets the outermost sphere in motion, or rather we should say he is the eternal cause of its motion. Similarly each of the circular motions, of which the composite movements of the heavenly bodies are the resultant, is produced by its own proper *Mover* which is a pure form or spirit. The world itself is uncreated and eternal and is not subject to destruction.

We may here return to the treatment of this view by Maimonides. He accepts most of the Aristotelian conception and develops it particularly in connexion with his views of Angels. The motions of the heavenly spheres cannot be purely 'natural', that is unconscious, like that of the elements, for if they were so, they would stop on reaching their natural place as do the elements. Nor are these spheres mere irrational creatures, such as animals, for if so their motions would cease as soon as they attain the object of their desire or escape that which they would avoid.

Now such attainment or escape cannot be effected by circular motion, for in that motion the thing approached is ever fled and the thing fled is ever approached. To account for this circular motion we must suppose the spheres endowed with reason, and the motion expresses the desire to attain the object of their contemplation. God, says Maimonides, following Aristotle, is the object of the contemplation of the spheres. The love of God, to whom the spheres desire to become similar, is the cause of their motion. This can only be circular, for circulation is the only possible continuous act and is the simplest bodily motion. Hence arose the medieval dictum, ' 'Tis love that makes the merry (i.e. pleasant, well ordered) world go round', a saying strangely perverted in later ages when medieval philosophy became but a memory.

The Scottish poet, William Dunbar (1465–1520) has put what is, in effect, the Maimonidean scheme into his poem *On the Nativity of Christ*.

> Archangellis, angellis and dompnationis,[1]
>   Tronis,[2] potestatis,[3] and marteiris seir,[4]
> And all ye hevinly operationis,
>   Ster, planeit, firmament and spheir,
>   Fire, erd,[5] air and water cleir,
> To Him gife loving,[6] most and lest,
>   That come in to so meik maneir.

A like scheme was in the mind of Joseph Addison (1672–1719) when he wrote his well-known hymn based on the nineteenth Psalm:

> The spacious firmament on high,
> With all the blue ethereal sky,
> And spangled heavens, a shining frame,
> The great Original proclaim.
>
> . . . . .
>
> In reason's ear they all rejoice,
> And utter forth a glorious voice;
> Forever singing as they shine,
> "The hand that made us is divine".

Aristotle invoked some fifty-six Intelligences as acting on these spheres. Maimonides identified these *Intelligences* with the angels of the biblical narrative. Many medieval drawings are extant in which this Maimonidean conception is literally interpreted, and angels are shown turning the world 'for the love of God' (Fig. 25).

---

[1] Dompnationis = dominations.
[2] Tronis = thrones.
[3] Potestatis = powers.
[4] Seir = various.
[5] Erd = earth.
[6] Loving = praising in the Middle English religious vocabulary.

The Nature of the Jewish Factor

The development of knowledge that had taken place since the time of Aristotle had, in the opinion of Maimonides, enabled all cosmical movements to be explained by the action of four heavenly spheres instead of the Aristotelian fifty-six. In this Maimonides relied on the teaching of the Muslim Platonist, Avempace of Saragossa (*d.* 1138), of whom he was a pupil's pupil. Maimonides supposes only four active spheres. These, from within outward, are the spheres of the moon, of the sun, of the other planets, and of the fixed stars. The sphere of the moon acts on water, that of the sun on fire, that of the fixed stars on earth, and that of the planets on air. Beyond them all and embracing all is an uttermost sphere which gives movement to all. This is the *Primum Mobile*. A slightly more complex but very similar scheme is familiar to readers of Dante, who was deeply affected by Hebraeo-Arabian thought (Fig. 24, p. 195).[1]

The four active spheres of Maimonides are governed by four special *Intelligences*. There is, however, also an *Intelligence* that governs the yet lower sphere—known also as the sublunary sphere—of the elements. This according to Maimonides, following Avicenna's interpretation of Aristotle (p. 189), is the *Active Intellect* which is not only responsible for the various processes in sublunary life in general, but also in particular is the cause of our mind passing from potentiality to actuality.

Maimonides holds that in a general way the views of Aristotle are compatible with the Bible. What Aristotle calls the *Intelligences* the Bible calls *Angels*. These are pure and incorporeal entities. Their rationality is indicated in the nineteenth Psalm, 'the Heavens declare the glory of God'. That God rules the world through these angels or Intelligences is evident, according to him, from many passages in Bible and Talmud. The plural number is used in such passages, e.g. 'Let *us* make man in *our* image, and after *our* likeness' (Gen. i. 26), or 'Let *us* go down and confound their language' (Gen. xi. 7). This plural,

[1] See pp. 169-170 and p. 276.

Maimonides tells us, is explained in the Talmud by the very peculiar statement that 'The Most High never does anything without *contemplating* the celestial host'.[1]

There are in this phrase recorded by Maimonides two words of exceptional interest. The nature of this interest Maimonides himself clearly perceived. That he did so is an illustration of his very remarkable acumen. The word *contemplating* is the actual expression used by Plato when he says that God *contemplates the world of Ideas* and produces the Universe. This use of the word by the Talmudic writer was most probably of Alexandrian origin. The other word which we translate *host* is a transliteration of the Latin, or, as Maimonides calls it, the 'Greek' word, *familia*. It may seem strange to call *familia* Greek, but Maimonides is quite right. The word had, in fact, passed very early from Latin into Greek, as is now known from inscriptions, and it became part of the vocabulary of Byzantine Greek. The primary meaning of *familia* is *the slaves in a household*, or *a household establishment*, and it is not the equivalent of our term *family*. The application of the word *familia* to the *Angels* or *Intelligences* governing the spheres is evident. Maimonides would hold that it gives a sense to such biblical phrases as 'Behold, he put no trust in his servants; and his angels he charged with folly' (Job iv. 18), or 'Thou hast made him a little lower than the angels' (Psalm viii. 5).

The aspect of the philosophy of Maimonides that had most effect on the West and is of the greatest importance for our purpose, was his treatment of the problem of creation. Creation he holds to be one of the necessary dogmas of Religion. Maimonides developed the Aristotelian philosophy so as to include a God external to the universe, who created it *out of nothing*.

In taking up this standpoint Maimonides placed himself

[1] This phrase, quoted by Maimonides from the Talmud, is not in the versions of the Talmud that have come down to our time.

in opposition not only to certain orthodox Aristotelians among the Arabic writers, who regarded the *Intelligences* that governed the outer sphere of the Universe as uncreated, but also to his great contemporary Averroes. The discussion turns round the question of motion. Now, according to Aristotle, motion in its purest form, as encountered in the heavenly bodies, is not subject to beginning and end, since it is always circular. Similarly, the prime substance that is common to the four elements, and is therefore the basis of matter as we know it, is not subject to generation and destruction, processes which are themselves of the nature of motion of the lower and linear type (p. 196). To this and many other Aristotelian arguments Maimonides rejoins that Aristotle's belief in the eternity of motion and of the upper World, is based on the erroneous assumption that the World as a whole must have come into being in the same way as its parts now appear to do. This, however, presupposes Natural Law. But Natural Law, according to Maimonides, is itself a creation and had to be produced in the process of *creation out of nothing*.

But the discussion may be carried farther. Maimonides perceives that the difference between belief in an eternal world and belief in a created world may ultimately be resolved into a basic difference between belief in impersonal mechanical law, as an explanation of the universe, and belief in an intelligent being acting with a particular design. Aristotle's resolution of all motions below the lunar sphere in terms of an impersonal mechanical law is successful, Maimonides admits. It is in the outer spheres that Aristotle fails, though we need not follow Maimonides into the details of his failure. Yet, since outer and inner spheres are intimately connected, failure in explaining the one involves failure in explaining the other. The mechanistic explanation of the world, which excludes free will, miracle, and efficacy of prayer, must therefore be rejected.

For the mechanistic hypothesis Maimonides must find an

alternative. It is that of intelligent purpose and design so dear to the heart of Galen (A.D. 130–200), the physician to the philosopher Emperor Marcus Aurelius (A.D. 121–180). With the work of Galen, Maimonides, who was also a physician, was quite familiar. For Maimonides as for Galen, *Design* takes the place of *Natural Law*, and as Maimonides develops it, is but another name for Natural Law. That there were rules of wide application in nature Maimonides could not deny; that these rules depended for their working on certain underlying series of events he also accepted; but ultimately these rules depended, he held, on the action of an intelligent being who was working to an intelligible end. Maimonides did not make the enormous claims of Galen that these ends were wholly known or discoverable by man, but his system implies something like this while it leaves room for prophecy and miracle. Despite the fact that he brought whole departments of thought—including religious observances, ethics, and psychology—under rational interpretation, Maimonides is thus not fundamentally a rationalist. He is essentially a religious thinker.

II. TRANSMISSION OF THE JEWISH FACTOR

§ 3. *Transmission in the Earlier Middle Ages*

During the earlier Middle Ages there were many interesting contacts between Western Christian and Jewish thought which we must pass over in silence. Judaism was certainly a real—and to a much larger extent an alleged—influence on the form of many heresies, Albigensian, Waldensian, Passagian, Hussite, and the rest. In this place, however, we must be content with a consideration of the impact of Jewish thought on the main body of Latin Catholic development. Here Jewish influence was primarily exerted by the translations of Jewish works or Judaized works into Latin. The active process of translation into Latin of works exhibiting Jewish thought begins in

Transmission of the Jewish Factor

Spain at the end of the earlier medieval period.[1] Its opening is thus earlier than Averroes (died 1198) and Maimonides (died 1204).

The brilliant episode of Spanish Judaism under Muslim rule is the most attractive and romantic in post-biblical Jewish history. Especially were the reigns of Abd-ur-Rahman III (912–961) and his son Al-Hakim, the golden era for the Spanish

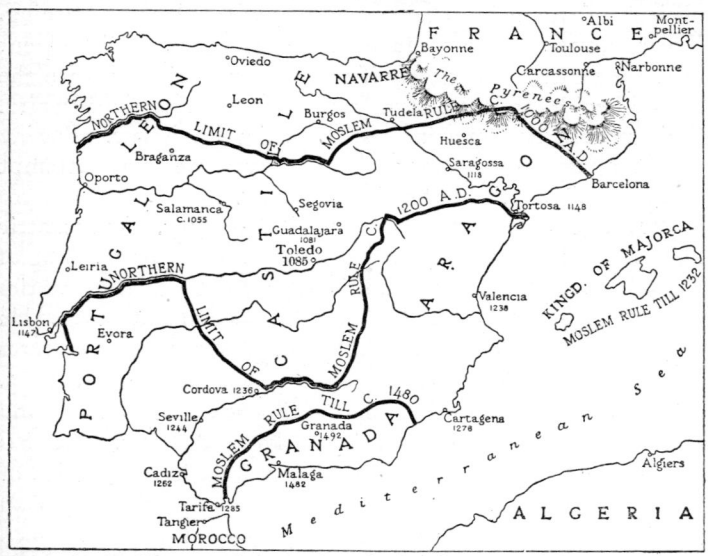

FIG. 26. To illustrate the recession of Islam in Spain. The figures after the names of the towns are the dates of their conquest by Christendom.

Jews, and for Jewish science. As the Muslim power receded the Jews came under less tolerant Christian rule. Jewish learning lost by the recession of the Arabic language which was its main literary reservoir. The retreat of Islam meant the substitution for learned purposes of Latin for Arabic. For

[1] There are yet earlier Jewish translations, e.g. the astrological treatise associated with the name 'Alcandrius', dating from about 950 (p. 289), and the versions of Isaac's medical writings by Constantine the African of about 1080. These earlier works are, however, unimportant for our present purpose.

the Jews, however, Latin could not take the place of Arabic, since Latin, unlike Arabic, was essentially a ritual tongue, representing a religious point of view opposed to their own Hebrew.

From the beginning of the twelfth century a certain number of adventurous Latin scholars from the North sought to make their way into Spain to gain something of the Arabian learning. Their efforts became gradually more successful. It is evident that the process was largely if not mostly carried on with the aid of Jewish students, often recent converts to Christianity. This process has long interested medieval scholars. Piecing together accounts from various sources we may attempt a thumbnail sketch of the circumstances.

We are at the beginning of the twelfth century. An eccentric and restless European student, dissatisfied with the teaching of the schools of his native land, is attracted by floating stories of the wonders of Arabian learning and wisdom and power. He determines to try his fortune in Spain. After many adventures he arrives at Toledo, which passed to Christendom in 1085. The country is in disorder, and fighting between Moslems and Christians is still going on in outlying districts. He has crossed the frontier from the Spanish march, having evaded or bribed the sentries. He brings with him a letter, from a patron in his own land, to an official of the native Church. Such officials are all in a state of nervous apprehension, for the Moslem rule is a recent memory. Our student seeks to establish his credentials. His host can converse with him in Latin, but only with difficulty for their pronunciations differ greatly.

Even when our student is accepted for what he is, his troubles have but begun. The very last thing he is likely to get from his clerical friend is any help with the accursed science of the Infidel. For one thing the poor man knows nothing of it. It stands to him for all that is abominable; it is 'black magic', accursed, unclean. Moreover, the language of these Mozarabs,

Fig. 27. TOLEDO SEEN ACROSS THE TAGUS

or native Christians, is a non-literary patois, of mixed Arabic and Latin origin, and quite useless for the investigation of Arabian philosophy. It is the patois, not the literary tongue, which our student picks up while looking round him for more efficient aid. At last he sees where help may be found.

The Spanish Jews of that age had entered with far greater spirit than the Spanish Christians into the philosophical and scientific heritage of Islam. While ignorant of Latin, with which they have not the same spiritual link as their Christian fellows, many speak and write good literary Arabic. Our student, now with some command of the vernacular, makes the acquaintance of a Jew of this type, and arranges a series of secret meetings in some back attic of the Jewish quarter. He soon finds, however, that the vernacular patois, with which he has still but an imperfect acquaintance, is an inadequate means for scientific discussion. Help from another source must be invoked. A none too reputable native Christian with a knowledge of Latin is asked to join the pair. He is of the 'Vicar of Bray' type, a man who was a Muslim before the land had been re-won by the Christians. Meetings are arranged at even more secluded lodgings, for none of the three is anxious for the matter to become known to his own people.

Now they can get to work, but all kinds of difficulties arise. The Mozarab convert reads Arabic with difficulty for he was never an enthusiastic Muslim. He knows the patois, however, and he has acquired a smattering of Latin since his conversion. The Jew reads Arabic fluently. He is no great philosopher and hardly understands the matter, but he can eke out his knowledge from his Hebrew studies. He too is well acquainted with the patois. Of Latin he knows only a few words. The European member of the conspiracy is by far the most intelligent of the three. He knows no science nor any philosophy save logic, but he is eager to learn and has a turn for languages. In the absence of a grammar, however, the classical Arabic is too hard for him, and he can make little of the constant discussion that goes on in the patois between the Mozarab and the Jew.

The work is very laborious. The Mozarab and the Jew painfully turn the Arabic text sentence by sentence into the patois. The three then beat out the meaning between them, and get it into some kind of Latin. What kind of Latin those accustomed to read medieval translations know only too well!

This is no greatly overdrawn picture of the making of a translation in twelfth-century Spain. Naturally in the course of such a process many words and phrases became unintelligible. Some were left by the translators in very weariness. Especial difficulty was encountered with technical terms. The meaning of some of these may well have been unknown to the Jewish member of the conspiracy and, like enough, to all three members. Such words were often simply carried over into the Latin, being transliterated from the Arabic, and they frequently take most absurd forms. Early Arabic-Latin translations are full of Semitic expressions, the Hebrew origin of some of which often betrays the fact that the Jew was sometimes really working not on an Arabic version but on a Hebrew translation from the Arabic. The medieval astronomical, alchemical, and medical vocabulary thus became stocked with Semitic words, many of which, e. g. *zero*, *azimuth*, *zenith*, *alembic*, *azure*, *nucha*, have come down to the speech, or at least the literary language, of our own time. Music too was affected, as the Semitic origin of *lute*, *guitar*, *rebeck*, *tabor*, *shawm*, and *fanfare* still bears witness. Where one of these Semitic words has survived, scores have perished, done to death by the linguistic purists of Renaissance humanism!

An interesting and typical character who may be supposed to have worked in the way we have described is ADELARD OF BATH. We have a considerable number of his writings which, when placed in chronological order, exhibit his increasing acquaintance with Arabic. Thus in his *Rules of the Abacus*, an early effort written about 1100, there is no trace of Arabian

FIG. 28. A STREET IN OLD TOLEDO

factors. In his work *On the Unchangeable and the Changeable*[1] of about 1106 he is still young, but has ventured into Southern Italy and has an inkling of Greek but not of Arabic. He is getting bitten by philosophy. Not much later is Adelard's *Physical problems* (Quaestiones naturales) which borrows its psychological theory from Latin translations from the Arabic by Constantine the African (died 1087).[2] Adelard's translation from the Arabic of the *Astronomical Tables* of al-Kwarizmi (fl. *c*. 830) is perhaps of 1126. He must have already stayed in Spain for some time. Of about the same date is his translation of al-Kwarizmi's *Introduction to the Art of Astronomy*, which exhibits some acquaintance with Hebrew chronology. A version from the Arabic of Euclid's *Elements* followed.

In addition to foreigners, such as Adelard, there were also natives who devoted themselves to the task of translation. Men of Jewish origin were very conspicuous among this band of native workers. Perhaps the earliest of them was one PETRUS ALPHONSI. This man came of a Jewish family and was born in 1062, somewhere in the Arabic-speaking zone, for he had an expert knowledge of Arabic. He would have been twenty-two years old at the fall of Toledo in 1085. He was converted to Christianity, and baptized at Huesca in Aragon in 1106, being then forty-three. His godfather was Alfonso I of Aragon, and his name implies that he was ' Alfonso's Peter '.

There are several works connected with Petrus Alfonsi. At an early age he wrote an astronomical work in Hebrew or Spanish. It was after his conversion that he wrote in Latin

[1] *De eodem et diverso*. It is a dialogue between Philosophy (the unchangeable, *de eodem*) and Philocosmy (changeable knowledge, *de diverso*). It is dedicated to the Bishop of Syracuse.

[2] This Constantine, born a Muslim or perhaps a Jew in North Africa, came to Salerno in South Italy about 1070 and was there converted to Christianity. He was the first who occupied himself in Italy with translation from the Arabic. The works he thus translated were largely of Jewish origin.

his *Dialogues with a Jew* and his *Training-school for the clergy*. The *Dialogues* are between 'Moses' and 'Peter'. Moses was Peter's name before he became a Christian, and the dialogues represent conversations of Petrus before conversion and Petrus after conversion. They are not without merit. The *Training-school for the clergy* contains all kinds of entertaining fables which were often used for homiletic purposes. It was the channel by which many Eastern folk-tales passed to the West. Translations of it were made into French, Spanish, and German. Some of the stories are printed at the end of Caxton's English *Aesop* of 1483. A number are incorporated into the medieval collection of tales known as the *Gesta Romanorum*. This work is the source of many of the stories in Chaucer and Shakespeare. It was first printed, about 1510, by Wynkyn de Worde. The edition survives in but a single copy, but was reprinted in 1577. Shakespeare probably read this later issue.

Petrus was of an adventurous and restless nature. After his conversion he came to England, where we hear of him acting as physician to Henry I. Here he attracted the attention of the learned. In 1120 Walcher, Prior of Malvern, brought out a translation of his astronomical work. As it is quite unlikely that Walcher knew the language of the original, it seems probable that Petrus himself helped him with the task. The work used certain mathematical refinements not previously known in the West. The collaboration of Petrus and Walcher represents the first impact of Arabian learning in England.

Another Spanish Jew who visited England in the twelfth century was the theologian, philosopher, mathematician, and astrologer, ABRAHAM BEN EZRA (1092–1167, p. 190). This remarkable man was in London in the year 1158, and while there wrote a work, the *Foundation of Religion*, which gives a description of the state of learning of the Jews of England at the time. Several of the mathematical works of Ben Ezra were translated into Latin, one in the twelfth century and others in 1274 at Malines in the house of Henri Bate (pp. 235-236). These were edited by Peter of Abano (pp. 275-276). Browning, who knew well the writings of Abraham Ben Ezra, puts into the mouth of the Rabbi many stanzas appropriate to one who had at once the clear view of the inevitability of material events that comes from astrology and the conviction of the freedom of the soul that comes of the philosophy that he professed.

> All that is, at all,
> Lasts ever, past recall;
> Earth changes, but thy soul and God stand sure:
> What entered into thee,
> *That* was, is, and shall be:
> Time's wheel runs back or stops: Potter and clay endure.
>
> He fixed thee mid this dance
> Of plastic circumstance,
> This Present, thou, forsooth, wouldst fain arrest:
> Machinery just meant
> To give thy soul its bent,
> Try thee and turn thee forth, sufficiently impressed.

Browning, too, puts some characteristic and not ignoble words into Ben Ezra's mouth in his *Holy Cross Day*, when Jews were forced to attend a sermon on the truths of the Christian religion. Rabbi Ben Ezra suffered terribly in body and spirit and he may well have spoken even thus:

> God spoke, and gave us the word to keep,
> Bade never fold the hands nor sleep
> 'Mid a faithless world,—at watch and ward,
> Till Christ at the end relieve our guard.
> By His servant Moses the watch was set:
> Though near upon cock-crow, we keep it yet.
> Thou! if thou wast He, who at mid-watch came,
> By the starlight, naming a dubious name!
> And if, too heavy with sleep—too rash
> With fear—O Thou, if that martyr-gash
> Fell on Thee coming to take thine own,
> And we gave the Cross, when we owed the Throne—
> Thou art the Judge. We are bruised thus.

Transmission of the Jewish Factor

> But, the Judgment over, join sides with us!
> Thine too is the cause! and not more thine
> Than ours, is the work of these dogs and swine,
> Whose life laughs through and spits at their creed!
> Who maintain Thee in word, and defy Thee in deed![1]

But to return to Abraham Ben Ezra's native land of Spain. The best-known of the native Spanish translators was Johannes Hispalensis, whose Arabic name, ibn Daud (ben David) was corrupted by the schoolmen into AVENDEATH.[2] In the bulk of his work Avendeath is excelled by only one translator from the Arabic, Gerard of Cremona (1113–1187).

Avendeath (c. 1090–c. 1165) was born a Jew at Toledo, soon after that city fell into Christian hands in 1085. He became converted to Christianity, lived into the second half of the twelfth century, and acquired an effective knowledge of Latin. At first he collaborated with a clerical colleague, DOMINICUS GUNDISSALINUS, Archdeacon of Segovia. Working thus, he turned Avicenna *On the soul* into Spanish, and Gundissalinus turned it thence into Latin. This commentary on the great philosophical treatise of Aristotle was of wide influence in the Latin West. Other writings of Gundissalinus are not translations but are treatises of a philosophical or astrological nature, which exercised considerable influence on the Latin West. They lean heavily, however, on Arabian writings, and in them also we may see the hand of Avendeath. Avendeath and Gundissalinus together turned into Latin besides Avicenna *On the soul*, Algazel's philosophical works, and Avicebron's *Fountain of Life*, all destined to be much read by the Latins.

Avendeath also produced translations of a whole host of astronomical and astrological books. The varied sources of

[1] Dr. Abrahams was of the opinion that Browning had not an individual Ben Ezra in his mind but that he uses the name in his poems as that of a sort of generalized medieval rabbi.

[2] The identification of Johannes Hispalensis with Avendeath is not quite certain.

these illustrate the manner in which the Spanish Jewish translators were pouring the garnered learning of the East into the libraries of the West. Among these astronomical translations of Avendeath are the works of Albumasar (786–886) of Bagdad, of Omar ibn al-Farrushan (died *c.* 932) the Persian, of Thabit ben Kurra (826–901) the 'Sabian' of Harran, of Messahala (died 815) the Jew of Bassorah, of Messahala'a pupil Albohali (died 835), of Alfraganus (died *c.* 880) of Fargan in Transoxania, and the *Centiloquium* ascribed to Ptolemy (*c.* 180). Avendeath thus provided a large proportion of the mathematical, astrological, and astronomical works in the medieval library.

The most popular of Avendeath's works was his version of part of the *Secretum secretorum*, a work falsely ascribed by the Middle Ages to Aristotle. This curious document he rendered into Latin for a Spanish Queen, Tharasia. It was one of the most popular works ever written. Copies, variants, and translations of it exist in many hundreds of manuscripts in many languages, Hebrew among them. It greatly influenced the Latins and Roger Bacon wrote notes upon it. It was frequently edited after the invention of printing, and parts of it appear to this day in debased form in a certain low type of print. More philosophical were Avendeath's translations of the works of the contemporary Turkish writer al-Farabi, *On the Divisions of Philosophy* and *On the Origin of the Sciences*.

Most important and interesting of all Avendeath's translations is that of the work of the Persian Muhammad ibn Musa al-Kwarizmi (fl. *c.* 830). In it our so-called *Arabic* numerical notation, in which the digits depend on their position for their value, is used in a Latin work for the first time. The Arabic numerals displaced the clumsy and laborious old Latin numerals. The new method was but slowly accepted, and the work of incorporation into our system was hardly complete until the sixteenth century. Yet this new method has had an almost incalculable influence on our mode of thought and seems to us

FIG. 29. Detail of a synagogue at Toledo. It was completed in 1357 by Samuel Abulafia (1320–1360). The building stands intact to this day. Since the expulsion of the Jews from Spain at the end of the fifteenth century, it has been used as a church and known as *El Transito*. The Hebrew and Arabic inscriptions form so essential a part of the design that they have been allowed to remain despite the prejudice against them in a Christian place of worship. There are three horizontal bands of Hebrew inscriptions. Arabic inscriptions may be seen on the capitals of the columns, in two horizontal bands, one above and one below the basal ornament, and in an intricate scrollwork connecting these two horizontal bands. The basal ornament consists of floral and heraldic designs. The whole is an admirable example of the very distinctive Hebraeo-Arabic art which had its centre in the Iberian peninsula.

now implicit in our ideas of number. The whole of modern mathematics may be said to date back to this translation by Avendeath. The word *Algorism*, used in the Middle Ages as the equivalent of what we now call Arithmetic, conceals the name of al-Kwarizmi, i. e. the 'man of Kwarism', the town we now call Khiva.

Avendeath was highly esteemed by his brother translators. A book was dedicated to him, for instance, by his contemporary, the Italian, PLATO OF TIVOLI. This Plato of Tivoli was, next to Gerard of Cremona and Avendeath himself, the most active of the Spanish group of the twelfth century. His seat of activities was Barcelona, and the period of his flourishing about 1130–1150.

Plato did not work alone, but in conjunction with a Jew, Abraham ben Hiyya, called SAVASORDA (Sahib al-Schurta, i. e. 'foreman of those who perform the rites of the dead'). Savasorda's own work on Geometry was translated by Plato in 1145. This is important as the first introduction of Arabian Trigonometry and Mensuration to the West. The work is noteworthy too for the impression that it made on Leonardo of Pisa (flourished 1225), himself the most widely read mathematician of the Middle Ages. The influence of Savasorda is the more remarkable when we remember that he was but a minor synagogue official.

Over the most industrious of all the translators, GERARD OF CREMONA (1114–1187), we must pass lightly. He came from Italy to Toledo to acquire Arabic with the express purpose of translating Ptolemy's *Almagest*, and he remained all his life engaged on translations from Arabic and Hebrew writings. His main assistant was a native Arabic-speaking Christian but he had occasionally a Hebrew helper. He translated the works of many Jewish authors, among whom were Messahala and Isaac Judaeus.

With the twelfth century the pioneer period of translation from the Arabic is over. From now on such work is conducted by better-known writers who carry on a tradition already established.

§ 4. *Transmission in the Later Middle Ages*

a. In the Sicilies

During the thirteenth century the rate at which translations come to the Latin West is greatly accelerated. Their

FIG. 30. Italy in the first half of the thirteenth century.

preparation becomes almost a recognized profession. Enlightened rulers are specially associated with the work. We have now to do with the Italo-Sicilian zone as well as Spain. There is, moreover, another complicating factor. Western Jews in the thirteenth century were becoming less familiar with Arabic, and there arose a need for translation from Arabic into Hebrew, the only learned language generally understood by Jews. These Arabic-Hebrew translations were produced in large numbers. Moreover many translations of Arabic works into Latin, prepared during this period, were made not directly from the Arabic but indirectly through these Hebrew versions.

For the first two-thirds of the thirteenth century, under the Hohenstaufen, the brilliant FREDERICK II, the *Stupor Mundi* (1194–1250), and his son Manfred (1232–1266), Oriental learning flourished in the kingdom of the Sicilies. The Emperor was himself a scholar, master of six languages and very eager for the new learning. Despite some of his edicts, which express a contrary tendency, he was, in fact, very tolerant of Muslims and Jews. At Palermo, Naples, Salerno, and elsewhere we hear much of their intellectual activity. Translation was aided by the polyglot character of the country, for Greek, Latin, and Arabic were all recognized for legal purposes, especially in Sicily, the 'many-tongued isle' (Fig. 31). Under Frederick arose an important group of translators of Arabian philosophy and science into Hebrew and Latin. This school had considerable influence on the subsequent course of scholasticism. The best representative of the Sicilian Hebrew translators is Jacob Anatoli, and the best representative of the Sicilian Latin translators Michael Scot.

JACOB ANATOLI (1194–1256) was born at Marseilles, and married into a family distinguished for its scholarship. His father-in-law was the first translator of the *Guide* of Maimonides into Hebrew. Anatoli had many learned Hebrew relatives throughout Provence. Frederick invited him to Naples, where he had established a University in 1224. Lectures in Hebrew were being given in the town at the time. In the event the new University was a failure, though it had St. Thomas Aquinas among its pupils. St. Thomas and Anatoli may well have come in contact at Naples, and it may be that it was there that St. Thomas first learned of the philosophy of Averroes.

However this may be, Anatoli was the first man to translate the philosophy of Averroes. He turned it into Hebrew, and this partly explains the extraordinary influence that Averroes had upon Jewish thought. There can be little doubt that much

FIG. 31. From an early thirteenth-century South Italian manuscript now in the Civic Library at Berne. The scene is laid in Palermo. It illustrates the current use of the three languages, Greek, Arabic, and Latin, which were employed not only colloquially but also in the courts and for general legal and commercial purposes. In the left panel are bearded *notarii Greci*. In the middle panel are turbaned *not[arii] Saraceni*. In the right panel are clean-shaven *not[arii] Latini*. The costume of the figures varies with their head-dress and facial adornment. The Greek-, Arabic- and Latin-speaking lawyers are, however, all alike engaged in writing on their tablets.

of the text of Averroes current in Latin during the Middle Ages was translated from the Hebrew. Anatoli also translated many astronomical works. A particular interest attaches to a volume of Hebrew sermons that he produced. In the course of these he gives allegorical suggestions which, he tells us, were made by the Emperor Frederick II. He cites also with very great respect a Christian sage who may have been Michael Scot.

Anatoli was a great admirer of Maimonides. We have seen that the *Guide to the perplexed* of Maimonides was translated into Hebrew by the father-in-law of Anatoli during the lifetime of its author. Soon after a second Hebrew translation of this work was made, perhaps by Judah Harisi. Early in the thirteenth century this second Hebrew version was turned into Latin, and it has been suggested that this was the joint work of Anatoli and Michael. In any event, there was personal contact between the two men, and Michael derived much from Anatoli.

MICHAEL SCOT (died *c.* 1235), after leaving England, adventured first into Spain to learn Arabic. To this period certainly belongs his version of Alpetragius (al Bitrugi) *On the sphere* (1217). Michael came to Italy about 1220, and, turning south, joined the court of Frederick II about 1228. He rose to high and trusted position, and occupied himself largely with the work of translation. Many writings were subsequently printed in his name. Of these, perhaps the most interesting is his version of the great Aristotelian biological works, and it may be that he rendered them not from Arabic but from Hebrew. This contribution was among the most important of all the works of translation, for the biological works, more than any other of Aristotle's scientific treatises, are based on first-hand observation. They profoundly affected Albertus Magnus and through him the other schoolmen. Michael Scot certainly had Jewish help, and Roger Bacon tells us that he did not know Arabic well but that his work was chiefly done by a Jew named Andrew.[1] Roger links the name of Herman the German (died 1272), his own teacher, in the same statement. There can be no doubt of the importance of the works that Michael Scot has left behind.

---

[1] It has been suggested that the name Andrew is a mistake or misreading for Anatoli. Such a misreading is possible in some scripts of the thirteenth century.

Among them were the *Metaphysics* of Aristotle and a work *On the Secrets of Nature* from a number of Greek, Arabic, and

FIG. 32. Thirteenth-century synagogue of South Italian type at Trani on the Adriatic in the heel of Italy. Trani was a prosperous seaport in the Middle Ages and was especially important during the Crusades. The large Jewish population there and elsewhere in the heel and toe of Italy suffered greatly from the crusaders. The harbour of Trani has now silted up and the place has become quite insignificant.

Hebrew sources. A letter from Pope Gregory IX, written in 1227, states that Michael Scot had a knowledge of both Arabic and Hebrew.

Translators of the type of Michael Scot were widely held by the ignorant Middle Ages to be magicians and sorcerers. It was known that they conversed with Muslims and Jews. It was known that they worked at astronomy, astrology, alchemy, and other mysterious crafts that savoured alike of heresy and of black magic. Some, like Michael himself, had allied themselves with Frederick II, the foe of the Papacy, who, as one exasperated monk records, 'even took baths on Sundays'. Magic and spells, blessings and curses and ever-filled purses, were among the weapons with which the medieval imagination equipped such men. The vulgar attitude toward them is faithfully reflected in the *Lay of the Last Minstrel*:

> Thus spoke the Monk, in solemn tone:
> 'I was not always a man of woe;
> For Paynim countries I have trod,
> And fought beneath the Cross of God:
>
> . . . .
>
> In those far climes it was my lot
> To meet the wondrous Michael Scott;
> A Wizard of such dreaded fame,
> That when, in Salamanca's Cave,
> Him listed his magic wand to wave,
> The bells would ring in Notre Dame!
> Some of his skill he taught to me;
> And, Warrior, I could say to thee,
> The words that cleft Eildon hills in three,
> And bridled the Tweed with a curb of stone,
> But to speak them were a deadly sin,
> And for having but thought them, my heart within
> A treble penance must be done.
>
> . . . .
>
> When Michael lay on his dying bed,
> His conscience was awakenèd;
> He bethought him of his sinful deed,
> And he gave me a sign to come with speed.
> I was in Spain when the morning rose,
> But I stood by his bed ere evening close.'

The interest of Frederick II in Oriental learning was inherited by his son and successor in Sicily, MANFRED (1232-1266). A number of translations from Hebrew and Arabic were prepared under Manfred's direction. One is peculiarly interesting, as it has been thought that the king himself had a hand in it. This is the curious pseudo-Aristotelian philosophical dialogue, the *Book of the Apple*. A version of it was either written in or translated into Hebrew by a Jew, Abraham ben Hasdai, and from Hebrew it was turned into Latin under Manfred's supervision or perhaps with his direct aid. It is indeed not at all improbable that Manfred had some knowledge of Hebrew.

The influence of Jewish learning in the South Italian zone did not cease with the Hohenstaufen, but was continued under the Angevin sovereigns. CHARLES OF ANJOU (1220-1285), after the death of Manfred in 1266, seized the whole Sicilian kingdom. Coming from the North, he was eager to win access to a civilization that was stranger to him than to a native of the country, such as Manfred. To render the Arabic works into Latin he too employed Jewish translators, of whom the best known is Faraj ben Salim of Girgenti, known to the Latins as Farrachius or Farragut.

FARRACHIUS must have been a very industrious worker. He is the first man of Jewish faith to appear on the stage as a professional translator occupied exclusively with turning works into Latin. His greatest achievement is the rendering into Latin of the enormous medical treatise known to the medievals as the *Liber continens* of Rhazes of Khorasan (died 932). This Rhazes was, scientifically speaking, the ablest of all the Arabian physicians, and the translation of Rhazes by Farrachius was still being read in the days of printing. The *editio princeps* (Brescia, 1486) has the somewhat doubtful distinction of being one of the largest and heaviest of fifteenth-century books! A good specimen weighs about twenty-two pounds! The actual work of translation was completed by Farrachius on the 13th of February 1279.

A particular interest attaches to a manuscript of this translation written in 1282. In it we have several representations of the translator. In one he receives the Arabic text from an Eastern potentate. In another he hands the finished product to Charles. These are the first portraits of a Jew, other than caricatures (Fig. 33). They are interesting as expressing the feeling for Oriental learning similar to that expressed by a contemporary artist in the death-bed scene of William the Good of Sicily (1152–1189, Fig. 34).

Charles of Anjou had translators specially trained for their task. The Jew, MOSES OF PALERMO, was thus educated in Latin by his order for this purpose. From this Moses we have a Latin version of a pseudo-Hippocratic work on the diseases of horses. About the same time it was also turned into Italian with reference to the Greek original.

Active interest in translation persisted in South Italy till the fourteenth century. Thus, Robert the Good, of Anjou, who reigned there from 1309 to 1343, ordered the Jew Kalonymus ben Kalonymus of Arles to translate the *Destructio destructionis* of Averroes (p. 192). The work of Kalonymus was completed in 1328.

b. *In Castille*

In Spain activity in production of translations from Arabic in the thirteenth century was even greater than in the Sicilies. ALFONSO X OF CASTILLE, called *El Sabio*, or 'the wise' (1252–84), ascended the throne when the transference of Eastern thought to the West was in active progress. He secured some of this material for his country through vernacular translations. Politically, Alfonso's position was weakened by his Imperial aspirations, and he made fruitless sacrifices for that end. Despite these he held the greater part of the peninsula until his final defeat at Seville. His Jewish subjects reached a high state of intellectual development. The King, himself an author, was interested in philosophy and astronomy, and employed a number of Jewish

FIG. 33. FROM A MANUSCRIPT (A.D. 1282) OF THE LATIN TRANSLATION OF RHAZES BY FARRACHIUS

On the left Farrachius delivers his translation to Charles of Anjou. On the right Farrachius receives the Arabic original of Rhazes from an Eastern Potentate. For description see pp. xxiii and 222

FIG. 34. From an early thirteenth-century South Italian manuscript now in the Civic Library at Berne. The scene is the death of the Norman King, William II of Sicily (died 1189). The central panel shows the king on his death-bed and wearing his crown. The curtain is flung aside to give him air while a nurse keeps flies from him with a fan. Above the king is written *Rex W[ilelmus] egrotans*. Sitting at the foot of the bed is a bearded attendant in oriental dress and wearing a turban. Above him is written the word *astrologus*. A great star shines in the sky, and the astrologer is about to take its elevation with an astrolabe which hangs from his left hand. In his right he holds an astrological book. By the head of the bed is another bearded and turbaned figure who holds a phial in his hand. Above him are written the words *achim medicus*. The word *achim* is the transcribed form of *hakim*, Arabic for *wise* or *learned*. It is applied by Muslims to their physicians just as we call ours *doctors*. The whole picture reflects the oriental atmosphere of medieval Sicily.

translators. The translations into the Castillian language which they made for him provide an important chapter in the history of Spanish literature.

The most permanent and remarkable of the scientific works executed in the reign of Alfonso X were certainly the so-called *Alfonsine Tables*. These celebrated lists of planetary movements form the basic document of modern scientific astronomy. They were prepared under the wise king's direct command by two learned Jews of Toledo, JUDAH BEN MOSES COHEN, a physician, and ISAAC BEN SID, a *Hazan*, or synagogue precentor. These important tables continued in great repute for centuries. They are to be found in numerous manuscripts, and long continued to be reprinted. They were still being consulted by Kepler and Galileo in the seventeenth century. The last edition of the tables for practical use appeared at Madrid as late as 1641.

In the preface to the Alfonsine tables we learn that they were prepared by Judah Cohen and Isaac Hazan 'in the first decade of the fourth century of the second millennium after the era of Caesar' (generally called the *Spanish era* and dating from the 1st January, 38 B.C.), and 'two hundred years after the publication of the work of *Arzarchel*'. This would date the work between 1262 and 1272. Ibn al-Zarkali, known as Arzarchel, was a Cordovan astronomer of the twelfth century, whose astronomical tables had already been rendered into Latin by Gerard of Cremona. The originals of these tables of Arzarchel, together with the Latin translation of them, have disappeared, but they are known in a Spanish version of Jewish origin prepared also for Alfonso X.

The preface of the Alfonsine tables tells us that since computed positions were often found to differ from those obtained by astronomical observation, King Alfonso collected instruments (Figs. 35 and 37) and directed observations to be taken at Toledo. Acting on his instruction the writers, Judah Cohen and Isaac

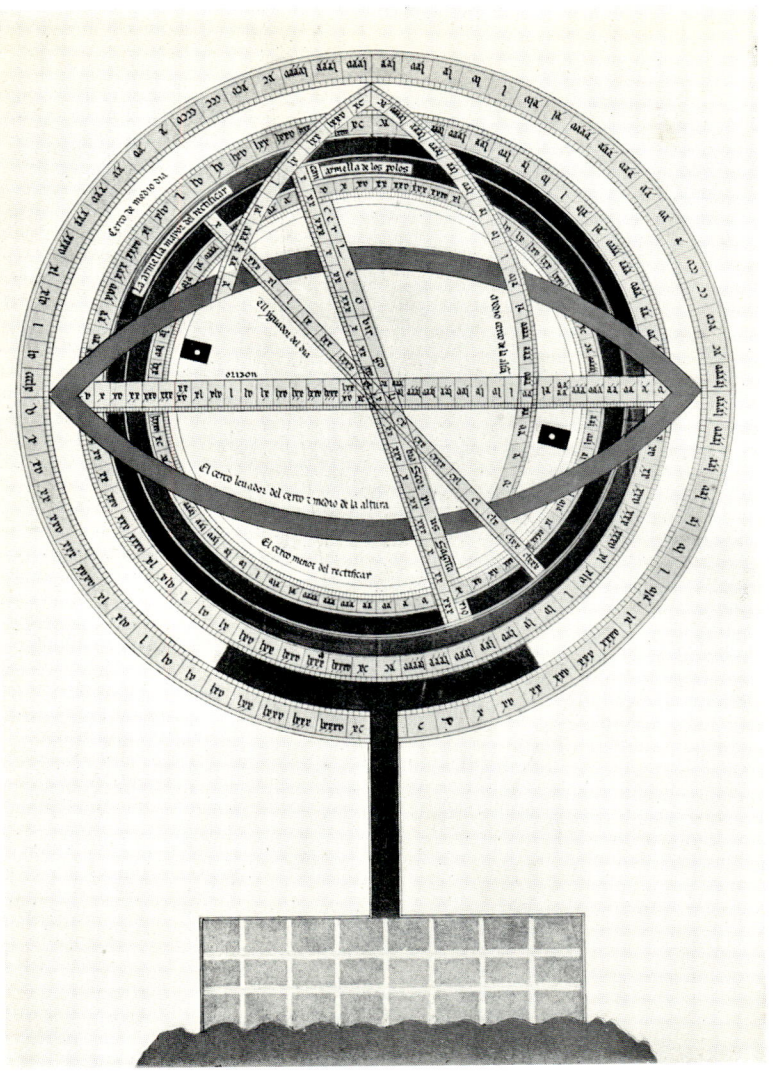

FIG. 35. ARMILLARY SPHERE CONSTRUCTED FOR ALFONSO THE WISE BY JUDAH COHEN AND ISAAC BEN SID

From a XIIIth-century manuscript

For description see p. xxiii

Transmission of the Jewish Factor 225

Hazan, say that they have therefore observed the sun throughout an entire year, particularly at the equinoxes and solstices, and at the middle of the signs of Taurus and Scorpio, Leo and Aquarius. They have also observed conjunctions of planets both with each other and with fixed stars. They have, moreover, taken observations of lunar and solar eclipses. Of some of the

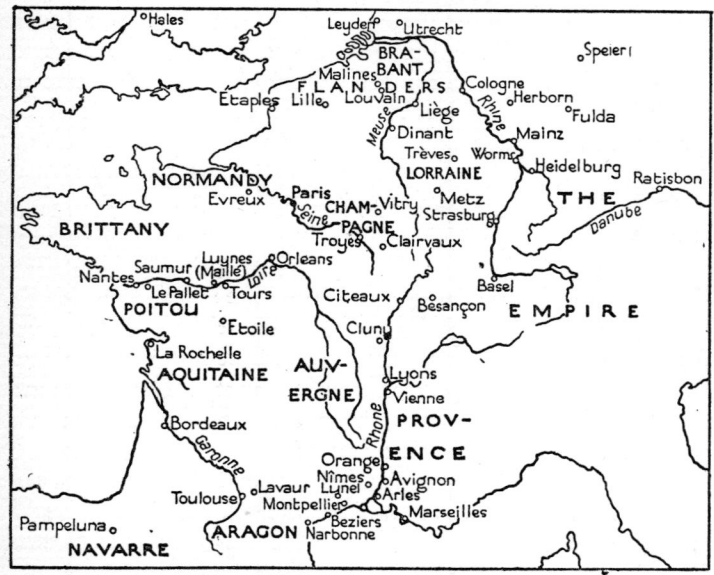

FIG. 36. France at the beginning of the fourteenth century.

observations that they took we learn from another Jewish source, for a Hebrew treatise written in 1310 refers to observations made by Isaac Hazan of the solar eclipse of 5 August 1263, and of two lunar eclipses in the years 1265 and 1266. Both the authors of the Alfonsine tables produced many other important astronomical, mathematical, and mechanical works in Spanish, and constructed a number of astronomical instruments (Figs. 35 and 37).

c. In Aragon

Alfonso's patronage of Arabian learning was copied by his neighbours, the monarchs of Aragon. Thus the Jew Astruc Bonsenior of Barcelona was secretary and interpreter to King Jaime I of Aragon (1208–1276) and of considerable service to him in his campaigns. Astruc died in 1280, and his son Judah succeeded him. This JUDAH BONSENIOR became afterwards interpreter both to Alfonso III of Aragon (1265–1291) and to his successor Jaime II (1260–1327). In 1287 Alfonso III took him on his expedition to Minorca. In 1294 he was placed in a peculiar office by Jaime II. Arabic-speaking merchants who had business documents translated into Spanish were directed to have them authenticated by appearing before Judah Bonsenior or some person nominated by him. In 1305 Bonsenior visited Provence with a royal passport, and there are many other records of the extension of royal favour to himself and his family. Among the literary works of Judah Bonsenior is a series of aphorisms in Catalan drawn from a variety of Hebrew and Arabic sources. Many saws and wise sayings taken from this book are in use to this day in Catalonia.

The Jewish astronomers of Castille had their counterpart in the Jewish geographers of Aragon. For the use of Aragonese merchants who visited the coasts of the Mediterranean, sailing books known as *portolani* were prepared. These contained descriptions of coasts, harbours, anchorages and so forth. Towards the end of the thirteenth century the portolani began to be provided with charts. These *portolano maps* differed from the medieval *mappae mundi* in being confined in the first instance to the Mediterranean, of which they gave a fair outline, and in giving the directions and sailing distances between different ports. They are thus the predecessors of modern charts. The best-known *portolano maps* were made in the island of Majorca, and here a very important school of Jewish map-makers sprang up.

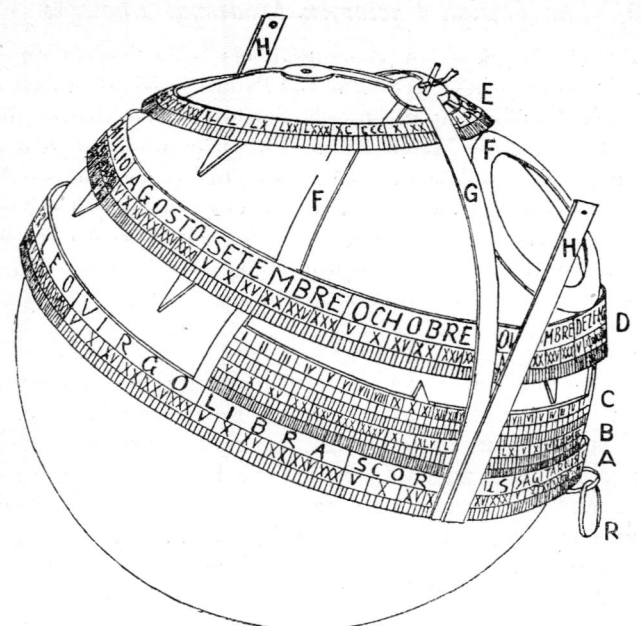

FIG. 37. Spherical astrolabe of Alfonso the Wise of Castille, constructed for him by his Jewish astronomers and described and figured by them. It is here exhibited as reconstructed. The sphere itself is not an essential part of the instrument, which is complete provided all the circles and bands are present. A is a circle marked with the twelve signs of the zodiac, each of which is graduated into thirty divisions. B C is a band of variously graduated quadrants. D is a calendarium bearing the Castillian names of the months, each of which is graduated into the appropriate number of days. E is the equator. F is a connecting piece used to give mechanical strength. G is the so-called *Alidad*, that is to say the movable part of the astrolabe that carries a *sight*. The Alidad rotates around an axis and the amount of rotation can be read off against the quadrants and circles. The sights themselves are seen as small holes in the projecting pieces H H. One of these pieces is attached to the Alidad G. R is the ring from which the astrolabe is suspended.

The Jewish Catalan chartographers drew largely on the Arabic geographers. It was at Las Palmas in Majorca that the Jew Cresques drew up in 1375 the first world map that set forth the discoveries of Marco Polo. This map was sent as a gift from the King of Aragon to Charles VI of France, and is still in existence (Figs. 38 and 39). Cresques long continued his chartographical activities, and in 1419 he was summoned to Portugal by Prince Henry the Navigator (1394–1460), to assist in the establishment of an astronomical observatory.

d. *In North Italy*

By the middle of the thirteenth century the two original gates of entry of Oriental learning are ceasing to serve. In the Iberian peninsula, now organized into Christian kingdoms, the vernaculars Catalan, Castillian, and Portuguese begin to be used even for learned purposes. The cultural and political importance of the Sicilies is on the decline. The rise of the Universities in North Italy and France has determined the future intellectual centres of gravity. Islam is in retreat in the

---

Note to maps opposite.

Portions of a Portolano map in the *Bibliothèque nationale* at Paris prepared by the Jewish cartographer, Cresques of Majorca, in 1375. Fig. 38 is Spain marked CHASTEL, i. e. Castille. Fig. 39 is Great Britain marked ANGILTERA. The outline of Spain is much the more accurate of the two. The more important towns of both countries are provided with banners or depicted as towers or castles. Lettering is usually to be read from the north.

In Spain we see Cordova, Seville (Sibillia), Burgos, Leon, Segovia (Seguia), Valencia (Vallancja), Barcelona, Tortosa, Saragossa, &c. Granada bears a banner with an Arabic emblem indicating that it is still Moslem. Toledo is represented as entirely surrounded by water.

In Great Britain London (Londer) bears a banner, as does Edinburgh (Endenborg) in Scotland (Schocja). Among the ports are Milford (Miraforda) and Bristol (Bristo). Lundy Island is clearly marked and named (Londey). Note the curious way in which the Orkney Islands are represented as a rosette.

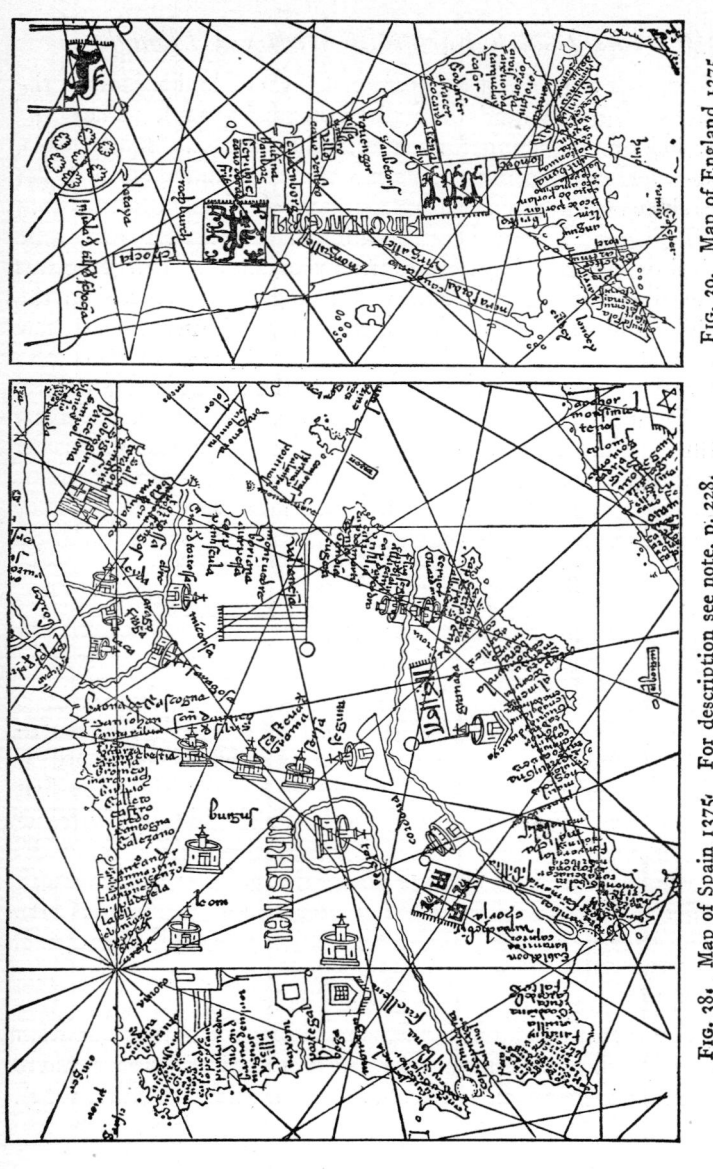

FIG. 38. Map of Spain 1375. For description see note, p. 228.

FIG. 39. Map of England 1375.

West, and at its heart has sustained the irreparable blow of the Mongol invasion and the sack of Bagdad (1227). The great period of translation from the Arabic is past. The process, however, still continues for some centuries, and the prestige of Arabian philosophy and science is not yet lessened in Europe.

Padua had by now become an important medical school, the rival of Bologna. By reason of its proximity to Venice, it was linked with the East. Paduan learning stamped itself on the philosophical and medical thought of Italy during the next few centuries and soon spread also to southern France. The Jews were powerful and numerous at Padua, as in the neighbouring Venice.

For Padua the *Lay of the Last Minstrel* again reflects faithfully the medieval feeling. In that poem is pictured a wizard who had

> Learned the art that none may name,
> In Padua, far beyond the sea.
> Men said he changed his mortal frame
> By feat of magic mystery;
> For when in studious mood he paced
> St. Andrew's cloister'd hall,
> His form no darkening shadow traced
> Upon the sunny wall!

We may glance at a few typical products of Paduan learning, though we can produce no such wondrous work as this! At Padua in 1265 the Jew BONACOSA made the first important North Italian contribution to the library of Arabic-Latin medical translation. It was the treatise known to the Latins as *Colliget* (Arabic *Kulliyyat*, i.e. 'General [medical] rules'), the work of the great Averroes himself (pp. 190–192). This treatise was still being studied in the days of printing, and the last edition appeared at Padua in 1560. It was also translated twice into Hebrew from Arabic.

Another product of the Paduan school was a Latin translation from the Hebrew version of the *Theiçir* (Arabic *Taysir*, i.e. Aid to health), of the Spanish Muslim, Avenzoar (died in Seville, 1162).

This was written by Avenzoar for his friend Averroes. It was one of the most widely read medical works during the Middle Ages and was early translated into Hebrew. From Hebrew it was turned into Latin in 1280 by a Paduan doctor in practice

FIG. 40. Fourteenth-century synagogue at Siena of the North Italian type, with later additions.

at Venice. He worked with a converted Jew, an immigrant from the south, one JACOB OF CAPUA. This Jacob of Capua also rendered into Latin from Hebrew the work *On Hygiene* by Maimonides, and a book of Indian fables. Both of these have an interesting history. The *Hygiene* of Maimonides had been turned into Hebrew from Arabic at Marseilles in 1244. It was one of the first pieces of secular prose to be thus translated outside the Arabic-speaking zone. The other work is the so-called *Fables of Bidpai*, a collection of stories of Indian origin, that have become extraordinarily widespread, largely through Jewish agency. The collection is said to have been translated into thirty-eight languages and twelve different versions, and to have passed into about one hundred and eighty editions. The English version is well known and is derived from the Spanish, which was taken from the Latin, which was taken from the Hebrew, through Arabic, through Pehlawi, and ultimately from the Sanskrit!

Another strange document connected with the Paduan school is the most popular of all the medieval books on remedies, the *Canones generales*, bearing the name of *Mesue*. Mesue is a well-known Arabic medical writer, but there can be no doubt that the ascription of this work is a fiction. The work is a compilation, and there is evidence that parts of it were taken from the Hebrew. Now at the end of the thirteenth century one Samuel ben Jacob of Capua, perhaps the son of the Jacob of Capua above discussed, wrote, composed, or translated part of this document into Hebrew. The Latin version in its complete form was subsequent to this and from a Hebrew source. It became very popular and was printed more than thirty times, the last occasion being as late as 1581. It can be shown to have influenced the modern pharmacopoeias, including that of England.

A translator who links North Italy with South France was the Christian, SIMON CORDO of Genoa. Cordo worked with a Jew, ABRAHAM BEN SHEMTOB of Tortosa, whose father Shemtob ben Isaac of Marseilles was a well-known translator into Hebrew from Arabic. In 1290 Cordo and Abraham between them produced in Latin the very popular drug list associated with the name of *Serapion junior*. This mysterious person, like the spurious Mesue, is unmentioned by the Arabic historians. He was perhaps invented by Cordo and Abraham to cover a drug list of miscellaneous Arabic and Hebrew origin. The work ascribed to Serapion was frequently printed. As with the case of Mesue, it can be shown to have influenced the modern pharmacopoeias. The partnership between Simon Cordo and Abraham Shemtob produced several other medical translations.

e. In France and Flanders

We now pass from Italy to Southern France. Jews were here settled in large numbers and were particularly active in the practice of medicine, notably at Avignon. Montpellier had been a medical centre since the early twelfth century. Despite the strength of the Jewish element in the town itself and neighbourhood, no conclusive evidence has yet been adduced that the University came under direct 'Arabian' influence until the second half of the thirteenth century. At that period Montpellier received a new medical tradition from Bologna and Padua. The first Montpellier physician who can be proved to have collaborated with a Jew came from North Italy. In 1263 John of Brescia, working with the Jew Jacob ben Makir, translated from Arabic into Latin at Montpellier the astronomical tables of Arzarchel (see p. 224).

This JACOB BEN MAKIR (died 1308) was born at Marseilles, studied at the great Talmudic seminary in Lunel, and practised as a physician at Montpellier. After assisting John of Brescia he busied himself with translation from Arabic into Hebrew and in presenting the philosophy of Maimonides in that language. He is best known for a Hebrew work that he wrote in 1288 on the astronomical instrument, the quadrant, into which he introduced certain improvements. The form which he here advocates was spoken of as the 'Jewish quadrant' (*quadrans judaicus*), or the 'new quadrant' (*quadrans novus*). The translation of this important work from the Hebrew into Latin was made no less than three times, on the first occasion by an Englishman named John, who was making a stay at Montpellier about the year 1308, and on the second occasion about 1314 by Armengaud of Montpellier. The well-known surveying instrument usually called *Jacob's staff* may be named after Jacob ben Makir. The first description of it that we have is, however, by his countryman Gersonides (pp. 236–237).

Jacob ben Makir was an able and many-sided man. The extent of his interests is shown by the many translations that he executed into Hebrew from the Arabic. Among them were Euclid's *Elements*, Alhazen's *Astronomy*, a commentary on Euclid, the works of Autolycus and of Menelaus *On the Sphere*, a compendium of the *Logic* of Aristotle, the *De partibus animalium* and the *De generatione animalium* of Aristotle in the version of Averroes, and a philosophical work of Algazel. Jacob's work was appreciated in both Latin and Hebrew circles. He is quoted repeatedly by the two founders of modern astronomy, Copernicus in his great work *On the Revolutions of the Celestial Orbs*, which appeared in 1543, and Kepler in the seventeenth century.

With Jacob ben Makir is associated the equally versatile Christian student Armengaud (died 1314), certain writings of whom he or his pupils turned into Hebrew. The physician ARMENGAUD BLASII (i. e. son of Blaise) of Montpellier attended Philip the Fair and earned a reputation for his knowledge of Arabic. He rendered a number of works into Latin, but all seem to have been made with the aid of Hebrew versions. Among other works Armengaud turned into Latin writings of Maimonides. There can be little doubt that Armengaud was helped by Jacob ben Makir and his pupils.

In 1305 Armengaud, while at Barcelona in attendance on Jaime II of Aragon, occupied his spare time by turning into Latin the very curious *Cantica* of Avicenna, and the medical work of Maimonides *On the treatment of poisoning*. Both were already available in Hebrew versions. The manner in which he relied on Hebrew rather than Arabic is an instance of a widespread practice in the scholastic ages. The reciprocal relationship in which Jacob ben Makir stood to Latin translators is also of interest. The relationship was probably much commoner than appears on the surface.

In 1305 Armengaud was displaced in his attendance on Jaime II by ARNALD OF VILLANOVA (1235–1311). There must be few medieval figures whose lives would give a better opportunity to a romantic writer than that of this man. After a youth of hardship, Arnald became a student at Naples and Salerno, and a traveller in Italy, Sicily, France, and Spain. He taught at Montpellier, and both there and at Barcelona was associated with Armengaud. He was one of the early European writers on Alchemy. He wrote voluminously on philosophical subjects in an heretical vein. He is thought to have had a good knowledge of both Hebrew and Arabic, and at least had access to helpers who had such knowledge. He served as medical adviser to the Papal court both at Rome and at Avignon. He was employed as ambassador on more than one special mission, and he ended his adventurous life at sea. It is very difficult to determine the authenticity of works that appear in Arnald's name, but he certainly translated from the Arabic a work of Avicenna on the heart, and he seems to have rendered from the Hebrew a work of Avenzoar on diet. Both were still being reprinted in the sixteenth century. On the other hand, Arnald's own works were much read in Hebrew, into which language about ten of them were translated.

By the second half of the thirteenth century activity in translation from Arabic had spread northward, and had reached Paris and Flanders. The earliest patron of these northern translators of whom we have tidings was the Fleming, Henri Bate, a student of Paris and a disciple of Albertus Magnus (1193–1280).

HENRI BATE (1244–*c.* 1310) came into occupation of an ecclesiastical benefice at his birthplace at Malines in 1273. In the following year he took part in the Council of Lyons. There he met William of Moerbeke (died 1285), the translator from the

Greek of the writings of Aristotle, whose work was inspired by St. Thomas Aquinas (1227-74). In 1269 Bate obtained ecclesiastical preferment and became a canon at Liége. In the years 1273 and 1274 a French Jew named Hayyim made in Bate's own house at Malines a translation into French of several works of the Spanish Jew Abraham Ben Ezra (1092-1167, see pp. 209-211). These translations influenced Bate's later writings, and notably his treatise on the astrolabe, which he produced in 1274 on the suggestion of William of Moerbeke.

During the first half of the fourteenth century the French Jews displayed a good deal both of philosophic and scientific activity. The leading representative of this movement is Levi ben Gerson or GERSONIDES (1288-1344). He lived at Avignon and Orange, and wrote largely on philosophical subjects. Gersonides is of some importance in the general history of philosophy and especially in relation to certain aspects of the thought of Spinoza. A man of great scientific and philosophic ability, as well as moral courage, his effectiveness suffered from the poorness of his linguistic equipment. He could read neither Arabic nor Latin, so that he was thrown back on Hebrew as his only learned language. The extent, the variety, and the depth of knowledge of this great thinker bear testimony to the development of medieval Hebrew literature.

Gersonides was an enthusiastic Aristotelian, who did not hesitate to interpret what he regarded as the words of his master in opposition alike to current Judaism and to the Averroism of the schools. He regarded himself as a complete rationalist. His philosophy was largely banned by his own people. His work that most affected the world in which he lived was astronomical and written in Hebrew. A passage from it dealing with 'Jacob's staff' was translated into Latin in 1342, during the lifetime of Gersonides, on the order of Pope Clement VI under the title *The instrument that reveals secrets*. Later the whole work was rendered into Latin. It deservedly enjoyed a high reputation, and was still esteemed in the seventeenth century, when Kepler gave himself much trouble to secure a copy. Kepler quotes Gersonides several times and refers to three separate works by him. The work turned into Latin by order of Clement VII is in essence an attempt to demonstrate the falseness of the homocentric theory of the structure of the Universe,[1] set out by Alpetragius. Thus Gersonides is a predecessor of Copernicus.

Some idea of the interests of Gersonides can be gathered from a list of his writings. Many were on theological and rabbinic topics. Apart from the astronomical treatise mentioned above he also wrote an important philosophical treatise, the *Wars of the Lord*—called by his more orthodox opponents, *Wars against the Lord*—commentaries on various biblical books, a treatise on the syllogism, a commentary on Averroes afterwards translated into Latin by Jacob Mantino and printed in the standard Latin edition of Averroes, a commentary on Euclid, an astrological work, and a note on the treatment of gout.

The philosophical work of Gersonides, the *Wars of the Lord*, is divided into six parts, which deal respectively with the soul's immortality, prophecy, God's omniscience, providence, the nature of the heavenly spheres, and the eternity of matter. The most interesting part is the third. While God's thought, according to Gersonides, embraces all the *laws* which regulate the evolutions of nature, yet the detailed happenings of the phenomenal world are hidden from His Spirit. Not to know these details, however, is not imperfection, since in knowing the universal conditions of things He knows that which is essential—and consequently that which is good—in the individual.

f. In England

English writers played a very important role in the transmission of Arabian learning. For the most part, however, as with

[1] That is, the theory that all the heavenly bodies move about the same centre.

Adelard of Bath (pp. 206-208) and Michael Scot (pp. 218-220),[1] they worked on the Continent. We have already referred to the relations of Petrus Alphonsi and Walcher, and to the visit of Abraham Ben Ezra at an earlier period (pp. 208-210). Few translations from Arabic were actually made in England. It is possible that ALFRED THE ENGLISHMAN, who knew Arabic, worked in his own country. About 1210 he produced his curious treatise *On the motion of the heart*, which refers to many Arabian authors, among them Avicebron and Isaac. The book influenced Roger Bacon (pp. 271-272). It exhibits the theory of emanations and many Neoplatonic features. Alfred dedicated it to ALEXANDER NECKAM, Abbot of Cirencester (died 1217), who had access to Latin versions of Hebrew origin, among them the works of Algazel and Isaac.

Perhaps the most popular work on physical science written during the Middle Ages was that *On the properties of things*, produced in 1240 by the Franciscan, BARTHOLOMEW THE ENGLISHMAN. This encyclopaedia is a mere collection taken mainly from translations of the Arabian literature but depending primarily on Neckam. It was translated into English, in its turn, in 1398 by the Cornishman, John of Trevisa (1326-1402). Trevisa's version was very widely read, and was printed in an entertainingly illustrated edition by Wynkyn de Worde in 1495. This was most quaintly re-edited in 1582 as *Batman upon Bartholome ... taken foorth of the most approved Authors ... profitable for all Estates as well for the benefite of the Minde as the Bodie*. Batman was studied by Shakespeare, who thus inherited the traditions of Hebraeo-Arabic science.

§ 5. *The Link with the Renaissance*

The later fourteenth century and nearly all the fifteenth show a depression in the activities with which we are concerned. The political and social conditions of the Jews are steadily

[1] Both of them, however, visited England after acquiring Arabic.

deteriorating, a process culminating with their expulsion from Spain, Sicily, and Sardinia in 1492. It must not, however, be concluded that the Hebrew-Arabic element that had already entered Latin thought grows less important. The main philosophical reading of the West continued in fact to be affected by Hebrew-Arabic literature far into the time of printing, and even to the seventeenth century.

Of later Jewish translators one of the more important was ELIJAH DELMEDIGO (1463–1497) of Padua. A good Hebrew, Latin, and Italian scholar, he applied himself to philosophy and took part in the activities of the University. Among his students was Pico della Mirandola (1463–1494) at whose request much of his work of translation was performed. Delmedigo's writings are very bulky. They are mostly Latin renderings of various treatises by Averroes. He also produced original philosophical works. It is interesting to observe that he differs from Pico in that he exhibits a strong bias against Cabalism.

In great contrast to Delmedigo is JUDAH VERGA of Lisbon, who died there under torture about 1490. He was a Cabalist but his secular work was of an exclusively scientific nature. Among his scientific writings, which are all in Hebrew, is a description of an astronomical instrument which he invented to determine the sun's meridian. The account of it was written at Lisbon about 1457.

The Cabala to which Verga devoted so much attention had been steadily rising in favour among the Hebrew reading public since the great classic of that literature, the *Zohar*, had been introduced about the year 1300 by Moses de Leon (died 1305). In the present state of scholarship it is still impossible to give a final judgement as to the extent to which Moses de Leon himself compiled this document from more ancient sources. At first affecting exclusively Jewish circles, the *Zohar* began in the fifteenth century to spread beyond them.[1] In 1450

---

[1] On the Cabala and its history see pp. 324–332.

a group of converted Jews in Spain issued Latin and vernacular compilations, based on the Cabala, for the purposes of proving the superiority of their new religion to their old.

It is strange how two seeming incompatibles, Cabalistic and scientific interests, often occur in the same individual. This was the case with a fifteenth-century translator, GUGLIELMO RAIMONDO of Girgenti. He was a Jew converted to Christianity in 1467, who later became a bishop. From him we have a translation of an astronomical work of the Arab mathematician Alhazen of Basra (965–1038). The dedication cites the Talmud and Ben Ezra (pp. 209–211). Raimondo prepared about 1477 a number of eclipse tables, and he translated into Latin sections of the Kuran. The fact that he also collected a number of Cabalistic works reflects the attention now given to that subject in the Latin West.

Kindred interests were exhibited later in the century by PAUL RICI, a Jew of German origin who acted as physician to the Emperor Maximilian. Rici translated Cabalistic treatises. Later he became professor of medicine at the University of Pavia and he is mentioned favourably by Erasmus. In 1519 he issued the only Latin edition that we possess of the medical treatise of the well-known Spanish Muslim, Albucasis (1013–1106). The book is interesting as an early instance of copyright.[1] On its title-page it bears a threat of excommunication by Leo X and punishment by the Emperor Maximilian, of any who shall reprint it or sell a reprinted copy within six years. The group of Christian Cabalists with Pico della Mirandola (1463–1494) at their head comes outside our field.[2]

Translation from the Arabic was now becoming a rarity. Among the last of the Jewish translators was ABRAHAM DE BALMES, who died at Venice in 1523, being then about one hundred years old. Abraham de Balmes lived long in Padua, and lectured there

---

[1] On the Jewish factor in the introduction of a law of copyright see p. 401.
[2] See article by Prof. Box, pp. 319–324.

Transmission of the Jewish Factor

on philosophy. He taught Hebrew to the Christian, Daniel Bomberg, who set up in Venice the most important of all Hebrew presses, and printed the first Hebrew 'Rabbinic Bible'[1] (1516), and the first complete Talmud by order of Leo X. The huge work appeared in fifteen volumes (1520–1523). Abraham de Balmes was physician to Cardinal Grimani. To him he dedicated a Latin translation of Avempace of Saragossa (died 1138, p. 199) from the Hebrew, and a work of the Arab mathematician Alhazen of Basra (965–1038) also from the Hebrew.

The very last of the Jewish translators that can rightly be termed medieval, JACOB MANTINO, was also connected with Padua. He was born in Spain, whence his parents brought him as an infant when the Jews were expelled thence in 1492. He studied philosophy and medicine at Bologna and Padua, and devoted most of his life to translation from Hebrew into Latin. He settled in Venice and attracted the attention of Clement VII as well as that of many scholars.

When Henry VIII of England was seeking to get rid of his wife, Catherine of Aragon, he sought to obtain a verdict on the basis that their marriage was contrary to biblical law. His emissary came to Italy, and Mantino was consulted as a learned Hebraist. Mantino gave his opinion against Henry and thus earned himself many enemies. His eventful life was marked by his holding office as physician to Pope Paul III and by disputes with the Messianic visionary, Solomon Molko (1500–1532).

Mantino rendered into Latin from Hebrew works of Averroes, Gersonides, Maimonides, and Avicenna. He is best remembered, however, as the editor of the monumental and standard Latin edition of Averroes which was published at Venice in 1553, soon after his death. This edition was much

---

[1] The work known as the *Biblia Rabbinica* is the Hebrew Bible with commentaries and three Aramaic versions or 'Targums' (p. 336). The first complete Hebrew Bible had been printed by Soncino at Bologna as early as 1488. On Bomberg and the Christian printers of Hebrew see pp. 335–340.

studied, especially at Padua. It was the basis of the Averroistic philosophical school which flourished at Padua well into the seventeenth century, and had some not undistinguished exponents, among them being the Englishman, William Harvey (1578–1657), discoverer of the circulation of the blood. Mantino died in 1549. The last flicker of the medieval Hebraeo-Arabic movement in Italy may be perceived in the Averroist, Cesaro Cremonini, professor of philosophy at Padua, who died there of the plague in 1631.

It is interesting to observe that the decline of what we may call the Hebrew-Arabic-Latin scientific movement is contemporary with the advent of a Jewish element in the new 'Renaissance' science. The event is illustrated by the careers of two Jewish astronomers, Abraham Zacuto and Joseph Vecinho. These men were involved in the opening up of new worlds by Vasco da Gama and Columbus.

ABRAHAM ZACUTO (1450–1510) taught astronomy at the Universities of Salamanca and Saragossa. Later he settled in Lisbon and became astronomer to John II. He was consulted and gave advice on the expedition of Vasco da Gama. That commander's vessels were fitted out with astrolabes designed by Zacuto, with the improvements that he introduced. In 1473, while still at Salamanca, Zacuto wrote in Hebrew a *Perpetual Almanack*. This was translated into both Latin and Spanish by his pupil Joseph Vecinho. The work was printed at Leiria in Portugal by a Jewish printer in 1496. Manuscript copies of this almanack were carried in the fleets of Vasco da Gama, Cabral, João de Nova, and Albuquerque.

JOSEPH VECINHO, a pupil of Zacuto, was also in the service of John II of Portugal, who sent him to the coast of Guinea to take measurements of the solar altitude. When the plan of Columbus for Western exploration was laid before the King he submitted it to a committee of five. The members were the Bishop of Ceuta, the court physician, the German chartographer, Martin

Behaim, a Jewish mathematician named Moses, and Joseph Vecinho. Joseph appears to have been the leading member of the committee which, in the event, reported against the expedition. Despite this Columbus retained a high respect for Vecinho. In the margins of one of his books, which still exists at the 'Columbina' at Seville, Columbus has inscribed this note: 'In the year 1485, the King of Portugal sent Master Joseph, his physician and astronomer, to determine the altitudes of the sun throughout Guinea, all of which he performed. And he reported to the King, in my presence, that he found the Island of Idols near Sierra Leone was exactly 5 degrees distant from the Equator, and he attended to this with the utmost diligence. Afterwards the King often sent to Guinea and other places, and always found the results to accord with those of Master Joseph. Whereby I have certainty that the Castle of Mine is under the Equator.' In another marginal note Columbus states that he himself, during various voyages to Guinea, had taken altitudes of the sun, and that his results always agreed with those of Vecinho.

COLUMBUS (1446–1506) had, in fact, much intercourse with Jewish men of science, and was acquainted with Zacuto as well as Vecinho. Almost the first financial assistance that he secured was from the Jewish statesman and Bible commentator, Isaac Abravanel (1437–1508), and in his will he left a legacy to a Lisbon Jew. At least five Jews accompanied him on his first expedition, and he valued them specially as interpreters. The first landing was effected on 15 October 1492, and on 2 November Columbus sent out his first expedition on American soil. It consisted of two men. One of them was the Jew, Luis de Torres. This Torres is believed to have been the first European to tread American soil and the first European to try the effects of tobacco. He settled and died in Cuba.

The Jewish friendships of Columbus had a peculiar sequel. He visited Jamaica in 1494 and 1505, and it became, in part, the property of his family who continued his relations with the Jews.

The island was colonized by an expedition sent out by his son Diego in 1509. In 1537 Luiz, eldest son of Diego and grandson of Christopher Columbus, was created Marquis of Jamaica with large rights in the island. These, in 1576, passed to the female line of the house of Braganza, who also remained in contact with Jewish families.

Jamaica was one of the very few places under Spanish or Portuguese rule where the Inquisition could obtain no foothold. A small group of unavowed Jews, mostly of Portuguese rather than Spanish origin, found it possible to live there, little noticed and comparatively unmolested, while their brethren were being hunted and burnt in other parts of the Spanish and Portuguese dominions. The British made attacks on Jamaica in 1596 and 1636 and had some success which they failed to follow up. With the more vigorous foreign policy of Cromwell things were changed. To undermine the power of Spain Cromwell formed an alliance with Portugal. With the same object he opened up communication with the Jamaican Jews, availing himself of their natural fear of the Inquisition and enmity to Spain. These negotiations led to the readmission of the Jews to England. Jamaica was captured by the British in 1655. The Spaniards were expelled in 1658. The Jews, however, who were in fact Portuguese and not Spanish, were allowed to remain and to declare their religion openly. In the security of British rule the Jamaican Jewish colonists prospered. Their descendants reside in the island to this day and form a link with the great discoverer.

In 1662 Catherine of Braganza came to England to marry Charles II. There were several unavowed Jews in her suite who declared their religion on reaching these shores. One at least remained in her service and that of the King until his death. The descendants of this man, and those of many other Jews who came to England at the time, are well-known citizens in various parts of the country at the present day.

There is also a curious bypath of modern English literary history which leads back by the same route to the medieval Jewry of Spain and Portugal. Part of Catherine's dowry was Tangiers, which had the same value for English sea-power that Gibraltar has now. When the district came under British rule, Jews from the Spanish and Portuguese dominions took refuge there from the Inquisition. Lancelot Addison (1632–1703), father of the essayist, went out as chaplain to the governor. He became greatly interested in Jewish affairs, and wrote a very able and knowledgeable account of the Jews from first-hand observation. This work was the first of its kind to appear in English.[1]

III. CHARACTERISTICS OF MEDIEVAL LATIN THOUGHT

§ 6. *The Course of Scholastic Philosophy*

IN the history of thought among the Latins, during the vast stretch of time included under the term *Middle Ages*, we may discern four divisions or periods. These we may distinguish by the relatively true statements; that during the first period the value of coherent and consecutive thought was seldom recognized; that during the second period a rational discipline of the mind became a part of education; that during the third period this rational discipline developed as philosophy but was regarded as the handmaid of theology; and that during the fourth period philosophical thought gained a position independent of theology. To make these statements either intelligible or justifiable some qualification and amplification is needed.

The *first period* ends about the year 1100. During the centuries before the twelfth the Western mind was hardly coherent. Among the few writers of the earlier Middle Ages who present

---

[1] It was published in London in 1675 as *The present State of the Jews (more particularly relating to those of Barbary) wherein is contained an exact account of their customs, secular and religious. To which is annexed a summary discourse of the Misna, Talmud and Gemara*. It ran into several editions.

us with a complete system of thought was John Scot Erigena (*c.* 800–*c.* 880). According to Erigena the power of Reason, working with its own instruments, evolves a system of the universe identical with that imparted by Scripture. Now most men, being unlike Erigena, do not by nature rejoice in the use of reason, the exercise of which, painful and difficult now, was even more painful and difficult then. While, therefore, the unity of the results reached by faith and by reason might delight an exceptional mind, in fact, in the age of Erigena, men preferred the way of faith.

Our *second period* is fairly bounded by the frontiers of the twelfth century. With that century the thought of the schools of the Christian West began to take on an appearance of variety, due to the intake of new ideas from the Orient. The thinkers of the time, we observe, in contrast to those of the later scholastic age, constantly name Plato as their master. To such typical writers, for example, as Adelard of Bath (*c.* 1130, see pp. 206–208), Isaac of Etoile (died 1169, p. 256), and Alan of Lille (died 1202), it is Plato who is *the philosopher*, a title which in the following centuries is always reserved for Aristotle. This attitude is associated with the advent into Europe of the earliest translations from the Arabic emanating from Spain. Important names connected with that pioneer work are Adelard (pp. 206–208), Avendeath (pp. 211–214), Gundissalinus (p. 211), and Gerard (p. 214), of all of whom we have already spoken. The material that thus became available during the twelfth century included a number of genuine Aristotelian works among which we note the *De coelo et mundo*, the *De generatione et corruptione* and the *Meteorologica*. On the Neoplatonic side very important was the translation into Latin of the *Fountain of life* of Avicebron. Other Neoplatonic works that came in during the twelfth century were those entitled *Theologia Aristotelis* and *De Causis*. The former puts forward the views of Plotinus, the greatest of the Neoplatonic teachers, the latter is closely linked with the work of Avicebron, whose philosophical writings found their way into Latin during the twelfth century. The same period saw the arrival in the West of the philosophical writings of Isaac the Jew. Much of this new knowledge suggested a view of the universe inconsistent with the contemporary presentation of religion.

With the thirteenth century the rate of advent of this material was accelerated and the *third period* opens. The triumph of that period was the absorption of the Arabian version of Aristotelian philosophy into Western thought, and its adjustment to theological demands. A certain amount of Aristotle came in also direct from the Greek. The third period practically covers the thirteenth century, during which medieval thought attained to what was in some respects its highest and in most respects its typical development. The thought of this third age was, however, influenced not only by versions and translations of works of Greek antiquity that thus reached it. Within the Arabic speaking world, as we have seen, philosophy and science had attained a very high level. Many of the compositions in which this true Arabian development was enshrined were also conveyed to the West in Latin dress. Arabian philosophy thus had a profound effect on Latin thought which seized on many of its most characteristic ideas and used them as generally and with as great avidity as it did the texts of Aristotle. Of the Arabian authors whose ideas were thus incorporated into the body of Christian thought, the most important were Averroes, Maimonides, Avicebron, and Algazel. Two of these, Maimonides and Avicebron, were themselves Jews. The other two, Averroes and Algazel, were perhaps the most widely discussed of all philosophers among the Jews, and their presentation to the West was largely by Jewish hands. It is therefore the case that, even apart from their role in the direct transmission of texts, the Jews were of importance in moulding the Western outlook in the period of high scholasticism.

248 *The Jewish Factor in Medieval Thought*

We now turn to the *fourth period* of medieval thought. By the end of the thirteenth century Aristotle had become Christianized. The system of St. Thomas Aquinas that was based upon him had gained wide acceptance. Reason and Faith had kissed each other and a harmony had been reached. Few doctrines were held as beyond the sphere of Reason. The new movement, however, is now at hand. Its herald is Duns Scotus (1265 ?–1308). He held that though Reason and Revelation are independent sources of knowledge, yet there was no true knowledge not ultimately based on Revelation. He even rejected the view of St. Thomas that the existence of God was capable of being proved by the sole exercise of Reason. It might perhaps be imagined that the followers of Duns would succeed in the further subordination of philosophy to theology. In fact it was discord that they sowed. The withdrawal of one doctrine after another from the domain of reason led to what was in effect a philosophic revolt. Men had now acquired the habit of dialectic. The rise of the Universities had encouraged this to an enormous extent, and the appetite grew by what it fed on. The union, that had promised so fairly, became intolerable to both parties. Philosophy and Theology at length separated.

An important figure in this process of separation is William of Ockham (died 1349) who announces the dissolution of Scholasticism by his dictum that no theological doctrine can be rationally demonstrated. Scholasticism (which may be defined as a close alliance between Theology and Philosophy, with Philosophy in the subordinate position) was doomed, and great was the fall of it. Decay was slow but sure. The cause may be traced to her own builders, for her house was upon the sand. It was not attacks from without that brought about her ruin.

This fourth period of medieval thought, lasting from about 1300 till the end of the fifteenth century, may be regarded

Characteristics of Medieval Latin Thought

as the probationary period of philosophical independence leading up to the humanist supremacy. It is related, too, to the great movements of Reformation and Renaissance. In this last medieval period there was less Jewish influence. This diminished influence was exerted on the one hand by positive scientific thinkers with an Aristotelian bent, of whom Gersonides is the most prominent example, and on the other by the works of Neoplatonic mystics of the type of Avicebron and Ben Ezra and by the Cabala. The Cabalistic and Neoplatonic influence had hardly attained its height at the very end of our period. The termination of the Middle Ages was moreover associated with a revival of Averroist philosophy with strong Jewish associations. In the humanist movement itself, however, the Jews played but a minor part.

§ 7. *The Medieval Latin Aristotle*

The whole modern system of thinking can be traced back very clearly to the acceptance of the writings of Aristotle in the Middle Ages. The arrival of these writings is, therefore, an event of first-class importance, and it happens also to be nearly connected with the theme that we are discussing. We therefore digress to treat the subject briefly.

Some of the Aristotelian logical works had been available in ancient Latin translations (direct from the Greek) made at the very commencement of the Middle Ages. Except for these, the writings of Aristotle reached the West in Latin form between the second quarter of the twelfth and the third quarter of the thirteenth century. They came partly from Arabic and partly from Greek. Moreover, the Aristotelian works were not only read in translations of the text, but even more in translations of commentaries rendered from the Arabic. A full and accurate account of the conditions under which these various documents were studied would be very long and very complex. It will, however, be enough to state here : (*a*) that the overwhelming majority of medieval readers received Aristotle only through translations of Arabian commentators on Averroes, often rendered from the Hebrew; (*b*) that the majority even of discerning medieval readers received Aristotle mainly in these commentaries, but partly in translations of Arabic versions of his work; and (*c*) that it was only a very small minority even of discerning medieval readers who studied any part of Aristotle (except the Logical works) in translations direct from the Greek.

Among the more interesting events in connexion with the introduction of the Aristotelian writings is the series of interdicts placed upon them. In 1210 there was a heresy hunt at Paris (p. 256). At a synod held there the works of David of Dinant were condemned to be burned and the body of Amalric (died 1207), his comrade in error, was ordered to be dug up and placed in unconsecrated ground. These men had taught the newly recovered Aristotelian texts or commentaries. More disagreeable to the victims was the handing over to the stake or perpetual imprisonment of a number of persons believed to be followers of David and Amalric. At the same time it was forbidden to read the books of Aristotle on Natural Philosophy and the current (i.e. the Averroan) commentaries on Aristotle were forbidden for three years. This edict was really directed against Averroistic thought in general and against certain versions of Averroes in particular.

In 1215 Statutes for the University of Paris were drawn up by the Papal legate. In these regulations the Physical and Metaphysical works of Aristotle were specifically forbidden. This time it was the version of Avicenna that was the real objective. At the same time an oath was imposed on candidates for degrees in Arts not to read the works of David of Dinant and of certain others, among whom Averroes was included.

In 1231 these prohibitions were renewed by Gregory IX ' until the works shall have been examined and purged of all heresy'. The papal prohibition was repealed by Urban IV in 1263, but it seems to have been a dead letter. At any rate long before the middle of the century Aristotle's *Metaphysics*, in a translation from the Arabic, was being openly studied. By 1254 nearly the whole range of Aristotelian writings had become part of the University curriculum. The actual texts studied for long remained, however, translations from the Arabic and commentaries thereon.

IV. RECEPTION OF THE JEWISH FACTOR

§ 8. *Jewish Elements in Twelfth-Century Scholasticism*

Having traced in barest outline the general history of thought in the Middle Ages, we now turn to consider it in connexion with the advent of the Arabian elements and especially of the Jewish factor. To speak first of the 'positive' sciences of Mathematics and Medicine. As the Arabic works on these topics became available in Latin—mostly in the thirteenth century—they were at once absorbed into the general European system. They early shed their Arabian or Jewish dress—if such studies can be described as wearing so temporal a cloak— and they became lost in the gathering throng of knowledge. With the department of philosophic thought, however, the course was more subtle and intricate. Here the material, on its arrival among the Latins, had already been impressed by specifically Arabian or Jewish ideas, even when these were not recognized as such by the scholastics. These Arabian and Jewish ideas continue to bear the marks of their origin in greater or less degree, and it is our final and most difficult task to trace them through the intricacies of Latin scholastic philosophy.

It is very necessary here to preserve perspective and to avoid over-emphasis of the role of the Arabian and Jewish thought. It must be stated at once that Latin Scholasticism developed a wider range of subjects than specifically Jewish Scholasticism, and no less wide a range than Arabian Scholasticism as a whole. Much discussion has raged round the question of the relative importance of the Hebraeo-Arabic element in thirteenth-century European thought. Now we are here dealing with matters in which quantitative estimates are as yet impossible. If Science be Measurement, then we are here surely out of the range of science and in the department of mere opinion. Making all allowance, however, for the regrettable and often unnecessary inexactness of methods of literary research, we cannot doubt that certain exceedingly important aspects of Christian medieval philosophy were closely related to the Arabian and notably to Jewish thought. Foremost among these we place the fact that it was largely owing to Jewish writings that Aristotelian teaching could be accommodated to biblical doctrine. After all, orthodox Jewish doctrine (save where the Nature of God and His relations to man were concerned) was largely identical with orthodox Christian doctrine. On such great topics as Creation, Revelation, Prophecy, the Field of Reason, Psychology, the Eternity of Matter, the Structure of the Heavens, there was no intrinsic reason why the two faiths should differ. These matters had been discussed on philosophical grounds by Jewish writers for centuries before the West became scholastic.

Before we turn to more detailed consideration of the actual impact of Jewish teaching on Christian thought, we would pause to take up again a theme to which we have already referred. A modern man trained in scientific method, turning to these scholastic discussions, finds them lacking in reality, tedious, verbose; and it is a fact that an undue proportion of medieval philosophical discussion can be described as mere froth. Yet there is surely another point of view from which to look at medieval thought. In his own age and in his own way is not the Scholastic fighting the battle of concrete coherent thought, or if you will of 'Reason', of which 'Science' is but

Fig. 41. CHURCH AND SYNAGOGUE ON JESSE TREE
From a XIIth-century Bible written in England

For description see p. xxiv

one expression ? Is not the attempt to establish the authority of the Faith by argument the first step to the acceptance of the authority of Reason ? Is it not the first sign of intellectual coherence ? What an advance on the patristic position ! *Credo quia absurdum est* said Tertullian (*c.* 145–*c.* 222). Anselm (1033–1109) had reached at least as far as *Credo ut intelligam*. The *Summa* of St. Thomas (1225–1274) is but a way of saying *Intelligo et credo*, for which the modern man of science would but change a letter or two and say, with Descartes (1596–1650), *Intelligo ergo credo*. The actual change of those letters was made when Science was founded in the sixteenth century and is outside the range of our discussion, but in thought as in time St. Thomas is far nearer to Descartes than to Tertullian.

The three Jewish authors who provided material that enabled the Latins to take the characteristic Scholastic point of view were Isaac, Avicebron, and Maimonides. Avicebron's *Fountain of life* was translated from Arabic by Avendeath and Gundissalinus about 1150. Parts of Isaac's philosophical works became available soon after in Latin translations by Gerard (died 1187). The *Guide for the perplexed* by Maimonides was rendered into Latin in the early part of the thirteenth century.

We now turn to Latin Philosophy itself, which we must be content to follow in the writings of a few typical exponents. We shall examine the work of these men from the point of view of their debt to Hebraeo-Arabic thought.

We may begin with the famous Breton scholar ABELARD OF PALLET (1079–1142), who is known to every reader for his relations with Héloise. Abelard lived just a little too early to be directly dependent on the Hebraeo-Arabic philosophical writings, though he has an inkling of the contents of one of the works of Avicenna. Abelard's works, however, point the direction that scholastic philosophy was to take in the next century under Arabian influence. As a thinker he is remarkable, too, for bringing Ethics into line with other philosophical topics, a matter in which he passed all but a few of the very boldest of the later Scholastics. He prepares us, moreover, for the displacement of Plato by Aristotle, the leading philosophical event of the century that followed him. Until Abelard's time only the presentation of certain Aristotelian logical works by Boethius (480–524) was available. During the twelfth century, however, practically the whole logical Canon became accessible, mostly in translation from the Arabic. We note that in his *Dialogue between a Philosopher, a Christian and a Jew* Abelard laments the prevalent ignorance of the Hebrew language.

The first work in Latin which conveyed any formal treatment of Jewish thought as distinct from the general mass of Arabian science, was the Neoplatonic *Fountain of life* of Avicebron translated into Latin by Avendeath collaborating with Gundissalinus about 1140 (p. 211). It was important in moulding Western thought. GUNDISSALINUS was himself the author of several philosophical works which lean heavily on the Arabian material. These treatises are the earliest Latin independent philosophical writings which fully exhibit Arabian influence. We may date them from about 1130 to about 1150 not much overpassing the latter year. Gundissalinus stands in place, time, and circumstance on a frontier position. As a dignitary of the Church he has full access to the Latin literature. Through his friend, the converted Jew AVENDEATH, he has access to the Hebraeo-Arabic literature. Living in Spain he is in natural contact with both Latin and Arabian culture. He is at a parting of the ways of time. The fading memories of his youth are in the Dark Ages. His life is lived in the Scholastic dawn.

The earliest independent work of Gundissalinus is *On the Soul*. It is based on a Latin translation by Avendeath from an Arabic Neoplatonic treatise by Avicebron. Later Gundissalinus produced a short encyclopaedia of the knowledge of his time. He opens his *Introduction* to this encyclopaedia with a discussion of the distinction between 'natural' and 'divine' knowledge. He here relies on Isaac (p. 187), Avicenna (pp. 188–189), Algazel (p. 192), and Alfarabi. Arabic works by all these authors except the first had been rendered into Latin by one or both of the Avendeath-Gundissalinus partnership (pp. 211–214). The debt of Gundissalinus to early Latin authors is insignificant in this section. The sources of the sections on *Logic*, *Geometry*, *Astrology*, and *Astronomy* are much the same as those of the Introduction, with Euclid added. The work of Euclid had already been rendered into Latin from Arabic by Adelard of Bath (p. 208). In great contrast to these sections are those on *Poetry* and on *Rhetoric*. These rely exclusively on the old Latin sources. Intermediate between these two groups are the sections on *Arithmetic*, *Music*, and *Medicine*, which rely on Arabic and old Latin sources in about equal proportions. The section on *Medicine* is peculiarly instructive, both for what it includes and for what it excludes. It has no reference to certain translations from the Arabic that had been made in the late eleventh and early twelfth centuries. These works were evidently little known and were not yet circulating in Spain. Gundissalinus, however, exhibits in this medical section a good many parallels to the old Latin work of Isidore of Seville and also some to the medical *Canon* of Avicenna (pp. 188–189), which was translated into Latin at Toledo by Gerard of Cremona (died 1187). It was one of Gerard's latest works (p. 214). The preparation of this vast treatise must, however, have occupied Gerard for years, and Gundissalinus may have seen it in an early stage. His contacts with it are in fact with the earlier parts.

The last work of Gundissalinus is *On the Immortality of the Soul*. It is based on the same Arabian material as his previous productions. It exhibits contact also with Aristotle's *Posterior Analytics* which was being translated in his time. This treatise of Gundissalinus was the channel by which certain very important doctrines passed to Christendom. The soul, according to it, has its own activity independent of the body and is immaterial and indestructible, desiring its own completion and happiness, independent of the body. Reason is the process of raising to the intelligible; it is without bodily organ though it requires the brain for its expression. The position of the human soul is in the scale of being between pure spirit and the souls of animals and plants that are steeped in matter. Its powers are thus partly mortal, partly immortal. No kind of destruction can affect the soul since it consists of both matter and form. In all this we may see the hand of Avicebron but the voice of Gundissalinus acting to the West as the interpreter of Arabian Neoplatonism.

The first outside Spain to exhibit the influence of Gundissalinus is ISAAC OF ETOILE in Poitou (p. 246), who became abbot of that place in 1147, and died in 1169. In his *Letter on the Soul* he borrows from a work of Gundissalinus, quoting almost its very words. Another philosopher who lived in the late twelfth century and appears to have been indebted to the works of Gundissalinus was DAVID OF DINANT (p. 250). His works and those of a similar writer, AMALRIC OF BENA (died 1207), have disappeared. Fragments of them seem to indicate that they exhibited an emanationist pantheism ascribed to Aristotle, but derived not improbably from such works of Jewish origin as the *Fountain of life* and certain other works of Avicebron. In the event, these heretical writers, David and Amalric, had but little effect on the Scholastic age. ALAN OF LILLE (1128–1202), a Cistercian teacher at Paris who took part in the propaganda of the Albigenses, also knew of certain works of Avicebron and Gundissalinus but was little affected by them. To discern the real influence of Avicebron and Gundissalinus we must turn to the next century.

§ 9. *Jewish Elements in Thirteenth-century Scholasticism*

a. *The Preparation for St. Thomas Aquinas*

Latin Scholasticism as a philosophical system came to flower in the thirteenth century. It was roughly about two generations later than the great period of Arabian thought on which it directly depends.

A movement of vast importance for the West was the foundation of the mendicant religious orders, the activities of which largely replaced those of the monastic Benedictines. Two among the new orders came to dominate philosophic thought. These were the *Dominicans* or Black Friars, founded in 1215 by the austere and orthodox Dominic (1170–1221), and the *Franciscans* or Grey Friars, founded in 1209 by the gentle and loving Francis of Assisi (1181–1226). During the thirteenth century these two orders provided most of the great university teachers, especially at Paris, the most important scholastic centre. The thought of both orders exhibits many elements of Jewish origin. The chief Jewish thinkers available to them were Maimonides and Avicebron. On the whole Maimonides was more used by the Dominicans, Avicebron by the Franciscans.

The first important teacher at Paris to exhibit this Jewish influence was WILLIAM OF AUVERGNE (died 1249). He was at Paris in the years in which the works of Aristotle were forbidden. In 1228 he became Bishop of Paris, continuing to take an active interest in the University. William was the author of a series of philosophical writings which reveal him as a pioneer in the adaptation of the Arabian philosophy to the service of Christian theology. One work by him *On the Immortality of the Soul* is in effect a redaction of the treatise by Gundissalinus bearing the same title and deeply influenced by Avicebron. Others of his works bear evidence of Arabian influence of the same type.

William of Auvergne introduced Maimonides to the circle

of Latin philosophers. In a number of his works William attacks the Jews in terms which show that he had some direct contact with their writings. Thus he raises the question as to whether the supernal world (i.e. the world above the sphere of the moon) consists of one or more beings endowed with soul. This is the old discussion of the unity of the intellect versus the persistence of individual souls (p. 192). It represents the difference between the school of Averroes and that of Maimonides, both of whom were, be it remembered, older contemporaries of William. From this discussion William digresses to tell us that the Jews once believed in the prophets but later took to superstitious practices, now followed by all save those few Jews who mix with Saracens and study philosophy. He here betrays his sources, for he quotes among the superstitions certain Talmudic ideas which Maimonides instances as *not* believed by any sensible Jew! William, in fact, constantly relies on the *Guide for the perplexed* of Maimonides. He does not speak of him by name, though he refers to him on one occasion as 'a man whom they [i. e. the Jews] call wise, but who is corrected by one of their own philosophers'. Among William's many debts to Maimonides are: (*a*) a discussion as to whether the *Empyrean*, or 'sphere of fire' of the Aristotelian system (p. 196), is formed of ordinary matter; (*b*) the view that Aristotle is infallible only in matters of *Natural Law*, i. e. the laws governing the sublunary world; and (*c*) the symbolism of the sacrifices. In these discussions he quotes almost literally from Maimonides, whom he both plagiarizes and attacks.

Very different is William's attitude to the 'theologian' Avicebron, 'whose name, and style of writing', he tells us, 'are Arabic, but who, I think, must be a Christian, as history tells us that not long ago the whole Moslem realm [of Castille] was converted to Christianity'. He thinks Avicebron the only Arabic author who accepts the Christian doctrine of the *Logos* as against the *Emanation* theory of Avicenna (pp. 188–189). William cites Avicebron's *Fountain of life* and admires its doctrine of the Divine Will which is equated with the *Active Word of God*. He feels called on to deny the characteristic view of Avicebron that the soul consists of Matter and Form, yet he tells us that Avicebron has succeeded by his philosophical powers in reaching spiritual heights attained by no other man.

Perhaps more influential as a thinker than William of Auvergne was his slightly younger contemporary, the Englishman, ALEXANDER OF HALES (c. 1170–1245), who entered the Franciscan order in 1231. Alexander studied at Paris, where he earned great distinction as a teacher. He excelled especially in dialectic, and became known among the scholastics as the *doctor irrefragibilis*. In his *Summa universae theologiae* he exhibits complete familiarity with the Latin translations of the *Fountain of life* of Avicebron and the *Guide* of Maimonides. He adopts the characteristic attitude of Avicebron in reference to 'spiritual substance', while he follows Maimonides in many details of biblical interpretation. Alexander is conspicuous among the scholastic teachers for his tolerant attitude toward the Jews, maintaining that their preservation is enjoined by Holy Writ.

Another writer of the first half of the thirteenth century who exhibited the same tolerant attitude was the great bishop of Lincoln, ROBERT GROSSETESTE (c. 1175–1253). By his eloquent protests and vigorous action he saved groups of Jews from massacre in England. He exhibited his enlightenment in the field of learning by his attempt to introduce the study of Greek at Oxford. He was the teacher of Roger Bacon, but was less well acquainted with the Hebraeo-Arabic philosophy than such of his contemporaries as Alexander of Hales and Albertus Magnus.

The most learned of the scholastic doctors was unquestionably the Dominican, ALBERTUS MAGNUS (1193–1280). Not only the wealth of knowledge but also the variety of interests of this remarkable man were greater than those of any other medieval thinker. A fair claim too may be made for him as the father of modern biological science. A German by birth, he studied at Padua, where in 1223 he joined the Dominicans. From 1228 to 1245 he taught in Germany, mainly at Cologne. Between 1245 and 1248 he lectured at Paris and there began to compile his great encyclopaedia. This was probably completed in 1256, but he continued to revise it until his death. In 1248 he returned to Cologne. From 1254 to 1257 he was Provincial of his Order in Germany. From 1260 to 1263 he acted, against his will, as Bishop of Ratisbon, where there was a synagogue of which a substantial record has come down to us (Figs. 42 and 43). In 1263 he resigned his office to devote the rest of his life to study which he pursued at Cologne and Paris.

The enormous works of Albert placed before the medieval reader the whole sum of knowledge and of thought developed from Aristotle and his Arabian commentators. He is well acquainted with the works of Averroes, Isaac, Avicebron, and Maimonides. He exhibits no effective knowledge of the Talmud, though, like William of Auvergne, he took part in the conclave at Paris in 1240 on the advice of which Innocent IV ordered the Talmud to be burnt. In this matter, he, like the other members of the conclave, relied for his judgement on the converted Jew, Nicholas Donin of La Rochelle (pp. 294–295), who had become a Franciscan. Albert occasionally copies citations of the Talmud from Maimonides.

Albert constantly cites with understanding Hebraeo-Arabic scientific writers. Thus, for instance, he quotes three Arabian commentaries on Ptolemy, and works by Zachel,[1] Messahala, Avendeath, and many other Jewish mathematical writers. Albert's great biological work, *De animalibus*, is entirely based on Michael Scot, whose work was prepared with Jewish aid

---

[1] Zachel, i.e. the Jewish astronomer Sahl ben Bishr who lived *c.* 820, has often been confused with the Moslem astronomer Arzarchel, i.e. Abu Ishak Ibrahim ben Yahya al-Zarkali of Cordova, who lived *c.* 1080 and who was a source of the Jewish astronomers of Alfonso the Wise. See p. 224.

FIG. 42. VESTIBULE OF XIIIth-CENTURY SYNAGOGUE
AT RATISBON

As it existed during the Bishopric of Albertus Magnus

For description see p. xxv

Fig. 43. INTERIOR OF XIIIth-CENTURY SYNAGOGUE
AT RATISBON

As it existed during the Bishopric of Albertus Magnus

For description see p. xxv

(pp. 218–220). In the *De animalibus* Albert quotes from Averroes, Avicenna, Constantine the African, Costa ben Luca, Hippocrates, Isaac, Josephus, Nicholas of Damascus, Plato, Ptolemy, Rhazes, and Serapion, works of all of whom came to him through Jewish channels. The other work on which his scientific reputation is based is his *De vegetabilibus*. It relies on a very similar set of writers but includes also Maimonides.

The two leading philosophers in Albert's view are Isaac and Maimonides. In the sphere of psychology, Albert hesitatingly disagrees with Isaac's view that plants have, in addition to their *vegetative soul*, a certain degree of *sensitive soul*, without, however, possessing consciousness. Reason, Albert considers, following Isaac's phraseology, is the power of uniting the judgement with that which is judged. He also cites and agrees with Isaac, who, like St. Augustine, calls the *rational soul* of the Aristotelians the specific human soul, and distinguishes it from the *angelic soul*.

The Heavens, Albert tells us, 'have a soul, as Maimonides and Isaac teach'. To the latter Albert refers the belief in the *music of the spheres*, a very ancient idea which, however, is not to be found in such of Isaac's works as have come down to us. Considering the knowledge of angels to be a matter of Revelation and of Faith, Albert opposes the doctrine held 'firstly by Epicureans, then by Stoics, from whom also Isaac, Maimonides and other Jewish philosophers derive', that the Intelligences are identical with the Angels (p. 198). Albert enters into discussion with these Jewish philosophers as to the knowledge of the powers higher than man. 'Isaac, Maimonides, and some Arabian philosophers', he says, 'attribute to the Angels that move the spheres only the knowledge of *Universals*, holding that they have no knowledge of *Particulars*.'

Albert is the first Latin to oppose Avicebron, regarding him as an opponent of Aristotle. He had no conception that he was a Jew and shows considerable misunderstanding of him, though he devotes much space to discussing his views. In treating Avicebron as an anti-Aristotelian, however, he is not very far wrong.

Albert often exhibits surprising independence of the Arabian commentators Averroes and Avicenna, who are constantly used by him. He is not afraid to oppose even Aristotle at times, as, for instance, in the question of the eternity of the world. Here Albert is closely dependent on Maimonides. He follows Maimonides too, and opposes Averroes, in holding that God's foreknowledge extends to individuals of the sublunary world. These views deeply affected his theological outlook and through him that of Catholic Christianity. Albert did not, however, lean on Maimonides so much in works of pure philosophy, still less in those of natural science. These subjects were, indeed, rather outside the purpose of the *Guide*, which Maimonides had composed for those perplexed Jews whose faith was threatened by the new Aristotelianism. We may trace Maimonides most clearly in the views of Albert on matters where Aristotle conflicts with biblical teaching. This subjugation of 'Aristotle' to religious needs is the most characteristic Scholastic development. Here Maimonides was invaluable, and was in fact the only helpful guide that the Latin thinkers could find among all the older writers.

We turn now to the specific doctrines derived by Albert from Maimonides and other Arabians.

(i) *The Nature of God*. The ontological proof of the existence of God, i.e. the *a priori* argument that the existence of the idea of God of necessity involves the existence of God, was derived by Albert primarily from Anselm, and beyond him from Ambrose and Augustine. The idea of God as the immovable mover of the moving spheres (p. 191) he had, however, from Aristotle via the versions of Averroes. On the other hand, from Maimonides came the recognition of God through negative attributes (p. 193). He agrees with Maimonides that if attributes be predicated of both Creator and created, then the predication must be in wholly different senses. He accepts too the Maimonidean teaching that while no name is adequate for the Divinity, that which is *Ineffable* (i.e. the Tetragrammaton) is the least inadequate. On the other hand, Albert accepts the emanation theory of Alfarabi and Avicenna (pp. 188–189) and discounts the objections of Maimonides to that view as 'theologizing'. Albert cites from Maimonides the basic doctrine of medieval physics, namely, that all motion, whether of the upper, i.e. supralunar, or of the lower, i.e. sublunar spheres, is caused, in the physical sense, by the outermost heaven, the *primum mobile* (pp. 195 and 199).

(ii) *Problem of Creation.* Maimonides, like Augustine and other philosophers who believed in creation in time, held all creation to have been a simultaneous act. In this matter they were at variance with Averroes, who was here a true follower of Aristotle (p. 191). Now it is on the topic of creation that there is the most marked difference between the Bible and Aristotle. As Maimonides said, it was not so much definite biblical passages that made the difficulty as the fact that Jews felt the entire incompatibility of Aristotle's idea of an external world with their view of God and of the Universe. Biblical textual difficulties could be explained as allegories, a treatment that had long been meted out to the anthropomorphisms. But the essential Hebrew view of the creation could not be thus evaded. Here Maimonides was in conflict with Aristotle. This he recognized, and Albert consciously follows him into opposition. Albert not only uses Maimonides in his argument against the eternity of the world but often repeats his very words.

(iii) *Angels.* Maimonides, as we have seen (pp. 199–200), sought to rationalize the biblical teaching concerning angels and to equate these beings with the *Intelligences* of the spheres, as had Isaac before him. Albert, however, was against this identification, which he regarded as heretical though he borrowed something from it. The conception, too, that the only activities of the angels were through forces obeying them, which he ascribes to Maimonides and to 'philosophers who adhere to the Old Testament', he also regards as heretical.

(iv) *Prophecy*. Maimonides regarded certain prophetic visions as internal events, and transfers them from the realm of *sensibilia* to the spiritual life of the prophets. He thus sought to put aside that which is offensive to reason without departing from the ideal significance of the prophecy. Albert, as a keener theologian, prefers to rely on Faith as the key to prophecy. Nevertheless, in a lengthy discussion of miracles and prophecies Albert is influenced very deeply by Maimonides both in a positive and negative sense.

b. St. Thomas Aquinas

The greatest of the Scholastic teachers is universally held to be ST. THOMAS AQUINAS (1225–1274), the 'doctor angelicus' of the schoolmen. He was born at Aquino, in the kingdom of Naples, of a noble family. It may be recalled that this pillar of the Church was distantly related to Frederick II, its greatest scourge. His education began at Monte Cassino where, in the eleventh century, the earliest work of translation from the Arabic had been performed. His studies were continued at the University of Naples, which had been founded in 1224 by Frederick II. At Naples Arabian and Hebrew influence was rife (pp. 215–222). In 1244 St. Thomas departed to study under Albert at Cologne. In the following year he went to Paris, and was there or at Cologne till 1261, when he was called to Italy, where he taught at various centres, notably Bologna and Rome. From 1269 to 1272 he was again in Paris. His last teaching place was also his first, Naples, which he left in 1273 to attend the Council of Lyons. On his way thither he fell ill, and next year he died. He was canonized in 1323, and in 1567 he was made by Pius V the fifth Doctor of the Church, thus ranking after St. Ambrose, St. Augustine, St. Jerome, and St. Gregory the Great.

There is at Pisa a picture painted in 1345 which represents well the position occupied by St. Thomas in the minds of medieval churchmen (Fig. 44). He is sitting with four books in his lap. These are the four parts of his *Summa contra gentiles*. In his hand he holds the open Bible, displaying Prov. viii. 7. *For my mouth shall speak truth, and wickedness is an abomination to my lips*. Above sits the enthroned Christ, from whom rays descend on the Saint. From the mouth of Christ rays pass also to each of the six biblical teachers, Moses, St. John, St. Mark, St. Paul, St. Matthew, and St. Luke, and from them on to illuminate St. Thomas. On the right of St. Thomas stands Aristotle holding his *Ethics*. On his left is Plato presenting his *Timaeus*. From these two also rays go to the Saint. From the books of St. Thomas rays pass to illuminate the faithful, habited as Dominicans, who are placed right and left below. Among the rays on the left may be read the text *He hath found out all the way of knowledge* (Baruch iii. 37), and among the rays on the right the text *A teacher of the Gentiles in faith and verity* (1 Tim. ii. 7). Between the groups of the faithful lies the prostrate Averroes, whose *wickedness is an abomination to the lips* of the sainted teacher. Averroes wears the Jewish badge upon each shoulder! By the side of Averroes is flung the great *Commentary*, emblem of Averroan abomination, transfixed by a lightning ray, not of illumination but of refutation, from the Thomistic works.

Thomas was essentially a codifier and a teacher. He accepts the Church's judgement concerning the Jews, and tries to justify it on a rational basis, at the same time giving it a milder turn. He was no fanatic and, unlike William of Auvergne and Albert, he shows no personal feeling against them. St. Thomas was very adverse to their forcible conversion. Unlike St. Augustine and St. Jerome, and later on, Duns Scotus, he deprecated baptism of Jewish infants against the wish of their parents.

At the time of Aquinas public disputations with Christians

were sometimes forced on the Jews (see p. 294). These gatherings were a fruitful source of disorder, for the mob was easily inflamed against teaching represented as blasphemous. The Jews themselves were naturally anxious to avoid such discussions, which they entered only under duress. Such compulsory debates were, in fact, a thinly disguised means of persecution. It was said that they helped to confirm Christians in their faith. Since the arguments that the Jews were permitted to use were only such as were *not* objectionable to Christian opinion it may be that this was indeed the case! St. Thomas regarded public disputation as a sinful method for a Christian to adopt in order to strengthen his own faith, but he held it to be a laudable method of conversion. He considered, however, that Jews should have freedom of worship, since their religion contains the germs of Christianity. It was his view that intercourse with the Jews should be forbidden to the unlearned, lest they become perverted to Judaism. He considered that in places where the Jews have no right to own Christian slaves such right should not be given them, but where they have already such right it should not be withdrawn. Nevertheless, a convert to Christianity should, on conversion, be freed from his Jewish owner.

As regards usury, Thomas held that no one must be tempted to sin by being asked to lend at interest, but if he wish to do this, the borrower may take advantage of the convenience. It may be recalled that even St. Bernard of Clairvaux in 1146 had deprecated the destruction of the Jews by the Crusaders, on the ground that without them there would be worse extortion by Christian usurers. St. Thomas held that special taxation of the Jews was justifiable, down to, but not beyond, their necessities of life.

St. Thomas shows no knowledge of the Talmud. His occasional quotations from it are always from Maimonides. It is noteworthy that in his *Summa contra gentiles* he hardly distinguishes between Jews and other opponents of Christianity. In

FIG. 44. ST. THOMAS TRIUMPHS OVER AVERROES
Altar-piece by Francesco Traini in Sta Catarina at Pisa

For description see p. 265

his works he cites only three Jewish writers, Isaac—from whom he takes only a few logical definitions—Avicebron—whom he does not know to have been a Jew—and Maimonides. To Avicebron he exhibits great opposition, and by doing so reveals the strength of the Avicebron party in contemporary Christian thought. St. Thomas devotes considerable space to a refutation of Avicebron's doctrine that spiritual substance, like corporeal substance, is made up of prime matter and of form. In the view of St. Thomas, whereas Avicebron postulated matter everywhere, Avicenna postulated matter only in corporeal bodies which all had the same substratum, while Averroes and Maimonides, being more orthodox Aristotelians, held that the heavenly bodies had a different material substratum from that of the elements.

To Maimonides, on the other hand, the debt of Aquinas is very great. In general it is the same in kind but greater in degree than that of Albert, his teacher. It may be considered under its various headings.

(i) *Relation of Reason to Revelation.* Thomas here owes almost everything to Maimonides. Not merely details in the structure but the very bases of his system are to be found in the Jewish philosopher. St. Thomas tells us that Revelation not only gives mankind truths inaccessible to the human intellect, but also gives to all men difficult truths that only a few would reach by their intellect. This line of thought is in the Jewish writer Saadia (892–942), whence it was adopted by Maimonides. In great detail also St. Thomas cites the reasons given in the *Guide for the perplexed* for the need of Revelation to lead mankind to the knowledge of God.

(ii) *Divine Attributes.* St. Thomas adopted the doctrine of Maimonides that Human Reason can attain to the recognition of the Existence of God, but neither to a knowledge of His Nature, nor to a recognition of the identity of His Nature with His Existence. St. Thomas also agrees with Maimonides that the Attributes of God cannot be regarded as something added to

His Nature, since that would suggest that Accidents distinct from His Nature could be added thereto, and such a conception would impart plurality to His single Nature.

Maimonides says that the Divine attributes can be neither identical with God's Nature nor can they define it. For that reason the only suitable name for God is the ineffable Tetragrammaton which is associated with no attribute. The attributes of God can be regarded either as expressions of His activity or as mere negation. St. Thomas, giving a different turn to the argument of Maimonides, regards the Divine attributes as identical with the Divine Nature. On the other hand, he adopts without reservation the repudiation by the Jewish philosopher of the attribution to God of human passions.

(iii) *God's Knowledge.* A fundamental part of the teaching of St. Thomas is his doctrine concerning God's knowledge and this doctrine is based on the *Guide for the perplexed.* Starting from Aristotle as interpreted by Averroes, Maimonides declares that, since the Knower must in some sort contain that which is known, God could not have knowledge of the individual details of accidents—good and evil—within this universe, but only of universe itself. Thus, He knows now that which has not yet come into existence. Our difficulty in accepting such a belief arises, he held, from our mistaken view of the Divine Thought, as though it were comparable to our thought. The matter becomes clear, he explains, when we regard God's knowledge of His universe as akin to the artist's knowledge of the work he has conceived. The details are implicit in the conception, but have no separate part in the artist's thought. St. Thomas follows these lines, and especially elaborates the conception of the Supreme Artist. This pregnant idea of God as artist, as presented by St. Thomas, made an especial appeal to the men of the Renaissance and is well presented, for example, by such a typical figure as Andreas Vesalius, the father of Anatomy (1514–1564).

(iv) *Providence*. In the matter of God's Providence, St. Thomas again follows Maimonides. The Middle Ages considered that Aristotle limited the manifestation of God's Providence to the Heavenly Spheres, 'not penetrating below the sphere of the Moon', as Alexander Aphrodisias (third century) had expressed it. (Works by Alexander were available to Maimonides in Arabic dress and to St. Thomas in Latin translations from the Arabic, prepared by Gerard in the twelfth century.) Maimonides emphatically declares that the Divine Providence extends also to this sublunary sphere—nay to each inhabitant thereof—in the proportion that he has cultivated the spirit, and has thus attained to union with God. St. Thomas, while adopting the argument of Maimonides, stigmatized as heresy the limitation of God's Providence, which he declared was exercised on all things on earth, and was not limited to those beings who had cultivated the spirit.

(v) *Omnipotence*. St. Thomas also adopted the argument of Maimonides that logical absurdities are outside the range of God's omnipotence. Thus God cannot make a thing at the same time exist and not exist, nor can He enable Matter to exist without Form, nor overthrow the fundamental laws of Logic or of Mathematics, which are part of His thought.

(vi) *Creation*. In no matter did Maimonides show more power and originality than in his doctrine of Creation, which formed the greater part also of the teaching on the subject by St. Thomas. Maimonides regards the Doctrine of Creation in Time as a matter rather for Faith than Reason. While, on the one hand, declaring that proof on such a subject is beyond the power of human reason, he points out, on the other hand, that Aristotle can adduce no proof of the eternity of the world, which indeed he puts forward merely as a hypothesis. In this absence of proof for either view, acceptance of the Creation of the world in Time is inevitable, not so much on account of the text of the Bible, which is susceptible of more than one interpretation, as because the whole religious sentiment of mankind is firmly based on this belief.

The ingenuity of Maimonides in the interpretation of Bible texts was very great, and often led him to strain and pervert the sense. Thus in his remarks on the biblical narrative of Creation, he declares that by *darkness* in the opening verses of Genesis is meant *fire*, so that the four Aristotelian elements may all be found there. In the same passage for the *Spirit* of God hovering on the waters, he would substitute *wind* to avoid the anthropomorphism. 'The *Earth* was without form, and void; and the darkness [*Fire*] was upon the face of the deep. And the Spirit [*Air* or wind] of God moved upon the face of the *Waters*.' Again the explanation by Maimonides of the omission after the second day of the divine approbation ' And God saw that it was good' (*Genesis* i. 8) is as follows. The second day saw only the beginning of the separation, which was not consummated until the third day; or the omission may be because the people could not appreciate the importance of ten Separations; or again the omission may be due to the Firmament (or ordinary foggy atmosphere) not being primarily an eternal or truly existing part of the Universe! Exegesis on such absurd lines is adopted by St. Thomas direct from Maimonides.

(vii) *Structure of the Universe*. The conception of the structure of the Universe adopted by St. Thomas accords less completely with that of Maimonides. St. Thomas accepts the analogy drawn by Maimonides between the Prime Mover in the heavens and the heart in the animal body, but he cannot follow Maimonides in the endowment of the heavenly bodies with souls. Nor could St. Thomas adopt the view of Maimonides that the Universe was not created solely for man's sake. He believed, rather, in the perpetual renewal of creation and ever for the benefit of man.

(viii) *Angels and Prophecy*. Here St. Thomas could get little help from Maimonides, who limited the number of angels and identified them with the 'separated Intelligences' of the Spheres. His interpretation of angels in many Bible texts, as signifying divinely inspired men, was no more congenial to St. Thomas than was the rationalizing Maimonidean interpretation of prophecy. Some conceptions concerning both angels and prophecy St.Thomas did, however, accept from Maimonides. Thus, following him, St. Thomas considered that a greater measure of the gifts of Freewill and Reason had been bestowed on these angels than on mankind. St. Thomas also accepted the view of Maimonides that prophetic revelation was accomplished by the agency of angels. He also adopted the Maimonidean classification of the grades of prophecy, and fully accepted the view of the unique character of the prophecy of Moses.

(ix) *Biblical Law*. It was the attempt of Maimonides to rationalize biblical law by symbolic interpretation that particularly scandalized his Jewish contemporaries. By his Christian followers, on the other hand, his doctrine on this subject commanded complete approval. St. Thomas accepted his distinction between Ceremonial and Judicial Law and his generalizations of the classes of sin most strongly condemned in the Bible. The Maimonidean rationalizations of the biblical view of sin and punishment were also adopted by St. Thomas and passed into the Scholastic system.

c. *The Later Thirteenth Century*

The Franciscan, ROGER BACON (1214–1294, Fig. 46), the 'doctor mirabilis', is the first great exponent of the methods of the positive sciences. If we seek for the fruits of the scientific method in his writings it must be confessed that we shall meet with some disappointment. It is, perhaps, chiefly in the department of language that Roger was able to apply his method. His knowledge of Hebrew and his attitude to the Jews we discuss elsewhere in this volume (pp. 299–301). His great interest in the calendar, however, led him to investigate the Jewish method of reckoning time, and it may well be that for this and for his Hebrew studies he had Jewish assistance. He mentions certain Jewish astronomers, such as Zachel (p. 260, note).

Bacon's earliest writings were probably his *Questions on the Physics of Aristotle*, and his *Questions on the Metaphysics of Aristotle*. These were composed in 1245, before he entered the Franciscan order. They exhibit familiarity with the Gundissalinus-Avendeath literature, and quote Avicebron frequently.[1] Bacon's work *On Metaphysics* was written in 1266. Only a fragment has survived, but it quotes Isaac Israeli and Petrus Alfonsi. Despite his broad-minded and noble utterances on the treatment of Jews, and despite his knowledge of the Hebrew language, it cannot be said that Roger Bacon, in his later writings, was under any profound debt to Jewish thought, though his work is permeated throughout by the influence of the Jewish translators.

While in Roger's own works Jewish philosophy is in the background, it comes very much to the fore in that of a pupil. The *Summa philosophiae*[2] of such an one is packed with Hebraeo-Arabic elements. He gives a short history of philosophy in which is a very interesting list of those whom he regarded as modern thinkers. He discusses 'the most famous Arabic, that is to say Spanish, philosophers'. He enumerates about thirty, with most of whom we have already dealt. He ends with Rabbi Moses, i.e. Maimonides, and is so completely satisfied with his teaching that he assures us that this sheet-anchor of Jewish theology was converted to Christianity and wrote a work against

[1] These *Questions* are as yet unpublished, and the information concerning them has been supplied by Mr. R. R. Steele.

[2] The *Summa philosophiae* in question has been edited in the name of Roger Bacon's teacher, Robert Grosseteste. L. Baur, *Die philosophischen Werke des Grosseteste*, Munich, 1912. It is, however, certainly later than Grosseteste, and in Mr. R. R. Steele's opinion, is probably the work of a pupil of Roger Bacon.

Judaism and in defence of the Catholic faith ! It is the more easy for him to think this since there are elements in the work of this pupil of Roger that do more than border on the heretical.

We have not space to consider heretical movements in general and their relation to Jewish thought. A curious position is, however, occupied by the heretical writer SIGER OF BRABANT (*c.* 1230–1290), who taught at Paris in the seventh and eighth decades of the thirteenth century and led an opposition to the mendicant orders there. Siger was an ardent Averroist of the type to which the writings of the orthodox St. Thomas were regarded as the best antidote. That 'Averroism' had a very strong following we know from the fact of Siger's candidature for the rectorship of the University of Paris in 1271, and the strife occasioned by the appointment of another. In 1277 there was a special condemnation of Averroism in the University coupled with the name of Siger. He fled to Italy where he is said to have died a violent death. Dante, oddly enough, places him in his Paradise.[1] Siger's works were of the most daring kind, and discussed freely the most radical problems, such as, for instance, the existence of God. He relied mainly on Averroes. His extreme Averroism is a foretaste of the Paduan philosophy of the fifteenth and sixteenth centuries. Among works of Jewish or Hebraeo-Arabic origin, Siger quoted Alfarabi, Algazel, Alkindi, Avempace, Averroes, Avicebron, Avicenna, Isaac, Maimonides, and the anonymous Neoplatonic treatise known as the *Liber de causis* (p. 246). Against Siger St. Thomas wrote a special work.

The Majorcan RAYMOND LULL (1235–1315), the 'illuminated doctor', is one of the most striking and also one of the most difficult of medieval thinkers. He was of noble birth, married, and a father of children, but renounced everything at the age of thirty for a life of devotion. He set himself two tasks in

[1] There is, however, doubt whether the Siger of Dante is the Siger here discussed.

life, to convert the heathen and to obtain martyrdom. In the first he failed; in the second he succeeded after many efforts.

Lull's greatest interest was the training of missionaries with a knowledge of Oriental languages. In the promotion of this object he visited Paris, Rome, Avignon, Montpellier, Genoa, Pisa, Naples, Cyprus, Tunis, Asia Minor, and Morocco. The fall of Acre in 1291 sealed the fate of the Crusades and the two centuries of effort that they represented. Christendom was deeply impressed. The circumstances enforced the abandonment of violent methods with Islam and pacific counsels, being in fact imperative, were proclaimed as more in accord with Christian principles. With the Jews, however, from whom Christendom had nothing to fear, Lull was in favour of far bolder measures. In his fantastic work *On the interpretation of the dreams of James II of Aragon* Lull gives excellent reasons for this violence. Jews, he says, are universally entrusted by the great with the care of their health. Nor is even the Church free from this abomination, for nearly every monastery has its Jewish physician. The custom is accursed.

The remedy for all this was, in Lull's opinion, renewed missionary effort. He propounded a scheme for the foundation of colleges for the study of Oriental languages and the establishment of chairs of Arabic and Hebrew for missionary instruction. His linguistic projects were only partially successful. He himself obtained a good knowledge of Arabic.

Lull was under strong Neoplatonic influence, and into Neoplatonic thought he was able to fit Cabalistic developments. The Cabala, in his opinion, began where Plato left off, and the later Christian Cabalists have been regarded as the spiritual descendants of Raymond Lull. He was probably acquainted with Hebrew, and it seems very likely that he had personal contact with Jews, whence came his Cabalistic knowledge.

Raymond Lull produced a long and wildly mystical series of writings, which are not made more intelligible by the use of

Reception of the Jewish Factor

a logical machine which he invented. In using it logical premises were to be put in, as it were, at one end, and conclusions came out at the other. An actual specimen of this machine has recently been described. Lull himself hoped that it would do away with all heresy, if only he could get heretics to agree as to the premises! The difficulty was to persuade the heretic or infidel to entrust his beliefs to the working of the machine. This very reluctance did but prove how active was the Devil and how necessary it was to combat him with vigour.

Despite his missionary fervour, Lull's own spiritual athletic feats were of such an order that he was obliged to obtain repeated certificates of orthodoxy. His books were in fact prohibited, because they subjected to reason—or at any rate to his reasoning machine—certain principles which, it was held, were not a matter of reason but of faith. His intellectual activity was vast, and extended into many departments. In philosophy he takes the position of an ardent opponent of Averroism, but in taking up this position he draws but little from Jewish thought save on the Cabalistic side.

The heretical PETER OF ABANO (1250–1318) was a professor at Padua and earned a reputation as a magician which has been commemorated in an interesting but difficult poem of Browning. Peter's natural death saved him from the hands of the Inquisition. His body was exhumed and burnt. Peter had a knowledge of Greek acquired at Constantinople. His greatest and best-known work, the *Conciliator of the differences of the philosophers*, is an attempt to mediate between the older Arabian and the newer Greek school, which was just beginning to appear. The *Conciliator*, which for long was very widely read and ran into scores of editions, is crammed with quotations from Jewish authors. Peter has been credited with translating a collection of works of Abraham Ben Ezra (pp. 209–210) from the Hebrew, but it is evident that he rendered them from the French.

DANTE (1265–1321) is the very summation of the medieval

spirit. He presents us in his works with the development of the philosophical system of St. Thomas. Thus the sources of St. Thomas may also be regarded as the sources of Dante. Apart from this indirect channel there can be no doubt that Dante's own reading brought him into direct contact with the Arabian literature, and that he draws largely on the Orient. He quotes works of Avicebron, as well as Avicenna, Averroes, and Algazel. It has been pointed out that close parallels to Dante's journeys into the other world are to be found in Arabic writers who preceded him.[1] These had not been translated in his time, and it is a problem how news of them could have reached him. Now there can be no doubt that Dante entertained friendly relations with certain Jews. It should be remembered, too, that Dante's friend and councillor, Brunetto Latini (c. 1210–1294), had visited the court of Alfonso X of Castille, where translation from the Arabic and Hebrew, especially by Jews, was being actively prosecuted. It may be through his Jewish acquaintances and through Brunetto that certain important hints on Arabian thought came to Dante. We note that Dante puts Averroes in the 'first circle' of the Inferno among the 'virtuous pagans'.

§ 10. *The End of the Middle Ages*

The last stage in medieval thought, the break-up of the scholastic alliance between Theology and Philosophy, is ushered in by the work of DUNS SCOTUS the 'doctor subtilis'. In this last stage we shall find Jewish influence on the wane.

Duns (1265–1308) became a Franciscan early, and studied at Oxford. Shortly before his death he removed to Paris where he exerted much influence. He was one of the most important figures among the Schoolmen, and led a reaction against the movement represented by Albertus Magnus and St. Thomas Aquinas. It is not unreasonable to represent this movement

[1] See article by Professor Guillaume, pp. 169–170.

under Duns as presaging that upheaval in Latin Christendom which ultimately developed into the Reformation.

The only Jewish works that Duns mentions are the *Fountain of life* of Avicebron and the *Guide for the perplexed* of Maimonides. That he had, however, direct contact with a Jew or a converted Jew comes out in a peculiar way. In one of his works he cites a certain *Rabbi Barahoc*. No such Rabbinic name is known. The statement he makes, however, is taken from the section of the Talmud known as *Berakoth*, i.e. 'Blessings'! Such an absurd error can only have arisen from a misunderstanding by Duns of a statement by one familiar with the Talmud.

Duns shows a sharp break with St. Thomas in his determination to separate Theology from Philosophy. In this he opposes Maimonides as much as St. Thomas. Nevertheless, he uses Maimonides considerably in details. The general cosmology of Duns is, however, from Avicebron. Matter and Form constitute for him both spiritual and corporeal world. Every created thing consists of Actuality and Potentiality. Matter as such is indeterminate Potentiality, and as we encounter it, has Actuality added. The higher the Actuality of a Form, the more it is pervaded by Matter, and the more complete is the fusion of Matter and Form. In spiritual things the fusion is most complete. Thus angels and the Rational Soul, though they consist of Matter and Form, do not come into the category of *Quantity*. Matter and Form are more completely fused in them, and most completely in God, in whom absolute unity is reached and from whom all things issue as do numbers from unity. As numbers must be less simple than Unity, so must the creatures be less simple than the Creator; but the nearer it reaches to the Divine Unity, the greater must be the degree of unity of the creature. In all this Duns declares himself an adherent of Avicebron.

As regards the relation of Faith and Reason, Duns follows Maimonides rather than Avicebron. The doctrine of the existence and Unity of God was revealed to the Israelites. Though this doctrine must have been apparent to their reason, it was Revelation, he holds, that made it impossible for them to ignore it. Nevertheless, Duns opposes the doctrine of Creation in Time, which he holds cannot be proved in the manner that St. Thomas sets forth. In doing this he does not realize that he is putting himself in opposition to Maimonides, whom he professes to follow. He definitely ranges himself with Maimonides, however, in his treatment of prophecy, in his discussion of the nature of Revelation, and in his division of commands into *ceremonial* and *legal*. His treatment of Divine attributes is peculiar. He regards them, when not negative, as due to the action of God Himself, and this, he thinks, is the opinion of Avicenna and Maimonides. He also cites Maimonides to the effect that God's activity is a necessity of His Nature.

WILLIAM OF OCKHAM (died *c.* 1349) was a Franciscan, who studied first at Oxford. He was summoned to Avignon in 1324 by Pope John XXII to answer charges of teaching heretical doctrine in his lectures at Oxford. While at Avignon he became interested in the question of evangelical poverty and papal claims. He escaped in 1328 to take part in the struggle of the Emperor, Louis V of Bavaria, against the Papacy. Ockham was the most prominent intellectual leader of his time. His writings announce the disintegration of Scholasticism, and they are of interest to us for that reason. They contain, however, few Jewish elements save those which he had derived indirectly from his brother Scholastics. His doctrine that all theological doctrine can have as basis only faith, not reason, is manifestly inconsistent with the position alike of St. Thomas and of Maimonides.

In the fifteenth century Latin writers develop an interest in Jewish writings from two opposing points of view. On the one hand there is a revival of Cabalism which affects such thinkers as Nicholas of Cusa. On the other hand there is a revival of Averroism which draws such firm Aristotelians as

Pomponazzi. We may consider briefly these two writers, as typical of the two movements.

The work of the remarkable thinker, NICHOLAS OF CUSA (1401–1464), who became a Cardinal, typifies in some ways the change from the Middle Ages to the Renaissance. This change brought with it the end of the supremacy of Aristotle. It was associated with a preference for mysticism coloured by Neoplatonism and often by the Cabala. In this process Maimonides passed into the shadow. Nicholas regarded Scholasticism as more harmful than helpful to theology. His basis was the counterfeit 'Dionysius the Areopagite', whom Erigena had translated, as well as the works of Erigena himself (p. 246). He relied also on the German mystics, especially Eckhard (1260 ?–1327 ?). Nicholas had little direct knowledge of the Hebrew mystical writers, but he had heard of them through personal intercourse with Jews.

Nicholas says that he has not found Jews so hard to convince of the Trinity, but that they were absolutely stiff-necked concerning the Incarnation of the Son of God. The Jews, he tells us, like the Saracens, believe in the coming of the Messiah. He is much surprised that the Jews believe in resurrection, though they refuse to believe in the resurrection of Jesus Christ. They must believe in the future life, however, he remarks, though it is not mentioned in their Law, for clearly otherwise they would not suffer martyrdom.

Nicholas reached very remarkable philosophical conclusions in contemplating the various religions around him. He tries through Wisdom to reach a concord of all faiths, declaring that there is only ' one religion with many manifestations '. God, he considered, sent diverse prophets to diverse peoples to teach them religion in diverse ways. The peoples only separated into different religions because they forgot the content of the teaching of their prophets owing to their pre-occupation with its form. Greek, Latin, Arab, Jew, and Scythian all worship the same truth. Even polytheists reverence one Godhead in all their gods. The difference in different faiths is only in expression and form. Therefore it would be easy to fuse them, allowing different forms. Even circumcision and idolatry should be permitted, provided that their symbolism is always remembered. Among the Jewish writers that he quotes in developing his argument are Ben Ezra, Isaac, Avicebron, and Jacob ben Makir. In his famous *De docta ignorantia* Nicholas frequently cites the *Guide for the perplexed*. The passages he selects are always those in which Maimonides is leaning not on Aristotle, but on the Neoplatonists.

JACQUES LEFÈVRE of Étaples (c. 1455–1537) was one of the most learned men of his time and an enthusiastic humanist. He is interesting as linking Nicholas of Cusa with the Reformation. He was ordained priest, taught at Paris, and edited many works of Aristotle. Later he devoted himself to theological and biblical topics and his views soon brought him into conflict with the Church. Lefèvre translated the Bible into French, and his work, so far as New Testament and Apocrypha is concerned, formed the basis of the vernacular version subsequently adopted by the French Reformed Church.

A pupil of Lefèvre, one CHARLES DE BOUELLES (c. 1470–1553), on a visit to Rome in 1507, made acquaintance with BONET DE LATTES, the Jewish physician of Pope Alexander VI. This Bonet had invented an astronomical dial by which stellar and solar altitudes could be taken, and the time determined with great precision, both by night and by day. De Bouelles tells how one day he went for a stroll in Rome and met Bonet in the Jewish quarter. It happened that the description of Bonet's dial had been republished by Lefèvre, and de Bouelles had read it. De Bouelles now asked to see the dial and they went together to Bonet's residence. There, at the top of the house, de Bouelles found a room, fitted as a synagogue, which he describes minutely. De Bouelles goes on to give an account of theological and philosophical arguments which he put before those whom he found there. The whole story conjures up a very vivid and not unpleasing picture of the intellectual relations of Jews and Christians of the time, and is interesting as providing a link between Jewish thought and the Reformation.

PIETRO POMPONAZZI (1462–1524) is the last Latin writer of first-class importance who can be treated as medieval. He exhibits vigour and originality of thought, and cannot be wholly omitted from any History of Philosophy. He taught at Padua, Bologna, and Ferrara, and devoted his life entirely to the disinterested pursuit of truth. He earned a great reputation as a teacher. It is remarkable that, living when and where he did, and with philosophy as his sole interest, he exhibits not the slightest trace of Renaissance influence.

Even to the men of his own day Pomponazzi was remarkable for his isolated position. On the one hand, he refused to accept the argument for the immortality of the soul that St. Thomas professed to elicit from Aristotle. On the other, he rejected the construction put upon Aristotle by Averroes, which provided for mankind as a whole an immortality in which that of the individual was sunk and lost. Thus the two great Scholastic lines of thought were alike abhorrent to him, and though a pure Scholastic he exhibits Scholasticism *in articulo mortis*. Jewish philosophy has little interest for him; on the rock of his self-confident and self-contained intellect the waves of Hebraeo-Arabic thought beat in vain.

Jewish philosophical influence did not however quite die with the fifteenth century. In Cabalistic form on the one hand, and in Averroistic form on the other, it long influenced certain schools. These schools were, however, anachronisms. In more subtle and less direct forms Jewish influence can be traced through Spinoza into the thought of our time. There are surely no clear divisions in the history of the human spirit. Yet it is fair to say that with the end of the fifteenth century the great Hebraeo-Arabic system of thought had spent its force, and its treatment by Pomponazzi illustrates its bankruptcy. With the noonday of the Renaissance we lay down our pen. With it the historian of Jewish thought must begin a new chapter. CHARLES AND DOROTHEA SINGER.

SOME BOOKS OF REFERENCE

General works on medieval Jewish thought: M. Steinschneider, *Jewish Literature*, London, 1857; J. Winter and A. Wünsche, *Die Jüdische Litteratur seit Abschluss des Kanons*, Trier, 1894–6; H. Graetz, *History of the Jews*, English trans., London, 1901; M. Güdemann, *Geschichte des Erziehungswesens und der Cultur der abendländischen Juden*, Vienna, 1880–8; I. Abrahams, *Jewish Life in the Middle Ages*, Philadelphia, 1911.

Arabian thought: C. Brockelmann, *Geschichte der Arabischen Literatur*, Weimar, 1898–1902; Carra de Vaux, *Les Penseurs de l'Islam*, Paris, 1921–6; De L. O'Leary, *Arabic Thought*, London, 1922. Jewish Literature in Arabic: M. Steinschneider, *Die arabische Literatur der Juden*, Frankfurt, 1902; I. Husik, *History of Mediaeval Jewish Philosophy*, New York, 1916. Studies of individual philosophers are J. Guttmann, *Die philosophischen Lehren des Isaac ben Salomon Israeli*, Munich, 1911; S. S. Wise, *Ibn Gebirol on the Improvement of the Moral Qualities*, New York, 1901; M. Friedländer, *Guide for the Perplexed of Maimonides*, 2nd edition, London, 1904; I. Abrahams and D. Yellin, *Maimonides*, London, 1903; Carra de Vaux, *Avicenne*, Paris, 1900; S. van den Bergh, *Epitome der Metaphysik des Averroes*, Leyden, 1924; and E. Renan, *Averroès et l'Averroïsme*, 3rd edition, Paris, 1866. The link with the Renaissance: J. Burckhardt, *Kultur der Renaissance in Italien*, 12th edition, Leipzig, 1919.

The transmission of Jewish thought to the West: M. Steinschneider, *Hebräische Übersetzungen des Mittelalters*, Berlin, 1893; and *Europäische Übersetzungen aus dem Arabischen*, Vienna, 1904–5; L. Thorndike, *History of Magic and Experimental Science*, New York, 1923; C. H. Haskins, *Studies in the History of Medieval Science*, Cambridge, Mass., 1924.

The medieval Aristotle: C. and A. Jourdain, *Recherches critiques sur l'âge et l'origine des traductions latines d'Aristote*, 2nd edition, Paris, 1844; M. Grabmann, *Forschungen über die lateinischen Aristoteles-Übersetzungen des XIII. Jahrhunderts*, Munich, 1916; P. Mandonnet, *Siger de Brabant*, Louvain, 1908–11; A Loewenthal, *Pseudo-Aristoteles über die Seele*, Berlin, 1891.

Jewish elements in scholastic thought: A series of works by J. Guttmann, notably *Scholastik des dreizehnten Jahrhunderts in ihren Beziehungen zum Judenthum*, Breslau, 1902; C. Baeumker, *Beiträge zur Geschichte der Philosophie des Mittelalters*, Munich, 1891 (26 vols.); L. J. Newman, *Jewish Influence on Christian Reform Movements*, New York, 1925; R. Seyerlen, *Beziehungen zwischen der abendländischen und morgenländischen Wissenschaft*, Jena, 1899.

FIG. 45. NICHOLAS OF LYRA

From a manuscript written in 1402 in the Franciscan
monastery of Pesaro in North Italy

FIG. 46. ROGER BACON

From a manuscript written about 1450 in Northern France

HEBREW SCHOLARSHIP IN THE MIDDLE AGES AMONG LATIN CHRISTIANS

§ 1. *The Hebrew Glosses and Glossaries*

AMONG the more interesting aspects of the contact of the Jews with their non-Jewish neighbours during the Middle Ages is the question of the accessibility of the literary medium of the one people to the other. This matter may be approached either from the Jewish or from the non-Jewish side.

The Jews, though accustomed to the vernaculars for the ordinary purposes of life, used Hebrew in their writings, but they constantly needed terms that did not exist in their literary medium. These were naturally taken from the language of the country in which the writers dwelt. Often such words presented difficulties for the Hebrew readers who might perhaps speak another vernacular. The vernacular words or passages (written in Hebrew characters) were therefore sometimes *glossed* or explained in Hebrew by the scribe. In other cases the reader's acquaintance with Hebrew was imperfect, and glosses in the vernacular were provided for him by more competent Hebrew scholars. The best known of the Hebrew writers who habitually employed the method of glossing for the purpose of explanation was the great French Hebrew scholar, Rabbi Solomon ben Isaac of Troyes, usually known as RASHI [1] (1040–1105). His Biblical and Talmudic commentaries contain over three thousand passages, of which an explanation is given in French spelt in Hebrew characters.[2] This practice of Rashi was followed by his pupils.

---

[1] The name RASHI is formed from the initial letters of his Hebrew name RAbbi SHelomo ben Isaac. This method of forming names or titles is common in Hebrew literature, for instance, Maimonides, i. e. RAbbi Moses Ben Maimon, is spoken of as RAMBAM and Nachmanides (pp. 295–7), i.e. RAbbi Moses Ben Nahman as RAMBAN.

[2] An account of the glosses of Rashi is given by M. Liber, *Rashi*, translated by A. Szold, Philadelphia, 1906, p. 99.

At an early date the glosses of Rashi and other writers were collected and added to and thus actual vocabularies or *glossaries* were prepared. The vocabularies or *glossaries* are usually written in the Hebrew script, more rarely partly in Hebrew and partly in the Latin script. They are, in effect, dictionaries. On the one side we have the foreign phrase or word, on the other is given the Hebrew equivalent. There are a number of these Hebrew glossaries known, dating from the tenth century onward. Most of them deal with Old French words, but Latin, Arabic, Spanish, Italian, and Slavonic glosses and glossaries also occur. These glosses and glossaries, especially those in French, are of very great philological interest. They often give the modern scholar a means of determining or checking the pronunciation of the French or other language at the date at which the glossary was made. Conversely, such word-lists may also be helpful in determining the contemporary pronunciation of Hebrew.[1]

The French explanations given by Rashi are of quite peculiar interest. Hebrew for the French Jews, like Latin for the Christians, was merely the language of literature and liturgy. Thus Rashi needed French most for the discussion of passages dealing with common acts of daily life. Now it happens that we possess very few eleventh-century specimens of the *langue d'oïl* or Old Northern French from which modern French is descended, and those few belong mostly to the Norman dialect and the language of poetry. The speech of Rashi was, however, a much purer form of the *langue d'oïl*. It was that spoken in Champagne and was between the dialect of the Ile-de-France

---

[1] The earliest Hebrew glossary is of Gershom of Metz (970–1040), edited by L. Brandin, *Revue des Études Juives*, xlviii, p. 48, Paris, 1901. The most extensive of the glossaries is edited by M. Lambert and L. Brandin, *Glossaire Hébreu-Français du XIIIᵉ siècle*, Paris, 1905. Earlier than these is a Latin-Arabic glossary by a converted Jew, with many Hebrew words. It is Visigothic. C. F. Seybold, *Glossarium Latino-Arabicum*, Berlin, 1900, dates it eleventh century, but tenth is more likely. It is the earliest known Latin MS. on paper.

and that of Lorraine. Moreover, the words he gives are mainly those which designate matters of common knowledge or things of daily use among the people. Thus the French glosses of Rashi provide a document of the highest importance for the reconstruction of the Old French language. In the case of many of these words their appearance in Rashi is the earliest known. The Old French grammatical forms which he preserves are no less interesting than his vocabulary. It should, perhaps, be added that Rashi's outlook was essentially French. He knew no Arabic and was unaffected by the Hebraeo-Arabic literature.

As time went on the written vernaculars of the various countries developed sufficiently for learned purposes, and were soon freely used by Jews. Indeed, in some respects Jews were disposed to use the written vernacular more than their Christian neighbours, for, unlike them, they had no religious tie with Latin.[1]

It is however with the approach to Hebrew from the non-Jewish side that we are chiefly concerned, for it was the non-Jewish approach that directly influenced medieval thought.

§ 2. *The Earlier Middle Ages*

Interest and curiosity as to the nature of the Hebrew language prevailed among Latin Christians from a very early date. Some suggestions were derived from the writings of St. Ambrose (340–397).[2] Most of the little knowledge of Hebrew in the Dark Ages came through St. Jerome. Throughout the Dark Ages some interest in Hebrew was fostered by Calendarial disputes.

ST. JEROME (337–420) had begun his study of Hebrew in Rome under a baptized Jew and continued it in Palestine

[1] On the employment of the vernacular by Jewish writers see A. Neubauer, *Jewish Quarterly Review*, iv, p. 7, London, 1892 ; M. Kayserling, *Bibliotheca Española-Portugueza-Judaica*, 1890 ; and M. Steinschneider, *Die italienische Litteratur der Juden*, Frankfurt, 1901.

[2] Ambrose on Ps. cxviii gives 'interpretations' of the Hebrew letters. They are from a lost work of Philo. D. H. Müller, *Sitzungsb. d. K. Akad. der Wissensch.*, Phil.-Hist. Kl. Bd. clxvii, Abh. 2, Vienna, 1911.

where he had several competent Jewish teachers. He even travelled with Jews to become better acquainted with biblical sites. He learned, moreover, Aramaic from his Jewish friends, that he might examine the Jewish literature in that language that bore on Biblical study.[1] By the year 600 St. Jerome's Latin version of the Bible, now known as the *Vulgate*, had replaced all older translations in the West. Many of the Hebrew words and names in the Vulgate and in other writings of St. Jerome were a subject of discussion in the Latin West in later centuries. On the other hand, St. Jerome's importance was recognized by Jewish authors of the Middle Ages, and he is sometimes quoted by them.

Apart from the Vulgate the works of Jerome that exerted most influence on the course of Hebrew learning among the Latins were *On the interpretation of Hebrew names*,[2] and *On the position and names of places in Holy Writ*.[3] These biblical lexicons or vocabularies excited a good deal of curiosity during the Dark and Middle Ages. Much of what has been supposed to be independent medieval Hebrew learning among the Latins has again and again been traced directly or indirectly to these and other works of Jerome. Thus for instance he is the source of Hebrew words found in certain English and Irish documents of the eighth century.[4]

---

[1] See article by Professor Burkitt, pp. 91 and 92.

[2] This work, of which early versions are known in Latin, Greek, Syriac, Arabic, Armenian, Ethiopic and Bulgar, has been submitted to scientific analysis by F. Wutz, *Onomastica sacra, Untersuchungen zum Liber interpretationis nominum hebraicorum des hl. Hieronymus*, 2 vols., Leipzig, 1914–15.

[3] These two works, of which the second was based on Eusebius, are conveniently edited by P. de Lagarde, *Onomastica sacra*, 2nd edition, Göttingen, 1887.

[4] e.g. J. H. Hessels, *An eighth century Latin-Anglo-Saxon Glossary*, Cambridge, 1890, p. 3, and *A Late eighth century Latin-Anglo-Saxon Glossary*, Cambridge, 1906, pp. 26 and 221. Hebrew words selected from Jerome are to be found also written on the fly-leaf of the *Book of Kells* (c. 700).

For centuries during the Dark Ages the Hebrew alphabet and language stood for something odd, strange, and difficult. They were often invested with a magical quality. Thus St. Isidore of Seville (560–636), exhibits a naïve curiosity concerning Hebrew,[1] but betrays no trace of Hebrew knowledge save what he derived from Jerome. Again in the sixth and seventh centuries there were produced in the British Isles a very peculiar series of semi-magical documents, which scholars have entitled the *Hisperic Literature*. In these extraordinary compositions, though the language is Latin, the vocabulary is drawn from the most out-of-the-way sources. A few words artificially derived from Hebrew are included. These words may have been obtained from wandering Syrian or Byzantine travellers.[2] There are also a few purely magical formulae of about the ninth or tenth century that seem to exhibit Hebrew elements.

On a higher plane than such magical incantations is the little Hebrew knowledge displayed by the Venerable BEDE (673–735). His acquaintance with the language, though exceedingly elementary, was real. In this he was superior to Alcuin (735–804), who was commissioned by Charlemagne to produce an improved text of the Bible.[3] Alcuin had no knowledge of Hebrew, although Jews were available at the court of the Great King. When sending an embassy to the Caliph, Harun-al-Rashid, Charlemagne included one, probably as an interpreter. This was no isolated case of Jewish intervention between East and West, but one further instance will suffice. A description of Jewish activities in travelling between the Orient and Occident has come down to us from the pen of the postmaster-general of the Caliph of Bagdad in the year 847. In this *Book of Ways* we

[1] e. g. *Etymologiae*, vii, §§ 1, 9, and ix, §§ 7 and 8.

[2] C. Singer, 'The Lorica of Gildas the Briton,' in *The Proceedings of the Royal Society of Medicine*, 1919, xii (*Section of the History of Medicine*, p. 124), and *Early English Magic and Medicine*, Oxford, 1920.

[3] On Bede's and Alcuin's knowledge of Hebrew see S. Hirsch, *A Book of Essays*, London, 1905, p. 5.

get a picture of constant Jewish movement from France and Spain to Egypt, Syria, and Arabia and back.[1]

It is, however, with the West that we are concerned. Soon after the death of Charlemagne, the great Abbot of Fulda RABANUS MAURUS (776–856), sent in the year 829 to a brother ecclesiastic a commentary on the *Book of Kings*, in the preparation of which, he says, he had 'inserted sections containing Hebrew traditions, by a Jew of our own time who is learned in the knowledge of the Law'. The passages are in fact taken from a work *On Hebrew questions in the Books of Kings and Chronicles*.[2] This treatise long passed under the name of St. Jerome. There can, however, be no doubt that it is by a converted Jew of a much later date than Jerome. The writer of this work was fairly conversant with Talmudic matters. We can hardly suspect the direct statement of Rabanus that he came in contact with a learned Jew. This man was therefore presumably the unknown author of the Latin work in question, the first genuine product of medieval Judaeo-Christian scholarship. Rabanus himself seems to have had some elementary knowledge of what he calls the Hebrew, though it really more resembles the Samaritan script.[3] It is significant, too, that the earliest Hebrew alphabet in an English manuscript that has yet come to light is annexed to a work of Rabanus. Very oddly it resembles the script of monuments at Palmyra (Fig. 47, cols. 3 and 5).

A number of Hebrew alphabets in Latin manuscripts are

---

[1] A translation of the passage in question by ibn Khurdadbih is given by J. Jacobs, *Jewish Contributions to Civilization*, New York, 1919, p. 194.

[2] See J. B. Halblitzel, *Hrabanus Maurus, Ein Beitrag zur Geschichte der Mittelalterlichen Exegese*, Freiburg, 1906, and Rieger, ' Wer war der Hebräer dessen Werke Hrabanus Maurus benutzt hat ? ' in the *Monatschrift für Geschichte und Wissenschaft des Judentums*, lxviii, p. 66, Frankfurt, 1924.

[3] See Migne, *Patrologia latina*, vol. cxii, columns 1579 and 1580. The Samaritan alphabet there given is substantially identical with that of MSS. of the Bibliothèque Nationale (see following note) and reproduced here in Fig. 47.

known of an early date, some of them accompanied by Greek and other letters. Two ninth-century manuscripts, one written in 822, have also the Samaritan letters (Fig. 47).[1] The letters of the Hebrew alphabet provided a permanent source of interest to the simple minds of the men of the Dark Ages, prompted thereto perhaps by the alphabetical Psalms. At a later date the numerical value of the Hebrew letters became of interest in connexion with astrology and magical prediction of the 'Pythagorean' type.

In the tenth century we have clear evidence of the existence of Jewish aid in the investigation of the Hebrew language. The most direct is the attempt to transliterate Hebrew into Latin letters. Such an effort is to be found in a manuscript at Chartres. In this the scribe thus transliterates the last few verses of Psalm ii (verses 8–12).

Saal mime ni ethna goim nahelathecha ua aHuzadcha afce arez teroaem beseuet barzel ki chli jocer tnape ce m uaatta malachim Hazkilu hiueçru softe arez aiuedu eth adn birea uegrlu bi reada nascu bar pen je naf uethoduedu derech ki jiuear ki maat apo asre col Hoçe bo.[2]

Any one with a slight acquaintance with the language will easily be able to check this transliteration against the Hebrew text.

From a later period in the tenth century comes to us the very remarkable Latin document called the *Mathematica Alcandrii*. This curious work, which exists complete in only a single manuscript, is devoted to astrology of a very complex type. The name *Alcandrius* is probably a form of *Alexander*. The author of this work writes a number of words in Hebrew script, and the Hebrew names for the planets and constellations are familiar to him. He uses too the common Rabbinic habit of

[1] Bibliothèque Nationale, lat. 11505, folio 213 verso, and lat. 152, folio 30. The latter MS. is of the year 822.

[2] S. Berger, *Quam notitiam linguae hebraicae habuerint Christiani medii aevi temporibus in Gallia*, Paris, 1893.

Description of Fig 47.

HEBREW AND SAMARITAN ALPHABETS IN EARLY LATIN MANUSCRIPTS

The Semitic alphabets in early Western Latin manuscripts fall into two groups. One group, of which examples are shown in columns 4 and 5, exhibits affinities with the Palmyrene Hebrew script. The author believes that the resemblance of columns 4 and 5 to Palmyrene is due to St. Ambrose of Treves (*c.* 340–397), Bishop of Milan. St. Ambrose wrote a commentary on the alphabetical Psalm 119 (the 118th psalm of the Vulgate). There is evidence that the early manuscripts of this commentary contained a Palmyrene Hebrew alphabet. The other group, of which examples are shown in columns 7 and 8, exhibits affinities with the Samaritan script. For the Samaritan affinities of columns 7 and 8 it is difficult to make any reasonable suggestion. The list of these Samaritan alphabets in Latin manuscripts might be largely increased. It is not improbable that they all derive from an early manuscript of the *De inventione linguarum* of Rabanus Maurus (776–856), abbot of Fulda, who was in contact with a learned Jew (p. 288). Even if these alphabets were thus traced, it will not, however, explain their Samaritan character.

Column 3 is from a Palmyrene inscription of about 300 A.D. (M. Lidzbarski *Handbuch der nordsemitischen Epigraphik*, Weimar, 1898).

Column 4 is from a Latin manuscript in a French hand of the ninth century (Bibliothèque nationale, Lat. 152).

Column 5 is from a Latin manuscript in an Anglo-Saxon hand of about the year 1000 A.D. (Exeter Cathedral Library, MS. 3507).

Column 6 is mainly from a Samaritan Pentateuch written in the year 1219 (Oriental Series XXVIII of the Palaeographical Society). The letters *He, Waw, Zayin, Heth, Teth, Nun, Samekh, Sin,* and *Taw* are, however, taken from the alphabet used by J. H. Petermann (in his *Brevis linguae Samaritanae ... Chrestomathia*, Berlin, 1873).

Column 7 is from a Latin manuscript in a French hand of the year 822 A.D. (Bibliothèque nationale, Lat. 11505).

Column 8 is another alphabet from the same manuscript as Column 4.

1	2	3	4	5	6	7	8
	Square Hebrew Letters	Palmyra c.300 A.D.	French IX.th Cent.	English c.1000 A.D.	Samaritan	French 822 A.D.	French IX.th Cent.
'Alĕph	א						
Bêth	ב						
Gimĕl	ג						
Dālĕth	ד						
Hē	ה						
Wāw	ו						
Záyĭn	ז						
Ḥêth	ח						
Têth	ט						
Yôd	י						
Kaph	כ						
Lāmĕd	ל						
Mêm	מ						
Nûn	נ						
Sāmĕkh	ס						
'Ayĭn	ע						
Pê	פ						
Ṣādê	צ						
Qôf	ק						
Rêš	ר						
Śîn	ש						
Tāw	ת						

FIG. 47. For description see page opposite.

combining initial letters into symbolic words (see note p. 283). His astrological system is largely based on the numerical values of the letters of the Hebrew alphabet. These numerical values were of constant interest to Cabalistic Hebrew writers, and it is evident that he has some acquaintance with the Hebrew language.[1]

§ 3. *The Twelfth Century*

From the eleventh century the line of Jewish contact with the Latin West becomes more continuous. In the later eleventh and early twelfth centuries we get definite news of Jewish aid effectively invoked for the study of the Scriptures. In fact attempts at revision of the Vulgate were undertaken very early,[2] whereas the New Testament had to wait for Erasmus. The first scholar of whom we have a record in this connexion is the Englishman, Stephen Harding.

STEPHEN HARDING (*c.* 1060–1134), second abbot of Citeaux, and the real founder of the Cistercian order, wrote a copy of the Bible for the use of his monks. He revised the Latin text with the help of some Jews who told him of the meanings of Hebrew words. The original manuscript seems to have existed as late as the end of the eighteenth century. It cannot now be found, but there still exists a copy made by one of his monks in 1109.[3] In it we read that 'I, Abbot Stephen, perceiving variations in the text in our books, visited certain Jews who were expert in their scripture, and I questioned them in the

---

[1] The MS. is at the Bibliothèque nationale at Paris, Lat. 17868. Some description of it has been given by F. Cumont in the *Revue archéologique* for 1916. The above account is drawn from the author's own examination of the MS.

[2] The so-called 'First Bible of Alcala' (Madrid, Bibl. Univ. MS. 31) is a Vulgate version written at Toledo in the ninth century. It contains Hebrew and Arabic marginal notes. These were not written by a professing Jew since they are violently anti-Jewish. Unfortunately these notes have not been dated.

[3] The manuscript is in the Public Library at Dijon, MS. 9, folio 150 verso.

vernacular (*lingua romana*) concerning all those passages in Scripture'. He goes on to say that 'in my presence these Jews turned to their numerous books, and, as I asked them, so they expounded to me in the vernacular the Hebrew or Chaldaean (i. e. Aramaic) readings'.

It is evident that Stephen was in a *Yeshiba* or Rabbinical College, of which many are known to have existed in Eastern France at this time. The great Jewish exegete Rashi (1040–1105, see pp. 283–285) was Stephen's contemporary. A Jewish meeting-house, erected in 1034 on much more ancient foundations, still stands almost intact at Worms, where for a time Rashi resided.[1] By means of that building we can picture the scene (Fig. 48, p. 294 and Fig. 53, p. 314). The senses and readings that Stephen had expounded to him in the *Yeshiba* are to be found, he says, in few or no Latin books, and it is on that account that he sets them down. To give one instance. He refers to Job ii. 10, and says that, 'In certain Latin texts there here stands *as one of the foolish women*, but in the Hebrew the word *women* is not there'. This is correct. The Vulgate and both Authorized and Revised versions read *women*, but this word does not occur, though it is clearly implied, in the Hebrew. In a number of other cases he was able to detect passages that had found their way without authority into some of the Latin codices.

Another early medieval scholar who dipped into Hebrew was known as NICHOLAS OF MANJACORIA. His date is not certain, and no such place as Manjacoria is known. We may, however, hazard a guess that he was French and lived towards the end of the twelfth century, at the town of Luynes near Tours.[2] The method of Nicholas of Manjacoria was much like that of Stephen Harding. He certainly had Jewish help, he refers to Jewish traditions, and he had access to the writings of Rashi, which he

---

[1] The so-called 'Rashi chapel' at Worms is, however, of much later date.
[2] Until the seventeenth century the town of Luynes was known as Maillé and is spoken of in the Latin documents as *Manjacorilla*.

used for the purpose of biblical interpretation. He says, in a letter that has survived, that he had access to a library of Hebrew books, and that he was thus able to correct the Vulgate text of the Bible by reference to the Hebrew original.[1]

We know of several other twelfth-century Christian workers who applied thus to Rabbis for information on the interpretation of scriptural passages. Sometimes these workers prepared Hebrew glossaries. In these the Hebrew was written in Latin letters, thus differing from those of Jewish origin. Several of these Latin-Hebrew glossaries of the twelfth century have survived.[2]

Besides the study of the Bible there was another motive that led Christian writers of the Middle Ages to the study of Hebrew. It was the conversion or refutation of the Jews. This motive became far more potent in the following century. Even in the twelfth century, however, a beginning was made, and we hear, for instance, of Peter the Venerable (*c.* 1092–1156), Abbot of Cluny, making an investigation of the Talmud with the aid of Jewish converts.[3]

§ 4. *Disputations between Jews and Christians in the Thirteenth Century*

The advent into France of the writings of Maimonides in the early years of the thirteenth century, caused a rift in Jewish circles. The orthodox party opposed the philosophizing tendency of the great Jewish thinker in much the way in which, among Christians, the entry of the Aristotelian writings was resisted (p. 250). The aid of the Friars was invoked. In 1233 the papal legate at Montpellier caused works of Maimonides and his school to be burned, and the example was too good to be lost.

In or about 1235 NICHOLAS DONIN, a native of La Rochelle, was converted from Judaism to Christianity and later became

[1] On Nicholas of Manjacoria see Berger, *loc. cit.*, p. 12.
[2] e. g. at Avranches and Tours. See Berger, *loc. cit.*, p. 17.
[3] Migne, *Patrologia Latina*, vol. clxxxix, col. 602 *et seq*.

FIG. 48. SYNAGOGUE AT WORMS. BUILT 1034
(See p. 293 and Fig. 53, p. 314)

Further details are given on p. xxvi

a Franciscan. Donin drew the attention of Pope Gregory IX to various passages in the Talmud and other Hebrew works which, he alleged, contained passages contemptuous of Christianity. The Pope ordered that on a certain Saturday, when the Jews would be in their synagogues, all their books were to be seized and held for investigation by the Friars. The event gave rise to a public debate between Jews and Christians. This disputation was the first of its kind and took place at Paris in 1240 before Louis IX and his court. The Friars depended for their interpretation of Hebrew passages chiefly on Nicholas Donin and on one Therebald, Sub-prior of Paris, who was also a converted Jew. Therebald prepared translations of passages for his colleagues. Albertus Magnus (pp. 259 ff.) and William of Auvergne (pp. 257–258) were present. The disputation resulted in a vast bonfire of Hebrew books. The entertainment became popular—at least with Christian disputants—and the experiment was frequently repeated in many parts of Europe. Little can be gained by recording the history or the details of this sordid practice which has resulted in incalculable losses to learning and is responsible for the great rarity of early Hebrew manuscripts. The disputations did, however, diffuse a certain knowledge of Hebrew among Christians.[1] We shall refer to only one other public disputation.

The philosophical views of Maimonides which, as we have seen, created much opposition among the Jews of France, found their ablest opponent in Spain in Moses ben Nahman Gerondi (i.e. *of Gerona*, a town near Barcelona), who is known more usually as NACHMANIDES (1194–*c*. 1270). This learned Talmudist was the recognized religious leader of the Jews of Catalonia who, by their geographical position and community of dialect,

[1] The subject of religious disputations between Jews and Christians is reviewed by I. Loeb, *La controverse religieuse entre les Chrétiens et les Juifs au Moyen Âge*, Paris, 1888, and I. Ziegler, *Religiöse Disputationen im Mittelalter*, Frankfurt, 1894.

were in close touch with their brethren in Provence. Circumstances brought Nachmanides into relation with a Dominican named Paul who was a converted Jew.

It happened that the Provincial of the Dominican Order, Raymond of Pennaforte,[1] took interest both in Hebrew studies and in Hebrew souls. He sent Paul on a missionary expedition to the Jewish congregations of Provence. Paul returned in 1263. At the instance of Raymond, King James of Aragon ordered a public disputation between Paul and Nachmanides. This was the first of many performances of the kind in Spain and was held in the presence of King, Court, and Ecclesiastical dignitaries who evidently greatly enjoyed it. It lasted four days; its echoes reverberated for centuries. Freedom of speech was demanded and granted. The condition was loyally observed—for the four days. The suppression of opinion that followed this disputation affected a score of unborn generations that never heard of it.

The subjects for discussion were of a simple if comprehensive character. It was debated (a) whether the Messiah had or had not already appeared; (b) whether the Old Testament prophecies predicted a Messiah of divine or human birth. Needless to say both sides claimed the victory, nor will it be unexpected by the reader that one side only suffered the penalties of defeat. It would not be useful to narrate the details of the discussion. The Latin protocol is available,[2] and the account by Nachmanides himself has been translated under the elegant title of *The Devil's Fiery Darts*.[3]

[1] Raymond of Pennaforte is not to be confused with the contemporary Catalan Dominican Hebrew scholar Raymund Martin who is discussed on p. 305, and with the contemporary Catalan Franciscan Raymond Lull who is discussed on pp. 274–275.

[2] The Latin protocol 'Instrumentum disputationis de fide cum quodam Rabbi Moyse' is edited by H. Denifle in the *Historisches Jahrbuch des Goeres-Gesellschaft*, Munich, 1887, viii, p. 231.

[3] Johan Christopher Wagenseil, *Tela ignea Satanae*, Altdorf, 1681.

The modern reader of the debate will probably regard it as inconclusive. Nachmanides lived to form the opposite opinion. Certain passages in his account were represented as blasphemous and he was arraigned on a capital charge. The King, who had evidently now acquired a taste for public disputation, ordered this trial also to take place in his presence. It does not astonish the judicious historian, nor did it surprise Nachmanides, that he should be found guilty. It is, however, evidence of the entrancing nature of this form of diversion that the punishment of so good a performer was commuted to banishment and fine.[1]

This victory of the Dominicans was ably followed up. They secured the right to examine and censor Hebrew books. More drastic measures by Royal or Papal decree followed in 1267, 1286, and 1299. By the fourteenth century the Inquisition was contributing efficiently to the establishment of faith and to the disestablishment of learning and of freedom.

§ 5. *Hebrew Learning among the Latins in the Early Thirteenth Century*

In the thirteenth century arose a small school of Christian writers who may be looked on as actual Hebrew scholars. Early in the century some converted Jew, probably of French origin, prepared a literal Latin translation of the whole Hebrew Bible, direct from the original. The name and all the circumstances of this man are unknown, nor have we the original draft of the work. We have however substantial fragments of a copy made by an English scribe or scribes, during the second half of the thirteenth century. The text is in Hebrew script. Each Hebrew word has its literal Latin translation written above. The Vulgate version is written at the side. Nicholas Donin taught at Paris and had a good knowledge of Rabbinic Hebrew. His name naturally comes to mind in this connexion, but there

[1] An account of the disputation between Paul and Nachmanides is given by A. Lukyn Williams, *Church Quarterly Review*, cii, p. 68, London, 1926.

is nothing known at present to connect him with the preparation of this translation. The absence of all information as to the author of the work is to be the more regretted as the chain of thirteenth-century Hebrew scholars seems to descend directly from him.

One of the early links in the chain of thirteenth-century Hebrew scholarship was the great bishop of Lincoln, the Franciscan, ROBERT GROSSETESTE (1175–1253, p. 259), the teacher of Roger Bacon. Grosseteste is especially remembered for having introduced the study of Greek at Oxford. As with many later scholars his motive in learning Hebrew was in large part the conversion of the Jews. We know that he possessed a copy of the mysterious literal translation discussed in the paragraph above.[1] The existence, in excellent preservation, of the 'Jew's House' at Lincoln (Fig. 49), the oldest stone house in the country and one of the best surviving specimens of medieval English domestic architecture, is a reminder of the relations of this great and humane scholar with the Jewish inhabitants of his diocese.

Another scholar of the time was one Odo, an Englishman, of whom we know nothing, save what is contained in a single manuscript, an *Introduction to Theology*.[2] This work contains the Ten Commandments in pointed Hebrew with Latin translation. A number of Messianic scriptural passages are similarly treated in it.

[1] Nearly all the information available concerning the English Hebraists is to be found in the works of S. Hirsch, *The Greek Grammar of Roger Bacon and a fragment of his Hebrew Grammar* (with E. Nolan), Cambridge, 1902; *A Book of Essays*, London, 1905; *Transactions of the Jewish Historical Society of England*, vii, London, 1915; and a separate article in A. G. Little's *Roger Bacon, Commemorative Essays*, Oxford, 1914.

[2] The manuscript in question is in Trinity College, Cambridge, and has been described by S. Hirsch, *Transactions of the Jewish Historical Society of England*, vii, p. 9, London, 1915.

FIG. 49. THE 'JEW'S HOUSE', LINCOLN. XIITH CENTURY
The oldest stone house in England
For further description see p. xxvi

§ 6. *Roger Bacon*

By far the best known of Grosseteste's pupils was the Franciscan, ROGER BACON (1213?–1294? Fig. 46, opp. p. 282). In numerous passages in his writings Roger urges the needs of proper linguistic study, laying especial stress on Greek, Hebrew, Arabic, and 'Chaldaean'. These four languages are important, he thinks, because all significant texts, whether in theology, philosophy, or science, are written in them. Hebrew and Greek are also necessary because words derived from them are of value in interpreting liturgical and religious terms. All four languages may be of use in diplomacy and trade. In the case of Greek and Arabic there are certainly great difficulties, for Greeks and Saracens are hard to come by. In the case of Hebrew and Chaldaean (that is Aramaic), however, these difficulties should be easily overcome, he thinks, for 'Jews are to be found everywhere'. Only when Hebrew was properly learned could the errors which overrun the Vulgate text be removed.

But the main motive for learning the Hebrew language is for Roger a spiritual one. He makes an impassioned protest against force on the part of Christians in dealing with unbelievers.

'In the hands of the Latins', says Roger, 'resides the power of converting. And so among us infinite numbers of Jews perish because no one knows how to preach to them or to interpret the Scriptures in their language, nor argue and dispute with them according to the literal meaning. . . . What unspeakable loss of souls, though it would be easy for countless Jews to be converted. And it is still worse because from them began the foundation of our faith and we ought to consider that they are of the seed of the patriarchs, and prophets, and, what is more, from their stem the Lord was born, and the glorious Virgin, and apostles, and saints innumerable have descended.'[1]

---

[1] *Opus Majus*, iii, § 13. Translation by A. G. Little, *Studies in English Franciscan History*, Manchester, 1917, p. 210.

Roger was firmly convinced that Hebrew was the language in which God had revealed to mankind His will, and His wisdom.

'God has revealed philosophy to His saints to whom also he gave the Law. He did so because philosophy was indispensable for the understanding, the promulgation, the adoption and the defence of the Law. It was for this reason that it was delivered in all its details in the Hebrew language . . . to the patriarchs and the prophets. They possessed wisdom in its entirety before the infidel sages obtained it. . . . All their information about heavenly bodies, about the secrets of nature and the superior sciences, about religions, God, Christianity, the beauties of virtue . . . were derived from God's saints. . . . Adam, Solomon, and the others testified to the truth of the faith not only in Holy Writ, but also in books of philosophy long before there were any philosophers so-called.'[1]

The attitude of Roger Bacon in regarding the Hebrews as the first philosophers seems extraordinary to us. Yet it was the general view of his time, nor was he wholly without ancient authority for this fantastic view. The Jew Aristobulus, who perhaps worked in Alexandria about 150 B.C., is said to have written that Moses was the father of Greek philosophy, and that Pythagoras, Socrates, and Plato were indebted to him! These statements are preserved by Eusebius (c. 260–340).[2] Aristotle himself, according to the medieval account, was no less indebted to Hebrew forbears. There are versions of the medieval Aristotle legend that would even have us believe that Aristotle was born a Jew or became a proselyte to Judaism!

No wonder that with thoughts such as these in his mind Roger Bacon was not deterred from seeking to learn a difficult

---

[1] *Opus tertium*, x, p. 32, and xxiv, p. 79, slightly modified from translation by S. Hirsch in A. G. Little, *Roger Bacon Commemorative Essays*, Oxford, 1914, p. 137.

[2] Eusebius, *Praeparatio evangelica*, xiii. On Aristobulus, see E. Schürer, *History of the Jewish People in the Time of Jesus Christ*, English translation, 5 vols., London, 1890, iii, p. 239; and W. Christ, *Geschichte der griechischen Litteratur*, Munich, 1890.

and obscure language. Of Roger's own efforts we have some indication in the fragment of his Hebrew grammar that has survived and in several manuscripts of certain of his other works (Figs. 50 and 51 overleaf). His views are characteristic of the Franciscan school, and when in a thirteenth- or fourteenth-century manuscript we find any evidence of Hebrew knowledge we may suspect a Franciscan origin.

The idea that hidden away in the library of Hebrew books is to be found the source of all philosophy, science, and learning, and notably that of Aristotle and the Greeks, persisted long after Bacon and far beyond the limits of the Middle Ages. It was quite seriously held throughout the fifteenth, sixteenth, and seventeenth centuries and only died out even among the learned in the eighteenth century. A legend arose that such a collection of books was still in existence in the East, perhaps on Mount Ararat! The story is recounted, for instance, in the *Two Bookes of Epigrammes* of the English poet Thomas Bancroft, published in 1639, and otherwise interesting as containing references to Shakespeare by a younger contemporary. Bancroft wrote:

> On this faire Mountaine, spherical & high
> Stands, as fame goes, *a precious Library*
> *Where Livy's whole work, Enoch's Oracles,*
> *Salomon's Physicks, and some mysteries else*
> *That did survive the Flood*, entreasur'd lye
> Insulting o're Time's wasteful tyranny.
> O could I thither reach! Then should I stand
> High in the Muses' grace, and all command.

§ 7. *The School of Roger Bacon and the Later Thirteenth Century*

An acquaintance with Hebrew sometimes shows itself in medieval lists of biblical corrections, the so-called *Correctoria*.[1] Among these documents is one of importance by Roger's contemporary, the Franciscan WILLIAM DE MARA (*fl. c.* 1282).

[1] H. Denifle, 'Die Handschriften der Bibel-Correctorien des 13 Jahrhunderts,' in the *Archiv für Litteratur und Kirchengeschichte*, 1888, iv, pp. 263 and 471.

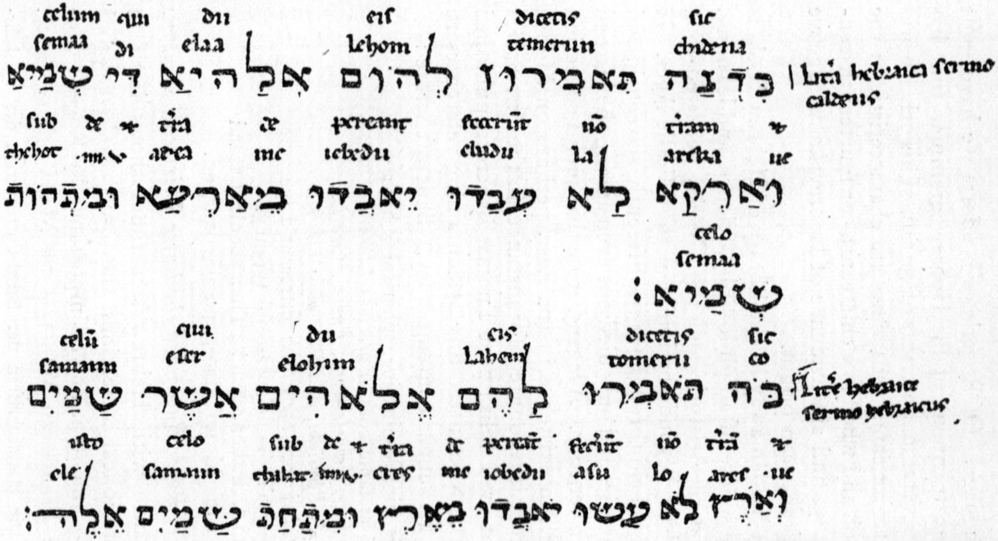

FIG. 50. From a manuscript at the Vatican, written about 1300, of the *Opus Majus* of Roger Bacon. It shows a passage in Aramaic and in Hebrew with transliteration and Latin translation. The lines transcribed are Jeremiah x. 11, 'Thus shall ye say unto them, The gods that have not made the heavens and the earth these shall perish from under the earth and under the heavens'. The Vulgate renders it, 'Sic ergo dicetis eis: Dii qui coelos et terram non fecerunt pereant de terra et de his quae sub coelo sunt'. This verse in the original text is written not in Hebrew but in Aramaic. It is a gloss which is out of place between verses 10 and 12. As the Targum indicates, it was designed to furnish the Jews with an answer to those who urged them to participate in idolatry.

celum semaa	qui di	dii elaa		peream iebedu	eis lehom	dicetis temerun	sic chidena	
אֲשְׁמַיָּא	דִּי	אֱלָהַיָּא		יֵאבַדוּ	לְהוֹם	תֵּאמְרוּן	כִּדְנָה	Litera hebraica sermo caldeus
sub de et thehot mi u		terra de area me		peream iebedu	fecerunt ebadu	non la	terram et areka ve	
מִתְּחוֹת		מֵאַרְעָא		יֵאבַדוּ	עֲבַדוּ	לָא	וְאַרְקָא	
							celo semaa	
							אֲשְׁמַיָּא	
celum samaim	qui eser	dii elohim	terra de eres me		eis lahem	fecerunt asu	sic co	
שָׁמַיִם	אֲשֶׁר	אֱלֹהִים	אֶרֶץ		לָהֶם	עָשׂוּ	כֹּה	Litere hebraice sermo hebraicus
isto ele	celo semaim		terra de eres me	pereant iobedu		non lo	terra et ares ue	
אֵלֶּה	שָׁמַיִם		אֶרֶץ	יֹאבֵדוּ		לֹא	וְאָרֶץ	

Fig. 51. Exact transliteration into modern type of the lines in Latin, Aramaic, and Hebrew of the Vatican manuscript of the *Opus Majus* of Roger Bacon. The fact that the Hebrew script is written from right to left and the Latin from left to right makes a special difficulty in word for word translation and especially in the matter of the Hebrew and Aramaic prefixes and suffixes. Above the scribe has given the Aramaic as it appears in the Biblical text. Below he has translated it into Hebrew. Both Hebrew and Aramaic versions contain a number of errors which we have preserved in our transliteration.

In this William some have seen Roger's Hebrew instructor. He was certainly his correspondent.

There was at least one other important Hebrew scholar associated with the Baconian movement. Among the most interesting of the documents of the later thirteenth century that exhibit Hebrew scholarship is a collection at Toulouse of Latin correspondence in which various questioners ask for information on a variety of Hebrew topics and are answered by a respondent. The questioners seem to have been without effective Hebrew knowledge but were occupied as lecturers who read single books of the Bible to their pupils. The respondent in these letters, however, was something of a Rabbinic scholar and particularly acquainted with the works of Rashi. He knew French perfectly and he had lectured probably at Paris. He had had Hebrew books sent to him by a learned Jew in Germany, who knew him by reputation, and with whom he carried on a regular correspondence in the Hebrew language. He had long sought these books and had written for them in vain to a Jew in Toledo.

We have some evidence as to what these Hebrew books were. They were mathematical or rather calendarial works. One was by Abraham ben Hiyya, known as Savasorda (*c.* 1116, p. 214), who not only helped Plato of Tivoli but himself wrote in Hebrew as well as in Spanish.[1] Another was a Hebrew translation of a work by Maimonides.

It has been thought that the authoritative Christian Hebraist who conducted the Toulouse correspondence could be identified with William of Mara. This now seems to be impossible but, whoever he may have been, it is most remarkable that his letters have actually been used by a modern scholar for the correction of the Hebrew text of Rashi! Such use of the writing of a medieval Christian Hebraist for the correction of the text of a Rabbinic author is a unique event, and in itself speaks highly

[1] Steinschneider in *Bibliotheca mathematica*, New Series, x, p. 34, Stockholm, 1896.

for the learning and accuracy of this unknown letter-writer, who was the most learned Hebrew scholar of the Middle Ages.[1]

Among the very few Spanish Christians of the thirteenth century who showed capacity in the study of Hebrew was the Dominican RAYMUND MARTIN, who was a Catalan by birth and died some time after 1284. In 1250 he was selected to study Oriental languages at a Dominican college, specially founded for the training of missionaries among Jews and Muslims. He lived long at Barcelona, and in 1264 he was commissioned with certain other Dominicans to examine Hebrew manuscripts so that they might delete passages regarded as offensive to Christianity. They took the Talmud especially in hand. In his *Pugio fidei* Martin tells us that many passages in the Talmud he found, in fact, to be confirmatory of Christianity. His works, which were long used as a source for Dominican polemics, show him to have been a good Hebrew scholar and well read in Rabbinic writings. The *Pugio fidei* cites the convert from Judaism of the previous century, Petrus Alfonsi, who is known for his book of anecdotes, his mathematical works, and his travels in England (pp. 208–209).

The policy that Roger Bacon had initiated in the thirteenth century bore but little fruit, or rather we should perhaps say that the ripening of the fruit was delayed till the Renaissance. Towards the end of the thirteenth and at the beginning of the fourteenth century, several Popes made attempts to get Hebrew chairs established at the more important universities, such as Oxford, Paris, Salamanca, and Bologna. These schemes were, however, a failure. Despite the efforts of their best minds, such as St. Thomas and Albert, the medieval universities were far too absorbed in philosophical discussion to take heed of philology and thus secure the bases on which their discussions

[1] S. Hirsch, *Transactions of the Jewish Historical Society of England*, vii, p. 16, London, 1915; and H. H. E. Craster in *Bodleian Quarterly Record*, iii, p. 68, Oxford, 1920.

could be conducted. It is this neglect of philology which proved in the end one of the causes of the downfall of Scholasticism. How could men discuss Aristotle, St. Paul, or the prophets unless they knew what they had really written?

At the beginning of the fourteenth century a converted Jew was lecturing on Hebrew and Aramaic at Paris, but on the whole the study languished. At Oxford the efforts of the Popes towards founding a Hebrew chair seem to have met with even less response. A tax of a farthing in the pound on ecclesiastical goods was imposed in the province of Canterbury in 1320 'for the stipend of the convert teaching the Hebrew tongue at Oxford', and in 1325 a contribution of $17\frac{1}{2}d$. was received from the Abbot of Westminster out of the revenues of one of his churches 'for the expenses of the masters lecturing in the Hebrew, Arabic, and Chaldean languages at the University'. No later references have been found. The Universities afforded the most meagre soil for such studies.[1]

§ 8. *Nicholas of Lyra and Paul of Burgos*

Despite the failure of the Universities there were other sources of Hebrew learning. At the end of the thirteenth and the beginning of the fourteenth century, there was considerable intercourse between Christian and Jewish scholars, particularly in Southern France. Concrete results of this were the works of Armengaud of Montpellier and Arnald of Villanova (see pp. 234–235). These Christian scholars both worked on medical and scientific texts. Both of them, together with the Majorcan, Ramond Lull, have been considered elsewhere (pp. 274–275). It is very difficult to estimate their knowledge of Hebrew, but it is fairly certain that they always worked with Jewish aid.

A younger contemporary of Lull, Armengaud, and Arnald was the scholar, NICHOLAS OF LYRA (Fig. 45, opp. p. 282). He

---

[1] See A. G. Little, *Studies in Early Franciscan History*, Manchester, 1917, from whom the previous passage is taken.

Nicholas of Lyra

was born in 1279, at Lyre near Evreux in Normandy and, according to a late and unreliable tradition, was of Jewish descent. He early gave himself to Hebrew studies, and must certainly have received competent Rabbinic aid. In 1291 he entered the Franciscan order. He studied at Paris and taught at the Sorbonne till 1325, when he was appointed Provincial of his Order for Burgundy. He died in 1340.

The most influential work of Nicholas of Lyra was on Biblical exegesis, and he lays great stress on the exact literal sense. For this purpose he constantly refers to the Hebrew text itself. In interpretation he depends on Rabbinic sources, and especially on Rashi, whom he sometimes translates almost word for word. By his critics he has been called the 'ape of Rashi'. Lyra's works, however, were much read and appreciated in the later Middle Ages, and were seven times printed, on the first occasion at Rome in 1471, and on the last at Paris in 1660.

Nicholas of Lyra is extremely important as one of the links between the Middle Ages and the Reformation. His system of Biblical interpretation had long been taught at the university of Erfurt, when Martin Luther (1483–1546) entered his name as a student in the year 1501. The foundation of Luther's knowledge of Hebrew was thus laid by Nicholas whom he calls 'a fine soul; a good Hebraist and true Christian'.[1] There is no doubt that Luther depended on Lyra and the well-known jingle may have an element of truth:

> Si Lyra non lyrasset,
> Luther non saltasset.
>
> If Lyra had not piped,
> Luther had not danced.

A contemporary Franciscan in England who exhibited some knowledge of Hebrew was Henry of Costessy who was Master of the Friars at Cambridge about 1330. In 1336 he wrote an

[1] Martin Luther, *Von den letzten Worten Davids*, ed. Erlangen, xxxvii, p. 4.

exposition of the Psalms in which he quotes a number of Rabbinic authorities, among them the Talmud, Rashi, and the *Guide for the perplexed* of Maimonides. He refers to and controverts the opinions of Nicholas of Lyra, and adds a note on Hebrew orthography. It is not easy to say how Henry of Costessy obtained his knowledge of the authors that he names, but it is fairly evident that his knowledge of Hebrew was but slight.

In the second half of the fourteenth century a trilingual Bible in Hebrew, Greek, and Latin was prepared by an Oriental Roman Catholic, Simon Atumano.[1] His work was, however, without perceptible influence.

PAUL OF BURGOS (1351–1435) was the only effective medieval successor in Hebrew scholarship to Nicholas of Lyra among Latin Christian writers. Paul was born of a good Jewish family and had a sound Rabbinical training. He travelled and visited London. A letter of his, written at the time, shows that he was then in close contact with Jewish friends and a keen observer of Jewish ritual.[2] Paul was converted to Christianity in 1391, convinced by the works of St. Thomas Aquinas. His brothers and children were baptized with him, but not his wife who died as a Jewess. Paul studied in Paris and took a degree in theology. He became archdeacon of Trevino and later Bishop of Cartagena, and tutor to the son of King Henry of Castille. He afterwards became a member of the regency of Castille and Archbishop of Burgos. In the latter office he was succeeded by his son.

Soon after his conversion Paul wrote *additiones* to the Biblical Commentary of Nicholas of Lyra. They betray a good deal of scholarship and have often been printed, but do not add substantially to the work of Nicholas. Paul wrote also violent works directed against the Jews or designed for their conversion. One of them, the *Scrutinium Scripturae*, written when he was

---

[1] See article by Professor Burkitt, p. 93.

[2] I. Abrahams, 'Paul of Burgos in London', *Transactions of the Jewish Historical Society*, ii p. 149, London, 1896.

more than eighty years of age, shows much Hebrew learning. It was printed at Rome in 1470, being one of the first works of the sort to issue from the press.

§ 9. *Medieval Translations of the Old Testament from the Hebrew*

We have already discussed the mysterious literal Latin translation of the Old Testament made from the Hebrew of which a copy was in the possession of Grosseteste (p. 298). But Latin was not the only language used for the purpose. Particularly interesting examples of Hebrew scholarship among Christians in the Middle Ages are the attempts to render the Bible into Castillian. Though most of these translations were made from the Latin, a certain number go back to the Hebrew. Of these the most ancient is a version of the Psalter ascribed to Herman the German, the teacher of Bacon. It must have been undertaken between about 1240 and 1256. The manuscript of the work tells us that it is ' according to that which is in the Hebrew '. This does not mean a translation direct from the Hebrew but a translation from the Latin of the so-called ' Hebrew version ' of St. Jerome. Nevertheless, Herman does, in fact, several times correct the Latin by an appeal to the actual Hebrew text.[1] In the following centuries, as we shall see, there were several more complete Castillian attempts to render the Old Testament direct from the original tongue.

During the thirteenth, fourteenth, and fifteenth centuries there were efforts to translate the Bible into various European languages. Those in English, French, and German were made without reference to the Hebrew original.[2] Spanish, and to a

[1] See S. Berger, *Romania*, xxviii, p. 389, Paris, 1889.

[2] The most convenient work to consult on the French translations of the Bible is S. Berger, *La Bible française au moyen âge*, Paris, 1884; on the Italian: J. Carini, *Le versioni della Bibbia in volgare Italiano*, 1890: on

less extent Italian, is in a different position. We have glanced at the appeal by Herman the German to the Hebrew text of the Psalter (p. 309). In the fourteenth and fifteenth centuries real attempts were made to translate the Old Testament as a whole direct from the Hebrew into Castillian.

Several manuscripts of these versions have survived.[1] One of them, of the fifteenth century, at the Library of the Escorial, is illustrated by pictures, which some have thought the work of a Jewish artist. It contains the entire Old Testament. It is obviously of Jewish origin, for many parts of it are divided in the way adopted in the Jewish liturgy. Many of the personal names have their Hebrew form. There is much other evidence of Hebrew contact. In the case of the Psalms this work is nothing else than a revision, with further reference to the Hebrew, of the Castillian version of the thirteenth century by Herman.

Another manuscript containing a Castillian translation of the Bible is at Evora and was written in 1429. It is less complete than the Escorial manuscript discussed above, but is essentially the same version. This Castillian translation has a surprising subsequent history, for it, or a version derived from it, is still to some extent in use, though not in the land in which it was prepared. When the Jews were expelled from Spain at the end of the fifteenth century they took with them to the Eastern Mediterranean the language of the country of their birth. Spanish is still spoken by the Jews of Salonica, Constantinople, Smyrna, and other parts of the Near East. These people needed a Bible, and it was first printed for them in Ferrara in 1553. The Ferrara Bible is based on the old Castillian written in Hebrew characters. Many editions have since appeared, and a version of the Ferrara Bible is current in the East to this day.

the English: H. W. Hoare, *Evolution of the English Bible*, London, 1906; on the German: W. Walther, *Die deutsche Bibelübersetzung des Mittelalters*, 1889–92.

[1] S. Berger, *Romania*, xxviii, p. 408, Paris, 1899.

Medieval Old Testament Translations

The interest of the other Castillian versions, however, pales before the splendid *Bible of the House of Alba*. The translation, of which this manuscript is the record, was begun in 1422. It was prepared at the direction of Don Luis Guzman, Lord of Algaba and Grand Master of the Military Order of Calatrava, who wished to read the Bible in his native language. The translator was the Jew, MOSES ARRAGEL of Guardalfajara, one of Don Guzman's vassals. It goes direct to the Hebrew. The translator was aided or advised by certain Franciscans. The work of translation was completed in 1430, and was presented as a magnificently illuminated codex to Don Luis at Toledo. The volume still exists, and contains an account both of the transactions leading up to the preparation of the work and of the circumstances of its presentation.

The translation by Moses Arragel is based on the Latin of Jerome. Where Jerome differs from the Hebrew, Moses Arragel follows the Hebrew. When the text, as thus interpreted, comes in conflict, in the translator's opinion, with Christian doctrine, Moses Arragel says 'this is the opinion of the Christians, but the Jews hold the opposite view'. Don Luis, in his original directions to Moses Arragel had written, 'We wish to possess a Bible with glosses and comments'. These Arragel provided, not infrequently citing in them the views of Don Luis himself. In the comments Arragel quotes many Jewish authorities, among them the Talmud, Rashi, Ibn Ezra, Maimonides, and certain Kabbalistical writers. It is evident that he was well read in secular literature for he quotes Aristotle, Euclid, Ptolemy, and Pliny. The latter he must have read in Latin. Among Christian scholars he refers to Nicholas of Lyra and St. Bernard of Clairvaux. There is evidence that Arragel used the previous attempts in Castillian.

No less interesting than the text are the numerous miniatures. Some have a strong Jewish element. It has been suggested that for these Arragel himself gave directions. One reproduces the interior of a synagogue. In the frontispiece Arragel is shown presenting the manuscript to Don Luis. Arragel wears the Jewish badge, and by his side stand a Dominican and a Franciscan. In the same scene knights of the order of Calatrava are seen feeding hungry Jews and attending to others that are sick.

This interesting and valuable volume, a pleasing monument of toleration and mutual understanding between Jews and Christians (Fig. 52), passed into the hands of the Inquisition. In 1624 the then Grand Inquisitor gave it to the fifth Duke of Alba, in recognition of the services for the Faith that his father had rendered in the Dutch wars. It is still possessed by the family, and is now the property of the Duke of Berwick and Alba.[1]

The first Bible printed in Italian appeared at Venice in 1471. It was derived from the Vulgate, and was due to the Camaldulian monk Nicolo di Malermi. A revision of this, with notes, rubrics, and *résumés*, largely after Nicholas of Lyra, was made by the Dominican Marine de Veneto, and was printed at Venice in 1477.

§ 10. *The Transition in Hebrew Studies from the Middle Ages to the Renaissance*

In the fifteenth century began another revival of Hebrew studies among Christians. There are one or two Hebrew scholars of the time who really belong rather to the Renaissance than to the Middle Ages. Such was Gianozza Manetti (1396–1459). He learned both Greek and Hebrew from servants speaking those languages whom he kept in his house. He became secretary to Pope Nicholas V and made for him a special translation of the Psalms. He wrote polemical works against Judaism. The Pope had offered a large prize for the discovery

---

[1] *Biblia (antigua testamento) traducida del Hebreo al Castellano por Rabi Mose Arragel de Guadalfajara* (1422–33 ?). *Y publicada por el Duce de Berwick y de Alba*, 2 vols., 1920.

A PAGE FROM THE BIBLE OF THE HOUSE OF ALBA

FIG. 52. A MEDIEVAL DEMONSTRATION IN FAVOUR OF RELIGIOUS TOLERATION

Rabbi Moses Arragel presents his Spanish translation of the Bible to his liege lord, Don Luis de Guzman, Grand Master of the Order of Calatrava. Knights of the Order, each wearing his cross, stand on either side. In the background the knights feed (*comer*), give drink (*beuer*), shoe (*calcar*), clothe (*vestir*), visit the sick (*visitar*), comfort (*consolar*) and bury (*entercar*) Jews. A Dominican and a Franciscan contemplate the scene. See pp. 311 and 312.

Transition to the Renaissance

of the original Hebrew of the text of St. Matthew. In his search for this he collected many Hebrew manuscripts which are now at the Vatican.[1]

Thus Hebrew was brought into the service of the Church. In the later fifteenth century a Camaldulian monk, Ambrogio Traversari, also learnt it, and Pope Sixtus IV, who built the Sistine chapel of the Vatican and became the second founder of the Vatican library by many purchases, found also funds for Latin, Greek, and Hebrew *scriptores*. These offices still exist. The study of the Hebrew language by Christians became now less rare. Hebrew manuscripts were collected in many libraries. The printing of Hebrew books began in Italy in 1475, and made the language more accessible. A chair of Hebrew was founded at Bologna in 1488 and one was established at Rome in 1514.

Among all those who busied themselves with Hebrew in the fifteenth century the most remarkable was Pico della Mirandola (Fig. 55, opp. p. 320). But the new interest in Hebrew studies is part of the general revival of learning that itself forms part of the movement known as the *Renaissance*. The story of that great movement is outside the scope of this chapter.

Looking back on the history of the knowledge of Hebrew in the Middle Ages, one is struck by its excessive rarity. During that period languages were never acquired save by the spoken word,—hence the rarity of linguistic accomplishment of a scholarly character. Despite the obvious importance of ascertaining the exact meaning of the words of Scripture, only four Latin Christians in the Middle Ages have left records which show that they attained to anything that can be called real Hebrew scholarship. These were (*a*) the unknown translator of the thirteenth-century Bible of Robert Grosseteste; (*b*) the unknown correspondent of the Toulouse manuscript; (*c*) Nicholas

[1] On Manetti see many references in J. Burckhardt, *Die Kultur der Renaissance in Italien*, 12th edition, 2 vols., Leipzig, 1919.

of Lyra; (*d*) Paul of Burgos. Of these (*d*) certainly and (*a*) probably were converted Jews. Thus Nicholas of Lyra and the Toulouse writer remain as almost the sole repository of Hebrew learning among the Latins in all those hundreds of years. We reflect on the relative accessibility of philological as distinct from other forms of scientific knowledge. No better illustration could be given of the extreme incompetence of the Middle Ages where scientific method was demanded than this utter helplessness in a matter of straightforward scholarship.

CHARLES SINGER.

FIG. 53. Interior of Synagogue at Worms, built 1034: see description of Fig. 48, p. xxvi.

Fig. 54. ERASMUS BY HOLBEIN

See also p. xxvii

HEBREW STUDIES IN THE REFORMATION PERIOD AND AFTER: THEIR PLACE AND INFLUENCE

§ 1. *Introduction*

THE revival of Hebrew studies, which is so striking a feature of the fifteenth and sixteenth centuries, and the influence of which has remained as an important element in sacred learning and, to some extent, in the humanities ever since, was one of the results of that mighty quickening of the human spirit that goes under the name of the Renaissance. Whatever else the Renaissance meant, it was accompanied by a vast enrichment of human life on the cultural side; new interests and new institutions were created—manuscripts were collected and copied and libraries founded; new universities were established and new studies, especially of Greek, inaugurated. This expansion of culture was vastly increased by the invention of printing. But, perhaps, the most significant result was the emergence of a new view of the universe—of man and of nature—which was inspired by the Greek spirit, which sought to rationalize everything in an atmosphere of truth and reality, which abhorred the *a priori* method and sought rather to base results on a careful survey and co-ordination of facts and relevant phenomena; in a word, which adopted what we should now call the method of science and induction.

Hebrew studies had not been wholly neglected in the earlier period. The names of Roger Bacon and Nicholas de Lyra will occur to the reader in this connexion.[1] But the study of Hebrew had certainly not become, in the earlier period, a recognized part of general culture. This place was only secured to Hebrew study by the advent of the 'new learning', which was

[1] The matter is fully discussed in Dr. Singer's Essay (pp. 283–314).

one of the early results of the Renaissance-spirit. A striking illustration of the difference, in this respect, between the medieval and later periods is to be seen in the fact that whereas, in the days of Becket, the *trilinguis eruditio* meant a knowledge of Latin, French, and English, to Erasmus, writing three centuries later, a *trilinguis homo* was one who knew Latin, Greek, and Hebrew.[1]

The Renaissance-spirit often produced a polite scepticism about the Christian religion and sometimes came to expression in a frank neo-paganism, which even invaded high ecclesiastical circles. More than one representative of this type is pictured vividly by Charles Reade in *The Cloister and the Hearth*. Nor is the novelist's representation exaggerated. The more serious and religious side of the Renaissance is to be seen not in Italy, but north of the Alps. 'It was in the Teutonic countries— Germany, Holland, England—' says Professor Hearnshaw, 'rather than in the Latin countries, that the Renaissance took the form of the Reformation.'[2]

§ 2. *Erasmus*

The most perfect embodiment of the humanistic spirit, allied to sincere moral purpose, is to be seen in ERASMUS. The whole of his wonderful literary career illustrates this. Such works as the *Enchiridion* (1516 and following years—often reissued), the *Novum Instrumentum* (i.e. the 1516 edition of the Greek Testament printed at Basel), the *Paraphrases of Scripture*[3] (1517 and following years), not to mention others, show how

[1] C. Jenkins, *The Monastic Chronicler and the Early School of St. Albans*, London, 1922, p. 89.

[2] F. J. C. Hearnshaw, *Social and Political Ideas during the Renaissance*, London, 1924, p. 23.

[3] The *Paraphrases of Scripture* is the title given to the English version based (probably) on the Latin version which accompanied the Greek Testament of Erasmus. These *Paraphrases* were very popular in England. They were ordered to be set up in churches and have survived in one or two.

sincere was the moral purpose that spurred his literary activities. Indeed it would be true to say that all the work of Erasmus was produced in an atmosphere of urgency. Great scholar as he was, he was yet by no means a recluse working slowly under conditions of ample leisure : his studies were not of the arm-chair type, far removed from the dust and conflict of everyday life. On the contrary; he brought his learning to the market-place, and thus kept himself in touch with the realities of ordinary life in all its varied moods. In consequence his work possesses a vitality and sincerity that grip the reader at once. He achieved a marvellous success in popularizing scholarship on the largest scale, so that his name became a household word throughout Europe. His attitude toward the Bible and biblical studies vividly illustrates the point of view of the New Learning. Behind the mystic and allegorical meaning it was necessary to penetrate to the literal and original meaning of the writers. To gain the real meaning of the text it was necessary to study the originals in the original languages, i.e. Hebrew and Greek. One of the frankest expressions of this point of view occurs in the letter prefixed by Erasmus to his edition of Laurentius Valla's *Annotations upon the New Testament* (Paris, 1505). Here he pointed out that

'in many passages the Vulgate was manifestly at fault. It was a bad rendering of the original Greek or had itself been corrupted. Should any reply that the theologian is above the laws of grammar, and that the work of interpretation depends solely upon inspiration, that were, indeed, to claim a new dignity for divines. Were they alone to be allowed bad grammar ? He quoted from Jerome to show that he claimed no inspiration for the translator ; and asked how would it have served for Jerome to have given directions for the translation of Holy Scripture if the power of translating depended upon inspiration ? Again, how was it that Paul was evidently so much more at home in Hebrew than in Greek ?

Finally, he urged, if there be errors in the Vulgate, is it not lawful to correct them ? Many indeed, he knew would object to change any word in the Bible, since fancying that in every letter is hid some mystic meaning. Were it so, would it not be the more needful that the exact original text be restored?'[1]

Here we have a clear and bold enunciation of the principles of biblical criticism. In this respect it is noteworthy how extraordinarily modern is the point of view of Erasmus. On his principles Erasmus must have realized fully the importance of a knowledge of Hebrew for the correct interpretation of the Old Testament Scriptures. And in fact he puts this among the special requirements for the Scripture student in the prefatory remarks with which, in 1516, he introduced the *Novum Instrumentum*, his Greek and Latin version of the books of the New Testament:

'A fair knowledge of the three languages, Latin, Greek and Hebrew', he says, ' is of course the first thing. Nor let the student turn away in despair at the difficulty of this. If you have a teacher and the will, these three languages can be learned with hardly more labour than is spent every day over the miserable babble of one mongrel language under ignorant teachers. . . . As to the Schoolmen, I had rather be a pious divine with Jerome than invincible with Duns Scotus. Was ever heretic converted by their subtleties? Let those who like follow the disputations of the schools; but let him who would be instructed rather in piety than in the art of disputation, first and above all apply himself to those writings which flow immediately from the fountain-head.'[2]

It is certainly strange that despite this explicit avowal, Erasmus himself made no serious attempt to acquire Hebrew. For long his efforts were concentrated on Greek, and he was probably never able to find sufficient leisure to master Hebrew.[3] He never failed, however, to recognize the importance of a knowledge of the language and was careful to avail himself of the

[1] Quoted with slight alterations from H. E. Seebohm, *Oxford Reformers*, London, 1906, p. 178.

[2] Seebohm, *op. cit.*, p. 329 f.

[3] Colet, also, writing in 1497, speaks of the impossibility of coming to an accurate understanding of the meaning of what Moses wrote without a knowledge of Hebrew and access to Hebrew commentaries, ' which Origen, Jerome, and all really diligent searchers of the Scriptures have appreciated.' Seebohm, *op. cit.*, p. 48.

help of such a Hebraist as Reuchlin in editing Jerome. Nor must the difficulties of learning Hebrew at this time be underestimated. Grammatical aids hardly existed as yet and the student was almost wholly dependent upon the services of a good teacher, who was by no means easily found. Nevertheless Hebrew played a great part in the Reforming movement. Both Luther and Calvin studied Hebrew, and the latter's knowledge of the Hebrew of the Old Testament was considerable.

It is not surprising, perhaps, that the adherents of the old order should have regarded these new-fangled studies with grave suspicion. To them the Latin of the Vulgate and of the Schoolmen was the sacred language. The study of Hebrew and Greek was the pastime of heretics. To scoff at the Schoolmen, as Erasmus scoffed, and to criticize the Vulgate 'were the surest proofs of ignorance as well as impiety'. This attitude is satirized in the first part of the notorious *Epistolae Obscurorum Virorum* which appeared in 1516–1517 and is full of expressions of the monkish hatred of Reuchlin and the Jews.

§ 3. *Pico della Mirandola and Johann Reuchlin*

The two most outstanding figures among the early humanists who seriously added Hebrew to their other studies, are PICO DELLA MIRANDOLA (1463–1494) and JOHANN REUCHLIN [1] (1455–1522).

A member of the famous group that gathered at Florence around the Medicis, which included the first translator of Plato (Ficinus) and the first translator of Homer (Politian), Pico was distinguished as the first Christian student of the Jewish Cabala. When, at the age of twenty-three, he published at Rome his notorious *Nine hundred theses* [2]—which so much scandalized the orthodox theologians of the time—he had

---

[1] See Fig. 56, facing p. 340.

[2] *Conclusiones Philosophicae, Cabalisticae et Theologicae*, Rome, 1486. For a sketch of Pico della Mirandola with special reference to his importance for Hebrew studies, see a Paper by Dr. Israel Abrahams in the *Hebrew Union College Jubilee Volume*, Cincinnati, 1875–1925.

already acquired a considerable knowledge of the Cabala. One of the theses ran : 'There is no science that can more firmly convince us of the divinity of Christ than magic and Cabala.'

Pico received his training in cabalistic lore from JOCHANAN ALLEMANNO, who had been born in Constantinople, and from thence migrated to Italy. Allemanno was himself an expert student of the Cabala, and was also widely read in the Greek and Arabic philosophers. He was the author of several books, among others a treatise on immortality and a cabalistic commentary on the Torah (Pentateuch). He was a man of great versatility and accomplishment, and we can well understand how congenial the friendship of Pico with his master must have been. Allemanno helped Pico to collect a valuable library of Jewish works, largely cabalistic in character. Pico also translated cabalistic books into Latin.[1] But perhaps the most important part of his activity was the influence he exercised over Reuchlin (Fig. 56, opp. p. 340), and through Reuchlin over the Christian religious world.

Reuchlin interviewed Pico in Florence in 1490, and was impressed by what he heard as to the importance of cabalistic studies. It was not, however, till 1492, at the age of thirty-seven, that he was able to begin the study of Hebrew. His first teacher was Jacob Loans (died 1506), physician to the Emperor Frederick III ; later he had the advantage of a distinguished scholar as his second teacher, OBADIAH SFORNO (1475–1550). Reuchlin became an ardent student of Hebrew, and in 1497–1499, when he was again in Rome, he seized the opportunity to pursue his researches into Talmud and Cabala. In 1494 appeared at Basel his *De Verbo mirifico*, based upon the Cabala. In this work a Jewish sage (Barachias), a Christian scholar (Capnion), and a Greek philosopher enter into a discussion the result of

[1] Viz., a commentary on the Pentateuch by Menahem Recanati, the *Hokmath ha-nefesh* (*Scientia Animae*) of Eleazar of Worms, and the *Sefer ha-ma'aloth* of Shem-tob of Falaquera.

Fig. 55. GIOVANNI PICO DELLA MIRANDOLA
From a portrait by an unknown artist in the Uffizi Gallery at Florence

Reformation Period and After

which is to suggest that Jewish wisdom and the Hebrew language occupy the first rank. Another important work was published by him at Pforzheim in 1506, the *Rudimenta Hebraica*, the first Hebrew grammar by a Christian. As a first attempt in its own line it is, of course, imperfect and inadequate, but it marked a beginning.

In 1510 Reuchlin became involved in the famous controversy—the *cause célèbre* of the time—with Pfefferkorn, a baptized Jew of Cologne. This person, who was attached to the Dominican friars, had obtained in 1509, from the Emperor Maximilian, an order authorizing the destruction of all Hebrew books found in the possession of the Jews of Cologne and Frankfort. The Jews appealed against this order, and Reuchlin was asked to give an opinion on the merits of the case. His verdict was favourable to the Jews, and as a consequence the Emperor rescinded his edict, 23 May 1510. Reuchlin at this time held a judicial office at Tübingen. The grounds on which he based his decision are as follows:

'He divided the Jewish literature into seven classes, in one of them being the Old Testament, and judging these classes singly, he arrived at the conclusion that the Talmud, the . . . Zohar, the commentaries of Rashi, the Kimhis, Ibn Ezra, Gersonides, Nahmanides &c., should not be burned, as they were useful for theology and science, and no heresy was contained in them; but books which contained blasphemies against Jesus, such as the "Toledoth Jeshu", he considered ought to be destroyed. Furthermore, the Jews being as such under the protection of the German Empire, could not be accused of heresy against Christianity.'[1]

There followed a violent controversy with the Dominicans, and a conflict which involved practically the whole educated world. On one side were ranged with Reuchlin the humanists, on the other the clericals with the universities of Louvain, Cologne, Erfurt, Mayence, and Paris. A considerable controversial literature followed. In 1511 Reuchlin published his

[1] See *Jewish Encyclopaedia*, x. 389 *ab*.

Augenspiegel in reply to Pfefferkorn's *Handspiegel*. In the following years (1512-1514) the controversy was continued. Jacob van Hoogstraten, the Dominican prior in Cologne, was especially prominent in opposition to Reuchlin, who published during this period an important work entitled *Clarorum virorum Epistolae Latinae, Graecae, et Hebraicae variis temporibus missae ad J. Reuchlinum* (Tübingen, 1514). In 1513 Hoogstraten ordered Reuchlin to appear before the Dominican court at Mayence, to answer a charge of heresy, based upon the *Augenspiegel*. The hearing was, however, suspended by order of the archbishop Uriel von Gemmingen, and the case was remitted, by order of the Pope, to the Bishop of Speyer, who decided in favour of Reuchlin. The Dominicans appealed against this decision to Pope Leo X, who finally in 1520 decided against Reuchlin and condemned the *Augenspiegel*. This decision was influenced by political considerations and by the fact that by this time the Reformation had begun to spread in Germany.

Meanwhile, during these crowded and exciting years, Reuchlin had found time to make contributions to Hebrew studies by the publication in 1512 of a book for beginners, containing the Hebrew text of the seven penitential Psalms, with a word for word Latin translation and grammatical explanations. It was partly from this manual that Luther learnt Hebrew. In 1518 there appeared another work of Reuchlin dealing with Hebrew linguistics, *De accentibus et orthographia linguae hebraicae*. Meanwhile, in 1517 he had published at Hagenau one of the most famous of his cabalistic treatises, the *De arte cabalistica*, with a preface addressed to Leo X. In dialogue form between a Jew, a Muhammadan, and a Pythagorean, the Jewish Cabala is represented as the primeval revelation made to Adam through the medium of an angel, and continued by an unbroken tradition down to the time of the men of the Great Synagogue, and afterwards until the secrets of the upper world were transmitted to

Reformation Period and After

the Talmudic teachers. The agreement of the Cabala with the Pythagorean philosophy is strongly asserted, and examples are given of the various cabalistic methods of manipulating words. In February 1520 he was appointed Professor of Greek and Hebrew at the University of Ingolstadt. Reuchlin was now sixty-five years of age, and lectured once again to a large body on Aristophanes and on Kimhi's Grammar. Among his pupils at Ingolstadt was the Hebraist Johann Forster. In the spring of 1521 he was forced by the advent of the plague to migrate to Tübingen where he died in June 1522.

Reuchlin taught Hebrew before he became a professor, and was the first scholar to introduce Hebrew into the curriculum of the university. Among his pupils for this study are some bearing famous names. They include Melanchthon, Christopher Schilling of Lucerne, John Oecolampadius, John Cellarius, and Bartholomäus Caesar, besides Johann Forster already mentioned.

Forster (1496–1558, known also as Föster, Forsthemius and Vorster) was a distinguished Lutheran divine. He was a most diligent student of the Hebrew language, and produced two important works bearing on Hebrew studies: (1) his great Hebrew-Latin Lexicon, the *Dictionarium hebraicum novum* (1st ed., Augsburg 1557; 2nd ed., 1564); and (2) *Meditationes hebraicae* (Cologne 1558).

In this connexion should be mentioned also Nicholas Ellenborg (1480 or 1481–1543), son of a physician Ulrich Ellenborg. Nicholas spent five years (1497–1502) at Heidelberg, where Oecolampadius was a fellow-student. Narrowly escaping death from the plague, he determined to enter a monastery, and became a monk at Ottobeuren, where he was ordained priest in 1506. In 1505 he began Greek and in 1508 Hebrew. Together with certain patristic works he speaks of reading Pico della Mirandola. Ellenborg was a diligent student and was encouraged in his studies by his Abbot, who allowed him to collect Hebrew books, and wrote to Reuchlin asking him to find a converted Jew who could act as teacher.

Another interesting link with Reuchlin is TRITHEMIUS (1462–1516), the learned Abbot of Spanheim. Here he built up a famous library, containing Greek manuscripts and Hebrew works. 'There seems to be little doubt', says Dr. Seton Watson,[1] 'that the collection was almost unique in Germany at that time, and it naturally helped to spread the fame of Trithemius, not only among all scholars, but among those princes who were affected by humanistic influence.' He was an intimate friend of Bishop Dalberg that 'prince of humanists', who in 1496 led Reuchlin and a party of friends to inspect some important libraries, viz., that founded by Nicholas of Cusa (died 1464) at Cues, and the collection at Spanheim. 'Their course was from Worms to Oppenheim ... by boat to Coblenz and up the Moselle to Cues; then over the hills to Dalberg, and finally to the abbey of Spanheim, near Kreuznach, where they admired the rich collection of manuscripts in five languages formed by ... Trithemius.'[2]

Trithemius did not himself contribute any works important for the study of Hebrew—he wrote largely on ecclesiastical matters. But he produced two books of a magical and mystical kind: the *Polygraphia* (1507) and *Chronologica mystica* (1508). These deal largely with the mystical meaning of numbers, secret ciphers, and the influence of the planets. It is not to be wondered at that he acquired the reputation of being a magician. But it must be remembered to his honour that when, in 1510, the Jews were publicly accused of the absurd charges of profaning the sacred elements in the Eucharist and of ritual murder, Trithemius protested, and raised his voice against senseless persecution and plunder. Perhaps here he was influenced by Reuchlin.

§ 4. *The Cabala*

The Cabala has been frequently mentioned in the pages of this volume. It exercised a profound influence on Christian thinking during the fifteenth, sixteenth, and seventeenth centuries. To understand its nature it is necessary to say something of its history.

Cabala is the general name for the mystical type of thought that finds expression in Jewish literature. The word means 'tradition', that is to say the received or traditional law. It is the specific term used for 'the esoteric or mystic doctrine concerning God and the universe, asserted to have come down as a revelation to elect saints from a remote past and preserved only by a privileged few'. At first the elements embraced in

---

[1] In *Tudor Studies*, London, 1924. 'The Abbot Trithemius,' p. 79.
[2] P. S. Allen, *Age of Erasmus*, Oxford, 1914, p. 31.

the tradition were simple, but under the influence of the Neoplatonic and Neopythagorean philosophy it gradually assumed a speculative character.

A considerable Hebrew literature of the Cabalistic-mystical type was current as early as the Geonic period (A.D. 589–1038).[1] Some of these books have survived. One of the most remarkable is that known as *Shi 'ur Komah*, an extraordinary treatise on the bodily dimensions of God. It exists in fragments, the largest of which is included in the cabalistic book *Sepher Raziel*. It was apparently current in the eighth and following centuries as an independent work, and in its present form may have been redacted, at the latest, in the eighth century. In substance, however, it is much older, having affinities with the early Gnostic systems of thought.

Closely allied to this, and in its present form probably belonging to the same period, is the 'Hekaloth' literature, a number of fragments treating of the heavenly 'Halls' (Hekaloth) which, according to Hai Gaon of Pumbeditha (died 1038), originated with the mystics who experienced the heavenly chariot-ride (*Yôrĕdê Merkabah*).[2] These, according to the same authority, ' brought themselves into a state of entranced vision by fasting, asceticism, and prayer, and imagined that they saw the seven [heavenly] halls, and all that is therein, with their own eyes, while passing from one hall into another.'[3]

---

[1] The title *Gaon*, 'Excellency' (plural *Geonim*, hence *geonic*), is the title given in Jewish literature to the heads of the two great Babylonian academies that were established at Sura and Pumbeditha. Their activity covered a period of about 450 years, from 589 to 1038. The Geonim, as directors of these academies, continued the activities of the *Amoraim* and the *Saboraim*. The Amoraim, by their interpretation of Jewish tradition, gave rise to the mass of Jewish lore and teaching known as the *Talmud*. Their activities, which were carried on both in Palestine and Babylonia, lasted for 280 years, from A.D. 219 to 500. They were followed by the Saboraim of Babylonia, who completed the editing of the Talmud during the following 88 years.

[2] Compare the article in this volume by Professor Guillaume, p. 172.

[3] There is an interesting *psychological* parallel to the seven halls of

The most remarkable literary production of this kind, however, is the *Sepher Yeṣirah* ('Book of Creation') which, in its present form, may belong to the Geonic period. This work enjoyed so great a reputation in the ninth century that Saadia wrote a commentary on it. It forms the link between the earlier mystic literature and the later Cabala. The *doctrine of emanations*, which played so prominent a part later,[1] as well as the mystic power of the letters of the Hebrew alphabet, are here enunciated in an early form. The *Ten Sephiroth*, according to this book, constitute the fundamentals of all existence. They are the ten principles that mediate between God and the universe. They include the three primal emanations that proceed from the Spirit of God, viz. (1) spiritual air, (2) primal water, (3) fire. Six others consist of the three dimensions (height, length, breadth) extended to the left and to the right. These nine, together with the Spirit of God, form the ten 'Sephiroth', which are eternal. The first three are the ideal prototypes of Creation, which became possible when infinite space, represented by the six other Sephiroth, was produced.

While the three primal elements constitute the *substance* of things, the twenty-two letters of the Hebrew alphabet constitute the *form*. The letters hover, as it were, on the boundary-line between the spiritual and the physical world; for the real existence of things is knowable only by means of language, i.e. the human capacity for conceiving thought. As the letters

heaven in Teresa's 'The Interior Castle'. God 'showed her a most beautiful globe of crystal, in the shape of a castle with seven rooms, the seventh, situated in the centre, being occupied by the King of glory resplendent with the most exquisite brilliancy, which shone through and adorned the remaining rooms' (Introduction, p. xviii; Eng. ed. of 1906). This raises the question of the influence of the Cabala on the mysticism of St. Teresa and of Spain in general, especially in view of the intensity of Jewish development in Spain.

[1] The later developments of this doctrine are discussed by Dr. and Mrs. Singer, pp. 187–189.

resolve the contrast between the substance and the form of things, they represent the solvent activity of God; for everything that is exists by means of contrasts, which find their solution in God. So, for instance, among the three primal elements, the contrasts between fire and water are resolved into *ruaḥ*, that is 'air' or 'spirit' ('spiritual air').

The doctrine of emanations is, of course, really Neoplatonic. It attempts to answer the question, how the finite can be brought into touch with the infinite, by the view that all existing things are an outflowing which ultimately proceeds from God. God embraces them all, animate and inanimate.

The *Sepher Yeṣirah* prepared the way for the medieval Cabala. The doctrine of the ten Sephiroth has obvious affinities with the later representation in the *Zohar* and allied literature, though there are important points of difference. Its importance is obvious, for it brings us into the heart of Jewish mysticism.

The revival of Cabalistic literature that took place in the Geonic period makes it certain that many scholars belonging to the Babylonian schools cultivated the mystic lore. Some of the Geonim themselves were deeply interested in these studies, and it is not without significance that certain Cabalistic works, even though they may have been compiled at a later time, were ascribed to the authorship of particular Geonim.

Another remarkable fact is that the German Cabala owes its origin to Babylonia. It was a Babylonian Jew, Aaron ben Samuel ha-Nasi, who, emigrating to Italy in the first half of the ninth century, carried with him these teachings, and imparted them to the famous Jewish family of the Kalonymides, who carried them to Germany about 917. They were not published till nearly three centuries later, when Judah the Pious (died 1217), himself a member of the family, commissioned his pupil, Eleazar of Worms, to introduce the oral and written cabalistic doctrine into larger circles. This explains the very strange fact that the German Cabala is a direct continuation of the Geonic and

Babylonian type of mysticism. In Italy and Germany it has remained untouched by foreign influence.

On the other hand, in Arabic-speaking countries, the Graeco-Arabic philosophy reacted upon the cabalistic tradition; and, in particular, the influence of the philosophical doctrines of Solomon ibn Gabirol (1021–1058), the great exponent of Neoplatonism, was marked.[1] Thus the three sources from which the Cabala of the thirteenth century was derived were the esoteric tradition of the Talmud, the Geonic mysticism, and the Arabic Neoplatonic philosophy.

During the thirteenth century and onward these studies, which had been more or less confined to small circles, received a great impetus and became widely diffused. They gave rise to an extensive literature, written in a peculiar dialect of Aramaic and grouped around a new holy book—the *Zohar*—which suddenly made its appearance, but claimed to be a work of great antiquity, its reputed author being the famous second-century Rabbi Simeon ben Yochai. This Cabalistic literature grew up, to some extent, in opposition to the Talmud.[2]

§ 5. *The Cabala and its place in Christian Thought of the XVIth and XVIIth centuries*

The Jewish Cabala exercised—especially through Reuchlin—a considerable influence in the Christian world. It helped to leaven the religious movements identified with the Reformation, and the cabalistic literature was diligently studied by Christian scholars during the sixteenth and seventeenth centuries. When in 1517 Reuchlin's *De arte cabalistica* appeared, Erasmus sent a copy of it to Bishop Fisher, with a letter asking

[1] See article by Dr. and Mrs. Singer, p. 189.

[2] For the above paragraphs see W. O. E. Oesterley and G. H. Box, *Short Survey of the Literature of Rabbinical and Mediaeval Judaism*. London, 1920, pp. 235 ff.

his opinion upon it. Colet saw the book, and in the last letter of his that has survived (to Erasmus) gives the following shrewd judgement :

'I dare not express an opinion on this book. I am conscious of my own ignorance, and how blind I am in matters so mysterious, and in the works of so great a man. However, in reading it, the chief miracles seemed to me to be more in the words than the things; for according to him, Hebrew words seem to have no end of mystery in their characters and combinations.'[1]

Something may usefully be said at this point about the cabalistic doctrines that exercised so great a fascination for many Christian scholars. The Zohar, which sums up the cabalistic ideas that had been developed up to the time of its appearance, was published in its present shape in the thirteenth century by Moses de Leon (1250–1305). Its name (*Zohar*), which means 'Brightness', was derived from Dan. xii. 3 : 'They that be wise shall shine as the brightness of the firmament.' Written partly in Aramaic and partly in Hebrew, it is in form a commentary on the Pentateuch, but in reality a compendium of cabalistic theosophy. It belongs to the large class of pseudepigraphical writings, purporting to be the record of a divine revelation made to R. Simeon ben Yochai (second century C. E.), who is represented as imparting it in a series of utterances to his disciples. It is in fact, however, a composite work, drawn from many sources, some of which are really ancient.

This remarkable compilation became not only the text-book of cabalistic doctrine, but also the canonical holy book of the cabalists. The doctrine of the *Ten Sephiroth* ('emanations', see above, p. 326 f.) is throughout assumed as axiomatic. As in all mystical systems, the soul occupies a dominant place in the theology of the *Zohar*, and the ideas concerning it (e. g. its constitution as a trinity) reflect the influence of the Platonic psychology. The doctrine of soul-transmigration plays a leading

[1] Seebohm, *op. cit.*, p. 413.

part, as well as that of the four worlds. These are (*a*) the *Azilutic* world (or world of 'emanation') which contains the Sephiroth; (*b*) the *Beri'atic* world (or world of 'creative ideas'), which contains the souls of the pious, the divine throne and the divine halls; (*c*) the *Yesiratic* world (or world of 'creative formations') which is the abode of the *ten classes of angels* with their chiefs, presided over by *Metatron*, who was changed into fire; (*d*) the '*Asiyyatic* world (or world of 'creative matter') in which are certain angelic powers (the *Ophannim*), the angels that receive the prayers and control the actions of men, and wage war against the embodiment of evil *Sammael*. There seems to be no doubt that these worlds were at first conceived realistically, but were later interpreted in an idealistic or mystical sense.

On its ethical side the Cabala teaches that love is the highest relation of the soul to God and that it transcends knowledge and will. Ethics is indeed part of religion to the cabalists. On this point a leading authority [1] says:

'The connexion between the real and ideal world is brought about by man, whose soul belongs to heaven, while his body is earthy. Man connects the two worlds by means of his love to God which ... unites him with God. The knowledge of the law in its ethical as well as its religious aspect, is also a means towards influencing the higher regions; for the study of the law means the union of man with the divine wisdom. ... The ritual also has a deeper mystical meaning, as it serves to preserve the universe and to secure blessings for it.' [2]

Pico discovered in the Cabala all the doctrines of Christianity. It represents the mystical side of Judaism, and marks the reaction against a dry and arid scholasticism. As such it naturally appealed to the leaders of the Reformation movement, especially in the German countries where it was largely a protest

---

[1] L. Ginzberg, article 'Cabala' (in *Jewish Encyclopaedia*).

[2] The summary given above of the Zohar doctrines is based upon *A Short Introduction to the Life of Rabb and Medieval Judaism*, pp. 247–250.

against the medieval scholastic theology. Mystical movements found in the Cabala a potent ally. Reuchlin's whole philosophical system is based upon it. He distinguished between cabalistic doctrines, cabalistic art, and cabalistic perception. Its central doctrine, for him, was the Messianology, around which all the other doctrines grouped themselves. And as the cabalistic doctrine originated in divine revelation so was the cabalistic art derived immediately from divine illumination. By means of this illumination man is enabled to gain insight of the contents of cabalistic doctrine through the symbolic interpretation of the letters, words, and contents of Scripture—hence the Cabala is symbolic theology. Whoever would become an adept in the cabalistic art, and thereby penetrate the cabalistic secrets, must have divine illumination and inspiration. The cabalist must, therefore, first of all purify his soul from sin, and order his life in accord with the precepts of virtue and morality.[1]

This interest in Jewish Cabala was shared by other Christian scholars, notably by H. C. Agrippa of Nettesheim (1487–1535), who, however, was specially interested in the magical side. His chief work, *De occulta philosophia* (Paris, 1528), expounds the *Sephiroth*, and the doctrine of the four worlds, modelled upon the doctrine summarized above. Mention may also be made in this connexion of Francesco Zorzi (1460–1540), author of *De Harmonia Mundi*, of the German Theophrastus Paracelsus (1493–1541), of the Italian Hieronymo Cardano (1501–1576), of Johann Baptist van Helmont (1577–1644), a native of Holland, and of Robert Fludd (1574–1637), a much-travelled Englishman, who possessed a remarkable knowledge of the Cabala acquired in his wanderings. Translations of cabalistic books were produced by Joseph de Voisin (1610–1685), Athanasius Kircher (1602–1684), and Knorr Baron von Rosenroth (1636–

---

[1] See L. Ginzberg in *Jewish Encyclopaedia*, iv. 471.

1689). The cabalistic literature was regarded as containing treasures of ancient wisdom.

The extraordinary influence of cabalistic studies at the time of the Reformation calls for remark. As has already been pointed out this phenomenon was due partly to the reaction against the medieval scholastic theology. This showed itself also in the growth of certain mystical movements, especially in Germany, where it was exemplified by Jacob Boehme (1575–1624) and others. In fact the atmosphere of the time was congenial to such tendencies.

Various judgements have been passed upon the Jewish cabalistic doctrines and literature. Some of their harshest critics have been certain Jewish scholars who, like Graetz, were, by temper and training, naturally antipathetic to any forms of mystical thought. 'The unlovely features of the whole literature have been seized upon—its weird and fantastic ideas, its irrationality, and its superstitious elements—to discredit the whole.' This is really an unfair method. There is much of real spiritual value in the literature. As a Jewish writer justly remarks: 'Nowhere in Jewish literature is the idea of prayer raised to such a pitch of sublimity as it is in the lives and writings of the Jewish mystics. If it is true to say that Judaism here and there suffers from too large an element of formalism and legalism and externalism, it is equally true to say that many of these drawbacks are corrected, toned down by the contributions of mysticism.'[1] Some of the most exquisite prayers and liturgical poems of the synagogue liturgy are the productions of the cabalists. By their sheer beauty and devotional power they have won their way into practically universal use in the synagogue and have left their mark outside it.

Mention has already been made of Jacob Loans, the Jewish teacher of Reuchlin, who refers to him affectionately as 'humanissimus praeceptor meus, homo excellens'. Loans died at Linz about 1506, and with two other more famous Jews, Elias Levita (1468–1549), and Obadiah Sforno (1475–1550, see p. 320), must be allowed a large share in influencing the Protestant Reformation.

[1] J. Abelson, *Jewish Mysticism*, London, 1913, p. 12, and cf. I. Abrahams, *Jewish Life in Middle Ages*, London, 1896, p. 423.

§ 6. *Rise of the Scientific Study of Hebrew*

ELIAS LEVITA (1468–1549), who may be regarded as the real founder of modern Hebrew grammar, was the teacher of many Christians. The episode of his relations with the liberal-minded Cardinal Aegidius of Viterbo, general of the Augustinian order, is well known and furnishes an attractive story. It was in 1509 that Levita arrived in Rome, after losing everything in the sack of Padua, and, hearing that the cardinal was studying Hebrew, called upon him, with the result that an arrangement was made by which he was to give lessons in Hebrew and receive lessons in Greek by way of exchange. He lived in the cardinal's palace as an honoured guest and friend for a period of thirteen years, giving and receiving lessons. During this time he produced some important books, dealing with Hebrew grammar.

In 1527, after the sack of Rome, Levita migrated to Venice, where he became a proof-reader for the Christian printer of Hebrew, Daniel Bomberg (died 1549, see p. 335 f.). At Venice Levita returned to his teaching work. Among his pupils was the French Ambassador, George de Selve, afterwards Bishop of Lavaur, who was a generous benefactor to his teacher. Levita's famous work *Masoreth ha-Masoreth* was published at Venice in 1538. In this treatise he proved that the 'points' used in the Hebrew Bibles were invented by the Masoretic scholars not earlier than the fifth century of our era. This excited angry protest from the orthodox Jews, with whom Levita's activities as a teacher of Hebrew had already made him suspect and unpopular. This attitude can be understood when some Christians openly confessed that their object in learning Hebrew was to confute the Jews by arguments derived especially from the Cabala. In his preface to the *Masoreth ha-Masoreth*, Levita replied to these criticisms that he had only taught the elements of the language and had never taught the Cabala at all. He also pointed out that the Christian Hebraists defended the Jews against fanatical anti-Semitic attacks. Levita's views as to the modern origin of the Hebrew points also excited lively interest among Christian scholars, and the question continued to be debated for three centuries. A new edition of the *Masoreth ha-Masoreth* was prepared by Sebastian Münster and published at Basel in 1539. In it the introductions appeared in Latin.

When Bomberg's printing press was closed, Levita, though an old man, left wife and children and departed to Isny in Würtemburg, at the invitation of Paul Fagius, to superintend the Hebrew printing-press there. While with Fagius he published several grammatical and lexicographical works, among them *Tishbi*, a dictionary of Talmudic and Midrashic words, and one on Targumic words. He died at Venice in 1549.

Among Christian Hebraists of this period may be mentioned SEBASTIAN MÜNSTER (1489–1552), a German Protestant, who distinguished himself as a Hebrew grammarian. He taught Hebrew in the university of Basel (1529). Elias Levita had been his teacher, and Münster edited and translated his grammatical works. He also issued a new edition of Reuchlin's *Rudimenta Hebraica* and himself produced important works dealing with Hebrew grammar, namely the *Epitome Hebraicae Grammaticae* in 1520 and the *Institutiones Grammaticae* in 1524. But perhaps his most important piece of work was the publication in 1534 of a Hebrew Bible with a Latin translation—the first diglot text of the sort to be issued by a Christian. Among his other works are a grammar of Aramaic or 'Chaldaic' (1527), another of Rabbinic Hebrew (1542), and an edition and translation of *Yosippon* (1541). He was also the first to issue a Hebrew translation of any part of the New Testament, viz. the Gospel of St. Matthew which appeared at Basel in 1537.

Hebrew lexicography of the period is represented by the work of Pellicanus (died 1556) and Pagninus (died 1541). Another interesting name is that of the Spanish priest ARIAS MONTANUS (1527–1598). He was the editor of the Antwerp

Polyglot Bible, which was published at Antwerp in the years 1568–1572, under the title *Biblia Sacra Hebraice Chaldaice Graece et Latine*, under the patronage of Philip II. Arias, who was a good Hebraist and Orientalist, also edited a work on the Masorah, translated Benjamin of Tudela's *Travels* into Latin, and was the author of other works, including a Book on Jewish Antiquities (Leyden, 1593). He was a regular 'reader' for the great printing firm Plantin at Antwerp. Memorials of him may still be seen in the Plantin Museum in that city.

§ 7. *Some Hebrew Printers of the XVIth century*

An enormous impetus was given to the diffusion of learning by the invention of printing, which, in contrast to the reception given to it in certain other quarters, was from the first welcomed by the Jews. The craft was regarded by the Jewish printers as 'holy work'.

During the earliest period (1475–1500) Hebrew printing was confined to Italy, Spain, and Portugal. The first part of the Old Testament to be printed in Hebrew was the Book of Psalms with Kimhi's Commentary (1477). In 1488 the first complete Hebrew Bible appeared in folio at Soncino. Another edition was issued in 1494 at Brescia. The latter was used by Luther and his copy is still preserved in the Royal Library at Berlin.

The close connexion between the great printing houses—especially those engaged in the production of Greek and Hebrew texts—and the best scholarship of the time may be illustrated in the case of two famous names, those of Bomberg and Froben.

DANIEL BOMBERG (died 1549), a Christian born at Antwerp, learnt the art of printing and type-founding from his father, Cornelius. Having acquired a knowledge of Hebrew, Bomberg went to Venice, where from 1517 to 1549 many important Hebrew works were issued from his famous press. Among these were the first Rabbinic Bible, containing the Hebrew text with the Jewish commentaries and Targums, edited by Felix Pratensis in 1517–1518; the second edition, edited by Jacob ben Chayyim, was issued in 1524–1525 and contains the *Masorah Magna*; the third edition was issued 1546–1548. A most important event in the history of Hebrew scholarship was the publication of the first complete edition of the Babylonian Talmud in fifteen volumes which came from Bomberg's press in 1520–1523. The pagination of this *editio princeps* has been followed in all subsequent editions. It is interesting to note that the publication was under the patronage of Pope Leo X. Other publications of the famous press included important editions of the Midrashim (*Mekilta*, *Sifra*, and *Sifre*), tractates of the Mishnah, as well as grammatical and lexicographical works, treatises dealing with philosophical and ethical subjects, and liturgical works.

Some famous Jewish scholars were employed by Bomberg for the production of these works. One of the best known and most remarkable was Jacob ben Hayyim Ibn Adonijah, who was mainly responsible for the *editio princeps* of the Rabbinic Bible, and wrote the Introduction to it. His connexion with Bomberg began perhaps as early as 1517, for he partly edited the Babylonian Talmud which was published 1520–1523, as well as the *editio princeps* of the Palestinian Talmud (published 1522–1523), and R. Nathan's Concordance (1523). 'It is perfectly amazing', says Dr. C. Ginsburg,[1] 'to find that the editing of these works ... was simply the recreation of Jacob ben Hayyim; and that the real strength of his intellect, and the vast stores of his learning were employed at that very time in collecting and collating manuscripts of the Masorah, and in preparing for the press the Rabbinic Bible ... which was the most powerful auxiliary to the then commencing Reformation.' The four folio volumes of this appeared in 1524–1525. The relations between printer and scholar were friendly and cordial in the highest degree, and ben Hayyim found his employer ready to spare no expense in facilitating the editor's work. 'When I explained to Bomberg', he

[1] C. D. Ginsburg, *Jacob Ibn Adonijah's Introduction to the Rabbinic Bible* (1867), p. 5 f.

Reformation Period and After

tells us, 'the advantage of the Masorah, he did all in his power to send into all the countries in order to search out what may be found of the Masorah; and, praised be the Lord, we obtained as many of the Masoretic books as could possibly be got. He was not backward, and his hand was not closed, nor did he draw back his right hand from producing gold out of his purse, to defray the expenses of the books, and of the messengers who were engaged to make search for them in the most remote corners, and in every place where they might possibly be found.'[1]

Bomberg was keenly interested in the publication of these great works, and lavished care and money on their production. It is interesting to note that he secured the help of the most famous Hebraist among the Jewish scholars of the time—Elias Levita (p. 333 f.)—to contribute an epilogue to the great Rabbinic Bible, in the form of a poem which celebrates the praises of the munificent publisher, of the learned editor, and of the work itself. Levita at this time was living in Rome under the protection of Cardinal Aegidius of Viterbo. Two years later (6 May 1527) Rome was sacked by the Imperialists under Charles V, and Levita, having lost all he possessed, arrived at Venice in a destitute condition, and was at once employed by Bomberg as joint corrector of the press and as editor. 'Thus the two learned Hebraists, Jacob ben Hayyim and Elias Levita, who were the great teachers of Hebrew to the greatest men of Europe, at the commencement and during the development of the Reformation, now became co-workers in the same printing-office.'[2]

Jacob ben Hayyim appears to have died in 1537 and to have embraced Christianity some years before his death. This may serve to explain his disappearance from the activities of Bomberg's press. As the books issued were intended largely for Jewish readers, it would have been inexpedient to employ one who had become a convert to Christianity.

Among others who assisted Bomberg was the Jew Cornelius ben Baruch Adelkind, who from 1524 to 1544 worked as scholar-printer in the press at Venice; he was of German descent, and assisted in the production of texts of the Bible, Hebrew commentaries and prayer-books. He worked for other publishers after 1544, and in 1553 left Venice for Sabionetta, where he was active till 1555.[3] The Jewish

---

[1] Ginsburg, *op. cit.*, p. 8.   [2] Ginsburg, *op. cit.*, p. 9.

[3] His son Daniel Adelkind was active at Venice in the printing and publishing of Hebrew Books in the years 1550–1552.

scholar Hiyya ben Meir, who was dayyan of Venice 1510–1520, was employed in Bomberg's press after 1520 in editing various works.

Felix Pratensis, who edited the *Biblia Veneta* (Venice, 1518), was a Jew who became converted to Christianity in 1518. Bomberg was his pupil. He joined the Augustinian order, and devoted himself to the work of Jewish conversion. He died at Rome in 1539. It is interesting to note that in his pre-Christian days Felix published a Latin translation of the Psalms entitled *Psalterium ex Hebraeo ad verbum translatum* (Venice, 1515).

The close relations existing at this time between printing and scholarship may further be illustrated by the history of Froben's press at Basel. When in 1514 Erasmus visited this printer's house, it had already been in existence more than thirty years (since 1475). Its founder, who at this time was still alive, was JOHANN AMORBACH. Froben (Fig. 57, opp. p. 340) had been taken into his establishment that he might have an able successor. His own three sons had been instructed in Latin, Greek, and Hebrew, to qualify them for the work of carrying on the traditions of their father's house. Amorbach was a man of some scholarship, and had taken his M.A. in Paris. He devoted his energies to the production of good books. It was his particular ambition to produce worthily the four Doctors of the Church. Ambrose appeared in 1492, Augustine in 1506, and Jerome followed. 'Reuchlin helped with the Hebrew and Greek, and spent two months in Amorbach's house in the summer of 1510 to bring matters forward. Subsequently his province fell to Pellican, the Franciscan Hebraist, and Johann Cono, a learned Dominican of Nuremburg, who had mastered Greek at Venice and Padua, and had recently returned from Italy with a store of Greek manuscripts copied from the library of Musurus.'[1] The circle also included the famous Beatus Rhenanus, a young scholar of great ability and wealth, who endeared himself to his friends, and was attached to Froben's press, as was also Gerard Lystrius, who had been

---

[1] P. S. Allen, *The Age of Erasmus*, Oxford, 1914, p. 147.

trained for the medical profession, and possessed a good knowledge of Greek and Hebrew. In 1511 Johann Cono began to teach Greek and Hebrew to the printer's sons, and any one else who wished might attend these lessons. Thus the printer's house at Basel became a veritable academy worthy to be compared with that of Aldus at Venice.

JOHANN FROBEN (1460–1527) is described as:

'a man after [Amorbach's] own heart: open and easy to deal with, but of dogged determination and with great capacity for work. He was not a scholar. It is not known whether he ever went to a University, and it is doubtful whether he knew any Latin; certainly the numerous prefaces which appear in his books under his name are not his own, but came from the pens of other members of his circle. So the division came naturally, that Amorbach organized the work and prepared manuscripts for the press, while Froben had the printing under his charge. In later years, after Amorbach's death, the marked advance in the output of the press as regards type and paper and title-pages and designs may be attributed to Froben, who was man of business enough to realize the importance of getting good men to serve him—Erasmus to edit books, Gerbell and Oecolampadius to correct the proofs, Graf and Holbein to provide the ornaments.'[1]

For thirteen years Froben was the printer of practically everything that Erasmus wrote. Froben and Erasmus were intimate friends, and the printer took a real pride in producing good books. When he died in 1527 Erasmus paid a warm tribute to his memory.[2]

It will be clear from these two examples how profoundly affected were the printing presses of the time with the prevailing

---

[1] *Op. cit.*, p. 152.

[2] Similarly in Zürich, in the very first year of Zwingli's preaching there (1519), the bookseller Christopher Froschauer came to the city and placed his printing-press at the service of the new Reform movement. 'Round Zwingli and him there gathered ... a literary circle comparable to that already assembled at Basel round Erasmus and Froben.' (Hastings, *Encyclopaedia of Religion and Ethics*, xii. 873 *b*).

spirit. Daniel Bomberg's press at Venice existed primarily for the production of Hebrew works; but some of the most important of these were issued under the direct patronage of Pope Leo X, who may be regarded as one of the leaders of the humanist movement in Italy. Froben's press at Basel, on the other hand, did not specialize in Hebrew books, but fully recognized the position of Hebrew as sharing a place equally with Greek and Latin in the category of the classical languages.

The close connexion of Hebrew studies with the Reformation emerges in Germany and Northern Europe in the person of Reuchlin, and was destined to become all-important. On the other hand, in the earlier period of the Italian Renaissance, the learning of Hebrew became a fashionable study—Jewish tutors were busy all over Italy.[1] It was not specially associated there with movements in the Church, but rather with the development of philosophical studies mainly through the Cabala.

§ 8. *Humanism and Hebrew Studies*

The humanistic movement gave a great impetus to the establishment of new centres of learning. Thus the University of Basel was founded in 1460, and Luther's University of Wittenberg in 1502. Chairs for the promotion of the new learning were founded and endowed and schools sprang up for the teaching of the same subjects. The advent of the new learning meant a great enrichment of cultural life—and in all of these developments Hebrew had an honourable, if not always a prominent, place.

Thus Hieronymus Buclidius, the friend of Erasmus, established a chair of Hebrew at Louvain, at a cost of 20,000 francs.

---

[1] Cardinal Grimani, and other men eminent both in Church and State, studied Hebrew and Cabala with Jewish teachers. Even the soldier Guido Rangoni began to study Hebrew with the aid of Jacob Mantino (1526). The relations between Elias Levita and Cardinal Aegidius of Viterbo have already been referred to.

Fig. 56. JOHANN REUCHLIN, 1455–1522

Fig. 57. JOHANN FROBEN, 1460–1527

A similar chair was established at the University of Paris. The famous Jewish scholar Elias Levita was invited to occupy it by Francis I, but felt bound to decline the honour as his co-religionists were still excluded from the city of Paris.[1] The mere fact that a non-Christian Jew was invited to fill such a position at all in a Christian university is remarkable enough. In England chairs for the promotion of the new learning were established by Henry VIII at Cambridge in 1540, the five Regius Professorships being those of Divinity, Civil Law, Physic, Hebrew, and Greek.

Similarly a number of schools came into existence in England which were designed to foster the new learning. The oldest of these, which was humanistic in origin, is St. Paul's School, founded by Dean Colet in 1512. One of the foremost pioneers of Greek study in England, William Lily, was appointed its first 'High Master'. Other schools founded under humanistic influences include Christ's Hospital, Westminster, and Merchant Taylors. The last mentioned of these was founded in 1561, and possesses the distinction of having taught Hebrew, by the side of Greek and Latin, from the first, a tradition still maintained there. The following account of an examination held in 1572 will illustrate this fact, as well as the methods of examination employed in the sixteenth century.

'About eight o'clock in the morning of the 10th June [1572], Horne, Bishop of Winchester; Nowell, Dean of St. Paul's; Goodman, Dean of Westminster; Watts, Archdeacon of Middlesex; Young, Rector of St. Magnus's; Robinson, President of St. John's College, Oxford; Russell and Case, senior fellows of the said College, the Master, Wardens, and assistants of the company, and many others assembled at the school.' After speeches, &c., 'they all went into the chapel. . . . Before this venerable assembly the head scholars of the school presented them-

---

[1] It is worth noting that the Italian Jerome Aleander in 1508 came to Paris and lectured in Greek, Latin, and Hebrew. He afterwards became Rector of the University. Returning to Rome in 1516, he became librarian of the Vatican and in 1538 was created a Cardinal.

selves for examination, and after one of them had briefly enumerated the several books they were learning in Latin, Greek, and Hebrew, Nowell began the examination by directing the lowest of that form to declare the sense and construction of a particular Ode of Horace; "*which from one to another he prosecuted throughe the whole number, untill the captayn, requiringe diversytie of phrases and varitie of words and finally obmyttinge nothinge which might seeme neadful for the tryall of their lerninge in the Latyn tongue.*" After him Watts examined the same boys in Homer, as to their skill in Greek, which was his favourite language. And then Horne tried them in the Hebrew Psalter. In all which exercises they were well allowed.' [1]

§ 9. *The Reformation and Hebrew Studies*

'In Germany, during the earlier half of the sixteenth century, the alliance between humanism and the Reformation was real and intimate. The paramount task which the New learning found in Germany was the elucidation of the Bible.' [2] This is reflected partly in the desire—fostered by the new learning—to study the Scriptures in the light of their original languages, Hebrew and Greek; and partly in a more rational approach to the study of the text of Scripture itself. This for ages had been wrapped up in the swaddling clothes of the traditional 'fourfold sense' of Scripture, including the allegorical exegesis.[3] The position, too, assigned by the Reformers

---

[1] *Memorials of the Guild of Merchant Taylors* (London, 1875), p. 408.

[2] Sir R. Jebb in the *Cambridge Modern History*, i, p. 573.

[3] 'The four-fold sense of scripture' which prevailed in the Middle Ages is summed up in the Latin jingle

'*Litera gesta docet ; quid credas allegoria ;*
  Moralis quid agas ; quo tendas anagogia,'

that is, (1) the literal, (2) the allegorical, (3) the moral, (4) the anagogic. Dobschütz (Hastings, *Dictionary of Religion and Ethics*, ii. 598) cites the following example. Luke ii. 21. 'And when eight days were accomplished for the circumcising of the child, his name was called Jesus, which was so named of the angel before he was conceived in the womb.' This means (1) verbally, Jesus was circumcised on the eighth day ; (2) allegorically, the eight parts of Holy Scripture ; (3) morally, the eight stages of repentance ;

to the Bible itself marks a complete revolution. Instead of an Infallible Church, speaking with divine authority through its Head on earth, the Vicar of Christ, there is now the Infallible Word of God, as revealed in the Sacred Scriptures of the Old and New Testaments. The accent and emphasis are now on the Bible, rather than the Church. Even where, as in the Anglican Communion, the historic continuity of the Church, as a visible body, is insisted upon, the authority of Holy Scripture is still paramount. The formula: 'the Church to teach, the Bible to prove' is typically Anglican.

Whatever else the Reformation meant, it greatly stimulated Biblical studies. The diffusion of the Scriptures in vernacular versions based upon the Hebrew and Greek originals, was immensely developed by the Reformation. Hebrew study and Hebrew scholarship came to play an all-important part.[1]

The distinctive feature in the exposition of Scripture by the Reformers generally was their insistence on the literal sense. This principle can already be detected at work in LUTHER in his early *Observationes in Psalmos* (1519). Melanchthon and Calvin are more consistent in their application of the same principle. Not that any of these leaders possessed any real idea of the principles of Biblical Criticism—that development was to come later—but it was really implicit in the application of humanistic principles to ancient texts. Luther, indeed, in the free and unguarded moments of his Table-talk, uttered many shrewd *obiter dicta* about the Bible, which are on the lines of rational criticism. He drew distinctions of a marked and definite kind between one part of Scripture and another.

---

(4) anagogically, the octave of the Resurrection, the eight ages of the world, the eight blessings of future salvation.

[1] We have already seen that Bomberg's press had in the early part of the sixteenth century published not only the Hebrew text of the Old Testament, but also the Hebrew commentaries of the great Jewish exegetes. These exercised an important influence later.

Thus in the New Testament he strongly preferred the Fourth Gospel to the Synoptics, and he considered the Epistle to the Romans the book of greatest value, while the Epistle of James was relegated to the lowest rank. As regards the Old Testament, he asked what it mattered if Moses were not the author of Genesis.

'He saw the essential superiority of the Books of Kings over those of Chronicles as an historical record, and did not hesitate to pronounce the former more credible. He discerned the dramatic character of the Book of Job, and compared its structure to that of the Comedies of Terence. The Book of Ecclesiastes, he thought, was not the production of Solomon, but of Sirach, and belonged to the time of the Maccabees. He wished that the Second Book of Maccabees and that of Esther did not exist, partly for their too Jewish tendency, partly because they contain much heathen folly. He points out that the prophecies of Jeremiah, as we have them, are not in chronological order, and hence infers that they were made into a book, not by the prophet himself, but by a compiler.'[1]

With regard to certain other matters he expressed free and critical opinions. Thus he regarded the predictive function of prophecy as relatively unimportant, and he doubted whether miracles were of any great value in producing conviction. Miracles, apart from faith, were useless. Luther's approach to the Bible was fresh and original, and far removed from the dull and mechanical view which regards all parts of Scripture as on exactly the same level, without distinction of worth or of inspiration.

Among the great figures of the Reformation period who were directly inspired by the spirit of humanism, we must not omit to mention HULDREICH ZWINGLI (1484–1531). His school days were spent at Basel and at Bern; then followed two years at the University of Vienna, and again four years at Basel, where he eagerly pursued the studies of the day.

'It was at Basel, already a centre of busy literary activity, that he fell under the influence of Thomas Wyttenbach, one of those grave

---

[1] C. Beard, *The Reformation*, London, 1883, p. 157 f.

scholars of the Rhineland who found the keenest admiration of ancient literature not inconsistent with an earnest Christian faith, and who directed his pupil to the study of the Scriptures apart from scholastic commentary. At a later period he learned for this purpose first Greek and then Hebrew, copying out with his own hand all the Epistles of Paul, that he might know them through and through. But he was not on this account untrue to his first classical preferences. He learned Valerius Maximus off by heart. Thucydides and Aristotle, Plutarch and Lucian were familiar to him. He thought Plato had drunk at the fountain of Divine Wisdom; he extolled the piety of Pindar; he gave the great heroes and poets of pagan antiquity a place in the Christian heaven. When Luther, in the first ardour of his Biblical soul, was forswearing all philosophy, Zwingli was burying himself in the speculations of Pico della Mirandola.' [1]

It may be noted here that Zwingli took a considerable share in the production of a complete German Bible for German Switzerland. Luther's New Testament was being printed in Zürich in 1524. The historical books of the Old Testament followed soon after. An independent translation of the rest of the Old Testament was then begun. The complete Bible was issued at Zürich in six volumes in 1529, and the one volume edition in 1530, several years before the privilege was enjoyed in Germany.

Of Zwingli's disciples the most prominent was Heinrich Bullinger (1504–1575). He has left a most interesting account of the methods employed at Zürich in 1524–1525 in the congregational study of the Scriptures, from which it will be seen how thoroughly the text of the Old Testament was compared with the ancient versions, and how the Jewish commentators were diligently studied. The following extract will illustrate these points.[2]

'This gathering began with intercessions. Uniting in common forms of prayers they supplicated the almighty and merciful God, whose word

[1] C. Beard, *op. cit.*, p. 231 f.
[2] Translated from the Latin text given by B. J. Kidd, *Documents illustrative of the Continental Reformation*, i. 449.

is a lantern unto our feet and a light unto our paths, to open and lighten our mind that we might understand his oracles purely and holily, and be transformed into that which we had rightly understood, and that in this we might in no way displease his majesty, through Christ our Lord.

After prayers, a very young man, a scholar of the church, read over side by side with the Vulgate, which they call Jerome's version, that passage at which they had, in the due progress of exegesis, arrived for discussion. It should be said that persons of good and promising intelligence are supported by a payment from the ecclesiastical chest, and educated in arts, languages and sacred literature, that they may one day repay the church by whom they are supported and be of the greatest service in the sacred offices ...

When the young man had read in Latin the passage which came up for discussion, a Hebrew reader rose and repeated the passage in Hebrew, occasionally pointing out the idioms and peculiarities of the language, sometimes giving a rendering of the sense, sometimes translating word for word, and moreover reading the comments of the Grammarians and Rabbis. Ceporinus [1] used to perform the task, now Dominus Pellicanus Rubeaquensis [2] does it with the greatest conscientiousness, breadth of learning and depth of devotion. He is distinguished alike in his knowledge of languages, his devotion and his scholarship.

The Greek reader followed the Hebrew. He ran through the Septuagint, or whatever Greek translation it might be, compared it with the Hebrew, and showed how far it differed from it. Sometimes too he emended it, and always fixed his attention on it with unflagging carefulness. Zwingli himself discharged this office as long as he lived. After comparing the two languages and translating the Greek text, he at last proceeded to the task of exegesis, which hitherto had given precedence to that of interpretation.

The words which had now been read in Latin, in Greek and in Hebrew were enunciated with the utmost conscientiousness and complete good faith. He showed how the present passage had been treated by the old writers, what the Jewish commentators had thought about it and what the Catholic. He taught what it had in common with sacred literature, the putting together, coherence and force of the words, the sublimity and high morality of their meanings, the strength of substance and delicacy of style to which everything must be referred —in short, he expounded the real meaning, and also the profit and use

---

[1] Jakob von Wisendangen, Professor of Hebrew at Zürich, 1525–1526.

[2] Conrad Kurschner, of Ruffach in Elsass (1478–1556), succeeded Ceporinus as Professor of Hebrew at Zürich.

of this passage, and how a lesson in faith, devotion, piety, justice and loyalty might be learned from it.'

JOHN CALVIN (1509–1564), the most acute mind among the Reformers, belongs to a later period of the Reformation than Luther and Zwingli. In his commentaries on the Old Testament, especially in those on Isaiah (1550–1570) and on the Psalms (1557), we have the best examples of the exegesis of the sixteenth century. The influence of Hebrew studies, especially of the study of grammar and philology, is shown in the increased attention given to these subjects by Christian scholars. Calvin was himself a careful and exact Hebraist.[1]

The ' discovery of the Bible ' was one of the firstfruits of the humanistic movement, and the diffusion of knowledge of the Bible was made possible, in the first instance, by the publication of the original texts, some of the early printed editions of which have been referred to above. Here may be conveniently mentioned the first of the great Polyglot Bibles to be published, viz. the Complutensian, which appeared in six folio volumes, dated 1514–1517. The work was printed and published at the expense of Cardinal Ximenes. The first four volumes, which are devoted to the Old Testament, give the Hebrew text, the Targums and LXX, all with Latin translations.

But the most important factor in spreading the knowledge of the Bible was the printing and publication of vernacular translations of the Scriptures, and especially those which were based upon the original

---

[1] The following are the most important of Calvin's exegetical works on the Old Testament. In some cases they were prepared by pupils or friends from notes taken at lectures, and afterwards revised by Calvin himself:

(1) *Commentarii in Jesaiam Prophetam*: first published 1550: later revised and enlarged by Calvin, and dedicated by him to Queen Elizabeth. Further enlarged by Gallasius (its original editor) and published 1570.

(2) *Praelectiones in Jeremiam et Lamentationes*, 1561.

(3) *Praelectiones in librum . . . Danielis*: 1st ed. 1553; 2nd ed. 1570.

(4) *Commentarium in Librum Psalmorum*, 1557.

(5) *Praelectiones in XII Prophetas . . . Minores*, 1559.

(6) *Homiliae in I librum Samuelis* (published for the first time after Calvin's death).

(7) *Conciones in librum Jobi*, 1593.

(8) *Praelectiones in Ezechielis viginti capita priora*, 1563.

languages. Only one or two of the more important of these can here be referred to.

Luther's German translation of the New Testament was made directly from the Greek text of the edition of Erasmus, and was published in 1522. The translation of the Old Testament was a much more difficult undertaking. In the preparation of it Luther was assisted by a number of friends, especially by Melanchthon, Aurogallus, Roerer, and Foerster. It is interesting to recall that the young humanist, Melanchthon, who was an accomplished scholar in the classical languages (including Hebrew), was a nephew of the famous Reuchlin, and owed no small part of his training to that great scholar. The translation appeared in parts, and was not complete till 1532. That of the Apocrypha appeared two years later. Of the English versions the work of William Tyndale (1477–1536) is most significant in this connexion. A good scholar, well versed in Greek and Hebrew, he had come under humanistic influences (he translated the *Enchiridion* of Erasmus into English). Tyndale began by rendering the New Testament into English. He found it expedient to cross to the Continent in 1524 and succeeded in issuing a printed edition in 1525. A third edition was issued at Antwerp in 1526. Tyndale then proceeded with the Old Testament, which was printed and issued in parts as far as Deuteronomy. There is some reason to believe that he actually completed the translation of the Old Testament, and that it was utilized in Miles Coverdale's version.[1] The importance of Tyndale's Old Testament work is that it was rendered direct from the Hebrew. The Geneva Bible (1558–1560) was also an important English version, translated from the original languages, as also was the Bishops' Bible (published 1568). The 'King James's Bible', or *Authorized Version*, which appeared in 1611, will be referred to in a later section.

It is curious to notice the effect of the Reformation on Art. With the emphasis laid on the Bible in Protestant circles there came in a tendency to restrict sacred themes for painting to the Bible proper. Thus Rembrandt, good Calvinist as he was, rigidly limits his pictures of this kind to purely Biblical subjects.

---

[1] In Matthew's Bible (1537) the entire New Testament and the Old as far as the end of Chronicles are Tyndale's.

§ 10. *The Buxtorfs*

The career of the elder Buxtorf—JOHANNES BUXTORF I (1564–1629) marks a new epoch in the study of Hebrew among Christians. The study of the Rabbinical literature was widely extended under his inspiration and with the aid of his invaluable works. The orientalist Humphrey Prideaux (1648–1724) did not overstate his claims when he said:[1] 'The world is more beholden to Buxtorf for his learned and judicious labours than to any other man that lived in his time, and his name ought ever to be preserved in honour in acknowledgement of it.' He was educated at Marburg and later at Herborn, where Johann Piscator persuaded him to learn Hebrew. He afterwards went to Heidelberg, Basel, Zürich, and Geneva, where he enjoyed the instruction of Grynaeus, Hospinian, Bullinger, and Beza. In 1591 he was appointed Professor of Hebrew at the University of Basel, a post which he retained till his death thirty-eight years later.

Buxtorf, by his philological and other works, opened up the subject of Rabbinics to Christians and put these studies on a scientific basis. He produced his famous Rabbinical Bible in two folio volumes (Basel, 1618–1619), with a supplement entitled *Tiberias, Commentarius Masorethicus*, a work which has become a classic. The *Synagoga Judaica* first appeared in German in 1603; then in Latin, 1604. His best-known grammatical work was first published at Basel in 1605 under the title *Praeceptiones Grammaticae de Lingua Hebraea* (afterwards altered to *Epitome Grammaticae Hebraeae*), went through numerous editions, and was translated into English (London, 1656). But perhaps his most important contribution to scientific study is the great *Lexicon Chaldaicum Talmudicum et Rab-*

---

[1] H. Prideaux, *The Old and New Testament connected in the history of the Jews and neighbouring nations*, first published, London, 1716; quoted from eighth edition.

binicum, which, originally begun in 1609, was completed by his son in 1639. This great work put the study of the Post-biblical Literature of the Jews upon a sound basis, and marked a real advance. A new edition, edited by B. Fischer, was published in 1875. Other invaluable pioneering works are Buxtorf's *Bibliotheca Rabbinica*, a bibliographical list of Rabbinical writings, arranged according to the letters of the Hebrew alphabet; his book on Hebrew abbreviations (*De abbreviaturis Hebraicis*), published at Basel, 1613 and 1640, and in later editions; and his *Institutio Epistolaris Hebraica* (Basel, 1610 and 1629), a collection of family and other letters, the Hebrew text being given and partly furnished with a Latin translation.

Buxtorf utilized for the last-mentioned work the material embodied in the *Ma'yan Gannim* ('the Fountain of Gardens') of the Italian Jewish grammarian and poet Archevolti (sixteenth century). The *Ma'yan Gannim* (published at Venice, 1553) was a collection of fifty metrical letters, designed as models for composition by students. Another important work was a Hebrew grammar, published at Venice, 1602,[1] under the title '*Arugath ha-bosem* ('Bed of Spices'). The book was divided into thirty-two chapters, the last of which (dealing with New-Hebrew metre) was translated into Latin by the younger Buxtorf, and appended to his edition of the *Cuzari* (1660).

The son of the above, JOHANNES BUXTORF II (1599–1664), was born and died at Basel. He succeeded his father in the chair of Hebrew at Basel in 1629, and closely followed in his footsteps. He devoted some of his energies to preparing new editions of his father's works. He was the author of some well-known treatises—notably the *De linguae Hebraicae origine et antiquitate* (Basel, 1644), and the *Florilegium Hebraicum* (Basel, 1648). He also translated into Latin the *Moreh* of Maimonides (*Doctor Perplexorum*, Basel, 1629) and the *Cuzari* of Judah ha-Levi (*Liber Cosri*, Basel, 1660), and wrote a number of dissertations, which appeared in various forms (some appended to *Liber Cosri*, some in Ugolino's *Thesaurus*, vol. xxv).

[1] Reprinted at Amsterdam, 1730.

The Buxtorfs, father and son, maintained the antiquity of the Masoretic system of vowel-points, in spite of the views expressed by Elias Levita on the subject (p. 333 f.). In 1624 an anonymous work was published at Leyden under the title *Arcanum punctationis revelatum* which maintained that the Hebrew vowel-points and accents were unknown to the Biblical writers, and were introduced some centuries after the commencement of the Christian Era. The authorship of this revolutionary publication was soon acknowledged by Ludovicus Cappellus (1586–1658), Professor of Hebrew at the Academy of Saumur in France. Cappellus was a learned and independent scholar, deeply interested in the history of the text of the Old Testament. His views, which were condemned by the leading Hebraists of the time, have long since been accepted by all scholars. Cappellus produced another important work entitled *Critica sacra* (Paris, 1650), in which he showed that the official text of the Old Testament is often faulty. The views propounded in this treatise were regarded as so dangerous that publication only took place sixteen years after the book had been written. He was also the author of *Templi Hierosolymitani delineatio triplex* and *Chronologia sacra* printed in the Prolegomena to the London Polyglot, as well as of other works.

§ 11. *French Hebraists of the early XVIIth century*

The seventeenth century is rich in names of eminent scholars who advanced Hebrew and Biblical studies in various directions. Hebrew had now a secure place beside Latin and Greek in the culture of the time. Perhaps the most striking example of the fusion of the different elements in one personality—and that of a man of supreme genius—is John Milton (1608–1674) in whom the Hebraic and the Greek streams unite in a perfect union.

A curious example of the position of Hebrew is afforded by a Dictionary—*Linguae Romanae Dictionarium Luculentum Novum* (A New

Dictionary in Five Alphabets: English-Latin, Classical Latin, Latin Proper Names, Barbarous Latin and Law Latin), published at Cambridge, 1693. Here, in the Classical Latin part, the Greek and Hebrew equivalents are regularly given. It is interesting to notice that this work is based partly upon 'a large manuscript in three volumes of Mr. John Milton'. Milton, of course, knew Hebrew.

The names of Morin, Brian Walton (of the Paris and London Polyglots), of Pococke, Lightfoot, Castell, Hyde, Cocceius, l'Empereur, Leusden, Abendana, Surenhusius, Hackspan, Plantavit, Selden, Spencer, and Reland form a brilliant galaxy indeed.

The learned JEAN MORIN (1591–1659) was educated as a Protestant, but in 1618 joined the Roman Church, becoming a Father of the Oratory in Paris. He published a Prolegomena to an edition of the Septuagint in 1628, some discourses on the Samaritan Pentateuch in 1631, and an edition of the text of the same which was included in the Paris Polyglot (ten volumes, 1645).

'Morinus' work', says Dr. C. H. H. Wright,[1] 'was in many ways important, although in the interests of the Church, he maintained the superiority of the texts of the LXX, Vulgate, and Samaritan to that of the Hebrew, and maintained that God would have the Hebrew Scriptures written without points, in order that men might learn to submit to the judgement of the Church, instead of following their own private judgement.'

Another convert to Romanism was JEAN PLANTAVIT, Sieur de la Pause (1576–1651). Born of a noble Protestant family in the diocese of Nîmes, he became pastor of Béziers, where in 1604 he joined the Roman Church, and in 1625 became Bishop of Lodeve. He was one of the most learned Hebraists of the age. He spent thirty years in the preparation of a vast *Thesaurus synonymus Hebraico-Chaldaico Rabbinicus* (Lodovae, 1644–1645). In this work under each general term are grouped the related words in six columns; the first and second give the Hebrew

---

[1] *Introduction to the Old Testament*, London, 1890, p. 4.

and Aramaic synonyms, with a Latin explanation; the third
and fourth give references to the Old Testament for examples
to illustrate each point, with Latin translation; and the fifth
and sixth give the Rabbinic synonyms, with Latin explanations.
There are even now very few works which deal systematically
with Hebrew synonyms. Plantavit was also the author of other
works, including a *Florilegium Rabbinicum* (Lodovae, 1645).

Any survey of the seventeenth century would be incomplete which
failed to record the really wonderful work of Samuel Bochart (1599–
1667), the great ornament of the French Reformed Church. Bochart
received a thorough theological training, and also studied the Oriental
languages. He is the author of two monumental works: *Geographica
sacra seu Phaleg et Chanaan* (1646), and *Hierozoicon . . . opus
de animalibus sacrae Scripturae* (1663), an amazing production surveying everything contained in classical and Oriental literature relating
to the animals mentioned in the Bible. Much that is contained in
these books is still valuable.

§ 12. *English Hebraists of the XVIIth century*

Among the brilliant group of scholars who flourished during
the middle years of the seventeenth century, the names of
Pococke and Lightfoot stand conspicuous. EDWARD POCOCKE
(Fig. 59 overleaf) (1604–1691) was born in Oxford. He graduated
there in 1622. In 1628 he became a Fellow of Corpus Christi
College and was ordained.[1] He took up the study of Oriental
languages, especially Hebrew and Arabic, and in this department
became one of the foremost scholars of his time. One of his earliest
works was an edition of the hitherto unpublished Syriac text of
2 Peter, 2 and 3 John, and St. Jude. Shortly after this he became Chaplain to the Turkey merchants at Aleppo, where he
remained for six years (1630–1636). During this period he
extended his knowledge of Oriental languages, and with the
financial assistance of Archbishop Laud purchased a large num-

---

[1] There is a valuable note on Rabbinic Studies in Oxford in the early
seventeenth century by G. W. Wheeler in *Bodleian Quarterly Record*, iii,
p. 144, Oxford, 1921.

ber of Oriental and Greek manuscripts, now embodied in the splendid Pococke collection in the Bodleian Library. On his return to Oxford in 1636 Pococke was appointed to the newly founded Laudian Chair of Arabic of which he was the first holder. He again visited the East, spending several years in Constantinople and its neighbourhood (1637–1640). During this period he made the acquaintance of Cyril Lucar, the Patriarch of Constantinople. In 1643 he became incumbent of Childrey in Berkshire. In 1647 he resumed his chair of Arabic, and in 1648 was appointed Regius Professor of Hebrew and Canon of Christ Church. In 1650, owing to political troubles, he was ejected from the canonry as a Royalist, but was allowed to retain his Professorship till his death.

Pococke was a really great Orientalist. Of his share in the work of the great London Polyglot his biographer says: 'From the beginning scarce a step was taken in that work [not excepting even the *Prolegomena*] till communicated to Mr. Pococke, without whose assistance it must have wanted much of its perfection.'[1] He took an active share in preparing the Arabic text of the Pentateuch, and lent to the editors engaged in the work several of his own manuscripts, including a Syriac manuscript of the entire Old Testament, an Ethiopic manuscript of the Psalms, two Syriac manuscripts of the Psalms, and a Persian manuscript of the Gospels.

In 1655 appeared Pococke's *Porta Mosis* containing six sections of Maimonides's Commentary on the Mishnah, the original Arabic text being printed in Hebrew characters, and accompanied by a Latin translation. This is the first book to be printed in Hebrew characters in Oxford. It is a strikingly able piece of work and is still valuable. Pococke's work as a Hebraist is reflected in a series of commentaries in English on some of the Minor Prophets, *Micah* and *Malachi* (1677), *Hosea* (1685), and *Joel* (1691). These are remarkable examples

[1] *Life*, by Leonard Twells, in the collected edition of his works.

Fig. 58. JOHN SELDEN, 1584–1654

Fig. 59. EDWARD POCOCKE, 1604–1691

of exposition of the text of Scripture, based upon exact knowledge of Hebrew with all the aids of Jewish and Christian learning. In the Preface to the *Micah* the authorities cited fill three columns, and include the ancient versions (with the Arabic), the ancient Jewish commentators, and Christian commentators down to the author's own time (e. g. Pellicanus, Sebastian Munster, Calvin). The following extract from the Preface to *Micah* will illustrate his method and command of illustrative aids :

'Those that we especially make use of, are *Rabbi Salomo Jarchi, R. Abraham Ezra, R. David Kimchi,* and *Isaac Abarbinel* ... who are all well known by name, as being printed and given account of by *Buxtorf* and others, whose expositions, where they might seem to the purpose, I have as far as I could, laboured to give a faithful account of, though to prolixity, that if we be not alwaies directly holpen by them in finding the truth, we might see how and wherein they err from it, and so by the discovery thereof, be more earnestly stirred up to seek after it and embrace it. Besides these, the Reader will find often cited one *R. Tanchum,* an *Hierosolymitan,* who is less known, because never yet printed, although as far as I can judge, he might as well deserve to be so as some of the rest, as as much conducing in divers places to the understanding of the text as any of them. He wrote Notes in the Arabick Language on the whole Old Testament (as himself declares): though I have not had the happiness to see them on divers of the Books thereof, on the Prophets (all but *Isaiah*) I have. When he lived I know not, only it appears he was after the time of *Moses Maimonides,* whom he often cites and follows in many things. To these may be added *Yalkut,* a Book so called, being a collection of divers Allegorical Expositions on the Scripture. What other Hebrew Books are cited, and are Printed, I shall not need give particular account of, seeing any that desires it may have it in *Buxtorfes Bibliotheca Rabbinica.*'

During his long residence in the East (the greater part of the years 1630–1640) Pococke was on friendly terms with Jews, especially in Aleppo and Constantinople (where he studied with Judah Romano).[1]

[1] See I. Abrahams, *Transactions of the Jewish Historical Society of England*, viii. 105.

JOHN LIGHTFOOT (1602–1675), the greatest of the Christian Rabbinical scholars, received a thorough training in Greek and Latin at school and afterwards at Cambridge. It was only after he had been ordained that he took up the study of Hebrew. While at Norton-under-Hales in Staffordshire he was induced by Sir Rowland Cotton—himself a Hebraist—to learn Hebrew. Sir Rowland took Lightfoot into his house as his chaplain. Subsequently he moved to Stone in Staffordshire, thence to Hornsey, and later to the living of Ashford in Staffordshire to which he was presented by his old friend Cotton. Here he built himself a small house not far from the parsonage, consisting of a study below and a sleeping room above, where he spent most of his time, visiting his family once a day. Thus he remained during the troubles that ensued on the execution of Charles I and the establishment of the Commonwealth. He became a member of the Westminster Assembly (1643) where his scholarship exercised a moderating influence. The same year (1643) he was appointed Rector of Much-Munden in Hertfordshire, a living which he retained till his death. He also became Master of Catherine Hall, Cambridge. In 1653 he became Vice-Chancellor of the University. He did not allow his University duties to lead to the entire neglect of his country parish, where he spent as much time as he was able. At the Restoration he was confirmed in his appointments, and before his death in 1675 was appointed to a prebendal stall in Ely Cathedral.

Lightfoot was a remarkable scholar. He aimed at introducing scientific method and order into the study of Scripture. With this in view, he wrote a work on the chronology of the Bible (*Harmonia, Chronica et Ordo Veteris Testamenti*, 1647, and *Harmonia, etc. Nov. Test.*, 1655), and another on the Four Gospels in the shape of a Harmony (*Harmonia Quattuor Evangelistarum*, 1644–47–50). But Lightfoot's most significant and important activity was in the domain of Rabbinic literature, his profound knowledge of which laid the foundations of work of permanent value. His *Descriptio Templi Hierosolymitani* (1650), his *Ministerium Templi quale erat tempore nostri Salvatoris* (1649), and above all his *Horae Hebraicae et Talmudicae* to the Four Gospels, the *Acts of the Apostles and 1 Corinthians* (1658–1678) are works of great importance, which have been supplemented but not superseded. His *Horae* in particular is a splendid piece of work, and here Lightfoot shows himself immensely superior to his successors in this type of work— Schöttgen (1687–1781), Meuschen (1680–1743), and Nork (Selig Korn), a converted Jew (1803–1850). His description, too, of Herod's Temple and its services, so far as it embodies Jewish tradition, is a work of permanent value. Lightfoot also took a share in the production of Walton's Polyglot, for which he revised the Samaritan Pentateuch, and contributed a description of the Geography of Palestine to that work; he was consulted also by Edmund Castell in the preparation of the *Lexicon Heptaglotton* which forms an Appendix.

Mention may here conveniently be made of two distinguished scholars who belong to the seventeenth century, and who made important contributions to the study of Hebrew archaeology and institutions—Selden and Spencer.

JOHN SELDEN (Fig. 58, fac. p. 354) (1584–1654) was by profession a lawyer, by taste an antiquary, and by application one of the most learned men of the age. He was a voluminous writer, and possessed an extensive knowledge of Hebrew and Hebrew antiquity. He was the author of *A treatise on the Jews in England* (1617). In the same year he produced a pioneering work on the study of Phoenician and Syrian mythology, the *De diis Syris*. In *Marmora Arundelliana* (1629) a small collection of Hebrew Inscriptions is translated. An important series of works deals with matters of Jewish law—*De successione in bona Defunctorum ad Leges Ebraeorum* (1631), *De successione in Pontificatum Ebraeorum* (1636) dedicated to Laud, the *De jure naturali et Gentium .. libri septem* (1640). In the last-mentioned work Selden treats of the so-called 'laws of Noah' which are of universal application and obligation, and the laws which were specifically obligatory on Jews. An elaborate treatise on the marriage and divorce laws of the Jews, *Uxor Ebraica*, was published by Selden in 1646, and a massive collection of material entitled *De Synedris*, dealing with the Jewish Sanhedrin and law courts. Much of Selden's work is of permanent value. He was himself an ardent adherent of the Parliamentary cause, and a convinced Protestant. He often found in Hebrew antiquity arguments to confirm his views, and it is interesting to note that Hebrew studies were specially congenial to his Protestant mind.

JOHN SPENCER (1630–1695), who belonged to a younger generation, has been called 'the founder of the science of Comparative Religion'. He received his academic training at Cambridge, where he became Fellow, and later Master of Corpus Christi College. At the age of thirty-three he proceeded to the degree of D.D., and in 1677 he was made Dean of Ely. Spencer's great work, which has made his name famous, was published in 1685 under the title *De legibus Hebraeorum Ritualibus et earum Rationibus*. This was afterwards enlarged.[1] Spencer recognizes that many of the Jewish laws are derived or modified from pagan rites and customs. It is from this point of view that he discusses in a most interesting and suggestive way the origins of sacrifice and of purifications, the commemoration of the New Moons, the Ark and the Cherubim, the Temple, the Urim and Thummim, and the Scapegoat. The enlarged edition treats also of rites and customs derived from pagan sources which are without divine sanction, and contains a dissertation on phylacteries. It may be noted here, as an example of Spencer's interest in purely Hebrew studies, that he took an

[1] A posthumous edition containing the author's latest additions and corrections was published in 2 vols., folio, in 1727; and another edited by Pfaff, 2 vols., folio, at Tübingen in 1732. This edition has a dissertation by the editor on Spencer's life and a critical estimate of his work.

active share with Cudworth, Lightfoot, and George Bright in reading the manuscript of Isaac Abendana's Cambridge Mishnah, as is attested by certain memoranda, dated at various times in 1671.

A word must be said here about the career of BRIAN WALTON (1600–1661), the learned editor of the *London Polyglot*—the most important of the Polyglot Bibles which have appeared. Walton was educated at Cambridge, but it was at Oxford (1639 and later), where he had taken refuge in consequence of the political troubles of the time, that he formed the idea of producing the Polyglot, and made preparations for it. The first volume of the *Polyglot* was published in 1654, the whole being completed by the end of 1657. It contains the Hebrew text, the Samaritan Pentateuch, the Samaritan Version, the Septuagint with various readings, the Vulgate together with fragments of the so-called *Old Latin Version*, the Syriac and the Arabic versions; the Targums, the Ethiopic version of Psalms and Canticles, and a Persian rendering of the Pentateuch—all with Latin translations. The books of the Apocrypha are also included, and it is interesting to note that in the case of the Book of Tobit two Hebrew versions are given, one by Paul Fagius (p. 334), and the other by Sebastian Munster (p. 334). Walton's own *Prolegomena* is prefixed to the work, and is notable among the earlier works of Introduction to the Old Testament.[1]

Among the eminent scholars who contributed to the great work edited by Walton—who included Lightfoot and Capellus —none is more eminent as an Orientalist than EDMUND CASTELL (1606–1685), whose *Lexicon Heptaglotton (Hebraicum, Chaldaicum, Syriacum, Samaritanum, Aethiopicum, Arabicum conjunctim, et Persicum separatim)* appeared in two folio volumes, as a supplement to the Polyglot Bible, in 1669. This gigantic undertaking, in spite of the fact that he received assistance and

---

[1] Afterwards issued separately by Heidegger (1673), Dathe (1777), and by F. Wrangham (Cambridge, 1828).

co-operation from various scholars, involved its author in enormous labour and expense. He was at work upon it from 1651 to 1669. Castell, whose academic career had been spent at Cambridge, was appointed Professor of Arabic in that University in 1666, and to a prebendal stall in Canterbury Cathedral in 1667; he also became chaplain to King Charles II, and at various times held livings in Essex and Bedfordshire. He held the living of Higham Gobion in the latter county at the time of his death.[1]

Castell assisted Walton not only by preparing the Lexicon, but also in many other ways, especially in the editing of the Syriac, Arabic, and Ethiopic versions for the Polyglot. The Lexicon itself reveals how extensive his knowledge of Hebrew and Aramaic was. He cites from the Targums, the two Talmuds, and the medieval Jewish commentators. In 1787 the well-known scholar J. D. Michaelis published in separate form the Syriac portion in two volumes, quarto, and later the Hebrew section in similar form. Castell was in close touch with other eminent scholars of his time—he refers particularly to the help he received from the Orientalists Beveridge (afterwards Bishop), Murray, and Wansleb, as well as to that from Pococke and Lightfoot. To the latter especially he expresses gratitude.[2] He bequeathed all his Oriental manuscripts (which included several Hebrew ones) to the University of Cambridge.

A distinguished Hebraist, who was active in the latter part

[1] In the chancel of Higham Gobion church there is a monument to the memory of Castell, placed by himself in the year 1674, with an inscription in Latin, followed by a line in Arabic.

[2] He was at various times in correspondence with several eminent foreign scholars. In one of his letters he says: 'Besides some among ourselves, I have a Golius, a Buxtorf, a Hottinger, a Ludolfo, &c., in foreign parts, that both by their letters and in print have not only sufficiently—but too amply and abundantly for me to communicate—expressed their over-high esteem of that which finds but a prophet's reward here in its close' (quoted by Dr. P. Holmes).

of the seventeenth century, was THOMAS HYDE (1636–1703). Hyde was for a time a student of Arabic and Persian in Cambridge under Wheelock. In 1658 he migrated to Oxford, and in 1665 became chief librarian at the Bodleian; in 1691 he became Professor of Arabic, and in 1697 Regius Professor of Hebrew. In 1691 there appeared an edition by him of the *'Iggereth 'orḥoth 'olam* of Abraham Peritsol (Farissol, 1451–1526), which he translated into Latin under the title *Itinera Mundi*. This was published as a supplement to Abulfeda's Arabic Geography. Three years later (1694) Hyde issued a remarkable treatise under the title *De ludis orientalibus*, which contains three Hebrew compositions on chess. In the preparation of both these works he appears to have been assisted by the learned Jew Isaac Abendana (born sometime before 1650 and died about 1710), of whose career something must be said.

ISAAC ABENDANA—brother of the famous Jacob Abendana (1630–1695), who was called to London to become Rabbi of the congregation of Spanish and Portuguese Jews in 1680—was an active influence on Hebrew studies, both in Cambridge and Oxford, during the latter part of the seventeenth century. Both brothers had friendly relations with contemporary Christian Hebraists.[1] To Isaac Abendana belongs the credit of having been the first to translate the entire Mishnah into Latin—a work accomplished between the years 1663 and 1675 at Cambridge, and which still exists in manuscript in the Library of that University. Dr. Israel Abrahams has told the story of these activities.[2] The first complete translation of the Mishnah in any language was the Spanish version made by Isaac's brother Jacob. Surenhusius made use of Jacob's work (which is still only in manuscript) in preparing his edition of the

[1] Jacob Abendana was known to Buxtorf in Basel, Cocceius and Golius in Leyden, and Anton Hulsius. The last mentioned was greatly assisted in his Oriental studies by Abendana.
[2] *Transactions of the Jewish Historical Society of England*, viii, pp. 98–122.

Mishnah, which was published in six volumes at Amsterdam in the years 1698–1703.

During the second half of the seventeenth century the desire for a translation of the Mishnah had been several times expressed at Cambridge. Dr. Abrahams writes: 'Isaac Abendana came to the rescue of the Cambridge Hebraists. He was certainly in Cambridge in 1663, for the payments of six pounds annually made to him by Trinity College began in the last quarter of that year. . . . He must have been commissioned to translate the Mishnah soon after his arrival, probably in 1663.' Abendana appears to have completed the manuscript of the work as it now exists in 1675, and left Cambridge soon afterwards. As with his brother's Spanish version, this Latin version was never printed.

In 1689 [1] Isaac Abendana was employed in Oxford as a Lecturer in Hebrew, and continued in this work down to 1699. As a Rabbinical authority he was welcomed by several distinguished Oxford scholars, among them Thomas Hyde (1636–1703), whose relations with Isaac Abendana have already been referred to (p. 361)—Anthony Wood, Dr. Jonathan Edwards (1629–1712), Principal of Jesus College (from 1686), Dr. Roger Mander, Master of Balliol, 1687–1704. The Jewish scholar had also as a patron Dr. John Hough (1651–1743), then Bishop of Oxford. Another generous Oxford friend was Arthur Charlett (1655–1722), Master of University College.

In 1692 Abendana issued through the University Press the first of his 'Jewish Kalendars', the series being regularly continued down to 1699. They are curious productions, containing besides the Jewish calendars proper, much miscellaneous information. They excited a good deal of interest at the time of their appearance, and seem to have been much sought after. A comprehensive work, based upon these calendars, was issued by Abendana in 1706 entitled *Discourses on the Ecclesiastical and Civil Polity of the Jews*.

[1] Between 1676 and 1689 he stayed for some time in London.

§ 13. *The Transition to Modern Scholarship*

Another great scholar of the latter part of the seventeenth century, who must not be passed over in this connexion, is CAMPEGIUS VITRINGA (1659–1722). Vitringa, who was successively Professor of Oriental Languages and Theology at Leyden, and of Theology at Franeker, has left behind some massive and important works, among them his commentary on Isaiah (2 vols., folio: 1st ed., 1714–1720).[1] Another great work is the *De Synagoga vetere* (1696), which even now no serious student of the subject can afford to neglect.[2] He also produced a commentary on Zechariah, and one on the Apocalypse (1705), besides two volumes of *Observationes Sacrae*, which last has passed through various editions, that of 1723, edited by Werner, having a life of the author prefixed. All this great scholar's works are important and valuable. Finally, a word must be said about that remarkable man RICHARD SIMON (1638–1712). Simon, who was a member of the congregation of the Oratory in Paris, was a scholar of great originality and power, possessed of great boldness, both in thought and action. A fine Hebraist, he published in 1678 his *Histoire Critique du Vieux Testament*, which on its appearance provoked a storm, and was suppressed. All copies of the book were ordered to be destroyed, but some escaped.[3] Dr. C. H. H. Wright [4] thus describes it:

'It was a work of learning and research, and its conclusions, though then generally regarded with horror, would be now on many points considered conservative. According to Simon, the Pentateuch in its present shape is not the work of Moses. His theory ... is as follows: In all Eastern states there have been official historiographers, and a

[1] After his death an improved edition, edited by Schultens, was published at Basel in 1732.

[2] An English work based on Vitringa (much abridged) was published in London in 1842 by J. L. Bernard.

[3] Various editions appeared in countries outside France. An English edition was issued in 1682.

[4] *Introduction to the Old Testament* (1890), p. 4 f.

similar class existed among the Hebrews since the days of Moses. In the case of the Hebrews their historiographers were, however, inspired prophets. These recorded not only what was of importance in their own day, but altered, abridged, and enlarged the works of their predecessors. All such writings were collected by Ezra and his successors; and from the material so brought together, the books of the Old Testament were arranged in the form in which they are now extant.'

Simon also produced some important books on the New Testament.

Other distinguished Hebrew scholars who belong to the seventeenth century, and who must be passed over briefly here, are Constantine L'Empereur (1571–1648), the author of a *Clavis Talmudica* (1634) and other works; Johann Cocceius (1603–1667), a profound Hebrew and Rabbinical scholar, the author of numerous commentaries and of a Hebrew Lexicon which had a wide circulation (he also edited some Rabbinical texts); John Henry Hottinger (1620–1667), the friend of Ussher, Pococke, Selden, and Wheelock, was an excellent Semitic scholar, and the author of many important philological works (the manuscripts are preserved in the library of Zürich where they fill fifty-two volumes); Ralph Cudworth (1617–1688), the Cambridge Platonist who was also Regius Professor of Hebrew; John Leusden (1624–1699), Professor of Hebrew in his native city of Utrecht, was a renowned Biblical scholar, and the author of numerous works on the Bible (critical, introductory, and exegetical). He was the first Christian scholar to issue a critical text of the Hebrew Bible (1667): he also published editions of the Greek Testament and of the LXX, and issued a Hebrew Lexicon (1688) and an elementary Hebrew grammar, as well as many other philological, introductory, and exegetical works. He published an edition of Lightfoot's works in Latin. Here, too, we must mention Johann Andreas Eisenmenger (1654-1704), the notorious author of *Entdecktes Judenthum* (' Judaism Unmasked '). Eisenmenger became a diligent student of Hebrew and (with the assistance of some Jews) of the Rabbinical literature. The book, which was first published in 1700, became the favourite manual for anti-Semites, and to this day is used as an armoury of facts and arguments against the Jews. Eisenmenger's contemporary, J. C. Wagenseil (1633–1705), also a Christian Hebraist, devoted his learning and energies to the task of collecting Jewish anti-Christian treatises. He published a collection of these in a well-known work, *Tela ignea Satanae* (Altdorf, 1681); at the same time he was not violently anti-Semitic—he defended the Jews against the charge of ritual murder. From 1674 to 1697 he was Professor of Oriental Languages at the University of Altdorf; he wrote several other works. John Frederick Breithaupt (1639–1713), a Christian Hebraist and Rabbinical scholar, published an edition of Yosippon with a Latin version under the title *Josephus Gorionides* (Gotha, 1707), and also a Latin translation of the commentary of Rashi in three volumes (Gotha, 1710–1713). This is a most useful edition, provided with excellent notes.

Before an attempt can be made to sum up the significance of the seventeenth century for Hebrew learning, a word must be said about two important Jewish figures who played a conspicuous part during this time—Manasseh ben Israel and Baruch Spinoza.

MANASSEH BEN ISRAEL (Fig. 61 overleaf) (1604–1657), the famous author of the *Conciliator*, and the friend and correspondent of many well-known Christian as well as Jewish scholars, played a conspicuous and honourable part in the affairs of his time. About 1622 he became the Rabbi of a Jewish congregation in Amsterdam. He corresponded at various times with Isaac and Dionysius Vossius, Hugo Grotius, and several other prominent scholars. He started the first Hebrew printing-press to be set up in Holland. He had been much influenced by the Cabala, and was deeply interested in Messianic questions. As is well known, he took a prominent part in the discussion of the question of the readmission of the Jews into England, and himself came over to England from Holland on a mission to Cromwell on the matter. The petition that he presented to Oliver Cromwell still exists and is reproduced in facsimile between p. 406 and p. 407 of this volume (Fig. 67). The house where he sojourned in London may be seen in Fig. 60 overleaf. Manasseh ' was a prolific writer, and his books show undeniable evidence of very wide reading and extraordinary industry. He cites not only Jewish writers like Ibn Gebirol and Maimonides, but also Euripides and Virgil, Plato and Aristotle, Duns Scotus and Albertus Magnus. Poets and legalists, mystics and rationalists, he had an appreciation of all, if not always a very intelligent appreciation.'[1] In 1640 he was appointed to a teaching post in the upper department of the Amsterdam Jewish school—the *yeshibah*—and it was here that he came into contact with Spinoza, who was a pupil at the school.

BARUCH SPINOZA (Fig. 70, fac. p. 450) (1632–1677) occupies a unique position in the history of European philosophical thought. His reputation has slowly and steadily grown during the last two and a half centuries, and to-day he is recognized as belonging to the small band of the world's greatest thinkers. It is no part of our task to attempt to expound or estimate Spinoza's system of philosophy,[2] but something must be said of his debt to Judaism and his Jewish upbringing.

Spinoza was by birth and training a Jew. He belonged to a family which was prominent among the 'Sephardic' community, i.e. the section of Spanish and Portuguese origin, at Amsterdam, and he was educated in the Jewish communal school of that city, in the upper department of which he had for his teachers, not only Manasseh ben Israel, but also the well-known scholar Saul Morteira.

'There he studied from eight to eleven in the morning, and from two to five in the afternoon, Hebrew, Bible, Talmudic literature, and toward the end of his course, some of the Jewish philosophers, certainly Maimonides, Gersonides, and Hasdai Crescas. It was probably during this period that he studied also Abraham Ibn Ezra's commentaries. The amount of his cabalistic knowledge is somewhat doubtful, but both Manasseh ben Israel and Morteira were adepts in Cabala. Spinoza was attracted by the atmosphere of free thought characteristic of the Dutch capital. He learned Latin, immediately after leaving school, from Franz van den Ende ... under him he studied as well mathematics, physics, mechanics, astronomy, chemistry, and the medicine of the day. Spinoza likewise acquired a knowledge of the scholasticism developed in the school of Thomas Aquinas.'[3]

[1] A. Wolf, *Spinoza*, p. xxvii.
[2] The place of Spinoza is discussed in the article by Dr. Roth, p. 449.
[3] Article *Spinoza* in *Jewish Encyclopaedia*, xi. 511 *b*.

FIG. 60. HOUSE IN 'THE STRAND', LONDON, WHENCE MANASSEH ISSUED HIS PETITION TO OLIVER CROMWELL

See Fig. 67 between pp. 406 and 407

FIG. 61. MANASSEH BEN ISRAEL, 1604–1657

We need not pursue the story of his quarrel with the synagogue and his subsequent excommunication. The breach was inevitable. But nevertheless his Jewish training exercised—as it was bound to do—a large influence over his character and thought. His fearless pursuit of truth for its own sake, his fine ethical sense, his moral courage and lofty idealism, were largely a legacy from his Jewish antecedents. In his system of thought he was certainly much influenced by Maimonides and the Jewish philosopher Hasdai Crescas. 'The insistence of Spinoza upon the love of God as the highest quality of human reason is undoubtedly influenced by Crescas's original view that love rather than knowledge was the divine essence.' In the *Tractatus Theologico-politicus* the influence of Maimonides and Gersonides is especially apparent, and—in the part that deals with Biblical Criticism—that of Abraham ibn Ezra. . . . Spinoza thus owed not a little to his Jewish antecedents. Apart from a due appreciation of these, it is impossible to understand either the man or his work. Nevertheless Spinoza was very far from being a typical Jew or specifically Jewish. He is still regarded by the orthodox as an 'Epikouros' or atheistic freethinker—though to a Novalis he is a 'God-intoxicated Jew'. We shall not attempt to answer the question whether it is possible to reconcile his system of thought with Judaism in any sense of the word. We may, however, sum up in the words of a Jewish thinker : [1]

'In any case Spinoza's thought is so definitely connected either by derivation or by opposition with that of the Jewish medieval thinkers that it must be regarded either as the consummation or the evisceration of Jewish philosophy.'

By the end of the seventeenth century, as we have seen, Hebrew studies and Hebrew learning had not only established a firm position, as a definite element in culture, by the side of Latin and Greek, but also had achieved work of the greatest

[1] In *Jewish Encyclopaedia*, xi. 520 b.

importance. The opening years of the century made an indelible mark alike upon our thought and our speech by the production of the *Authorized Version* of the Bible, which has long since secured its place as one of the great classics of our literature. From our present rather special point of view it is important to observe that the translation of the Old Testament in the Authorized Version is an achievement of Hebrew scholarship: and this included a knowledge of the traditional Jewish exegesis, the influence of David Kimhi being especially apparent. Another great achievement was the production of the *London Polyglot Bible* and Castell's *Lexicon* that accompanied it. The enlargement of Hebrew studies, so as to embrace the cognate languages, is a feature; and it is a notable fact that Hebrew and cognate studies had not yet been divorced from classical studies generally. Rabbinical learning flourished, and was brought to bear upon the illumination of the New Testament. When the work of such men as John Spencer, John Lightfoot, Edward Pococke, Brian Walton, and Edmund Castell is surveyed, we can understand how it was possible to coin the phrase which perhaps first became current during this century: *Clerus Anglicanus stupor Mundi!*

§ 14. *The Rise of Modern Biblical Criticism*

With the rise of modern Biblical criticism—of which Spinoza, in the *Tractatus Theologico-politicus*, may be regarded as the harbinger, and which steadily developed in the eighteenth century—interest in the wider aspects of Hebrew studies, as these had been hitherto understood, began to wane. The study of Hebrew began to assume a more specialized form and to be divorced from Jewish tradition. Its association with humane learning, too, became weakened. But these tendencies did not become pronounced till towards the end of the century. Some distinguished names remain which shine in the afterglow of the preceding century; and with the consideration of some of the most representative of these—as it is no part of our task to attempt to trace the development of the Higher Criticism—we bring this essay to a conclusion.

The following list will, perhaps, be sufficiently representative: Reland, Hody, Prideaux, Michaelis, Wolf, Wetstein, Schultens, Ugolino, Kennicott, and Lowth.

HADRIAN RELAND (1676–1718), the author of many well-known works, was Professor of Oriental Languages and Antiquities at Utrecht, where he died. Among his best known books are the *Analecta Rabbinica* (1713), which is still useful, and *Palestina ex monumentis veteribus illustrata* (2 vols. 1714), which long remained the standard work on the geography of Palestine, and marked a great advance.

HUMPHREY HODY (1659–1706) greatly distinguished himself as a Biblical scholar at Oxford. He was elected to a Fellowship at Wadham College in 1684, and became Regius Professor of Greek in 1698. His memory is perpetuated at his old college by the scholarships he founded for the promotion of Greek and Hebrew. Hody was a brilliant scholar, and at the age of twenty-two published a Dissertation on the *Letter of Aristeas*, in which he argued that the story embodied in it is a Jewish legend intended to enhance the credit of the Septuagint. The book was severely criticized by the famous Isaac Vossius, and this led Hody to devote himself to his great work *De Bibliorum Textibus Originalibus* (Oxford, 1704). This is a great contribution, and occupied its author, in the labour of its production, nearly twenty years. It deals with the history of the Septuagint and of the original Hebrew texts as well as of the Latin Vulgate and of the later Greek versions (Aquila, Symmachus, Theodotion, Origen's *Hexapla*).

Humphrey Prideaux (1648–1724), the author of the well-known *Connexion of the Old and New Testaments*, a work which has often been republished, deserves a word of recognition. His range of learning included a sound knowledge of classical languages and literature, and of Hebrew and Rabbinic.

Several members of the family of Michaelis were distinguished as Biblical scholars; but the one who rendered, on the whole, the greatest services to Hebrew learning was JOHN HENRY MICHAELIS (1668–1731), who became Professor of Oriental Languages and (later) of Divinity in the University of Halle. His most important work was an edition of the Hebrew Bible in two volumes (1720). Kennicott, referring to this, says: 'This edition was the first which contained any various readings collected from Hebrew manuscripts by a Christian editor.' He also edited a large commentary on the *Hagiographa*, accompanied by a critical text. The most famous member of the family was John David Michaelis (1717–1791), who forms a link between the old orthodoxy and the new rationalism. The learning of John David Michaelis ranged over a wide field, embracing a knowledge of several Semitic languages and New Testament subjects as well as Old. He gained a great reputation, and received many marks of distinction both at home and abroad. Early in his career he formed a friendship with Bishop Lowth.[1] In 1745 he published a Hebrew grammar at Halle, and in the following year migrated to Göttingen, where he became Professor of Philosophy and Oriental Languages, and where he remained for the rest of his life. In 1789 he was elected a Fellow of the Royal Society in England.

Michaelis was a voluminous writer, and his books exercised a wide influence. The best known and most valuable are: (1) The *Mosaisches Recht* (6 vols. 1770–1775; 2nd ed. 1776–1780). Under the title *Commentaries on the Laws of Moses* this work was translated into English by Dr. Alexander Smith, and published in four volumes (1814). (2) The *Introduction to the New Testament*, translated into English from the fourth German edition (1788; 1st German ed., 1750).[2] The appearance of this work in England excited much controversy. An

---

[1] He contributed some notes to Lowth's *Sacra Poesis Hebraeorum*.
[2] This English edition appeared in 1823.

Introduction to the Old Testament was planned, but Michaelis did not live to carry it out. Michaelis is really the 'stormy petrel' of the new criticism, though in his encyclopaedic range his affinities are rather with the older type of scholarship.

JOHANN CHRISTOPH WOLF (1683–1739), at one time Professor of Oriental Languages at Hamburg (1712–1715), was an indefatigable scholar and writer. His best known work is the *Bibliotheca hebraea* (4 vols. Hamburg, 1713–1733), a collection of material about Hebrew writers and institutions. It provided a basis for Steinschneider's catalogue of Hebrew books in the Bodleian Library. Wolf was on friendly terms with the eminent scholars of the time, such as Vitringa, Surenhuis, and Reland.

A scholar who knew how to combine the new learning with the old, and who was a good Hebrew scholar, was J. J. WETSTEIN (1693–1754). Born at Basel, he went later in life to Holland and became Professor of Church History in the Remonstrant Gymnasium at Amsterdam. His name has become famous in connexion with his splendid edition of the New Testament (2 vols. folio, Amsterdam, 1751–1752). This work, which has not yet lost its value, is remarkable for the wealth of illustrative material that is gathered together within its pages. Hebrew illustrations are frequently given.

Another Dutch scholar, who has been called 'the father of modern Hebrew grammar', must be mentioned here—ALBERT SCHULTENS (1686–1750). He was a pupil of Reland, and settled at Leyden, where he became Curator of the Manuscripts of the Warner Oriental Collection. Schultens was a fine Hebraist, and distinguished himself as a grammarian, being the first among modern scholars to use Arabic in a scientific way to illustrate Hebrew. His most important grammatical works are *Institutiones* (Leyden, 1737) and *Vetus et Regia Via Hebraizandi* (1738). He also published an elaborate commentary on Job (2 vols. quarto, 1737) and one on Proverbs. The former was translated into German and English.

The most monumental work on Hebrew literature and antiquities of the century was edited and published by the Italian scholar BLASIO UGOLINO (? 1700–1770). In the *Thesaurus Antiquitatum Sacrarum* (34 vols. Venice, 1744–1769) the editor has collected and republished a number of treatises on Jewish subjects by Bochart, Bonfrère, Buxtorf, Carpzov, Lowth, Reland, Selden, Spencer, Wagenseil, besides enlisting the help of new scholars and himself contributing translations (into Latin) especially of Midrashic texts. This vast work deals with the following subjects: festivals (vol. i); antiquities (ii–iv); geography (v–vi); priests and temple (vii–xiii); Midrashim (xiv–xvii); Talmud (xvii–xx); synagogue worship (xxi); sects and proselytes (xxii); heathen deities (xxiii); Jewish law (xxiv–xxvii); numismatics (xxviii); costume, marriage, and medicine (xxix–xxx); poetry and music (xxxi–xxxii); death and burial (xxxiii); indexes (xxxiv). Ugolino is said to have been a converted Jew. It must be admitted that some of his Latin translations of obscure texts (e. g. that of *Sifra*) are sometimes more obscure than the originals. But the work, as a whole, is an amazing achievement.

With two names of eminent English Hebraists—Kennicott and Lowth—we will bring this sketch to a close.

BENJAMIN KENNICOTT (1718–1783) received his academic training at Wadham College, Oxford, where he lived for the rest of his life. He ultimately became a canon of Christ Church. He devoted himself to the study and criticism of the Hebrew text of the Old Testament, and published an important series of dissertations entitled *The state of the Printed Text of the Old Testament considered* (2 vols. 1753, 1759), in which, among other things, he examines the text of the Samaritan Pentateuch, and indicates its superiority in certain cases. He also gave a catalogue of a hundred Hebrew manuscripts, and cited some of their various readings. He ultimately published his splendid edition of the Hebrew Bible with variant readings: *Vetus*

Testamentum Hebraicum cum variis Lectionibus, 2 vols. folio (Oxford, 1776, 1780). Kennicott was assisted by other scholars and over 600 Hebrew manuscripts (besides 116 Samaritan) were collated, either wholly or partially. The results, however, did not fully realize expectations. Kennicott wrote other notable works on Bible text and criticism, and may be regarded as one of the best equipped Hebraists of the century.[1]

ROBERT LOWTH (1710–1787) has established a unique place for himself in the annals of Hebrew scholarship by his masterly lectures on the poetry of the Hebrews, which appeared in 1753 under the title *Praelectiones Academicae de sacra poesi Hebraeorum*. In this work the different kinds of parallelism which characterize Hebrew poetry were defined, and analysed. Lowth's treatise laid down the lines for the treatment of its subject which have been followed ever since. It has passed through many editions, both at home and abroad, and has been translated into English, French, and German. His other great work is *Isaiah : a new translation ... with notes critical, philological and explanatory*. This brilliant monograph has by no means lost its value even now, and is always worth consulting. It is an admirable example of the combination of Hebrew with other forms of classical learning. Textual criticism is a strong point as well as the illustrative matter. The translation, too, is a fine piece of work, aiming as it does to reproduce the poetical impression of the original. It was published in 1778, when Lowth was Bishop of London.[2]

It is interesting to note that the father of Bishop Lowth, viz. Dr. William Lowth (1661–1732), was himself a good Hebraist. He had been educated at Merchant Taylors' School, London, where, it will

---

[1] A sum of £10,000 was raised in subscriptions to enable Kennicott to carry out the work necessary for the edition of the Hebrew text. Among the subscribers was Dr. Thomas Secker (1693–1768), Bishop of Oxford and afterwards Archbishop of Canterbury, himself a good Hebraist.

[2] The thirteenth edition is dated 1842.

be remembered, Hebrew had been taught as a classical language, and he went thence as a scholar to St. John's College, Oxford. He was widely read, and published several books, but nothing worthy to be compared with his son's work.

Here our survey, though very far from complete, must be broken off. With the growth of modern specialism Hebrew has ceased to play the part it maintained for a time—in fact from the Renaissance down to the end of the eighteenth century. The study of Hebrew, as we have seen, was an essential element in the Humanistic Movement, which aimed at recovering reality and life. As one of the two Biblical languages, a knowledge of Hebrew was regarded as indispensable for the serious study of the Bible. The Reformation owed not a little to the pursuit of the *Hebraica veritas*. Moreover it has long been evident that the two permanent and fundamental factors in our culture are the Hebrew and the Greek. Neither can be neglected, or unduly exaggerated, at the expense of the other, without grave consequences. The leaders of the sixteenth, seventeenth, and eighteenth centuries recognized this, and in this respect we have much to learn from them. Efforts are being made to correct the limitations of too narrow a specialism by enlarging the horizons of study. It is much to be desired that this enlargement of outlook may sooner or later lead to the rehabilitation of Hebrew studies as occupying an essential place in sound learning, and above all in studies which have the Bible as their foundation.

Any survey of the vast range of Hebrew scholarship, and of its relation to humanistic studies during the last two centuries, is beyond the range alike of this article and of this volume. It is nevertheless not unfitting to say here a few words concerning him who planned this book. Dr. Israel Abrahams, Fig. 62, who died in October 1925, was admittedly the greatest Jewish scholar that this country has produced. He united in himself the widest humane culture with scientific method and caution,

FIG. 62. I. ABRAHAMS, 1859–1925

Reformation Period and After   375

and he was able to bring these faculties to bear on an immense and detailed knowledge of Hebrew and Rabbinic literature and history. We are too near him in time to place him exactly in the history of scholarship and it would not be appropriate merely to enumerate here his many learned and inspiring works. It can, however, be said that his two brilliant volumes, *Studies in Pharisaism and the Gospels*, show in masterly fashion the way in which the early Christian literature can be illustrated from Rabbinic sources. They exhibit a combination of sympathetic insight and profound learning, as well as a freedom from prejudice, which is as infrequent as it is welcome.

G. H. Box.

Fig. 63. Ornamental Hebrew Letters from the Rabbinic Bible of Daniel Bomberg (Venice, 1517–18).

FIG. 64. Book-plate designed by Dürer for the *trilinguis homo* (see p. 316) Willibald Pirckheimer (1470–1530). This German humanist and bibliophile was friend of Erasmus, Reuchlin, and Pico Della Mirandola. His library was thrown open to all students and was a centre of the humanist movement in Germany. He chose as the motto of his book-plate the words from Psalm cxi. 10, *The fear of the Lord is the beginning of wisdom*, in the three learned languages, Hebrew, Greek, Latin.

FIG. 65. SHRINE FOR SCROLLS OF THE LAW. MODENA, 1472

For description see p. xxviii

THE INFLUENCE OF JUDAISM ON WESTERN LAW

A Gift inter vivos

RATHER than of a legal legacy of Israel we should perhaps speak of a gift *inter vivos*, for living Israel has never ceased from bringing contributions to the fund of legal ideas in the Western world. There is no allusion here to the work of those judges and legislators, lawyers and writers, who have happened to be Jews. The contributions referred to are those of Israel as a people. Not only have Jews been living under the ' Law ' throughout medieval and modern times; they have expanded and developed their law to meet all kinds of new conditions, including subjection to local laws; they have philosophized about their law; and they have brought their Christian neighbours into many contacts with it. Though the Jews could not eat or drink or pray with these neighbours, they did buy with them, sell with them, walk with them, talk with them.

There have, of course, been times and countries in which artificial barriers have hindered the interchange of legal ideas, but these barriers have never been sky-high or water-tight. At the very moment when the barrier assumes the extreme form of economic elimination or expulsion of the Jews of a country, we find that country taking over their documents, their records, their credit devices, their methods of doing business, in short their legal institutions. The statutes and ordinances that open with the avowed purpose of isolating Jews from their Christian neighbours not only bear witness to their intercourse, but end with a recognition of the Jewish community ordering its own internal affairs. Thus Jewish law becomes a part of the content of the law of the land and available as a model for some new purpose. At the same time the literary and traditional influences of Judaism are at work, sometimes quite independently of the efforts of post-Biblical Jews, but, more frequently than may be suspected, with their help. Though the ideas that reach Western Europe in this way are not always branded as legal, no system of filtration can be devised by which theological, philosophical, political, and economic ideas can be let in and legal ideas kept out. Let us take as an example a view of life that has influenced both Judaism and Western civilization : the ' common ancestry of mankind ' is an anthropological theory ; the ' brotherhood of man ' is the same thing in a religious garb ; that ' all men are born equal ' is a bit of political philosophy which amounts to the same thing ; and ' equality before the law ' is the juristic aspect of the same doctrine. The law is merely one expression of life. No adequate survey of the influence of one people on another can be made unless we are willing to break down such artificial compartments as that which is commonly supposed to contain the law as an entity in itself.

In the case of Judaism and Western Law, this task is rendered exceedingly difficult by the popularity of a generalization that divides modern civilization rather too sharply into three distinct parts. To Greece it attributes the origin of the humanities, to Judea the origin of modern religion, and to Rome the foundations of modern law. Each part of the generalization is, of course, subject to reservations ; but the last in particular is subject to so many that it may be well to dispose of it entirely before entering upon the discussion of a subject that it has long tended to obscure.

In the first place, not all of the Western world has submitted to a reception of Roman law. England succeeded in warding it off by developing its own institutions early. The Scandinavian countries escaped through the lateness of their development. Of those countries that were influenced by it in a greater measure, some modified it unwittingly and others deliberately. In all of them Romanists have at one time or another been opposed by those who would emphasize the service and the claim of native law. All of them find it necessary to supplement their Roman or Romanesque code with special codes, particularly Commercial Codes, to bring them into harmony with the needs of modern times, for Roman law knew nothing of negotiable instruments, of the modern principles of agency, of the use of corporations for private business. Either within the code or outside of it they must develop a non-Roman modern public law, constitutional, international, and in a large measure criminal, too. They depart entirely from Roman precedents in family law, including marriage, divorce, domestic relations, inheritance. The very meagre Roman law of private wrongs has broken down under a pressure that has at the same time crystallized modern social legislation, differing not only in content but in spirit from anything in the Roman law books. In many of these instances, even in the laws of Roman law countries, it is easier to trace a kinship with Judaism than with the civilization of the Roman world. In the Roman world itself, it must be remembered, we are not confronted with a homogeneous system. It is a matter of heated controversy whether the influence of two centuries of Christian emperors is great or little in the compilations of Justinian. But there is hardly room for doubt that the Greek, Semitic, and Slavic Orient furnished not only some of the leading exponents of the law, but so many important ideas that the adjective 'Roman' when applied to those compilations must be understood as meaning 'Eastern Roman' or 'Byzantine'. Yet writers turn piously to the city of Rome when confronted with an institution antedating the memory of man. Blackstone attributes the invention of the corporation to Numa Pompilius. The Latin maxims that Coke spun are commonly displayed to give a Roman setting to un-Roman ideas. The Civil Law countries can turn to Rome, except in the departments of law already indicated, with a little more hope of discovering the truth, but the difference is only one of degree. A Roman lawyer of the classical period would be scarcely more at home in an Italian court to-day than in an English court. In fact he would see very little difference between the two and very little resemblance in either of them to the tribunals with which he was familiar.

Conscious imitation of the Bible not generally effective

If we get rid of the illusion that modern law is essentially a legacy of one ancient people, we shall incidentally be relieved of the necessity of picking out petty exceptions, the point of which may be that here a little or there a little suggests a relationship with another ancient people. Coke is more amusing than convincing when he traces the practice of sending judges on circuit to the habit of the prophet Samuel, or when he traces the twenty-fifth section of Magna Carta on weights and measures to the influence of the twenty-fifth chapter of Deuteronomy, or the treatment of political refugees to the provision in Deuteronomy as to fugitive slaves, or the size of a jury to the Biblical fondness for the number twelve, or *livery of seisin*[1] to the formalities of a transfer in the Book of Ruth. Blackstone agrees with him in tracing the *law of deodands* to the goring ox of the Bible.[2] Here are similarities indeed, but it is mere trifling to assume that every resemblance is based on imitation.

---

[1] *Livery of seisin* or delivery of seizance is a legal term for the delivery of property into the corporal possession of a person; in the case of a house, by giving him the latch or key of the door; in the case of land, by delivering him a twig, turf, or the like.

[2] *Law of deodands.* The word is derived from the medieval Latin *deodandum*, i.e. *Deo dandum*, 'that is to be given to God'. In English Law a personal chattel which had been the occasion of death of a human being was given to God as an expiatory offering, i.e. forfeited to the Crown to be applied to some pious use. This law was abolished only in 1846.

The student of Comparative Law may well learn a lesson from the etymologist. True relationships are frequently found between words with scarcely a letter left in common, while words that sound alike and have similar meanings can frequently be shown to be unrelated. And so it is with legal institutions. Mere appearances would never lead one to think of the jury system of England as a very close kin of the Inquisition in Spain. On the other hand no one has seriously attempted to explain the striking similarities between the Salic Law and the Code of Hammurabi by any theory of imitation. There have, of course, been several attempts in the history of Western civilization to copy the laws of Israel: in Alfred's code, in Calvin's theocratic State, in Puritan England and America. To say that nothing has come of all these attempts is a little misleading. Perhaps in King Alfred's case the attempt was more apparent than real. It may be that his long quotation from the Ten Commandments and the Book of the Covenant in Exodus with his curious substitution of Christian for Hebrew and Christ for God, was never intended as anything more than a learned gloss or an exhortation to goodness. Certainly the *Leges Barbarorum*, put into writing under missionary influence, make free with the Bible. The Anglo-Saxon Laws quote all five books of Moses, Kings, Job, Psalms, and Proverbs, besides Apocryphal and New Testament books.

In American colonial days the judges of Massachusetts, Connecticut, the New Haven colony, and West New Jersey had been commanded to inflict penalties according to the 'Law of God'. The gradual reception of the Common Law of England and the disappearance of this 'Law of God' led to the remark of Washington Irving that the New Englanders had seen fit to be governed by the laws of God until they could make better laws for themselves. Of course the reasons for the reception of English Law are not hard to find. English rules were brought over as stowaways hidden in the English language. Men talked of wills, of sheriffs, of juries, of towns and counties. Without seeking any Biblical warrant they soon found themselves making wills, appointing sheriffs, conducting trials by juries, and organizing towns and counties after English patterns. When questions arose about these institutions they found little comfort in the Bible, but naturally enough they found the English law ready with a reasonable answer to their most natural queries. There are several instances of Biblical rules in the other colonies. In Pennsylvania, for example, the eldest son at one time inherited a double portion. These experiments with Biblical ideas were not only shortlived; they were frequently very sad experiences. They led to the Sunday Blue Laws, to the expulsion of heretics, to the hanging of witches, and to such trials and awarding of punishments by the Elders as are described in Hawthorne's *Scarlet Letter*.

When the juristic notions for which the Bible has been quoted are considered, one may be tempted to take the side of those Rabbis who opposed the teaching of the Torah to Gentiles! 'To deny the possibility, nay, actual existence,' says Blackstone, 'of witchcraft and sorcery, is at once flatly to contradict the revealed word of God, in various passages both of the Old and New Testament. . . . The civil law punishes with death not only the sorcerers themselves, but also those who consult them, imitating in the former the express law of God: "Thou shalt not suffer a witch to live." And our own laws, both before and since the Conquest, have been equally penal; ranking this crime in the same class with heresy, and condemning both to the flames.' In like manner we find Biblical precedents cited in favour of slavery and against the emancipation of women, against the development of divorce laws—here it is the attitude of New Testament times that is reflected—against the prohibition of liquor traffic, against the disestablishment of State churches, in favour of capital punishment, in favour of polygamy, and against every effort to mitigate ruthlessness in war.

In none of these cases has the Biblical argument scored a complete victory. As to some of them we may say with Antonio, 'The devil can cite Scripture for his purpose.'

Fortunately the example of Jewish law has frequently, perhaps generally, predisposed Western Europe in favour of what might be called the better rule. Coke is probably right in his suggestion that the isolation of lepers in medieval Europe was based on Jewish law. If so, its influence can be traced farther into the modern laws of quarantine and other public measures to prevent the spread of disease. In an American case upholding the constitutionality of a Public Health Act, the court said: 'Measures to prevent the spread of dangerous diseases and to provide for the isolation and segregation of those diseased are practically as old as history. . . . The law of Moses segregated the lepers, and their forced cry of "Unclean! Unclean!" was the forerunner of the modern warning placard.'[1] The deep concern of Jewish law for the stranger, the afflicted, the widow and the orphan, its humanitarian measures reaching to the ox that treadeth the corn and to the mother-bird, its concern for the labourer toiling in the vineyards, the hired man awaiting his reward, the poor debtor—all this has given inspiration as well as aid and comfort to reformers even when their proposed Bills copied none of the phraseology of the Bible.

Post-Biblical Hebrew and Christian ' Natural Law '

More important, however, than any number of single provisions of Western Law in which Jewish influence may be detected, is the underlying jurisprudence or general theory of law that was developing in Judea in the days that gave birth to Christianity. The Jews developed a *ius naturale et gentium*. They referred to it as the ' Seven Commandments for the

[1] Rock *v.* Carney, 216 Michigan Reports, 280.

Descendants of Noah'. They taught that the righteous among the Gentiles who obeyed these Seven Commandments would share in the World to Come. There was a disinclination, however, to any sharing of the special laws of Israel with the Gentiles. Thus a point of view suggested often in the New Testament is quite Jewish. In the Epistle to the Romans the second chapter turns on the theory that Jews are subject to their received law and Gentiles to the law of nature. The Rabbinic conception of the content of the law of nature and of nations varies slightly according to different teachers. The classical reference is a passage in the Babylonian Talmud:[1] 'Seven Commandments were imposed on the *Descendants of Noah* (i.e. the whole human race), concerning justice between man and man, the prohibition of idol worship, of blasphemy, of incest, of murder, of theft, and the prohibition of eating parts cut from living animals.'

This doctrine or one of its variants is considerably older than the Gemara. We can easily detect a garbled or mistranslated form of it in the 'Testament of Noah' in the Book of Jubilees of the first or second century before the Christian era. The Church Fathers seem to retain a reminiscence of the doctrine. Tertullian talks of the law of nature among the Patriarchs and Eusebius quotes Midrashic views about the laws that Abraham observed. Jerome sees a reference to natural law in Isaiah xxiv. 5. He insists that Adam and Eve and Cain and Pharaoh were conscious of sinning against this natural law. Ambrose discourses on the pre-Mosaic natural law reflected in Romans v, and makes a classification of natural law that suggests the Jewish division: between Man and God; between Man and Man. Though more specific allusions to the Jewish law of nature are rare in early Christian literature (they are all noted in the tenth chapter of Selden's great work), it seems that the early Christians mastered this notion thoroughly enough to lay

[1] Sanhedrin, folio 57.

Western Law

a foundation for the acceptance and rejection of parts of Biblical law in accordance with the principle that came to prevail eventually in the Roman Catholic Church, that so much of the Old Testament as was declaratory of 'natural law' was still binding. Thus the Ten Commandments are saved. Chrysostom sees in them a codification of natural law. The forbidden degrees of consanguinity and affinity pass from the Levitical law into the Canon Law of the Roman Catholic Church and eventually into the secular systems of Western Europe. Finally this principle opened the pages of the Jewish Bible for discussion in spite of the sweeping repudiation of the old law in many Christian texts. There was always the possibility that a point of natural law was involved.

Was the Hebrew conception of natural law destined to play a role in the development of the natural law of the Middle Ages and early modern times? It must be borne in mind that in spite of the disrepute into which the idea has fallen in recent years and in several other stages in the history of jurisprudence, no other single force has been so potent in the shaping of modern European law as the notion that there was a discoverable law of nature in the universe. Every great legal name from the beginning of modern times to the middle of the eighteenth century is connected with this assumption. Its height is reached when Grotius makes it the foundation of International Law. The climax of its pretensions comes in the work of a man who calls himself *Professor Generis Humani*, Christian von Wolf (1679–1754), the author of *Institutiones Juris Naturae et Gentium in quibus ex ipsa hominis natura continuo nexu omnes obligationes et jura omnia deducuntur*, that is: 'Institutes of the Law of Nature and of Nations in which, by an unbroken argument, all obligations and all laws are deduced from the nature of man itself.'

In England this natural law was the formative principle in the development of Equity. On the Continent it was the basis of the dissertations on which the legislation and codification of the nineteenth century was founded. In the American colonies it furnished the Bills of Rights of the various Constitutions. The appeal of the Declaration of Independence is to 'the laws of Nature and of Nature's God'.

Just what was the Hebraic contribution to this conception of natural law? The most learned man of the seventeenth century tried to make it the basis of the whole thing. John Selden in his controversy with Grotius on the freedom of the seas expressed great dissatisfaction with the latter's Romanism—though Grotius, too, is fond of Biblical and Rabbinical authority. He himself sought light on the Law of Nature in the writings of the Hebrews. Some years later he published his *De Jure Naturali et Gentium juxta Disciplinam Ebraeorum*, that is to say, 'The law of nature and of nations according to the Hebrews.' But natural law is not made by erudition. Even Selden brought back from the Hebrews a mere confirmation of the law of his own country. He found that dominion could be gained over a part of the sea as his countrymen contended, and that judges trained in law could sit in judgement over priests but not priests over judges, that tithes were subject to secular control, and so on.

On the Continent it was a sublimated Roman law that passed as natural law. Yet Hebrew ideas furnished a constant check on all extremists and a common element in all systems. Hebrew materials were drawn on more and more heavily as natural law came to be identified with Divine Law. This was sought in the Bible quite regardless of one's theory as to how it got there, always subject to the fundamental doctrine of Jewish and Christian jurisprudence, that some of the Biblical matter was natural law and some of it was the particular law of the Hebrews. Accordingly the contemporaries of Blackstone expected such sentiments at the following in any discussion of law : ' As man depends absolutely upon his Maker for everything, it is necessary that he should in all points conform to his Maker's will. This will of his Maker is called the law of nature. ... No human laws are of any validity, if contrary to this. ... Divine Providence ... hath been pleased at sundry times and in divers manners, to discover and enforce its laws by an immediate and direct revelation. The doctrines thus delivered we call the revealed or divine law, and they are to be found only in the Holy Scriptures.'

More lip-homage than serious attention has been given to these theories. Yet they have made of the Jewish law a most persuasive body of quotations for use in court, and help to account for its frequent use and misuse already discussed in connexion with legislative reforms. Among the discoveries of this natural law that have a Judeo-Christian rather than a Roman appearance are the equality of all men before the law—'Ye shall not respect persons in judgement, ye shall hear the small and the great alike'—the concept of law as a means of protecting the individual against the tyranny of the State, and a recognition of the place of the Church or of Churches in or beside the State.

Jewish foundations of Medieval Constitutional Law :

a. Church and State

The last of these achievements, the establishment of a *modus vivendi* between Church and State, deserves in this connexion a little more attention. It reflects the motive at the heart of the great struggles, intellectual and juristic, as well as military, of the Middle Ages. The foundations for the struggle, and also for the several solutions that have been reached in modern times, go back to Palestinian days when men were puzzled over the question whether it was lawful to pay tribute to Caesar. The answer of Jesus—'Render unto Caesar the things that are Caesar's and unto God the things that are God's'—epitomizes the hard-earned wisdom of centuries of Jewish history. Israel had already had a long experience in the task for which it takes the first place in history, preserving the essentials of its mode of life under adverse governments. It had made these beginnings in a world that knew no distinction between religion and law. During the Babylonian captivity its dilemma might very easily have led to such a charge as this: 'There is a certain people scattered abroad and dispersed among the peoples in all the provinces of thy kingdom; and their laws are diverse from those of every people; neither keep they the king's laws.' And all this in spite of an honest attempt to follow the advice of the prophet Jeremiah: 'Seek the peace of the city whither I have caused you to be carried away captive and pray unto the Lord for it.'

Between those sad days and the period, eight or nine centuries later, when it becomes proverbial among Jews that the law of the land prevails in certain matters, there is a long development. It is somewhere in the course of this development that the early Christians take up the burden of the Jews and manage to struggle through several centuries during which Christianity is an outlaw religion. For this end essentials had to be distinguished from local and temporary provisions and customs; a rough cleavage between ecclesiastical law and ordinary civil law had to be invented. The task of Christianity was eventually simplified by declaring more things Caesar's than the Jews were willing to concede. Yet it did not get rid of its relics of Jewish law without a struggle. The Church Fathers complain of those Christians who persist in adhering to Jewish customs. Jerome laments that 'the Jewish laws appear to the ignorant and the common people as the very ideals of wisdom and human reason'. The 'Judaizers' are put down with a strong hand. Yet the Church does not emerge from the struggle without being for ever impressed with a 'natural law' idea that gives Europe its constitutional law. The medieval Church is destined to be *imperium in imperio*. Spiritual right is to be opposed to temporal power.

b. *The Constitution of the Church*

When Christianity becomes a lawful religion it is already equipped with a definite constitutional law and a growing body of private law and customs. It is quite inevitable that the State that accepts it must make room for its idea of marriage and the family, for its treatment of a slave as a fellow man, and for its existence as an organized body. Roman law does change to make room for these ideas that had their origin in the realm of thought of the Jewish *halakah*.

The early Churches were congregations that differed but little from the Jewish 'schools'. The puzzled pagans could hardly conceive of them as places of worship. The heads were teachers. The Christian clergy quite naturally took on the constitution of the Jewish rabbinate of its day. It was not an hereditary priesthood like that of the Bible. Its members were to be qualified by learning and to be ordained by the laying on of hands. They were to function as judges. Their difficult questions were to be settled in synods. The independence of this body was not to be surrendered in making peace with the powers of this world, else the legalization of Christianity would seem to have been bought too dearly. Biblical texts were soon found to justify the reproving of kings and the exemption of clerics from political control. Verses from the Psalms were torn from their context to establish benefit of Clergy: 'He reproved kings for their sakes, saying, Touch not mine anointed and do my prophets no harm.' Texts were found to justify the claims of the popes even to temporal power.

Of course, the wars of the great Italian parties had more to do with the final outcome than did the battle of the books. But it is wholly to misunderstand the medieval mind if we measure the influence of disjointed texts on it by our own reaction to them. Whatever might happen to these extreme claims and the Pope's armies, the Church could not be expected to surrender the great weapon that it had developed or rather taken from the Jews in its early outlaw days—excommunication. Beginning no doubt with the Biblical ban, it had grown among the Jews, perhaps in part because of their political impotence, until it had become a system of 'putting out of the synagogue' that John mentions, and of refusing to keep company with an offender as laid down in Corinthians. These Christian records suggest that several stages of 'putting out'—censorship, anathema, and excommunication—were already growing into some such system as that reflected in the Babylonian Talmud.[1]

The early Church depended for its charity and other funds on freewill offerings such as the Jews had been in the habit of collecting in their dispersion and sending to Jerusalem. In course of time it demanded taxes from its adherents. It introduced *tithes*. So successful was this device that in Selden's day it was almost universally believed that the payment of tithes to the Church went back to the earliest Christian days, and that Christian tithes had been based directly on Jewish precedents. Selden showed that there had been a long gap between Jewish and Christian tithes. Churchmen had undoubtedly urged at a very early day that they were entitled *jure divino* to an income similar to that enjoyed by the ancient Hebrew priests and Levites. No doubt their urgings had had some effect here and there. The actual legal recognition of the Church's claim begins with Charlemagne. There follows a long series of enactments throughout Europe, imposing and changing and commuting tithes, until very little is left of them to suggest the Biblical model that had given them so much of their vitality, if not their life.

[1] Tractate *Mo'ed Katon*.

c. The State

If the Church gets its legal powers from Judaism, the State is not far behind in reaping similar advantages from the same source of constitutional law. The doctrine of the divine right of kings is not exclusively of Jewish origin. But wherever it appears independently of Judaism it seems to take the form of a claim of descent from the gods for the reigning family. In Rome it took on the further aspect, not uncommon in antiquity, of teaching that the emperor himself was a kind of deity or was shortly to become one. Such doctrines of divine right could hardly go hand in hand with Christianity. But the Jewish idea of an 'anointed of the Lord' readily took its place, and has served as the literary defence of kingship ever since. Long before the divine right of kings is questioned—in England it is thoroughly outlawed in Blackstone's day—the Jewish aspect of it furnishes a little consolation to the downtrodden subject, for it follows that the king, who is an instrument of God, owes obedience to God's law. Some question has been raised of the authenticity of such passages in medieval law books as Bracton's sermon to the King about his answerability to God; but it seems likely that they were taken for granted, hell-fire and all, as a kind of legal-literary commonplace in which nothing personal was intended or understood. Not only kings, but feudal lords based their claims to consideration on Scripture, for Coke tells us that the statutes of *scandalum magnatum* are based on the words: 'Thou shalt not curse a ruler of thy people.'

d. The Canon Law

With the main lines of the constitution drawn so that Church and State divide jurisdiction over men's affairs, there is still the hopelessly detailed problem of ascertaining just what are the things that are Caesar's and what are God's. Every State, every age, has drawn this jagged dividing line differently. In

England, for example, probate and divorce matters were under the jurisdiction of ecclesiastical courts until 1857. Defamation passed from the Church's jurisdiction into the King's courts in the seventeenth century. The beginning of that century finds Lord Coke vigorously combating all special jurisdictions that compete with the King's courts. If we go back to Chaucer's day we find an archdeacon boldly at work—

> In punisshinge of fornicacioun,
> Of wicchecraft, and eek of bauderye,
> Of diffamacioun, and avoutrye,
> Of chirche-reves, and of testaments,
> Of contractes, and of lakke of sacraments,
> And eek of many another maner cryme
> Which nedeth nat rehercen at this tyme.

One could write a history of the law of almost any European country in terms of the struggle of ordinary courts to wrest jurisdiction from special courts and particularly from those of the Church. In this struggle the Church was fortified at first by a monopoly of learning, but eventually it came to depend more and more on Biblical texts. The crime which happened to be a sin as well as a crime—such as perjury or defamation, or usury or simony, perhaps we should have read on with Chaucer —it claimed as its own.

In course of time when the State took over from the Church fragments of its jurisdiction it took over its legal principles as well. Many of these were of Jewish origin. Thus in the law of wills we still have a two-witness rule, unknown in the Common Law, because the Church gave some weight to the Biblical requirement in certain cases of two witnesses. When mortgages were dealt with by courts of law and of equity they allowed a redemption for land, such as Church courts had ordered on the basis of Biblical law. The Church had taken part in ordeals—was not the Biblical ordeal performed by the priest?—and when the Fourth Lateran Council forbade the clergy to participate in ordeals, the State never ventured to conduct ordeals of its own. We have already seen how the forbidden degrees within which one may not marry passed through the Canon Law into the Common Law with very little change. Heresy passed from Ecclesiastical Law into the Common Law with the penalty of burning attached, but was given back after the Restoration to the keeping of ecclesiastical courts with no power to punish except by ecclesiastical correction for the good of the soul. The Canon Law took over the Biblical prohibition of usury in the sense of even the slightest amount of interest. European countries that have legalized interest-taking have, of course, had to begin with this as their Common Law. In like manner divorce first makes its appearance in civil courts with the limitations based on a New Testament Midrash. Genesis is quoted: 'They shall be one flesh.' 'So then,' it is argued, 'they are no more twain but ONE FLESH. What therefore God hath joined together let no man put asunder.' In the Sermon on the Mount an exception is made where the ground is fornication.

A moment's digression may be useful in correcting a widespread false impression of the relation of Jewish law to the controversy that gave rise to the very serious difficulties faced by Western Europe and particularly Catholic countries in handling the divorce problem. The general impression is, I believe, that the Pharisee questioners are entirely satisfied with the rule they attribute to Moses giving the husband practically unlimited power to send away his wife. The impression needs correction in several particulars. In the first place, far from being satisfied with the received text, they realize that this question is something of a 'poser' for a teacher in their day. To endorse freedom of divorce is utterly out of the question, and they know it. For a long time their leaders have taken care of that by imposing a burden of alimony through a clause in the standard marriage contract. Just how far the Rabbis have gone by this time in making divorce requirements so technical that the whole process is converted into a judicial procedure and subject to the personal supervision of the learned, we do not know. Certainly a few generations later the Mishnah records precept upon precept, about witnesses, about writing and signing between sunset and sunset, about who may write and on what and with what, about dates and names and conditions. And they go on in the same spirit in the Gemaras and the later authorities until the procedure becomes not only judicial and public, but almost prohibitive. The freedom of the husband is curtailed and a right on the part of the wife to demand a divorce is developed.

We do not know how much of this could have been in the minds of these Pharisees. Certainly they knew they were not asking an innocent question that could be answered by a simple yes or no. It was difficult to see how any 'modern' man could do otherwise than accept the improvements of the Pharisaic tradition in these matters, whether man-made or God-made. A steady progress had been made since the Deuteronomic code had 'suffered' the continuance of an old institution. The word 'suffered' ($\epsilon\pi\iota\tau\rho\epsilon\pi\epsilon\iota\nu$), attributed to the Pharisees in Mark x. 4 and to Jesus in Matthew xix. 8, is more descriptive of the famous passage in Deuteronomy xxiv than any words suggestive of a new command. Modern scholarship is almost unanimous in preferring the traditional Jewish interpretation of this passage in Deuteronomy to the rendering of the Authorized and Revised Versions of the English Bible. The meaning seems to be that if a man divorce his wife and she become the wife of another, he shall never marry her again. The same idea is expressed in the third chapter of Jeremiah. What is new is not the institution of divorce nor the bill of divorcement but a check upon freedom of divorce and remarriage. The same code contains at least two other similar limitations. In other words, here as in so many other cases the sole object of the

Scriptural legislation is to mitigate a Common Law evil, and those who later sit in the seat of Moses carry on the work of mitigation in the same spirit. Thus it is the post-Biblical development rather than the Biblical stage of the law that touches Western Europe most.

There is at least one instance in which European law went back to the Common Law of the Hebrews, or possibly to a universal heathen practice, rather than to the Biblical amendment. In Exodus it is said of the murderer, 'Thou shalt take him from Mine altar, that he may die.' Joab was not spared when he fled to the tent of the Lord and 'caught hold on the horns of the altar'. Adonijah likewise had caught hold on the horns of the altar. And in the story of Athaliah we are told that the priest said, ' Let her not be slain in the house of the Lord.' Some idea of asylum probably lingered among the Hebrews. In fact the Mekilta remarks that removal from the altar applies only to cases involving the death penalty. At any rate medieval Europe sees a revival of the right of sanctuary. In England it leads to a great deal of law about the right of the confessed criminal, who has taken sanctuary, to abjure the realm. In course of time the right was subjected to many restrictions in all the countries of Europe, beginning in fact in the Roman Empire and lasting until the end of the eighteenth century, when the right disappeared entirely and the European lawgivers subscribed to the wisdom of their Jewish predecessors. An intermediate stage in England is marked by a curious Biblical imitation. By the reforming Act of 1540 Henry VIII established seven cities as places of refuge or privilege. It is hardly correct to attribute the whole idea of sanctuary, as is often done, to the influence of Jewish law. Yet the widespread notion that it was related to Jewish law gave it a place in Canon Law and kept it alive long after it had become a general nuisance.

Indirect Importations of Jewish Legal Doctrines

Religion was the vehicle through which most of this Jewish matter, both Biblical and early post-Biblical, was brought into Europe. Whether it was seized upon by Churchmen or statesmen for their own particular ends, it was accompanied by the argument that it represented the revealed will of God. There were, however, several other ways in which Jewish legal ideas came in and were accepted without being thought of as having a religious sanction. In the first place, some of them were just taken for granted. A few of these had become associated with some early Christian story or doctrine or formula, and so were handed down to modern times quite accidentally. 'No man can serve two masters' seems at the outset to have been a legal doctrine. In Leviticus it is argued that the children of Israel may be dealt with as hirelings but never as ordinary servants (or slaves), 'for', says the Lord, 'unto me the children of Israel are servants.' 'My document takes precedence,' says one commentator. In the Sermon on the Mount the idea is used to drive home a religious teaching. It reappears in modern law books in connexion with the absolute loyalty and fidelity exacted from the agent to-day.

Another illustration may be drawn from the law of agency. Its central doctrine to-day, both in English and in Continental law, is the doctrine of representation: *Qui facit per alium, facit per se*. The notion is not a doctrine of Roman law. The Latin expression is one of a bouquet of such sayings in the *Liber Sextus Decretalium*, a part of the Canon Law. Whence the Canon Law took it, is not easy to say—but may it not have drawn its legal notion of vicarious action and responsibility from the same sources as those which supplied its theological doctrines of vicarious sin and atonement? At least to the Talmudists it was a matter of universal knowledge that *sheluho shel adam kemotho*, 'one's messenger is equivalent to one's self.' Even a prayer may carry a legal notion down through the centuries. 'As we forgive our debtors' is a phrase redolent of the Jewish law of the Sabbatical year and the Jubilee, rather than of anything in Roman law. From time to time relief Acts have been passed in Europe for poor debtors. Is it not possible that a thought which came into a prayer out of the law found expression again and again in related laws?

The taking over of Jewish Activities and Laws

A second aspect of Jewish influence in which the will of the Church was even less involved was the taking over of Jewish practices and with them Jewish law. It is generally conceded—though there are gaps in the evidence—that negotiable paper was introduced into Europe by the Jewish money-lenders. Blackstone has given currency to the notion that the Star Chamber had received its name from the Jewish Starrs (i.e. *shetaroth*, documents) that he supposes were kept there. The early name *Camera Stellata* seems, however, to point to a different origin. There is evidence, at any rate, that Jews were employing bills of exchange between Russia and England in the twelfth century, and vague traces have been discovered indicating that Jews had something to do with the introduction of similar documents in other places several centuries earlier. The codified Roman law knows of no documents of indebtedness save certain Greek bankers' chirographs. The Mishnah on the other hand takes them for granted. It talks of losing and finding them, singly and in bundles. Recent studies of Babylonian clay tablets coming from the banking house of the Egibis and the temples suggest pretty clearly that the Jews were not the inventors of bills and notes and cheques and endorsements. They found them in the everyday life of the boulevards of Babylon. The Gemara indicates openness to suggestions from without in such matters [1] where it lays down

[1] Gittin, folio 10.

the rule that all documents registered in the non-Jewish courts, excepting bills of divorcement and emancipation, are valid in all respects.

In all of the business conducted by Jews they found it necessary to devise extraordinary means for the safeguarding of credit. This necessity was dictated not merely by their lack of access to the ordinary courts but by the failure of those ordinary courts to make any provision for the collection of simple debts. In any event the Jews would have been helpless but for the king's heavy interest in their gains. That interest was the motive behind the improvement of the machinery of the law for the enforcement of promises. The Jews were familiar with both pledges and mortgages or rather gages. Their law books discuss schemes whereby the creditor pays himself out of the use of the debtor's property. They had experimented with *shetaroth* that were practically judgements of courts from the outset. All of these devices they helped to carry from land to land, though it must not be supposed that they invented all of them or that Jews were indispensable to the introduction of any one of them here or there.

One device should perhaps be singled out because of its vast development in modern jurisprudence. It is the keeping of public records of private transactions. Here again the motive is simple, the protection of claims in the face of the dangers from fire, mobs, theft. On the king's side there is an obvious advantage in publicity or at least in access to information of all transactions. There is no need of asking who invented the device. The Babylonians were in the habit of depositing copies of their business contracts in the temples before the Jews came into contact with them. In 1194 provision was made in England that all ' deeds, pledges, mortgages, lands, houses, rents and possessions of the Jews should be registered '. Contracts with Jews were to be made in duplicate in certain towns where *archae,* or treasury-chests, were to be kept for them. The word 'archa' probably meant simply 'chest' to the outside world, but one wonders if it did not suggest something else to the Jews: it is the very word used in the Mishnah for the place of recording *shetaroth*. 'All *shetaroth* issuing from non-Jewish *Archaoth* are valid', says the Mishnah.[1] In the Gemara[2] there are references to the recording of a deed for a house and of a bill of sale for a slave in the '*Archaoth* of the Gentiles'. At all events the idea was not new in Jewish legal history, though it apparently was in English legal history. The next year we find an official regulation issued with regard to the formalities of recording the *feet of fines*, that is, records of agreements made in Common Pleas, and we are told that 'from that day until their abolition by statute in 1833 the records of fines are complete'.

Such remarkable readiness in putting a legal device imported by the Jews into general use is rarely seen. The nearest approach to it comes perhaps when a country applies the principles worked out for its Jews to foreigners whom it sees fit to admit. The internal organization of the English Jewry with its own presbyter, with a kind of joint liability of the whole community for the deeds of each, with courts on which Jews are represented, with protection or a charter from the king, all paid for by a large percentage of the profits, is practically the organization offered to foreigners when they first come to England to do business. Their *staple towns* correspond to the Jewish *archa towns*. It is impossible to state positively that the plans worked out between the Jews and the kings were consciously used as models in dealing with groups of foreign merchants, but no other model suggests itself, and the resemblance is quite close. The sad part of the story is that the Jews were frequently excluded from trades that they had developed, and that others were invited to take their places together with all their devices and methods. Thus the Lombards took the place of the Jews in England, and were soon occupied with pledges and mort-

[1] Second Mishnah of the fifth chaper of Gittin. [2] Gittin (folio 44 a).

gages, with the improved devices of the courts to safeguard credit, with records and internal organization and special contracts with the king. The Jewish devices became the property of others, and with them went a Jewish contribution to the law of the land.

It is always interesting to watch the growth of a transplanted legal institution once it has taken root. It may develop into new things undreamed of in the system from which it was taken. We have already alluded (p. 381) to the fact that the English jury trial sprouted from a shoot brought over from the Continent, namely, the royal *inquisitio* or prerogative of demanding information from subjects under oath. In like manner the Jewish idea of a body allowed to trade in a country under a bargain with its king, under special supervision and restrictions and yet highly autonomous, discriminated against and yet protected, was applied by the English to several new situations as they arose. The Jews were compelled to leave England in 1290. In the next century we find the foreign groups of merchants fitting into the shell that they left behind. Eventually groups of Englishmen take the places of these foreigners and want to be similarly organized, especially to act outside of England. The first trading companies, the East India Company, the Muscovy Company, the Hudson Bay Company, are groups that make bargains with the Crown in which they are licensed individually as well as collectively to do business, and by which they are given some powers of self-government, special limitations, and special protection. Is it going too far to say that they inherit from the foreign merchants the shell of the old Jewry? And may we not discern in the crude devices that necessity invented for the Jews in the early Middle Ages the prototype of the modern business company on the one side and of the chartered colony, through which Englishmen have done so much in the world, on the other?

Post-Biblical Jewry has met a number of problems for which

it has developed its own juristic solutions. Some of these were developed for Jewry and the rest of the world contemporaneously, as for example, copyright law, I might say 'international copyright' law. The centuries following the invention of printing raised the questions. The sixteenth and seventeenth centuries saw them debated and a few feeble attempts made through censorship and special grants of monopolies to protect the rights of an author or publisher. True copyright law begins at the beginning of the eighteenth century. At random I turn to my copy of the *Turim* with the *Bayith Hadash* printed in Frankfort within a few years of the first English statute on the subject, that statute which led the way to a general solution of the problem in Europe. I find, in the place of a copyright notice, a *haskamah* of Samuel Schotten, president of the Rabbinate, which after praising the editor for having brought the book through the press, recites the latter's fear that others will 'remove his boundary' (the modern Hebrew equivalent of infringement), and pronounces a ban against any one who raises a hand to reprint this work within fifteen years of the date of the completion of the current printing.

This type of clause was practically universal in Hebrew books of this time. The first occurrence of it is said to go back to the Grammar of Elias Levita (see p. 332), printed in Rome in 1518. The period of copyright varies from three to twenty-five years according to circumstances. Frequently the ban applies to purchasers and readers as well as publishers. In the development of this law the Rabbis searched Scripture and the Talmud and occasionally resorted to deliberate legislation. In fact, recent developments under pressure of governmental interference with the use of the ban have made the copyright law operate automatically by implication. In the early days of printing, Jews were in direct contact with non-Jews who were confronted with the very same problem. Many of the Hebrew books, the one I first referred to in this connexion, for example, were printed by Christians. They must have learned that the Jews had an effective device to prevent the pirating of books. Did they borrow from the Jews the idea of making the censorship of the State and the Church serve incidentally as a device for the protection of the private interests of authors and publishers?

In more recent times the solution of Jewish problems has resulted more directly in the improvement of the general laws. In the struggle for emancipation that has made up a good part of recent Jewish history, no claims have been made for Jews that would not, upon being granted, redound to the advantage of other groups similarly situated. These episodes belong rather to politics than law. We need only mention, as an example and a climax, the fight for minority rights in the new countries of Europe in which representative Jews took a leading part at Versailles.

The Value of Jewish Experience under the Law

The history of Israel's contribution to Western Law might end here, but a beginning has been made in an additional chapter, the trend of which ought to be sketched. It is the discovery that Israel's juristic experiences are a part of the world's history, and that they have accordingly a value and a meaning for the world. Students of Comparative Law, who had searched the darkest corners of the earth for data, have been surprised quite recently to learn that in their own towns life was going on under a system that had its roots in the Bible. What they have not learned, although researches in this field are being carried on with reasonable success, is that this system has shown an adaptability no less remarkable than its vitality.

The notion that Jewish law reached its zenith in the Old Testament and its nadir in the Talmud has been so successfully taught by religious propagandists that the scholar hardly knows what to do with evidences of effective Jewish social engineering when they come into his hands. The late Eugen Ehrlich of Czernowitz came across a Jewish custom in his seminar of living law. Jewish tenants respected each other's tenant-right, or *hazakah*, so that they could not be made to compete with each other effectively. Learning that this law was not in the Talmud, he set it down as due to a misunderstanding of their traditional law by the Jews. There was no misunderstanding, however, when the Rabbis of the Middle Ages turned their attention to the artificially hastened housing problem wherever ghettoes existed. In some places they read the requirements of the day into the Biblical text that prohibited the removal of ancient boundaries. In others they found a Talmudic principle bearing on the case involved in the saying : ' If a poor man is turning a cake, he who takes it from him is wicked.' In still other places they called together representative assemblies for communities or groups of communities to legislate on the subject, or even legislated themselves. Thus the principle of *hazakah* for the benefit of tenants was developed by means of Legal Fictions, Equity, and Legislation.

The reasonableness of the arrangement commended it to the Popes, who made it binding on the Christian landlords of the ghetto, with the result that Jewish tenants had a kind of perpetual leasehold interest that they could sell or hand down or give away, and for which compensation was made to them in Rome when ghetto property was taken over for State purposes. Since the war other parts of the world have felt the pinch of housing shortages and have drawn up legislation recognizing a kind of *hazakah* for the tenant in possession. In the United States the constitutionality of such laws was challenged, and it is interesting to note that in the arguments before the Supreme Court the experience of the Jews was cited as an illustration of the reasonableness, nay the inevitableness, of such provisions in the face of a housing shortage.

As the living law of thousands of residents in Western

European countries, Jewish law has occasionally attracted the attention of the courts and legislatures. Sometimes this attention has been unfriendly, as in the attempts to prohibit the Jewish mode of slaughter. Sometimes it has been friendly, as in those American States that have passed statutes to prevent the misuse of the word 'kosher', by which is meant ritually clean in the Jewish sense and especially applied to food. Such a law has just been upheld by the Supreme Court of the United States, though it was pointed out in argument that it involved the enactment of the whole of the Jewish law bearing on the ritual cleanliness of food into an American code by reference. More frequently the attention is merely that neutral type involved in the Conflict of Laws, where the intention of men who speak with a certain law in view cannot be ascertained without a study of that law. In one instance, for example, a Jewish marriage contract came up for examination, and after hearing the experts, the judge concluded that it did not mean exactly what it said—at least he would not interpret it as a prenuptial agreement to limit the wife's alimony.

In a few of the larger Jewish communities of America, municipal judges have encouraged the reference of Jewish disputes to a Jewish court arranged for that purpose. Occasionally a clash with civil authorities brings a question of Jewish ritual or civil law into prominence. It was such a provocation that led Zacharias Frankel to carry out his exhaustive studies of the Jewish law of oaths and testimony, misconceptions and misrepresentations as to which had kept alive the infamous rules of the oath *more judaico* in civilized countries until his day. A similar need inspired some of the finest studies of Leopold Zunz. It was the threat of the Prussian Government to restrict Jews to Biblical names, as Austria had done, that induced him to publish his history of Jewish names, in which he demonstrated the non-existence of an alleged tradition. A number of monographs on Jewish marriage and divorce, and on the Jewish mode of slaughter, and recent ones on the use of wine in the synagogue and on autopsies, owe their inspiration to similar conditions. The most extensive contributions by Jews, however, have been chiefly of an apologetic nature and have tended rather to prove that Jewish law is not unethical nor unduly harsh with Gentiles than to open the treasury of Jewish legal experience.

What a treasury it is may be surmised when we realize how hard facts have compelled Jewish law to deal with topics growing out of their preternaturally crowded, intensely urban communities long before such topics forced themselves on the attention of the Western world. Already in the Talmud the Jews are concerned with party-walls, with the ownership of upper stories in houses dissociated from the ownership of the land and of the lower stories, with the protection of the right of privacy (for ' damage by peering in is damage '), with insurance contracts in which the insured wants monetary compensation whereas the association is merely willing to give him a new animal or a new ship. They even have a case of labourers striking, and the solution is not without merit: the strike is valid provided it is called only after consulting learned men! In the Middle Ages they become acquainted with the necessity of curbing competition to preserve goodwill, an interest which modern commercial law is just beginning to understand. Their practically autonomous community organization, and particularly their administration of charities, anticipated many of the problems of modern civic society. In most of these respects their experiences are beyond the ken of modern jurists. Now and then they reached a happy solution that may still prove suggestive. Of course even the less happy solutions may convey valuable lessons to humanity. Their living law is scattered in some fifteen hundred printed volumes of *Responsa* and endless manuscripts, scarcely indexed in the codes and commentaries. When this storehouse is opened through the progressive work of scholars, encouraged by a better understanding among men, and perhaps stimulated by the experiment in Palestine, a new chapter may be added to the influence of Judaism on Western Law.

NATHAN ISAACS.

FIG. 66. From an edition of Gratian's *Concordia discordantium Canonum* printed at Lyons in 1509. The Jewish and Christian fathers of Canon Law are allegorically set forth.

For further description see p. xxix.

To His Highnesse Oliver Lord Protector of the
Commonwealth of England, Scotland, and Ireland, & the Dominions thereof

The Humble Petition of The Hebrews at Present
Residing in this citty of London whose names ar Underwritten

Humbly Sheweth

That Ack:[nowledg]ing The Manyfold favours and Protection yo[u]r Highnesse hath bin pleased to grant us, In order that wee may with security meete privatly in our particular houses to our Devotions, And being Desirous to be favoured more by yo[u]r Highnesse, wee pray with all Humblenesse yt by the best meanes which may be such Protection may be granted us in Writing as that wee may thereoff meete at our sayd private Devotions in our Particular howses without feare of Molestation, either to our persons familles or estates, our desire of Being to live Peaceably under yo[u]r Highnesse Government, And being neere att all mortall evers a like Humain from yo[u]r Highnesse to graunt us Lycence that those which may Dey of our nation may be buryed in such place out of the cittye as wee shall thinck Convenient with the Proprietors Leaves in whose Land this place shall bee, and soe wee shall as well in our lifetyme as at our Death be highly favoured by yo[u]r Highnesse for whose Long Life and Prosperity wee shall continually pray to the Almighty God &c

Menasseh ben Israel
Samuell Abrabanel

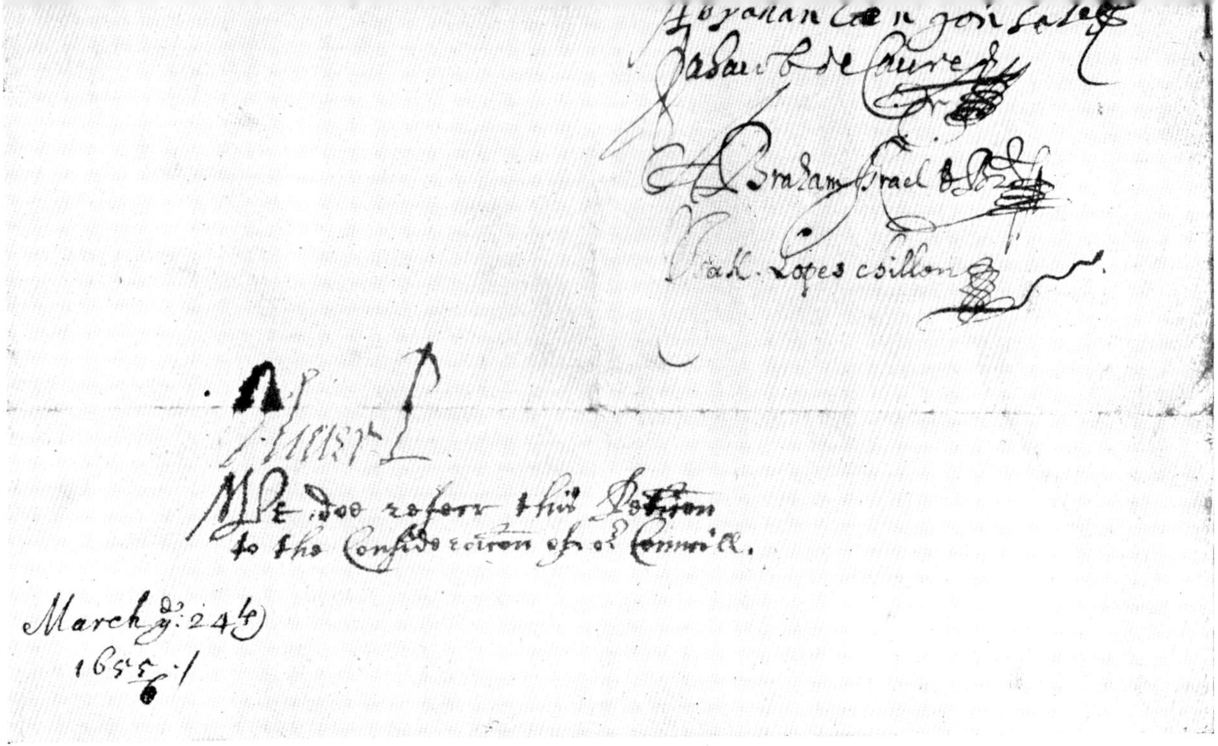

Fig. 67. JEWISH PETITION TO OLIVER CROMWELL, 1656

It led to the legalization of Jewish residence in England

A full description and transcript will be found on pp. xxix–xxx

THE INFLUENCE OF THE OLD TESTAMENT ON PURITANISM

IN his *Short History of the English People* John Richard Green characterizes the temper of Puritan England in the following terms: 'No greater moral change ever passed over a nation than passed over England during the years which parted the middle of the reign of Elizabeth from the meeting of the Long Parliament. England became the people of a book, and that book was the Bible. It was as yet the one English book which was familiar to every Englishman: it was read in churches and read at home and everywhere its words, as they fell on ears which custom had not deadened, kindled a startling enthusiasm.' What the revival of classical learning had done on the Continent was done in England in a far profounder fashion by the translation of the Scriptures. It came at a psychological moment in the moral and political development of our people. It not only entered into the warp and woof of our literature, but seemed to give point, emphasis, and expression to the new ethical, social, and religious impulses with which the country was at that time stirred.

The real representatives of Protestantism in this country, both in its political and religious aspects, were the Puritans. First within the borders of the Anglican Church, and afterwards as Separatists from it, they found their inspiration in the new knowledge of the Scriptures made available in translations, and from them derived their ideals. In their use of the Bible they were altogether uncritical. Old and New Testaments alike were regarded as equally inspired of God and every precept and sentiment they contained became a divine command and rule of life. They had little or no conception of the Hebrew Bible as the thousand-years-long record of a people's history, nor did they see in it any movement or development of thought. It was all the Word of God and the work of the Holy Ghost. They accepted the new English version in its baldest and most literal sense. It moulded their speech, their thoughts, and their lives, and on it they built all their hopes of a better future both in this world and the next. In the bitter experiences of persecution and of civil war they found in the Old Testament in particular, language and sentiments which exactly fitted their mood and suited their occasions.

The Puritans were not, of course, blind to the finer elements in the Old Testament, nor were they deaf to its lyric appeals. They felt its call to personal and national righteousness, but they knew nothing, at all events by experience, of the Jews' own attitude to their sacred books. During the whole Puritan period there were either no Jews at all in England or they were so few as to be negligible. Hence the Puritans relied entirely on the letter of prescriptions many of which the Jews had long ago come to regard as obsolete. For example, Western educated Jews had entirely abandoned the belief in witchcraft at the time when English courts were still condemning witches to death. It must be remembered, therefore, that in speaking of the Hebrew Bible we have in view not what the Jews made of it, but what it meant to Puritans whose understanding of the Book was limited, and who knew nothing of the people of the Book.

The Puritans shared to the full the extraordinary awakening which came to the English people after the defeat of the Spanish Armada. It was as if a cloud had been lifted from the whole nation. The change was like the coming of spring after a long and dark winter, and, with the spring, came a great outburst of thought, speech, and song. To many Englishmen the defeat of Spain was the defeat of the Roman Catholic Church. Protestantism took a new lease of life and asserted itself more boldly than ever before. Its real representatives within the English Church were the Puritan party, and they took heart of grace from the belief that the English people were the chosen people of God, distinguished among the nations of the earth by the signal mercies they had received at His hands. They found a close analogy between their fortunes and those of Israel of old, and no language could express it more fitly than that used by the prophets and psalmists. It is not indeed surprising, when we consider the temper of the times, that the Old Testament should have taken a very firm hold of the imaginations of religious men. Life in Elizabethan England was pretty crude; manners were rough and the moral standard was none too high. Would-be reformers were therefore naturally attracted by the corrective which they derived from the clear-cut commands and prohibitions of the Old Testament legalism, and by the dire penalties attached to every form of transgression. Speaking generally, too, there can be no doubt of the attraction presented by the vivid historical narratives of the Old Testament with their deep sense of God's power and presence and their intense human interest. As time went on and many of the Puritans were forced into separation from the Church of their fathers and ultimately to take up arms in civil warfare, they found in the prophetic and apocalyptic writings of the New Testament, as well as the Old, the best possible expression for their hopes and fears, and in the wars of Israel against her numerous foes a fitting parallel for their own beleaguered position. The Old Testament became to them a book of the Wars of the Lord. Their God was Jehovah of Hosts who would help them to smite Philistines and Amalekites hip and thigh. It was a very real experience of religious and political strife and persecution which gave point and verisimilitude to the Old Testament imagery and made them use its names and language as the fittest vehicle for their tumultuous thoughts. In the fortunes of God's chosen people from the days of their slavery in Egypt onwards they found a rich vein of suggestion and consolation for their own evil case. Mr. Chesterton's treatment of English history is perverse and highly imaginative, but he is not far from the truth when he characterizes the later Puritans as men ' to whom the wreck of the Armada was already a legend of national deliverance from Popery, as miraculous and almost as remote as the deliverances of which they read so realistically in the Hebrew Books now laid open to them. The august accident of that Spanish defeat may perhaps have coincided only too well with their concentration on the non-Christian parts of Scripture. It may have satisfied a certain Old Testament sentiment of the election of the English being announced in the stormy oracles of air and sea which was easily turned into that heresy of a tribal pride that took even heavier hold upon the Germans. It is by such things that a civilized state may fall from being a Christian nation to being a chosen people.' [1] So far as this is true it shows again how little those who entertain such a view have realized the true Hebraic conception of a chosen people.[2]

Before we come to deal in detail with the influence of the Old Testament on Puritan ideas and life it will be well to attempt some general estimate of the extent to which it moulded their religious outlook. As we have said already, there was much in the Old Testament which met their peculiar needs and provided a congenial atmosphere for their thought.

---

[1] *A Short History of England*, p. 164.

[2] Cf. Dr. Abrahams's volume of annotations on the Hebrew Daily Prayer Book, pp. x and xi. ' Israel is the Chosen People called to a special service commissioned to receive and propagate the Law, to testify to God's truth by its own example and by its message to the world. " You only have I singled out of all the families of the earth, *therefore* I will visit upon you all your iniquities " (Amos iii. 2). The choice carried with it the obligation to be God's servant in the work of establishing the divine kingdom throughout all the earth.'

It was not that they in any way neglected the New Testament, though they certainly used it more as an armoury of texts for their ecclesiastical conflicts than as a guide either for theology or ethics. Their theology was in the main Calvinistic and their God, with his sovereign power and arbitrary decrees, was more easily conceivable in terms of Jehovah the Lord of hosts than of the God and Father of our Lord Jesus Christ. The Calvinistic doctrine of redemption, with its background of original sin derived from Adam, was expressed largely in terms of Old Testament legalism. This doctrine was no doubt derived from St. Paul rather than directly from the Old Testament. As Dr. Tennant says, 'The Old Testament books of later date than the Jahvist document supply no evidence of a doctrine of the Fall having been extracted out of Genesis.' [1]

Later Judaism made but little use of the Adam story. It looms larger in Paulinism than in the Rabbis. The Calvinistic theologians perhaps understood Paulinism as little as they did Rabbinism. To Calvinism the dominant idea was that of a Covenant to which God and His people were parties and the terms of which, however inconsistently, included Grace, Faith, and Predestination. It was a grim creed, but it met certain obvious needs of the time and it made strong men. By exalting their conception of God and driving them back upon His will, it quickened their moral consciousness and put iron into their blood. The *leitmotiv* of their whole theology was 'The Lord our Righteousness' rather than 'God is Love'. They rested little on the strength and tenderness of Micah's ideal, 'What doth the Lord require of thee, but to do justly and love mercy and walk humbly with thy God?'—the perfect ideal of religion as Huxley termed this great text. But the Puritan adopted its strength without its tenderness. No

[1] *The Sources of the Doctrines of the Fall and Original Sin.* Cambridge, 1903, p. 94.

better illustration of this temper can be found than Milton's *Paradise Lost*. As Mark Pattison says, 'a Puritan poet in a Puritan environment' could do no other than choose his subject and treat it as he did. 'He had not to create his supernatural personages; they were already there. The Father, and the Son, the angels, Satan, Baal and Moloch, Adam and Eve were in full possession of the popular imagination and more familiar to it than any other set of known names. Nor was the belief accorded to them a half-belief, a bare admission of their possible existence, such as prevails at other times or in some countries. In the England of Milton, the angels and devils of the Scriptures were more real beings and better vouched for than any historical personages could be. The old chronicles were full of lies but this was Bible truth.'[1]

An examination of a large number of Puritan sermons shows that the subjects of them were chosen indiscriminately from both Testaments and that in about equal proportion, but in all of them illustrations are freely drawn from the history of Israel. Both preachers and audiences are obviously at home in the Old Testament atmosphere. They, too, are God's people and in covenant relations with their Lord. They must keep his statutes and commandments if they are to secure his favour. In a sermon by Thomas Playfere, Lady Margaret Professor of Divinity at Cambridge in the time of Queen Elizabeth, we have a good example of their method. The sermon is entitled 'The Pathway to Perfection', and is based on Phil. iii. 14. The preacher begins by saying that as Solomon went up six steps to his great ivory throne so we must ascend six degrees on the way to perfection. He therefore divides his discourse into six parts. In one of these he argues, 'wherefore though thou have conquered kingdoms yet crake not of it as Sennacherib did : though thou hast built Babel yet brag not of it as Nebuchadnezzar did : though thou hast rich

[1] *Life of Milton*, p. 185.

treasures yet show them not as Hezekiah did: though thou hast slain a thousand Philistines, yet glory not in it as Samson did: though thou give alms yet blow not a trumpet.'[1]

In the multitude of pamphlets, tracts, broadsheets, and manifestoes issued in the latter half of the sixteenth century and the whole of the seventeenth the Old Testament plays a conspicuous part. The polemical writers of those days had no buttons on their foils. Puritans and Anglicans alike vied with each other in the bitterness of their vituperation and both found in the Old Testament vocabulary weapons fitted to their hands. Every Puritan hated the Church of Rome. It was true of them, as Baxter sadly confessed, *contra ecclesiam nemo pacificus*. Roman ceremonies, images, and vestments were all roundly condemned as idolatry, and visited with all the penalties attaching to the worship of idols in the Old Testament scriptures. To Bishop Jewel vestments were ' relics of the Amorites ' and he only very reluctantly assumed them when he was consecrated Bishop of Salisbury. To the Reformers generally Rome was Babylon, the great enemy of the people of God. Compare a tract issued in 1623 by one M. Pattenson, ' The image of both Churches, Hierusalem and Babel, unitie and confusion, obedience and sedition.'

In the prolonged controversies between Puritans and Anglicans as to the right methods of Church government and organization, while the main arguments are derived from St. Paul and the Acts of the Apostles, the Old Testament is also called into service, and that by both parties. The following titles of pamphlets tell their own tale. ' The Perpetual Governement of Christe's Church. Wherein are handled: The fatherly superioritie which God first established in the Patriarkes for the guiding of his Church, and after continued in the tribe of Levi and the Prophetes: and lastlie conformed in the New Testament to the Apostles and their successours,' by

[1] Cf. *Puritan Preaching in England*, by Rev. John Brown, D.D., p. 61.

T. Bilson, 1593. 'Salomon on a treatise declaring the state of the kingdome of Israel, as it was in the daies of Salomon, whereunto is annexed another treatise of the Church, or more particularly of the right constitution of a church,' by T. Morton, 1596. 'The Reformation of religion by Josiah a commendable example for all Princes professing the Gospel to follow, with a warning to all faithfulle and true-hearted subjects, to encourage their princes in so happie a course.' Anon., 1600. 'Historie of Corah, Dathan and Abiram, applied to the Prelacy, Ministerie and Church Assemblies of England,' by J. Penry, 1609. 'A brief exposition of the whole book of Canticles, a work very usefull and seasonable to every Christian: but especially such as endeavour and thirst after the setling of Church and State according to the rule and pattern of the word of God,' by J. Cotton, 1692. 'Eschol: a cluster of the fruit of Canaan brought to the borders, or rules of direction for the walking of the Saints in Fellowship according to the order of the Gospel,' by J. Owen, 1648. 'The doome of Heretiques; or a discovery of subtle foxes who were tyed tayle to tayle and crept into the Church to doe mischiefe,' by Z. Smith, 1648. Examples of this kind of thing might be multiplied almost indefinitely, but these will suffice to show with what naïve assurance these controversialists accepted and used the Old Testament scriptures as the Word of God for their own times and purposes.

Among the more positive and salutary results of Old Testament theology has been reckoned the Puritan love of liberty. Their belief in the sovereignty and supremacy of God had the effect of both exalting and abasing their conception of human nature. Man might be the most miserable and sinful of beings, but he was responsible to God alone and possessed therefore certain rights and dignities of his own. In the vindication of God's cause revolt against human tyranny was always justifiable.

the Old Testament on Puritanism 415

Lecky puts the point as follows : ' It is at least an historical fact that in the great majority of instances the early Protestant defenders of civil liberty derived their political principles chiefly from the Old Testament and the defenders of despotism from the New. The rebellions that were so frequent in Jewish history formed the favourite topic of the one—the unreserved submission inculcated by St. Paul of the other.'[1] The antithesis is here put rather too sharply and it may be questioned whether the facts are quite as stated. In Scotland, under John Knox and his followers, where, as we shall see in other connexions, Puritan principles were carried to the utmost bound of their logic, the analogy of the prophets was most frequently used to justify the assertion of liberty and rebellion against earthly powers. Knox certainly claimed for himself and for the ministers of the Kirk of Scotland the privilege of the prophets to utter a ' Thus saith the Lord '. In one of his letters to the faithful he writes (1554) : ' The prophets of God sometimes may teach treason against kings, and yet neither he, nor such as obey the word spoken in the Lord's name by Him, offends God.' Among English Puritans, too, this sense of a prophetic vocation was not uncommon and seemed to justify their attitude to secular authority.

One of the most definite effects of Old Testament teaching on the minds of Protestants generally and of Puritans in particular was the justification it provided for persecution and for taking vengeance on their enemies. That this is not merely lawful but right and praiseworthy is seriously argued by Protestant writers of the sixteenth and seventeenth centuries. Most of them rest their case on the Old Testament. But they did not realize that the Old Testament speaks with two voices. Implicit in Hebraism lay a belief in human brotherhood which cannot be reconciled with racial or sectarian enmities. Indeed it may be said that the world as a whole has not yet risen to

[1] *The Rise and Influence of Rationalism in Europe*, vol. ii, p. 172.

the height of this great Hebraic argument. The parts of the Old Testament in which the Puritans rejoiced were those in which God is represented as a jealous God whose wrath is a terrible reality. He hates idolatry and suffers his people to punish idolaters, and Himself sends plagues on those who do despite to his will.

To the Puritans both in England and Scotland this example was one to be followed and they had therefore no hesitation in burning, hanging, and imprisoning those whom they regarded as enemies of God. Here again we find that it is by Knox that the doctrine is stated in its most extreme form. He writes in 1557: 'I would your Honours should note for the first time that no idolater can be exempted from punishment by God's Law. The second is, that punishment of such crimes as are idolatry, blasphemy and others that touch the Majesty of God doth not appertain to king and chief rulers only, but also to the whole body of that people, and to every member of the same, according to the vocation of every man and according to that possibility and occasion which God doth minister to avenge the injury done against His Glory, what time that impiety is manifestly known.'[1]

Though it is true that the Puritans persecuted somewhat less than did their opponents and that the first traces of a more tolerant spirit may be found among them, especially under Cromwell and the Independents and also among the Anabaptists, their general attitude on the subject shows how entirely they were dominated by what they conceived to be Old Testament standards. It is very remarkable that men familiar with the Old Testament should forget such texts as Job's splendid protest, 'If I rejoiced at the destruction of him that hated me, or lifted up myself when evil found him: yea I suffered not my mouth to sin by asking his life with a curse' (Job xxxi. 29, 30). It is even more remarkable that men with the New Testament in their hands should have been so blind

[1] Cf. *John Knox and the Reformation*, by Andrew Lang, pp. 82 and 83.

to its teaching in regard to mercy and love for one's enemies.[1] It was not merely that they accepted the ideas of their time, for they showed on occasion that they could transcend them. Rather was it that their conception of God had not yet reached the true level, and in this they were not alone.

The Puritan attitude to witchcraft and the cruelties which it sanctioned have often been cited as evidence of their bondage to the letter of the Old Testament. But it must be remembered that in this matter they were but men of their time and only strengthened in their fanaticism by the Old Testament ban on all forms of divination and magic and by such positive injunctions as 'Thou shalt not suffer a witch to live'. The belief in witches and in their powers for evil was certainly not peculiar to them. Though the Jews themselves had largely abandoned it, it was shared not only by the common people in England but by the intellectual leaders of the time. Shakespeare, Bacon, Selden, Sir Walter Raleigh, and Sir Thomas Browne all believed in witches. Laws against witchcraft were passed under Henry VIII, Elizabeth, and James I. They were enforced with the utmost stringency and breaches of them were visited with atrociously cruel punishments. In the years 1691 and 1692 there was a fierce outburst of feeling against witches in Massachusetts, New England, largely under the influence of Cotton Mather. It led to the arrest and trial of many hundreds of innocent people, and of those condemned some twenty were put to death. The writings and sermons of Mather fanned the flame of popular superstition and form a notable

[1] The nearest approach to this is 'A soldier must love his enemies as they are his enemies and hate them as they are God's enemies', one of the heads of the soldier's pocket Bible. This is a selection of texts for soldiers published in 1643 in which passages from the Old Testament predominate. It is sometimes called Cromwell's Soldier's Bible, though there is no evidence that Cromwell had anything to do with it. Its author was probably Robert Ram of Spalding who also wrote the Soldier's Catechism, though it was issued under the imprimatur of Richard Calamy.

example of the way in which the Puritans gave religious sanction to the suppression of what was otherwise regarded as a real social menace. Incidentally in this connexion we find evidence of the belief entertained by the Puritan leaders in America that their mission was to set up a theocracy in place of the kingdom of Satan which had, as they imagined, dominated the New World before their arrival. The activity of witches was put down to the efforts of the powers of evil to reassert themselves under the new régime. This idea of setting up a theocratic system over against the kingdom of the powers of darkness was undoubtedly derived from Old Testament analogies, and was to a certain extent shared by some of the more extreme Puritans in the Old Country. At the same time it should be remembered that, ' It was not in their use of the Old Testament to justify acts of intolerance and cruelty that the Puritans differed from their countrymen at large, but in the application of its other lessons. The God of the Israelites was primarily a god of justice. Merciful he could be, but his mercy was reserved for the penitent : to the sinner he was a God of wrath. In common with all their nation, his denunciation of the heathen they applied to their enemies, his promises of reward they appropriated to themselves ; but it is to their lasting honour that taking the promises, they were also willing to assume the corresponding obligations.' [1]

The Puritan attitude to war was also largely regulated by Old Testament ideas. Cromwell's Ironsides believed themselves to be wielding the sword of the Lord and of Gideon. To smite the Amalekites and slaughter Baalites was at once their duty and their privilege. Cromwell himself, his chaplain tells us, never went into battle without a text upon his lips, and where they have been recorded these texts are mostly from the Old Testament. The Psalms of David provided the

[1] Douglas Campbell, *The Puritan in England, Holland, and America*, vol. ii, p. 145.

troops with songs of encouragement before a fight and songs of triumph after it. Here is a typical picture, ' In the rout of the enemy, and in their flying and scattering about, many of them ran most frightedly and amazedly to the place where some of the regiments of horse of the Parliament side were standing on their guard and all or most of their riders were religiously singing Psalms, to whom as the aforesaid runaways of the enemy came near and by their singing of Psalms perceiving who they were, they all most fiercely fled back again and cryed out : " God damn them, they had like to have been taken by the Parliament Roundheads." For they only knew them, I say, to be Parliament soldiers by their singing of Psalms, a blessed badge and cognizance indeed.' [1] The longer the civil war lasted, the more implacable became the spirit of the Puritan soldiery and the more intense their consciousness that they were fighting the battles of Jehovah of Hosts. ' Dark and fierce were the prayers and outpourings of heart with which the Ironsides sought the Lord as the second civil war gathered round them. The fiery words of the Hebrew prophets had heated their brains : and the Biblical notions of " atonement " and " the avenger of the blood " had grown into sacred moral obligations. To their morbid fanaticism the curse of blood guiltiness lay upon the land until he on whose door-post it rested had atoned for his sins.' [2] The Ironsides would have felt their occupation gone had they been reminded of the hope expressed in Isaiah and Micah of a time coming when nations should learn war no more (Isaiah ii. 4).

In the hey-day of the Puritan protest this use of the ideas and language of the Hebrew scriptures was natural and sincere. But it did not always remain so. Of nothing is it more true than of Puritanism that *corruptio optimi pessima*. From being

[1] Quoted by Sir C. H. Firth in *Cromwell's Army*, p. 333.
[2] Frederick Harrison's *Oliver Cromwell*, p. 118 ; cf. also Calvin's *Commentary on Ps. 137*.

'one of the noblest heroisms ever transacted on this earth' it sometimes descended to a very pitiful hypocrisy. A man must be very strong and very humble to carry off successfully the conviction that he is an instrument in the hands of Almighty God. A Cromwell perhaps could do it, but many of his followers were not big enough for their self-appointed task. In the ravings of Levellers and Fifth Monarchy men we have Puritan Bibliolatry at its worst. The use of Scripture language in writing and conversation continued long after it ceased to represent anything real in life or conduct and so brought the whole movement into contempt.

Much the same may be said of that moral strictness which to the outsider is the most characteristic feature of the Puritan régime. While at first it represented an altogether healthy protest against corruption it afterwards degenerated into a pose. But all the time it drew its inspiration from Old Testament ideals and was a genuine attempt to reconstruct society on the basis of Hebrew legalism. Such was the inevitable result of the teaching of Calvin. 'Calvinism,' says J. A. Froude, 'as it existed at Geneva, and as it endeavoured to be wherever it took root for a century and a half afterwards, was not a system of opinion, but an attempt to make the will of God as revealed in the Bible an authoritative guide for social as well as personal direction. Men wonder why the Calvinists being so doctrinal, yet seemed to dwell so much and so emphatically on the Old Testament. It was because in the Old Testament they found, or thought they found, a divine example of national government, a distinct indication of the laws which men were ordered to follow, with visible and immediate punishments attached to disobedience. At Geneva, as for a time in Scotland, moral sins were treated after the example of the Mosaic law, as crimes to be punished by the magistrate.'[1] The moral stringency of the Puritan régime in England was due to the belief in God

[1] Froude's *Short Studies*, vol. ii, p. 53.

as a lawgiver. If men were really to please Him their lives must be regulated by the commands and ordinances which He has given, and any failure in this respect would bring its appointed penalty. It should be remembered in extenuation of their strictness that the moral conditions with which the early Puritans had to contend were exceedingly bad. The usual representation of them as gloomy kill-joys is only true of their decadence. They were not at first enemies of the lighter side of life. But they did raise a much needed protest against the immorality and debauchery that accompanied all forms of popular amusement in their day. The mistakes they made were the inevitable result of dealing with the situation in a purely legalistic spirit. They regarded themselves as in a similar position to the Israelites in Canaan. They were God's chosen people in a land of godlessness and idolatry, and the best service they could render to their God was to compel men to do His will. So in the very spirit of the Jewish Law they hedged life round with ' Thou shalt ' and ' Thou shalt not '. The end of it all was great moral confusion. The failure to discriminate between the use and abuse of pleasure and the good things of life led to the creation of artificial sins and a spirit of sour censoriousness. Here again the splendid moral idealism of the early Puritans degenerated into that temper of mind which tithes mint, anise, and cummin and neglects the weightier matters of the Law. They failed to realize that at this very time Jews themselves were being delivered from this error by their Synagogue tradition.

The crowning instance of this spirit is to be found in the Puritan treatment of Sunday. Under the Church of Rome Sunday was kept as a festival. After early mass the day was given up to recreation and work was not forbidden. The first indication of a stricter observance is found in a *Treatise on the Sabbath* issued by Dr. Richmond Bound in 1595. Its argument was to the effect that for the proper regulation of the Christian

Sunday we must look to the Old Testament precepts regarding the Jewish Sabbath. These precepts were meant for all time and the command to keep holy the Sabbath day was one which Christians were bound to obey. Any form of work or recreation on Sunday was therefore unlawful. God meant man to give up to Him a seventh of his time and this was to determine his use of every seventh day. This doctrine was not altogether new. In England the Jewish name Sabbath had been used for Sunday in a public proclamation in 1580 and in an Act of Parliament in 1585, but it was not until Puritanism had attained a measure of strength that strict Sabbatarianism was enjoined upon all Christian people. The injunction resulted in reducing Sunday to a day of gloom and idleness and in the creation of a number of artificial sins. It was in Scotland again under the direct influence of Geneva that Sabbatarianism was carried to extremes. From the latter half of the seventeenth century the kirk sessions exercised an atrocious tyranny over men's hearts and lives, meting out drastic punishment for every breach of what they regarded as divine commands. Citations for breaking the Sabbath are very frequent in the records. It became a sin for mothers to kiss their children on Sunday or for ministers to shave. The following are typical: 'Cite Isobell Balfort, servant to William Gordone tailyeor, beeing found sleeping at the Loche syde on the Lord's Day in tyme of Sermon.' 'It was reported that Margaret Brotherstone did water her kaill upon the Sabbath day, and was thairupon ordained to be cited.' 'Complained Margaret Brotherstone, and confessed her breach of Sabbath in watering of her kaill and thairupon ordained to give evidence in public of her repentance the next Lord's Day.' There is a very curious parallel in all this to Rabbinical regulations about the Sabbath which became so great a feature in later Judaism. We see the spirit of Old Testament legalism working itself out to the same ends under very different conditions and among very different people. In this respect, among others, the Puritan influence has been very persistent. In many sections of the Christian Church to-day the attitude towards Sunday observance savours far more of the spirit of Puritanism than of the teaching of Him who said: 'The sabbath was made for man, not man for the sabbath.'[1] A good example of the temper of the Scottish Presbyterians is to be found in their treatment of Quaker doctrine at the time of the visit of George Fox in 1647. The ministers were so much alarmed at the spread of his teaching that they drew up a number of curses which were to be read aloud in the churches and to which the people were called to say 'Amen' after the manner of the Israelites on Mount Ebal, e.g. 'Cursed is he that saith, "Every man hath a light within him sufficient to lead him into salvation;" and let all the people say Amen. Cursed is he that denieth the Sabbath Day, and let all the people say Amen.' Though it is not necessary for our argument it should perhaps be pointed out that the Sabbath as observed by the Jews themselves is not what the Puritans conceived it to be. To the Jews it is a day of happiness. The synagogue liturgy of the Sabbath is full of the joyous note. It is marked by gay dress, sumptuous meals, and a general sense of exhilaration. The Puritans knew little or nothing of synagogue worship or of Jewish homes. They had no experience of 'the joy of the commandment'—a phrase often on Jewish lips and in Jewish hearts. They interpreted the Scripture injunctions in their own dour spirit.

We now turn to a less questionable indication of the influence of the Old Testament on Puritan thought, viz. the part played by the Book of Psalms. There is no surer witness to the mind of a people than that given by its songs, and the songs of the Puritan were derived almost entirely from the Hebrew Psalter. We have already had occasion to refer to the psalm-singing of

[1] St. Mark ii. 27. On a Rabbinic parallel to this text see I. Abrahams, *Studies in Pharisaism and the Gospels*, First Series, p. 130.

Cromwell's soldiers on the field of battle. There is ample evidence of their habit in this respect both as a celebration of victory and as an encouragement before going into the fight. The Protestant Reformation on the Continent had given a great impetus to sacred psalmody and this was not without its parallel in this country. As early as 1539 Miles Coverdale had issued his *Goostly Psalms and Spiritual Songs*, mostly from the Old Testament and largely based on Luther. This was followed by Sternhold and Hopkins's version of the Psalms and by the collection of *Gude and Godlie Ballatis* in Scotland. All of these had a very considerable part in shaping Protestant thought in the British Isles. Later on, however, the Puritans objected to Sternhold and Hopkins as not being a sufficiently accurate rendering of the original. The hold which the Psalter had over them is evidenced by the fact that several attempts were made to render the Hebrew into the same rhythm in English for use in public worship. Among these is the very interesting Bay Psalm Book of the New England Puritans (1640). This superseded the version of Henry Ainsworth of Amsterdam. In 1649 the Long Parliament set up a committee to produce a metrical Psalm Book, and their labours resulted in the Scottish Version which has remained in use to the present day.

It would hardly be possible to exaggerate the influence of these various versions of the Psalms in shaping Protestant thought in England and Scotland. The use of them for purposes of devotion and worship was by no means confined to the Puritans. Jeremy Taylor and Archbishop Laud give abundant evidence to the contrary. But the epithet Psalm-singing quite justly characterized the Puritans, who found in the Psalter the best expression of their hopes, fears, and ideals, and turned to it on all occasions for encouragement and inspiration. John Milton began his career as a poet by translations from the Psalms, and echoes of their language are to be found in all his writings. Bunyan, too, found in the Psalms a perpetual fountain of consolation in the miseries of his spiritual state and used them freely to illustrate the ways of God with men. This is even more marked in the case of Cromwell. Lord Ernle says of him: 'The spirit that he read into the Psalms governed his actions at each supreme crisis of his stormy life: the most striking stages in his career are marked by quotations from the Psalms: in his private letters, his public dispatches, his addresses to Parliament, the imagery, metaphors and language of the Psalms drop from his lips or from his pen, as if by constant meditation he had made their phraseology a part of his very life.'[1] Thus in one of his earliest extant letters he writes: 'Truly then, this I find: that He giveth springs in a dry, barren wilderness where no water is. I live, you know, where—in Meshec, which they say signifies *prolonging*: in Kedar which signifies *blackness*: yet the Lord forsaketh me not. Though He do prolong, yet He will, I trust, bring me to His tabernacle, to His resting place.' In opening his second Parliament his speech was largely taken up with an exposition of the 85th and 46th Psalms. In his speech to the Rump Parliament he expounded Psalm lxviii: 'And indeed the triumph of that Psalm is exceeding high and great, and God is accomplishing it. And the close of it, that closeth with my heart and I do not doubt with yours, the Lord shaketh the hills and mountains and they reel, and God hath a hill too: an high hill as the hill of Bashan: and the chariots of God are twenty thousand, even thousands of angels: and God will dwell upon this hill for ever.' Instances of this kind might be multiplied indefinitely. It is sometimes suggested that Cromwell's use of scriptural language was only a concession to his supporters and was part of the deep-seated hypocrisy of the man. But the whole thing is too natural to admit of any such explanation. There is no doubt at all that his view of life, of

[1] *The Psalms in Human Life*, p. 242.

himself, and of his mission was shaped and moulded by his study of the Old Testament. Its language came unbidden to his lips and was the natural and inevitable expression of his thought.

Turning to Scotland once more we find that the thought of the Reformed Church there was largely shaped by the Old Testament and the Psalter. In his *Bible in Scots Literature* Dr. Moffat notes that as early as the middle of the sixteenth century 'the Old Testament was becoming dominant in the thought of the period, and that the book of Psalms was particularly popular'.[1] He thinks it may be assumed that the Bible was being widely read and there is evidence that even the more recondite details of the Old Testament story were familiar. The *Gude and Godlie Ballatis*, to which we have already referred, were steeped in the language of the Old Testament and of the Psalms. Later on in the days of the troubles the Psalms became the song-book of those who stood for the solemn League and Covenant against a world of enemies. On the scaffold and at the stake their martyrs died with the words of the Psalter on their lips. Isabel Alison and Marian Harvie, who were hanged at Edinburgh in 1680, died singing the 23rd Psalm, and Margaret Wilson as the waters closed over her at Blednoch sang—

> My sins and faults of youth
>   Do thou, O Lord, forget;
> After Thy mercies think on me,
>   And for thy goodness great.

In their field conventicles the Covenanters found help and strength in singing

> Thou art my hiding place, Thou shalt
>   From trouble keep me free.
> Thou with songs of deliverance
>   About shalt compass me.

---

[1] Pp. 90 and 104.

And when they sallied forth to scatter Claverhouse's dragoons at Drumclog it was to the words

> In Judah's land God is well known,
>   His name's in Israel great:
> In Salem is His tabernacle:
>   In Zion is His seat.
> There arrows of the bow he brake,
>   The shield, the sword, the war;
> More glorious thou than hills of prey
>   More excellent art far.

It is little wonder that the Psalms should have remained until this day the chief poetic expression of the religion of Scottish Presbyterianism. Their part in shaping it can hardly be over-estimated.

The same thing is true of the French Huguenots. De Remond writes of them: 'It was the book of Psalms which fostered the austere morals of the Huguenots, and cultivated those masculine virtues which made them the pick of the nation. It was that book which supported fainting courage, uplifted downcast souls, inspired heroic devotion. Their affirmations were *certes* or *en vérité*: they were enemies of luxury and worldly follies: they loved the Bible or the singing of spiritual songs and psalms better than dances and hautboys. Their women wore sober colours and in public appeared as mourning Eves or penitent Magdalenes: their men, habitually denying themselves, seemed struck by the Holy Spirit.'

Another and very striking example of the influence of the Bible and especially of the Old Testament in seventeenth-century England is to be found in the Quaker movement. Although George Fox and his friends were stout opponents of Puritanism in many of its forms, it is quite true, as Dr. Thomas Hodgkin suggests, that their doctrine ' required a Puritan *nidus* to work in '.[1] Indeed it may be said that in the life and teaching

---
[1] Cf. *Life of George Fox,* p. 121.

of the founder of Quakerism we have the Puritan spirit both at its best and at its worst. There is an intense consciousness of the presence and guiding hand of God coupled with a narrow individualism and an arrogant sense of perfection if not of infallibility. Fox's doctrine of the inner light and sense of his divine mission may be traced back ultimately to his study of the Old Testament prophets. Like Amos, Hosea, and Isaiah he had heard the divine call and on him lay the burden of the Lord. Like them, too, he was constrained to testify against a crooked and perverse generation and all his work was carried out in obedience to a 'Thus saith the Lord'. His whole life was regulated by the consciousness of a direct mandate from heaven. Like the Puritans Fox regarded the Bible as the infallible word of God and a sure guide for life. He used the Old Testament as freely as the New, though at times he distinguished between them more clearly than any of his contemporaries. For example, on one occasion when he was put on trial for refusing to take an oath and his accuser quoted against him the words in Jeremiah, ' Ye shall swear in truth and righteousness,' he replied, ' Aye, it was written so in Jeremiah's time, but that was many ages before Christ commanded not to swear at all : but where is it written so since Christ forbade all swearing ? I could bring as many instances for swearing out of the Old Testament as thou, and it may be more ; but of what force are they to prove swearing lawful in the New Testament, since Christ and the Apostle had forbade it ? ' This may be paralleled by his teaching on war which was based entirely on the New Testament and breathed a very different spirit from that of the Soldier's Bible. On the other hand Fox was saturated with the thought of the Old Testament and quite naturally made use of its words to defend his positions. Even in regard to swearing he argues : 'The world saith, " Kiss the book," but the book saith, " Kiss the Son, lest He be angry." And the Son saith, " Swear not at all ".' So in regard to the Quaker refusal to take off the hat, the following scene is typical. It was the occasion of Fox's trial before the Chief Justice of England in Launceston. 'Then said the Judge, "The court commands you to put off your hats." Then I spoke and said, " When did ever any magistrate, king or judge from Moses to Daniel command any to put off their hats when they came before them in their courts, either amongst the Jews, the people of God, or amongst the heathen? And if the law of England doth command any such thing, show me that law either written or printed." After some wrangling the judge went on, " Come, when had they hats from Moses to Daniel? Come answer me. I have you fast now." I replied, " Thou mayest read in the third of Daniel that the three children were cast into the fiery furnace by Nebuchadnezzar's command, with their coats, their hose and their hats on." This plain instance stopped him, so that, not having anything else to say to the point, he cried again, "Take them away, gaoler."' It was the uncompromising Biblicism of Fox and the early Quakers that earned them their reputation of crazy fanatics. But there was method in their madness, and if they shared the general belief of Protestants in the infallibility of Scripture as a guide for life, they were a little more discriminating than most in their use of it and they faced the inevitable consequences of their logic with unshaken courage.

In conclusion, the Puritan emphasis on the Old Testament has had very far-reaching effects on the religion of the Protestant Churches generally, and remains with them even to this day. In the war against the Central Powers it became evident in this country as well as in Germany that the God many worshipped was a national deity and that men thought of Him very much as Israel at one time did of Jehovah. He was invoked on both sides as a God of battles fighting on behalf of his own people, and their enemies were his. So, too, there is a tendency on the part of all the Churches to regard themselves as God's own people. He is with them in a sense in which He is not with those who differ from them, and in their own opinion they have a better chance of salvation than have others who do not share their privileges. In many respects their attitude savours more of the more primitive Old Testament particularism than of the broad universalism of the teaching of the second Isaiah, reinforced by the spirit of Christ and the teaching of St. Paul. This is even more true of the Theology of the Churches. In recalling the religion of his boyhood Bishop Lawrence of Massachusetts draws a picture which was true of all the evangelical Churches fifty years ago and remains true of many of them still. He says, 'While the Jesus of the Gospels was a vivid story, the chief emphasis was upon the Old Testament, and of course both Old and New Testaments, being inspired, were true to the word and letter. The world was created in six days in the year 4004 B.C., for Genesis and the date on the margin of the family Bible said so. Adam and Eve, the serpent, Noah and the flood destroying everything and everybody on the earth but the family and the animals entering the ark two by two, Jonah and the whale, Joshua and the sun, Daniel and the lions' den, the three young men in the fiery furnace, were facts as real as anything that happened yesterday. God from out of heaven sent His word or put out His hand and stopped the sun or the plagues, did anything that He wanted to : and by His miracles showed that He was God. These were the leading ideas in a boy's religion : whoever denied or questioned any of them was a sceptic or an atheist and liable to be damned.'[1] It may be said that all this was not peculiar to the Old Testament and that we have changed it now, and to a very large extent it is true. But how far we are from a complete rejection of these views is shown by the narrow and unprogressive temper that still characterizes many sections of the Christian Church in these days.

[1] *Fifty Years*, by William Lawrence, p. 10.

the Old Testament on Puritanism

In its crude Bibliolatry, Puritanism left to the Churches an inheritance the ill effects of which are still felt. Nevertheless it played a noble part in shaping our history and moulding the character of our people. Its religious fervour, its love of liberty, and its vivid sense of the presence of God in human affairs, were derived from its reverence for the Scriptures as well as were some of those more doubtful features on which we have dwelt. Its treatment of the Old Testament was arbitrary and one-sided, and coloured always by the peculiar temper of the people and the necessities of the times. There are in the Old Testament splendid incentives to peace, humanity, and spiritual religion which the Puritans either ignored or set in the background. For this it is they and not Hebraism that must bear the blame. But their errors in this respect must not be allowed to obscure the positive advantages they obtained from their familiarity with the Scriptures. The legacy of Judaism was to them a real inspiration, and they have handed it on to their posterity in an intensity of religious devotion and a passion of moral fervour for which the whole world is still in their debt.

W. B. Selbie.

Fig. 68. Medal to commemorate grant of religious liberty to Protestants and Jews of Hungary by the 'Patent of Tolerance', 1781.

FIG. 69. SPOILS OF THE TEMPLE

The details of the Triumphal Procession with Temple Spoils on the Arch of Titus are now much obliterated by ill usage (see Fig. 5 and description, p. 28). The monument was, however, carefully studied in the seventeenth century by the artist-engraver Pietro Santo Bartoli (1635–1700). His representation is reproduced of the triumphal procession with Temple spoils. It shows clearly many points now obliterated, such as the form of the table and the trumpets. Other details which survive on the Arch prove that Bartoli made a faithful copy.

JEWISH THOUGHT IN THE MODERN WORLD

Introduction: Jewish Thought and the Renaissance

THE close of the fifteenth century saw Hebrew established as one of the three languages of higher education, and the result may be traced in both theological and humanistic spheres. Luther on the one hand, Pico della Mirandola on the other, exemplify its influence and importance. But whereas the theologians saw in the Hebrew language only the means to the interpretation of the Bible, the humanists believed that in it they had found the key to the secrets of creation. Ideas derived from the Hebrew mystical books powerfully aided the new movements of thought. Telesio and Patrizzi, typical Renaissance philosophers, reproduce their theories of the creative light and of the nature of matter and space;[1] while pioneers of the experimental sciences like Agrippa and Paracelsus may well have drawn from them their sense of the unity and continuity of nature which became one of the main factors in the new outlook. A favourite philosophical book of the age was the *Dialoghi di Amore*[2] of 'Leon the Hebrew' ('Leone Ebreo' = Don JUDAH ABRAVANEL, ? 1465–1530); while some essential doctrines of Giordano Bruno have been traced back to the *Fountain of Life* of the medieval Jewish thinker IBN GABIROL (eleventh century).

---

[1] See A. Franck, *Philosophes modernes* (1879), p. 111 f. Through Henry More, the Cambridge Cabalist, these ideas reached Newton.

[2] Written about 1502, first published 1535; also in contemporary versions in French, Spanish, and Latin; re-edited by Gebhardt as vol. iii of the *Bibliotheca Spinozana* (Oxford and Heidelberg, 1927). The English reader will know it from the 'third partition' of the *Anatomy of Melancholy* and Borrow's *Lavengro* (cap. 50).

In this way both mystical and scientific tendencies of the Renaissance were nourished from Jewish sources,[1] and 'the enlargement of Japhet' was found 'in the tents of Shem'.

It would be an easy, although voluminous, task thus to trace out the influence of individual Jewish thinkers. Our problem, however, is not that, but the disentangling of a specifically Jewish factor from their thought. We are met at once with the difficulty which faces every inquiry involving abstract terms. How is one to arrive at the general class without a study of particular instances? And yet, without a knowledge of the characteristics of the class, how are the particular instances to be selected? Unless we can define exactly what we mean by Judaism or *Jewish* thought, it is dangerous to fix on any particular points and declare them to constitute the Jewish 'legacy'. If, however, we do set out from any one definition, we run a grave risk of its being partial or preconceived. The only way in which a criterion can be established is to examine the primary documents themselves. It is necessary therefore to go back to the Hebrew Bible and to see what points of philosophical interest it presents. We shall then be in a position to estimate the Hebraic quality of the contributions to modern thought made by the Jewish philosophers. A survey of the Biblical data is the more germane to our task since we are to start from the epoch of the Reformation.

I. *Some characteristics of Biblical Hebraism*

The charter of monotheism is comprised in articles not of metaphysical theory but of ethical precept. Its sole dogma, that of the unity of God, is not offered (was possibly never understood) as theoretic creed. Polytheism involved a variety of moral standards, that is to say, no standard at all. Monotheism substituted the principle of unity, one 'judge of all

---

[1] For details as to the influence of the Cabala see article by Canon Box, pp. 324–332.

Characteristics of Biblical Hebraism 435

the earth'[1] with 'one law'[2] for all. Much is said of the 'particularism' of the chosen people and the 'transcendence' of the chosen God; yet in the moral life, emphasized alike by legislator and prophet, the place of both is seen. 'And a stranger shalt thou not oppress: *for ye know the heart of a stranger, seeing ye were strangers* in the land of Egypt'[3]—it is only through personal experience that the universal can be reached. 'He judged the cause of the poor and needy. ... *Was not this to know me?* saith the Lord'[4]—the 'hidden God'[5] of the physical universe is revealed in the moral life.

How it came about that the ancient Hebrews laid such stress on conduct is a difficult question. We only know that Canaan is said to have 'vomited forth its inhabitants'[6] not for erroneous beliefs but for immoral practices; that Ahab was denounced not for Baal-worship but for the murder of a poor man;[7] that it was the '*doings* of the land wherein ye dwelt' and the '*doings* of the land whither I am bringing you', not their doctrines, which the Israelites were forbidden to follow;[8] that the original choice itself of Abraham was conditional on his 'commanding his children after him to *keep the way of God*', that is, 'to *do justice*'.[9] The idea of God seems in fact to have meant, whatever else, justice and moral order.

It is easy to understand how it is only within monotheism that the conception of the unity of mankind is attained. Polytheism rends the earth into fragments, each autonomous with separate tribe and private deity; even the aspirations of a Plato rose no higher than the dream of a united Greece.[10]

---

[1] Gen. xviii. 25.   [2] e.g. Num. xv. 15–16; Isa. xlii. 4.
[3] Exod. xxii. 21, xxiii. 9; Deut. x. 19, xxiv. 17–22.   [4] Jer. xxii. 16.
[5] Pascal's *Deus absconditus* (*Pensées*, iv. 242) from Isa. xlv. 15.
[6] Lev. xviii. 24–30, xx. 22–23.
[7] 1 Kings xxi. 17 f.; 2 Kings ix. 25–26.
[8] Lev. xviii. 3.   [9] Gen. xviii. 19.   [10] *Rep.* 469 f.

Within monotheism the earth and its people are one, 'the children of the Ethiopians' as much as 'the children of Israel'.[1] Monotheism unites; polytheism divides.

A similar tendency may be traced in the spheres of logic and metaphysics. Polytheism involves, although it is not of course identical with, what would now be called a pluralism. It pre-supposes, that is, the existence of a number of coordinate wills, each equally active in the government of the world. This is the obvious or 'common-sense' theory and has been accepted and justified by some philosophers. But whatever one may think of the nature and origin of Biblical monotheism, it clearly demands precisely the opposite view. It has no place for any doctrine but that of unity of source—'in the beginning God created both heaven and earth'; and the doctrine of unity of *source* involves that of unity of *control*. That feature of pluralism which William James was fond of calling 'tychism'—the reign of chance—is thus overcome. Sporadic or magical interference is at once put out of court. Only one supreme God is concerned in the government of things, not many minor deities. Power is concentrated in one hand. First the importance, then the reality, finally the very possibility, of miracles not wrought by the one God is denied; and even the miracle-working 'false prophet' is declared to be sent by God to test a credulous generation.[2] The greatest of God's miracles, however, lies in the way in which he once for all controlled the rebellious chaos: 'set a bound to the sea', 'fixed the earth on its foundation', so that 'seed-time and harvest, summer and winter, day and night, shall not cease'.[3] These 'ordinances of heaven and earth'[4] are thus at once the index of God's power and the expression of his sole wisdom.

This complete dependence of all things on God, itself source of the ethical doctrine of the divine impartiality which

[1] Amos ix. 7.
[2] Deut. xiii. 1–5.
[3] Gen. viii. 22.
[4] Jer. xxxiii. 25.

Maimonides and his School

is the highest justice, opens up wider vistas than the narrowly human. The Hebrew Bible, although it gives full measure to the claims of the human heart, is notoriously theocentric. Man is neither the measure nor the centre of things. The cattle of Nineveh,[1] the farmer's ox and ass,[2] the very trees of the forest,[3] are of account to the Maker of all; and the 'God in his holy habitation' who is 'father of the fatherless and judge of the widow'[4] gives the raven its food[5] and waters the grass of the 'wilderness in which there is no man'.[6] In this firm sense of totality lies the unique character of the Biblical account. Its universality is thoroughgoing. It holds the scales equal between all the various parts of creation. Nothing is small; nothing is great. 'They wait all upon thee.'[7]

II. *The Medieval Development and Modern Thought*

Importance of Maimonides and his school

Jewish philosophy proper, so far as it has made itself felt in modern European thought, emerges, for the first time after PHILO,[8] with the medievals, beginning with ISAAC JUDAEUS (855–955)[9] and SAADIA (892–942)[10] and reaching its highest point in MOSES MAIMONIDES (1135–1204).[11] There were of course many divergent streams in the movement, and one important current approached its problems from a different direction altogether; but Maimonides holds a unique position not only because of his intrinsic pre-eminence, but also because, up to the opening of the eighteenth century, he was the main channel through which

---

[1] Jonah iv. 11. [2] Exod. xxiii. 12; Deut. v. 14, xxv. 4, &c.
[3] Hab. ii. 17. The command of Deut. xx. 19 against destroying fruit-trees was developed notably by the Rabbis into a unique prohibition of any form of destruction.
[4] Ps. lxviii. 5. [5] Ps. cxlvii. 9. [6] Job xxxviii. 26.
[7] Ps. civ. 27, cxlv. 15. [8] See above, pp. 42–63. [9] Above, p. 187.
[10] Above, p. 267. [11] Above, pp. 192–202, 257–282.

post-Biblical Hebraism reached the non-Jewish world. The remarks which follow, necessarily short as they are, are made therefore with central reference to him and his school, and concern themselves with the question of the contribution made by them to the store of modern thought, and of the relation in which that contribution stands to the older Hebraism.

§ 1. *Logic and Metaphysics : Unity of God and Unity of Nature*

In the Hebrew Bible God is conceived as being not only the sole but also the immediate cause of each single thing or event. It is true that he alone can perform miracles and that his greatest miracle is the establishing of order in the world. Within the world itself, however, there is little idea of reciprocal interaction. Traces of the appearance of this view may be seen in those passages in which the operation of secondary causes is emphasized—the lifting up of the sea through a strong wind; the feeding of Elijah by the agency of ravens; the sheltering of Jonah by means of a gourd. Still, such passages are few and probably not representative. Biblical writers are so full of the majesty of God that in each single phenomenon they see the immediate consequence of a particular act of his will.

When one considers the character of scientific inquiry, however, it is clear that this simple doctrine fails to satisfy. Chance has been banished from the world and in its place the wisdom of God has been enthroned. But unless the acts of God's wisdom constituting nature are such as we can understand, we can never penetrate into the heart of things. The interpretability of nature depends on its being one whole, any part of which theoretically is explicable in terms of the rest. This great development of the implications of monotheism was clearly enunciated by the medieval Jewish thinkers, particu-

Unity of God and of Nature

larly Maimonides. Through them in various ways (the principal being the philosophy of Spinoza) it reached the modern world. The Bible had declared that the whole of nature had one Creator. They added the corollary that created nature is one.

To the recognition of the ethical weakness of polytheism is thus explicitly added that of the logical. Polytheism is seen to involve a chaos in science as well as in morals; or rather, it is seen to preclude the very possibility of science, as formerly it had been seen to preclude the very possibility of morality. If there is no unity of control in nature there is no standard of conduct. If there is no unity of structure in nature there is no such thing as ordered knowledge. The establishing of this position is the central point in the argument of the masterpiece of the whole movement, Maimonides' *Guide for the Perplexed*.[1] The clarity with which it is seized is remarkable. God is a 'free cause', but a rational one; and his rationality lies in the homogeneity of his creation.

The point is so important as to merit the closest attention. The world is treated as one individual whole, and it is one because the God who made it is one. The position achieved is not that of monism, since it insists on a transcendent creator; but it has come to the doctrine of the unity and harmony of the *structure* of things from a sense of the unity of their *source*. Hence Hebraic monotheism is not originally a *scientific* theory, arising, as among the Greek philosophers, from the contemplation of the unitary character of natural phenomena;[2] rather the unitary character of natural phenomena is a deduction from the primary intuition of religion. But, the result once arrived at, the *religious* theory proved much more thoroughgoing

[1] Available in an English translation by M. Friedländer. The standard edition is that of S. Munk, *Le Guide des Égarés* (Paris, 1856–1866).

[2] For an interesting comparison between Greek metaphysical and Hebrew ethical monotheism, see H. F. Hamilton's *People of God* (Oxford, 1912), vol. i, cap. i. The book suffers from the usual disadvantage of neglecting the post-Biblical Jewish data.

than the *scientific*. Greek metaphysics never threw off the polytheistic taint. Both Plato and Aristotle believed in the existence of a real contingency in Nature. Such a doctrine, however, is inconceivable to a philosophy arising from monotheism. Monotheism can have no more dealings with 'errant causes', 'chance' or 'fortuitousness' in science, than with a host of co-ordinate controls in morals. And its emotional appeal is immeasurably more powerful than that of contemplative analysis. To the religious mind, even when turned towards science, the spirit of God still moves upon the face of the waters.

It is impossible here to follow out fully the consequences of this doctrine, and to show how, by the transference of emphasis from the unity of God to the unity of nature, scientific inquiry (the inquiry into the uniformities of the structure of things) was raised to the supreme religious duty. Search after truth in the sciences was even held to have been a high and essential step in the grades of wisdom culminating in the illumination of the prophet. Theories of prophecy apart, however, the position as a whole remains striking. Theism is not a confession of ignorance but the expression of knowledge. God, in Biblical phrase, is not only 'justice' but 'wisdom', and his service is in the intellectual as well as in the moral life.

This bold setting of science in the very shrine of religion is the chief contribution to the modern world of the medieval Jewish thinkers, since it was this lesson which, impressed three and a half centuries later on the mind of Spinoza, was set by him in the very heart of his system. Whether they were right in deducing it, as they did, from Biblical Hebraism is an interesting question. It is noteworthy, however, that not only this idealizing of scientific endeavour, but also the very background of modern scientific ideology, is Hebraic. As a matter of history this derives not from the empirical monism of Greece but from the transcendental monotheism of Israel. The ideal

Ethics and Politics

of absolute cosmic regularity, so far as it has reached general thought, is of theological origin. 'Laws of Nature' are originally decrees of God. At least one most important strand in their history can be traced back through the Deism and Rational Theology of the seventeenth and eighteenth centuries to Spinoza, and back from Spinoza to his Jewish predecessors.[1] Detail apart, however, the whole conception derives all its force from the 'words' and 'commandments' of God whereby the universe is created and sustained. Hebraism, in fact, far from being the enemy of science, is the rock from which its philosophy was hewn.[2]

§ 2. *Ethics and Politics: the theory of the Covenant and its Outcome*

A remarkable feature in the whole movement of philosophical Hebraism was the freedom with which the most various doctrines were entertained, a fact to be connected with the traditional lack of interest in speculation as such. What mattered was not theory but practice. So long as the conduct was right, any extravagance of theory could be, if not welcomed, at least condoned. It was this flexibility which formed the strength of the whole tradition. Few indeed were the doctrines which could not find some support in a judicious selection and interpretation of Biblical phrase. The written word remained the standard, but the way in which it was understood varied. Hence, under the semblance of uniformity the greatest diversity of opinion prevailed. Never within the bounds of a religious system was freedom of thought so widely offered or so curiously

---

[1] The famous sixth chapter 'On Miracles' of the *Tractatus Theologico-Politicus* can be documented verbally from Maimonides. See M. Joel, *Spinozas Theologisch-Politischer Traktat* (Breslau, 1870), p. 57 f.

[2] I am glad now to be able to refer in support of the above to the similar point urged by Professor Whitehead in his recently published Lowell Lectures, *Science and the Modern World* (Cambridge, 1926), p. 17 f.

disguised; nor, so long as the historical and poetical portions only of the Bible were allegorized away, was there much harm done.

It became obvious, however, even in the time of Philo, that the code of conduct stood in danger. Religious discipline, in both Alexandrian and Arabist periods, speedily decayed as a consequence of this 'creative' interpretation, and, as ever, the resulting antinomianism refused to confine itself to rejection of ceremonial alone. It became an urgent social problem to provide a justification of the whole system of conduct which should not be affected by the symbolical use of the text of the code.

The solution was found in the reference to history. Habits of conduct, we learn, are not capable of an *a priori* deduction. Objections against them based on *a priori* grounds are therefore invalid. Whatever the origin of the practice may be, its validity depends on its acceptance as a part of a whole system. The people entered freely, that is, in agreement with its native character, into a 'covenant', and bound itself to follow definite ways of life. The obligation to retain them lies therefore in the self-consistency of the people's character. In the working out of this theory [1]—Biblical through and through, and sustained by powerful arguments from Rabbinical literature—there emerged three ideas of far-reaching importance for the modern age: the theory of a universal moral code, the 'comparative method', and the problem of values, human and divine.

---

[1] It is repeated by Spinoza (*Theol.-Pol.*, cap. v) and to all intents and purposes by Mendelssohn (see below, p. 458 f.). The *ethical* character of the covenant lay of course in the freedom of its acceptance (see the remarks of Robertson Smith in *Prophets of Israel* (1882), pp. 161 f., 169, and 175, and in a similar connexion, *Religion of the Semites* (1889), p. 42). This is well brought out in the Rabbinic comment on Deut. xxxiii. 2, which asserts that God offered the Torah to all the other nations before giving it to Israel; they all refused it, however, on the ground that its moral demands conflicted with their accustomed way of life.

Theory of the Covenant

(i) *Contract and 'natural' religion*

It would be paradoxical to affiliate so separatist a doctrine as that of a national covenant with the theory of a universalistic morality, if we did not remark the obvious point that contracts are binding only on the contracting parties. 'No positive law whatsoever', as Locke puts the argument in the first of his *Letters on Toleration*, ' can oblige any people but those to whom it was given. "Hear, O Israel" sufficiently restrains the obligation of the law of Moses only to that people.' Jewish tradition, from the very earliest times of which we have record, stressed the uniqueness of the ceremonial law to the Jews.[1] For the non-Jew a simpler code was held to exist, a code the universality of which is marked by its being associated with the ancestors, not of the Jews specifically, but of all mankind, the ' sons of Noah '.

We need not enter into the sources of this doctrine as the whole subject is treated elsewhere in this volume.[2] We need only remark that obedience to the 'Noachide laws' constituted 'righteousness' for the 'nations of the world', and conferred upon them, just as much as did adherence to the Sinaitic covenant upon Jews, a 'portion in the world to come'. From the point of view of general religious thought it is important to observe the interpretation involved herein of the doctrine of 'election'. The divine choice of Israel entails not rights but special duties;[3] Israel is after all only the 'first born'[4] of the family of nations. But in addition, one

---

[1] Exegetically, the point was made to depend on the Pentateuchal differentiation between 'judgements' and 'statutes', e. g. in Lev. xviii. 4. 'Judgements' are the universal moral laws which 'if they had not been written down, would have had to be written down', i.e. laws the validity of which is not *merely* legal; 'statutes' are the seemingly arbitrary points of ceremonial (*Babli Joma*, 67 b).

[2] *The Influence of Judaism on Western Law*, above, pp. 383–387.

[3] So already in the famous outburst of Amos (iii. 2). It is, of course, central in the 'servant' passages of Isaiah. [4] Exod. iv. 22.

point in the detail of the 'Noachide code' invites special comment. It contains no creed, no theoretic statement about the nature of God, belief in which is the condition of salvation. It consists solely of such articles of practical morality as are an essential condition of civilized life. This twofold characteristic is reflected in the use made of it in the sixteenth and seventeenth centuries.[1] In the hands of the jurists it became one of the main elements in the foundation of the edifice of universal, international law; while thinkers like Bodin [2] made it part of the theoretic basis for the general plea for tolerance of dissent in religion.

(ii) The 'reasons for the commandments' and the science of cultural anthropology

More significant even than this is the place which these discussions hold in the rise of the 'comparative' outlook, the characteristic mark of the modern as opposed to the ancient and medieval spirit. They came to a head in the *Guide for the Perplexed* of Maimonides, the first part of the third and last book of which offers a masterly exposition of Pentateuchal law from this point of view. The attempt there developed to find an explanation of the customs of Israel in those of neighbouring peoples gradually broadened in the hands of later inquirers into the study of the customs of all early and primitive

---

[1] Spinoza's unfortunate reference (*Tract. Theol.-Pol.*, cap. v) is set right by M. Joel, *op. cit.*, pp. 55-6; and Hermann Cohen, *Spinoza über Staat und Religion*, now reprinted in his *Jüdische Schriften* (Berlin, 1924), vol. iii, pp. 345 ff. The general question is dealt with in the latter's *Nächstenliebe im Talmud* (*Jüd. Schrift.*, vol. i, pp. 145 ff.).

[2] For the relation of Bodin to Jewish thought reference should be made to Jacob Guttmann's long and important essay in the *Monatsschrift für Geschichte und Wissenschaft des Judentums* for 1905. It is noteworthy that, like Montaigne and L'Hôpital, Bodin had one Jewish parent.

Theory of the Covenant

races.¹ The influence on general thought of this comparative study, particularly in the spheres of morals and religion, is incalculable. Yet behind it lies not only an old Jewish problem but also an old Jewish answer. John Spencer's work on the *Laws of the Hebrews* (1685), according to the testimony of Robertson Smith,² laid the foundations of the whole science; but the portly folios of the Cambridge orientalist and theologian who was 'so much before his time that his work was not followed up', rest directly and confessedly on the pregnant chapters of the *Guide* of Maimonides (1190).

(iii) *Values human and divine*

The return to the Biblical idea of covenant and the consequent stress on the historical character of the detail of Pentateuchal legislation led to the enunciation of a third and more specifically metaphysical concept. The justification through history of the validity of habits of conduct necessarily drew attention, as we have seen, to their empirical origin. The argument is now thrown out wider and joins the treatment of the great problem of the divine attributes.³ Validity in general is validity for us. Ultra-personal experience, expressed in the revelation on Sinai, may determine what for us is finally valid, finally consonant, that is, with the wider structure of human life as apprehended by prophetic insight or social discovery. We are not then driven to the desperate chaos of a relativity in morals. Yet for all that, moral values and standards of conduct, although final to man (or rather,

---

[1] For some interesting remarks in this connexion see Sir James Frazer's preface to his *Folklore of the Old Testament*.

[2] *Religion of the Semites*, Pref. p. vi. (The special point of Spencer's dependence on Maimonides is worked out in Julius Guttmann's essay in *Festschrift Simonsens* (Copenhagen, 1923), pp. 258–276.)

[3] See David Kaufmann's *Geschichte der Attributenlehre in der jüdischen Religionsphilosophie des Mittelalters* (Gotha, 1877).

because final to man), are final for man only. Human categories of good and evil are not applicable to the universe as a whole. God himself, we are told, is called 'good', as He is called 'wise', 'living', even 'existent', only *homonymously*, 'as the constellation (*canis*) is called by the same name as the animal, dog'.[1] Ethics is then a specifically human science, and its principles hold only for humanity.

We would seem to be on the way to a pure naturalism, and in a certain sense this is the case. To interpret the universe as a whole in the light of human opinions or human needs— the presentation to the mind of 'all that is unintelligible in the world as a glorified image of itself'[2]—is to Hebraism the ultimate blasphemy, and the development by Maimonides of this old Biblical theme is only reproduced in Spinoza's famous attacks on anthropomorphism. Yet, since ethical principles *are* valid *for men*, arising as they do out of man's place in the universe, Maimonides (therein again to be followed by Spinoza) reverts to the old answer to the difficulties aroused by the doctrine of the transcendence of God. God's 'glory' may not be known, but his 'ways' are,[3] and his 'ways' are the ways of the moral life. It is only through the practice of 'lovingkindness, judgement, and righteousness'—'*on this earth*', as

---

[1] The conventional example given by Maimonides (*Introduction to Logic*, cap. 13) and repeated by Spinoza (*Cog. Met.* ii. 11, § 3 and *Eth.* i. 17 sch.).

[2] I borrow the phrase from Mr. Lowes Dickinson's characterization of Greek religion in his *Greek View of Life* (1898), p. 7.

[3] The reference is to the famous passages in Exod. xxxiii. 17–23, xxxiv. 5–8 which had already been expounded in this sense in *Guide*, I, liv. For Spinoza see *Theol.-Pol.* xiii, § 22; xiv, §§ 25 and 30; and for the significance of the doctrine of the *exemplar humanae vitae* in his finished system, *Eth.* iv, Pref. [For the Rabbinic use of this Greek conception see Abrahams's *Studies in Pharisaism and the Gospels*, Second Series, Cambridge, 1924, pp. 138–182. The Jewish contribution to the doctrine lies, as usual, in the ethical turn given to it.] It is important to note that both for Maimonides and Spinoza ethical perfection comes first. A man must be good before he can be wise.

Theory of the Covenant

they are careful to complete the quotation [1]—that the final perfection of man can be attained.

If we ask wherein this perfection lies we are met with a noble appeal to disinterestedness. 'Rewards and punishments' are not external judgements on, but natural developments of, actions; the very promises and threats of the Scriptures are only statements of these intrinsic consequences. The 'end' then is not the attainment of some thing or goal outside of ourselves but the perfecting of the mind. The supreme command to '*know* the God of thy father' [2] through his works has its end only in the pure ideal of knowledge. 'Say not: "I shall study in order that I may become rich"'—so Maimonides, in the words of the Talmud, concludes the introductory book of his digest of Rabbinic law—'Say not: "I shall study in order that I may be called learned, or in order that I may receive reward in the world to come." The command that thou shouldst love God [3] means that thou shouldst do nothing except from love. . . . Only children and the uneducated are taught to serve from fear of punishment or from the hope of reward; and as their intelligence becomes more developed, we must gently accustom them to the thought of serving from love. . . . We love God through the knowledge which we have of him, and as the measure of the knowledge so is the measure of the love. We must therefore devote ourselves to the study of those sciences which, so far as is given to man at all, offer him knowledge of his Maker.' [4]

---

[1] Jer. ix. 24 (Maimonides, *Guide*, III, liv, end; Spinoza, *Theol.-Pol.*, xiii, § 21).

[2] A favourite motto adopted from David's last charge to Solomon (1 Chron. xxviii. 9). Critics pointed out drily, much as Pascal did long after, that the 'dieu des savants' was not the same as the 'God of Abraham, Isaac and Jacob'.   [3] e.g. Deut. vi. 5.

[4] *Treatise on Repentance*, x, § 4 f. (available in a rather poor English translation by Soloweyczik, London, 1863, and in Bernard's *Selections from Yad Hachazakah*, Cambridge, 1832).

The position is saved from degenerating into an egoistic intellectualism by the profound Hebraic appreciation of the social character of human life, an appreciation which is most clearly manifested in the doctrine of the Messiah. To Maimonides, as to the essential Old Testament tradition, the Messiah is not so much a person as an age; or rather, emphasis is laid not so much upon the Messianic person as upon the age of which he is the initiator. This age, the last and highest in human history, is a kingdom of *this* world, and Maimonides recognized the advent of Christianity and Islam as stages in the evolution of its accomplishment. In it what are now the aspirations of the few will become the common heritage of all, and thus the conflict between wisdom and justice be reconciled in a human society patterned on the unity of God's name. 'They shall no more *teach*', he quotes,[1] 'every man his neighbour and every man his brother saying, Know the Lord; for they shall *all know* me from the least of them unto the greatest of them, for my Torah shall be in their *heart*.'[2] In this fusing of a naturalistic metaphysics with a positivistic ethics and politics in the religious enthusiasm of 'service in the heart',[3] medieval Jewish philosophy found its inspiration and consummation.[4]

---

[1] In the introduction to the attempted formulation of 'articles' of a 'Jewish creed' in his commentary to *Mishnah Sanhedrin*, xii (available in an English translation by J. Abelson in *Jewish Quarterly Review*, October, 1906).

[2] Jer. xxxi. 33-34.   [3] *Guide*, III, li (the phrase is Talmudic).

[4] The direct influence of this school on the widest circle of modern thought is not confined to the points we have noted already or to those in which it is followed by Spinoza. This is obvious from the numerous translations of Maimonides' philosophical works which appeared in the sixteenth and seventeenth centuries. We may instance among others the reprint of the old Latin version of the *Guide* (Paris, 1520); Buxtorf's new version (Basel, 1629); Pococke's *Porta Mosis* (Oxford, 1655); Voorst's *Foundations of the Law* (Amsterdam, 1680); Clavering's *Treatises on Education and Repentance* (Oxford, 1705). The result may be seen not only in the casual references of polymaths like Bayle but in the reasoned system of the Cambridge

III. *Spinoza*

With Lessing's historic declaration that 'there is no other philosophy than the philosophy of Spinoza', the Dutch Jew BARUCH (BENEDICT) SPINOZA (1632–1677) began to assume his place among the foremost thinkers of the world. Although himself alienated from his people and excommunicated[1] by the local congregation in which he had been educated and of which his father had been an elder, he yet retained throughout life so strong an impress of his early training that his mature system recalls, both in general feature and in detail, the work of his Jewish predecessors.

By this statement is not intended any depreciation of Spinoza's originality, or any denial of his debts to non-Jewish sources. Spinoza is in the line of the Hebraic tradition because he brought to the problems of his age a mind steeped in the outlook of that tradition. The very passage in which he tells us of the impulse which drove him to philosophical reflection sets him within it at once. 'After experience had taught me that the common occurrences of ordinary life are vain and futile, and I saw that all the objects of my desire and fear were in themselves nothing good nor bad save in so far as the mind was affected by them; I determined at length to search out whether there were not something truly good and communicable to man, by which alone, all other things being set aside, his spirit might be affected; yea, whether there were anything through the discovery and acquisition of which I might enjoy continuous and perfect happiness for ever.'[2] The problem is not one of theory, the

Platonists. In this connexion the series of penetrating comments and summaries made by Leibniz during his study of the *Guide* (printed in Foucher de Careil's *Leibniz, la Philosophie juive, et la Cabale*, Paris, 1861) is of especial interest. [1] See below, p. 452, n. 3.

[2] *On the Improvement of the Understanding*, cap. i. The passage is set at the head of Mr. Bridges's anthology, *The Spirit of Man*, and I have used his translation.

discovery of an abstract truth. It is the old Hebraic problem of practice, the finding of a way of life.

The contention that Spinoza is a *Jewish* philosopher, Jewish, that is, not only in origin but in inspiration, needs to be limited carefully. 'Spinozism', it has been happily remarked, 'is not a system but a habit of mind.'[1] Now it is this 'habit of mind', not any specific system of doctrine, which divergent opinion in the modern world has found valuable in Spinoza, and it is this 'habit of mind', again apart from any question of specific doctrine, which Spinoza derived from the Hebraic tradition. Like any other thinker he took over the detail of problems, often indeed solutions, from many sources; but his way of looking at the most general problem of all, the problem of life itself, was that of his Jewish predecessors.[2] His 'vision', to use the term of William James, is natively Hebraic, and it is this 'vision' which appeals.

The complex elements making up the human world may be summed up under the two heads of moral and intellectual. Ethics and science, the practical and the theoretical, divide between them the universe of human problems, and no one of the wider syntheses, if it hopes to maintain a permanent hold, can afford to relinquish either. Most systems, whether of philosophy or of religion, stress one of these primary factors at the expense of the other, or cover up an unresolved opposition by the device of a one-sided disparagement. Spinoza's philosophy is the most thoroughgoing and successful attempt we have to do justice to both.

To take one example, no other thinker has given in so small a space so suggestive an account of the possibilities of the

[1] Pollock, *Spinoza* (ed. 2, 1912), p. 381.

[2] Lack of space precludes a discussion of indebtedness on special points. An idea of the factors involved may be gained from Dunin-Borkowski's *Der junge De Spinoza* (Münster i. W., 1910); Prof. Wolfson's series of essays in *Chronicon Spinozanum*, i–iii (1921–1923), and Dr. Gebhardt's *Uriel da Costa* (Oxford and Heidelberg, 1922).

Fig. 70. BARUCH SPINOZA, 1632–1677

human body; but the recognition does not blind him to the equally existent powers of the human mind. He is enabled to follow out impartially both lines of reflection (how fruitfully in each case, later literature shows), because in his view specific human minds, no less than specific human bodies, are only 'modes', within parallel 'attributes', of the one reality. The complaint has been made that he reduces all mysteries into one great one; and in a sense this is true. But the very simplification is an advance, since all explanation consists in showing that any one puzzling phenomenon is only an instance of a wider puzzle; and the point is doubly important for our present inquiry because the simplification so effected is just that reference to unity which is the characteristic of Hebraism. The *Ethics* touches on all subjects connected with human conduct: psychology and the theory of Law and the State as well as practical moral precept; but the key-note of his theology, the rejection of the merely human point of view, is the general characteristic of the whole. Spinoza's work is an attempt to get rid of prejudice and preconception, and allow things to speak, as it were, for themselves. It offers a theory independent of the human spectator which should yet include the facts of the human. But this is only to set out explicitly what is implicit in the theocentricity of the Hebrew Bible. As Spinoza himself said: 'Some begin from created things and some from the human mind. I begin from God.'[1]

It is sometimes thought that the seventeenth century was unique in its interest in nature, and that therefore its great thinkers had to start completely afresh with problems never faced before. Nothing could be farther from the truth. Research has shown that Descartes himself was a medieval (the best of the medievals were very modern); and a glance at Steinschneider's monumental work on the Hebrew trans-

[1] *ap.* Stein, *Leibniz und Spinoza* (Berlin, 1890), p. 283.

lations of the Middle Ages[1] shows the burning interest in contemporary scientific theory of medieval Jewry. It is not then a matter for surprise that the religio-philosophical synthesis elaborated within the earlier epoch should have sufficed, when passed through a rich and appreciative mind, for the later. Spinoza had not to fashion, he had only to absorb, the 'vision of all reality as one' which students recognize as the informing principle of his outlook.[2] He had only to repeat the conception that God is not a mere 'refuge of ignorance' but a unity of intellect and will; that theology therefore must rest on physics, and both on the 'eternal verities' recognized by the human mind. It was within the philosophy of the Jewish Schoolmen that the profoundest stress on conduct had been combined with the realization that human norms are no more than human; theirs too was the commonplace that the highest worship was that arising from the study of the systematic unity of Nature. Further, the explicit equation of God with Nature was formulated in the history of Jewish thought long before Spinoza. It could not indeed have appeared strange to the minds which treasured the 104th Psalm.

It is so often thought that the famous excommunication of Spinoza was due to his enunciation of this and similar 'heresies'[3]

[1] *Die hebräischen Übersetzungen des Mittelalters* (Berlin, 1893).

[2] Cf. Sorley in *Proc. Brit. Acad.*, 1917-1918, p. 477. So already Hegel in the first paragraph of his account of Spinoza in his *History of Philosophy*.

It was Hegel who wrote that to become a philosopher a student must first soak himself in Spinoza, a piece of advice which, with Fichte and Schelling in his own day and most great thinkers since, he certainly followed himself. Among his own debts to the master is the fruitful doctrine that 'the truth is the whole'.

[3] It was of course a 'political' move. The new community, itself hardly tolerated, was bound to dissociate itself from the holder of views which were becoming a scandal in the wider world and were likely to prejudice its own hardly won position.

The 'Synagogue', as one organized body like the Roman Church, never existed, and so could not as such at any epoch issue a general decree of

FIG. 71. SPINOZA'S WORK-ROOM AT RHIJNSBURG.
The instruments that Spinoza used for his work as a maker of lenses are on the table.

that it is worth while referring here to a curious event in the history of Jewish theology. About twenty years after Spinoza's death, a well-known scholar and thinker, DAVID NIETO (1654–1728), became Rabbi of the Spanish Jewish community in London. No mean philosopher in his own right (he published in Spanish a treatise *On Divine Providence*, and in Hebrew and Spanish a defence of tradition), he came into conflict with his congregation because both in class-room and pulpit he had asserted the identity of Nature with God. When called on to explain himself, he pointed out the scriptural authority for the doctrine, and availed himself of the distinction between 'particular natural things' (*natura naturata*) and 'Nature in general' (*natura naturans*). It seems to have been echoes of a recent millenarian upheaval which caused the controversy to be referred to the leading Jewish scholar of the day.[1] Far from expressing surprise at Nieto's thesis, he accepted it as genuinely religious and natively Jewish, and was even at pains to show, by reference to older literature, that it was a commonplace among thinkers of undoubted authority.[2] He is particularly in agreement with Nieto in his condemnation of those who denied the existence of a

excommunication. Apart from local theological amenities the only serious attempt at suppressing opinion was the (unsuccessful) attack made by a number of individual leaders of communities against Maimonides after his death, but the essence of their objection was that he was thought to have tried to make *opinion* the test of Judaism. The attack, repeated with all virulence by S. D. Luzatto in the last century, was not therefore on any one opinion, but rather on the attempt to make any one set of opinions authoritative and final. It was hence a condemnation not of any particular 'heresy' but of the idea of 'heresy' as such.

[1] Zevi Ashkenazi of Amsterdam (for the documents see *Chronicon Spinozanum*, i, pp. 278–282). Ashkenazi's ruling is the more interesting in that he had no pretensions whatever to philosophy, having earned his great reputation in the sphere of pure Talmudics.

[2] '*Antiqui omnes Hebraei*' as Spinoza himself remarked (to Oldenburg, *Ep.* lxxiii).

'general world-order', or who thought that the God-idea was saved by conceiving Nature as an intermediary between God and the objects of his providence.[1] There is no room left for doubt as to the significance of the doctrine for ethics as well as for physics. 'The reward of those who perform the commandments of God and the punishment of those who transgress them', he quotes approvingly from a favourite book of popular philosophy, 'are natural, since it is of the very nature of things that good should produce good.' God, then, is one with Nature in the profound sense that it is only through Nature and its workings that his providence, even in human affairs, is operative. Hence the old equation of suffering with sin. There are not two realms, one of nature, another of morality. Either nature is ultimately moral or morality is ultimately natural. The unity of things is such as to preclude the possibility of the workings of two distinct powers.

If this type of thought must be called by a name, it should be termed pan*en*theistic, because, in the Rabbinic phrase, although 'God is the place of the world', 'the world is not his place'.[2] Spinoza himself strongly protested [3] against the twisting of his doctrine to mean that the material world as we see it and tread upon it is God. In any case it is with him a cardinal point that the real is not confined within or exhausted by the two attributes of thought and extension which happen to be open to the understanding of men.

This widening of the boundaries repeats itself in the typical opposition between Spinoza's ethical teaching and that of pantheism proper. The pantheism of the Far East, at least, rests on negation, the denial of life and its values. The aim

---

[1] Nieto's position on this point is curiously like that of Berkeley some years later (see *Principles*, § 150).
[2] So already Philo (*De Somn.* i, 11, §§ 63–64; *Legum Alleg.* i, 14, § 44). For the interpretation of the phrase see *Guide*, I, lxx.
[3] *Ep.* lxxiii.

set before man is to rid himself of this world, to escape from illusion and to find consummation in disappearance. Spinoza's system rests throughout on affirmation. Human values are not denied but set in their place. It is not that nothing human is valuable but that everything else is as well. The result is an optimism which cries aloud for more and more activity, the 'transition from less to greater perfection' which is accompanied by joy. It is an error to suppose that the doctrine of the omnipresence of God stultifies human action. Human action is encouraged and stimulated by the knowledge that it is God's strength which is working within us. The 'immanent causality' of the *Ethics*, whatever else it may involve, is a reaffirmation of the individual essence, and everything alike, by the very fact of its existence, persists in that essence. The joy then which is the accompaniment of activity suffuses the whole of nature; and the motto 'to act well and to rejoice'[1] holds as well of the whole creation as of man.

In this universal affirmation the spirit of the new age finds its oracle. The cramping confines of the medieval world-scheme fade away. The 'attributes' of God whose essence is activity[2] are infinite, and the 'modes' appearing under the attributes are infinite too. How far soever we may broaden our vision, there are new continents ever spread before us. It is the voice of the new age and of its prophet, but the message is of the ancient wisdom. It is the adoration of the Psalmist: 'How manifold are thy works, O God!'; the challenge from the whirlwind: 'Where wast thou when I laid the foundation of the earth?'; the 'joy' of the pastures and the valleys, the 'clapping of the hands' of the trees of the field; the faith in the time when 'the earth shall be filled with the knowledge of the glory of God as the waters cover the sea'. The key-note of

[1] *Eth.* iv, 50 sch.

[2] 'Tam nobis impossibile est concipere Deum non agere quam Deum non esse' (*Eth.* ii, 3 sch.).

the practical philosophy is the same revulsion against other-worldliness. Life is for life. 'No deity', runs a famous passage,[1] 'nor any one save the envious, is pleased by my want of power or inconvenience, nor counts as virtuous our tears, sobs, fear, and other signs of weakness; on the contrary, the more we enjoy, the more we pass to a greater perfection, that is, the more we necessarily participate in the divine nature.' Or again we have the direct challenge to Augustinian Platonism: 'The free man thinks of nothing less than of death, and his wisdom is a meditation not of death but of life.' [2] Again, it is the very essence of the revolt of the new age, but the thought is far older than Spinoza: 'The heavens are the heavens of the Lord; but *the earth hath he given to the children of men.*' 'He created it not in vain; he formed it *to be inhabited.*' 'Behold, I set before you this day life and good and death and evil . . . and *thou shalt choose life* . . . that thou mayest *live.*' The 'living God' created in his own image, and his 'glory' is the 'fullness of the whole earth'.[3]

IV. *Some Later Thinkers*

So far we have been dealing with a fairly simple and coherent story. The older Hebraism presents certain definite characteristics which achieve their full implication in the medieval Jewish thinkers. These characteristics so developed form the permanent background of Spinoza's system, which therefore may be considered to be the principal channel of the entry of philosophical Hebraism into the modern world.[4] From now

---

[1] *Eth.* iv. 45, 2 sch.   [2] *Eth.* iv. 67.

[3] This joy in universal life, expressed so vividly in the creation hymn of Job xxxviii–ix, is strikingly symbolized in Blake's well-known 'invention'. (Cf. Fig. 74, fac. p. 472.)

[4] For the later history of Spinozism see Pollock, *Spinoza*, cap. xii; Grunwald, *Spinoza in Deutschland* (Berlin, 1897); Altkirch, *Maledictus*

on our task becomes more complicated. On the one hand we have individual Jewish thinkers, on the other the old tradition of Jewish thought; and it is often as difficult to specify Jewish characteristics in the former as it is impossible exactly to determine the bounds of the influence of the latter. Instead therefore of pretending to offer a complete account either of every modern Jewish thinker or of every ramification in the modern world of old Jewish thought, I propose to conclude the historical side of this survey with a brief note on two well-known men who in themselves combine both interests.

The first, MOSES MENDELSSOHN (1729–1786, Fig. 79, facing p. 502), was too much the popular philosopher of his day to be of especial significance to posterity, and although he holds an important place in the development of the science of aesthetic, his work in metaphysics is by now only the concern of the historian. In one great problem of more general interest, however, his contribution to thought was both permanently valuable and Jewish.

Forced into theological controversy by Lavater, Mendelssohn was compelled to declare publicly his views on religion in general and on Judaism in particular. He defined his position in the course of the original correspondence (1769–1770), his introduction to the German translation by Herz (1782) of Menasseh ben Israel's *Vindication of the Jews* to Cromwell, and finally in his *Jerusalem* (1783).[1] He maintained first, so far as the particular question of Judaism as a religious system is concerned, that it is a religion for the Jew. He proposed therefore to follow his conviction and remain a Jew, only asking from his non-Jewish friends the tolerance which he himself extended

---

und Benedictus (Leipzig, 1924); and various notices and essays in the *Chronicon Spinozanum* (Hague, 1921 ff.) and *Het Spinozahuis* (1900 ff.).

[1] All available to the English reader in the two volumes of the translation of the *Jerusalem* by M. Samuels (1838). A summary account of Mendelssohn's views is to be found in the posthumous *An die Freunde Lessings* (1788), pp. 28 ff.

to them. Secondly, and here he attacked the wider issue, he laid it down that the requirement of religion is not speculative theory but moral practice. 'There is not, amongst all the precepts and tenets of the Mosaic law, a single one which says, "Thou shalt believe this", or "Thou shalt not believe it"; but they all say "Thou shalt do" or "Thou shalt forbear". Faith is not commanded; for that takes no commands.'[1] In this appeal for a uniform standard not of creed but of conduct, Mendelssohn gave expression to what we have seen throughout to be one of the fundamentals of Hebraism. Creeds and theologies may vary in accordance with the varying tempers of peoples (this point was driven home by Mendelssohn's friend Lessing in his *Nathan the Wise*); but ' what *the Lord* requireth of thee' is ' to do justly, and to love mercy, and to walk humbly with thy God '.[2] The position [3] was so strange to eighteenth-century enlightenment as to arouse the wonder and admiration even of Kant, who, in a congratulatory letter (of 16 August 1783), was moved to express the wish, yet unfulfilled, that the lessons of the *Jerusalem* might be taken to heart by the religions of all the world.

The second of the two Jewish thinkers to whom special

[1] *Jerusalem* (Samuels's translation), vol. ii, p. 106.
[2] Mic. vi. 8.
[3] It is essentially the same as that held by Spinoza. See in particular the important chapter (xiii) of the *Tractatus Theologico-Politicus*, in which 'it is shown that Scripture teaches only the most simple things, and intends nothing but obedience; nor teaches anything concerning the divine nature except that which men can imitate by a certain way of living' (again the old Rabbinic notion of imitation of the ethical attributes of God, above, p. 446, n. 3). It is worthy of remark that, according to a well-known anecdote of Colerus, Spinoza's practice was in agreement with his theory: 'It happened one day that his landlady asked him whether he believed she could be saved in the religion she professed. He answered: "Your religion is a good one; you need not look for another, nor doubt that you may be saved in it, provided, whilst you apply yourself to piety, you live at the same time a peaceable and quiet life."'

attention should be directed is the great protagonist of Kantian studies in recent times, HERMANN COHEN (1842–1918). This thinker, the founder of the so-called 'Marburg school', sought to establish a theory on the basis of the Kantian which should yet dispense with the 'twofold root' of the Kantian account. In this he followed the path originally traced by another Jew, SOLOMON MAIMON (1754–1800, Fig. 72), who was the first to point out the dualism inherent in the Critical Philosophy and owes his very high place in the history of modern Idealism [1] to his attempt to rectify it. It is an interesting question whether we are justified in seeing in Maimon's reaction against dualism a new form of the old monotheistic protest.[2] But whatever may have been the case with Maimon there is no doubt at all about Cohen. He most certainly saw in his own reconstruction of Kant the workings of the monotheistic idea, and spared no pains to show the general affiliations of his thought with that of Biblical monotheism and its philosophical presentation in post-Biblical Jewish thinkers, particularly Maimonides. To link Kant with Maimonides is not so absurd as appears at first sight. The scholastic synthesis lived on till Kant, some would say after Kant, too; and in the making of that synthesis Maimonides, through the Latin version of the *Guide*, took a direct and leading part.[3] It is not then a matter for surprise that the material and arrangement of the 'transcendental dialectic' should reflect the structure of the *Guide*; the Kantian 'ideal of reason', the Maimonidean God of whom

---

[1] See Léon, *Fichte et son Temps* (Paris, 1922), i, pp. 226 ff.

[2] Maimon, like Mendelssohn and Cohen himself, was a great student of Maimonides. He named himself after him, and wrote a commentary in Hebrew on the *Guide*.

[3] See Kaufmann's essay *Der 'Führer' Maimûni's in der Weltliteratur* in Stein's *Archiv* for 1898 (reprinted in his *Ges. Schrift.*, Frankfurt, 1910, vol. ii, pp. 152–189); Guttmann's *Der Einfluss der maimonidischen Philosophie auf das christliche Abendland* (*Moses ben Maimon*, Leipzig, 1908, pp. 134–230); and Gilson's *Le Thomisme*, Paris, 1923.

FIG. 72. SOLOMON MAIMON, 1754–1800

FIG. 73. IMMANUEL KANT, 1724–1804

even the attribute of existence is predicated only *per analogiam*; the 'critical' inquiry itself, the discussion by Maimonides of the nature and instruments of knowledge. Whatever one may think, however, of the relation between the logic of the *Critique of Pure Reason* and that of philosophical monotheism,[1] it must be agreed that it needs no Philonian ingenuity to see in the Kant of the *Critique of Practical Reason* only a Moses speaking German. The kernel of Kant's doctrine, its ethical orientation, has seemed to many directly reminiscent of the (Hebraizing) Pietist movement in which he was brought up. The thunders from Sinai are only repeated in Kant's majestic formulation of the 'categorical imperative'. The Kantian 'ethical monotheism' (it has wittily been called 'ethical monatheism') which creates God as a pattern for morality, can take as its motto the precept 'Ye shall be holy for I the Lord your God am holy'.[2] The twofold appeal to 'the moral law within' and 'the starry heavens without' recalls the bringing together in the same apostrophe[3] of 'the heavens which declare the glory of God' and the 'Torah which restoreth the soul'. Kant's principle of universality is the first implication of a monotheistic code;[4] and the 'practical maxim' is Hillel's negative interpretation of the command[5] to love one's neighbour as oneself: 'Do not unto him what thou wouldst not have him do unto thee'. The ceremonial of Judaism exhibits an ethical significance valid for all time and all human societies. The institution of the Sabbath, for example, already singled out by Philo[6] as a unique contribution to the

---

[1] The point is taken up by DAVID NEUMARK (1866–1924) in his profoundly acute and suggestive, but unfortunately unfinished work on the History of Jewish Philosophy. See in particular his *Geschichte der jüdischen Philosophie des Mittelalters*, Berlin, 1907, vol. i, Book I, cap. 3; *Toldoth Hapilusophiah Beyisrael* (1921), i, 3; and essays in *Hatekufah* xi and xiv and in various periodicals.   [2] Lev. xix. 2.
[3] Ps. xix.   [4] Above, p. 434 f.   [5] Lev. xix. 18, 34.
[6] *De Vita Mosis* II, 4, § 17.

well-being of society, means the limitation of the hours of labour which lifts the labourer from the sphere of 'things', and restores to him the 'dignity' of a 'person'. The dogmas of Judaism (reduced in a passage of the Talmud[1] to one, the rejection of polytheism, and fundamentally no more than three: the belief in one God, in future 'reward and punishment', and in the coming of the Messianic age) express the essence of the moral life in its threefold aspect of ideal end, permanent striving, and assured attainment. In this stress on the moral life of reason Cohen saw the 'significance of Judaism for the religious progress of mankind',[2] and it is his great achievement forcibly to have turned men's minds back to the ethical aspect of the God of Israel. In him the struggle against mythology, which is of the essence of Hebraism, found a doughty protagonist over the widest fields of thought, and, the peculiar difficulties of his position both in general philosophy and his interpretation of Judaism[3] apart, it is remarkable with what sublimity he

[1] T. B. *Megil.* 13 a; cf. *Midr. Rab. Est.*, § 6.

[2] The title of a paper read by him before the World Congress of Religions in 1910, reprinted in *Jüd. Schrift.* i, pp. 18 ff. His fullest treatment of the whole subject is in his massive *Die Religion der Vernunft aus den Quellen des Judentums* (Leipzig, 1919).

[3] Kant's thought seems to have exercised a fascination over Jews (one need only recall the work of Marcus Herz and Lazarus Bendavid in its popularization, and Schleiermacher's remark that of every three educated Jews at least one was a Kantian), and Hermann Cohen was only the greatest representative of what may be called the Kantianizing movement in the interpretation of Judaism. The best introduction to this for English readers is Lazarus's *Ethics of Judaism* (English translation by Miss Szold, Jewish Publication Society of America, 1900–1901). [Cohen's onslaught on this work, now reprinted in his *Jüdische Schriften*, iii, pp. 1 ff., deserves to be kept in mind, as it would seem that much of what Cohen has to say against Lazarus is valid against Cohen himself.]

MORITZ LAZARUS (1824–1903) is famous as an introspective psychologist, and as the founder, together with his brother-in-law HEYMANN STEINTHAL (1823–1899), of the science of 'Völkerpsychologie' (racial psychology).

invested the age-worn wisdom of his people and with what subtlety he read its universal significance.

The historical side of our survey must now cease, and that for two reasons. In the first place, the number of contemporary Jewish thinkers is so large as to defy dismissal in a concluding paragraph; and secondly, in most cases their connexion, either explicit or implicit, with Judaism or Jewish thought is by no means clear. The attempt has been made, for example, to exhibit the philosophy of M. Bergson as a re-emergence of that side of Jewish thought which is represented in its history by Philo, Ibn Gabirol, and the Kabbala; and Mr. Alexander has been held to show atavistic leanings in his partiality for Spinoza. Again, much has been written about the source of the doctrine of Prof. Freud and other masters in the sphere of modern psychology, and it is certainly notable that the opening of the wider boundaries of the subject as a whole owed so much to men of Jewish origin such as Steinthal, Durkheim, and Münsterberg. In the same way, what is perhaps the most remarkable of modern intellectual movements, the development in mathematical physics, is largely the result of the labours of the Jews Michelson, Minkowski, Einstein, and Weyl, while its philosophical interpretation (as a part of a vast body of other fruitful work in the general history and evaluation of the sciences) is being furthered by the insight of Cassirer, Brunschvicg, and Meyerson. Yet truth is its own witness and its own judge, and it is absurd to discuss it in terms of its discoverers. Like many other pioneers these men are of Israel, but their work is for the whole world.

V. *The significance of Hebraism for modern thought*

§ 1. *Hebraism and Ethics*

Leaving history, we may now take a wider survey of the ground. Hebraism in all its manifestations has shown itself essentially concrete. We have already seen how the genius of the prophets actually defined the 'knowing of God' as 'judging the cause of the poor and needy'.[1] In the same way legislator and moralist alike offer, not a theory about the nature of justice, but the practical rule: 'Thou shalt not have divers weights.'[2] By the side of ancient and modern theosophy or the fifth book of the *Nicomachaean Ethics*, such texts seem banal; yet they contain in sum and in the simplest language lessons for society which the analytic mind never managed to evolve. The same note may be seen in the pictures of the golden age, visualized consistently by the whole Hebraic tradition as being an age for the future, not one which has had its day in the past.[3] The contemplative mind looks back; the active, forward. The will for right is not satisfied by the present state of society and seeks to realize (not dream about) better things. Hence, as prophet and philosopher clearly see, the Messianic age is not in another world; it is the improved state of this. Morality is not a matter of abstractions.

This realism may be taken as a second and cognate note of Hebraism. It accepts the facts and, after its first great flight, does not indulge in the transcendental. 'It is not in Heaven.'[4] In religion it has always laid stress on the discipline of 'works' in the everyday grind of matter-of-fact existence. In ethics it

---

[1] Above, p. 435. Cf. Spinoza in *Theol.-Pol.*, xiii, § 21.

[2] Deut. xxv. 13–15; Prov. xx. 10.

[3] It is perhaps worth remarking that in the Hebrew Bible the 'Garden of Eden' of the early chapters of Genesis only reappears in a few obscure passages. In any case the conception never coloured later thought.

[4] Deut. xxx. 12.

Hebraism and Ethics

gives us practical codes—the Pentateuch; the Talmud (it is a great loss to Europe that this complete system of civil and criminal legislation is not better known); Maimonides' digest of Rabbinic law; the hard sense of Spinoza's work on politics, with its endeavour ' not to laugh or to weep at human actions, but to understand them ' in the light of the ' common nature and condition of men '.[1]

To the notes of concreteness and realism we may add that of objectivity.[2] The message is given under the formula : ' Thus saith the Lord '; and the Lord of all, as the Psalmist reminds us,[3] just because He is Lord of all, takes no bribes. He is, in the better sense of a much misused word, impersonal, and man is expected to be the same. The demands of justice are absolute. Geiger [4] asked whether any other book of laws had achieved the moral sublimity of the precept ' not to favour a *poor* man in his cause '. Yet from the point of view of practical conduct it is not so fruitful as the repeated warning attached to ' all matters

---

[1] *Tract. Pol.*, i, §§ 4, 7. It is noteworthy that the very latest effort in constitution-making comes from the Jew Hugo Preuss.

[2] See the remarkable essay *Judaism and the Gospels* of Achad Ha-Am (*Essays on Zionism and Judaism*, translated by Leon Simon, London, 1922).

' ACHAD HA-AM ' (' One of the people ') = ASHER GINZBERG (1856–1927), the greatest modern Hebrew-writing Jewish thinker, exemplifies the practical tendencies of the Jewish mind in his contact with the social philosophy of Mill and the psychology of Tarde. In him, as in other Jewish thinkers, the note of ethical idealism is dominant, and though his concern is primarily with the specific problems of his own people, he has sought for their solution in the light of premisses which are of the widest applicability. In particular his re-statement of the prophetic synthesis between nationalism and ethical universalism deserves to rank as a permanent contribution to modern thought (see his *Selected Essays*, translated by Mr. Simon, Jewish Publication Society of America, 1912, and the translator's *Studies in Jewish Nationalism*, London, 1920).

[3] Ps. l. 9–12.

[4] *Judaism and its History* (English version by Newburgh, Bloch Publishing Co.), 1911, p. 37. The reference is to Exod. xxiii. 3 (= Lev. xix. 15), already remarked on by Philo (*De Spec. Leg.*, iv, § 72 = *De Judice*, 5).

given over to the heart ' (that is, the individual conscience) [1] :
' but thou shalt fear thy God '.[2] God is omnipresent and ever-present, and, omniscient witness, is sole judge. We may well contrast the ethical consequences of polytheism expressed, in however satirical a manner, in the verses of Euripides :

> 'Twas the will
> Of Cypris that these evil things should be,
> Sating her wrath. And this immutably
> Hath Zeus ordained in Heaven : *no god may thwart*
> *A god's fixed will* ; we grieve but stand apart.
> Else, but for fear of the great father's blame,
> Never had I to such extreme of shame
> Bowed me, be sure, as here to stand and see
> Slain him I loved best of mortality.[3]

Thus the polytheism of Hellas, tried in the acid test of human conduct, stands in persistent contrast to the monotheism of Israel. It remains fixed in pluralism. This is shown strikingly in its great positive contribution of art, for art is essentially individualistic.[4] Contemplative in essence, its interest lay not in conduct but in speculation; hence the legacy it left to the religion of Europe, the belief in the saving power of *opinion*.[5] Hebraism has chosen consistently a different standard. The Hebrew Bible, as we have seen, demands not thinking but doing, not creed but a moral way of life. In the medieval period again, one of the few storms in the history of

---

[1] The idea of conscience only entered Hellenic thought with the Jew Philo. For this ' solemn moment in the history of European ideas ' see Bréhier, *Idées philosophiques et religieuses de Philon d'Alexandrie* (ed. 2, Paris, 1925), p. 296 f.

[2] Lev. xix. 14, &c., with Rabbinic comments.

[3] *Hippolytus*, 1325 ff. (Murray's translation). The same criticism of polytheistic ethics is found in Plato, e.g. the *Euthyphro*.

[4] Cf. Collingwood, *Outlines of a Philosophy of Art* (Oxford, 1925), p. 23 f.

[5] See Hatch, *The Influence of Greek Ideas and Usages upon the Christian Church*. As he well remarks (ed. 6, p. 138), it has proved a *damnosa hereditas*.

Hebraism and Ethics

Jewish theology was roused by the attempt to confine Judaism within the bounds of a number of theoretic dogmas.[1] The point is significant in view of its analogue in the avowed philosophers. Spinoza[2] refused to sunder intellect and will, therein, as often, generalizing from his Jewish predecessors' doctrine of God. Maimonides reacts with amazing vigour against the Platonic doctrine that 'God first contemplated the ideas and then created the world'.[3] Ibn Gabirol, the medieval thinker who rose so far above his age and environment as to be able to be mistaken for a Christian Moor (his work is completely free from any references to authorities, apart from a few mentions of Plato and ' the wise '), yet betrays the native bent of his mind when he insists that knowledge must be accompanied by action before the mind can be ' freed from the captivity of nature ',[4] and deviates most profoundly from his Neoplatonic sources in his peculiar stress on the divine will. Even Philo knows that the 'words' of God are 'not merely words but deeds'.[5] Thought and action in all these great Jewish thinkers of the past (as in so many others of the present, as well as in Judaism as a religious system) are indissolubly connected. Consciously or unconsciously, it is the ultimate protest of Hebraic stress on conduct against Hellenic stress on opinion, ortho*praxy* against ortho*doxy*.

In the light of what has been said, the living interest of Hebraism in social problems is readily explained. Renan may have been over-emphatic in treating the prophets solely as sublime forerunners of Saint-Simon; but a great part of their burden was undoubtedly a protest against practical wrong, ' the

[1] Above, p. 452, note 3, end.

[2] *Eth.* ii. 49, with corollary and appendix; and constantly.

[3] *Guide*, II, vi.

[4] *Auencebrolis Fons Vitae* (Münster, 1895), p. 4, ll. 27 ff. For the Hebraic points in Ibn Gabirol's system see now Prof. J. Klausner's Introduction to the new Hebrew translation (Jerusalem, 1926).

[5] οὐ ῥήματα ἀλλὰ ἔργα (*De Dec.* 11, § 47).

joining of house to house and of field to field', 'the grinding of the face of the poor'. The same spirit lies behind the part played by individual Jews in more modern movements towards the embodying of justice in human institutions. So far as special theories of economics and politics are concerned, whether of the Left or of the Right, Hebraism has of course nothing to say, and as a matter of fact individual Jews are to be found on either side of most causes. Yet the determination not to abandon Justice to the realm of the abstract is independent of the machinery suggested for its establishment, and in so far as any movement sets before itself the task of bringing the good things of life within the reach of the masses it is carrying on the work of the prophets. This side of Hebraism, the passion for Justice in the concrete, far from being dead, is one of the living influences of our time. Indeed, some have thought that it is not living enough. ' It is one of the curiosities of our civilization ', remarks Dr. Moulton,[1] ' that we are content to go for our liberal education to literatures which, morally, are at an opposite pole from ourselves : literatures in which the most exalted tone is often an apotheosis of the sensuous, which degrade divinity, not only to the human level, but to the lowest level of humanity.... It is surely good that our youth, during the formative period, should have displayed to them, in a literary dress as brilliant as that of Greek literature—in lyrics which Pindar cannot surpass, in rhetoric as forcible as that of Demosthenes, or contemplative prose not inferior to Plato's—a people dominated by an utter passion for righteousness, a people whom ideas of purity, of infinite good, of universal order, of faith in the irresistible downfall of all moral evil, moved to a poetic passion as fervid, and speech as musical, as when Sappho sang of love or Aeschylus thundered his deep notes of destiny.'

[1] *Literary Study of the Bible*, ed. 2, Pref., pp. xii–xiii.

§ 2. *Hebraism and Science*

The place of Hebraism in ethics is generally acknowledged. It remains to consider its significance for science. The point to be noted is not only that that significance exists,[1] but that it is of precisely the same order, and arises from precisely the same source, as in ethics. Monotheism means not only the positive search for unity but also, negatively, the refusal to set man in the throne of God. Hence, as we have seen, its concreteness, its realism, its objectivity. Now the spirit of science is definable in terms of these very characteristics, and it is the great function of the second movement of Jewish thought, the movement of medieval Hebraism, explicitly to have deduced them in the study of nature from the monotheistic principle. We have seen that herein lies its principal importance for the modern world, since that part at least of its doctrine lives again in the thinker who has been called the 'philosopher of men of science'—Spinoza. Attention must now be drawn to the fact that the same spirit reappears, consciously or unconsciously, in the most recent work of thinkers of Jewish origin.

The theory of relativity, for example, which is in considerable part the work of Jews, is, according to the best of its interpreters,[2] and in spite of its unfortunate and misleading name, an attempt to get beyond the limited point of view of the individual observer, and hence is only a further step towards the depersonalization of our fundamental ideas which is the aim of all scientific thought. As such, however, it is clearly akin also to what we have seen to be so integral a part of the Hebraic tradition in metaphysics.[3] The affirmation that 'God's thoughts

[1] Above, pp. 436, 438 f.

[2] Russell, *The A B C of Relativity* (1925), caps. ii and xv; Whitehead, *Science and the Modern World* (1926), p. 167 f.

[3] It appears prominently in Mr. Alexander's philosophy, which itself has been declared, although not by way of compliment, to be a 'philosophy

are not ours'[1] throws emphasis not on human error but on God's truth. An ultimate standard is thus set up, equally valid from every and any point of view; or rather the standard set up is of such a character that before it individual points of view disappear. In the theory of relativity this anti-anthropomorphic tendency seems to have found its mathematical expression, and in it we have an important contribution to the store of modern thought not only coming from Jews but also unconsciously reflecting the familiar characteristics of the older Hebraism.

To take another example, it is remarkable that the three determined efforts of modern times to set the human intellect 'in its place' come from Bergson, Alexander, and Freud. Again, whether explicitly or implicitly, this effort is clearly linked with the Hebraic revulsion against anthropomorphism. Human thought is only one element in the universe. 'Minds', in Mr. Alexander's phrase,[2] 'are but the most gifted members known to us in a democracy of things.' It is the essence of Hebraism to *widen* the boundaries. In the vastness of creation we dare not claim for any one thing precedence over any other.

The significance of this point of view appears forcibly in the treatment offered by many Jewish thinkers, classical as well as modern, of one of the ultimate problems, that of the relationship between ethics and metaphysics. It is often proposed to elevate the requirements of the kingdom of human ends into a legislation controlling the cosmos, and thus to interpret the universe as a whole in the light of the moral ideals of humankind. Whence these ideals arose is a question upon which varying opinions have been held. But, except in the interests

---

for science' (*Proc. Arist. Soc.*, 1924–1925, pp. 59–60). 'It is not our human conceptions of things which metaphysics seeks to exhibit,' he remarks (*Space, Time and Deity*, i, p. 196), 'but the constitution of the world itself.'

[1] Isa. lv. 8.   [2] *Op. cit.*, i, p. 6.

of a special theory, it is difficult to maintain that man, or 'spirits' akin to him, comprise the whole of reality. It is hence an exaggeration of man's importance to look for the interpretation of reality solely in his aspirations. In the same way Hebraism has always looked with suspicion on any doctrine of 'final causes'. We cannot offer reasons *why* things are what they are. We can only, with all care and humility, note the fact of their existence and classify them as best we can. 'God made everything for its own end.'[1] Each thing merits scrutiny for its own sake, not with reference to the needs or imaginings of humankind.

VII. *Summary and Prospect*

Looking back on the ground so roughly surveyed and remembering the points which seem to be common to the whole, we may perhaps single out two primary tendencies which would appear to be fundamental. These are the sense for unity and the stress on the concrete. From the former comes the ethical doctrine of the unity of mankind and the scientific doctrine of the unity of nature; from the latter the determination not to suffer these doctrines to remain merely theoretic, but to work them out in the framing of ways of life for human societies and methods of investigation for natural facts. Whether or no we have herein traces of a 'national' ethos, is a question which will always arouse interest and controversy. It is curious, however, that, quite unwittingly, no doubt, some of the work of the most modern Jewish thinkers should recall peculiarities of the ancient Hebraic outlook, and that the message should often be voiced with an intensity reminiscent of the prophets

[1] Prov. xvi. 4, used pretty much in this sense, although in the alternative version, by Maimonides in *Guide*, III, xiii. The suggestion of empiricism is all the more remarkable in view of his clear realization of the nature and status of scientific hypothesis (II, xi; followed by Spinoza in *D. I. E.* § 57, n. 2, and *Ep.* ix).

of old. As has been well said of M. Bergson,[1] and as we saw earlier to be particularly true of Spinoza, they provide us 'not only with a theory but with a vision'.

Yet the debt of the world to Jewish thought is not exhausted by the contributions of the professed philosophers. A wider factor must be taken into account. Whatever idea of the spiritual has reached the masses of the European peoples is due to the Jewish view of the character of supreme reality. In the light of this achievement all else pales.

One last remark. It must be emphasized that we have been dealing throughout neither with one determinate system nor with one definite 'school' of thought.[2] However persistent mental tendencies may be, the matter and manner of their application are infinitely various. There have been, and still are, Jewish philosophers, men whose whole being is consumed with a passion to understand; but the link which binds them together is not one philosophical belief, but a belief in the value of philosophy. They are men of the spirit, but the spirit bloweth where it listeth. 'It is not a system but a habit of mind.' Jewish thinkers may yet create a fresh synthesis which is beyond and distinct from the old. Or, if we prefer to speak in more doubtful terms, the Jewish mind may well open up new paths. In any case, the future must be safeguarded from crippling preconceptions. The belief in unity is the supreme liberating influence, and a liberating influence must be left free.

LEON ROTH.

[1] *Proc. Arist. Soc.*, 1925–1926, p. 298.
[2] There is a certain continuity among the Hebrew-writing philosophers, of whom every age, including our own, has had a goodly number. But a discussion of their work is precluded by the limits of our subject.

FIG. 74. FROM BLAKE'S *JOB* (1825)

'When the morning stars sang together and all the sons of God shouted for joy'

For description see p. xxxi and p. 457

INFLUENCE OF THE HEBREW BIBLE ON EUROPEAN LANGUAGES

The influence of Hebrew on our language can never have been direct. Certainly it could not have been the result of personal intercourse, for when the western nations first came into contact with the Jews the latter spoke no longer Hebrew but Aramaic. To whatever extent the Jews in Rome had retained their mother tongue, the language thus preserved was not Hebrew. It follows, therefore, that the Hebrew influence at work has been entirely literary and springs wholly from the Bible. The study of Hebrew influence on our vocabulary becomes then the study of the effect wrought by the Bible.

Since we are dealing with a member of the Hebraeo-Phoenician group of Semitic languages, linguistically we should be justified in pausing here to set down such English words as were derived from the Phoenician—if there were any to be found. Judging from the important part played for centuries by the Phoenicians in world-trade and navigation it might have been thought that many a name they gave to their merchandise would have slipped into Greek and Latin, and passed thence into the modern languages of Europe. But a search for such words will bring scarcely one to light. Many terms current in civilized Europe were borrowed by Greek and Latin from Mediterranean tongues, but these languages were not Hebraeo-Phoenician—nor even Semitic; *wine* and *oil*, for instance, come from some lost language once spoken on Mediterranean shores. Only here and there some solitary word such as the coarse textile stuff called *sack*, and that article of dress called a *tunic* (from *tunica*, the Latin form of the word), can be traced back to the Hebraeo-Phoenician group of languages.

The influence on our vocabulary of the Bible—which is the only thing we need consider here—was, then, not direct, but filtered down through successive translations. The first of these was the ancient Alexandrine version—the so-called Septuagint—which was accomplished between the third and second centuries B. C. The many Jews then in Egypt, while closely adhering to their faith, had assimilated Grecian civilization; and the more highly educated of them—at any rate—wished to read in Greek their Sacred Books which, from that time onwards, were being gathered into a single collection. The translation which ensued was in the colloquial Greek dialect, plebeian perhaps, yet Greek in accidence and vocabulary, even if the modes of expression were frequently un-Greek and Hebraic. In it not a single Hebrew common noun has been fully transcribed, except technical terms such as *ephod* (Judges viii. 27; xvii. 5), otherwise the Greek retains only proper nouns and such words as have almost the property of proper nouns. So entirely at variance was Biblical from Greek thought that the Greek words employed to express the former had to be moulded anew to clothe ideas so foreign to them. Even the later translators into old Latin—with the original Hebrew before them—based their version on the model set by the Septuagint. Among the Latin words which were used to express the Hebrew there were two kinds: (1) Latin words undergoing the same modification as had their Greek equivalents; (2) Greek words, the meaning of which had already changed. As time went on all the languages of Europe followed along the same path, shaping themselves after the two models—the Greek and the Latin.

The significance of many Greek words in the Septuagint (and consequently in the diction of the Christian Church) is thus the result of a fusion between a Hebrew and a Greek word. At first sight we seem to have before us a word entirely Greek, but in reality the result of fusion of Greek and Hebrew elements. Seemingly wholly Greek, it owes to Hebrew the essence of its meaning. In this hidden way many a valuable element of the Hebrew tongue has been kept alive among us. Take, for instance, the Greek word *kyrios*; in a purely Greek text the word means 'chief', 'master', 'owner', and is not a term specifically religious. Now, the men who produced the Septuagint came across the tetragram JHWH, the Hebrew name for the whole being of God. As is well known, the ancient Hebrew text was written in consonants only.[1] The utterance of this Name was forbidden, and wherever the Jews encountered it they used instead a word meaning 'lord'. In the vocalized text of the Bible this is shown by the fact that the vowel-points in this word 'my Lord'—*Adōnai* according to the Massoretic pronunciation—have been imposed upon the consonants JHWH. The result of this is the fanciful form of the word often written *Jehovah*.

What the Septuagint had to render, however, was the word actually pronounced—that is, a word meaning 'lord'. The Greek for this is *kyrios*. But *Kyrios* used thus no longer means simply 'chief', 'master'; it has become transfused with a Hebrew word of the same sense, used as a substitute for the ineffable Name of God, and it has thus acquired a significance which its use in classical Greek would not justify; beneath a Greek mask it is, in this way, Hebrew.[2]

Where the Greek has *kyrios*, the Latin uses *dominus*. In those Romance languages where, as in French, the idea of

[1] The vowel-signs and pronunciation-marks were not added until many centuries after the Septuagint had done their work, by which time the pronunciation differed from that with which the first translators were familiar. There is no need to touch on this now, since we are concerned only with matters as they were before the Christian era.

[2] No doubt in the Hellenistic East the Greek word *kyrios* came to be attached to the names of divinities—*ho kyrios* Sarapis, &c. But this usage was not in its origin Greek, and the use of *ho Kyrios* by itself to designate 'God' would seem a peculiarity of the Greek translation of the Bible.

'master', 'lord', has been expressed by a new word, this word—*seigneur* in French—invests the concept of *dominus* with the significance of its Hebrew equivalent. The same thing has happened to the English *Lord*, and similar instances will be found in other European tongues. When we use *Lord* to mean God we do so because the Jews shunned the use of the Hebrew JHWH, so that a substitute had to be found for it.

In order to realize the effect of Hebrew—through the various translations of the Bible—on modern European languages, it will be sufficient to glance at one or two words in the Latin *Thesaurus*—at *benedico*, for example. Here the Latin corresponds to the Greek *eulogô*, of which it is the literal translation. In Old Latin, used by non-Christian writers, it means 'to speak well of', 'commend'. In later writers, influenced by Biblical concepts, it came to mean 'to pronounce a formula conveying spiritual beneficence', an idea rendered by *bénir* in French, *segnen* in German, *bless* in English. This second meaning is the result entirely of fusion with the Hebrew *brk*. As the Septuagint could not find a Greek symbol capable of interpreting the religious concept conveyed by *brk* they had recourse to *eulogô* and its derivatives, as the Latinists to *benedico*. The root *brk* passed neither into Greek nor Latin, nor, in consequence, into the languages of modern Europe; but its semantic essence is found in the French *bénir*, the German *segnen*, and the English *bless*. The French form is derived from the Latin *benedicere*; the German and English forms derive from other elements of the vocabulary. What elements go towards the formation of a word is a matter of indifference, the important thing is that, under diverse forms, the meaning of the root *brk* has been transmitted to the whole of modern Europe.

Among our commonest words and phrases there are many which show no signs of Hebrew, but which, without Hebrew, would either not have come down to us or would have retained quite another meaning than the one they bear. The two instances quoted are among the more obvious. But there are many words which would have borne quite another meaning if they had not absorbed the contents of Hebraic words and phrases. It will suffice if we give as an instance *curse* as against *bless*; or *abominate, abominable, abomination,* or *adore* and its derivatives. There are, moreover, words which seem derived from the Greek or Latin but which are, in significance, Hebrew.

Let us take the word *angel*. If you asked a philologist the etymology of *angel* he could only reply that it is a Greek word which has passed into Latin and thence into all the languages of Europe. But the Greek *angelos* meant simply 'messenger', it was a generic term applied to any one entrusted with a message, and had no ritual or judicial significance whatever. Without foreign intervention there is no reason to think that this simple, necessary word would have undergone any development. It has no technical sense, for pagan civilization did not require it. There was thus no need for it to pass from Greek to other languages. Latin of the pagan period, which borrowed freely from Greek, did not borrow *angelos*, and no ancient text, prior to Christianity, uses it. But, in the Bible, God frequently acts through messengers. In order to communicate with mankind he sends emissaries, whose outward appearance is never described and who are, as it were, manifestations of His Divinity conversing with humanity. The Hebrew word used for these Beings is *mal'āk*, 'messenger [of Jahweh]'. These Divine messengers formed a group of beings superior to man. In order to express such a concept—foreign to Greek thought but familiar to the Septuagint—the latter used the word *angelos*. The men who produced the Septuagint translate the Hebrew *mal'ak* JHWH ('messenger of Jahweh') by *angelos kyriou*, 'messenger of the Lord'; and simply *angelos* where the Hebrew has only *mal'ak*.

There entered then into Greek a new word, new in spite of its ancient form: *angelos* with the meaning of the Hebrew *mal'ak*; the result of a fusion between the original *angelos* and the Hebrew *mal'ak*. Although in its former sense there was no reason for *angelos* to pass into Latin—already provided with *nuntius*—the new *angelos* = *mal'ak* was a peculiar term for which the Latin had no equivalent. When Latin needed to express the Biblical concept the same process might have been followed as with the word 'Lord'. But *angelos* in its Biblical sense was now a word with a well-defined meaning and a meaning wholly unrepresented in Latin. The Latin translators took it just as it was, under the form *angelus*. Instead of attempting to translate the word, as was done in the case of Greek *kyrios* into Latin *dominus*, &c., the translators here lifted the word bodily from one language to another, so that from *angelos* come the French *ange*, the German *engel*, the English *angel*, &c.; words of which the phonetic elements are Greek, but the entire semantic essence is Hebrew.

The history of *devil* is closely similar to that of *angel*, though less simple. In Greek there was a noun *diabolos*, agent of the verb *diaballein*. This noun was applied to one who wounded with words—a calumniator. It was a word but rarely used and was of no great importance. Left to itself the word might possibly have fallen into disuse and certainly would not have been borrowed by another language. But the Septuagint required a name for a Biblical character known in Hebrew as Sātān. Every one knows the part played by this personage in, for instance, the Book of Job, where he presents himself before God and declares that Job's uprightness is only assumed, that if his goods are taken away from him he will prove but a reprobate. Greek thought had nothing approaching this. As this spirit always appears alone and is definitely brought out as a distinct personage, it was possible to make of his name a proper noun—Satan, or Satanâs. But the Hebrew word designating him was a common noun, and the Septuagint translators wished—particularly in the Book of Job—to translate it, so they had recourse to the Greek word *diabolos*. By the fusion of a valueless Greek term with an important Hebrew word there was formed, then, the word *diabolos*, which had nothing in common with the old word *diabolos* but its phonetic elements, yet which, in the diction of Christianity, is still endued with strong vitality.

It was not possible to translate into Latin either the Hebrew *sātān* or the Greek *diabolos*—they are both really the same thing. The Greek word was therefore simply taken over into Latin. From Greek and Latin it has passed into all the languages of Europe and gave us French *diable*, German *teufel*, English *devil*.

Up to this point the history of *diabolos*, *diabolus*, *devil* resembles that of *angelos*, *angelus*, *angel*, the only difference being that *diabolos* has more the character of a proper noun than *angelus*, and that the Greek *diabolos*, before its interfusion with Hebrew, was less used than *angelos*. But a second fusion occurred to complicate the history of the word and to give it yet a new significance. The Jews had conceived the idea of evil, impure spirits, which play an important part in the Gospels. These evil spirits are entirely different from *diabolos*. In Greek they were given the name *daimon*—or more often *daimonion* (plural *daimonia*). These evil spirits were looked on as the enemies of the angels—God's messengers. Neither in Greek nor in Old Latin were *diabolos*, *diabolus* ever confused with *daimonia* (Latin *daemones*, *daemonia*). The most that is apparent is that the *daemones* may have been considered as *angeli diaboli*—' the devil's messengers '. As time passed, however, this concept widened, there was no longer any distinction made between *diabolus* and *daemons* ; medieval thought regarded the *diaboli* as opposed to *angeli*. In modern languages the French word *diable*, the German *teufel*, the English *devil* are thus the result of two successive interfusions: one going back to the Septuagint (the Greek *diabolos* with the Hebrew *satan*); the others dating from the Middle Ages (the confusion of *diabolus* with *daemon*).

The word *paradise* has a remarkable history. It is a Greek word—*paradeisos*—but it was originally borrowed from a foreign language; it is an Eastern term, and was the name given to the enclosures or parks of the Persian kings and nobles. The Old Persian is *pairidaēza*, and the ancient Greeks used it, under the form *paradeisos*, to describe a Persian thing of which they themselves had no counterpart. The Septuagint found the word useful when they were trying to translate *gan*, by which was designated the great park, or Garden of Eden, referred to in Genesis ii. 8. From that time onwards the word which had held but a bare foothold in the Greek language played in it an important part, going from Greek into Latin (*paradisus*, with the Biblical meaning), and thence into all modern Europe. It is curious to see an Iranian word pass into Greek and flourishing in it because it was used to translate a Hebrew term. It is one of the most remarkable instances in the history of a vocabulary formed by the interfusion of words of diverse origin.

The above examples of the intermingling of Greek and Hebrew words have been chosen from among the more obvious. The delicate shade of meaning caused by the influence of the Hebrew on the Greek word used by the translators is often less apparent, but it should never be lost sight of. The Greek word *prophētēs* passed into Latin only to describe Eastern characters—as a rule the Jewish prophets. If the Greek *prophētēs* differed less from the Hebrew *nābhī* than *angelos* did from *mal'ak*, at least the meaning of *prophētēs* (and its Latin form *propheta*) which has survived is that of the Hebrew word.

In a language like English in which, for centuries, the Bible has been read and studied, many Hebrew words and phrases have passed into daily use. Moreover many of the words used

in the English version of the Bible that are not of Hebrew origin have caught from it some gleam of Hebraic meaning. Words and phrases which otherwise would astonish us have become familiar to all. The influence which began with the Septuagint was continued through the Latin versions and on through the Middle Ages by the language of the Church (based chiefly on Biblical diction) into ordinary use. It was further developed in English from the sixteenth century onwards, when the Bible became the people's daily companion. And it is hard to imagine what would be, without the Bible, the English tongue to-day.
A. MEILLET.

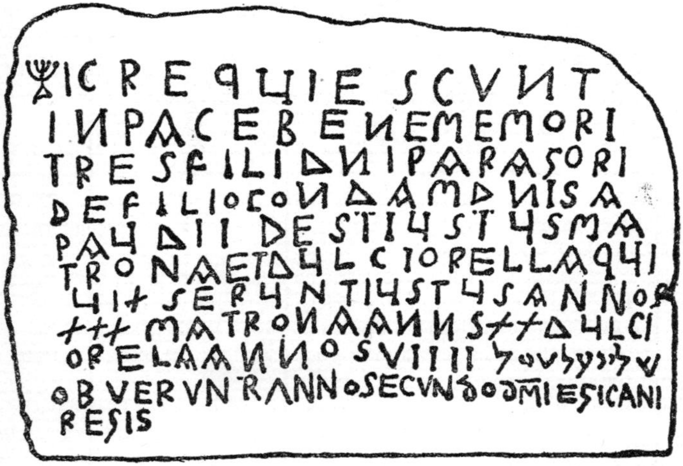

FIG. 75. The earliest dated inscription relating to the Jews of France. For interpretation see next page.

Description of Fig. 75 on p. 481

Tracing of an early dated inscription relating to the Jews of France, A. D. 689. It is on a tombstone at Narbonne and can be thus transcribed and expanded:

HIC REQUIESCUNT
IN PACE BENE MEMORI
TRES FILI DOMINI PARAGORI
DE FILIO CONDAM (quondam) DOMINI SA-
PAUDI ID EST IUSTUS MA-
TRONA ET DULCIORELLA QUI
VIXSERUNT IUSTUS ANNOS
XXX MATRONA ANNOS XX DULCI-
ORELA ANNOS VIIII שלום על ישראל
OBUERUNR (obierunt) ANNO SECUNDO DOMINI EGICANI
REGIS

The Latin is very peculiar and is becoming vernacular. It may be translated thus:

' Here rest in peace the three children of happy memory of Paragorus son of the late Master Sapaudus, to wit Justus, Matrona and Dulciorella. Justus lived 30 years, Matrona 20 years and Dulciorella 9 years. PEACE BE UPON ISRAEL (in Hebrew script). They died in the second year of our Lord the King Egicanus.'

Egicanus was a Visigothic sovereign who came to the throne in November 687. The Jewish character of this rudely cut tombstone is determined (*a*) by the use of the branched candlestick at the beginning, an emblem very commonly employed in Jewish inscriptions; (*b*) by the phrase in Hebrew script towards the end.

The names in the inscription are of considerable interest. They have been discussed most recently by M. Schwab, *Rapport sur les inscriptions hébraïques de la France*, Paris, 1904. Other Jewish inscriptions, some of which are more ancient, are described and figured by G. I. Ascoli, *Iscrizioni inedite o mal note di antichi sepolchri giudaici del Napolitano*, Turin and Rome, 1880. The most ancient Jewish inscriptions in Europe are, however, probably those in the catacombs at Rome, which date back to the first centuries of the Christian era. Many exhibit noteworthy Latin and Greek linguistic elements. See N. Müller, *Die jüdische Katakombe am Monteverde zu Rom*, Frankfurt, 1912.

C. S.

Fig. 76. SYNAGOGUE OF SPANISH AND PORTUGUESE JEWS IN LONDON, BUILT 1701
From an XVIIIth-century painting by M. Belisario

THE LEGACY IN MODERN LITERATURE

§ 1. *Words and Images*

THE legacy of Israel to the literature of modern Europe may be illustrated first by a comparison between two passages of English poetry. We select our examples from Arnold's *Sohrab and Rustum* and Tennyson's *Ulysses*:

(1) But as a troop of pedlars, from Cabool,
Cross underneath the Indian Caucasus,
That vast sky-neighbouring mountain of milk snow,
Winding so high, that, as they mount, they pass
Long flocks of travelling birds dead on the snow,
Choked by the air, and scarce can they themselves
Slake their parch'd thirst with sugar'd mulberries—
In single file they move, and stop their breath,
For fear they should dislodge the o'erhanging snows—
So the pale Persians held their breath with fear.

(2) How dull it is to pause, to make an end,
To rest unburnish'd, not to shine in use!
As tho' to breathe were life. Life piled on life
Were all too little, and of one to me
Little remains: but every hour is saved
From that eternal silence, something more,
A bringer of new things; and vile it were
For some three suns to store and hoard myself,
And this gray spirit yearning in desire
To follow knowledge like a sinking star,
Beyond the utmost bound of human thought!

Arnold's verses imitate the Greek style. The likeness found for the fearful Persians is elaborated, in the manner of an Homeric simile, by details of the climbing pedlars with whom they are compared, and the canvas is stretched to include more than the actual terms of the comparison. The birds dead on the snow, the sugar'd mulberries, and so on, are used to beautify the picture, without exact reference to parts of the original subject. Tennyson's poem, though its subject is Greek, is not composed in the Greek manner. The dozen lines quoted above are full of Biblical echoes. To make an end, breathing and living, little remains (Isa. vii. 13), eternal silence (Ps. cxv. 17), bringer of new things, yearning in desire, &c.—these turns of expression, and others, though not direct quotations from the Bible, are Biblical in form. To a sensitive ear, the Tennyson passage is as Hebrew as the Arnold passage is Homeric.

Take, again, the following sentences from the opening paragraph of George Eliot's *Romola*. She is writing of sunrise in Florence:

As the faint light of his course pierced into the dwellings of men, it fell, as now, on the rosy warmth of nestling children; on the haggard waking of sorrow and sickness; on the hasty uprising of the hard-handed labourer; and on the late sleep of the night-student, who had been questioning the stars or the sages, or his own soul, for that hidden knowledge which would break through the barrier of man's brief life. ... As our thought follows close in the slow wake of the dawn, we are impressed with the broad sameness of the human lot, which never alters in the main headings of its history—hunger and labour, seed-time and harvest, love and death.

No one could have written this who was not steeped in the language of the Old Testament. We may trace the superman idea, identical in Tennyson and George Eliot ('to follow knowledge like a sinking star', 'that hidden knowledge which would break through the barrier of man's brief life') to Elizabethan usage of the Renaissance heritage of Roman splendour, to Cicero's individualism reanimate through Petrarch and Machiavelli in Christopher Marlowe. But both passages, the verse and the prose, recall, as the Arnold passage does not, the familiar diction of the Bible, in Pss. xc, civ, cxxvi, and elsewhere.

A proof that this literary legacy is with us to this day is the familiarity of the diction. We climb the hill with the troop

Words and Images 485

of pedlars with a sense of strangeness and surprise. It is a grateful exercise to Hellenists to recognize the skill of the imitation, but it is not authentic English poetry. But we travel westward with Ulysses or watch the sun rise over Savonarola's Florence with all our senses attuned to our surroundings.

In a sudden disturbance of that harmony is a clue to some of the successes of modern literature, and this, too, is worth consideration in estimating the size of the Hebrew legacy. Byron, for instance, with his fame overnight, not only took us to new places but he took us by a new way. He relied partly for his early and more explosive effects on models hardly if at all subject to vernacular Biblical inspiration. The great line of Italian burlesque-satirists, from Luigi Pulci to Giovanni Casti, had little taste and less opportunity to train their style, which Byron imitated, on Italian versions of the Hebrew Bible; and when Carlyle bade the generation of 1830 to close its Byron and open its Goethe, he summoned it to a return to the Hebrew legacy. This return, by another surprise, was consummated in Swinburne, whose daring modernism in thought would have recommended him to a far narrower circle if it had not been married to a familiar Hebraism in diction.

Going back for a moment to the Arnold and Tennyson passages above, we may measure the distribution of the Hebrew legacy by another test. The Greek simile is foreign to English habits of speech, the Hebrew simile has become naturalized. Homer compares A with B, and elaborates B pictorially. The Hebrew poet compares A with B, and justifies the likeness by speaking of A in terms of B. The pale Persians (the A in the Arnold passage) could not be spoken of in the terms employed to elaborate the pedlars (B), since those terms were expanded into details which passed beyond the limits of the likeness. But knowledge (A) like a sinking star (B) in Tennyson could be pursued in stellar terms (terms of B) to the bounds of a star's horizon. And this is the familiar simile, shading into metaphor, of the Old Testament:

He (A) shall be like a tree (B) planted by the rivers of water, that bringeth forth his fruit in his season; his (A's) leaf also shall not wither.

The likeness of A to B is proved by the appropriateness of B's attributes employed to describe A. The green pastures and still waters of Ps. xxiii are extracted in the same way from the simile of the shepherd with his sheep. A particularly fine example of this usage in modern poetry is in Shelley's image of life (A), which,

> like a dome (B) of many-coloured glass
> Stains the white radiance of eternity,—

where A functions in terms of B, and the dome's action describes the course of human life.

If the legacy of style, or the use of words, transmitted to England through the Authorized Version, is so familiar as almost to escape notice, the words themselves are even more common. We are not referring now to English words directly derived from Hebrew, such as sabbath, camel, cabal, jot, manna, ebony, &c., but rather to words not Hebrew in origin yet Hebraized by their employment, as a servant takes the tone of his master's house.[1] We may select Prov. xxx and xxxi, and compute the debt of the English language to those sixty-four verses:

> Who hath gathered the wind in his fists?
> Neither poverty nor riches.
> Lest I be full, and deny thee.
> Lest I be poor, and steal.
> Pure in their own eyes.
> Their eyelids are lifted up.
> To devour the poor.
> The horseleach hath two daughters.

[1] Reference may be made to *Hebraisms in the Authorized Version of the Bible*, by William Rosenau, Ph.D., Baltimore, 1903.

The way of a man with a maid.
Little but wise.
They make their houses in the rocks.
The poor and needy.
A virtuous woman.
Her price is far above rubies.
She will do him good and not evil all the days of her life.
Food from afar.
Clothed with scarlet.
Silk and purple.
Known in the gates.
In her tongue is the law of kindness.
The ways of her household.
The bread of idleness.
Favour is deceitful.
The fruit of her hands.

The list is far from complete, but, even uncompleted, it is longer than any list of commonplaces that could be compiled out of an equal number of short sentences in any other piece of literature, ancient or modern.

This leads us to a further conclusion. The legacy of Israel in the English language is not merely a matter of words and phrases; it is a matter of the association of ideas. It is mental as well as mechanical, and thus, quite apart from the occurrence of occasional Hebraisms in our daily speech, it is intimate of our life and habits. We think and act *more Hebraico* without conscious imitation, as a son enjoying his patrimony does not pause to remember whence it came. Take the commonest ideas behind words—man, woman, bread, death, are four that suggest themselves at once; and take from the Bible some phrases embodying these ideas:

When I consider thy heavens, the work of thy fingers, the moon and the stars, which thou hast ordained; What is man that thou art mindful of him? and the son of man that thou visitest him? Ps. viii, 3, 4.

Man being in honour abideth not. Ps. xlix. 12.
Man goeth to his long home. Eccl. xii. 5.

Woman. Proverbs xxxi, above.
Man doth not live by bread only. Deut. viii. 3.
Thou feedest them with the bread of tears. Ps. lxxx. 5.
If ought but death part thee and me. Ruth i. 17.
The valley of the shadow of death. Ps. xxiii. 4.

The Hebrew associations of these names have entered into the heritage of modern literature. We need not pursue them in detail through the treasures of that storehouse, discovering the bread of tears in Heine, the faithfulness till death in Lovelace, the state of man in a dozen passages of Shakespeare. Our point is that we think in Hebrew images. There is a Hebrew background to our common mind. Our mind is full of Hebrew furniture, and unconsciously, from childhood upwards, we frame our ideas of common things after patterns supplied by the Jews of old. To a large extent, our ' Platonic ' ideas are laid up for us in the Hebrew Bible. Omar's image of a loaf of bread and a jug of wine in a wilderness *à deux* is much less instant to our consciousness than the Biblical summons not to live by bread only nor to eat the bread of idleness. The Bible standardized the loaf's spiritual value. In one word, it was the Hebrew way to associate moral ideas with the names of things: bread, wine, and the rest were not merely what the dictionary called them; they were sublimated, or consecrated, into a call to virtuous living. The literary legacy of the Hebrews is, in fine, a summons to conduct by the use of words. And conduct, rightly or wrongly, has been computed to be three-fourths of life.

§ 2. *Writers and Kinds*

(a) *to the Sixteenth Century*

This call to conduct, eloquent in the Bible, as Bishop Lowth, Professor of Poetry at Oxford, pointed out in the middle of the eighteenth century, has been heard in other and lesser books up and down the literary annals of Europe. In mentioning individual writers and the kinds of literature infected by Hebrew ideas we shall not find that all Jewish writers write recognizably Jewish books nor yet that all recognizably Jewish books are written by Jewish writers. The two classes most interesting to our inquiry are Jewish books written by Jewish writers and Jewish books not written by Jewish writers; for it is the Hebrew note in literature which we are pursuing, not the accident of Jewish birth in writers of non-Jewish books.

One note may be selected, however, partly because it was very early in appearance, and partly because, if it is Jewish, it is almost unique in its kind. Can we construct a Jewish man of letters out of the Sicilian writer on *The Sublime*, the inadequacy of whose discussion of that topic formed the starting-point of the famous treatise which bears (or bore till 1808) the name of Longinus? Suidas said that we could, and some modern critics, at least,[1] uphold the opinion of Suidas that this non-Roman rhetor from Calacte was a Jew by religion. If so, he may be deemed responsible for a passage in the classic treatise on *The Sublime*, which Robortello translated in 1554, Boileau in 1674, and which dominated English thought in the eighteenth century. The passage runs:

> Sublimity is the echo of greatness of soul. This is illustrated from Homer, in contrast with Hesiod; also from *the legislator of the Jews*, ... who wrote in the beginning of his Laws, *God said, Let there be light, and there was light; let there be land, and there was land*.[2]

We have no evidence that 'Longinus' did not draw this illustration of the Sublime out of his own resources; but if, as seems likely, it is a fossil deposited by the older writer, and if that writer, drawing from Genesis, was a Jew by religion, as Suidas said, then we have a striking example of the influence of Hebraism on the foundations of taste, a study to which the Jewish genius has been very rarely directed.

[1] See Schürer, *Geschichte des jüdischen Volkes*, iii. 629-633.
[2] See Sir J. E. Sandys, *History of Classical Scholarship*, i. 289.

Yet rarer interest attaches to the tradition that Fernando de Rojas, a converted Spanish Jew, was the author of the tragi-comedy *Celestina*. This novel written in dramatic form towards the end of the fifteenth century, and translated by James Mabbe in 1631, is of essential importance in the development of its kind. The authorship by Rojas was unchallenged from 1501 till 1900, when some doubts were cast upon it, though later editors are disposed to return to the traditional view, which, if upheld, would present us with what has been described as a resounding triumph of the Jewish genius.

Still, it would be an isolated triumph. The genius which went to make the 'Spanish bawd', who is in the line of ascent to Juliet's nurse, was not characteristically Jewish, and we recall our distinction, in respect to the Hebrew legacy, between books written by Jews who had assimilated the colours of their environment, and recognizably Jewish books. The former are legitimate sources of gratification to an historian of the Jews, but add no special note to modern letters; it is with the latter class of writings that the heirs of the legacy are concerned.

So we turn from this example—one of many—of a Jewish author of a non-Jewish book to the consideration of a *kind* of literature in which the Hebrew genius found typical expression. This kind is political philosophy. The 'holy nation' of Exod. xix. 6, had at one time national frontiers as well as a complete set of laws. The Mosaic code was devised in every article to build up civic liberties out of a slaves' revolt, and amplifiers of that code in modern Europe became Hebraists by intellectual inheritance. Thus, Bodin, whose *République*, 1577, appeared in a Latin version in 1586, and was in use at English universities when Hobbes was a young man, had to meet in his own lifetime the opprobious reputation of Jewish opinions and descent. But his 'Judaism' was a literary acquisition, derived from deep study of the Hebrew Bible, from frequent quotation from it, from willing discipline to the theocratic State, and from his perception that the Jewish revelation was intended, not for Palestine, but for mankind. The Old Testament became to political philosophers of the seventeenth century what the 'exemplaria Graeca' were to Horace, and what Horace in his turn became to English Augustans. This influence of Judaism on political thought is examined in another chapter of the present volume : here we remark how the impulse to those studies, communicated by the founders of political science, found native expression in the nineteenth century in the writings of the younger Disraeli, Ricardo, and others.

Very close to the science of politics is the utopia of politics, as the works of Plato and Francis Bacon stand to witness, and it is notable that the *New Atlantis*, despite its Greek derivation and Latin language, approximates in the English version of 1629 to the language of the Old Testament. The whale's belly and the jaws of death are obvious phrases for shipwrecked men to use. But a more remarkable feature of this romance is the introduction of Solomon's House, or the College of the Six Days' Work, 'whereby I am satisfied that our excellent King had learned from the Hebrews that God had created the world and all that therein is within six days' ; and of real significance is the fact that the visitor to Bensalem 'fell into straight acquaintance with a merchant of that city, whose name was Joabin. He was a Jew, . . . for they have some few stirps of Jews yet remaining among them, whom they leave to their own religion. . . . And for the country of Bensalem this man would make no end of commending it, being desirous by tradition among the Jews there to have it believed that the people thereof were of the generations of Abraham by another son, whom they called Nachoran ; and that Moses by a secret cabala ordained the laws of Bensalem which they now use ; and that when the Messiah should come, and sit in His throne at Jerusalem, the King of Bensalem should sit at His feet, whereas other Kings should keep a great distance. But yet, setting aside these Jewish dreams, the man was a wise man, and learned, and of great policy, and excellently seen in the laws and customs of that nation.' This learned Jew *of great policy* is surely a more faithful indicator of the literary value of the legacy of Israel than his contemporary, Shylock, on the stage. The usurer was the conventional presentment of a Jew; but the utopian, practising his own religion, dreaming his Jewish dreams, and selected to expound the laws of an ideal republic, was the child of a longer tradition.

We pass to another branch of letters in which the legacy is manifest, and which possesses some further historical interest. Compare the two following sets of stanzas:

(1) Zion, wilt thou not ask if peace's wing
 Shadows the captives that ensue thy peace,
 Left lonely from thine ancient shepherding?

 Lo! west and east and north and south—world-wide—
 All those from far and near, without surcease
 Salute thee: Peace and Peace from every side;

 And Peace from him that from the captive's fount
 Of tears, is giving his like Hermon's dew,
 And longing but to shed them on thy mount. . . .

 Lo! it shall pass, shall change, the heritage
 Of vain-crowned kingdoms; not all time subdues
 Thy strength; thy crown endures from age to age. . . .

 Happy is he that waiteth,—he shall go
 To thee, and thine arising radiance see
 When over him shall break thy morning glow;

 And see rest for thy chosen; and sublime
 Rejoicing find amid the joy of thee
 Returned unto thine olden youthful time.

(2) O dwelling of great might,
 Temple of lovely light incomparable,
 My soul that to thy height
 At birth aspired, what spell
 Doth in this dark, low prison-house compel? . . .

> O skyward lift your eyes,
> Unto this heavenly eternal sphere!
> And you will then despise,
> The vain delights that here
> Offers our life, its every hope and fear;
>
> Petty, if we compare
> The fleeting span of this low earthly scene
> With that great region where
> In noblest forms are seen
> What is and what shall be and what hath been. . . .
>
> Lo, here dwells sweet content,
> Peace reigns, and on a rich and lofty throne
> Sits holy love, and blent
> Together in its zone
> Delight and honour are evermore at one.

The first is translated from the Hebrew of Jehudah Halevi, who died in or near 1142, and the second from the Spanish of Luis de Leon,[1] who died in 1591. But this is not the whole of the story. It has been said that Luis de Leon had a Hebrew soul. True, his modern editor neutralizes that statement into the sense that de Leon was merely 'essentially a poet', but we may colour it afresh by a ray from another Spanish scholar, who tells us that 'the intellectual movement recommenced among the Jews' in the twelfth century, and that to Halevi may be traced 'one of the first essays in metre in Spanish'.[2]

A deeper tint is lent to this perception by the remark of a great Jewish historian that: 'If ever Spain could be brought to desist from estimating her great men by the standard of the Church, Jehudah Halevi would occupy a place of honour in her Pantheon.'[3] Thus, though Halevi and de Leon were separated by four and a half centuries of Spanish history, and

[1] See (1) Nina Salaman, *Selected Poems of Jehudah Halevi, translated into English chiefly from the Critical text of Heinrich Brody*, Philadelphia, 1924, and (2) *Luis de Leon: A Study of the Spanish Renaissance*, by Aubrey F. G. Bell; Oxford, 1925.

[2] James Fitzmaurice-Kelly, *Littérature espagnole*, Paris, Colin, 1913; p. 4.

[3] H. Graetz, *History of the Jews*, London, 1892; iii. 328.

were separate, too, in creed, yet they were joined across the centuries by affinities of blood and taste. In order to grasp the full significance of the curious, piercing likeness between the Hebrew poet's ode to Zion and the Spanish poet's *noche serena*, we must refer for a moment to the golden age of the Jews in Spain. De Leon, the Wordsworthian nature-poet, in whom Ticknor discovered a Hebrew soul, was alleged by some of his contemporaries to possess the worse property of a Hebrew body. Certainly, his birth occurred within forty years of the expulsion of the Jews, and there was a great-grandmother among his forbears who had been burnt for her faith. It is a reasonable inference that the native school of Spanish poetry, as distinct from the Italianate, was indebted to the example of Hebrew poets resident in Spain prior to 1492.

A light is cast on that early epoch by a contemporary Jewish writer. Rabbi Solomon ben Adreth was born in 1235 and died in 1310. His lifetime at Barcelona fell midway between the epoch of Halevi and the epoch of persecution which led to the harsh decree of Ferdinand and Isabella. The kingdom of Aragon in his time—the time of the chivalrous James I—was a fortunate land for Spanish Jews and for Jews who came to seek their fortune under his standard; and the 'Responses' of Rabbi Solomon to questions of public and private interest posed to him from all parts of Aragon amount to over three thousand, and form a unique source for the history of the Jews in Spain.[1] They reveal a state of prosperity and conditions of leisure and ease very favourable to learning and culture. We find Jew and Christian living together on terms of friendship and toleration unparalleled in Europe at that date and for many centuries after the expulsions. The Jews enjoyed complete freedom of residence, either mixing freely with their neighbours or concentrated in their own quarters, according to choice.

---

[1] See *The 'Responses' of Rabbi Solomon ben Adreth of Barcelona*, London, 1925; edited, with Introduction, by I. Epstein.

Theoretically, they were excluded from high office in the State, but practically, despite such prohibitions, their character recommended them to important posts, in which they were confirmed by local consent. Rabbi Solomon's 'Responses' deal with the problems that presented themselves to Jews in various walks of life. Most remarkable, however, is the record of the office of ' Sooltan ', with power of jurisdiction over Christians, being filled by a Jew. This was in fact in contravention to the codes of various Cortes.

Such, briefly, was the soil on which Judaism flourished in Spain in the eleventh, twelfth, and thirteenth centuries. It was a soil favourable to the seeds sown by the poets and scholars, whose legacy passed into common keeping. The influence of the Jews was tangible, and it worked for their country's good in the ratio in which their lot was more fortunate than elsewhere in Christendom. A German writer refers to the epoch as a ' dream of springtide ', and, indeed, this Jewish Arcadia, where Hebrew poets left their imprint on European letters, and Jewish thinkers taught the Schoolmen their first lessons, appeals to the specialist historian, undistracted by Roger Bacon's impatience of the defective grammar of some Jewish Latinists, as a country of romance, the complete inheritance of which is partly withheld from present enjoyment by the dead language of its exiled inhabitants.

Before quitting Spain, we may refer to another kind of literature which sprang up under Jewish hands in that hospitable soil. The Jews' service as agents of communication, by their Latin versions of Arabic renderings of Greek books, is discussed elsewhere in the present volume ; and, omitting here their contribution to philosophy, the record of Jews as folk-lorists merits more than passing mention. *Traduttore traditore*, says the proverb : ungratefully, in the country of the Renaissance ; and *translator, transplanter*, is a variant which the heirs of Jewish culture might adopt. Abraham ben Hasdai, for example, who flourished in Barcelona in the first half of the thirteenth century, won renown as a commentator on Maimonides, and is celebrated, too, as the transmitter of the Barlaam and Josaphat legend, which took hold of the imagination of Europe. Modern letters owe it, among other stories, the tale of the caskets in the *Merchant of Venice*,—an odd sidelight on the play which held a Jewish type up to derision. The Bidpai and Sindbad fables were likewise transferred from the East to the West wholly by Jewish mediation, and Aesop, too, would have been known much less fully and much less early except for the labours of Jewish scholars. One of these, Berachyah Nakdan, whose collection was of critical importance for the bestiaries of the Middle Ages, was probably writing in England towards the close of the twelfth century, and his relation to Alfred the Englishman has been compared with that of Andrew the Jew to Michael the Scot.[1] Song, too, like story, was adorned by Jewish practitioners in the Middle Ages; and particular mention is due to the German Minnesinger, Süsskind of Trimberg (Fig. 77), not only for the charm of the verse which he added to love-lyric in the thirteenth century, but likewise for his constant Jewish consciousness. An earlier Heine in this respect, Süsskind sang Israel's fate into German Minnesong. Medieval Jews, then, particularly in Spain, rendered signal service to modern literature in several departments of that art. Boccaccio selected a Jew as critic of the established religion; Francis Bacon, as we saw, chose a Jew to expound civil law; and these aspects of literary history, briefly examined in connexion with folk-lore, still await completer research and assimilation into general histories of literature.[2]

We would add one word at this point about the year 1492.

[1] See Joseph Jacobs, *Aesop*, 2 vols., London, 1889, *Barlaam and Josaphat*, London, 1896, and *Bidpai*, 1888; also the *Jewish Encyclopaedia*, s.v. Folk-Lore, by the same scholar.

[2] A good start is made in that direction by F. J. Snell, in *The Fourteenth Century* ('Periods of European Literature', vol. ii), p. 419 f.

Fig. 77. SÜSSKIND OF TRIMBERG

Singing before a Bishop, from a manuscript of about 1300

See p. 496 and for description p. xxxii

It was a fateful date in Jewish annals. Columbus sailed West in that year in the service of the Spanish King, preceded by Jewish navigators and charted by Jewish astronomers. In that year, Reuchlin, home from Italy, was seeking from Saxon Jews the keys to the northern Renaissance, and in 1492 Spain expelled her Jews. It is not for us to dilate on the irony of history: in the West, a stream of Jewish exiles, driven from their fertile fields; in the East, sowers of the Reformation, fetching their seeds from Hebrew barns. But we may add some notes to the record. First, the expulsion from Spain was one of a series: England, 1290; France, 1394; Portugal, 1496. Secondly, some of the Spanish fugitives undoubtedly reached our own shores: the number of Jews in England midway between Edward I and Cromwell is known to have been considerably increased by migration from Spain. Thirdly, a sombre note is due to the effects of this cumulative experience on the character of the Jews. We shall not attempt a computation of how much or how little of its darker side was directly caused by Christian treatment. Our point is, that the close of the fifteenth century closed a brilliant chapter in Jewish history. The type of Jew who had flourished in Spain in her liberal age represented humanity at its highest. The type of Jew who remained behind and hid his Judaism, or who was cast out and hugged it, inevitably deteriorated.

There was never another golden age. Individual Jews and communities of Jews, in Germany, England, and elsewhere, recovered from the effects of the expulsions, emerging out of the ghetto-walls and straightening out the ghetto-bend. But the sixteenth century did not fulfil the rich promise of the Middle Ages. There is a certain resemblance in method between the recourse taken to Hebrew books by the makers of the northern Renaissance, and the recourse taken to classical studies by Reuchlin's teachers in Italy. The Hebrew Bible, after all, was more essential to the making of the modern man than Cicero himself, and Reuchlin, going down the Jews' lane to search for Hebrew books, was repeating in another branch of Renaissance studies the toilsome journeys of the Italian humanists who went on pilgrimages to secluded monasteries seeking Latin manuscripts. Each sought a guide to present conduct, wrapped in the cerecloths of a dead civilization, and Reuchlin justly called his Hebrew grammar, written in 1506, *monumentum aere perennius*. But the likeness, finally, is illusory. The Jews, though custodians of their sacred books, were never or very rarely regarded as the authoritative repositories of the thought that those books preserved. They seemed even more remote from the classics of their own literature than the first Greek teachers in Florence—Boccaccio's Homeric tutor, for example—from the classical age of Hellas. Reuchlin might be sorry for the Jewish race, and even friendly to some of its members, as Boccaccio tolerated his uncouth tutor for the sake of the learning which he could impart. But toleration of Jews in the fifteenth and sixteenth centuries was much more than a social solecism: it was an offence against the Church; and deeper darkness descended on German ghettoes when the treasures which they held in keeping had been yielded up. The exodus of German Jews to Poland assumed even larger dimensions in and about the year 1503, when Luther was a student at Erfurt; and the Reformation, like the Renaissance, practically passed the Jews by. We should turn to Prague (see Fig. 14) and other cities for the history of the Jews in this age. Socially, and morally too, to some extent, it is a story of degraded conditions; linguistically, it was an age of jargon; and intellectually, the influence of Jews on literature and thought was either merely occasional or chiefly revived from earlier times. Spinoza, the only great exception, though largely a Maimonist by philosophic descent, was too much addicted to Latin studies for the convenience of Jewish exiles of the Inquisition, and he became Benedict where he had been Baruch.[1]

[1] On Spinoza see article by Dr. Roth, pp. 449-457.

FIG. 78. JEWISH HOUSE OF XIVTH CENTURY AT TOLEDO
The house is fortified and almost without windows
Built by Samuel Abulafia (1320–1360)

§ 2. *Writers and Kinds*
(b) *After the Sixteenth Century*

The legacy survived. It was preserved in every country by the vernacular Bibles, the direct influence of which was most marked in communities most responsive to the Reformation. The husbandman, the weaver and the traveller, invoked by Erasmus in a famous passage, which has been called ' a literary Rubicon ', were more likely to sing the Bible at their work in countries where Latin had been disused as the language of prayer, and so to win the further reward which Erasmus had in mind, of speaking the Bible in their hearts—learning it by heart, as the phrase goes—till its language became a part of their daily speech. Lutherans, Huguenots, and Puritans chiefly attained this greater consummation. The story told by such a book as *The Psalms in Human Life* [1] shows us how spontaneous was the appeal which the Psalter, among other sacred writings, made to the consciousness of reformers, and how deeply its forms of speech, in French, German, Dutch, and English, had bitten into their familiar vocabulary.

All this, with the further evidence derived from a study of the works of Guillaume du Bartas (1544–1590) in France, Joost van den Vondel (1587–1679) in Holland, Milton (1608–1674), and Bunyan (1628–1688) in England, is a commonplace of criticism. Less common, perhaps, is the perception that these immense literary riches were all ultimately extracted from the Hebrew Bible. There have been two universal languages in the course of the last six centuries: Latin, which Petrarch recovered, and the field of which was enlarged by Budé, Erasmus, More, the Latin playwrights and the rest; and Hebrew, which Mirandola and Reuchlin found indispensable to Renaissance studies.[2] The difference is that Latin was used

---

[1] By R. E. Prothero (Lord Ernle).

[2] On the Hebrew studies of Mirandola and Reuchlin see article by Prof. Box, pp. 319–324.

directly and Hebrew at one remove. Ardent Hebraists never compiled 'Nizolian Paper-books and figures and phrases', as Sir Philip Sidney described the Ciceronian treasuries of his day. There was no Bembo among the Hebraists. The stream overflowed the dykes, and the grammarians were lost in the commonalty. The language of the Bible became the daily speech of common folk, and the prophecy of Erasmus, referred to above, is matched by the hardly less eloquent passage of an historian of the English people : [1] ' as a mere literary monument the English version of the Bible remains the noblest example of the English tongue, while its perpetual use made it from the instant of its appearance the standard of our language.'

'The standard of our language.' Truly, the literary triumph of Hebrew resides in its permeation into every living tongue. After Lyly, it was said, all the world of fashion parleyed Euphuism; after Tyndale, Luther, and the Authorized Version, every one, we may say, parleyed Hebraism. We cannot follow in detail the stages of this conquest—for it amounted to nothing less.[2] A great literary critic tells of Milton's 'wonderful prose cadence, which we never find in English till the early translators of the Bible got it somehow from their originals and infused it into our literature for ever '.[3] The word 'infusion' is essential. The legacy of Israel in literature is not to be calculated or measured. It does not consist in so many words derived from Hebrew in our vocabulary, nor even in so many phrases which might be separated from the mass. It is, literally, an infused element, and, equally literally, it is a Jewish element. Those who recall from 1897 the wide spiritual effect of Mr. Kipling's *Recessional* are conscious that its appeal resided, not in saying new things, but in saying old

[1] J. R. Green, *History of the English People.* Opening of Book VII.

[2] An admirable summary is given by Prof. Albert Cook in ch. ii of vol. iv of the *Cambridge History of English Literature.*

[3] G. Saintsbury, *Cambridge History of English Literature*, vii. 127.

things in a new setting. It said in a new time the old things said by the Jewish author of the 51st Psalm, thus proving, at the end of the nineteenth century, and in the midst of an imperial display inconceivable to the writer of that poem, that the 'clean heart' and the 'right spirit', the 'broken spirit' and the 'contrite heart', were one and the same for ancient Jew and modern Christian, and that one language was common to both. That language, though English, was Hebrew: the Hebrew consciousness was infused in the English poet. We may take an even more contemporary example. During the recent war, there was a widespread demand, answered in *The Times* and other quarters, for Wordsworth's *Sonnets dedicated to Liberty*. These, too, are firmly founded on Hebrew teaching. No better epitome, for instance, of the doctrinal legacy of Israel—of the moral and domestic code of the Pentateuch—could be devised than is contained in five words of Wordsworth:

> Pure religion breathing household laws.

How close, again, to an old invocation never disused in the Hebrew liturgy, 'though our mouths were full of song as the sea,' in Wordsworth's apostrophe to Milton:

> Thou hadst a voice whose sound was like the sea.

Or read Lincoln and Whitman in America, Goethe in Germany, Chateaubriand in France, Leopardi in Italy, and a like debt to the same legacy is presented to us.

At certain periods in modern history, the Jews, scattered among the nations, recovered the liberty of expression, and regained that consciousness of identity with the peoples among whom they dwelt which had been rudely broken by expulsion in the thirteenth and fourteenth centuries. The policy of Napoleon was redintegratory. The Lutherans of Bavaria and the Catholics in Luther's Saxony were alike admitted to religious freedom, and the Jews throughout Napoleon's Empire were restored from the degradation of previous centuries. Their emancipation, completed in the nineteenth century, was founded by the Emperor of the French. It is remarked that the name of Schöntheil, adopted by some German Jews in this period, was a translation of Buonaparte, and in some of the ghettoes of eastern Europe a kind of Napoleon-legend grew up. In this light is to be read the romance of Heinrich Heine's career (Fig. 80). Heine was born of Jewish parents at Düsseldorf during the time of the French occupation, and was thirteen or fourteen years of age at the date of the Battle of Leipzig. Thus, he grew up in the period of disillusionment and broken hopes which followed the War of Liberation: the years 1815–1840 were, morally, a shattering experience. In Heine's verse we hear this double note—the sense of liberty and equal standing, and of a *patria* adequate to a poet's patriotism, and the mocking sense of closing-in walls, repressing the ardour of youth.

> Ich hatte einst ein schönes Vaterland . . .
> Ich grolle nicht, und wenn das Herz auch bricht . . .
> Ein Fichtenbaum steht einsam . . .
> Vorbei sind die Kinderspiele . . .

We need not extend these references. It was the tragedy of Heine's life to be a Jew thrust back by Metternich into a circle of the medieval Inferno, and therefore deprived of his country too. But through all his suffering, physical and intellectual, he never completely let go the vision revealed to Jehudah Halevi of the peace and healing of Jerusalem.

Napoleon was not the first benevolent despot who ruled for the people, though not by them, and the reign of Frederick the Great of Prussia likewise saw a renascence of Jewish influence on modern letters. Moses Mendelssohn (Fig. 78) died in the same year, 1786, as King Frederick, and Lessing, his friend, to whom he sat as model for Nathan, predeceased him only by

FIG. 79. MOSES MENDELSSOHN, 1729–1786

FIG. 80. HEINRICH HEINE, 1797–1856

wrote, 'God confers direct with men, and men with angels, face to face, as one friend confers with another.' But suppose they had not found what they sought, when Reuchlin, Luther's precursor, learned Hebrew in 1494. Suppose the text of the Bible, like that of Cicero's *De Republica*, had been restorable only in fragments, or its commentaries hidden away so safely as not to be recoverable. But for the Jewish contribution to the Reformation, Europe would surely have missed one-half of the harvest of Humanism. But the Book was there, and the commentaries were there, and the spirit invoked by Erasmus and inspired into Bunyan was already present in the soul of the children of the medieval ghettoes. There is a Hebrew legend or fancy that the soul of the unborn child is taught the Talmud every morning, and that the dip in the middle of his upper lip is caused by the angel's finger wiping out this knowledge at birth. Thus, it was not mere tattered scrolls which Reuchlin reclaimed by his Hebrew grammar for the use of the Renaissance in the North. He recovered an antiquity which was ever new, which was renewed in the souls of unborn children, and which German Jews before the Reformation had joyfully and freshly reanimated in no less than seventy-three living commentaries.

This, then, first: the constant influence of the Hebrew Bible as a factor of modern literature, and, secondly, the permeation of the Jews with the influence of their own Book. The wider aspects of Hebraism are not to be pursued in this place. We would not draw for the present generation the exact distinction between Hebraism and Hellenism which Matthew Arnold drew in 1869: 'The governing idea of Hellenism is *spontaneity of consciousness*; that of Hebraism *strictness of conscience*,' nor would we seek to cure the evils of our epoch by prescribing a larger dose of either virtue. We would rather say with Samuel Henry Butcher that 'henceforth it is in the confluence of the Hellenic stream of thought with the waters that flow from Hebrew sources that the main direction of the world's progress is to be sought'. For Hellenism and Hebraism are not contrary, but complementary; and if Plato could be called 'Moses Atticus' by a reader in the second century, A.D., readers in the twentieth century should be skilful to discern that modern literature is inextricably Greek and Hebrew, since it inherits and enhances the glory of Greece and the righteousness of Zion.

LAURIE MAGNUS.

FIG. 81. Printer's mark used by Gershon ben Moses Soncino from 1521 to 1526. The castle is the crest of Rimini where Soncino was at work during these years. He printed in Italian, Latin, Greek, and Hebrew.

EPILOGUE

THE previous essays contained in this volume have dealt with the spiritual contributions of value which 'Israel' in bygone years has given to the world. They have dealt with the past, and their authors have sought to discuss that past with as much objectivity as possible. They approached their various themes in the same spirit of scientific impartiality as the writers of the corresponding volumes upon Greece and Rome. They may have admired, but they have admired critically. They have told us, 'such and such, in our opinion, are the facts about the past, so far as Israel and its influence are concerned'.

For these writers 'Israel' might be in precisely the same category as Greece and Rome. Greece is still a country on the European map, and in that country live many Greeks. Rome is still a great city, and in it live a large number of Romans. But for the writers of the Legacies of Greece and Rome, Greece and Rome had ceased to be. It was another 'Greece' and another 'Rome' of which they were thinking, and *that* Greece and *that* Rome lay in the past. So, too, for the writers of the preceding essays in this volume, 'Israel' also might be as extinct and past as Greece and Rome. It might live only as Greece and Rome live: in its spiritual effects and issues which continue to influence the world. If, in the year 1900, it had so happened that all living Israelites, or, as we now call them, Jews, had been carefully killed, the preceding essays could have been written just as they have been written. The *contents* of their articles, at all events, would not have needed any alteration. Whether any Israelites were alive or no, the facts of the past and their right appraisement would be the same. And the writers discuss and assess them in a spirit of detachment. Israel may, indeed, exist to-day, but for *their* purposes it might as well be dead.

All of us, however, know that Israel is not dead. The Jews continue the Israel of the past in a very real sense : there is no definite break. Greece and Rome are now a totally different Greece and Rome from those with which the ' Legacy' volumes have to do. But, though the Israel of to-day is not the Israel of the sixth or the sixteenth century, it is as clearly, if not as closely, connected therewith as, for instance, the Catholic Church of to-day is connected with the Catholic Church of Innocent III. If Israel was a living religious community in the sixth and sixteenth centuries, Israel is a living religious community to-day. Strictly speaking, indeed, one may well talk about the *legacy* of Greece and Rome, for Greece and Rome (in the sense in which these terms are here used) have passed away. And a legacy is something left, or given, by somebody who has died. But one cannot so strictly and accurately speak of the *legacy* of Israel. For Israel has not passed away. Israel has not died. Israel lives.

It might, perhaps, be safer to call the attention of readers to this difference, and then to stop, so that this volume, like its companion volumes, should (in one sense) deal exclusively with the past. But it has been thought more just to add an Epilogue, which should take account of the difference, and should briefly allude to the future. Should such a chapter have been assigned to one who did, or to one who did not, himself belong to Israel ? One can see obvious objections both to the one assignment and to the other. And the present writer is keenly alive to the difficulties of his task. The Epilogue, then, is more or less concerned with the following questions. Is Israel negligible and dead, so far as spiritual influences are concerned ? Or is Israel still capable of giving ? Or again, if giving little or nothing *now*, may Israel still give something in the future ?

Epilogue

I imagine that most non-Israelites would say that Israel is neither giving now nor at all likely to give in days to come. It was, therefore, they would say, quite correct to entitle this volume 'The *Legacy* of Israel', for, from the spiritual point of view, as a religious community or as a people, Israel is negligible or dead. Such a presentation has at least the merit of adopting a mean between the worst estimate of Judaism as formed by its bitterest enemies and the best estimate of Judaism as formed by its most ardent friends. Most Jews, however, believe that Israel still has a spiritual task to fulfil. They believe that Israel is either giving or will give to the world, and by *giving* they mean something of value, an addition to the sum of truth and righteousness. On the other hand, the more vehement anti-Semites believe that Israel is, indeed, giving, but that it is only giving what is evil. They believe that the world would be spiritually better off if every Jew were to expire within the next two years. Between these two extremes, the great majority of educated Europeans would hold the view, I imagine, that Israel as such, i.e. apart from individuals, is giving, and is likely to give, very little either in the one way or in the other.

It would not enter into the scheme of this book to combat or even to discuss the view of the 'educated European' or of the 'vehement anti-Semite'. More especially is this so as regards the latter. For the 'Legacy' volumes must by their very nature treat of the beneficial elements which have been produced by the civilizations with which they deal. They are hardly even concerned with the defects of qualities—but only with those effects and influences which contributed to the enrichment and benefit of the world. This limitation is observed in the present volume. It would, for example, hardly be maintained even by the greatest admirer of the Hebrew Bible that its *total* effect upon religion and civilization has been *entirely* good. But 'legacy' has been generously and rightly interpreted to mean *legacy for good*. The volumes are the production of scientific men who are in a position to estimate that good. But there is a department of thought which is beyond the reach of science. That department is rightly presented, not in the book itself, but in an Epilogue. The Epilogue seeks to present to the educated and unprejudiced the Jewish view, and more especially one Jewish view, as it actually exists. This view, being actually held by a certain number of living persons, is itself a fact. To present it is to present a fact. Whether the view be true or false is quite another matter. To discuss that would involve argumentation, and such argumentation is outside the province of the Epilogue.

It has been held that the reader—the non-Israelite reader especially—may be interested in such a presentation. Perhaps, too, it is a fitting close to the 'legacy' of Israel that an Israelite should speak of present and future in the light of his faith and of his dreams. The Legacy of Greece and the Legacy of Rome could not have ended so. For, in the sense in which the words were used in those volumes, there is no Greek and no Roman living to act as speaker. But Israelite speakers there still are in plenty. It is, perhaps, then not unfitting that the difference should be marked in this way. What Israel has given in the past has been stated in the body of this volume. Let it now be stated what some Israelites believe that Israel may have yet to give.

It is clear that there can and will be no more gifts of the kind which are described in many of the previous essays in this volume. The Jews will no longer act even as intermediaries in philosophy or science. They will not influence Law or Scholarship, as they may have influenced it in the past. Individual Jews may, and doubtless will, play their part, and rise to eminence, but it is not as Jews that they will do so. Their Jewish religion or Jewish birth will be an accident. Some may hope that a Jewish philosopher may yet appear, whose philosophic and constructive Theism, based upon his Jewish faith, may prove a fresh contribution to the world's thought, but

Epilogue 511

beyond a hope we cannot go. The Old Testament will doubtless continue to exercise its influence and its power. But it would continue to do this even if all the Jews of the world were next year to die of the plague. Only in one particular department of scholarship and investigation may Jews as Jews still be of service to knowledge. So far as Biblical science is concerned and the knowledge of Hebrew, the leadership has passed from them. But in Rabbinic learning they still largely hold the field. And Rabbinic learning has still something to say in the interpretation of the New Testament and, more especially, of the first three Gospels. If the teaching of the Pharisees and of the Rabbis, if the true meaning and the true ideals of Jewish 'legalism' are more equitably and accurately set forth in many Christian books to-day than they were twenty years ago, that is largely due to the teaching of a few great Jewish scholars, of whom Israel Abrahams and S. Schechter may be more particularly singled out for praise. And there is still more work to be done in this department. The teaching of Jesus—its measure of originality, its true relation to the Rabbinic teaching of his age—has to be further discussed and investigated in the light which can still be thrown upon it from impartial and critical Rabbinic learning. Both Christians and Jews must share in this work, and it may be confidently expected that in the next fifty years some results of value will be achieved. Even two or three more scholars such as Abrahams and Schechter, though they are, it must be confessed, very unusual appearances, might be of considerable assistance. But, otherwise, the Jewish contribution to human civilization must be of a different kind.

It is, I think, true to say that there are two main—strongly contrasted and very different—views prevailing among Jews with regard to the future spiritual influence of Israel upon the world. These two views correspond with two main divisions into which the Jews can now be divided, namely, (1) nationalist and Zionist Jews, and (2) purely religious and non-Zionist Jews. As the present writer belongs to the second group, and is even regarded by many as a somewhat extreme representative of that group, it might have been fairer had there been two epilogues—one by a 'nationalist' Jew, and another by one who regarded himself as a Jew only by reason of his religion. But two epilogues would have tried the patience of the reader too sorely. I have, therefore, first of all, to say a few words as to the view of the nationalist group as impartially as I can, and for a fuller, more sympathetic and therefore more faithful representation of the nationalist view to refer the reader to specifically nationalist publications.

I fancy that the nationalist Jew holds that, under the conditions in which the Jews live at the present time, they have insufficient opportunity, as a group, to give anything of value to the world, nor would they ever be able to do so if these conditions continued. (Perhaps I ought parenthetically to state here that the gift of any individual artist or writer or scientist or statesman, who just happens to have been born and to remain a Jew, is obviously not a Jewish 'giving' such as that with which we are here concerned.) Nationalist Jews believe that, in order to give some distinctive spiritual gifts of value to the world—in order to enrich civilization by a fresh variety of spiritual culture—the Jews, or at least many Jews, must live in a country of their own. There must be at least a spiritual *centre*. The 'homeland' will provide such a centre, from which will radiate spiritual influences both to the Jews outside, and, gradually, to the world at large. Scattered Frenchmen and scattered Italians could not by themselves give the spiritual gifts of France and Italy to others. They could not by themselves enrich civilization. It is France and Italy which do this, or the Frenchmen and Italians who live in their own lands. Without France and Italy French and Italian culture could not be. So also, these nationalists hold, is it with the Jews.

Epilogue

They too must live as a compact body in their own land and develop naturally their own specific culture. The world, they believe, will be enriched by this new extra culture. And that enrichment, they think, will come simply and naturally without propaganda or proselytizing, just as the separate specific cultures of France, Italy, or England all contribute and add to the sum total of the spiritual wealth of mankind.

I fancy, too, that many nationalist Jews believe that non-nationalist, and more especially, 'liberal' Jews are inclined to limit the possible Jewish contribution to civilization too exclusively to *religion* in the narrower sense of the word. Jewish culture in the homeland, these nationalists would have us believe, while it will include religion, will be something much wider than religion, just as English or French culture is something wider. Nevertheless, many nationalist Jews are quite prepared to lay stress upon the ethical and religious portions and aspects of the culture. They may agree with their Jewish antagonists that it was in religion, and in the relation of religion to morality, that the great Jewish gift to mankind predominantly consisted in the days of old. They may also agree that it is in these matters that the future gift is specifically to consist. But they hold that with no homeland life there can and will be no such future gift. On the other hand, they consider that from the centre may come the light which may yet illumine the world. From the centre alone can the outer communities be spiritually fed. For in the homeland—in Palestine—there will, they believe, before very long, begin a great spiritual revival. And then from Palestine, as the issue of this revival, noble, spiritual products of utmost value—ethical and religious in the broadest sense of those two words—will be given to the world for its enrichment and purification. Then, truly, through Jewish agencies and Jewish life, *Torah* will go forth from Zion and the Word of the Lord from Jerusalem. Thus nationalist Jews, like their antagonists, possess their own faith and their own vision, and none can say that this faith and this vision are ignoble. Nor are they without points of connexion and kinship with the faith and vision of the other group of Jews to whose conception I must now turn.

In a sense, it is easier for me to deal with *their* faith because I share it, but, in a sense, it is also more difficult for the very same reason. For, in this Epilogue, this faith must be described in the most detached possible way, and as an informed outsider might describe it. But there is another difficulty. The non-nationalist or purely religious Jewish view about Jewish ' giving ' in the future, or about the function of Judaism both to-day and to-morrow, while depending upon facts, depends also upon an interpretation and assessment of those facts, and this interpretation and assessment are contentious. They might be partially accepted by some few persons detached from any branch of orthodox or liberal Christianity, but by most people they would be rejected. Hence the extra difficulty to which I have alluded, and the need for caution and restraint.

The non-nationalist, or purely religious, Jew regards the Jews as a religious community. So far as they are anything more, in his eyes, that more is of small value whether for themselves or for the world. If the Jews have anything to give, if they have any spiritual function or task, it must be in the sphere of religion, though religion must not be so narrowly defined as to exclude morality, more especially in its relation to religion. The non-nationalist, or purely religious, Jew assumes the continued existence of Jews as a distinct religious community, among the various nations of European descent, and it is the groups of Jews in these various countries rather than the Jews of Palestine, who, it is hoped, may render some religious service to Europe, though if Palestinian Jews help in that service, so much the better.

It is, perhaps, most straightforward to make at once the simple statement that the faith of this second division of Jews

Epilogue 515

is that Jews and Judaism may yet have some service to render to the cause of Theism, as they conceive and interpret Theism. It is, it must be confessed, a presumptuous faith, involving as it does, first, a belief that Jewish Theism has special and peculiar aspects of value and truth, and secondly, a belief that the tiny minority of Jews may exercise some religious influence outside their own borders. And it must be admitted that these beliefs are rash and strange.

It has been said that all argument must be avoided, and all attempts at rejoinder to very obvious and very pertinent objections. Yet to this rule one exception has to be made, for it would not be easy to get on and make things clear without it. It may, then, be justifiably asked by the critics of Judaism: 'What contribution did Judaism make to Theism and its development between A.D. 300 and the present day? What direct religious influence has it had in the last sixteen hundred years? Christianity has had its own history since Constantine made it the dominant religion of the Roman Empire. What have the Jews done to affect that history? If Jewish Theism is somehow distinctive and valuable, is there (apart from the Jews themselves) more of it than there would have been if the Jews in the year A.D. 326 had been entirely exterminated? Is it more widely accepted and believed in?' Some answers to these questions are to be found in previous chapters, but I want to speak, not of the past, but of the future.

Religious faith takes very long views; it thinks of Him in whose sight a thousand years are but as yesterday when it is passed, or as a watch in the night. So thinking, it can, and does, become yet more daring and presumptuous. Strange visions pass before the Jewish mind, nor could even the genius of a Browning in *Holy Cross Day* interpret them quite faithfully. It is not an Ibn Gabirol or a Maimonides, still less a Spinoza, who fulfilled the Jewish mission most truly, or rendered the greatest service to the Jewish cause. No. It was the many little obscure Jewish communities through the ages, persecuted and despised, who kept alive the flame of purest Monotheism and the supremacy and divineness of the Moral Law. The imageless synagogue was perhaps squalid; the services within it were often crude and undignified; there were certainly several untenable beliefs and also much superstition. But, withal, at the root there was something which has yet to come by its own, something very pure, something which at once can satisfy reason and transcends reason, something that is the seed of a future, preserved, it may be, in an uncouth and unattractive husk. Jewish faith is not perturbed if the witnessing was silent and passive, if the messengers have made, and still make, little stir, and have produced visible results that seem but small. Only let them hold fast, only let the 'witnesses' and the 'servants' remain faithful, in prosperity as in adversity, in new environments as in old, in freedom as in servitude, and the promise shall yet be fulfilled. The Lord's hand is not shortened that it cannot save. . . .

But a dream as to the future, in answer to searching and inconvenient questions as to the present, may seem fantastical. Let us return to the present, before we touch again upon the future.

If compelled to translate dreams, visions, and faith into baldest words, they who hold this faith, see these visions, and dream these dreams, would, I suppose, say that now and henceforward, when and where there is free intercourse between Jew and Gentile, when and where artificial barriers are broken down, and when and where unfettered interchange of thought and discussion is the rule, Judaism may exercise a more direct influence upon the world's religious future than it has done in the last sixteen hundred years. It is, for those who hold this view, an article of faith that their form of Theism, together with their conception of the relation of morality to religion and to God, has in it elements of value and of truth

Epilogue

which will ultimately prevail, or which, at any rate, in various modes and forms and embodiments, will be more and more widely accepted by mankind. This faith does not mean—at all events to Liberal Jews, of whose dreams and visions and beliefs I know most, because I know them from within—that the Jewish conception of God and of His relations to the world and to man has reached its term or limit of development. It does not mean that this Jewish conception cannot, and will not, expand and deepen. It does not mean that it contains all truth, or that it has not its own special difficulties and rough edges which the future will have to tackle and to overcome. But it does mean that this conception is believed to be fundamentally true and pure, with little to abandon and with much to keep. To set forth that conception in detail and fullness this is not the place, though incidentally, a word or two has to be said of it. Meanwhile, it has to be confessed that the Jewish view of what Israel has yet to give to the world is exceedingly daring and presumptuous, for it is nothing less than a faith that Israel has still something to say and to do as regards the world's attitude towards that which comes first and comes last in human thought, towards that on which all action and character do ultimately depend : the belief in God and in His relation to human righteousness and duty. If any part of this faith were to be fulfilled, how superb would be the Epilogue ! It would put much of the past ' Legacy ' into the shade. For this would be indeed a gift of value unassessable.

Once more, however, let me come down from these vague and shadowy hopes and anticipations, which none beyond Israel can fully share, and few even can adequately appreciate, to something more restricted and, perhaps, more generally approvable. Among the nations of Europe and among their descendants in the new worlds of America and Australia, Theism is accepted by many, and is held in several forms. Even within the Christian limits God is conceived in more ways than one, and greater emphasis is laid, here upon one aspect of His Being, there upon another. But, while Theism is the accepted faith of many, it is also being attacked, and perhaps, above all, it is being forgotten. It has its antagonists, from Pantheists on the one side to Atheists on the other, while there are many more to whom it seldom makes an effective appeal. Now, if only there could be enkindled a religious revival among the Jews, so that they took their religious mission and function more seriously, if only the flame of faith in Judaism and religion burnt more brightly and keenly, so that the drift towards indifferentism and agnosticism could be wholly stopped (I do not know—I have no adequate information—how serious or insignificant the drift may be), if one could count upon ten millions or more of eager and impassioned Theists in Europe and its offshoots, would not such a force for the cause of Theism be worth having? Would not even those who conceive the nature of God somewhat differently from Israel consider that such a band of allies would not be entirely negligible?

The matter may also be put thus; the Jewish conception of God and of His relation to man, the Jewish conception of the relation of religion to morality, are akin to Christian conceptions dealing with these same high themes. Yet while akin, they are not identical with them. In some respects the two sets of conceptions can be regarded as not so much antagonistic as complementary. And it may, perhaps, be truly said that the maintenance of these complementary conceptions (where the many-sided truth is too hard for man to grasp in its fullness) may be of value to mankind. The concurrent existence of certain one-sidednesses may tend to safety. They may enrich civilization instead of impoverishing it. Thus one can imagine a philosophic Christian recognizing that Israel may still have something to give, as an ally in an age-old struggle, and as clinging to and pressing, even if with some exaggeration, certain important aspects of an exceedingly complex whole.

Epilogue

It was stated that it would be impossible and out of place to give any portrayal here of Jewish Theism. But yet, in close connexion with the last paragraph, just this must be said. On the one hand, Jewish Theism is very independent of historical criticism ; the results of critical investigation upon the Old and the New Testaments will hardly affect it. Again, it is, as Jews think, a very pure Theism ; as non-Jews think, a very severe and abstract Theism, which, by rejecting the doctrine of the Incarnation, too utterly separates man from God and God from man, and makes relations between them impossible. On the other hand, Jewish Theism is a very simple Theism, or, as some would say, a very unphilosophic Theism. Its God is both far and near, without and within. It clings to two aspects of God, summed up in the twofold metaphor, which, though a metaphor, yet, as Judaism insists, describes a reality, ' Our Father, our King.' *Abhinu, malkenu*. So Judaism addresses its God, and it refuses to let go either term, either metaphor. What do the two metaphors imply? Do they show that the Jewish conception of God if, by its rejection of the Incarnation dogma, not anthropomorphic enough on the one hand, is yet, by its insistence upon the divine Kingship and Fatherhood, too anthropomorphic upon the other? I do not know. But may it not also be said that the anthropomorphism, and the rejection of anthropomorphism, are both needed in our conception of God, and may it not be that Judaism, which has its own special acceptances, and its own special rejections, of anthropomorphism, may, for that very reason, be of abiding value as a complement and an ally?

Or, yet again, may the matter be put thus? It is, I gather, often surmised that the least inadequate conception of God is one which most fully and harmoniously combines what is called the immanent and the transcendent aspects of Deity. Now there are times and eras when the one or other of these aspects is more in fashion, or is more heavily stressed. At present, it is the aspect of immanence which is to the fore. It consorts with various ideas that are pleasing to, or favoured by, our thoughts and our emotions, and it would appear as if the stress on immanence were likely to continue for an indefinite time. It harmonizes with certain mystical leanings and yearnings, on the one hand; it harmonizes also with a tendency to emphasize the 'divineness' of man, upon the other. And it harmonizes too with the tendency to insist on autonomous morality to a degree and to an intensity that makes morality something which has come to efflorescence in man, and is unknown beyond and outside him. Judaism is often said to overstress the transcendent aspect of Deity: if it does so, it may be that it provides and maintains a useful corrective, and that it errs (if indeed it errs) in good company. For that the conception of Deity in Mark, Matthew, and Luke is prevailingly transcendent can hardly be denied. The Gospel hero certainly accepted the 'Father and King' conception of God, and it may be part of the function and gift of Judaism to preserve this conception, in its childlike simplicity and purity, through the ages. It may be that the conception is one-sided and inadequate; but, perhaps, no one religion can either *do* everything or *possess* everything.

There is another connected point, which touches morality and its relation to religion. People decry the 'barren' transcendence of the Jewish God, and with that barren transcendence they connect that terrible bugbear—terrible more especially to Lutheran theologians—of Jewish legalism. Well, Jewish legalism, in the sense of belief in a perfect and divine code identified with the Pentateuch, must pass away. That belief is dissolved by historical criticism. If Judaism depended upon, and were inseparable from, *that* belief, it could, indeed have no gift to render, no function to fulfil. It must then dwindle and die. The Pentateuchal Code is not Mosaic, homogeneous and perfect; nor is it God-given and divine, in the sense in which all generations of orthodox Jews from the first to the twentieth century A.D. undoubtedly believed it to be. Judaism can emerge, and has emerged, from the narrowing shackles and bondage of this belief into a larger and freer air. Yet with this deliverance and freedom the conception of law in religion has not been entirely abandoned. Judaism still holds that whatever the human history and development of morality may be, morality has not arisen and developed by chance, nor are rightousness and love merely human creations. They have come to be in man because, before man was, they were in God. God is their Author and Source, God is their condition and guarantee. Moreover, man, mysteriously developed from the animal, and, risen above the animal into a kinship with the divine, strives towards, but can never reach, the perfect autonomy of God. Man ever needs an *Ought* and a *Must*; the acceptance and acknowledgement of a Law,—' Thou shalt ' and ' thou shalt not ',—is at once his limitation and his privilege. The Law is both within him and without him. He discovers it, and it is revealed to him. He accepts it as the law of his own being; he bows down before it as the law of God. It is his own and not his own: it is more and more to be made one with him, but it is to be ever recognized as greater and older and diviner than he. The old covenant and the new covenant are not inconsistent opposites: so far as man is concerned, he needs them both. Both are glorious and sublime. To the freedom of God—the new covenant in its perfection, autonomy in its perfection— he can never attain. For he is man and not God. And though he must strive towards that freedom, it remains his joy and privilege to recognize his *servitude*—he need not fear the word, for in that servitude is joy. Indeed the two covenants tend to merge into one. For the more man recognizes and joyously fulfils the Moral Law, the more he admits the fitness and glory of the old covenant; the more he acknowledges the propriety and grandeur of the Law without—God's law and his law in one—the more joyously and freely he admits and bows down before it in homage and reverence, the nearer has he drawn to the New Covenant, the closer has he come to the purest and the fullest self-realization and autonomy. And if it be said that 'Thy service is perfect freedom' is a Christian maxim, then the reply must be, first, that such Christianity is the purest Judaism, and, secondly, that such Christianity is surely somewhat enfeebled at the present time, and that many tendencies and beliefs, now in fashion, appear to oppose and contradict it. Here Israel may surely have something to give, not as antagonist, but as friend, and as a not quite insignificant ally.

> But all, in their unlikeness, blend
> Confederate to one golden end—
> Beauty: the vision whereunto,
> In joy, with pantings, from afar,
> Through sound and odour, form and hue,
> And mind and clay, and worm and star—
> Now touching goal, now backward hurled—
> Toils the indomitable world.[1]

[1] William Watson.

FIG. 82. Babylonian weight. See p. xxxiii.

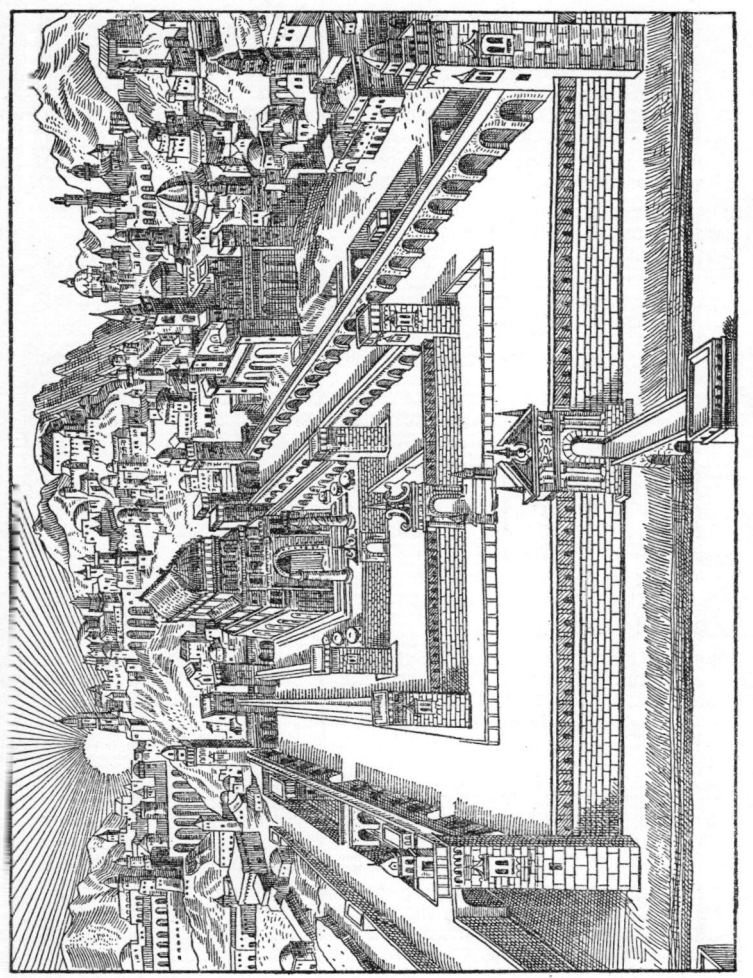

FIG. 83. A SEVENTEENTH-CENTURY VISION OF THE TEMPLE

GLOSSARY

ABACUS : from the Greek *abax* = 'a board' or 'slab', a calculating frame or table for the mechanical solution of arithmetical problems. While the old Roman system was in use and before the introduction of the decimal system of notation and of the so-called *arabic* numerals, an abacus was essential for arithmetical operations. The abacus remained in use in Europe until the end of the sixteenth century. See p. 206.

AGRAPHA : Greek = 'unwritten things', that is, records handed down from mouth to mouth. See p. 145.

ALIDAD : through Old French and Medieval Latin from Arabic *aladud* or *aladid* = 'the humerus' or 'upper arm' (which revolves in its socket). The alidad is that part of an astrolabe (see ASTROLABE) which carries the sights. See fig. 37, p. 227.

AMORA : plural *amoraim* = 'speaker' or 'interpreter' from the Hebrew *amar* = 'to speak'.

(1) The officer who stood at the side of the lecturer in the academy or at meetings for public instruction. He expounded at length, in a loud voice and in the vernacular, what the lecturer had just expressed briefly, in a low voice and in academic Hebrew.

(2) In a wider sense the whole body of teaching in Palestine and Babylonia in the period between the death of the Patriarch Rabbi Juda I (A. D. 219), the compiler of the MISHNA, and the completion of the Babylonian TALMUD (about A. D. 500).

(3) In plural *amoraim* the teachers who were engaged on the work of (2). See also TANNAIM and note, p. 325.

AMORAIM : plural of AMORA.

ARMILLARY SPHERE : through Old French from Late Latin *armilla* = 'a bracelet'. The armillary sphere was an astronomical instrument in wide use during the Middle Ages. The armillary sphere is a skeleton celestial globe consisting of metal hoops or rings representing the Equator, ecliptic, tropics, arctic and antarctic circles, &c., revolving on an axis. See fig. 35.

ASEH and LO TA-ASEH : Hebrew, literally = 'do' and 'thou shalt not do'. In Talmudic terminology used to describe positive and negative commands contained in the Law.

ASTROLABE : through Old French and Medieval Latin from Greek *astrolabon* = 'star-taking (instrument)', a widely used astronomical instrument employed for taking the altitudes of stars and for the solving of other problems of practical astronomy. A simple form of astrolabe is shown in use in fig. 34, p. 223. A much more complicated form of Jewish manufacture and used by Alfonso the Wise of Castille is shown in fig. 37, p. 227.

Glossary

BAWWAB: Arabic word = 'door-keeper' from *bab* = 'a door'.

BAYITH HADASH: Hebrew title of a commentary by the Polish rabbi Joel Sirkes (1561–1640) on the TURIM of Jacob ben Asher (flourished *c.* 1300).

CABALA: for derivation and description see pp. 324–8.

CABALIST and CABALISTIC: words formed from CABALA.

COVENANT OF ABRAHAM = rite of circumcision as enjoined on Abraham and his descendants, see Genesis xiv. 10–14.

DIASPORA: from the Greek *diaspora* = 'dispersion' or 'scattering about', or 'sowing' (as of seed). The *dispersion* or *diaspora* was the term used by the Hellenistic Jews for the whole body of Jews living dispersed among the Gentiles after the Captivity, see John vii. 35. The term was also used among the early Jewish Christians outside of Palestine, see 1 James i, and 1 Peter i. 1. The word originated in Deuteronomy xxviii. 25, where the SEPTUAGINT translates the phrase of the Revised Version 'thou shalt be *tossed to and fro among* all the kingdoms of the earth' by 'thou shalt be *a diaspora in* all the kingdoms of the earth'. Later the word *diaspora* is often used for the Jews outside Palestine throughout the ages.

DOCETIC = pertaining to the *Docetae*, a word derived from Greek *doke-ein* = 'to seem' or 'to appear'. The *Docetae* were an early sect of Christian heretics who held that the body of Christ was not human, but was either a phantom or was of real but celestial substance. See p. 143.

ELEMENTS: the word has a technical meaning in medieval thought different from that with which we now usually associate it. The *four elements*, earth, air, fire and water, are component parts of all matter in the medieval view, see especially p. 124.

EMEK HABAKHAH: Hebrew for *The Valley of Weeping*.

EMPYREAN: through medieval Latin from the Greek *empyros* = 'fiery'. The word Empyrean (used both as adjective and noun) was used in the Middle Ages to describe the sphere of fire or highest heaven. See p. 196 and fig. 24 on p. 195.

FIQH: Arabic = 'jurisprudence'.

FIRST SUBSTANCE: a translation of scholastic Latin *substantia prima*, itself a translation of the Greek *prōtē ousia* of the Aristotelian *Categories* = 'that which underlies phenomena', the permanent substratum of things. The term is used in the Latin translations of some Arabian Aristotelian philosophers as equivalent to *the Creator*.

GAON: see p. 325, note.

GEONIM: plural of GAON, see p. 325, note.

GHETTO: a word of unknown origin, perhaps an abbreviation of the *borghetto*, a diminutive of *borgo* = 'borough'. The quarter of a city to which the Jews were restricted. See p. 122 and figs. 13 and 14.

Glossary

GOLAH: a Hebrew word meaning 'emigration', 'exile', and used to designate the diaspora (see DIASPORA) in Babylonia during the first few centuries of the Christian era. See p. 114. The word is also sometimes used for the diaspora in general. See also RESH GALUTHA.

HADITH: Arabic = 'Traditions' as to what Muhammad said and did. All Islamic Law not already promulgated in the Kuran is theoretically based on *Hadith*.

HAGGADA: rabbinic Hebrew = 'tale', especially 'an edifying tale'. The word is used to describe that part of rabbinic literature that consists of legend, anecdote, parable, and the like. Hence it is applied to the legendary and fanciful element in the TALMUD as contrasted with the HALAKA, or body of precepts.

HAGIOGRAPHA, a Greek term, literally = 'sacred writings'. It is used to describe the last of the three great divisions of the Hebrew scriptures. This division is called in Hebrew *ketubim* = 'writings'. The *hagiographa* contains all the books not included in the other two divisions which are known as *the Law* and *the Prophets*. See p. 84.

HALAKA: from Hebrew *halak* = 'to walk', hence 'way (of acting)', 'custom', 'guidance for practice', 'precept'. The meanings of the word become:

(1) Precept or tradition.

(2) The whole legal part of Jewish tradition.

(3) Instead of the plural form *halakoth* for the whole body of precepts that form the Mishna. The *halaka* is often contrasted with the *haggada*. See HAGGADA and also TALMUD.

HALAKOTH: plural of HALAKA, see also TALMUD.

HASKAMAH is a Hebrew word with several very different meanings, one being for the permit or licence for the publication of a book. These permits or licences were issued by the Jewish authorities from about the middle of the sixteenth century. The primary object of these permits was to prevent the publication of a work likely afterwards to be destroyed by the Inquisition. Later they came to carry something of the nature of copyright. See p. 401.

HASMONEAN: the name given to the Levite family to which Judas Maccabaeus belonged, from an ancestor Hashmon. After the successful revolt led by Judas (fell in battle 161 B. C.) against the Seleucid (Macedonian) kings of Syria, the Hasmonean family became the ruling family in the Jewish state. The great-nephew of Judas (reigned 104 to 103 B. C.) assumed the title of *king*, which was borne by his successors till the dynasty was suppressed by Pompey in 63 B. C.

HAZAN: Hebrew = 'synagogue precentor'. The word, which is ancient, seems to have been borrowed from the Assyrian *hazanu* = 'overseer', 'director'. It was very early used as an 'overseer of the synagogue' who was expected to lead the prayers, and thus became a cantor.

Glossary

HEKALOTH : a type of Cabalistic literature. See p. 325.

HEKESH (better HIKKISH) : a Hebrew word implying the derivation of law by inference and analogy. The application of this principle has been most fruitful in Jewish law and has been freely imitated by the Arabs. See KIYAS.

HEXAPLA : Greek for 'sixfold', used for the sixfold text in parallel arrangement of the Old Testament made by Origen. See pp. 89–91.

HIJRA : Arabic = 'flight' or 'emigration' from country and friends. The flight of Muhammad from Mecca to Medina in the year A. D. 622. The Muhammadan era is reckoned from this event.

HOBAH : a Hebrew word meaning an obligatory religious duty and thus parallel with the Islamic *wajib* or *fard*.

HOMOCENTRIC : see p. 237, note.

IJMA' : an Arabic word = 'general consent'. The doctrine that what the Islamic community accepts as *de fide* is so, and that it can never agree in an error.

INQUISITION : this word is used in two senses in this volume :
   (1) An ecclesiastical tribunal officially styled *The Holy Office* for the suppression of heresy and the punishment of heretics. *The Congregation of the Holy Office* still exists and is chiefly concerned with heretical literature. See p. xvi and figs.
   (2) The Royal *Inquisition* or prerogative of demanding information from subjects on oath. See p. 400.

INTENTIO : the devotional intention ; the filial descendant of the Hebrew KAWWANA.

ISLAM : Arabic word, literally = 'surrender', hence 'resignation', 'surrender to God'. The religious system of Muhammad, Muhammadanism. The whole body of Muhammadans are called *Muslims* from the participle of the same verb.

ISSOR : a Hebrew word = 'binding', and used of a binding prohibition. In Muhammadan jurisprudence the equivalent of the actions classed as *haram*.

KA'BA : the sanctuary at Mecca that held the sacred Black Stone, an object of worship before the foundation of Islam. When Muhammad returned from Medina to Mecca, the images were removed from the Ka'ba. It became a sanctuary of Islam, and with the spread of that Faith it remained, and has continued an object of pilgrimage for the pious.

KABBALA : see CABALA.

KAFFARA : an Arabic word = Hebrew *kappara* = expiation. In Islam the sense is limited to an act of expiation.

KAWWANA: a Hebrew word meaning 'fixing the mind'. The Rabbis were the first to affirm that ritual acts were void of significance unless they were directed and accompanied by a devotional intention. This formulated doctrine is found in the INTENTIO of Latin Christianity and the NIYYA of Islam, whose founder is reported to have said that all actions will be judged by God according to the doer's *intention*.

KHALIL: in Hebrew and Arabic alike = friend [*sc.* of God] and especially used of Abraham.

KHUTBA: an Arabic word meaning the 'sermon' or 'address' in a Muhammadan service. The same is now often applied to the bidding-prayer.

KINAH: Hebrew = 'elegy', 'dirge'.

KIYAS: the Arabic equivalent of the Hebrew HIKKISH. The word means 'analogy' and is specially applied to the inferential deduction of law from existing law, precedent or custom.

KORBAN: a Hebrew word meaning 'offering'; used in Mark vii. 11, 13 of property consecrated to a sacred purpose and thereby not available for any other object.

KURAISH: the Arabian tribe to which Muhammad belonged.

KURAN: an Arabic word = 'recitation'. The sacred book of Islam, consisting of revelations orally delivered at intervals by Muhammad and collected in writing after his death. It contains 114 SURAS or chapters.

MAIMONIST: a word applied to a member of the rationalist party of the medieval Jews who were opposed by the old-fashioned traditionalists who restricted study to the Talmud and rejected Hellenized philosophy. See p. 113.

MANDUB = MUSTAHABB.

MARRANO: Spanish word of unknown origin applied in medieval Spain to a Jew or Moor who professed conversion to Christianity while continuing in secret to practise his former religion. The word was later used of Portuguese Jews in a similar position.

MASORA: represents Hebrew *masoreth*, a word occurring in Ezekiel xx. 37 where (by those scholars who do not regard the text as corrupt) it is interpreted as 'bond' (of the covenant) and referred to the Hebrew root *asar* = 'to bind'. The *Masora*, as now understood, is the body of traditional information relating to the text of the Hebrew Bible, compiled by Jewish scholars in the tenth and preceding centuries. The word *masora* is also used to describe the collection of critical notes in which this information is preserved.

MASORETIC: adjective formed from MASORA. The word is especially applied to the *Masoretic text* of the Hebrew Old Testament. See p. 84.

MEKILTA: an Aramaic word = 'measure', 'rule', used to describe a certain rabbinical commentary on a part of Exodus in the form of a

Glossary

halakic midrash (see HALAKA and MIDRASH). The name is given to this midrash because the comments and explanations that it contains are based on certain fixed rules of scriptural exegesis. The authorship of the Mekilta is doubtful, but its date is perhaps of the second century A. D.

MIDRASH : from Hebrew *darash* = ' seek ', ' enquire ', hence ' seek out the meaning ', hence substantive *midrash* = ' commentary '. The term *midrash* (plural *midrashim*) is applied to a rabbinic homiletic commentary, especially of the Hebrew Bible that makes free use of allegorical interpretation. *Midrashim* represent an endeavour to probe, beyond the literal sense, into the spirit of the Scriptures, and so to reach interpretations not immediately obvious.

MINHAG : a Hebrew word meaning ' custom '. It is applied :

(1) In general to any old and general usage or religious practice among Jews.

(2) In particular to the ritual of the synagogue which varies at different periods and in different Jewish settlements.

MISHNA : see TALMUD.

MIZVAH : a Hebrew word used as a general term for a ' commandment '. It also means a religious act, and especially in neo-Hebrew a good or meritorious deed. In this latter sense it resembles the Arabic MUSTAHABB.

MOZARAB : through old Spanish *mozárabe* a corrupt form of Arabic *mustarib* = ' would-be Arab '. The word was used to describe a Spanish Christian who, under Moorish rule, on condition of owning allegiance to the Moorish ruler, was allowed the exercise of his religion. More generally the word is used for an Arabic-speaking Spanish Christian.

MUADHDHIN : a transliteration of the Arabic word usually represented in English by MUEZZIN.

MUEZZIN : the participle of an Arabic verb meaning ' to make hear '. The word is especially used of the public crier who, in Muhammadan countries, proclaims the regular hours of prayer from the minaret or turret of a mosque.

MUFTI : an Arabic word meaning the giver of a decision on a point of law.

MUSLIM : see ISLAM.

MUSTAHABB : an Arabic word used by legists to describe actions, the doing of which is rewarded, but the omission of which is not punished. See MIZVAH.

NEOPLATONISM : a word used to describe certain schools of followers of Plato who have modified his teaching in various fashions. Those with which this volume is concerned are :

(1) A religious and philosophical system, based on the writings of Plato which originated in Alexandria and was elaborated in Italy by the

Egyptian Greek, Plotinus (A. D. 204–270). After Plotinus Porphyry (A. D. 232–c. 304) and Proclus (A. D. 410–484) were the chief exponents of Neoplatonism.

(2) The further development of (1) among Arabic writers of the Middle Ages.

(3) The development of (2) among the Latin writers of the Middle Ages.

(4) a small group of writers at Cambridge in the seventeenth century who derived from (1).

NIYYA : an Arabic word = 'intention'. Its content is somewhat wider than the Hebrew KAWWANA on which it is based; but it is a fixed principle that intention determines the divine judgement of man's acts.

PARNAS, plural PARNASSIM : a neo-Hebrew word of doubtful etymology used to describe the president, trustee, or warden of a Jewish congregation.

POGROM : a Russian word = 'destruction', 'devastation'. The word is used to describe an organized massacre in Russia for the destruction or annihilation of any class—chiefly applied to such massacres directed against Russian Jews.

PRIMUM MOBILE : see pp. 191, 197 *et seq.*, and 262–3 ; see also fig. 24, p. 195 and fig. 25, p. 199.

PTOLEMIES : the Macedonian Greek rulers of ancient Egypt from the death of Alexander the Great to Cleopatra. The Ptolemaic dynasty lasted from about 323–43 B. C. See pp. 37 and 40.

QUADRANT : an instrument, properly having the form of a graduated quarter-circle, used for making angular measurements, especially for taking altitudes in astronomy and navigation.

RABBINIC BIBLE : for the special meaning of this word see top of p. 336.

RESH GALUTHA : Hebrew for 'head of the emigration', the head of the Jewish community in Babylonia during the first few centuries of the Christian era. See GOLAH and p. 114.

RESHITH HOKMAH : Hebrew for 'the beginning of Wisdom' in allusion to Psalm cxi. 10 : 'The fear of the Lord is the beginning of Wisdom.'

RESHUTH : a Hebrew word = ' power ' or ' control ' ; used in the Talmud of acts which are optional and thus similar to the Muslim category of actions which are *jaiz* or *mubah*, i. e. ' permitted '.

SEPHIROTH : a late Hebrew word from a root meaning 'to number'. In the Cabala the Sephiroth are the ten Emanations or Divine Attributes by which the infinite enters into relation with the finite. See p. 326.

SEPTUAGINT : the translation into Greek of the Old Testament made in Egypt during the last three centuries B. C. It takes its name from the legend that when Ptolemy II wished a translation made of the Pentateuch, seventy (*septuaginta*) Jewish scribes were confined in seventy separate cells, and that each, by divine inspiration, produced a translation exactly similar to all the rest.

SHETAROTH : plural of Hebrew *shetar* = 'writing' used as equivalent to 'legal documents'. The term is ancient, but it is specially applied to medieval records of indebtedness to Jews. These were written in Hebrew, often accompanied by a Latin translation, and were deposited in the various Chancelleries. In medieval Latin these documents were called *starra*. The so-called 'Star Chamber' at Westminster probably earned its name because in it such starra were deposited. See p. 398.

SUBSTANCE, FIRST : see FIRST SUBSTANCE.

SUNNI : an Arabic word = 'lawful'. It is used to describe the orthodox Muhammadans who accept as of equal authority with the Kuran the *Sunna* = 'way', 'rule'. This Sunna is a body of traditional sayings and customs attributed to Muhammad and supplementary to the Kuran. The Sunna of Islam has obvious parallels to the Oral Law of Judaism. See TALMUD. The *Sunni* in Islam is contrasted to the opposing sect of the *Shia*.

SURA : an Arabic word designating a chapter of the Kuran.

TALMUD = 'instruction'. From the Hebrew root *lamad* = 'to teach'. The body of Jewish civil and ceremonial traditionary law, consisting of the *Mishna* (from the Hebrew root *Shāna* = 'to repeat', and in later Hebrew 'to learn' or 'to teach') and the *Gemara* (from the Aramaic root *gemar* = 'to be complete'). The Mishna comprises the body of *Halakoth* = 'precepts', or 'that by which one walks', from the Hebrew root *hālak* = 'to walk', the binding precepts of the elders additional to or developed from the Pentateuch, which together make up the Oral Law. The precepts of the Mishna were codified about the year A. D. 200. The Gemara consists of commentary on the Mishna, forming a complement, explanatory, illustrative, and discursive.

The term Talmud was originally applied solely to the Gemara, of which two recensions exist, known respectively as the Jerusalem or Palestinian Talmud (the *Yerushalmi*) and the Babylonian Talmud (the *Babli*).

In the Jerusalem Talmud each portion of the work is preceded by the Mishna text which is commentated. The Jerusalem Talmud reached its present form about the year 408 A. D., but large portions of it are now lost. The redaction of the Babylonian Talmud extended from about A. D. 400 to A. D. 500, and the term Talmud is in strict use confined to it. Nevertheless, the whole of the Mishna, including those portions on which there is no commentary, are included in the only complete manuscript of the Babylonian Talmud (or *Babli*) which is at Munich, and also in the printed editions. Cf. also p. 325, note.

TANNAIM : plural of *tanna*, a word derived from Aramaic *tani* = 'to teach'. The word designates in particular one of the teachers of the Torah whose teaching is contained in the Mishna (see TORAH and MISHNA). Some of the teaching of the Tanaim was collected in a series of *Baraitas* (a word derived from an Aramaic root meaning 'outside'). The period of the Tannaim was from about A. D. 10 to 220. They were succeeded by the *Amoraim* whose activities lasted from A. D. 220 to 500. The *Amoraim* were followed by the *Saboraim* or Babylonian teachers who completed the editing of the Talmud (see TALMUD and note on p. 325).

TOLEDOTH JESHU: Hebrew = 'generations' or 'history of Jesus'. Under this title there is a well-known Hebrew collection of legends concerning the life of Jesus, compiled during the Middle Ages.

TORAH: a Hebrew word = 'direction', 'instruction', 'doctrine', 'law'.
The word is primarily used to describe the teaching and instruction, as well as the judicial decisions given by the ancient Hebrew priests as a revelation of the Divine Will.

Secondarily, the word is used for the body of Jewish law, practice, and custom which is theoretically based upon the Pentateuch.

In a third and more restricted sense, and especially in the ritual of the synagogue, it is used to describe the Pentateuch itself.

TURIM: plural of Hebrew *tur* = 'order', 'row', the title of a work by Jacob ben Asher who died at Toledo before 1340. The *Turim* is a comprehensive treatise on Jewish law which was very widely read. See also BAYITH HADASH.

WAAD: Hebrew = 'council'. The *waad arba arazot* = council of four lands was the central body of Jewish autonomy in Poland from the middle of the sixteenth to the middle of the eighteenth century. See p. 114.

WAKF: an Arabic word meaning 'pious benefaction'.

YERUSHALAYIM: transliteration of the Hebrew name of Jerusalem.

YESHIBAH: a Hebrew word originally meaning a 'session' or meeting of scholars. Later the word came to signify 'a rabbinical school' or 'college'.

ZOHAR: see p. 329 for derivation and description.

INDEX

Dates are ANNO DOMINI unless otherwise stated.

Aaron ben Samuel ha-Nasi (9th cent.), Babylonian, 327.

'Abd Allah ibn Salam, Jewish convert to Islam (died 664), 134.

Abd-ur-Rahman III (reigned 912–961), caliph of Cordova, 203.

Abelard, Peter (1079–1142), of Pallet teacher, 253–4.

Abendana, Isaac (c. 1650–c. 1710), Anglo-Jewish orientalist, 352, 359, 361–2.

Abendana, Jacob (1630–1695), English rabbi, brother of the preceding, 361–2.

Aben-Ezra, see Ben Ezra.

Abrabanel, David, see Dormido.

Abraham de Balmes (c. 1423–1523), Jew of Padua and Venice, physician, translator, 240–1.

Abrahams, Dr. Israel (1859–1925), xxviii, 308; his views quoted, 66, 104–5, 211; on Isaac Abendana, 362; note on his knowledge of Hebrew and Rabbinic literature, 374–5; his contribution to the meaning and ideals of Jewish 'legalism', 511.

Abravanel, Isaac (1437–1508), Jewish statesman, philosopher, and rabbinical commentator, 243.

Abravanel, Judah (? 1465–1530), 'Leone Ebreo' (Leon the Hebrew), philosopher, 433.

Abulafia, Samuel (1320–1360), Castillian Jew, builder of synagogue now known as the church of El Transito, xxiii, 213, fig. 78 (facing 498).

Abulfeda (1273–1331), Arabic geographer and historian, 361.

Achad Ha-Am (Asher Ginsberg), (died 1927), Hebrew writer, 465.

Addison, Joseph (1672–1719), essayist, 198.

Addison, Lancelot (1632–1703), divine, father of the essayist, 245.

Adelard of Bath (12th cent.), translator from the Arabic, 206, 208, 238, 246, 255.

Adelkind, Cornelius ben Baruch (16th cent.), scholar-printer at Venice, 337.

Adelkind, Daniel (16th cent.), printer at Venice, son of the preceding, 337.

Aegidius of Viterbo (16th cent.), cardinal, 333, 337, 340.

Aelfric (10th cent), English abp., 503.

Aeschylus (5th cent. B.C.), tragic poet, 468.

Aesop (d. c. 564 B.C.), fabulist, 496.

Agrippa, Heinrich Cornelius (1487–1535), of Nettesheim, physician and theologian, 331, 433.

Ainsworth, Henry (1571–1623 ?), of Amsterdam, 424.

Aḳiba ben Joseph (d. c. 135), rabbi, 85–6.

Alan of Lille (1128–1202), Cistercian, teacher at Paris, 246, 256.

Alba, 5th duke of (17th cent.), 312.

Alba, Bible of the House of, xxvii, 312.

Albertus Magnus (1193–1280), Dominican, theologian, and philosopher, 259–64; other references, xxv, 218, 235, 265, 267, 276, 295, 305, 365.

Albigenses, the, 256.

Al Bitrugi, see Alpetragius.

Albohali (d. 835), pupil of Messahala, 212.

Albucasis (1013–1106), Spanish Moslem medical writer, 240.

Albumasar of Bagdad (786–886), 212.

Albuquerque, Alfonso (1453–1515), viceroy of the Indies, 242.

Alcalá (town near Madrid, birthplace of Cervantes), Bible of, 292.

Alcandrius (10th cent.), probably a form of Alexander, writer of the *Mathematica Alcandrii*, 203, 289, 292.

Alcuin (735–804), English poet, philosopher, and theologian, 287.
Aldus Manutius (d. 1515), printer at Venice, 339.
Aleander, Jerome (1480–1542), cardinal, 341.
Alexander, see Alcandrius.
Alexander the Great (356–323 B.C.), 30, 32, 34.
Alexander VI (c. 1430–1503), pope, 280.
Alexander, Samuel (b. 1859), philosopher, 463, 470.
Alexander Aphrodisias (3rd cent.), commentator on Aristotle, 269.
Alexander of Hales (c. 1170–1245), Franciscan, philosopher, 259.
al-Farabi (12th cent. A.D.), Turkish writer, 212, 255, 263, 273.
Alfonso, see Petrus Alphonsi.
Alfonso I (d 1134), king of Aragon, 208.
Alfonso III (1265–1291), king of Aragon, 226.
Alfonso V (1385–1458), king of Aragon, 228.
Alfonso X (1252–1284), *El Sabio* (the Wise), king of Castille, xxiv, 222–5, 227, 276, 524.
Alfraganus (d. c. 880), i.e. the man of Fargan a town in Transoxania, 212.
Alfred (849–901), king of the West-Saxons, 381.
Alfred the Englishman (13th cent.), writer and translator with a knowledge of Arabic, 238, 496.
Algazel (1058–1111), Muslim philosopher, 192, 211, 234, 238, 247, 255, 273, 276.
Al-Hakim (10th cent.), son of Abd-ur-Rahman III, 203.
Alhazen of Basra (965–1038), Arabian mathematician, 234, 240, 241.
Alison, Isabel (hanged 1680), 426.
Alkindi (c. 750–c. 850), Arabic mathematical writer, 273.
al-Kwarizmi, Muhammad ibn Musa (fl. c. 830), writer of astronomical tables, 208, 212, 214.
Allemanno, Jochanan (15th cent.), cabalist, author, and commentator, 320.

Allen, P. S., quoted, 324
Alpetragius, or Al Bitrugi, of Seville (fl. c. 1180), writer of a treatise on the sphere (translated into Latin in *Spherae Tractatus*, 1531), 218, 237.
Altdorfer, Albrecht (1488–1538), engraver, pupil of Dürer, xxvi.
Amador de los Rios, José (19th cent.), xxii.
Amalric of Bena (d. 1207), French philosopher, 250, 256.
Ambrose, St. (340–397), of Trèves, abp. of Milan, 285, 290 ; his works printed by Amorbach, 338 ; his views on law, 384 ; other references, xxix, 262, 264.
Amorbach, Johann (15th cent.), founder of Froben's press at Basel, 338, 339.
Anatoli, Jacob (1194–1256), Sicilian Hebrew translator, 216–18, 253.
Andrew (12th–13th cent.), Jew, said to have helped Michael Scot in translation, 218, 496.
Anselm, St. (1033–1109), abp. of Canterbury, 253, 262.
Antiochus III (223–187 B.C.), the Great, 36.
Antiochus IV (reigned 176–164 B.C.), Epiphanes, 33, 37, 38.
Apion (fl. 38 B.C.), Greek grammarian and anti-Jewish writer, 33.
Apollonius Molon (fl. c. 70 B.C.), Greek rhetorician and anti-Jewish writer, 33.
Aquila (3rd cent.), of Pontus, convert from Paganism to Christianity and from Christianity to Judaism, translated Old Testament into Greek, xi–xii, 66, 86, 87, 89–91, 369.
Aquinas, Thomas, St. (1227–1274), of Naples, scholastic theologian, 'doctor angelicus', 257, 264–71 ; other references, xxvi, 216–17, 236, 248, 253, 273, 275–8, 281, 305, 308, 366.
Arch of Titus, xv, xxxi, 28, 172, 432.
Archevolti (16th cent.), Italian Jewish grammarian and poet, 350.
Archimedes (287–212 B.C.), mathematician, 186.

Index

Arias Montanus (1527–1598), Spanish priest, editor of the Antwerp polyglot Bible, 334–5.
Aristobulus (fl. *c.* 150 B.C.), 300.
Aristophanes (5th–4th cent. B.C.), Greek comic poet, 323.
Aristotle (4th cent. B.C.):
— commentaries mentioned, 191, 211.
— disciples of, 31, 236, 267.
— his philosophy, 47, 269, 270.
— in the 13th cent., 246–8, 294.
— medieval and later ideas about, 300, 301.
— medieval Latin Aristotle, 249–51.
— monotheism of, 440.
— pantheism ascribed to, 256.
— translations of, 218, 234, 254, 255.
— Universe in the Aristotelian system, 194–202.
— and Albertus Magnus, 260, 261, 262.
— and Arragel, 311.
— and Avicenna, 188.
— and Averroes, 234.
— and Roger Bacon, 272.
— and Ben Israel, 365.
— and Jacques Lefèvre, 280.
— and Maimonides, 263.
— and Pomponazzi, 278, 281.
— and William of Auvergne, 257, 258.
— other references, 105, 109, 177, 181, 185, 186, 187, 193, 212, 265, 268, 306.
Armengaud Blasii (d. 1314), of Montpellier, physician, translator, 234–5, 306.
Arnald of Villanova (1235–1311), writer on Alchemy and philosophical subjects, translator, 235, 308.
Arndt, W., engraver, xxxi.
Arnold, Matthew (1822–1888), poet, 483–6, 504.
Arragel, Moses (15th cent.), of Guardalfajara, translated the *Bible of the House of Alba*, 311–12.
Arzarchel (12th cent., Ibn al-Zarkali), Cordovan astronomer, 224, 233, 260.
Ashkenazi, Zevi (1658–1718), chief rabbi of Amsterdam, 454.
Astruc Bonsenior, *see* Bonsenior.
Atumano, Simon, *see* Simon Atumano.

Augustine, St. (354–430), bp. of Hippo, xxix, 5, 76, 91, 92, 261–3, 264, 338.
Aurelian (3rd cent.), emperor of Rome, 82.
Aurelius Antoninus, Marcus (121–180), emperor of Rome, 202.
Aurogallus, Matthaeus (d. 1543), aids Luther in translating the Bible, 348.
Autolycus (4th cent. B.C.), mathematician, 234.
Avempace (d. 1138), of Saragossa, Muslim Platonist, 199, 241, 273.
Avendeath (*c.* 1090–*c.* 1165), Spanish Jew converted to Christianity, believed to be the same as Johannes Hispalensis whose Arabic name, Ibn Daud (ben David), was corrupted into Avendeath, 211–14; other references, 246, 253–5, 260, 272.
Avenzoar (d. 1162), Spanish Muslim, author of *Theisir*, 230–1, 235.
Averroes (1126–1198), Spanish Muslim physician and philosopher, 190–2.
— in the 13th cent., 247, 249, 250.
— in the 15th cent., 279.
— translations of, 217, 230, 239, 241.
— and Albertus Magnus, 260, 261, 262.
— and Aquinas, xxvi, 265, 267, 268.
— and Dante, 276.
— and Gersonides, 237.
— and Lull, 275.
— and Maimonides, 262, 263.
— and Pomponazzi, 281.
— and Siger of Brabant, 273.
— other references, 201, 231, 234, 258.
Avicebron, *see* Ibn Gabirol, Solomon.
Avicenna (980–1037), Arab physician and philosopher, 188–9.
— in the 13th cent., 250.
— translations of, 211, 234, 235, 241.
— and Albertus Magnus, 261, 262, 263
— and Aquinas, 267.
— and Aristotle, 194, 199.
— and Dante, 276.
— and Duns Scotus, 278.
— and Gundissalinus, 211, 255.
— and Isaac Israeli, 187.
— and Siger of Brabant, 273.
— and William of Auvergne, 258.

Bacon, Francis (1561-1626), Baron Verulam, philosopher, 491, 496.
Bacon, Roger (1214-1294), Franciscan, natural philosopher, 271-3, 299-305; other references, xxvii, 93, 212, 218, 238, 295, 298, 309, 315, 417, 495.
Bancroft, Thomas (fl. 1633-1658), English poet, 301.
Bar Kokeba (fl. 132), Jewish rebel leader, 34, 100.
Bartholomew the Englishman (fl.1230-1250), minorite friar, 238.
Bartoli, Pietro Santo (1635-1700), artist-engraver, 432.
Bate, Henri (1244-c. 1310), Flemish translator, 210, 235-6.
Batman on Bartholome, 238.
Baxter, Richard (1615-1691), divine, 413.
Bayle, Pierre (1647-1706), French encyclopaedist, 448.
Becket, Thomas à (1118?-1170), abp. of Canterbury, 316.
Bede (673-735), the Venerable, ecclesiastical historian, 287.
Behaim, Martin (d. 1506), German cartographer, 242.
Belisario,M.(18th cent.), painter, xxxii.
Bembo, Pietro (1470-1547), cardinal, 500.
Ben Adreth, Solomon (1235-1310), rabbi, 494-5.
Ben Asher, Jacob (fl. c. 1300), 525.
Ben David, *see* Avendeath.
Bendavid, Lazarus (1762-1832), German philosopher and reformer, 462.
Ben Ezra, Abraham (1092-1167), Spanish Jew, theologian, philosopher, mathematician, and astrologer, 209-11.
— and Arragel, 311.
— and Hayyim, 236.
— and Nicholas of Cusa, 280.
— and Peter of Abano, 275.
— and Reuchlin, 321.
— and Spinoza, 366, 367.
— other references, 93, 190, 238, 240, 249, 355.
Ben Hasdai, Abraham (13th cent.), Jewish Hebrew translator,221,495-6.

Ben Hayyim Ibn Adonijah, Jacob (16th cent.), editor of the Rabbinic Bible and other works printed by Bomberg, 336-7.
Ben Hiyya, Abraham (12th cent.), known as Savasorda, q.v.
Ben Isaac, Solomon, *see* Rashi.
Ben Israel, Manasseh (1604-1657), rabbi, Hebrew scholar, xxviii, xxx, 365-6, 458.
Ben Kurra, Thabit (828-901), the 'Sabaean' of Harran, 212.
Ben Makir, Jacob (d. 1308), Jewish Hebrew and Latin translator, 233-5, 280.
Ben Meir, Hiyya (16th cent.), dayyan of Venice, employed by Bomberg, 338.
Ben Shemtob, Abraham (13th cent.), of Tortosa, Jewish Latin translator, 232.
Ben Sira, writer of Ecclesiasticus, 85.
Benjamin of Tudela (d. c. 1173), rabbi, traveller, 335.
Bergson, Henri Louis (b. 1859), French philosopher, 463, 470, 471-2.
Bernard, St. (1091-1153), abbot of Clairvaux, 266, 311.
Bernard, J. L. (19th cent.), published a work based on Vitringa, 363.
Beveridge, William (1637-1708), bp. of St. Asaph, orientalist, 360.
Beza (1519-1605), prof. of theology at Geneva, 349.
Bidpai, Fables of, 232.
Bilson, Thomas (1547-1616), bp. of Winchester, 414.
Blackstone, Sir William (1723-1780), judge, 379, 380, 382, 386, 391, 397.
Blake, William (1757-1827), poet, xxxi-xxxii, 457.
Boccaccio, Giovanni (1313-1375), Italian novelist, 496, 498.
Bochart, Samuel (1599-1667), French theologian and orientalist, 353, 372.
Bodin, Jean (c. 1530-1596), French philosopher, 444, 490.
Boehme, Jacob (1575-1624), mystic, 332.
Boethius (480-524), philosopher, 254.

Index

Boileau-Despréaux, Nicolas (1636–1711), French poet and critic, 489.
Bomberg, Cornelius (15th cent.), printer and type-founder, father of Daniel Bomberg, 335.
Bomberg, Daniel (d. 1549), Christian printer of Hebrew at Venice, 335–8; other references, 240–1, 333, 334, 340, 343, 375.
Bonacosa (13th cent.), Jew of Padua, translator of Averroes, 230.
Bonet de Lattes (fl. c. 1490), Jewish physician, 280–1.
Bonfrère, Jacques (1573–1643), Jesuit, hebraist, 372.
Bonsenior, Astruc (d. 1280), Jew of Barcelona, translator, secretary and interpreter to Jaime I of Aragon, 226.
Bonsenior, Judah (13th–14th cent.), son of Astruc B., translator, interpreter to Alfonso III and Jaime II of Aragon, 226.
Borrow, George (1803–1881), 433.
Bouché-Leclercq, Auguste (b. 1842), French historian, 67.
Bound, Nicholas (d. 1613), puritan, 421.
Bracton, Henry de (d. 1268), ecclesiastic and judge, author of *De Legibus et Consuetudinibus Angliae*, 391.
Braganza, house of, 244.
Breithaupt, John Frederick (1639–1713), hebraist and rabbinical scholar, 365.
Bridges, Robert, poet laureate, 449.
Bright, George (17th cent.), dean of St. Asaph, 359.
Brito, Abraham Israel de (17th cent.), signed petition to Cromwell, xxxi.
Browne, Sir Thomas (1605–1682), physician and author, 53, 417.
Browning, Robert (1812–1889), 210, 275, 515.
Brunetto Latini (c. 1210–1294), friend of Dante, 276.
Bruno, Giordano (1550–1600), philosopher, 433.
Brunschvicg, Léon, philosopher, 463.

Buclidius, Hieronymus (16th cent.), friend of Erasmus, established chair of Hebrew at Louvain, 340.
Budé, Guillaume (1467–1540), philologist, &c., 499.
Bullinger, Heinrich (1504–1575), disciple of Zwingli, 345, 349.
Bunyan, John (1628–1688), 425, 499, 504.
Buonaparte, *see* Napoleon I.
Burton, Robert (1577–1640), 433.
Butcher, Samuel Henry (1850–1910), 504.
Buxtorf, Johannes, the elder (1564–1629), professor of Hebrew at Basel, 349–50, 355, 361, 372, 448.
Buxtorf, Johannes, the younger (1599–1664), prof. of Hebrew at Basel, 350–1.
Byron, George (1788–1824), 6th baron, poet, 485, 486.

Cabral, Pedro Alvarez (16th cent.), maritime discoverer, 242.
Cacares, Jahacob de (17th cent.), signed petition to Cromwell, xxx.
Caedmon (fl. 670), St., poet, 503.
Caesar, Bartholomäus (16th cent.), pupil of Reuchlin, 323.
Caesar, C. Julius, 36.
Calamy, Richard (fl. 1650), 417.
Calvin, John (1509–1564), reformer, 347; other references, 21, 319, 343, 355, 381, 419, 420.
Cappellus, Ludovicus (1586–1658), prof. of Hebrew at Saumur, France, 351, 359.
Cardano, Hieronymo (1501–1576), physician and mathematician, 331.
Carlyle, Thomas (1795–1881), essayist, 26, 485.
Carpzov, Johann Benedict II (1639–1699), German Christian hebraist, 372.
Carvajal, Abraham Israel, properly Antonio Fernandez Carvajal (c.1590–1659), signed petition to Cromwell, xxx.
Cassirer, Dr. Ernst (b. 1874), philosopher, 463.
Castell, Edmund (1606–1685), orienta-

list, 359-60; other references, 352, 357, 368.
Casti, Giovanni (1421-? 1804), Italian poet, 485.
Catherine of Aragon (d. 1536), queen of England, 241.
Catherine of Braganza (1638-1705), queen of England, 244, 245.
Caxton, William (1422 ?-1491), 209.
Cellarius, John (16th cent.), pupil of Reuchlin, 323.
Ceporinus, *see* Wisendangen, J. von.
Ceuta, bishop of (15th cent.), 242.
Charles I (742-814), the Great, king of the Franks, emperor of the Romans, 287, 288, 390.
Charles I (1220-1285), of the Angevin line, count of Anjou, king of Naples and Sicily, xxiii, 221, 222.
Charles I (1600-1649), king of England, 356.
Charles II (1630-1685), king of England, 244, 360.
Charles V (1500-1558), king of Spain, 114, 337.
Charles VI (1368-1422), king of France, 228.
Charlett, Arthur (1655-1722), master of University College, Oxford, 362.
Chasmah, Lā'zar, rabbi mentioned in the Talmudic treatise *Pirke Aboth*, 80.
Chateaubriand, François Auguste, Viscount de (d. 1848), French writer, 501.
Chaucer, Geoffrey (1340 ?-1400), 108, 209, 392.
Chesterton, Gilbert Keith (b. 1874), journalist and author, 410.
Chillon, Isak Lopes (17th cent.), signed petition to Cromwell, xxxi.
Chrysostom John, St. (*c.* 305-407), 34, 385.
Cicero, M. Tullius (106-43 B.C.), orator, 484, 498, 504.
Clavering, Robert (1671-1747), bp. of Peterborough, 448.
Clearchus (4th cent. B.C.), Greek philosopher, 31.
Clemens, Flavius (d. 95), convert to Judaism, put to death as a Christian, 101.
Clement, St. (1st cent.), bp. of Rome, 66, 77-82.
Clement VI (14th cent.), pope, 236, 237.
Clement VII (d. 1534), pope, 241.
Cocceius, Johannes (1603-1667), hebraist, rabbinical scholar, 352, 361, 364.
Cohen, Hermann (1842-1918), philosopher, 460-3.
Coke, Sir Edward (1552-1634), judge, 379, 380, 383, 391, 392.
Colerus=Jean Coler (fl. 1700), biographer of Spinoza, 459.
Colet, John (1467 ?-1519), dean of St. Paul's, 318, 329, 341.
Columbus, Christopher (1446-1506), maritime discoverer, 242, 243-4, 497.
Columbus, Diego (15th-16th cent.), son of the preceding, 244.
Columbus, Luiz (16th cent.), grandson of Christopher C., marquis of Jamaica, 244.
Cono, Johann (16th cent.), of Nuremburg, Dominican, 338, 339.
Constantine (d. 1087), the African, 203, 208, 261.
Copernicus, Nicolaus (1473-1543), astronomer, 94, 234, 237.
Cordo, Simon (13th cent.), of Genoa, Christian translator, 232-3.
Corfiato, Mr. Hector, artist, xxii.
Cornelius, the centurion, 73-7.
Cornutus, Julius (fl. 68), Latin stoic philosopher, 54.
Costa ben Luca (864-922), Christian mathematical writer in Arabic, 261.
Cotton, J. (fl. 1690), English theological writer, 414.
Cotton, Sir Rowland (17th cent.), hebraist, 356.
Covel, John (1638-1722), master of Christ's College, Cambridge, xvii.
Coverdale, Miles (1487-1568), bp. of Exeter, translator of the Bible, 348, 424.
Cremonini, Cesaro (d. 1631), professor of philosophy at Padua, 242.

Crescas, Hasdai (1340–1410), Jewish philosopher, 366, 367.
Cresques (14th cent.), Jewish cartographer, 228–9.
Cromwell, Oliver (1599–1661), protector: foreign policy of, 244.
— Jewish petition to, xxviii, xxix–xxxi, 365.
— his attitude to war, 418–20.
— his quotations from the Psalms, 425–6.
— Soldiers' Bible, 417.
— other references, 416, 458, 497.
Cudworth, Ralph (1617–1688), philosopher and divine, 359, 364.
Cyprian, St. (3rd cent.), bp. of Carthage, Christian Father, 88.
Cyril Lucar (1572–c. 1638), patriarch of Constantinople, 354.

Dalberg, Johann (1445–1503), bp. of Worms, 324.
Damasus (d. 384), bp. of Rome, patron of St. Jerome, 92.
Dante, Alighieri (1265–1321), poet and philosopher, 275–6; other references, 169–70, 195, 196, 199, 276, 503.
Dathe, Johann August (1731–1791), orientalist, 359.
David of Dinant (13th cent.), philosopher, 250, 256.
Davidson, Andrew Bruce (1831–1902), Scottish divine, 18.
De Bouelles, Charles (c. 1470–1553), pupil of Jacques Lefèvre, 280–1.
Delmedigo, Elijah (1463–1497), of Padua, Jewish writer and translator, 239.
de León, Luis (d. 1591), Spanish poet, 492–4.
Demosthenes (4th cent. B.C.), orator, 468.
De Remond, writer on French Huguenots, 427.
Descartes, René (1596–1650), philosopher, 253, 451.
Diocletian (245–c. 316), emperor of Rome, 82.
Disraeli, Benjamin (1804–1881), 1st earl of Beaconsfield, 491.

Dominic, St. (1170–1221), founder of Dominican Order, xvii, 257.
Donin, Nicholas (fl. 1235), of La Rochelle, converted from Judaism to Christianity, Franciscan, xviii, 260, 294–5, 297–8.
Dormido, David Abrabanel (fl. 1627–1663), signed petition to Cromwell, xxx.
Du Bartas, Guillaume de Saluste (1544–1590), French poet, 499.
Dürer, Albrecht (1471–1528), engraver, &c., xxv.
Dunbar, William (1465–1520), Scottish poet, 198.
Duns Scotus (1265–1308), Franciscan, 248, 276–8; other references, 265, 318, 365.
Durkheim, Émile (b. 1858), French psychologist, 463.

Eckhard (1260?–1327?), German mystic, 279.
Edward I (1239–1307), king of England, 497.
Edwards, Jonathan (1629–1712), controversialist, 362.
Egicanus (fl. 687), king of the Visigoths, 482.
Ehrlich, Dr. Eugen (b. 1862), of Czernowitz, jurist, 403.
Einstein, Albert (b. 1879), physicist, 463.
Eisenmenger, Johann Andreas (1654–1704), anti-Jewish writer, 124, 364.
Eleazar of Worms (12th cent.), cabalist, pupil of Judah the Pious, 320, 327.
Eliot, George (1819–1880), novelist, 484.
Elizabeth (1533–1603), queen of England, 347, 417.
Ellenborg, Nicholas (1480 or 1481–1523), priest at Ottobeuren, 323.
Ellenborg, Ulrich, physician, father of the preceding, 323.
Erasmus, Desiderius (1467–1536), Dutch classical scholar and theologian, xxvii, 316–19.
— his 'literary Rubicon', 499, 500.
— and Froben's press at Basel, 338, 339.

Erasmus and Luther, 348.
— and Reuchlin, 328–9.
— and Paul Rici, 240.
— other references, 292, 340, 376, 499, 504.
Erigena, John Scot (c. 800–c. 880), philosopher, 246, 279.
Ernle, Lord (R. E. Prothero), 425.
Euclid, geometrician (fl. c. 300 B.C.), 186, 208, 234, 237, 255, 311.
Euripides (5th cent. B.C.), Greek tragic poet, 365, 466.
Eusebius Pamphili (c. 260–340), bp. of Caesarea, ecclesiastical historian, 90, 300, 384.

Fagius, Paul (1504–1549), theologian, 334, 359.
Farissol, Abraham (1451–1526), rabbi, known as Abraham Peritsol, 361.
Farrachius (13th cent., Faradj ben Salim of Girgenti—known to the Latins as Farrachius or Farragut), Jewish translator, xxiii, 221–2.
Farradj ben Salim of Girgenti, see Farrachius.
Farragut, see Farrachius.
Felix Pratensis (d. 1539), Augustinian, editor of first rabbinic Bible, 336, 338.
Ferdinand V (1452–1516), king of Castille and Aragon, 494.
Fichte, Johann Gottlieb (1762–1814), philosopher, 452.
Fischer, B. (19th cent.), edited new ed. of Buxtorf's *Lexicon*, 350.
Fisher, John (1459–1535), bp. of Rochester, 328–9.
Fludd, Robert (1574–1637), physician, 331.
Föster, see Forster, Johann.
Forster, Johann (1496–1558), also known as Föster, Forsthemius, and Vorster, hebraist, Lutheran divine, pupil of Reuchlin, 323, 348.
Forsthemius, see Forster, Johann.
Fox, George (1624–1691), quaker, 423, 427–9.
Francis, St. (1181–1226), of Assisi, founder of Franciscan Order, 257.
Francis I (1494–1547), king of France, 341.

Frankel, Zacharias (1801–1875), German theologian, 404.
Franks, Sir A. Wollaston (1826–1897), Director of the British Museum, 172.
Frederick II (1194–1250), of the Hohenstaufen line, emperor of the Romans, king of Germany and of Sicily, 216, 218, 220, 264.
Frederick III (1415–1493), emperor of the Romans, king of Germany, 320.
Frederick II, the Great (1712–1786), king of Prussia, 502.
Freud, Sigmund (b. 1856), psychoanalyst, 463, 470.
Froben, Johann (1460–1527), printer at Basel, xxviii, 338, 339, 340.
Froschauer, Christopher (16th cent.), bookseller and printer at Zürich, 339.
Froude, James Anthony (1818–1894), historian, 420.

Galen (130–200), medical writer, physician to Marcus Aurelius, 186, 202.
Galilei, Galileo (1564–1642), astronomer, natural philosopher, 94, 189, 224.
Gallasius (16th cent.), editor of Calvin's *Commentarii in Jesaiam Prophetam*, 347.
Gama, Vasco da (1450–1525), maritime discoverer, 242.
Geiger, Abraham (1810–1874), Jewish orientalist, 465.
Gemmingen, Uriel von (16th cent.), abp., 322.
Gerard of Cremona (1114–1187), translator, 211, 214, 224, 246, 253, 255, 269.
Gerbell, Nicholas (16th cent.), proof corrector at Froben's press at Basel, 339.
Gershom (970–1040), of Metz, writer of the earliest Hebrew glossary, 284.
Gersonides (Lev ibn Gerson, 1288–1344), French Jew, philosophical writer, 236–7 ; other references, 234, 241, 249, 321, 366, 367.
Gibertuzzi, Ugolino Marini (15th cent.),

Index

completed a MS. of Nicholas de Lyra, xxvi.
Gildas (d. 570), of Britain, historian, 287.
Ginsberg, Asher, *see* Achad Ha-Am.
Ginsburg, Dr. C. D., on Jacob ben Hayyim and Elias Levita, 336, 337.
Goethe, J. W. von (1749-1832), poet, 15, 485, 501.
Golius, Jacob (1596-1667), orientalist, 361.
Gonzales, Abraham Coen (17th cent.), signed petition to Cromwell, xxx.
Goodman, Gabriel (1529 ?-1601), dean of Westminster, 341.
Grätz, Heinrich (1817-1891), Jewish scholar, 112, 332.
Gratian, Francis (fl. *c.* 1148), Camaldulian, monk; his *Decretum*, xxix 406.
Green, John Richard (1837-1883), historian, 407, 500.
Gregory, St. (*c.* 540-604), the Great, pope, xxix, 92, 264.
Gregory IX (d. 1241), pope, 219, 250, 295.
Grimani, Antonio (d. 1523), cardinal, 241, 340.
Grosseteste, Robert (1175-1253), bp. of Lincoln, Franciscan, xxvii, 259, 272, 298, 309, 314.
Grotius, Hugo (1583-1645), theologian and jurist, 365, 385, 386.
Grynaeus, Johann Jacob (1540-1618), prof. of theology at Basel and Heidelberg, 349.
Gundissalinus, Dominicus (12th cent.), archd. of Segovia, collaborated with Avendeath (q.v.), 211, 254-6 ; other references, 246, 253, 257, 272.
Guzman, Don Luis (15th cent.), lord of Algaba, 311.

Hackspan, Dietrich (1607-1659), orientalist, 352.
Hadrian (76-138), emperor of Rome, xi, 100.
Hai Gaon of Pumbeditha (d. 1038), 325-6.
Halevi, Jehudah (d. *c.* 1142), Hebrew poet, 492-4.
Halfpenny, Joseph (1748-1811), engraver, xviii.
Hameln, Glückel (1645-1724), Jewess, writer of an autobiography, 125-8.
Hammurabi, Code of, 381.
Handel, George Frederick (1685-1759), musical composer, 13.
Harding, Stephen (*c.* 1060-1134), abbot of Cîteaux, Cistercian, 292-3.
Harisi, Judah (13th cent.), Hebrew translator, 218.
Harley, Robert (1661-1724), first earl of Oxford, xvii.
Harnack, Adolf von (b. 1851), German biblical critic, 82.
Harun-ar-Rashid (d. 809), Caliph of Bagdad, 271.
Harvey, William (1578-1657), discoverer of the circulation of the blood, 242.
Harvie, Marian (hanged 1680), 426.
Hasdai Crescas, *see* Crescas.
Hasdai ibn Shaprut (10th cent.), Spanish physician, 101.
Hawthorne, Nathaniel (d. 1864), American novelist, 382.
Hayyim (13th cent.), French Jew, translator, 236.
Hearnshaw, Prof. F. J. C., quoted, 316.
Hecataeus (4th cent. B.C.), of Abdera, Greek philosopher, 31, 32.
Hegel, G. W. F. (1770-1831), philosopher, 105, 452.
Heidegger, Johann Heinrich (1633-1698), theologian, hebraist, 359.
Heine, Heinrich (1800-1856), poet, xxxiii, 488, 496, 502.
Helena, queen of Adiabene (d. *c.* 56), convert to Judaism, 101.
Helmont, Johann Baptist van (1577-1644), physician and chemist, 331.
Héloise (*c.* 1101-1164), pupil of Abelard, 253.
Henry I (1068-1135) king of England, 209.
Henry III (1375-1406), king of Castille, 308.
Henry VIII (1491-1547), king of England, 241, 341, 395, 417.
Henry of Costessy (14th cent.), Franciscan, master of the Friars at Cambridge, 307-8.

Henry the Navigator, Prince (1394–1460), 228.
Henry, Matthew (1662–1714), nonconformist divine and biblical commentator, author of a well-known work, *Exposition of the Old and New Testaments*, that is still in use, 22.
Heraclitus (5th cent. B.C.), Greek philosopher, 52, 57.
Herman the German (d. 1272), 218, 309–10.
Hermas (1st–2nd cent.), apostolical father, 77.
Hero of Alexandria (1st cent.), Greek geometer, 186.
Herz, Mark (1747–1803), German physician, 458, 462.
Hesiod (c. 700 B.C.), 489.
Hillel the Great, 80.
Hillel II (330–365), patriarch, 104, 461.
Hippocrates (460–c. 357 B.C.), medical writer, 186, 261.
Hobbes, Thomas (1588–1679), philosopher, 490.
Hodgkin, Thomas (1831–1913), historian, 427.
Hody, Humphrey (1659–1706), biblical scholar, 369.
Holbein, Hans (1498–1554), painter, xxvii.
Homer, 319, 489.
Hoogstraten, Jacob van (16th cent.), Dominican prior in Cologne, 322.
Hôpital, Michel de l' (d. 1573), chancellor of France, 444.
Hopkins, John, *see* Sternbold, Thomas.
Horace (65–8 B.C.), Latin poet, 101, 491.
Horne, Robert (1519?–1580), bp. of Winchester, 341.
Hospinian, Rudolph (1547–1626), pastor at Zürich, 349.
Hottinger, John Henry (1620–1667), hebraist, 364.
Hough, John (1651–1743), bp. of Oxford and of Worcester, 362.
Hulsius, Anton (17th cent.), orientalist, 361.
Huxley, Thomas Henry (1825–1895), man of science, 411.

Hyde, Thomas (1636–1703), orientalist, 352, 361, 362.

Ibn al-Zarkali, *see* Arzarchel.
Ibn Daud, *see* Avendeath.
Ibn Ezra, *see* Ben Ezra.
Ibn Gabirol, Solomon (c. 1021–c. 1058), known to the Latins as Avicebron, Spanish Jewish philosopher, 189–90.
— translations mentioned, 211, 238, 246–7, 253.
— and Albertus Magnus, 260–1.
— and Aquinas, 267.
— and Roger Bacon, 272.
— and Ben Israel, 365.
— and Giordano Bruno, 433.
— and Cabalistic tradition, 328.
— and Dante, 276.
— and Duns Scotus, 277.
— and Nicholas of Cusa, 280.
— and Siger of Brabant, 273.
— and William of Auvergne, 258–9.
— other references, 247, 249, 254, 256, 257, 463, 467, 515.
Ibn Habib (16th cent.), head of the college in Jerusalem, 115.
Ibn Honein (d. 911), of Bagdad, Syrian Christian, translator of Aristotle, 194.
Ibn Khodadbeh, translated a passage from the *Book of Ways*, 288.
Ibnu-l-Arabi (1165–1240), Spanish Arab, Muslim theologian, xxi, 170.
Ignatius, St. (died c. 1100–1107), bp. of Antioch, 82–3.
Innocent III (c. 1160–1254), pope, 121, 508.
Innocent IV (d. 1254), pope, 260.
Irenaeus, St. (2nd cent.), bp. of Lyons, 81, 87, 88.
Irving, Washington (1783–1859), American novelist and historian, 381.
Isaac of Etoile (d. 1169), 246, 256.
Isaac ben Sid Hazan (13th cent.), Spanish Jewish translator, 224–5.
Isaac Israeli (c. 855–955), of Kairouan, known to the Latins as Isaac Judaeus, Jewish physician and philosopher, 187.
— translations mentioned, 214, 238.

Index

Paul of Burgos (1351–1435), converted Jew, bp. of Cartagena, abp. of Burgos, 308–9, 314.
Pellicanus Rubeaquensis, Dominus, *see* Kurschner, Conrad.
Penry, John (1559–1593), Welsh puritan, 414.
Peritsol, Abraham, *see* Farissol.
Peter (*c.* 1092–1156), the Venerable, abbot of Cluny, 294.
Peter of Abano (1250–1318), heretical writer, professor at Padua, 210, 275.
Petrarch, Francis (1304–1374), poet, 484, 499, 503.
Petrus Alphonsi, or Alfonsi (b. 1062), Spanish Jewish writer, converted to Christianity, physician, 208–9, 238, 272, 305.
Pfaff, Christoph Matthaeus (1686–1760), theologian, 358.
Pfefferkorn (15th–16th cent.), baptized Jew of Cologne, 321, 322.
Philip II (1527–1598), king of Spain, 335.
Philip IV (1268–1314), the Fair, king of France, 234.
Philo (*c.* 20 B.C.–*c.* A.D. 45), of Alexandria, Jewish philosopher, 33, 40, 42–65, 67, 139, 285, 437, 455, 461, 463, 465, 466, 467.
Pico della Mirandola, Giovanni (1463–1494), cabalist, 319–24; other references, xxvii, 239, 240, 313, 330, 345, 376, 433, 499.
Pietro da Eboli (14th cent.), writer of *Liber ad honorem Augusti*, xxii.
Pindar (6th–5th cent. B.C.), poet, 468.
Pirckheimer, Willibald (1470–1530), bibliophile, xxviii, 376.
Piscator, Johann, (16th cent.), 349.
Pius V (1504–1572), pope, 264.
Plantavit, Jean (1576–1651), sieur de la Pause, bp. of Lodeve, hebraist, 352–3.
Plantin (16th cent.), firm of printers at Antwerp, 335.
Plato, in the Middle Ages, 177, 186, 246.
— 'Moses Atticus', 505.
— first translator of, 319.

Plato and Abelard of Pallet, 254.
— and Albertus Magnus, 261.
— and Ben Israel, 365.
— and Ibn Gabirol, 467.
— and Raymond Lull, 274.
— and Maimonides, 200.
— and Philo, 45, 47, 48, 57.
— and the *Zohar*, 329.
— other references, 41, 265, 300, 435, 440, 466, 468, 491, 529.
Plato of Tivoli (fl. *c.* 1130–1150), Italian, 214, 304.
Playfere, Thomas (1561?–1609), divine, 412.
Pliny, 311.
Plotinus (204–270), Neoplatonist, 177, 187, 246, 530.
Pococke, Edward (1604–1691), orientalist, xxviii, 352, 353–5, 360, 364, 368, 448.
Polo, Marco (1254–1324), traveller, 228.
Pompeius (106–48 B.C.), 526.
Pomponazzi, Pietro (1462–1524), Aristotelian, 279, 281–2.
Porphyry (232–*c.* 304), Neoplatonist, 530.
Posidonius (*c.* 130–50 B.C.), of Apamea, Greek stoic philosopher, anti-Jewish writer, 33.
Preuss, Hugo (b. 1860), political philosopher and politician, 465.
Prideaux, Humphrey (1648–1724), orientalist, 349, 369.
Proclus (410–484), Neoplatonist, 530.
Prothero, R. E., *see* Ernle, Lord.
Ptolemy II (283–246 B.C.), Philadelphus, 40, 530.
Ptolemy IV (fl. 217 B.C.), Philopator, 37.
Ptolemy VII (fl. 163 B.C.), Physcon (Euergetes II), 37.
Ptolemy, Claudius (fl. 126–61), astronomer, mathematician, and geographer, 212, 214, 260, 261, 311.
Pulci, Luigi (1431–1487), Italian poet, 485.
Pythagoras (6th cent. B.C.), philosopher, 300.

Rabanus Maurus (776–856), abbot of Fulda, abp. of Mentz, 288, 290.

Index

Raimondo, Guglielmo (15th cent.), of Girgenti, Jew converted to Christianity, translator, 240.
Raleigh, Sir Walter (1552 ?–1618), 417.
Ram, Robert (fl. 1643–1655), divine, 417.
Rambam = Maimonides, q.v.
Ramban = Nachmanides, q.v.
Rangoni, Guido(16th cent.),soldier, 340.
Rashi (1040–1105), properly Rabbi Solomon ben Isaac of Troyes, French Hebrew scholar, 113, 283–5.
— and Arragel, 311.
— and Stephen Harding, 293.
— and Henry of Costessy, 308.
— and Nicholas of Lyra, 307.
— and Nicholas of Manjacoria, 293.
— and Reuchlin, 321.
— and unidentified 13th cent. Hebrew scholar, 304.
— other references, xxvi, 102, 123, 365.
Rawlinson, Richard (d. 1755), nonjuring bp., xvii.
Raymond (13th cent.), of Pennaforte, provincial of the Dominican Order, 296.
Reade, Charles (1814–1884), English novelist and dramatist, 316.
Reland, Adrian (1676–1718), orientalist, 352, 369, 371, 372.
Rembrandt, H. van Ryn (d. 1669), painter, 348.
Reuchlin, Johann (1455–1522), German scholar and jurist, 319–24, 503, 504.
— in 1492, 497.
— his Hebrew Grammar, 94, 498, 504.
— and Jewish Cabala, 328, 331.
— and Amorbach, 338.
— and Erasmus, 328.
— and Jacob Loans, 332.
— and Melanchthon, 348.
— and Sebastian Münster, 334.
— other references, xxvii, 376, 498, 499, 503, 504.
Rhazes of Khorasan (d. 932), writer of the medical treatise known as the *Liber continens*, xxiii, 221, 261.
Rhenanus, Beatus (1485–1547), philologist, attached to Froben's press at Basel, 338.

Ricardo, David (1772–1823), English economist, 491.
Rici, Paul (15th–16th cent.), Jew of German origin, physician, translator, 240.
Robert of Anjou (*c.* 1275–1343), king of Naples, 222.
Robinson, John (d. 1598), president of St. John's College, Oxford, 341.
Robortello, Francisco (1516–1567), philologist, 489.
Roerer = Rorarius, Georgius (16th cent.), aids Luther in translating the Bible, 348.
Rojas, Fernando de (15th cent.), converted Spanish Jew, playwright, 490.
Romano, Judah (17th cent.), 355.
Rosenroth, Knorr Baron von (1636–1689), translator of cabalistic writings, 331.

Saadia or Saadya (892–942), Jewish philosophical writer, 267, 325, 437.
Sahib al-Schurta, *see* Savasorda.
Saint-Simon, Claude Henri de (1760–1825), philosopher, 467.
Salman the Persian, Jewish convert to Islam, 134.
Samuel ben Jacob (13th cent.), of Capua, Hebrew translator, 232.
Samuels, M. (19th cent.), translated Mendelssohn's *Jerusalem* (1838), 458.
Sappho, poetess, 468.
Saul of Tarsus (1st cent.), 131.
Savasorda (12th cent.), properly Abraham ben Hiyya (Sahib al-Schurta), writer on geometry, 214, 304.
Schechter, Solomon (b. 1847), talmudist, 511.
Schelling, Friedrich (1775–1854), philosopher, 452.
Schiller, Johann (1759–1805), poet, 503.
Schilling, Christopher (16th cent.), of Lucerne, pupil of Reuchlin, 323.
Schlegel, Friedrich von (1772–1829), poet, 503.
Schleiermacher, Friedrich (1768–1834), philosopher, 462.

Schöttgen, Christian (1687-1781), hebraist, 357.
Schotten, Samuel (18th cent.), president of the rabbinate, 401.
Schultens, Albrecht (1686-1750), orientalist, 363, 371.
Scot, Michael (d. *c*. 1235), Sicilian Latin translator, 218-20; other references, 216, 238, 253, 260, 496.
Secker, Thomas (1693-1768), bp. of Oxford, abp. of Canterbury, hebraist, 373.
Selden, John (1584-1654), jurist and antiquary, xxviii, 352, 357-8, 364, 372, 384, 386, 390, 417.
Selve, George de (16th cent.), bp. of Lavaur, pupil of Elias Levita, 333.
Serapion (fl. *c*. 350), said to be author of a popular Arabic drug list, 232, 261.
Sforno, Obadiah (1475-1550), scholar, 320, 332.
Shakespeare, William (1564-1616), 59, 108, 209, 417.
Shemtob of Falaquera (1225-*c*. 1290), cabalist, 320.
Shemtob ben Isaac (13th cent.), of Marseilles, Hebrew translator, 232.
Sidney, Sir Philip (1554-1586), statesman and poet, 500.
Siegfried, Karl (1830-1903), German theologian, 48, 67.
Siger (*c*. 1230-1290), of Brabant, heretical writer, not certainly the Siger spoken of by Dante, 270.
Silas (fl. 50), early Christian prophet and missionary, 74.
Simeon ben Yochai (2nd cent.), rabbi, reputed author of the *Zohar*, 328, 329.
Simon, Richard (1638-1712), hebraist, 363.
Simon Atumano (14th cent.), the Ottoman, Latin abp. of Thebes in Boeotia, prepared trilingual Bible in Hebrew, Greek, and Latin, 93, 308.
Sirkes, Joel (1561-1640), Polish rabbi, 525.
Sixtus IV (1414-1484), pope, 313.
Smith, Alexander (fl. 1814), Scottish minister, translated a work by J. D. Michaelis, 370.
Smith, William Robertson (1846-1894), encyclopaedic scholar, biblical critic and commentator; his most famous work is *Lectures on the Religion of the Semites* (first edition, 1889), 16, 442, 445.
Smith, Z. (fl. 1648), 414.
Socrates (5th cent. B.C.), philosopher, 300.
Soncino, Gershon ben Moses (16th cent.), printer of the first complete Hebrew Bible, xxxiii, 241, 505.
Spencer, John (1630-1695), theologian, hebraist, 352, 358-9, 368, 372, 445.
Speyer, bp. of, 322.
Spinoza, Baruch (Benedict) (1632-1677), philosopher, 366-8, 449-57,
— 'philosopher of men of science', 469.
— and Mr. Alexander, 463.
— and Gersonides, 236.
— other references, xxxi, 282, 439-42, 444, 446, 448, 459, 464, 465, 467, 471, 472, 498, 515.
Steinschneider, Moritz (1816-1907), Jewish bibliographer, 371, 451.
Steinthal, Heyman (1823-1899), psychologist, 462, 463.
Sternhold, Thomas (d. 1549), and Hopkins, John (d. 1570), versifiers of the Psalms, 424.
Strabo (b. *c*. 60 B.C.), Greek geographer and historian, 44, 65.
Süsskind of Trimberg (*c*. 13th cent.), minnesinger, xxxii, 496.
Suidas (? 10th cent.), Greek lexicographer, 489.
Surenhusius (17th cent.), hebraist, 352, 361, 371.
Swinburne, Algernon Charles (1837-1909), poet, 485, 503.
Symmachus, the Samaritan, convert to Judaism, translated the Old Testament into Greek (end of 2nd cent.), 86, 91, 369.

Tanchum (= Tanḥum ben Joseph Yerushalmi) (13th cent.), oriental philologist and exegete, 355.

Index

Tarde, Gabriel (1843-1904), French sociologist, 465.
Taylor, Jeremy (1613-1667), bp. of Down and Connor, 424.
Telesio, Bernardino (d. 1588), philosopher, 433.
Tennant, Frederick Robert (b. 1866), writer and lecturer on philosophy of religion, 411.
Tennyson, Alfred (1809-1892), 1st baron, poet laureate, 483-6.
Teresa, St. (1515-1582), of Spain, 326.
Tertullian (c. 145-c. 222), Latin father, 88, 89, 253.
Tharasia (12th cent.), Spanish queen, 212.
Theagenes (6th cent. B.C.), of Rhegium, Greek philosopher, 55.
Theodotion (2nd cent.), 86-91, 369.
Theophrastus (372-287 B.C.), of Eresus, Greek philosopher, 31.
Therebald (13th cent.), sub-prior of Paris, converted from Judaism to Christianity, 295.
Tiberius Alexander (1st cent.), governor of Alexandria under Vespasian, gives up the Jewish religion, 61, 105.
Ticknor, George (1791-1871), American educator and author, 494.
Timagenes (fl. 55 B.C.), of Alexandria, Greek historian, 33.
Titus, see Arch of Titus.
Tolstoy, Leo (1828-1910), Russian social reformer, 15, 503.
Torquemada (1420-1498), inquisitor, xvi.
Torres, Luis de (15th-16th cent.), Jew, believed to be the first European to tread American soil, 243.
Traini, Francesco (14th cent.), painter of an altar-piece at Pisa, xxvi, 265.
Traversari, Ambrogio (1386-1439), Camaldulian monk, 313.
Trithemius (1462-1516), abbot of Spanheim, 323-4.
Trogus (fl. c 20 B.C.), Gaulish historian, 33.
Tyndale, William (1477-1536), translator of the New Testament into English, 348, 500.

Ugolino, Blasio (?1700-1770), hebraist, 350, 372.
Urban IV (d. 1264), pope, 251.
Ussher, James (1581-1656), abp. of Armagh, 364.

Valla, Laurentius (15th cent.) classical scholar, 317.
Van den Ende, Franz (17th cent.), teacher, 366.
Van den Vondel, Joost (1587-1679), Dutch poet and dramatist, 499.
Vecinho, Joseph (15th cent.), Jewish astronomer, 242-3.
Verga, Judah (d. c. 1490), of Lisbon, Jewish scientific writer, 239.
Vesalius, Andreas (1514-1564), anatomist, 268.
Vespasian (7-79), Roman emperor, 100.
Virgil (1st cent. B.C.), Latin poet, 365.
Vitringa, Campegius (1659-1722), orientalist, 363, 371.
Voisin, Joseph de (1610-1685), translator of cabalistic writings, 331.
Voorst, — (17th cent.), *Foundations of the Law*, 448.
Vorster, see Forster, Johann.
Vossius, Dionysius (17th cent.), scholar, 365.
Vossius, Isaac (1618-1688), philologist, &c., 365, 369.

Wagenseil, Johann Christoph (1633-1705), hebraist, 364-5, 372.
Walcher, prior of Malvern, translated (1120) the astronomical work of Petrus Alphonsi, 209, 238.
Walton, Brian (1600-61), bp. of Chester, orientalist, editor of the *London Polyglot*, 352, 357, 359-60, 368.
Wansleb, Johann Michael (17th cent.), orientalist, 360.
Watson, Dr. Seton, quoted, 324.
Watson, Sir William (b. 1858), English poet, 522.
Watts, — (16th cent.), archd. of Middlesex, 341.
Werner, —, (17th-18th cent.), edited Vitringa's *Observationes Sacrae*, 363.
Wetstein, Johann Jacob (1693-1754), hebraist, 371.